KU-537-854

BURNS

Poems and Songs

ROBERT BURNS

Born Alloway, Ayrshire, 25 January 1759
Died Dumfries, 21 July 1796

BURNS

Poems and Songs

EDITED BY

JAMES KINSLEY

OXFORD UNIVERSITY PRESS

Oxford University Press, Walton Street, Oxford OX2 6DP

OXFORD LONDON GLASGOW
NEW YORK TORONTO MELBOURNE WELLINGTON
KUALA LUMPUR SINGAPORE JAKARTA HONG KONG TOKYO
DELHI BOMBAY CALCUTTA MADRAS KARACHI
IBADAN NAIROBI DAR ES SALAAM CAPE TOWN

This Oxford Standard Authors edition of Burns's Poems and Songs *is based on Professor Kinsley's Oxford English Texts edition (Clarendon Press, 1968) and was first published in 1969 and reprinted in 1970, 1975, 1978*

First issued as an Oxford University Press paperback 1971 and reprinted in 1978

Cased : ISBN 0 19 254164 1

Paperback : ISBN 0 19 281114 2

Printed in Great Britain
at the University Press, Oxford
by Vivian Ridler
Printer to the University

PREFACE

THE TEXT OF THIS BOOK has been set from corrected proofs of my three-volume edition published in the Oxford English Texts in 1968. It is based on Burns's holographs, and transcripts revised in his hand; the authoritative Kilmarnock (1786) and Edinburgh (1787–94) editions of his *Poems, chiefly in the Scottish Dialect* (some copies with autograph corrections and additions); Johnson's *Scots Musical Museum* (1787–1803) and Thomson's *Select Collection of Original Scotish Airs* (1793–1818); transcripts of manuscripts which are not at present accessible; and early printings in newspapers, periodicals, and tracts.

Due weight has been given to the 1786–94 editions of the *Poems*, and to the surviving parts of Burns's manuscript copy for the printer. In using these editions as copy-text, I have normally followed the first, collated with subsequent printings. Apparently authoritative variants from these have been admitted, and silently brought into conformity with the copy-text. The typography of titles, notes, and names of airs has been standardized; long 's' and merely typographical devices have been discarded. Interpolations from other manuscripts, and passages of dubious authority or not by Burns, are enclosed in square brackets.

The greater part of the text, however, is based on autographs. About 800 manuscripts, relating to rather more than two-thirds of the poems and songs, have been collated. This material is not only extensive but varied in bulk and character: isolated poems, fragments, drafts, fair copies for friends and editors; poems accompanying or included in letters; inscriptions in books, on windows, a goblet, and a bank-note; sets of poems haphazardly got together by collectors; gatherings made by Burns for his friends; and his commonplace books. Most of the songs survive in single manuscripts; but for some of the poems eight or more holographs have been collated. This edition, therefore, omitting the *apparatus criticus* and textual commentary of the Oxford English Texts edition, provides material only for an elementary study of Burns's craft. But it offers to the student and the general reader, for the first time, a complete text of Burns's acknowledged work—and of poems reasonably attributed to him—based on a critical review of all the accessible manuscripts and early printings.

The canon of Burns's work will probably never be fully established. The core is firm enough: it consists mainly of the Kilmarnock and Edinburgh editions, the signed contributions Burns made to the four volumes of *The Scots Musical Museum* which appeared in his lifetime, and original poems which were unpublished at his death but survive in holograph. Outside this core is a mass of lyric verse in manuscript, which is in some degree traditional; and the deliberate impersonality with which Burns reshaped Scottish folk-song in the traditional styles often throws his editor back on provisional, subjective judgements. But the editor who is rigidly exclusive will, more certainly, omit much that Burns had a hand in. Burns worked to recover and consolidate the native lyric tradition; and an edition of his songs is, inevitably, to some extent another 'Museum' of that tradition. Where there is no present certainty, I have thought it right to be cautiously liberal in admitting to the canon songs which survive in holograph. But for an assessment of the claims of many unacknowledged poems and songs to be partly or wholly Burns's work, readers of this book must refer to the Commentary in the Oxford English Texts edition.

The identifiable airs for the songs have been included in their eighteenth-century form. I have as far as possible copied those versions which Burns specifically recommended to his editors, James Johnson and George Thomson. But the versions in all the main song-books and music-books have been collated, and (where we have no directions from Burns) selected on two principles: melodic simplicity, and close correspondence with the poetic texts. I have made conservative copies, removing only instrumental flourishes: there is an obvious—and I hope acceptable—propriety in giving direct transcripts from eighteenth-century music-books to accompany an old-spelling text. The transcripts do not, of course, include all the minor variations that may be needed in working through complete songs; the singer must make his own accommodations, find his own key, and (for some songs or stanzas) provide a starting-note. It is advisable to follow Burns's own practice, and assimilate the air before trying to fit words to it. A number of tunes are sets for more than one song; for cross-reference, see the Index of Airs.

The Chronology, Bibliography, and Glossary are reduced from the Oxford English Texts edition. The Glossary includes all Scots words and 'terms of art' peculiar to Scotland; Scottish forms and spellings of English words, where these may cause difficulty or misunderstanding; English words which are obsolete, or are used in senses now obsolete; colloquialisms and cant terms.

JAMES KINSLEY

University of Nottingham
1969

CONTENTS

CHRONOLOGY OF ROBERT BURNS

1750 The poet's father, William Burnes (born in Kincardineshire, 1721) settles in Ayrshire as a 7-acre tenant at Alloway.

1757 William Burnes marries Agnes Broun of Maybole (1732–1820).

1759 25 January. Robert Burns born at Alloway (see **140**).[1]

1765 Robert and his brother Gilbert taught by John Murdoch at the village school established by their father and neighbours.

1766 William Burnes moves to Mount Oliphant, a 70-acre farm near Alloway.

1768 Murdoch leaves Alloway. William Burnes takes up his sons' education.

1774 Burns working on the farm; first commits 'the sin of Rhyme'.

1775 Burns at Hugh Rodger's school, Kirkoswald, to learn mathematics.

1777 William Burnes moves to Lochlie, Tarbolton, a 130-acre farm on the north bank of the Ayr.

1780 The Tarbolton Bachelors' Club founded by Robert Burns and others for 'diversion to relieve the wearied man worn down with the necessary labours of life'.

1781 Burns works as a flax-dresser in Irvine, with a 'grand view of settling in life'.

1782 Burns returns to Lochlie after the burning of the Irvine shop.

1783 April. The First Commonplace Book begun. A writ of sequestration served on William Burnes. Robert and Gilbert rent Mossgiel, a 118-acre farm near Mauchline, 'as an asylum for the family in case of the worst'.

1784 William Burnes dies. Robert moves to Mossgiel 'with a full resolution' and begins 'to be known in the neighbourhood as a maker of rhymes'; becomes Depute Grand Master of St. James (Tarbolton) Masonic Lodge (cf. **115**).

[1] References are to the poems as numbered in this edition. Quotations are from Burns's letters and journals.

1785 22 May. Birth of Elizabeth, Burns's daughter by his mother's servant-girl Betty Paton (see **46–8, 49, 60, 61, 80**).

Burns meets Jean Armour (see **42, 44, 62**. 63).

Burns begins 'to puzzle Calvinism with so much heat and indiscretion' as to raise 'a hue and cry of heresy' (cf. **39, 52, 53, 59, 63, 70**).

1786 3 April. Proposals for the Kilmarnock *Poems* sent to the printer; published 14 April. Proofs of Burns's affair with Jean Armour 'every day arising more and more to view', the lovers make up 'some sort of Wedlock'; Jean's father repudiates Burns as a son-in-law, late April.

14 May. Supposed date of Burns's parting from Mary Campbell (cf. **107, 274**).

June. Copy for *Poems* sent to the printer. Burns vainly tries to forget Jean in 'all kinds of dissipation and riot, Mason-meetings, drinking matches. . . : and now for a grand cure: the Ship is on her way home that is to take me out to Jamaica' (see **100, 115–16**).

9 July. Burns's first penance for fornication (cf. **119B**). James Armour's writ issued against Burns in late July, 'to throw me into jail till I find security for an enormous sum'. *Poems* published at Kilmarnock.

3 September. Twins born to Jean Armour (see **126**). The 'feelings of a father' urge Burns to postpone and then to abandon his plan to emigrate.

27–29 November. Burns travels to Edinburgh (cf. **135**) to 'try a second edition'.

9 December. *Poems* reviewed by Henry Mackenzie in the *Lounger*; a week later, subscription bills issued for a second edition.

1787 February. Burns commemorates the Edinburgh poet, Robert Fergusson (**142–4**).

April. Second Commonplace Book begun. 17 April, *Poems* published by William Creech (see **154**).

5 May–1 June. Burns tours the Border with his lawyer friend, Robert Ainslie.

First volume of James Johnson's *Scots Musical Museum* published (preface dated 22 May).

late June. Excursion into the West Highlands as far as Inverary (**159**) and Arrochar.

25 August–16 September. Burns tours the Highlands with an Edinburgh schoolmaster, William Nicol (cf. **184**). See *Journal*, ed. J. C. Ewing, 1927. Poems relating to the tour are: **165–6, 168, 169, 170, 172, 173, 174, 175, 177.**

4–20 October. Burns tours Stirlingshire with Dr. Adair, and visits Sir William Murray of Ochtertyre (**179, 180**). Returns to Edinburgh to live with William Cruikshank, to whose daughter **213** and **271** are addressed. First London edition of *Poems* published. Burns begins his sustained contribution to *The Scots Musical Museum.*

4 December. Burns meets Mrs. McLehose, 'Clarinda' (see **187, 214, 217, 219**).

1788 14 February. Second volume of *The Scots Musical Museum* published.

18 February. Burns returns to Ayrshire and Jean Armour, despite the 'prophanity' of comparing her with Clarinda.

late February. Burns visits Ellisland, near Dumfries, offered to him on lease by Patrick Millar of Dalswinton.

3 March. Twins born to Jean Armour. After a brief visit to Edinburgh and Clarinda, Burns prepares to settle at Ellisland.

April. Jean given 'a *legal* title to the best blood in my body; and so farewell Rakery!'

June. Burns goes to Ellisland (to be followed by Jean in December).

14 July. Burns commissioned as an exciseman (cf. **230**). Friendship with the Riddell family begins (see **223**).

1789 June–July. The Riddells introduce Burns to Captain Grose (see **275, 322**), for whom *Tam o' Shanter* (**321**) was written.

18 August. Burns's son Francis Wallace born.

1 September. Burns begins work in the Excise (see **265**), at a salary of £50.

October. The Dumfries election (**269, 270**).

1790 Burns 'ill . . . the whole winter. An incessant head-ache, depression of spirits, and all the truly miserable consequences of a deranged nervous system'; struggling with his farm, and riding 'on my Excise matters at least 200 miles every week'; but 'I have not by any means given up the Muses'.

February. Third volume of *The Scots Musical Museum* published. Burns involved in the Dumfries theatre (see **315**).

July. General election (see **318**).

1 November. *Tam o' Shanter* completed.

1791 30 January. Death of Burns's patron, the Earl of Glencairn (see **334**).

31 March. Burns's daughter Elizabeth born to Anne Park, Dumfries (see **320**).

9 April. Burns's son William Nicol born at Ellisland.

25 August. Burns's crops auctioned at Ellisland in a notable scene of drunkenness, 'about thirty people engaged in a battle . . . for three hours' after the roup.

10 September. Burns renounces the lease of Ellisland in favour of full-time excise work.

November. Burns goes to Edinburgh, and says farewell to Clarinda (**336, 337**).

1792 February. Burns appointed to the Dumfries Port division of excise at £70 a year, with the prospect of perquisites worth at least £15.

April. A new edition of *Poems* planned (published by Creech in February 1793).

August. Fourth volume of *The Scots Musical Museum* published; sixty of the hundred songs written or communicated with some revision by Burns.

16 September. Burns agrees to contribute to George Thomson's *Select Collection of Original Scotish Airs* (1793–1818).

21 November. Burns's daughter Elizabeth Riddell born. Mrs. Burns 'seems determined to make me the Patriarchal leader of a band'.

December. Burns accused of political disaffection during revolutionary commotion in Dumfries. The blast overblown by 5 January, but 'I have set, henceforth, a seal on my lips, as to these unlucky politics'.

1793 February. Second Edinburgh edition of *Poems*.

May. First set of Thomson's *Select Collection* published.

19 May. Burns moves to Mill Vennel, Dumfries.

late July–2 August. Burns tours Galloway with John Syme (see **415**; *Robert Bruce's March*, **425**, is associated with this trip).

late December. Burns quarrels with the Riddells. His antipathy is expressed in **443, 448, 452, 486**.

1794 February. Burns sends 41 songs to Johnson, despite a winter of 'low spirits and blue devils'.

20 April. Death of Robert Riddell (**445, 446**).

12 August. Burns's son James Glencairn born.

November. Burns looks out English songs for Thomson's collection (**460, 465, 469**).

December. Burns appointed acting supervisor of excise. Correspondence with Maria Riddell resumed.

1795 January. Burns and Mrs. Dunlop estranged. Burns joins in organizing the Dumfries Volunteers (see **484**).

Spring. Patrick Heron election candidate for Kirkcudbright (see **491–4**).

September. Burns's daughter Elizabeth Riddell dies.

December. Burns ill with rheumatic fever.

1796 January–March. Famine and unrest in Dumfries. 'The *Swinish Multitude* . . . threaten daily.'

4 July. Burns struggling, in his last illness, to keep up a supply of songs for Thomson; vainly appeals to Thomson (12 July) for a loan of £5 to meet a debt.

21 July. Burns dies at Dumfries.

25 July. Burns's funeral. His son Maxwell born.

December. Fifth volume of *The Scots Musical Museum* published.

SELECT BIBLIOGRAPHY

MANUSCRIPTS

The main collections of poetical manuscripts are in: the Burns Cottage Museum, Alloway (about 160 holographs); the Pierpont Morgan Library, New York, Dalhousie MSS. (more than 100 songs sent in letters to George Thomson) and Lochryan MSS. (nearly 40 poems sent in letters to Mrs. Dunlop); the British Museum, notably the Hastie MSS. (nearly 200 songs and fragments sent to James Johnson); the National Library of Scotland, notably the Glenriddell MS. containing 52 poems (mainly autograph); the Henry E. Huntington Library, San Marino, California (60 poems, including 17 epigrams sent to Creech); and the Burns Monument Museum, Kilmarnock. For a fuller account, see the O.E.T. edition, vol. iii, pp. 964–9.

EARLY EDITIONS

Poems, chiefly in the Scottish Dialect, Kilmarnock, July 1786 (44 poems and songs); Edinburgh, 17 April 1787 (22 additional poems, minor omissions); Edinburgh, 2 vols., February 1793 (19 additional poems), reprinted 1794. The first London edition, and two pirated Irish editions, appeared in 1787.

The Scots Musical Museum, edited by an Edinburgh engraver, James Johnson, was published in 6 vols. (1787, 1788, 1790, 1792, 1796, 1803); it includes about 200 songs and fragments (and some airs) written, revised, or communicated by Burns. *A Select Collection of Original Scotish Airs for the Voice*, edited by an Edinburgh clerk, George Thomson, was published in 8 parts (1793, 1798, 1799, ?1799, 1802, 1803, 1805, 1818); it includes more than 70 songs by Burns, many of them mangled by Thomson.

For a full description of these, and of early printings in broadsheets and tracts, see J. W. Egerer, *A Bibliography of Robert Burns*, 1964; supplemented in my review in *The Library*, xxi (1966), 76–9, and by G. Ross Roy in *Modern Philology*, lxiv (1967), 357–61.

The main nineteenth-century editions are: *Works*, ed. James Currie, 4 vols. (1800; 2nd edn., 1801); *Poems Ascribed to Robert Burns*, ed. Thomas Stewart (1801; 2nd edn., 1802); *Poems*, ed. Thomas Duncan, 1801; *Reliques of Robert Burns*, ed R. H. Cromek, 1808; *Works*, ed. James Hogg (The Ettrick Shepherd) and William Motherwell, 5 vols., 1834–6; *Works*, ed. Allan Cunningham, 8 vols., 1834; *Life and Works*, ed. Robert Chambers, 4 vols. (1851; revd. William Wallace, 1896); *Works*, ed. W. Scott Douglas, 6 vols., 1877–9; *Poetry*, ed. W. E. Henley and T. F. Henderson, 4 vols., 1896.

BIOGRAPHY

The main sources are: Burns's *Letters*, ed. J. De Lancey Ferguson, 2 vols., 1931 (now under revision by G. Ross Roy); the First Commonplace Book (ed. J. C. Ewing and Davidson Cook, in facsimile, 1938); the journals of the tours of the Border (ed. J. De L. Ferguson in R. T. Fitzhugh, *Robert Burns: His Associates and Contemporaries*, 1943) and the Highlands (ed. J. C. Ewing, in facsimile, 1927); and contemporary impressions and reminiscences gathered by the earlier editors (see above), often with credulousness and sometimes in malice. The first separate biographies are by Robert Heron (1797; reprinted as an appendix in Hans Hecht's biography, 1950) and J. G. Lockhart (1828). There is a wealth of material in the annual *Burns Chronicle* (1892–). The best modern biographies are by F. B. Snyder (1932), Hans Hecht (1936; transl. Jane Lymburn, 1950), J. De Lancey Ferguson (1939).

CRITICISM

J. D. Ross, *Early Critical Reviews*, 1900; the nineteenth-century editions listed above; Thomas Carlyle, *Edinburgh Review* (December 1828) and *On Heroes, Hero-Worship and the Heroic*, 1841, v; R. L. Stevenson, *Familiar Studies of Men and Books*, 1882; Auguste Angellier, *Robert Burns: La Vie, les Œuvres*, 2 vols., 1893.

Good recent critical studies are: David Daiches, *Robert Burns*, 1952; Robert Dewar's essay in *Scottish Poetry: A Critical Survey*, ed. J. Kinsley, 1955; Kurt Wittig, *The Scottish Tradition in Literature*, 1958, ch. vii; Thomas Crawford, *Burns: A Study of the Poems and Songs*, 1960; David Craig, *Scottish Literature and the Scottish People 1680–1830*, 1961, pt. I.

SOCIAL BACKGROUND

An indispensable handbook is *Ayrshire at the Time of Burns*, ed. John Strawhorn, 1959 (Collections of the Ayrshire Archaeological and Natural History Society, no. 5), which contains a chronology, a gazetteer and directory of Ayrshire (with Armstrong's map), a bibliography, and an anthology of contemporary social comment. Standard general studies are H. G. Graham, *The Social Life of Scotland in the Eighteenth Century* (1899; 4th edn. reprinted 1950) and *Scottish Men of Letters in the Eighteenth Century*, 1908; Marjorie Plant, *The Domestic Life of Scotland in the Eighteenth Century*, 1952. See also: J. E. Handley, *Scottish Farming in the Eighteenth Century*, 1953; Stuart Maxwell and Robin Hutchison, *Scottish Costume 1550–1850*, 1958; Henry Hamilton, *An Economic History of Scotland in the Eighteenth Century*, 1963; David Daiches, *The Paradox of Scottish Culture: The Eighteenth-Century Experience*, 1964.

I. Early Poems 1774–1784

LOCHLIE AND MOUNT OLIPHANT

1. *O once I lov'd*

O ONCE I lov'd a bonnie lass,
  An' aye I love her still,
An' whilst that virtue warms my breast
  I'll love my handsome Nell.

As bonnie lasses I hae seen,
  And mony full as braw,
But for a modest gracefu' mein
  The like I never saw.

A bonny lass I will confess,
  Is pleasant to the e'e,
But without some better qualities
  She 's no a lass for me.

But Nelly's looks are blythe and sweet,
  And what is best of a',
Her reputation is compleat,
  And fair without a flaw;

She dresses ay sae clean and neat,
  Both decent and genteel;
And then there 's something in her gait
  Gars ony dress look weel.

A gaudy dress and gentle air
  May slightly touch the heart,
But it 's innocence and modesty
  That polishes the dart.

'Tis this in Nelly pleases me,
'Tis this enchants my soul;
For absolutely in my breast
She reigns without controul.

2. *Song, composed in August*

Tune, I had a horse, I had nae mair

I

Now westlin winds, and slaught'ring guns
Bring Autumn's pleasant weather;
The moorcock springs, on whirring wings,
Amang the blooming heather:
Now waving grain, wide o'er the plain,
Delights the weary Farmer;
The moon shines bright, as I rove at night,
To muse upon my Charmer.

II

The Pairtrick lo'es the fruitfu' fells;
The Plover lo'es the mountains;
The Woodcock haunts the lanely dells;
The soaring Hern the fountains:
Thro' lofty groves, the Cushat roves,
The path o' man to shun it;
The hazel bush o'erhangs the Thrush,
The spreading thorn the Linnet.

III

Thus ev'ry kind their pleasure find,
  The savage and the tender;
Some social join, and leagues combine;
  Some solitary wander:
Avaunt, away! the cruel sway,
  Tyrannic man's dominion;
The Sportsman's joy, the murd'ring cry,
  The flutt'ring, gory pinion!

IV

But PEGGY dear, the ev'ning 's clear,
  Thick flies the skimming Swallow;
The sky is blue, the fields in view,
  All fading-green and yellow:
Come let us stray our gladsome way,
  And view the charms o' Nature;
The rustling corn, the fruited thorn,
  And ilka happy creature.

V

We'll gently walk, and sweetly talk,
  While the silent moon shines clearly;
I'll clasp thy waist, and fondly prest,
  Swear how I lo'e thee dearly:
Not vernal show'rs to budding flow'rs,
  Not Autumn to the Farmer,
So dear can be, as thou to me,
  My fair, my lovely Charmer!

3. *I dream'd I lay, &c.*

I DREAM'D I lay where flowers were springing
  Gaily in the sunny beam,
List'ning to the wild birds singing,
  By a falling, chrystal stream;
Streight the sky grew black and daring,
  Thro' the woods the whirlwinds rave;
Trees with aged arms were warring,
  O'er the swelling, drumlie wave.

Such was my life's deceitful morning,
  Such the pleasures I enjoy'd;
But lang or noon, loud tempests storming
  A' my flowery bliss destroy'd.
Tho' fickle Fortune has deceiv'd me,
  She promis'd fair, and perform'd but ill;
Of mony a joy and hope bereav'd me,
  I bear a heart shall support me still.

4. *Song*

Tune, My Nanie, O

I

BEHIND yon hills where Lugar flows,
  'Mang moors an' mosses many, O,
The wintry sun the day has clos'd,
  And I'll awa to Nanie, O.

II

The westlin wind blaws loud an' shill;
  The night's baith mirk and rainy, O;
But I'll get my plaid an' out I'll steal,
  An' owre the hill to Nanie, O.

III

My Nanie's charming, sweet an' young;
  Nae artfu' wiles to win ye, O:
May ill befa' the flattering tongue
  That wad beguile my Nanie, O.

IV

Her face is fair, her heart is true,
  As spotless as she 's bonie, O;
The op'ning gowan, wat wi' dew,
  Nae purer is than Nanie, O.

V

A country lad is my degree,
  An' few there be that ken me, O;
But what care I how few they be,
  I'm welcome ay to Nanie, O.

VI

My riches a's my penny-fee,
  An' I maun guide it cannie, O;
But warl's gear ne'er troubles me,
  My thoughts are a', my Nanie, O.

VII

Our auld Guidman delights to view
  His sheep an' kye thrive bonie, O;
But I'm as blythe that hauds his pleugh,
  An' has nae care but Nanie, O.

VIII

Come weel come woe, I care na by,
  I'll tak what Heav'n will sen' me, O;
Nae ither care in life have I,
  But live, an' love my Nanie, O.

5. *A Penitential thought, in the hour of Remorse —Intended for a tragedy*

In my early years nothing less would serve me than courting the tragic Muse.—I was, I think, about eighteen or nineteen when I sketched the outlines of a Tragedy forsooth; but the bursting of a cloud of family Misfortunes, which had for some time threatened us, prevented my farther progress.—In those days I never wrote down anything; so, except a speech or two, the whole has escaped my memory.—The following, which I most distinctly remember, was an exclamation from a great character—great in occasional instance[s] of generosity, and daring at times in villainies.—He is supposed to meet with a child of misery, and exclaims to himself——

ALL devil as I am, a damned wretch,
A harden'd, stubborn, unrepenting villain,
Still my heart melts at human wretchedness;
And with sincere tho' unavailing sighs
I view the helpless children of Distress.
With tears indignant I behold th' Oppressor,
Rejoicing in the honest man's destruction,
Whose unsubmitting heart was all his crime.

Even you, ye hapless crew, I pity you;
Ye, whom the Seeming good think sin to pity;
Ye poor, despis'd, abandon'd vagabonds,
Whom Vice, as usual, has turn'd o'er to Ruin.
O, but for kind, tho' ill-requited friends,
I had been driven forth like you forlorn,
The most detested, worthless wretch among you!

O injur'd God! Thy goodness has endow'd me
With talents passing most of my compeers,
Which I in just proportion have abus'd;
As far surpassing other common villains
As Thou in natural parts hadst given me more—

6. *Song*—

Tune, Invercald's reel—Strathspey

CHORUS

TIBBY I hae seen the day
Ye wadna been sae shy
For laik o' gear ye lightly me
  But trowth I care na by—

Yestreen I met you on the Moor
Ye spak'na but gaed by like stoor
Ye geck at me because I'm poor
  But fien' a hair care I.—

[When comin' hame on Sunday last
Upon the road as I cam' past
Ye snufft an' gae your head a cast
  But trouth I caretna by.—]

I doubt na lass, but ye may think
Because ye hae the name o' clink
That ye can please me at a wink
  Whene'er ye like to try—

But sorrow tak' him that 's sae mean
Altho' his pouch o' coin were clean
Wha follows ony saucy Quean
  That looks sae proud and high—

Altho' a lad were e'er sae smart
If that he want the yellow dirt
Ye'll cast your head anither airt
  An' answer him fu' dry—

But if he hae the name o' gear
Ye'll fasten to him like a breer
Tho' hardly he for sense or lear
  Be better than the ky—

But Tibby lass tak' my advice
Your daddie's gear mak's you sae nice
The de'il a ane wad speir your price
  Were ye as poor as I—

[There lives a lass beside yon park
I'd rather hae her in her sark
Than you wi' a' your thousand mark
  That gars you look sae high—

An' Tibby I hae seen the day
  Ye wadna been sae shy
An' for laik o' gear ye lightly me
  But fien' a hair care I.]

7. *A Fragment—*

Tune, John Anderson, my jo—

ONE night as I did wander,
  When corn begins to shoot,
I sat me down to ponder
  Upon an auld tree root:
Auld Aire ran by before me,
  And bicker'd to the seas;
A cushat crouded o'er me,
  That echoed thro' the braes.

8. *Song*

Tune, Corn rigs are bonie

I

IT was upon a Lammas night,
  When corn rigs are bonie,
Beneath the moon's unclouded light,
  I held awa to Annie:

The time flew by, wi' tentless heed,
  Till 'tween the late and early;
Wi' sma' persuasion she agreed,
  To see me thro' the barley.

II

The sky was blue, the wind was still,
  The moon was shining clearly;
I set her down, wi' right good will,
  Amang the rigs o' barley:
I ken't her heart was a' my ain;
  I lov'd her most sincerely;
I kiss'd her owre and owre again,
  Amang the rigs o' barley.

III

I lock'd her in my fond embrace;
  Her heart was beating rarely:
My blessings on that happy place,
  Amang the rigs o' barley!
But by the moon and stars so bright,
  That shone that hour so clearly!
She ay shall bless that happy night,
  Amang the rigs o' barley.

IV

I hae been blythe wi' Comrades dear;
  I hae been merry drinking;
I hae been joyfu' gath'rin gear;
  I hae been happy thinking:
But a' the pleasures e'er I saw,
  Tho' three times doubl'd fairly,
That happy night was worth them a',
  Amang the rigs o' barley.

CHORUS

Corn rigs, an' barley rigs,
  An' corn rigs are bonie:
I'll ne'er forget that happy night,
  Amang the rigs wi' Annie.

9. *Song*

Tune, Gilderoy

I

FROM thee, ELIZA, I must go,
  And from my native shore:
The cruel fates between us throw
  A boundless ocean's roar;
But boundless oceans, roaring wide,
  Between my Love and me,
They never, never can divide
  My heart and soul from thee.

II

Farewell, farewell, ELIZA dear,
  The maid that I adore!
A boding voice is in mine ear,
  We part to meet no more!
But the latest throb that leaves my heart,
  While Death stands victor by,
That throb, ELIZA, is thy part,
  And thine that latest sigh!

10. *Winter, A Dirge*

I

THE Wintry West extends his blast,
And hail and rain does blaw;
Or, the stormy North sends driving forth,
The blinding sleet and snaw:
While, tumbling brown, the Burn comes down,
And roars frae bank to brae;
And bird and beast, in covert, rest,
And pass the heartless day.

II

'The sweeping blast, the sky o'ercast,'*
The joyless *winter-day*,
Let others fear, to me more dear,
Than all the pride of May:
The Tempest's howl, it *soothes* my soul,
My *griefs* it seems to join;
The leafless trees my fancy please,
Their *fate* resembles mine!

III

Thou POW'R SUPREME, whose mighty Scheme,
These *woes* of mine fulfil;
Here, firm, I rest, they *must* be best,
Because they are *Thy* Will!
Then all I want (Oh, do thou grant
This one request of mine!)
Since to *enjoy* Thou dost deny,
Assist me to *resign*!

* Dr. Young.

11. *Song*

Tune, If he be a Butcher neat an' trim

ON Cessnock banks a lassie dwells;
  Could I describe her shape and mien;
Our lassies a' she far excels,
  An' she has twa sparkling, rogueish een.

She 's sweeter than the morning dawn
  When rising Phœbus first is seen
And dew-drops twinkle o'er the lawn;
  An' she has twa sparkling, rogueish een.

She 's stately, like yon youthful ash
  That grows the cowslips braes between
And drinks the stream with vigour fresh;
  An' she has twa sparkling, rogueish een.

She 's spotless, like the flow'ring thorn
  With flow'rs so white and leaves so green
When purest in the dewy morn;
  An' she has twa sparkling, rogueish een.

Her looks are like the vernal May
  When ev'ning Phœbus shines serene,
While birds rejoice on ev'ry spray;
  An' she has twa sparkling, rogueish een.

Her hair is like the curling mist
   That climbs the mountain sides at e'en,
When flow'r-reviving rains are past;
   An' she has twa sparkling, rogueish een.

Her forehead 's like the show'ry bow
   When gleaming sun-beams intervene
And gild the distant mountain's brow;
   An' she has twa sparkling, rogueish een.

Her cheeks are like yon crimson gem,
   The pride of all the flowery scene,
Just opening on its thorny stem;
   An' she has twa sparkling, rogueish een.

Her teeth are like the nightly snow
   When pale the morning rises keen,
While hid the murmuring streamlets flow;
   An' she has twa sparkling, rogueish een.

Her lips are like yon cherries ripe
   Which sunny walls from Boreas screen;
They tempt the taste and charm the sight;
   An' she has twa sparkling, rogueish een.

Her breath is like the fragrant breeze
   That gently stirs the blossom'd bean,
When Phœbus sinks behind the seas;
   An' she has twa sparkling, rogueish een.

Her voice is like the ev'ning thrush
   That sings on Cessnock banks unseen,
While his mate sits nestling in the bush;
   An' she has twa sparkling, rogueish een.

But it 's not her air, her form, her face,
   Though matching beauty's fabled Queen;
'Tis the mind that shines in ev'ry grace,
   An' chiefly in her rogueish een.

12. *To Ruin*

I

ALL hail! inexorable lord!
At whose destruction-breathing word,
  The mightiest empires fall!
Thy cruel, woe-delighted train,
The ministers of Grief and Pain,
  A sullen welcome, all!
With stern-resolv'd, despairing eye,
  I see each aimed dart;
For one has cut my *dearest tye*,
  And quivers in my heart.
    Then low'ring, and pouring,
      The *Storm* no more I dread;
    Tho' thick'ning, and black'ning,
      Round my devoted head.

II

And thou grim Pow'r, by Life abhorr'd,
While Life a *pleasure* can afford,
  Oh! hear a wretch's pray'r!
No more I shrink appall'd, afraid;
I court, I beg thy friendly aid,
  To close this scene of care!
When shall my soul, in silent peace,
  Resign Life's *joyless* day?
My weary heart it's throbbings cease,
  Cold-mould'ring in the clay?
    No fear more, no tear more,
      To stain my lifeless face,
    Enclasped, and grasped,
      Within thy cold embrace!

13. *A Prayer, in the Prospect of Death*

I

O THOU unknown, Almighty Cause
  Of all my hope and fear!
In whose dread Presence, ere an hour,
  Perhaps I must appear!

II

If I have wander'd in those paths
  Of life I ought to shun;
As *Something*, loudly, in my breast,
  Remonstrates I have done;

III

Thou know'st that Thou hast formed me,
  With Passions wild and strong;
And list'ning to their witching voice
  Has often led me wrong.

IV

Where human *weakness* has come short,
  Or *frailty* stept aside,
Do Thou, ALL-GOOD, for such Thou art,
  In shades of darkness hide.

V

Where with *intention* I have err'd,
  No other plea I have,
But, *Thou art good*; and Goodness still
  Delighteth to forgive.

14. *Stanzas on the same Occasion*

WHY am I loth to leave this earthly scene?
  Have I so found it full of pleasing charms?
Some drops of joy with draughts of ill between;
  Some gleams of sunshine mid renewing storms:
Is it departing pangs my soul alarms?
  Or Death's unlovely, dreary, dark abode?
For guilt, for guilt, my terrors are in arms;
  I tremble to approach an angry GOD,
And justly smart beneath his sin-avenging rod.

Fain would I say, 'Forgive my foul offence!'
  Fain promise never more to disobey;
But, should my Author health again dispense,
  Again I might desert fair Virtue's way;

Again in Folly's path might go astray;
  Again exalt the brute and sink the man;
Then how should I for Heavenly Mercy pray,
  Who act so counter Heavenly Mercy's plan?
Who sin so oft have mourn'd, yet to temptation ran?

O Thou, Great Governor of all below!
  If I may dare a lifted eye to thee,
Thy nod can make the tempest cease to blow,
  Or still the tumult of the raging sea:
With that controuling pow'r assist ev'n me,
  Those headlong, furious passions to confine;
For all unfit I feel my powers to be,
  To rule their torrent in th' allowed line;
O, aid me with Thy help, *Omnipotence Divine*!

15. *A Prayer*, *Under the Pressure of violent Anguish*

O THOU great Being! what Thou art,
  Surpasses me to know:
Yet sure I am, that known to Thee
  Are all Thy works below.

Thy creature here before Thee stands,
  All wretched and distrest;
Yet sure those ills that wring my soul
  Obey Thy high behest.

Sure Thou, Almighty, canst not act
  From cruelty or wrath!
O, free my weary eyes from tears,
  Or close them fast in death!

But if I must afflicted be,
  To suit some wise design;
Then, man my soul with firm resolves
  To bear and not repine!

16. [*Though fickle Fortune has deceiv'd me*]

THOUGH fickle Fortune has deceiv'd me,
She promis'd fair and perform'd but ill;
Of mistress, friends, and wealth bereav'd me,
Yet I bear a heart shall support me still.—

I'll act with prudence as far 's I'm able,
But if success I must never find,
Then come Misfortune, I bid thee welcome,
I'll meet thee with an undaunted mind.—

17. [*O raging Fortune's withering blast*]

O RAGING Fortune's withering blast
Has laid my leaf full low! O
O raging Fortune's withering blast
Has laid my leaf full low! O
My stem was fair my bud was green
My blossom sweet did blow; O
The dew fell fresh, the sun rose mild,
And made my branches grow; O
But luckless Fortune's northern storms
Laid a' my blossoms low, O
But luckless Fortune's northern storms
Laid a' my blossoms low, O.

18. *Extempore*

O WHY the deuce should I repine,
And be an ill foreboder;
I'm twenty-three, and five feet nine,
I'll go and be a sodger.

I gat some gear wi' meikle care,
I held it weel thegither;
But now its gane, and something mair,
I'll go and be a sodger.

19. *The First Psalm*

THE man, in life where-ever plac'd,
  Hath happiness in store,
Who walks not in the wicked's way,
  Nor learns their guilty lore!

Nor from the seat of scornful Pride
  Casts forth his eyes abroad,
But with humility and awe
  Still walks before his GOD.

That man shall flourish like the trees
  Which by the streamlets grow;
The fruitful top is spread on high,
  And firm the root below.

But he whose blossom buds in guilt
  Shall to the ground be cast,
And like the rootless stubble tost,
  Before the sweeping blast.

For why? that GOD the good adore
  Hath giv'n them peace and rest,
But hath decreed that wicked men
  Shall ne'er be truly blest.

20. *The* First Six Verses *of the Ninetieth Psalm*

O THOU, the first, the greatest friend
  Of all the human race!
Whose strong right hand has ever been
  Their stay and dwelling-place!

Before the mountains heav'd their heads
  Beneath Thy forming hand,
Before this ponderous globe itself
  Arose at Thy command:

That Pow'r which rais'd and still upholds
  This universal frame,
From countless, unbeginning time
  Was ever still the same.

Those mighty periods of years
  Which seem to us so vast,
Appear no more before Thy sight
  Than yesterday that's past.

Thou giv'st the word; Thy creature, man,
  Is to existence brought;
Again Thou say'st, 'Ye sons of men,
  'Return ye into nought!'

Thou layest them with all their cares
  In everlasting sleep;
As with a flood Thou tak'st them off
  With overwhelming sweep.

They flourish like the morning flow'r,
  In beauty's pride array'd;
But long ere night cut down it lies
  All wither'd and decay'd.

21. *Song*

Tune, The Weaver and his shuttle O

My father was a farmer upon the Carrick border O
And carefully he bred me, in decency and order O
He bade me act a manly part, though I had ne'er a farthing O
For without an honest manly heart, no man was worth regarding. O

Chorus Row de dow &c.

Then out into the world my course I did determine. O
Tho' to be rich was not my wish, yet to be great was charming. O
My talents they were not the worst; not yet my education: O
Resolv'd was I, at least to try, to mend my situation. O

In many a way, and vain essay, I courted fortune's favor; O
Some cause unseen, still stept between, and frustrate each endeavor; O
Some times by foes I was o'erpower'd; sometimes by friends forsaken; O
And when my hope was at the top, I still was worst mistaken. O

Then sore harass'd, and tir'd at last, with fortune's vain delusion; O
I dropt my schemes, like idle dreams; and came to this conclusion; O
The past was bad, and the future hid; its good or ill untryed; O
But the present hour was in my pow'r, and so I would enjoy it, O

No help, nor hope, nor view had I; nor person to befriend me; O
So I must toil, and sweat and moil, and labor to sustain me, O
To plough and sow, to reap and mow, my father bred me early, O
For one, he said, to labor bred, was a match for fortune fairly, O

Thus all obscure, unknown, and poor, thro' life I'm doom'd to wander, O
Till down my weary bones I lay in everlasting slumber; O
No view nor care, but shun whate'er might breed me pain or sorrow; O
I live today as well 's I may, regardless of tomorrow, O

But chearful still, I am as well as a Monarch in a palace; O
Tho' fortune's frown still hunts me down with all her wonted malice: O
I make indeed, my daily bread, but ne'er can make it farther; O
But as daily bread is all I heed, I do not much regard her. O

When sometimes by my labor I earn a little money, O
Some unforeseen misfortune comes generally upon me; O
Mischance, mistake, or by neglect, or my good-natur'd folly; O
But come what will I've sworn it still, I'll ne'er be melancholy, O

All you who follow wealth and power with unremitting ardor, O
The more in this you look for bliss, you leave your view the farther; O
Had you the wealth Potosi boasts, or nations to adore you, O
A chearful honest-hearted clown I will prefer before you. O

22. *Fragment—*

Tune—Galla water—

Altho' my bed were in yon muir,
Amang the heather, in my plaidie,
Yet happy, happy would I be
Had I my dear Montgomerie's Peggy.—

When o'er the hill beat surly storms,
And winter nights were dark and rainy;
I'd seek some dell, and in my arms
I'd shelter dear Montgomerie's Peggy.—

Were I a Baron proud and high,
And horse and servants waiting ready,
Then a' 'twad gie o' joy to me,
The sharin 't with Montgomerie's Peggy.—

23. *John Barleycorn*. A Ballad*

I

THERE was three kings into the east,
Three kings both great and high,
And they hae sworn a solemn oath
John Barleycorn should die.

II

They took a plough and plough'd him down,
Put clods upon his head,
And they hae sworn a solemn oath
John Barleycorn was dead.

III

But the chearful Spring came kindly on,
And show'rs began to fall;
John Barleycorn got up again,
And sore surpris'd them all.

IV

The sultry suns of Summer came,
And he grew thick and strong,
His head weel arm'd wi' pointed spears,
That no one should him wrong.

V

The sober Autumn enter'd mild,
When he grew wan and pale;
His bending joints and drooping head
Show'd he began to fail.

VI

His colour sicken'd more and more,
He faded into age;
And then his enemies began
To show their deadly rage.

* This is partly composed on the plan of an old song known by the same name.

VII

They've taen a weapon, long and sharp,
  And cut him by the knee;
Then ty'd him fast upon a cart,
  Like a rogue for forgerie.

VIII

They laid him down upon his back,
  And cudgell'd him full sore;
They hung him up before the storm,
  And turn'd him o'er and o'er.

IX

They filled up a darksome pit
  With water to the brim,
They heaved in John Barleycorn,
  There let him sink or swim.

X

They laid him out upon the floor,
  To work him farther woe,
And still, as signs of life appear'd,
  They toss'd him to and fro.

XI

They wasted, o'er a scorching flame,
  The marrow of his bones;
But a Miller us'd him worst of all,
  For he crush'd him between two stones.

XII

And they hae taen his very heart's blood,
  And drank it round and round;
And still the more and more they drank,
  Their joy did more abound.

XIII

John Barleycorn was a hero bold,
  Of noble enterprise,
For if you do but taste his blood,
  'Twill make your courage rise.

XIV

'Twill make a man forget his woe;
'Twill heighten all his joy:
'Twill make the widow's heart to sing,
Tho' the tear were in her eye.

XV

Then let us toast John Barleycorn,
Each man a glass in hand;
And may his great posterity
Ne'er fail in old Scotland!

24. *The Death and Dying Words of Poor Mailie, The Author's only Pet Yowe, An Unco Mournfu' Tale*

As Mailie, an' her lambs thegither,
Was ae day nibbling on the tether,
Upon her cloot she coost a hitch,
An' owre she warsl'd in the ditch:
There, groaning, dying, she did ly,
When **Hughoc* he cam doytan by.

Wi' glowrin een, an' lifted han's,
Poor *Hughoc* like a statue stan's;
He saw her days were near hand ended,
But, waes my heart! he could na mend it!
He gaped wide, but naething spak,
At length poor *Mailie* silence brak.

'O thou, whase lamentable face
Appears to mourn my woefu' case!
My *dying words* attentive hear,
An' bear them to my *Master* dear.

Tell him, if e'er again he keep
As muckle gear as buy a *sheep*,
O, bid him never tye them mair,
Wi' wicked strings o' hemp or hair!

* A neibor herd-callan.

But ca' them out to park or hill,
An' let them wander at their will:
So, may his flock increase an' grow
To *scores* o' lambs, an' *packs* of woo'!

Tell him, he was a Master kin',
An' ay was guid to me an' mine;
An' now my *dying* charge I gie him,
My helpless *lambs*, I trust them wi' him.

O, bid him save their harmless lives,
Frae dogs an' tods, an' butchers' knives!
But gie them guid *cow-milk* their fill,
Till they be fit to fend themsel;
An' tent them duely, e'en an' morn,
Wi' taets o' *hay* an' ripps o' *corn*.

An' may they never learn the gaets,
Of ither vile, wanrestfu' *Pets*!
To slink thro' slaps, an' reave an' steal,
At stacks o' pease, or stocks o' kail.
So may they, like their great *forbears*,
For monie a year come thro' the sheers:
So *wives* will gie them bits o' bread,
An' *bairns* greet for them when they're dead.

My poor *toop-lamb*, my son an' heir,
O, bid him breed him up wi' care!
An' if he live to be a beast,
To pit some havins in his breast!
An' warn him, what I winna name,
To stay content wi' *yowes* at hame;
An' no to rin an' wear his cloots,
Like ither menseless, graceless brutes.

An' niest my *yowie*, silly thing,
Gude keep thee frae a *tether string*!
O, may thou ne'er forgather up,
Wi' onie blastet, moorlan *toop*;
But ay keep mind to moop an' mell,
Wi' sheep o' credit like thysel!

And now, *my bairns*, wi' my last breath,
I lea'e my blessin wi' you baith:
An' when ye think upo' your Mither,
Mind to be kind to ane anither.

Now, honest *Hughoc*, dinna fail,
To tell my Master a' my tale;
An' bid him burn this cursed *tether*,
An' for thy pains thou 'se get my blather.'

This said, poor *Mailie* turn'd her head,
An' clos'd her een amang the dead!

25. *Poor Mailie's Elegy*

LAMENT in rhyme, lament in prose,
Wi' saut tears trickling down your nose;
Our *Bardie*'s fate is at a close,
Past a' remead!
The last, sad cape-stane of his woes;
Poor Mailie 's dead!

It 's no the loss o' warl's gear,
That could sae bitter draw the tear,
Or make our *Bardie*, dowie, wear
The mourning weed:
He 's lost a friend and neebor dear,
In *Mailie* dead.

Thro' a' the town she trotted by him;
A lang half-mile she could descry him;
Wi' kindly bleat, when she did spy him,
She ran wi' speed:
A friend mair faithfu' ne'er came nigh him,
Than *Mailie* dead.

I wat she was a *sheep* o' sense,
An' could behave hersel wi' mense:
I'll say 't, she never brak a fence,
Thro' thievish greed.
Our *Bardie*, lanely, keeps the spence
Sin' *Mailie* 's dead.

Or, if he wanders up the howe,
Her living image in *her yowe*,
Comes bleating to him, owre the knowe,
For bits o' bread;
An' down the briny pearls rowe
For *Mailie* dead.

She was nae get o' moorlan tips,
Wi' tauted ket, an' hairy hips;
For her forbears were brought in ships,
Frae 'yont the TWEED:
A bonier *fleesh* ne'er cross'd the clips
Than *Mailie*'s dead.

Wae worth that man wha first did shape,
That vile, wanchancie thing—*a raep*!
It maks guid fellows girn an' gape,
Wi' chokin dread;
An' *Robin*'s bonnet wave wi' crape
For *Mailie* dead.

O, a' ye *Bards* on bonie DOON!
An' wha on AIRE your chanters tune!
Come, join the melancholious croon
O' *Robin*'s reed!
His heart will never get aboon!
His *Mailie*'s dead!

26. [*Remorse*]

I intirely agree with that judicious Philosopher Mr Smith in his excellent Theory of Moral Sentiments, that Remorse is the most painful sentiment that can embitter the human bosom. Any ordinary pitch of fortitude may bear up tolerably well, under those calamities, in the procurement of which, we ourselves have had no hand; but when our own follies or crimes, have made us miserable and wretched, to bear it up with manly firmness, and at the same time have a proper penitential sense of our misconduct,—is a glorious effort of Self-command.—

OF all the numerous ills that hurt our peace;
That press the soul, or wring the mind with anguish;
Beyond comparison the worst are those
That to our Folly, or our Guilt we owe.
In ev'ry other circumstance the mind
Has this to say, it was no deed of mine:
But, when to all the evil of misfortune
This sting is added, blame thy foolish self;
Or worser far, the pangs of keen remorse:
The tort'ring, gnawing consciousness of guilt—
Of guilt, perhaps, where we've involved others;

The young, the innocent, who fondly lov'd us;
Nay more, that very love their cause of ruin—
O! burning Hell! in all thy store of torments
There's not a keener LASH—
Lives there a man so firm who, while his heart
Feels all the bitter horrors of his crime,
Can reason down its agonizing throbs,
And, after proper purpose of amendment,
Can firmly force his jarring thoughts to peace?
O happy, happy, enviable man!
O glorious magnanimity of soul!

27. *Song*

Tune, Prepare, my dear Brethren, to the tavern let's fly, &c.

I

No Churchman am I for to rail and to write,
No Statesman nor Soldier to plot or to fight,
No sly Man of business contriving a snare,
For a big-belly'd bottle's the whole of my care.

II

The Peer I don't envy, I give him his bow;
I scorn not the Peasant, tho' ever so low;
But a club of good fellows, like those that are here,
And a bottle like this, are my glory and care.

III

Here passes the Squire on his brother—his horse;
There Centum per Centum, the Cit with his purse;
But see you the Crown how it waves in the air,
There a big-belly'd bottle still eases my care.

Song. 11 the Crown] "*D'en haut" *Huntington Library MS with a note:* *D'en haut) the motto of Sir J. Whiteford's arms, hung in Mauchline, as a tavern-sign to J. Dow, of bibipotent fame.

IV

The wife of my bosom, alas! she did die;
For sweet consolation to church I did fly;
I found that old Solomon proved it fair,
That a big-belly'd bottle 's a cure for all care.

V

I once was persuaded a venture to make;
A letter inform'd me that all was to wreck;
But the pursy old landlord just waddl'd up stairs,
With a glorious bottle that ended my cares.

VI

'Life's cares they are comforts*'—a maxim laid down
By the Bard, what d'ye call him, that wore the black
gown;
And faith I agree with th' old prig to a hair;
For a big-belly'd bottle 's a heav'n of care.

A Stanza added in a Mason Lodge:

Then fill up a bumper and make it o'erflow,
And honours masonic prepare for to throw;
May ev'ry true Brother of th' Compass and Square
Have a big-belly'd bottle when harass'd with care.

28. *On Ja^s Grieve, Laird of Boghead, Tarbolton*

HERE lies Boghead amang the dead,
In hopes to get salvation;
But if such as he, in Heav'n may be,
Then welcome, hail! damnation—.

28A. *On an Innkeeper in Tarbolton—*

HERE lies 'mang ither useless matters,
A. Manson wi' his endless clatters.—

* Young's Night Thoughts.

On Ja^s Grieve. Holograph in a copy of Poems *1787 subtitled* A sanctimonious rascal of the first water.

29. *Song.—In the character of a ruined Farmer—*

Tune, Go from my window, Love, do!—

I

THE sun he is sunk in the west;
All creatures retired to rest,
While here I sit, all sore beset,
With sorrow, grief, and woe:
And it's O, fickle Fortune, O!

2

The prosperous man is asleep,
Nor hears how the whirlwinds sweep;
But Misery and I must watch
The surly tempest blow:
And it's O, fickle, &c.

3

There lies the dear Partner of my breast;
Her cares for a moment at rest:
Must I see thee, my youthful pride,
Thus brought so very low!
And it's O, fickle &c.

4

There lie my sweet babies in her arms;
No anxious fear their little hearts alarms;
But for their sake my heart does ache,
With many a bitter throe:
And it's O, fickle &c.

5

I once was by Fortune carest;
I once could relieve the distrest:
Now life's poor support, hardly earn'd,
  My fate will scarce bestow:
And it 's O, fickle &c.

6

No comfort, no comfort I have!
How welcome to me were the grave!
But then my wife and children dear—
  O, whither would they go!
And it 's O, fickle &c.

7

O whither, O whither shall I turn!
All friendless, forsaken, forlorn!
For in this world, Rest or Peace,
  I never more shall know!
And it 's O, fickle Fortune, O!

30. *Mary Morison*

Tune, Duncan Davison

O MARY, at thy window be,
  It is the wish'd, the trysted hour;
Those smiles and glances let me see,
  That make the miser's treasure poor:
How blythely wad I bide the stoure,
  A weary slave frae sun to sun;
Could I the rich reward secure,
  The lovely Mary Morison!

Yestreen when to the trembling string
  The dance gaed through the lighted ha',
To thee my fancy took its wing,
  I sat, but neither heard, nor saw:
Though this was fair, and that was braw,
  And yon the toast of a' the town,
I sigh'd, and said amang them a',
  'Ye are na Mary Morison.'

O Mary, canst thou wreck his peace,
  Wha for thy sake wad gladly die!
Or canst thou break that heart of his,
  Whase only faute is loving thee!
If love for love thou wilt na gie,
  At least be pity to me shown;
A thought ungentle canna be
  The thought o' Mary Morison.

II. Poems 1784–1785

MOSSGIEL

31. *Epitaph on my own friend, and my father's friend, Wm Muir in Tarbolton Miln—*

AN honest man here lies at rest
As e'er God with his image blest.
The friend of man, the friend of truth;
The friend of Age, and guide of Youth:
Few hearts like his with virtue warm'd,
Few heads with knowledge so inform'd:
If there 's another world, he lives in bliss;
If there is none, he made the best of this.—

32–37. *Epitaphs*

32. *On a Celebrated Ruling Elder*

Here Sowter **** in Death does sleep;
   To H–ll, if he 's gane thither,
Satan, gie him thy gear to keep,
   He'll haud it weel thegither.

33. *On a Noisy Polemic*

Below thir stanes lie Jamie's banes;
   O Death, it 's my opinion,
Thou ne'er took such a bleth'ran b–tch,
   Into thy dark dominion!

34. *On Wee Johnie*

Hic jacet *wee* Johnie

Whoe'er thou art, O reader, know,
That Death has murder'd Johnie;
An' here his *body* lies fu' low—
For *saul* he ne'er had ony.

35. *For the Author's Father*

O ye whose cheek the tear of pity stains,
Draw near with pious rev'rence and attend!
Here lie the loving Husband's dear remains,
The tender Father, and the gen'rous Friend.

The pitying Heart that felt for human Woe;
The dauntless heart that fear'd no human Pride;
The Friend of Man, to vice alone a foe;
'For ev'n his failings lean'd to Virtue's side.*'

36. *For R. A. Esq;*

Know thou, O stranger to the fame
Of this much lov'd, much honor'd name!
(For none that knew him need be told)
A warmer heart Death ne'er made cold.

37. *For G. H. Esq;*

The poor man weeps—here G——N sleeps,
Whom canting wretches blam'd:
But with *such as he*, where'er he be,
May I be *sav'd* or *d——'d*!

* Goldsmith.

38. *A Fragment*

The Earl of Glencairn's

I

WHEN *Guilford* good our Pilot stood,
An' did our hellim thraw, man,
Ae night, at tea, began a plea,
Within *America*, man:
Then up they gat the maskin-pat,
And in the sea did jaw, man;
An' did nae less, in full Congress,
Than quite refuse our law, man.

II

Then thro' the lakes *Montgomery* takes,
I wat he was na slaw, man;
Down *Lowrie's burn* he took a turn,
And *C–rl–t–n* did ca', man:
But yet, whatreck, he, at *Quebec*,
Montgomery-like did fa', man,
Wi' sword in hand, before his band,
Amang his en'mies a', man.

III

Poor *Tammy G–ge* within a cage
Was kept at *Boston-ha'*, man;
Till *Willie H––e* took o'er the knowe
For *Philadelphia*, man:
Wi' sword an' gun he thought a sin
Guid Christian bluid to draw, man;
But at *New-York*, wi' knife an' fork,
Sir Loin he hacked sma', man.

IV

B–rg––ne gaed up, like spur an' whip,
  Till *Fraser* brave did fa', man;
Then lost his way, ae misty day,
  In *Saratoga* shaw, man.
C–rnw–ll–s fought as lang 's he dought,
  An' did the Buckskins claw, man;
But *Cl–nt–n*'s glaive frae rust to save
  He hung it to the wa', man.

V

Then *M–nt–gue*, an' *Guilford* too,
  Began to fear a fa', man;
And *S–ckv–lle* doure, wha stood the stoure,
  The German Chief to thraw, man:
For Paddy *B–rke*, like ony Turk,
  Nae mercy had at a', man;
An' *Charlie F–x* threw by the box,
  An' lows'd his tinkler jaw, man.

VI

Then *R–ck–ngh–m* took up the game;
  Till Death did on him ca', man;
When *Sh–lb–rne* meek held up his cheek,
  Conform to Gospel law, man:
Saint Stephen's boys, wi' jarring noise,
  They did his measures thraw, man,
For *N–rth* an' *F–x* united stocks,
  An' bore him to the wa', man.

VII

Then Clubs an' Hearts were *Charlie*'s cartes,
  He swept the stakes awa', man,
Till the Diamond's Ace, of *Indian* race,
  Led him a sair *faux pas*, man:
The Saxon lads, wi' loud placads,
  On *Chatham's Boy* did ca', man;
An' Scotland drew her pipe an' blew,
  'Up, Willie, waur them a', man!'

VIII

Behind the throne then *Gr–nv–lle* 's gone,
  A secret word or twa, man;
While slee *D–nd–s* arous'd the class
  Be-north the Roman wa', man:

An' *Chatham*'s wraith, in heav'nly graith,
(Inspired Bardies saw, man)
Wi' kindling eyes cry'd, '*Willie*, rise!
'Would I hae fear'd them a', man!'

IX

But, word an' blow, *N–rth, F–x, and Co.*
Gowff'd *Willie* like a ba', man,
Till *Suthron* raise, an' coost their claise
Behind him in a raw, man:
An' *Caledon* threw by the drone,
An' did her whittle draw, man;
An' swoor fu' rude, thro' dirt an' blood,
To mak it guid in law, man.

* * * * * *

39. *Address to the Unco Guid, or the Rigidly Righteous*

My Son, these maxims make a rule,
And lump them ay thegither;
The Rigid Righteous *is a fool,*
The Rigid Wise *anither:*
The cleanest corn that e'er was dight
May hae some pyles o' caff in;
So ne'er a fellow-creature slight
For random fits o' daffin.
SOLOMON.—Eccles. ch. vii. vers. 16.

I

O YE wha are sae guid yoursel,
Sae pious and sae holy,
Ye've nought to do but mark and tell
Your Neebours' fauts and folly!
Whase life is like a weel-gaun mill,
Supply'd wi' store o' water,
The heaped happer 's ebbing still,
And still the clap plays clatter.

II

Hear me, ye venerable Core,
As counsel for poor mortals,
That frequent pass douce Wisdom's door
For glaikit Folly's portals;

I, for their thoughtless, careless sakes
  Would here propone defences,
Their donsie tricks, their black mistakes,
  Their failings and mischances.

III

Ye see your state wi' theirs compar'd,
  And shudder at the niffer,
But cast a moment's fair regard
  What maks the mighty differ;
Discount what scant occasion gave,
  That purity ye pride in,
And (what 's aft mair than a' the lave)
  Your better art o' hiding.

IV

Think, when your castigated pulse
  Gies now and then a wallop,
What ragings must his veins convulse,
  That still eternal gallop:
Wi' wind and tide fair i' your tail,
  Right on ye scud your sea-way;
But, in the teeth o' baith to sail,
  It maks an unco leeway.

V

See Social-life and Glee sit down,
  All joyous and unthinking,
Till, quite transmugrify'd, they're grown
  Debauchery and Drinking:
O would they stay to calculate
  Th' eternal consequences;
Or your more dreaded h–ll to state,
  D–mnation of expences!

VI

Ye high, exalted, virtuous Dames,
  Ty'd up in godly laces,
Before ye gie poor *Frailty* names,
  Suppose a change o' cases;
A dear-lov'd lad, convenience snug,
  A treacherous inclination—
But, let me whisper i' your lug,
  Ye're aiblins nae temptation.

VII

Then gently scan your brother Man,
  Still gentler sister Woman;
Tho' they may gang a kennin wrang,
  To step aside is human:
One point must still be greatly dark,
  The moving *Why* they do it;
And just as lamely can ye mark,
  How far perhaps they rue it.

VIII

Who made the heart, 'tis *He* alone
  Decidedly can try us,
He knows each chord its various tone,
  Each spring its various bias:
Then at the balance let 's be mute,
  We never can adjust it;
What 's *done* we partly may compute,
  But know not what 's *resisted.*

40. *The Ronalds of the Bennals*

In Tarbolton, ye ken, there are proper young men,
  And proper young lasses and a', man:
But ken ye the Ronalds that live in the Bennals,
  They carry the gree frae them a', man.

Their father 's a laird, and weel he can spare 't,
  Braid money to tocher them a', man,
To proper young men, he'll clink in the hand
  Gowd guineas a hunder or twa, man.

There 's ane they ca' Jean, I'll warrant ye've seen
  As bonie a lass or as braw, man,
But for sense and guid taste she'll vie wi' the best,
  And a conduct that beautifies a', man.

The charms o' the min', the langer they shine,
  The mair admiration they draw, man;
While peaches and cherries, and roses and lilies,
  They fade and they wither awa, man.

If ye be for Miss Jean, tak this frae a frien',
  A hint o' a rival or twa, man,
The Laird o' Blackbyre wad gang through the fire,
  If that wad entice her awa, man.

The Laird o' Braehead has been on his speed,
  For mair than a towmond or twa, man;
The Laird o' the Ford will straught on a board,
  If he canna get her at a', man.

Then Anna comes in, the pride o' her kin,
  The boast of our bachelors a', man:
Sae sonsy and sweet, sae fully complete,
  She steals our affections awa, man.

If I should detail the pick and the wale
  O' lasses that live here awa, man,
The faut wad be mine, if she didna shine
  The sweetest and best o' them a', man.

I lo'e her mysel, but darena weel tell,
  My poverty keeps me in awe, man,
For making o' rhymes, and working at times,
  Does little or naething at a', man.

Yet I wadna choose to let her refuse,
  Nor hae 't in her power to say na, man,
For though I be poor, unnoticed, obscure,
  My stomach 's as proud as them a', man.

Though I canna ride in weel-booted pride,
  And flee o'er the hills like a craw, man.
I can haud up my head wi' the best o' the breed,
  Though fluttering ever so braw, man.

My coat and my vest, they are Scotch o' the best,
  O' pairs o' guid breeks I hae twa, man:
And stockings and pumps to put on my stumps,
  And ne'er a wrang steek in them a', man.

My sarks they are few, but five o' them new,
  Twal'-hundred, as white as the snaw, man,
A ten-shillings hat, a Holland cravat;
  There are no mony poets sae braw, man.

I never had freens weel stockit in means,
  To leave me a hundred or twa, man,
Nae weel-tocher'd aunts, to wait on their drants
  And wish them in hell for it a', man.

I never was cannie for hoarding o' money,
  Or claughtin 't together at a', man,
I've little to spend and naething to lend,
  But devil a shilling I awe, man.

41. *The Tarbolton Lasses*

If ye gae up to yon hill-tap,
  Ye'll there see bonie Peggy:
She kens her father is a laird,
  And she forsooth 's a leddy.

There 's Sophy tight, a lassie bright,
  Besides a handsome fortune:
Wha canna win her in a night
  Has little art in courtin.

Gae down by Faile, and taste the ale,
  And tak a look o' Mysie;
She 's dour and din, a deil within,
  But ablins she may please ye.

If she be shy, her sister try,
  Ye'll may be fancy Jenny:
If ye'll dispense wi' want o' sense—
  She kens hersel she 's bonnie.

As ye gae up by yon hillside,
  Spier in for bonnie Bessy:
She'll gie ye a beck, and bid ye light,
  And handsomely address ye.

There 's few sae bonny, nane sae guid
  In a' King George' dominion;
If ye should doubt the truth o' this—
  It 's Bessy's ain opinion.

42. *Song—*

Tune—Bonie Dundee—

IN Mauchline there dwells six proper young Belles,
The pride of the place and its neighbourhood a',
Their carriage and dress a stranger would guess,
In Lon'on or Paris they 'd gotten it a':
Miss Miller is fine, Miss Murkland 's divine,
Miss Smith she has wit and Miss Betty is braw;
There 's beauty and fortune to get wi' Miss Morton,
But ARMOUR's the jewel for me o' them a'.—

43. *O leave novels &c.*

O LEAVE novels, ye Mauchline belles,
Ye're safer at your spinning wheel;
Such witching books, are baited hooks
For rakish rooks like Rob Mossgiel.
Your fine Tom Jones and Grandisons
They make your youthful fancies reel;
They heat your brains, and fire your veins,
And then you're prey for Rob Mossgiel.

Beware a tongue that 's smoothly hung;
  A heart that warmly seems to feel;
That feelin heart but acks a part,
  'Tis rakish art in Rob Mossgiel.
The frank address, the soft caress,
  Are worse than poisoned darts of steel,
The frank address, and politesse,
  Are all finesse in Rob Mossgiel.

44. *A Fragment—*

Tune, I had a horse and I had nae mair—

WHEN first I came to Stewart Kyle
  My mind it was nae steady,
Where e'er I gaed, where e'er I rade,
  A Mistress still I had ay:
But when I came roun' by Mauchlin town,
  Not dreadin' any body,
My heart was caught before I thought
  And by a Mauchlin Lady—

45. *Green grow the Rashes. A Fragment*

CHORUS

Green grow the rashes, O;
Green grow the rashes, O;
The sweetest hours that e'er I spend,
Are spent amang the lasses, O.

I

THERE'S nought but care on ev'ry han',
In ev'ry hour that passes, O:
What signifies the life o' man,
An' 'twere na for the lasses, O.
Green grow, &c.

II

The warly race may riches chase,
An' riches still may fly them, O;
An' tho' at last they catch them fast,
Their hearts can ne'er enjoy them, O.
Green grow, &c.

III

But gie me a canny hour at e'en ,
My arms about my Dearie, O;
An' warly cares, an' warly men,
May a' gae tapsalteerie, O!
Green grow, &c.

IV

For you sae douse, ye sneer at this,
Ye're nought but senseless asses, O:
The wisest Man the warl' saw,
He dearly lov'd the lasses, O.
Green grow, &c.

V

Auld Nature swears, the lovely Dears
Her noblest work she classes, O:
Her prentice han' she try'd on man,
An' then she made the lasses, O.
Green grow, &c.

46. *Song*—

Tune: Black Joke—

My girl she 's airy, she 's buxom and gay,
Her breath is as sweet as the blossoms in May;
  A touch of her lips it ravishes quite.
She 's always good natur'd, good humor'd and free;
She dances, she glances, she smiles with a glee;
  Her eyes are the lightenings of joy and delight:
Her slender neck, her handsome waist,
Her hair well buckl'd, her stays well lac'd,
Her taper white leg with an et, and a, c,
For her a, b, e, d, and her c, u, n, t,
  And Oh, for the joys of a long winter night!!!

47. *Epistle to J. R******, Enclosing some Poems*

O rough, rude, ready-witted R******,
The wale o' cocks for fun an' drinkin!
There 's monie godly folks are thinkin,
          Your *dreams** an' tricks
Will send you, Korah-like, a sinkin,
          Straught to auld Nick's.

* A certain humorous *dream* of his was then making a noise in the country-side.

Ye hae sae monie cracks an' cants,
And in your wicked, druken rants,
Ye mak a devil o' the *Saunts*,
An' fill them fou;
And then their failings, flaws an' wants,
Are a' seen thro'.

Hypocrisy, in mercy spare it!
That *holy robe*, O dinna tear it!
Spare 't for their sakes wha aften wear it,
The lads in *black*;
But your curst wit, when it comes near it,
Rives 't aff their back.

Think, wicked Sinner, wha ye're skaithing:
It 's just the *Blue-gown* badge an' claithing,
O' Saunts; tak that, ye lea'e them naething,
To ken them by,
Frae ony unregenerate Heathen,
Like you or I.

I've sent you here, some rhymin ware,
A' that I bargain'd for, an' mair;
Sae when ye hae an hour to spare,
I will expect,
Yon *Sang** ye'll sen 't, wi' cannie care,
And no neglect.

Tho' faith, sma' heart hae I to sing!
My Muse dow scarcely spread her wing:
I've play'd mysel a bonie *spring*,
An' *danc'd* my fill!
I'd better gaen an' sair't the king,
At Bunker's hill.

'Twas ae night lately, in my fun,
I gaed a rovin wi' the gun,
An' brought a *Paitrick* to the *grun'*,
A bonie *hen*,
And, as the twilight was begun,
Thought nane wad ken.

* A *Song* he had promised the Author.

The poor, wee thing was *little hurt*;
I *straiket* it a wee for sport,
Ne'er thinkan they wad fash me for 't;
But, Deil-ma-care!
Somebody tells the *Poacher-Court*,
The hale affair.

Some auld, us'd hands had taen a note,
That *sic a hen* had got a *shot*;
I was suspected for the plot;
I scorn'd to lie;
So gat the whissle o' my groat,
An' pay't the *fee*.

But by my *gun*, o' guns the wale,
An' by my *pouther* an' my *hail*,
An' by my *hen*, an' by her *tail*,
I vow an' swear!
The *Game* shall Pay, owre moor an' *dail*,
For this, niest year.

As soon 's the *clockin-time* is by,
An' the *wee powts* begun to cry,
L—d, I 'se hae sportin by an' by,
For my *gowd guinea*;
Tho' I should herd the *buckskin* kye
For 't, in Virginia!

Trowth, they had muckle for to blame!
'Twas neither broken wing nor limb,
But twa-three *draps* about the *wame*
Scarce thro' the *feathers*;
An' baith a *yellow George* to claim,
An' *thole* their *blethers*!

It pits me ay as mad 's a hare;
So I can rhyme nor write nae mair;
But *pennyworths* again is fair,
When time 's expedient:
Meanwhile I am, respected Sir,
Your most obedient.

48. *Lines Addressed to Mr. John Ranken*

AE day, as Death, that grusome carl,
Was driving to the tither warl',
A mixie-maxie motely squad,
And mony a guilt-bespotted lad;
Black gowns of each denomination,
And thieves of every rank and station,
From him that wears the star and garter
To him that wintles in a halter:
Asham'd himself to see the wretches,
He mutters, glow'ring at the bitches,
'By G–d I'll not be seen behint them,
'Nor 'mang the sp'ritual core present them,
'Without, at least, ae honest man,
'To grace this damn'd infernal clan.'
By Adamhill a glance he threw,
'L—d, G–d!' quoth he, 'I have it now,
'There 's just the man I want, in faith,'
And quickly stopped Ranken's breath.

49. *Verses*

Addressed to the above J. Ranken, on his writing to the Poet, that a girl in that part of the country was with child by him.

I AM a keeper of the law
In some sma' points, altho' not a';
Some people tell gin I fa',
  Ae way or ither,
The breaking of ae point, tho' sma',
  Breaks a' thegither.

I hae been in for 't ance or twice,
And winna say o'er far for thrice,
Yet never met with that surprise
  That broke my rest,
But now a rumour 's like to rise,
  A whaup 's i' the nest.

50. *Lines*

Wrote by Burns, while on his death-bed, to J—n R—k-n, Ayrshire, and forwarded to him immediately after the Poet's death.

HE who of R—k–n sang, lies stiff and dead,
And a green grassy hillock hides his head;
Alas! Alas! a devilish change indeed.

51. *Epistle to Davie, a Brother Poet*

January—

I

WHILE winds frae off BEN-LOMOND blaw,
And bar the doors wi' driving snaw,
  And hing us owre the ingle,
I set me down, to pass the time,
And spin a verse or twa o' rhyme,
  In hamely, *westlin* jingle.
While frosty winds blaw in the drift,
  Ben to the chimla lug,
I grudge a wee the *Great-folk*'s gift,
  That live sae bien an' snug:
    I tent less, and want less
      Their roomy fire-side;
    But hanker, and canker,
      To see their cursed pride.

II

It 's hardly in a body's pow'r,
To keep, at times, frae being sour,
  To see how things are shar'd;
How *best o' chiels* are whyles in want,
While *Coofs* on countless thousands rant,
  And ken na how to wair 't:
But DAVIE lad, ne'er fash your head,
  Tho' we hae little gear,
We're fit to win our daily bread,
  As lang 's we're hale and fier:

Epistle to Davie. Title in Adam MS An Epistle to Davy, a brother Poe Lover, Ploughman and Fiddler. Jan: 1785.

'Mair spier na, nor fear na,'*
  Auld age ne'er mind a feg;
The last o't, the warst o't,
  Is only but to beg.

III

To lye in kilns and barns at e'en,
When banes are craz'd, and bluid is thin,
  Is, doubtless, great distress!
Yet then *content* could make us blest;
Ev'n then, sometimes we'd snatch a taste
  Of truest happiness.
The honest heart that 's free frae a'
  Intended fraud or guile,
However Fortune kick the ba',
  Has ay some cause to smile:
    And mind still, you'll find still,
      A comfort this nae sma';
    Nae mair then, we'll care then,
      Nae *farther* we can *fa'*.

IV

What tho', like Commoners of air,
We wander out, we know not where,
  But either house or hal'?
Yet *Nature*'s charms, the hills and woods,
The sweeping vales, and foaming floods,
  Are free alike to all.
In days when Daisies deck the ground,
  And Blackbirds whistle clear,
With honest joy, our hearts will bound,
  To see the *coming* year:
    On braes when we please then,
      We'll sit and *sowth* a tune;
    Syne *rhyme* till 't, we'll time till 't,
      And sing 't when we hae done.

V

It 's no in titles nor in rank;
It 's no in wealth like *Lon'on Bank*,
  To purchase peace and rest;
It 's no in makin muckle, *mair*:
It 's no in books; it 's no in Lear,
  To make us truly blest:

* Ramsay.

If Happiness hae not her seat
  And center in the breast,
We may be *wise*, or *rich*, or *great*,
  But never can be *blest*:
    Nae treasures, nor pleasures
      Could make us happy lang;
    The *heart* ay 's the part ay,
      That makes us right or wrang.

VI

Think ye, that sic as *you* and *I*,
Wha drudge and drive thro' wet and dry,
  Wi' never-ceasing toil;
Think ye, are we less blest than they,
Wha scarcely tent us in their way,
  As hardly worth their while?
Alas! how aft, in haughty mood,
  GOD's creatures they oppress!
Or else, neglecting a' that 's guid,
  They riot in excess!
    Baith careless, and fearless,
      Of either Heaven or Hell;
    Esteeming, and deeming,
      It a' an idle tale!

VII

Then lest us chearfu' acquiesce;
Nor make our scanty Pleasures less,
  By pining at our state:
And, ev'n should Misfortunes come,
I, here wha sit, hae met wi' some,
  An 's thankfu' for them yet.
They gie the wit of *Age to Youth*;
  They let us ken oursel;
They make us see the naked truth,
  The *real* guid and ill.
    Tho' losses, and crosses,
      Be lessons right severe,
    There 's *wit* there, ye'll get there,
      Ye'll find nae other where.

VIII

But tent me, DAVIE, *Ace o' Hearts*!
(To say aught less wad wrang the *cartes*,
  And flatt'ry I detest)
This life has joys for you and I;
And joys that riches ne'er could buy;
  And joys the very best.
There 's a' the *Pleasures o' the Heart*,
  The *Lover* and the *Frien'*;
Ye hae your MEG, your dearest part,
  And I my darling JEAN!
    It warms me, it charms me,
      To mention but her *name*:
    It heats me, it beets me,
      And sets me a' on flame!

IX

O, all ye *Pow'rs* who rule above!
O THOU, whose very self art *love*!
  THOU know'st my words sincere!
The *life blood* streaming thro' my heart,
Or my more dear *Immortal part*,
  Is not more fondly dear!
When heart-corroding care and grief
  Deprive my soul of rest,
Her dear idea brings relief,
  And solace to my breast.
    Thou BEING, Allseeing,
      O hear my fervent pray'r!
    Still take her, and make her,
      THY most peculiar care!

X

All hail! ye tender feelings dear!
The smile of love, the friendly tear,
  The sympathetic glow!
Long since, this world's thorny ways
Had number'd out my weary days,
  Had it not been for you!
Fate still has blest me with a friend,
  In ev'ry care and ill;
And oft a more *endearing* band,
  A *tye* more tender still.

It lightens, it brightens,
The tenebrific scene,
To meet with, and greet with,
My Davie or my Jean!

XI

O, how that *name* inspires my style!
The words come skelpan, rank and file,
Amaist before I ken!
The ready measure rins as fine,
As *Phœbus* and the famous *Nine*
Were glowran owre my pen.
My spavet *Pegasus* will limp,
Till ance he 's fairly het;
And then he'll hilch, and stilt, and jimp,
And rin an unco fit:
But least then, the beast then,
Should rue this hasty ride,
I'll light now, and dight now,
His sweaty, wizen'd hide.

52. *The Holy Tulzie—*

Blockheads with reason wicked Wits abhor,
But Fool with Fool is barbarous civil war.—
Pope—

O a' ye pious, godly Flocks
Weel fed in pastures orthodox,
Wha now will keep you frae the fox,
Or worryin tykes?
Or wha will tent the waifs and crocks
About the dykes?

The twa best Herds in a' the west
That e'er gae gospel horns a blast
This five and fifty simmers past,
O dool to tell!
Hae had a bitter, black outcast
Atween themsel.—

The Holy Tulzie. Note in B.M. MS Egerton 1656: The following was the first of my poetical productions that saw the light.—I gave a copy of it to a particular friend of mine who was very fond of these things, and told him—'I did not know who was the Author, but that I had got a copy of it by accident.'—The occasion was a bitter and shameless quarrel between two Revd Gentlemen—Mr Moodie of Riccarton and Mr Russel of Kilmarnock.—It was at the time when the hue and cry against patronage was at the worst.

O Moodie man, and wordy Russel,
How could ye breed sae vile a bustle?
Ye'll see how New-light Herds will whistle,
And think it fine!
The L—d's cause gat na sic a twissle
Since I hae min'.—

O Sirs! wha ever wad expeckit
Your duty ye wad sae negleckit?
You wha was ne'er by Lairds respeckit,
To wear the Plaid;
But by the vera Brutes eleckit
To be their Guide.—

What Flock wi' Moodie's Flock could rank,
Sae hale and hearty every shank?
Nae poison'd Ariminian stank
He loot them taste;
But Calvin's fountain-head they drank,
That was a feast!

The Fulmart, Wil-cat, Brock and Tod
Weel kend his voice thro' a' the wood;
He knew their ilka hole and road,
Baith out and in:
And liked weel to shed their blood,
And sell their skin.—

And wha like Russel tell'd his tale;
His voice was heard o'er moor and dale:
He kend the L—d's sheep ilka tail,
O'er a' the height;
And tell'd gin they were sick or hale
At the first sight.—

He fine a maingie sheep could scrub,
And nobly swing the Gospel-club;
Or New-light Herds could nicely drub,
And pay their skin;
Or hing them o'er the burning dub,
Or shute them in.—

Sic twa——O, do I live to see 't,
Sic famous twa sud disagree't
And names like, 'Villain, Hypocrite,'
Each other giein;
While enemies wi' laughin spite
Say, 'Neither 's liein.'—

O ye wha tent the Gospel-fauld,
Thee, Duncan deep, and Peebles shaul,
And chiefly great Apostle Auld,
We trust in thee,
That thou wilt work them het and cauld
To gar them gree.—

Consider, Sirs, how we're beset;
There 's scarce a new Herd that we get
But comes frae 'mang that cursed Set,
I winna name:
I trust in Heaven, to see them het
Yet in a flame.—

There 's D'rymple has been lang our fae;
M^c^gill has wrought us meikle wae;
And that curst rascal ca'd M^c^quhey;
And baith the Shaws,
Wha aft hae made us black and blae
Wi' vengefu' paws.—

Auld Wodrow lang has wrought mischief,
We trusted death wad bring relief;
But he has gotten, to our grief,
Ane to succeed him;
A chap will soundly buff our beef
I meikle dread him.—

And mony mae that I could tell
Wha fair and openly rebel;
Forby Turn-coats amang oursel,
There 's Smith for ane;
I doubt he 's but a Gray-neck still
And that ye'll fin'.—

O a' ye flocks o'er a' the hills,
By mosses, meadows, moors and fells,
Come join your counsels and your skills
To cowe the Lairds,
And get the Brutes the power themsels
To chuse their Herds.—

Then Orthodoxy yet may prance,
And Learning in a woody dance;
And that curst cur ca'd Common Sense
Wha bites sae sair,
Be banish'd o'er the seas to France,
Let him bark there.—

[Then Shaw's and Dalrymples eloquence,
M'—ll's close nervous excellence,
M'Q——e's pathetic manly sense,
And guid M'——h,
Wi' S—th wha thro' the heart can glance,
May a' pack aff.]

53. *Holy Willie's Prayer—*

And send the Godly in a pet to pray—
POPE.

Argument.

Holy Willie was a rather oldish batchelor Elder in the parish of Mauchline, and much and justly famed for that polemical chattering which ends in tippling Orthodoxy, and for that Spiritualized Bawdry which refines to Liquorish Devotion.——In a Sessional process with a gentleman in Mauchline, a Mr Gavin Hamilton, Holy Willie, and his priest, father Auld, after full hearing in the Presbytry of Ayr, came off but second best; owing partly to the oratorical powers of Mr Robt Aiken, Mr Hamilton's Counsel; but chiefly to Mr Hamilton's being one of the most irreproachable and truly respectable characters in the country.—On losing his Process, the Muse overheard him at his devotions as follows—

O THOU that in the heavens does dwell!
Wha, as it pleases best thysel,
Sends ane to heaven and ten to h–ll,
A' for thy glory!
And no for ony gude or ill
They've done before thee.—

I bless and praise thy matchless might,
When thousands thou has left in night,
That I am here before thy sight,
For gifts and grace,
A burning and a shining light
To a' this place.—

What was I, or my generation,
That I should get such exaltation?
I, wha deserv'd most just damnation,
For broken laws
Sax thousand years ere my creation,
Thro' Adam's cause!

When from my mother's womb I fell,
Thou might hae plunged me deep in hell,
To gnash my gooms, and weep, and wail,
In burning lakes,
Where damned devils roar and yell
Chain'd to their stakes.—

Yet I am here, a chosen sample,
To shew thy grace is great and ample:
I'm here, a pillar o' thy temple
Strong as a rock,
A guide, a ruler and example
To a' thy flock.—

[O L—d thou kens what zeal I bear,
When drinkers drink, and swearers swear,
And singin' there, and dancin' here,
Wi' great an' sma';
For I am keepet by thy fear,
Free frae them a'.—]

But yet—O L—d—confess I must—
At times I'm fash'd wi' fleshly lust;
And sometimes too, in warldly trust
Vile Self gets in;
But thou remembers we are dust,
Defil'd wi' sin.—

O L—d—yestreen—thou kens—wi' Meg—
Thy pardon I sincerely beg!
O may 't ne'er be a living plague,
To my dishonor!
And I'll ne'er lift a lawless leg
Again upon her.—

Besides, I farther maun avow,
Wi' Leezie's lass, three times—I trow—
But L—d, that friday I was fou
When I cam near her;
Or else, thou kens, thy servant true
Wad never steer her.—

Maybe thou lets this fleshy thorn
Buffet thy servant e'en and morn,
Lest he o'er proud and high should turn,
That he 's sae gifted;
If sae, thy hand maun e'en be borne
Untill thou lift it.—

L—d bless thy Chosen in this place,
For here thou has a chosen race:
But G–d, confound their stubborn face,
And blast their name,
Wha bring thy rulers to disgrace
And open shame.—

L—d mind Gaun Hamilton's deserts!
He drinks, and swears, and plays at cartes,
Yet has sae mony taking arts
Wi' Great and Sma',
Frae G–d's ain priest the people's hearts
He steals awa.—

And when we chasten'd him therefore,
Thou kens how he bred sic a splore,
And set the warld in a roar
O' laughin at us:
Curse thou his basket and his store,
Kail and potatoes.—

L—d hear my earnest cry and prayer
Against that Presbytry of Ayr!
Thy strong right hand, L—d, make it bare
Upon their heads!
L—d visit them, and dinna spare,
For their misdeeds!

O L—d my G–d, that glib-tongu'd Aiken!
My very heart and flesh are quaking
To think how I sat, sweating, shaking,
And p–ss'd wi' dread,
While Auld wi' hingin lip gaed sneaking
And hid his head!

L—d, in thy day o' vengeance try him!
L—d visit him that did employ him!
And pass not in thy mercy by them,
Nor hear their prayer;
But for thy people's sake destroy them,
And dinna spare!

But L—d, remember me and mine
Wi' mercies temporal and divine!
That I for grace and gear may shine,
Excell'd by nane!
And a' the glory shall be thine!
AMEN! AMEN!

54. *Epitaph on Holy Willie*

HERE Holy Willie's sair worn clay
Taks up its last abode;
His saul has ta'en some other way,
I fear, the left-hand road.

Stop! there he is as sure 's a gun,
Poor silly body see him;
Nae wonder he 's as black 's the grun,
Observe wha 's standing wi' him.

Your brunstane devilship I see
Has got him there before ye:
But ha'd your nine-tail cat a wee,
Till ance you've heard my story.

Your pity I will not implore,
  For pity ye have nane;
Justice, alas! has gi'en him o'er,
  And mercy's day is gaen.

But hear me, Sir, de'il as ye are,
  Look something to your credit;
A coof like him wou'd stain your name,
  If it were kent ye did it.

55. *Death and Doctor Hornbook. A True Story*

SOME books are lies frae end to end,
And some great lies were never penn'd:
Ev'n Ministers they hae been kenn'd,
      In holy rapture,
A rousing whid, at times, to vend,
      And nail 't wi' Scripture.

But this that I am gaun to tell,
Which lately on a night befel,
Is just as true 's the Deil 's in h–ll,
      Or Dublin city:
That e'er he nearer comes oursel
      'S a muckle pity.

The Clachan yill had made me canty,
I was na fou, but just had plenty;
I stacher'd whyles, but yet took tent ay
      To free the ditches;
An' hillocks, stanes, an' bushes kenn'd ay
      Frae ghaists an' witches.

The rising Moon began to glowr
The distant *Cumnock* hills out-owre;
To count her horns, wi' a' my pow'r,
      I set mysel,
But whether she had three or four,
      I cou'd na tell.

I was come round about the hill,
And todlin down on *Willie's mill*,
Setting my staff wi' a' my skill,
To keep me sicker;
Tho' leeward whyles, against my will,
I took a bicker.

I there wi' *Something* does forgather,
That pat me in an eerie swither;
An awfu' scythe, out-owre ae shouther,
Clear-dangling, hang;
A three-tae'd leister on the ither
Lay, large an' lang.

Its stature seem'd lang Scotch ells twa,
The queerest shape that e'er I saw,
For fient a wame it had ava,
And then its shanks,
They were as thin, as sharp an' sma'
As cheeks o' branks.

'Guid-een,' quo' I; 'Friend! hae ye been mawin,
'When ither folk are busy sawin*?'
It seem'd to mak a kind o' stan',
But naething spak;
At length, says I, 'Friend, whare ye gaun,
'Will ye go back?'

It spak right howe—'My name is *Death*,
'But be na' fley'd.'—Quoth I, 'Guid faith,
'Ye're maybe come to stap my breath;
'But tent me, billie;
'I red ye weel, tak care o' skaith,
'See, there 's a gully!'

'Gudeman,' quo' he, 'put up your whittle,
'I'm no design'd to try its mettle;
'But if I did, I wad be kittle
'To be mislear'd,
'I wad na' mind it, no that spittle
'Out-owre my beard.'

* This rencounter happened in seed-time 1785.

'Weel, weel!' says I, 'a bargain be 't;
'Come, gies your hand, an' sae we're gree't;
'We'll ease our shanks an' tak a seat,
'Come, gies your news!
'This while* ye hae been mony a gate,
'At mony a house.'

'Ay, ay!' quo' he, an' shook his head,
'It 's e'en a lang, lang time indeed
'Sin' I began to nick the thread,
'An' choke the breath:
'Folk maun do something for their bread,
'An' sae maun *Death*.

'Sax thousand years are near hand fled
'Sin' I was to the butching bred,
'And mony a scheme in vain 's been laid,
'To stap or scar me;
'Till ane Hornbook 's† ta'en up the trade,
'And faith, he'll waur me.

'Ye ken *Jock Hornbook* i' the Clachan,
'Deil mak his king's-hood in a spleuchan!
'He 's grown sae weel acquaint wi' *Buchan*‡,
'And ither chaps,
'The weans haud out their fingers laughin,
'And pouk my hips.

'See, here 's a scythe, and there 's a dart,
'They hae pierc'd mony a gallant heart;
'But Doctor *Hornbook*, wi' his art
'And cursed skill,
'Has made them baith no worth a f—t,
'D—n'd haet they'll kill!

'Twas but yestreen, nae farther gaen,
'I threw a noble throw at ane;
'Wi' less, I'm sure, I've hundreds slain;
'But deil-ma-care!
'It just play'd dirl on the bane,
'But did nae mair.

* An epidemical fever was then raging in that country.

† This gentleman, Dr Hornbook, is professionally, a brother of the sovereign Order of the Ferula; but, by intuition and inspiration, is at once an Apothecary, Surgeon, and Physician.

‡ Buchan's Domestic Medicine.

'*Hornbook* was by, wi' ready art,
'And had sae fortify'd the part,
'That when I looked to my dart,
'It was sae blunt,
'Fient haet o't wad hae pierc'd the heart
'Of a kail-runt.

'I drew my scythe in sic a fury,
'I nearhand cowpit wi' my hurry,
'But yet the bauld *Apothecary*
'Withstood the shock;
'I might as weel hae try'd a quarry
'O' hard whin-rock.

'Ev'n them he canna get attended,
'Altho' their face he ne'er had kend it,
'Just sh— in a kail-blade and send it,
'As soon 's he smells 't,
'Baith their disease, and what will mend it,
'At once he tells 't.

'And then a' doctor's saws and whittles,
'Of a' dimensions, shapes, an' mettles,
'A' kinds o' boxes, mugs, an' bottles,
'He 's sure to hae;
'Their Latin names as fast he rattles
'As A B C.

'Calces o' fossils, earths, and trees;
'True Sal-marinum o' the seas;
'The Farina of beans and pease,
'He has 't in plenty;
'Aqua-fontis, what you please,
'He can content ye.

'Forbye some new, uncommon weapons,
'Urinus Spiritus of capons;
'Or Mite-horn shavings, filings, scrapings,
'Distill'd *per se*;
'Sal-alkali o' Midge-tail clippings,
'And mony mae.'

'Waes me for *Johnny Ged's-Hole** now,'
Quoth I, 'if that thae news be true!
'His braw calf-ward whare gowans grew,
'Sae white an' bonie,
'Nae doubt they'll rive it wi' the plew;
'They'll ruin *Johnie*!'

The creature grain'd an eldritch laugh,
And says, 'Ye needna yoke the pleugh,
'Kirk-yards will soon be till'd eneugh,
'Tak ye nae fear:
'They'll a' be trench'd wi' mony a sheugh,
'In twa-three year.

'Whare I kill'd ane, a fair strae-death,
'By loss o' blood, or want o' breath,
'This night I'm free to tak my aith,
'That *Hornbook*'s skill
'Has clad a score i' their last claith,
'By drap and pill.

'An honest Wabster to his trade,
'Whase wife's twa nieves were scarce weel-bred,
'Gat tippence-worth to mend her head,
'When it was sair;
'The wife slade cannie to her bed,
'But ne'er spak mair.

'A countra Laird had ta'en the batts,
'Or some curmurring in his guts,
'His only son for *Hornbook* sets,
'And pays him well,
'The lad, for twa guid gimmer-pets,
'Was Laird himsel.

'A bonie lass, ye kend her name,
'Some ill-brewn drink had hov'd her wame,
'She trusts hersel, to hide the shame,
'In *Hornbook*'s care;
'*Horn* sent her aff to her lang hame,
'To hide it there.

* The grave-digger.

'That 's just a swatch o' *Hornbook*'s way,
'Thus goes he on from day to day,
'Thus does he poison, kill, an' slay,
'An 's weel pay'd for 't;
'Yet stops me o' my lawfu' prey,
'Wi' his d–mn'd dirt!

'But hark! I'll tell you of a plot,
'Tho' dinna ye be speakin o't;
'I'll nail the self-conceited Sot,
'As dead 's a herrin:
'Niest time we meet, I'll wad a groat,
'He gets his fairin!'

But just as he began to tell,
The auld kirk-hammer strak the bell
Some wee, short hour ayont the *twal*,
Which rais'd us baith:
I took the way that pleas'd mysel,
And sae did *Death*.

56. [*On Tam the Chapman*]

As Tam the chapman on a day
Wi' Death forgather'd by the way,
Weel pleased, he greets a wight sae famous,
And Death was nae less pleas'd wi' Thomas,
Wha cheerfully lays down his pack,
And there blaws up a hearty crack:
His social, friendly, honest heart
Sae tickled Death, they could na part;
Sae after viewing knives and garters,
Death taks him hame to gie him quarters.

57. *Epistle to J. L*****k, An Old Scotch Bard*

April 1*st*, 1785.

While briers an' woodbines budding green,
An' Paitricks scraichan loud at e'en,
And morning Poossie whiddan seen,
Inspire my Muse,
This freedom, in an *unknown* frien',
I pray excuse.

On Fasteneen we had a rockin,
To ca' the crack and weave our stockin;
And there was muckle fun and jokin,
Ye need na doubt;
At length we had a hearty yokin,
At *sang about.*

There was ae *sang*, amang the rest,
Aboon them a' it pleas'd me best,
That some kind husband had addrest,
To some sweet wife:
It thirl'd the heart-strings thro' the breast,
A' to the life.

I've scarce heard ought describ'd sae weel,
What gen'rous, manly bosoms feel;
Thought I, 'Can this be *Pope*, or *Steele*,
Or *Beattie*'s wark;'
They tald me 'twas an odd kind chiel
About *Muirkirk*.

It pat me fidgean-fain to hear 't,
An' sae about him there I spier't;
Then a' that kent him round declar'd,
He had *ingine*,
That nane excell'd it, few cam near 't,
It was sae fine.

That set him to a pint of ale,
An' either douse or merry tale,
Or rhymes an' sangs he'd made himsel,
Or witty catches,
'Tween Inverness and Tiviotdale,
He had few matches.

Then up I gat, an' swoor an aith,
Tho' I should pawn my pleugh an' graith,
Or die a cadger pownie's death,
At some dyke-back,
A *pint* an' *gill* I'd gie them *baith*,
To hear your crack.

But first an' foremost, I should tell,
Amaist as soon as I could spell,
I to the *crambo-jingle* fell,
Tho' rude an' rough,
Yet crooning to a body's sel,
Does weel eneugh.

I am nae *Poet*, in a sense,
But just a *Rhymer* like by chance,
An' hae to Learning nae pretence,
Yet, what the matter?
Whene'er my Muse does on me glance,
I jingle at her.

Your Critic-folk may cock their nose,
And say, 'How can you e'er propose,
'You wha ken hardly *verse* frae *prose*,
'To mak a *sang*?'
But by your leaves, my learned foes,
Ye're maybe wrang.

What 's a' jargon o' your Schools,
Your Latin names for horns an' stools;
If honest Nature made you *fools*,
What sairs your Grammars?
Ye'd better taen up *spades* and *shools*,
Or *knappin-hammers*.

A set o' dull, conceited Hashes,
Confuse their brains in *Colledge-classes*!
They *gang in* Stirks, and *come out* Asses,
Plain truth to speak;
An' syne they think to climb Parnassus
By dint o' Greek!

Gie me ae spark o' Nature's fire,
That 's a' the learning I desire;
Then tho' I drudge thro' dub an' mire
At pleugh or cart,
My Muse, tho' hamely in attire,
May touch the heart.

O for a spunk o' ALLAN's glee,
Or FERGUSON's, the bauld an' slee,
Or bright L*****K's, my friend to be,
If I can hit it!
That would be *lear* eneugh for me,
If I could get it.

Now, Sir, if ye hae friends enow,
Tho' *real friends* I b'lieve are few,
Yet, if your catalogue be fow,
I'se no insist;
But gif ye want ae friend that 's true,
I'm on your list.

I winna blaw about *mysel*,
As ill I like my fauts to tell;
But friends an' folk that wish me well,
They sometimes roose me;
Tho' I maun own, as monie still,
As far abuse me.

There 's ae *wee faut* they whiles lay to me,
I like the lasses—Gude forgie me!
For monie a Plack they wheedle frae me,
At dance or fair:
Maybe some *ither thing* they gie me
They weel can spare.

But MAUCHLINE Race or MAUCHLINE Fair,
I should be proud to meet you there;
We'se gie ae night's discharge to *care*,
If we forgather,
An' hae a swap o' *rhymin-ware*,
Wi' ane anither.

The *four-gill chap*, we'se gar him clatter,
An' kirs'n him wi' reekin water;
Syne we'll sit down an' tak our whitter,
To chear our heart;
An' faith, we'se be *acquainted* better
Before we part.

Awa ye selfish, warly race,
Wha think that havins, sense an' grace
Ev'n love an' friendship should give place
To *catch-the-plack*!
I dinna like to see your face,
Nor hear your crack.

But ye whom social pleasure charms,
Whose hearts the *tide of kindness* warms,
Who hold your *being* on the terms,
'Each aid the others,'
Come to my bowl, come to my arms,
My friends, my brothers!

But to conclude my lang epistle,
As my auld pen 's worn to the grissle;
Twa lines frae you wad gar me fissle,
Who am, most fervent,
While I can either sing, or whissle,
Your friend and servant.

58. *To the Same*

April 21st, 1785.

WHILE new-ca'd kye rowte at the stake,
An' pownies reek in pleugh or braik,
This hour on e'enin's edge I take,
To own I'm debtor,
To honest-hearted, auld L*****K,
For his kind *letter*.

Forjesket sair, with weary legs,
Rattlin the corn out-owre the rigs,
Or dealing thro' amang the naigs
Their ten-hours bite,
My awkart Muse sair pleads and begs,
I would na write.

The tapetless, ramfeezl'd hizzie,
She 's saft at best an' something lazy,
Quo' she, 'Ye ken we've been sae busy
'This month an' mair,
'That trouth, my head is grown right dizzie,
'An' something sair.'

Her dowf excuses pat me mad;
'Conscience,' says I, 'ye thowless jad!
'I'll write, an' that a hearty blaud,
  'This vera night;
'So dinna ye affront your trade,
  'But rhyme it right.

'Shall bauld L*****K, the *king o' hearts*,
'Tho' mankind were a *pack o' cartes*,
'Roose you sae weel for your deserts,
  'In terms sae friendly,
'Yet ye'll neglect to shaw your parts
  'An' thank him kindly?'

Sae I gat paper in a blink,
An' down gaed *stumpie* in the ink:
Quoth I, 'Before I sleep a wink,
  'I vow I'll close it;
'An' if ye winna mak it clink,
  'By Jove I'll prose it!'

Sae I've begun to scrawl, but whether
In rhyme, or prose, or baith thegither,
Or some hotch-potch that 's rightly neither,
  Let time mak proof;
But I shall scribble down some blether
  Just clean aff-loof.

My worthy friend, ne'er grudge an' carp,
Tho' Fortune use you hard an' sharp;
Come, kittle up your *moorlan harp*
  Wi' gleesome touch!
Ne'er mind how Fortune *waft* an' *warp*;
  She 's but a b–tch.

She 's gien me monie a jirt an' fleg,
Sin' I could striddle owre a rig;
But by the L—d, tho' I should beg
  Wi' lyart pow,
I'll laugh, an' sing, an' shake my leg,
  As lang 's I dow!

Now comes the *sax an' twentieth* simmer,
I've seen the bud upo' the timmer,
Still persecuted by the limmer
Frae year to year;
But yet, despite the kittle kimmer,
I, Rob, am here.

Do ye envy the *city-gent*,
Behint a kist to lie an' sklent,
Or purse-proud, big wi' cent per cent,
An' muckle wame,
In some bit *Brugh* to represent
A *Baillie*'s name?

Or is 't the paughty, feudal *Thane*,
Wi' ruffl'd sark an' glancin cane,
Wha thinks himsel nae *sheep-shank bane*,
But lordly stalks,
While caps an' bonnets aff are taen,
As by he walks?

'O *Thou* wha gies us each guid gift!
'Gie me o' *wit* an' *sense* a lift,
'Then turn me, if *Thou* please, *adrift*,
'Thro' Scotland wide;
'Wi' *cits* nor *lairds* I wadna shift,
'In a' their pride!'

Were this the *charter* of our state,
'On pain o' *hell* be rich an' great,'
Damnation then would be our fate,
Beyond remead;
But, thanks to *Heav'n*, that 's no the gate
We learn our *creed*.

For thus the royal *Mandate* ran,
When first the human race began,
'The social, friendly, honest man,
'Whate'er he be,
' 'Tis *he* fulfils *great Nature's plan*,
'And none but *he*.'

O *Mandate*, glorious and divine!
The followers o' the ragged Nine,
Poor, thoughtless devils! yet may shine
In glorious light,
While sordid sons o' Mammon's line
Are dark as night!

Tho' here they scrape, an' squeeze, an' growl,
Their worthless nievefu' of a *soul*,
May in some *future carcase* howl,
The forest's fright;
Or in some day-detesting *owl*
May shun the light.

Then may L*****K and B**** arise,
To reach their native, kindred skies,
And *sing* their pleasures, hopes an' joys,
In some mild sphere,
Still closer knit in friendship's ties
Each passing year!

59. *To W. S*****n, Ochiltree*

May—1785.

I GAT your letter, winsome Willie;
Wi' gratefu' heart I thank you brawlie;
Tho' I maun say 't, I wad be silly,
An' unco vain,
Should I believe, my coaxin billie,
Your flatterin strain.

But I'se believe ye kindly meant it,
I sud be laith to think ye hinted
Ironic satire, sidelins sklented,
On my poor Musie;
Tho' in sic phraisin terms ye've penn'd it,
I scarce excuse ye.

My senses wad be in a creel,
Should I but dare a *hope* to speel,
Wi' *Allan*, or wi' *Gilbertfield*,
The braes o' fame;
Or *Ferguson*, the writer-chiel,
A deathless name.

(O *Ferguson*! thy glorious *parts*,
Ill-suited *law*'s dry, musty arts!
My curse upon your whunstane hearts,
    Ye Enbrugh Gentry!
The tythe o' what ye waste at *cartes*
    Wad stow'd his pantry!)

Yet when a tale comes i' my head,
Or lasses gie my heart a screed,
As whiles they're like to be my dead,
    (O sad disease!)
I kittle up my *rustic reed*;
    It gies me ease.

Auld COILA, now, may fidge fu' fain,
She 's gotten *Bardies* o' her ain,
Chiels wha their chanters winna hain,
    But tune their lays,
Till echoes a' resound again
    Her weel-sung praise.

Nae *Poet* thought her worth his while,
To set her name in measur'd style;
She lay like some unkend-of isle
    Beside *New Holland*,
Or whare wild-meeting oceans *boil*
    Besouth *Magellan*.

Ramsay an' famous *Ferguson*
Gied *Forth* an' *Tay* a lift aboon;
Yarrow an' *Tweed*, to monie a tune,
    Owre Scotland rings,
While *Irwin*, *Lugar*, *Aire* an' *Doon*,
    Naebody sings.

Th' *Illissus*, *Tiber*, *Thames* an' *Seine*,
Glide sweet in monie a tunefu' line;
But *Willie* set your fit to mine,
    An' cock your crest,
We'll gar our streams an' burnies shine
    Up wi' the best.

We'll sing auld Coila's plains an' fells,
Her moors red-brown wi' heather bells,
Her banks an' braes, her dens an' dells,
Where glorious Wallace
Aft bure the gree, as story tells,
Frae Suthron billies.

At Wallace' name, what Scottish blood,
But boils up in a spring-tide flood!
Oft have our fearless fathers strode
By Wallace' side,
Still pressing onward, red-wat-shod,
Or glorious dy'd!

O sweet are Coila's haughs an' woods,
When lintwhites chant amang the buds,
And jinkin hares, in amorous whids,
Their loves enjoy,
While thro' the braes the cushat croods
With wailfu' cry!

Ev'n winter bleak has charms to me,
When winds rave thro' the naked tree;
Or frosts on hills of *Ochiltree*
Are hoary gray;
Or blinding drifts wild-furious flee,
Dark'ning the day!

O Nature! a' thy shews an' forms
To feeling, pensive hearts hae charms!
Whether the Summer kindly warms,
Wi' life an' light,
Or Winter howls, in gusty storms,
The lang, dark night!

The *Muse*, nae *Poet* ever fand her,
Till by himsel he learn'd to wander,
Adown some trottin burn's meander,
An' no think lang;
O sweet, to stray an' pensive ponder
A heart-felt sang!

The warly race may drudge an' drive,
Hog-shouther, jundie, stretch an' strive,
Let me fair NATURE's face descrive,
And I, wi' pleasure,
Shall let the busy, grumbling hive
Bum owre their treasure.

Fareweel, 'my rhyme-composing brither!'
We've been owre lang unkenn'd to ither:
Now let us lay our heads thegither,
In love fraternal:
May *Envy* wallop in a tether,
Black fiend, infernal!

While Highlandmen hate tolls an' taxes;
While moorlan herds like guid, fat braxies;
While Terra firma, on her axis,
Diurnal turns,
Count on a friend, in faith an' practice,
In ROBERT BURNS.

Postscript

My memory 's no worth a preen;
I had amaist forgotten clean,
Ye bad me write you what they mean
By this *new-light*,*
'Bout which our *herds* sae aft hae been
Maist like to fight.

In days when mankind were but callans,
At *Grammar*, *Logic*, an' sic talents,
They took nae pains their speech to balance,
Or rules to gie,
But spak their thoughts in plain, braid lallans,
Like you or me.

In thae auld times, they thought the *Moon*,
Just like a sark, or pair o' shoon,
Woor by degrees, till her last roon
Gaed past their viewin,
An' shortly after she was done
They gat a new ane.

* A cant-term for those religious opinions, which Dr. TAYLOR of Norwich has defended so strenuously.

This past for certain, undisputed;
It ne'er cam i' their heads to doubt it,
Till chiels gat up an' wad confute it,
An' ca'd it wrang;
An' muckle din there was about it,
Baith loud an' lang.

Some *herds*, weel learn'd upo' the beuk,
Wad threap auld folk the thing misteuk;
For 'twas the *auld moon* turn'd a newk
An' out o' sight,
An' backlins-comin, to the leuk,
She grew mair bright.

This was deny'd, it was affirm'd;
The *herds* an' *hissels* were alarm'd;
The rev'rend gray-beards rav'd an' storm'd,
That beardless laddies
Should think they better were inform'd,
Than their auld dadies.

Frae less to mair it gaed to sticks;
Frae words an' aiths to clours an' nicks;
An' monie a fallow gat his licks,
Wi' hearty crunt;
An' some, to learn them for their tricks,
Were hang'd an' brunt.

This game was play'd in monie lands,
An' *auld-light* caddies bure sic hands,
That faith, the *youngsters* took the sands
Wi' nimble shanks,
Till *Lairds* forbad, by strict commands,
Sic bluidy pranks.

But *new-light herds* gat sic a cowe,
Folk thought them ruin'd stick-an-stowe,
Till now amaist on ev'ry *knowe*
Ye'll find ane plac'd;
An' some, their *New-light* fair avow,
Just quite barefac'd.

Nae doubt the *auld-light flocks* are bleatan;
Their zealous *herds* are vex'd an' sweatan;
Mysel, I've ev'n seen them greetan
Wi' girnan spite,
To hear the *Moon* sae sadly lie'd on
By word an' write.

But shortly they will cowe the louns!
Some *auld-light herds* in neebor towns
Are mind't, in things they ca' *balloons*,
To tak a flight,
An' stay ae month amang the *Moons*
An' see them right.

Guid observation they will gie them;
An' when the *auld Moon* 's gaun to lea'e them,
The hindmost *shaird*, they'll fetch it wi' them,
Just i' their pouch,
An' when the *new-light* billies see them,
I think they'll crouch!

Sae, ye observe that a' this clatter
Is naething but a 'moonshine matter;'
But tho' dull *prose-folk* Latin splatter
In logic tulzie,
I hope we, *Bardies*, ken some better
Than mind sic brulzie.

60. *A Poet's Welcome to his love-begotten Daughter; the first instance that entitled him to the venerable appellation of Father—*

THOU 's welcome, Wean! Mischanter fa' me,
If thoughts o' thee, or yet thy Mamie,
Shall ever daunton me or awe me,
My bonie lady;
Or if I blush when thou shalt ca' me
Tyta, or Daddie.—

Tho' now they ca' me, Fornicator,
And tease my name in kintra clatter,
The mair they talk, I'm kend the better;
E'en let them clash!
An auld wife's tongue 's a feckless matter
To gie ane fash.—

Welcome! My bonie, sweet, wee Dochter!
Tho' ye come here a wee unsought for;
And tho' your comin I hae fought for,
Baith Kirk and Queir;
Yet by my faith, ye're no unwrought for,
That I shall swear!

Wee image o' my bonie Betty,
As fatherly I kiss and daut thee,
As dear and near my heart I set thee,
Wi' as gude will,
As a' the Priests had seen me get thee
That 's out o' h———.—

Sweet fruit o' monie a merry dint,
My funny toil is no a' tint;
Tho' ye come to the warld asklent,
Which fools may scoff at,
In my last plack your part 's be in 't,
The better half o't.—

Tho' I should be the waur bestead,
Thou 's be as braw and bienly clad,
And thy young years as nicely bred
Wi' education,
As any brat o' Wedlock's bed,
In a' thy station.—

[Lord grant that thou may ay inherit
Thy Mither's looks an' gracefu' merit;
An' thy poor, worthless Daddie's spirit,
Without his failins!
'Twad please me mair to see thee heir it
Than stocked mailins!]

For if thou be, what I wad hae thee,
And tak the counsel I shall gie thee,
I'll never rue my trouble wi' thee,
The cost nor shame o't,
But be a loving Father to thee,
And brag the name o't.—

61. *The Fornicator. A New Song—*

Tune, Clout the Caldron

Ye jovial boys who love the joys,
  The blissful joys of Lovers;
Yet dare avow with dauntless brow,
  When th' bony lass discovers;
I pray draw near and lend an ear,
  And welcome in a Frater,
For I've lately been on quarantine,
  A proven Fornicator.

Before the Congregation wide
  I pass'd the muster fairly,
My handsome Betsey by my side,
  We gat our ditty rarely;
But my downcast eye by chance did spy
  What made my lips to water,
Those limbs so clean where I, between,
  Commenc'd a Fornicator.

With rueful face and signs of grace
  I pay'd the buttock-hire,
The night was dark and thro' the park
  I could not but convoy her;
A parting kiss, what could I less,
  My vows began to scatter,
My Betsey fell—lal de dal lal lal,
  I am a Fornicator.

But for her sake this vow I make,
  And solemnly I swear it,
That while I own a single crown,
  She 's welcome for to share it;
And my roguish boy his Mother's joy,
  And the darling of his Pater,
For him I boast my pains and cost,
  Although a Fornicator.

Ye wenching blades whose hireling jades
  Have tipt you off blue-boram,
I tell ye plain, I do disdain
  To rank you in the Quorum;

But a bony lass upon the grass
  To teach her esse Mater,
And no reward but for regard,
  O that 's a Fornicator.

Your warlike Kings and Heros bold,
  Great Captains and Commanders;
Your mighty Cèsars fam'd of old,
  And Conquering Alexanders;
In fields they fought and laurels bought
  And bulwarks strong did batter,
But still they grac'd our noble list
  And ranked Fornicator!!!

62. *The Vision. Duan First**

THE sun had clos'd the *winter-day*,
The Curlers quat their roaring play,
And hunger'd Maukin taen her way
      To kail-yards green,
While faithless snaws ilk step betray
      Whare she has been.

The Thresher's weary *flingin-tree*,
The lee-lang day had tir'd me;
And when the Day had clos'd his e'e,
      Far i' the West,
Ben i' the *Spence*, right pensivelie,
      I gaed to rest.

There, lanely, by the ingle-cheek,
I sat and ey'd the spewing reek,
That fill'd, wi' hoast-provoking smeek,
      The auld, clay biggin;
And heard the restless rattons squeak
      About the riggin.

* Duan, a term of Ossian's for the different divisions of a digressive Poem. See his Cath-Loda, Vol. 2. of M'Pherson's Translation.

All in this mottie, misty clime,
I backward mus'd on wasted time,
How I had spent my *youthfu' prime*,
An' done nae-thing,
But stringing blethers up in rhyme
For fools to sing.

Had I to guid advice but harket,
I might, by this, hae led a market,
Or strutted in a Bank and clarket
My *Cash-Account*;
While here, half-mad, half-fed, half-sarket,
Is a' th' amount.

I started, mutt'ring blockhead! coof!
And heav'd on high my wauket loof,
To swear by a' yon starry roof,
Or some rash aith,
That I, henceforth, would be *rhyme-proof*
Till my last breath—

When click! the *string* the *snick* did draw;
And jee! the door gaed to the wa';
And by my ingle-lowe I saw,
Now bleezan bright,
A tight, outlandish *Hizzie*, braw,
Come full in sight.

Ye need na doubt, I held my whisht;
The infant aith, half-form'd, was crusht;
I glowr'd as eerie 's I'd been dusht,
In some wild glen;
When sweet, like *modest Worth*, she blusht,
And stepped ben.

Green, slender, leaf-clad *Holly-boughs*
Were twisted, gracefu', round her brows,
I took her for some SCOTTISH MUSE,
By that same token;
And come to stop those reckless vows,
Would soon been broken.

A 'hare-brain'd, sentimental trace'
Was strongly marked in her face;
A wildly-witty, rustic grace
Shone full upon her;
Her *eye*, ev'n turn'd on empty space,
Beam'd keen with *Honor*.

Down flow'd her robe, a *tartan* sheen,
Till half a leg was scrimply seen;
And such a *leg*! my bonie JEAN
Could only peer it;
Sae straught, sae taper, tight and clean,
Nane else came near it.

Her *Mantle* large, of greenish hue,
My gazing wonder chiefly drew;
Deep *lights* and *shades*, bold-mingling, threw
A lustre grand;
And seem'd, to my astonish'd view,
A *well-known* Land.

Here, rivers in the sea were lost;
There, mountains to the skies were tost:
Here, tumbling billows mark'd the coast,
With surging foam;
There, distant shone, *Art*'s lofty boast,
The lordly dome.

Here, DOON pour'd down his far-fetch'd floods;
There, well-fed IRWINE stately thuds:
Auld, hermit AIRE staw thro' his woods,
On to the shore;
And many a lesser torrent scuds,
With seeming roar.

Low, in a sandy valley spread,
An ancient BOROUGH rear'd her head;
Still, as in *Scottish Story* read,
She boasts a *Race*,
To ev'ry nobler virtue bred,
And polish'd grace.

By stately tow'r, or palace fair,
Or ruins pendent in the air,
Bold stems of Heroes, here and there,
I could discern;
Some seem'd to muse, some seem'd to dare,
With feature stern.

My heart did glowing transport feel,
To see a Race* heroic wheel,
And brandish round the deep-dy'd steel
In sturdy blows;
While back-recoiling seem'd to reel
Their Suthron foes.

His Country's Saviour†, mark him well!
Bold Richardton's‡ heroic swell;
The Chief on *Sark*§ who glorious fell,
In high command;
And *He* whom ruthless Fates expel
His native land.

* The Wallaces. † William Wallace.

‡ Adam Wallace of Richardton, cousin to the immortal Preserver of Scottish Independence.

§ Wallace Laird of Craigie, who was second in command, under Douglas Earl of Ormond, at the famous battle on the banks of Sark, fought *anno* 1448. That glorious victory was principally owing to the judicious conduct and intrepid valour of the gallant Laird of Craigie, who died of his wounds after the action.

---

108 *additional stanzas follow in the Stair MS:*

With secret throes I mark'd that earth,
That cottage witness of my birth;
And near I saw, bold issuing forth,
In youthful pride,
A *Lindsay* race of noble worth,
Fam'd far and wide.

Where, hid behind a spreading wood,
An ancient, Pict-built Mansion stood, Sundrum
I spy'd, among an angel brood,
A female pair;
Sweet shone their high maternal blood,
And father's air.

An ancient *tow'r* to mem'ry brought,
How Dettingen's bold heroe fought; Stair
Still far from sinking into nought,
It owns a lord,
Who far in Western climates fought,
With trusty sword.

There, where a sceptr'd *Pictish** shade
Stalk'd round his ashes lowly laid,
I mark'd a martial Race, pourtray'd
In colours strong;
Bold, soldier-featur'd, undismay'd
They strode along.

†Thro' many a wild, romantic grove,
Near many a hermit-fancy'd cove,
(Fit haunts for Friendship or for Love,
In musing mood)
An *aged Judge*, I saw him rove,
Dispensing good.

* Coilus King of the Picts, from whom the district of Kyle is said to take its name, lies buried, as tradition says, near the family-seat of the Montgomeries of Coilsfield, where his burial place is still shown.

† Barskimming, the seat of the Lord Justice Clerk.

---

114 *additional stanza and note in Stair MS:*

Among the rest I well could spy
One gallant, graceful, martial boy;
The sodger sparkl'd in his eye,
A diamond water;
I blest that noble *Badge* with joy,
That own'd me frater.

One gallant { Captn Ja^{s} Montgomery, Master of St. James's Lodge, Tarbolton, to which the Author has the honor to belong.

120 *additional stanzas follow in Stair MS:*

[Nearby] arose a Mansion fine, Auchinleck
The seat of many a Muse divine;
Not rustic Muses such as mine,
With holley crown'd,
But th' ancient, tuneful, laurell'd Nine,
From classic ground.

I mourn'd the card that Fortune dealt,
To see where bonie Whitefords dwelt; Ballochmyle
But other prospects made me melt;
That village near; Mauchline
There Nature, Friendship, Love, I felt,
Fond-mingling dear!

Hail! Nature's pang, more strong than death!
Warm Friendship's glow, like kindling wrath!
Love, dearer than the parting breath
Of dying friend!
Not ev'n with life's wild devious path,
Your force shall end!

*With deep-struck, reverential awe,
The learned *Sire* and *Son* I saw,
To Nature's God and Nature's law
They gave their lore,
This, all its source and end to draw,
That, to adore.

* Catrine, the seat of the late Doctor, and present Professor Stewart.

The Pow'r that gave the soft alarms
In blooming Whiteford's rosy charms,
Still threats the tiny, feather'd arms,
The barbed dart,
While lovely Wilhelminia warms — Miss Wilhelminia Alexander
The coldest heart.

126 *additional stanzas follow in Stair MS to complete* Duan First*:*

Where Lugar leaves his moorland plaid, — Cumnock
Where lately Want was idly laid,
I marked busy, bustling Trade,
In fervid flame,
Beneath a Patroness's aid,
Of noble name.

Wild, countless hills I could survey,
And countless flocks as wild as they;
But other scenes did charms display,
That better please,
Where polish'd manners dwell with Gray, — Mr. Farquhar Gray
In rural ease.

Where Cessnock pours with gurgling sound; — Auchinskieth
And Irwine, marking out the bound,
Enamour'd of the scenes around,
Slows runs his race,
And name I doubly honor'd found, — Caprington
With knightly grace.

Brydone's brave ward, I saw him stand, — Colonel Fullarton
Fame humbly offering her hand,
And near, his kinsman's rustic band, — Dr. Fullarton
With one accord,
Lamenting their late blessed land
Must change its lord.

The owner of a pleasant spot,
Near sandy wilds, I last did note; — Orangefield
A heart too warm, a pulse too hot
At times, o'erran;
But large in ev'ry feature wrote,
Appear'd the Man.

BRYDON's brave Ward* I well could spy,
Beneath old SCOTIA's smiling eye;
Who call'd on Fame, low standing by,
To hand him on,
Where many a Patriot-name on high
And Hero shone.

Duan Second

With musing-deep, astonish'd stare,
I view'd the heavenly-seeming *Fair*;
A whisp'ring *throb* did witness bear
Of kindred sweet,
When with an elder Sister's air
She did me greet.

'All hail! *my own* inspired Bard!
'In me thy native Muse regard!
'Nor longer mourn thy fate is hard,
'Thus poorly low!
'I come to give thee such *reward*,
'As *we* bestow.

'Know, the great *Genius* of this Land,
'Has many a light, aerial band,
'Who, all beneath his high command,
'Harmoniously,
'As *Arts* or *Arms* they understand,
'Their labors ply.

* Colonel Fullarton.

133–8 *Stair MS has*

Duan the second.

All these in colours, strong imprest,
I marked chief among the rest,
While favor'd by my honor'd guest,
In converse sweet;
Who, as I said, in blushes drest,
Thus did me greet.
'All hail &c.

The rest of this Duan is exactly the same as the printed copies . . . .

'They SCOTIA's Race among them share;
'Some fire the *Sodger* on to dare;
'Some rouse the *Patriot* up to bare
'Corruption's heart:
'Some teach the *Bard*, a darling care,
'The tuneful Art.

' 'Mong swelling floods of reeking gore,
'They ardent, kindling spirits pour;
'Or, mid the venal Senate's roar,
'They, sightless, stand,
'To mend the honest *Patriot-lore*,
'And grace the hand.

'And when the Bard, or hoary Sage,
'Charm or instruct the future age,
'They bind the wild, Poetic rage
'In energy,
'Or point the inconclusive page
'Full on the eye.

'Hence, FULLARTON, the brave and young;
'Hence, DEMPSTER's truth-prevailing tongue;
'Hence, sweet harmonious BEATTIE sung
'His "Minstrel lays;"
'Or tore, with noble ardour stung,
'The *Sceptic*'s bays.

'To lower Orders are assign'd,
'The humbler ranks of Human-kind,
'The rustic Bard, the lab'ring Hind,
'The Artisan;
'All chuse, as, various they're inclin'd,
'The various man.

'When yellow waves the heavy grain,
'The threat'ning *Storm*, some, strongly, rein;
'Some teach to meliorate the plain,
'With *tillage-skill*;
'And some instruct the Shepherd-train,
'Blythe o'er the hill.

'Some hint the Lover's harmless wile;
'Some grace the Maiden's artless smile;
'Some soothe the Lab'rer's weary toil,
'For humble gains,
'And make his *cottage-scenes* beguile
'His cares and pains.

'Some, bounded to a district-space,
'Explore at large Man's *infant race*,
'To mark the embryotic trace,
'Of *rustic Bard*;
'And careful note each op'ning grace,
'A guide and guard.

'*Of these am I*—COILA my name;
'And this district as mine I claim,
'Where once the *Campbells*, chiefs of fame,
'Held ruling pow'r:
'I mark'd thy embryo-tuneful flame,
'Thy natal hour.

'With future hope, I oft would gaze,
'Fond, on thy little, early ways,
'Thy rudely-caroll'd, chiming phrase,
'In uncouth rhymes,
'Fir'd at the simple, artless lays
'Of other times.

'I saw thee seek the sounding shore,
'Delighted with the dashing roar;
'Or when the *North* his fleecy store
'Drove thro' the sky,
'I saw grim Nature's visage hoar,
'Struck thy young eye.

'Or when the deep-green-mantl'd Earth,
'Warm-cherish'd ev'ry floweret's birth,
'And joy and music pouring forth,
'In ev'ry grove,
'I saw thee eye the gen'ral mirth
'With boundless love.

'When ripen'd fields, and azure skies,
'Call'd forth the *Reaper*'s rustling noise,
'I saw thee leave their ev'ning joys,
'And lonely stalk,
'To vent thy bosom's swelling rise,
'In pensive walk.

'When *youthful Love*, warm-blushing, strong,
'Keen-shivering shot thy nerves along,
'Those accents, grateful to thy tongue,
'Th' adored *Name*,
'I taught thee how to pour in song,
'To soothe thy flame.

'I saw thy pulse's maddening play,
'Wild-send thee Pleasure's devious way,
'Misled by Fancy's *meteor-ray*,
'By Passion driven;
'But yet the *light* that led astray,
'Was *light* from Heaven.

'I taught thy manners-painting strains,
'The *loves*, the *ways*, of simple swains,
'Till now, o'er all my wide domains,
'Thy fame extends;
'And some, the pride of *Coila*'s plains,
'Become thy friends.

'Thou canst not learn, nor I can show,
'To paint with *Thomson*'s landscape-glow;
'Or wake the bosom-melting throe,
'With *Shenstone*'s art;
'Or pour, with *Gray*, the moving flow,
'Warm on the heart.

'Yet all beneath th' unrivall'd Rose,
'The lowly Daisy sweetly blows;
'Tho' large the forest's Monarch throws
'His army shade,
'Yet green the juicy Hawthorn grows,
'Adown the glade.

'Then never murmur nor repine;
'Strive in thy *humble sphere* to shine;
'And trust me, not *Potosi's mine*,
    'Nor *King's regard*,
'Can give a bliss o'ermatching thine,
    'A *rustic Bard*.

'To give my counsels all in one,
'Thy *tuneful flame* still careful fan;
'Preserve *the dignity of Man*,
    'With Soul erect;
'And trust, the UNIVERSAL PLAN
    'Will all protect.

'*And wear thou this*'—She solemn said,
And bound the *Holly* round my head:
The polish'd leaves, and berries red,
    Did rustling play;
And, like a passing thought, she fled,
    In light away.

63. *Epistle to John Goldie in Kilmarnock, Author of, The Gospel recovered—*

August — 1785

O GOWDIE, terror o' the whigs,
Dread o' black coats and reverend wigs!
Sour Bigotry on his last legs
    Girns and looks back,
Wishing the ten Egyptian plagues
    May sieze you quick.—

Poor gapin, glowrin Superstition!
Waes me, she 's in a sad condition:
Fye! bring Black Jock* her state-physician,
    To see her water:
Alas! there 's ground for great suspicion,
    She'll ne'er get better.—

* The Rev[d] J. R--ss--ll — Kilm[ck]

Enthusiasm 's past redemption,
Gane in a gallopin consumption:
Not a' her quacks wi' a' their gumption
Can ever mend her;
Her feeble pulse gies strong presumption,
She'll soon surrender.—

Auld Orthodoxy lang did grapple
For every hole to get a stapple;
But now, she fetches at the thrapple
And fights for breath;
Haste, gie her name up in the Chapel*
Near unto death.—

It' s you and Taylor† are the chief
To blame for a' this black mischief;
But could the L—d's ain folk get leave,
A toom tar-barrel
And twa red peats wad bring relief
And end the quarrel.—

For me, my skill 's but very sma',
And skill in Prose I've nane ava;
But quietlenswise, between us twa,
Weel may ye speed;
And tho' they sud you sair misca',
Ne'er fash your head.—

E'en swinge the dogs; and thresh them sicker!
The mair they squeel ay chap the thicker;
And still 'mang hands a hearty bicker
O' something stout;
It gars an Owther's pulse beat quicker,
And helps his wit.—

There 's naething like the honest nappy;
Whare'll ye e'er see men sae happy,
Or women sonsie, saft and sappy,
'Tween morn and morn,
As them wha like to taste the drappie
In glass or horn.—

* Chapel — Mr Russel's kirk—
† Taylor — Dr Taylor of Norwich—

I've seen me daez't upon a time,
I scarce could wink or see a styme;
Just ae hauf-mutchkin does me prime,
(Ought less, is little)
Then back I rattle on the rhyme,
As gleg 's a whittle.—
I am &c.

64. *Man was Made to Mourn, A Dirge*

Peggy Bawn

I

WHEN chill November's surly blast
Made fields and forests bare,
One ev'ning, as I wand'red forth,
Along the banks of AIRE,
I spy'd a man, whose aged step
Seem'd weary, worn with care;
His face was furrow'd o'er with years,
And hoary was his hair.

II

Young stranger, whither wand'rest thou?
Began the rev'rend Sage;
Does thirst of wealth thy step constrain,
Or youthful Pleasure's rage?

Or haply, prest with cares and woes,
  Too soon thou hast began,
To wander forth, with me, to mourn
  The miseries of Man.

III

The Sun that overhangs yon moors,
  Out-spreading far and wide,
Where hundreds labour to support
  A haughty lordling's pride;
I've seen yon weary winter-sun
  Twice forty times return;
And ev'ry time has added proofs,
  That Man was made to mourn.

IV

O Man! while in thy early years,
  How prodigal of time!
Mispending all thy precious hours,
  Thy glorious, youthful prime!
Alternate Follies take the sway;
  Licentious Passions burn;
Which tenfold force gives Nature's law,
  That Man was made to mourn.

V

Look not alone on youthful Prime,
  Or Manhood's active might;
Man then is useful to his kind,
  Supported is his right:
But see him on the edge of life,
  With Cares and Sorrows worn,
Then Age and Want, Oh! ill-match'd pair!
  Show Man was made to mourn.

VI

A few seem favourites of Fate,
  In Pleasure's lap carest;
Yet, think not all the Rich and Great,
  Are likewise truly blest.
But Oh! what crouds in ev'ry land,
  All wretched and forlorn,
Thro' weary life this lesson learn,
  That Man was made to mourn!

VII

Many and sharp the num'rous Ills
  Inwoven with our frame!
More pointed still we make ourselves,
  Regret, Remorse and Shame!
And Man, whose heav'n-erected face,
  The smiles of love adorn,
Man's inhumanity to Man
  Makes countless thousands mourn!

VIII

See, yonder poor, o'erlabour'd wight,
  So abject, mean and vile,
Who begs a brother of the earth
  To give him leave to toil;
And see his lordly *fellow-worm*,
  The poor petition spurn,
Unmindful, tho' a weeping wife,
  And helpless offspring mourn.

IX

If I'm design'd yon lordling's slave,
  By Nature's law design'd,
Why was an independent wish
  E'er planted in my mind?
If not, why am I subject to
  His cruelty, or scorn?
Or why has Man the will and pow'r
  To make his fellow mourn?

X

Yet, let not this too much, my Son,
  Disturb thy youthful breast:
This partial view of human-kind
  Is surely not the *last*!
The poor, oppressed, honest man
  Had never, sure, been born,
Had there not been some recompence
  To comfort those that mourn!

XI

O Death! the poor man's dearest friend,
  The kindest and the best!
Welcome the hour, my aged limbs
  Are laid with thee at rest!

The Great, the Wealthy fear thy blow,
  From pomp and pleasure torn;
But Oh! a blest relief to those
  That weary-laden mourn!

65. *A Song.—On Miss P—— K——*

YOUNG Peggy blooms our boniest lass,
  Her blush is like the morning,
The rosy dawn, the springing grass,
  With early gems adorning:
Her eyes outshine the radiant beams
  That gild the passing shower,
And glitter o'er the chrystal streams,
  And chear each fresh'ning flower.

Her lips more than the cherries bright,
  A richer die has grac'd them,
They charm th' admiring gazer's sight
  And sweetly tempt to taste them:
Her smile is as the ev'ning mild,
  When feath'red pairs are courting,
And little lambkins wanton wild,
  In playful bands disporting.

Were Fortune lovely Peggy's foe,
  Such sweetness would relent her,
As blooming spring unbends the brow
  Of surly, savage winter.
Detraction's eye no aim can gain
  Her winning pow'rs to lessen;
And fretful envy grins in vain,
  The poison'd tooth to fasten.

Ye Pow'rs of Honor, Love and Truth,
    From ev'ry ill defend her;
Inspire the highly favor'd Youth
  The Destinies intend her;
Still fan the sweet connubial flame,
  Responsive in each bosom;
And bless the dear parental name
  With many a filial blossom.

66. *The Braes o' Ballochmyle*

THE Catrine woods were yellow seen,
  The flowers decay'd on Catrine lee,
Nae lav'rock sang on hillock green,
  But Nature sicken'd on the e'e.
Thro' faded groves Maria sang,
  Hersel in beauty's bloom the while,
And ay the wild-wood echoes rang,
  Fareweel the braes o' Ballochmyle.

Low in your wintry beds, ye flowers,
  Again ye'll flourish fresh and fair;
Ye birdies dumb, in with'ring bowers,
  Again ye'll charm the vocal air.
But here alas! for me nae mair
  Shall birdie charm, or floweret smile;
Fareweel the bonnie banks of Ayr,
  Fareweel, fareweel! sweet Ballochmyle!

67. [*Third Epistle*] *to J. Lapraik*

Sept. 13*th*, 1785.

GUID speed an' furder to you Johny,
  Guid health, hale han's, an' weather bony;
Now when ye're nickan down fu' cany
      The staff o' bread,
May ye ne'er want a stoup o' brany
      To clear your head.

May Boreas never thresh your rigs,
Nor kick your rickles aff their legs,
Sendin' the stuff o'er muirs an' haggs
      Like drivin' wrack;
But may the tapmast grain that wags
      Come to the sack.

I'm bizzie too, an' skelpin' at it,
But bitter, daudin showers hae wat it,
Sae my auld stumpie pen I gat it
      Wi' muckle wark,
An' took my jocteleg an' whatt it,
      Like ony clark.

It 's now twa month that I'm your debtor,
For your braw, nameless, dateless letter,
Abusin' me for harsh ill nature
On holy men,
While deil a hair yoursel ye're better,
But mair profane.

But let the kirk-folk ring their bells,
Let 's sing about our noble sels;
We'll cry nae jads frae heathen hills
To help, or roose us,
But browster wives an' whiskie stills,
They are the muses.

Your friendship sir, I winna quat it,
An' if ye mak' objections at it,
Then han' in nieve some day we'll knot it,
An' witness take,
An' when wi' Usquabae we've wat it
It winna break.

But if the beast and branks be spar'd
Till kye be gaun without the herd,
An' a' the vittel in the yard,
An' theekit right,
I mean your ingle-side to guard
Ae winter night.

Then muse-inspirin' aqua-vitæ
Shall make us baith sae blythe an' witty,
Till ye forget ye're auld an' gutty,
An' be as canty
As ye were nine year less than thretty,
Sweet ane an' twenty!

But stooks are cowpet wi' the blast,
An' now the sinn keeks in the west,
Then I maun rin amang the rest
An' quat my chanter;
Sae I subscribe mysel in haste,
Yours, Rab the Ranter

68. *To the Rev. John M'Math, Inclosing a copy of* Holy Willie's Prayer, *which he had requested*

Sept. 17*th*, 1785.

WHILE at the stook the shearers cow'r
To shun the bitter blaudin' show'r,
Or in gulravage rinnin scow'r
To pass the time,
To you I dedicate the hour
In idle rhyme.

My musie, tir'd wi' mony a sonnet
On gown, an' ban', an' douse black bonnet,
Is grown right eerie now she 's done it,
Lest they shou'd blame her,
An' rouse their holy thunder on it
And anathem her.

I own 'twas rash, an' rather hardy,
That I, a simple, countra bardie,
Shou'd meddle wi' a pack sae sturdy,
Wha, if they ken me,
Can easy, wi' a single wordie,
Louse h–ll upon me.

But I gae mad at their grimaces,
Their sighan, cantan, grace-prood faces,
Their three-mile prayers, an' hauf-mile graces,
Their raxan conscience,
Whase greed, revenge, an' pride disgraces
Waur nor their nonsense.

There 's *Gaun*, miska't waur than a beast,
Wha has mair honor in his breast
Than mony scores as guid 's the priest
Wha sae abus't him:
An' may a bard no crack his jest
What way they've use't him?

See him, the poor man's friend in need,
The gentleman in word an' deed,
An' shall his fame an' honor bleed
By worthless skellums,
An' not a muse erect her head
To cowe the blellums?

O Pope, had I thy satire's darts
To gie the rascals their deserts,
I'd rip their rotten, hollow hearts,
An' tell aloud
Their jugglin' hocus pocus arts
To cheat the crowd.

God knows, I'm no the thing I shou'd be,
Nor am I even the thing I cou'd be,
But twenty times, I rather wou'd be
An atheist clean,
Than under gospel colors hid be
Just for a screen.

An honest man may like a glass,
An honest man may like a lass,
But mean revenge, an' malice fause
He'll still disdain,
An' then cry zeal for gospel laws,
Like some we ken.

They take religion in their mouth;
They talk o' mercy, grace an' truth,
For what?—to gie their malice skouth
On some puir wight,
An' hunt him down, o'er right an' ruth,
To ruin streight.

All hail, Religion! maid divine!
Pardon a muse sae mean as mine,
Who in her rough imperfect line
Thus daurs to name thee;
To stigmatize false friends of thine
Can ne'er defame thee.

Tho' blotch't an' foul wi' mony a stain,
An' far unworthy of thy train,
With trembling voice I tune my strain
To join with those,
Who boldly dare thy cause maintain
In spite of foes:

In spite o' crowds, in spite o' mobs,
In spite of undermining jobs,
In spite o' dark banditti stabs
At worth an' merit,
By scoundrels, even wi' holy robes,
But hellish spirit.

O Ayr, my dear, my native ground,
Within thy presbytereal bound
A candid lib'ral band is found
Of public teachers,
As men, as Christians too renown'd
An' manly preachers.

Sir, in that circle you are nam'd;
Sir, in that circle you are fam'd;
An' some, by whom your doctrine 's blam'd
(Which gies you honor)
Even Sir, by them your heart 's esteem'd,
An' winning manner.

Pardon this freedom I have ta'en,
An' if impertinent I've been,
Impute it not, good Sir, in ane
Whase heart ne'er wrang'd ye,
But to his utmost would befriend
Ought that belang'd ye.

69. *To a Mouse, On turning her up in her Nest, with the Plough, November, 1785.*

WEE, sleeket, cowran, tim'rous *beastie*,
O, what a panic 's in thy breastie!
Thou need na start awa sae hasty,
Wi' bickering brattle!
I wad be laith to rin an' chase thee,
Wi' murd'ring *pattle*!

I'm truly sorry Man's dominion
Has broken Nature's social union,
An' justifies that ill opinion,
Which makes thee startle,
At me, thy poor, earth-born companion,
An' *fellow-mortal*!

I doubt na, whyles, but thou may *thieve*;
What then? poor beastie, thou maun live!
A *daimen-icker* in a *thrave*
'S a sma' request:
I'll get a blessin wi' the lave,
An' never miss 't!

Thy wee-bit *housie*, too, in ruin!
It's silly wa's the win's are strewin!
An' naething, now, to big a new ane,
O' foggage green!
An' bleak *December's winds* ensuin,
Baith snell an' keen!

Thou saw the fields laid bare an' wast,
An' weary *Winter* comin fast,
An' cozie here, beneath the blast,
Thou thought to dwell,
Till crash! the cruel *coulter* past
Out thro' thy cell.

That wee-bit heap o' leaves an' stibble,
Has cost thee monie a weary nibble!
Now thou 's turn'd out, for a' thy trouble,
But house or hald,
To thole the Winter's *sleety dribble*,
An' *cranreuch* cauld!

But Mousie, thou art no thy-lane,
In proving *foresight* may be vain:
The best laid schemes o' *Mice* an' *Men*,
Gang aft agley,
An' lea'e us nought but grief an' pain,
For promis'd joy!

Still, thou art blest, compar'd wi' *me*!
The *present* only toucheth thee:
But Och! I *backward* cast my e'e,
On prospects drear!
An' *forward*, tho' I canna *see*,
I *guess* an' *fear*!

70. *The Holy Fair**

A robe of seeming truth and trust
Hid crafty Observation;
And secret hung, with poison'd crust,
The dirk of Defamation:
A mask that like the gorget show'd,
Dye-varying, on the pigeon;
And for a mantle large and broad,
He wrapt him in Religion.—
Hypocrisy a-la-Mode.

I

UPON a simmer *Sunday morn*,
When Nature's face is fair,
I walked forth to view the corn,
An' snuff the callor air:
The rising sun, owre GALSTON muirs,
Wi' glorious light was glintan;
The hares were hirplan down the furrs,
The lav'rocks they were chantan
Fu' sweet that day.

II

As lightsomely I glowr'd abroad,
To see a scene sae gay,
Three *hizzies*, early at the road,
Cam skelpan up the way.
Twa had manteeles o' dolefu' black,
But ane wi' lyart lining;
The *third*, that gaed a wee aback,
Was in the fashion shining
Fu' gay that day.

III

The *twa* appear'd like sisters twin,
In feature, form an' claes;
Their visage—wither'd, lang an' thin,
An' sour as onie slaes:
The *third* cam up, hap-step-an'-loup,
As light as onie lambie,—
An' wi' a curchie low did stoop,
As soon as e'er she saw me,
Fu' kind that day.

* *Holy Fair* is a common phrase in the West of Scotland for a sacramental occasion.

IV

Wi' bonnet aff, quoth I, 'Sweet lass,
'I think ye seem to ken me;
'I'm sure I've seen that bonie face,
'But yet I canna name ye.—'
Quo' she, an' laughan as she spak,
An' taks me by the hands,
'Ye, for my sake, hae gien the feck
'Of a' the *ten commands*
A screed some day.

V

'My name is FUN—your cronie dear,
'The nearest friend ye hae;
'An' this is SUPERSTITION here,
'An' that 's HYPOCRISY:
'I'm gaun to ********* *holy fair*,
'To spend an hour in daffin;
'Gin ye'll go there, yon runkl'd pair,
'We will get famous laughin
At them this day.'

VI

Quoth I, 'With a' my heart, I'll do 't;
'I'll get my Sunday's sark on,
'An' meet you on the holy spot;
'Faith we'se hae fine remarkin!'
Then I gaed hame, at crowdie-time,
An' soon I made me ready;
For roads were clad, frae side to side,
Wi' monie a weary body,
In droves that day.

VII

Here, farmers gash, in ridin graith,
Gaed hoddan by their cotters;
There, swankies young, in braw braid-claith,
Are springan owre the gutters.
The lasses, skelpan barefit, thrang,
In silks an' scarlets glitter;
Wi' *sweet-milk cheese*, in mony a whang,
An' *farls*, bak'd wi' butter,
Fu' crump that day.

VIII

When by the *plate* we set our nose,
  Weel heaped up wi' ha'pence,
A greedy glowr *Black-bonnet* throws,
  An' we maun draw our tippence.
Then in we go to see the show,
  On ev'ry side they're gath'ran;
Some carryan dails, some chairs an' stools,
  An' some are busy bleth'ran
          Right loud that day.

IX

Here, stands a shed to fend the show'rs,
  An' screen our countra Gentry;
There, *Racer-Jess*, an' twathree wh-res,
  Are blinkan at the entry:
Here sits a raw o' tittlan jads,
  Wi' heaving breasts an' bare neck;
An' there, a batch o' *Wabster lads*,
  Blackguarding frae K*******ck
          For *fun* this day.

X

Here, some are thinkan on their sins,
  An' some upo' their claes;
Ane curses feet that fyl'd his shins,
  Anither sighs an' pray's:
On this hand sits a Chosen swatch,
  Wi' screw'd-up, grace-proud faces;
On that, a set o' chaps, at watch,
  Thrang winkan on the lasses
          To *chairs* that day.

XI

O happy is that man, an' blest!
  Nae wonder that it pride him!
Whase ain dear lass, that he likes best,
  Comes clinkan down beside him!
Wi' arm repos'd on the *chair back*,
  He sweetly does compose him;
Which, by degrees, slips round her *neck*,
  An 's loof upon her *bosom*
          Unkend that day.

XII

Now a' the congregation o'er,
  Is silent expectation;
For ****** speels the holy door,
  Wi' tidings o' d–mn–t—n:
Should *Hornie*, as in ancient days,
  'Mang sons o' G— present him,
The vera sight o' ******'s face,
  To 's ain *het hame* had sent him
      Wi' fright that day.

XIII

Hear how he clears the points o' Faith
  Wi' rattlin an' thumpin!
Now meekly calm, now wild in wrath,
  He 's stampan, an' he 's jumpan!
His lengthen'd chin, his turn'd up snout,
  His eldritch squeel an' gestures,
O how they fire the heart devout,
  Like cantharidian plaisters
      On sic a day!

XIV

But hark! the *tent* has chang'd it's voice;
  There 's peace an' rest nae langer;
For a' the *real judges* rise,
  They canna sit for anger.
***** opens out his cauld harangues,
  On *practice* and on *morals*;
An' aff the godly pour in thrangs,
  To gie the jars an' barrels
      A lift that day.

XV

What signifies his barren shine,
  Of *moral pow'rs* an' *reason*;
His English style, an' gesture fine,
  Are a' clean out o' season.
Like SOCRATES or ANTONINE,
  Or some auld pagan heathen,
The *moral man* he does define,
  But ne'er a word o' *faith* in
      That 's right that day.

XVI

In guid time comes an antidote
  Against sic poosion'd nostrum;
For *******, frae the water-fit,
  Ascends the *holy rostrum*:
See, up he 's got the Word o' G—,
  An' meek an' mim has view'd it,
While COMMON-SENSE has taen the road,
  An' aff, an' up the *Cowgate**
        Fast, fast that day.

XVII

Wee ****** niest, the Guard relieves,
  An' Orthodoxy raibles,
Tho' in his heart he weel believes,
  An' thinks it auld wives' fables:
But faith! the birkie wants a *Manse*,
  So, cannilie he hums them;
Altho' his *carnal* Wit an' Sense
  Like hafflins-wise o'ercomes him
        At times that day.

XVIII

Now, butt an' ben, the Change-house fills,
  Wi' *yill-caup* Commentators:
Here 's crying out for bakes an' gills,
  An' there, the pint-stowp clatters;
While thick an' thrang, an' loud an' lang,
  Wi' *Logic*, an' wi' *Scripture*,
They raise a din, that, in the end,
  Is like to breed a rupture
        O' wrath that day.

XIX

Leeze me on Drink! it gies us mair
  Than either School or Colledge:
It kindles Wit, it waukens Lear,
  It pangs us fou o' Knowledge.
Be 't *whisky-gill* or *penny-wheep*,
  Or onie stronger potion,
It never fails, on drinkin deep,
  To kittle up our *notion*,
        By night or day.

* A street so called, which faces the *tent* in ——.

XX

The lads an' lasses, blythely bent
  To mind baith *saul* an' *body*,
Sit round the table, weel content,
  An' steer about the *Toddy*.
On this ane's dress, an' that ane's leuk,
  They're makin observations;
While some are cozie i' the neuk,
  An' forming *assignations*
      To meet some day.

XXI

But now the L—'s ain trumpet touts,
  Till a' the hills are rairan,
An' echos back return the shouts,
  Black ****** is na spairan:
His piercin words, like highlan swords,
  Divide the joints an' marrow;
His talk o' H–ll, whare devils dwell,
  Our vera* 'Sauls does harrow'
      Wi' fright that day.

XXII

A vast, unbottom'd, boundless *Pit*,
  Fill'd fou o' *lowan brunstane*.
Whase raging flame, an' scorching heat,
  Wad melt the hardest whunstane!
The *half-asleep* start up wi' fear,
  An' think they hear it roaran,
When presently it does appear,
  'Twas but some neebor *snoran*
      Asleep that day.

XXIII

'Twad be owre lang a tale to tell,
  How monie stories past,
An' how they crouded to the yill,
  When they were a' dismist:
How drink gaed round, in cogs an' caups,
  Amang the furms an' benches;
An' *cheese* an' *bread*, frae women's laps,
  Was dealt about in lunches,
      An' dawds that day

* Shakespeare's Hamlet.

XXIV

In comes a gausie, gash *Guidwife*,
An' sits down by the fire,
Syn draws her *kebbuck* an' her knife;
The lasses they are shyer.
The auld *Guidmen*, about the *grace*,
Frae side to side they bother,
Till some ane by his bonnet lays,
An' gies them 't, like a *tether*,
Fu' lang that day.

XXV

Wae sucks! for him that gets nae lass,
Or lasses that hae naething!
Sma' need has he to say a grace,
Or melvie his braw claething!
O *Wives* be mindfu', ance yoursel,
How bonie lads ye wanted,
An' dinna, for a *kebbuck-heel*,
Let lasses be affronted
On sic a day!

XXVI

Now *Clinkumbell*, wi' rattlan tow,
Begins to jow an' croon;
Some swagger hame, the best they dow,
Some wait the afternoon.
At slaps the billies halt a blink,
Till lasses strip their shoon:
Wi' *faith* an' *hope*, an' *love* an' *drink*,
They're a' in famous tune
For crack that day.

XXVII

How monie hearts this day converts,
O' Sinners and o' Lasses!
Their hearts o' stane, gin night are gane
As saft as ony flesh is.
There 's some are fou o' *love divine*;
There 's some are fou o' *brandy*;
An' monie jobs that day begin,
May end in *Houghmagandie*
Some ither day.

71. *The Twa Dogs. A Tale*

'TWAS in that place o' *Scotland's* isle,
That bears the name o' auld king COIL,
Upon a bonie day in June,
When wearing thro' the afternoon,
Twa Dogs, that were na thrang at hame,
Forgather'd ance upon a time.

The first I'll name, they ca'd him *Ceasar*,
Was keepet for his Honor's pleasure;
His hair, his size, his mouth, his lugs,
Show'd he was nane o' Scotland's dogs;
But whalpet some place far abroad,
Whare sailors gang to fish for Cod.

His locked, letter'd, braw brass-collar,
Show'd him the *gentleman* an' *scholar*;
But tho' he was o' high degree,
The fient a pride na pride had he,
But wad hae spent an hour caressan,
Ev'n wi' a Tinkler-gipsey's *messan*:
At *Kirk* or *Market*, *Mill* or *Smiddie*,
Nae tawtied *tyke*, tho' e'er sae duddie,
But he wad stan't, as glad to see him,
An' stroan't on stanes an' hillocks wi' him.

The tither was a *ploughman's collie*,
A rhyming, ranting, raving billie,
Wha for his friend an' comrade had him,
And in his freaks had *Luath* ca'd him;
After some dog in **Highlan Sang*,
Was made lang syne, lord knows how lang.

He was a gash an' faithfu' *tyke*,
As ever lap a sheugh, or dyke!
His honest sonsie, baws'nt *face*,
Ay gat him friends in ilka place;
His *breast* was white, his towzie *back*,
Weel clad wi' coat o' glossy black;
His gawsie tail, wi' upward curl,
Hung owre his hurdies wi' a swirl.

* Cuchullin's dog in Ossian's Fingal.

Nae doubt but they were fain o' ither,
An' unco pack an' thick the gither;
Wi' social *nose* whyles snuff'd an' snowcket;
Whyles mice an' modewurks they howcket;
Whyles scour'd awa in lang excursion,
An' worry'd ither in *diversion*;
Untill wi' daffin weary grown,
Upon a knowe they sat them down,
An' there began a lang digression
About the *lords o' the creation.*

CEASAR

I've aften wonder'd, honest *Luath*,
What sort o' life poor dogs like you have;
An' when the *gentry*'s life I saw,
What way *poor bodies* liv'd ava.

Our *Laird* gets in his racked rents,
His coals, his kane, an' a' his stents;
He rises when he likes himsel;
His flunkies answer at the bell;
He ca's his coach; he ca's his horse;
He draws a bonie, silken purse
As lang 's my *tail*, whare thro' the steeks,
The yellow, letter'd *Geordie* keeks.

Frae morn to een it 's nought but toiling,
At baking, roasting, frying, boiling:
An' tho' the gentry first are steghan,
Yet ev'n the *ha' folk* fill their peghan
Wi' sauce, ragouts, an' sic like trashtrie,
That 's little short o' downright wastrie.
Our *Whipper-in*, wee, blastiet wonner,
Poor, worthless elf, it eats a dinner,
Better than ony *Tenant-man*
His Honor has in a' the lan':
An' what poor *Cot-folk* pit their painch in,
I own it 's past my comprehension.—

LUATH

Trowth, *Ceasar*, whyles they're fash'd eneugh;
A *Cotter* howckan in a sheugh,
Wi' dirty stanes biggan an dyke,
Bairan a quarry, an' sic like,

Himsel, a wife, he thus sustains,
A smytrie o' wee, duddie weans,
An' nought but his han'-daurk, to keep
Them right an' tight in *thack an' raep.*

An' when they meet wi' sair disasters,
Like loss o' health, or want o' masters,
Ye maist wad think, a wee touch langer,
An' they maun starve o' cauld an' hunger:
But how it comes, I never kent yet,
They're maistly wonderfu' contented;
An' buirdly chiels, an' clever hizzies,
Are bred in sic a way as this is.

CEASAR

But then, to see how ye're negleket,
How huff'd, an' cuff'd, an' disrespeket!
L—d man, our gentry care as little
For *delvers, ditchers*, an' sic cattle;
They gang as saucy by poor folk,
As I wad by a stinkan brock.

I've notic'd, on our Laird's *court-day*,
An' mony a time my heart 's been wae,
Poor *tenant-bodies*, scant o' cash,
How they maun thole a *factor*'s snash;
He'll stamp an' threaten, curse an' swear,
He'll *apprehend* them, *poind* their gear,
While they maun stand, wi' aspect humble,
An' hear it a', an' fear an' tremble!

I see how folk live that hae riches,
But surely poor-folk maun be *wretches*!

LUATH

They're no sae wretched 's ane wad think;
Tho' constantly on poortith's brink,
They're sae accustom'd wi' the sight,
The view o't gies them little fright.

Then chance an' fortune are sae guided,
They're ay in less or mair provided;
An' tho' fatigu'd wi' close employment,
A blink o' rest 's a sweet enjoyment.

The dearest comfort o' their lives,
Their grushie weans, an' faithfu' wives;
The *prattling things* are just their pride,
That sweetens a' their fire-side.

An' whyles, twalpennie-worth o' *nappy*
Can mak the bodies unco happy;
They lay aside their private cares,
To mind the Kirk an' State affairs;
They'll talk o' *patronage* an' *priests*,
Wi' kindling fury i' their breasts,
Or tell what new taxation 's comin,
An' ferlie at the folk in LON'ON.

As bleak-fac'd Hallowmass returns,
They get the jovial, rantan *Kirns*,
When *rural life*, of ev'ry station,
Unite in common recreation;
Love blinks, Wit slaps, an' social Mirth
Forgets there 's *care* upo' the earth.

That *merry day* the year begins,
They bar the door on frosty win's;
The nappy reeks wi' mantling ream,
An' sheds a heart-inspiring steam;
The luntan pipe, an' sneeshin mill,
Are handed round wi' right guid will;
The cantie, auld folks, crackan crouse,
The young anes rantan thro' the house—
My heart has been sae fain to see them,
That I for joy hae *barket* wi' them.

Still it 's owre true that ye hae said,
Sic game is now owre aften play'd;
There 's monie a creditable *stock*
O' decent, honest, fawsont folk,
Are riven out baith root an' branch,
Some rascal's pridefu' greed to quench,
Wha thinks to knit himsel the faster
In favor wi' some *gentle Master*,
Wha, aiblins, thrang a *parliamentin*,
For *Britain's guid* his saul indentin—

CEASAR

Haith lad, ye little ken about it;
For Britain's guid! guid faith! I doubt it.
Say rather, gaun as PREMIERS lead him,
An' saying *aye* or *no* 's they bid him:
At Operas an' Plays parading,
Mortgaging, gambling, masquerading:
Or maybe, in a frolic daft,
To HAGUE or CALAIS takes a waft,
To make a *tour* an' take a whirl,
To learn *bon ton* an' see the worl'.

There, at VIENNA or VERSAILLES,
He rives his father's auld entails;
Or by MADRID he takes the rout,
To thrum *guittarres* an' fecht wi' *nowt*;
Or down *Italian Vista* startles,
Wh–re-hunting amang groves o' myrtles:
Then bowses drumlie *German-water*,
To make himsel look fair an' fatter,
An' clear the consequential sorrows,
Love-gifts of Carnival Signioras.
For Britain's guid! for her destruction!
Wi' dissipation, feud an' faction!

LUATH

Hech man! dear sirs! is that the gate,
They waste sae mony a braw estate!
Are we sae foughten an' harass'd
For gear to gang that gate at last!

O would they stay aback frae courts,
An' please themsels wi' countra sports,
It wad for ev'ry ane be better,
The *Laird*, the *Tenant*, an' the *Cotter*!
For thae frank, rantan, ramblan billies,
Fient haet o' them 's illhearted fellows;
Except for breakin o' their timmer,
Or speakin lightly o' their *Limmer*;
Or shootin of a hare or moorcock,
The ne'er-a-bit they're ill to poor folk.

But will ye tell me, master *Cesar*,
Sure *great folk*'s life 's a life o' pleasure?
Nae cauld nor hunger e'er can steer them,
The vera thought o't need na fear them.

CESAR

L—d man, were ye but whyles where I am,
The *gentles* ye wad ne'er envy them!

It 's true, they needna starve or sweat,
Thro' Winter's cauld, or Summer's heat;
They've nae sair-wark to craze their banes,
An' fill *auld-age* wi' grips an' granes:
But *human-bodies* are sic fools,
For a' their Colledges an' Schools,
That when nae *real* ills perplex them,
They *mak* enow themsels to vex them;
An' ay the less they hae to sturt them,
In like proportion, less will hurt them.

A country fellow at the pleugh,
His *acre*'s till'd, he 's right eneugh;
A country girl at her wheel,
Her *dizzen*'s done, she 's unco weel;
But Gentlemen, an' Ladies warst,
Wi' ev'n down *want o' wark* they're curst.
They loiter, lounging, lank an' lazy;
Tho' deil-haet ails them, yet uneasy;
Their days, insipid, dull an' tasteless,
Their nights, unquiet, lang an' restless.

An' ev'n their sports, their balls an' races,
Their galloping thro' public places,
There 's sic parade, sic pomp an' art,
The joy can scarcely reach the heart.

The *Men* cast out in *party-matches*,
Then sowther a' in deep debauches.
Ae night, they're mad wi' drink an' wh-ring,
Niest day their life is past enduring.

The *Ladies* arm-in-arm in clusters,
As great an' gracious a' as sisters;
But hear their *absent thoughts* o' ither,
They're a' run-deils an' jads the gither

Whyles, owre the wee bit cup an' platie,
They sip the *scandal-potion* pretty;
Or lee-lang nights, wi' crabbet leuks,
Pore owre the devil's *pictur'd beuks*;
Stake on a chance a farmer's stackyard,
An' cheat like ony *unhang'd blackguard*.

There 's some exceptions, man an' woman;
But this is Gentry's life in common.

By this, the sun was out o' sight,
An' darker gloamin brought the night:
The *bum-clock* humm'd wi' lazy drone,
The kye stood rowtan i' the loan;
When up they gat, an' shook their lugs,
Rejoic'd they were na *men* but *dogs*;
An' each took off his several way,
Resolv'd to meet some ither day.

72. *The Cotter's Saturday Night. Inscribed to R. A****, Esq.*

Let not Ambition mock their useful toil,
Their homely joys, and destiny obscure;
Nor Grandeur hear, with a disdainful smile,
The short and simple annals of the Poor.
GRAY.

I

My lov'd, my honor'd, much respected friend,
No mercenary Bard his homage pays;
With honest pride, I scorn each selfish end,
My dearest meed, a friend's esteem and praise:
To you I sing, in simple Scottish lays,
The *lowly train* in life's sequester'd scene;
The native feelings strong, the guileless ways,
What A**** in a *Cottage* would have been;
Ah! tho' his worth unknown, far happier there I ween!

II

November chill blaws loud wi' angry sugh;
The short'ning winter-day is near a close;
The miry beasts retreating frae the pleugh;
The black'ning trains o' craws to their repose:

The toil-worn COTTER frae his labor goes,
This night his weekly moil is at an end,
Collects his *spades*, his *mattocks* and his *hoes*,
Hoping the *morn* in ease and rest to spend,
And weary, o'er the muir, his course does hameward bend.

III

At length his lonely *Cot* appears in view,
Beneath the shelter of an aged tree;
Th' expectant wee-things, toddlan, stacher thro'
To meet their *Dad*, wi' flichterin noise and glee.
His wee-bit ingle, blinkan bonilie,
His clean hearth-stane, his thrifty *Wifie*'s smile,
The *lisping infant*, prattling on his knee,
Does a' his weary kiaugh and care beguile,
And makes him quite forget his labor and his toil.

IV

Belyve, the *elder bairns* come drapping in,
At *Service* out, amang the Farmers roun';
Some ca' the pleugh, some herd, some tentie rin
A cannie errand to a neebor toun:
Their eldest hope, their *Jenny*, woman-grown,
In youthfu' bloom, Love sparkling in her e'e,
Comes hame, perhaps to show a braw new gown,
Or deposite her sair-won penny-fee,
To help her *Parents* dear, if they in hardship be.

V

With joy unfeign'd, *brothers* and *sisters* meet,
And each for other's weelfare kindly spiers:
The social hours, swift-wing'd, unnotic'd, fleet;
Each tells the uncos that he sees or hears.
The *Parents partial* eye their hopeful years;
Anticipation forward points the view;
The *Mother* wi' her needle and her sheers
Gars auld claes look amaist as weel 's the new;
The *Father* mixes a', wi' admonition due.

VI

Their Master's and their Mistress's command,
The *youngkers* a' are warned to obey;
And mind their labors wi' an eydent hand,
And ne'er, tho' out o' sight, to jauk or play:

'And O! be sure to fear the LORD alway!
'And mind your *duty*, duely, morn and night!
'Lest in temptation's path ye gang astray,
'Implore His counsel and assisting might:
'They never sought in vain, that sought the LORD aright.'

VII

But hark! a rap comes gently to the door;
Jenny, wha kens the meaning o' the same,
Tells how a neebor lad came o'er the muir,
To do some errands, and convoy her hame.
The wily Mother sees the *conscious flame*
Sparkle in *Jenny*'s e'e, and flush her cheek,
With heart-struck, anxious care enquires his name,
While *Jenny* hafflins is afraid to speak;
Weel-pleas'd the Mother hears, it 's nae wild, worthless *Rake*.

VIII

With kindly welcome, *Jenny* brings him ben;
A *strappan youth*, he takes the Mother's eye;
Blythe *Jenny* sees the *visit* 's no ill-taen;
The Father cracks of horses, pleughs and kye.
The *youngster*'s artless heart o'erflows wi' joy,
But blate and laithfu', scarce can weel behave;
The Mother, wi' a woman's wiles, can spy
What makes the *youth* sae bashfu' and sae grave;
Weel-pleas'd to think her *bairn* 's respected like the lave.

IX

O happy love! where love like this is found!
O heart-felt raptures! bliss beyond compare!
I've paced much this weary, *mortal round*,
And sage EXPERIENCE bids me this declare—
'If Heaven a draught of heavenly pleasure spare,
'One *cordial* in this melancholly *Vale*,
' 'Tis when a youthful, loving, *modest* Pair,
'In other's arms, breathe out the tender tale,
'Beneath the milk-white thorn that scents the ev'ning gale.'

X

Is there, in human-form, that bears a heart—
A wretch! a villain! lost to love and truth!
That can, with studied, sly, ensnaring art,
Betray sweet *Jenny*'s unsuspecting youth?

Curse on his perjur'd arts! dissembling smoothe!
  Are *Honor*, *Virtue*, *Conscience*, all exil'd?
Is there no Pity, no relenting Ruth,
  Points to the Parents fondling o'er their Child?
Then paints the *ruin'd Maid*, and *their* distraction wild!

XI

But now the Supper crowns their simple board,
  The healsome *Porritch*, chief of SCOTIA's food:
The soupe their *only Hawkie* does afford,
  That 'yont the hallan snugly chows her cood:
The *Dame* brings forth, in complimental mood,
  To grace the lad, her weel-hain'd kebbuck, fell;
And aft he 's prest, and aft he ca's it guid;
  The frugal *Wifie*, garrulous, will tell,
How 'twas a towmond auld, sin' Lint was i' the bell.

XII

The chearfu' Supper done, wi' serious face,
  They, round the ingle, form a circle wide;
The Sire turns o'er, with patriarchal grace,
  The big *ha'-Bible*, ance his *Father*'s pride:
His bonnet rev'rently is laid aside,
  His *lyart haffets* wearing thin and bare;
Those strains that once did sweet in ZION glide,
  He wales a portion with judicious care;
'*And let us worship* GOD*!*' he says with solemn air.

XIII

They chant their artless notes in simple guise;
  They tune their hearts, by far the noblest aim:
Perhaps *Dundee*'s wild-warbling measures rise,
  Or plaintive *Martyrs*, worthy of the name;
Or noble *Elgin* beets the heaven-ward flame,
  The sweetest far of SCOTIA's holy lays:
Compar'd with these, *Italian trills* are tame;
  The tickl'd ears no heart-felt raptures raise;
Nae unison hae they, with our CREATOR's praise.

XIV

The priest-like Father reads the sacred page,
  How *Abram* was the Friend of GOD on high;
Or, *Moses* bade eternal warfare wage,
  With *Amalek*'s ungracious progeny;

Or how the *royal Bard* did groaning lye,
  Beneath the stroke of Heaven's avenging ire;
Or *Job*'s pathetic plaint, and wailing cry;
  Or rapt *Isiah*'s wild, seraphic fire;
Or other *Holy Seers* that tune the *sacred lyre*.

XV

Perhaps the *Christian Volume* is the theme;
  How *guiltless blood* for *guilty man* was shed;
How HE, who bore in Heaven the second name,
  Had not on Earth whereon to lay His head:
How His first *followers* and *servants* sped;
  The *Precepts sage* they wrote to many a land:
How *he*, who lone in *Patmos*, banished,
  Saw in the sun a mighty angel stand;
And heard great *Bab'lon*'s doom pronounc'd by Heaven's command.

XVI

Then kneeling down to HEAVEN'S ETERNAL KING,
  The *Saint*, the *Father*, and the *Husband* prays:
Hope 'springs exulting on triumphant wing,'*
  That *thus* they all shall meet in future days:
There, ever bask in *uncreated rays*,
  No more to sigh, or shed the bitter tear,
Together hymning their CREATOR's praise
  In *such society*, yet still more dear;
While circling Time moves round in an eternal sphere.

XVII

Compar'd with this, how poor Religion's pride,
  In all the pomp of *method*, and of *art*,
When men display to congregations wide,
  Devotion's ev'ry grace, except the *heart*!
The POWER, incens'd, the Pageant will desert,
  The pompous strain, the sacredotal stole;
But haply, in some *Cottage* far apart,
  May hear, well pleas'd, the language of the *Soul*;
And in His *Book of Life* the Inmates poor enroll.

XVIII

Then homeward all take off their sev'ral way;
  The youngling *Cottagers* retire to rest:
The Parent-pair their *secret homage* pay,
  And proffer up to Heaven the warm request,

* Popes Windsor Forest.

That 'HE who stills the *raven*'s clam'rous nest,
'And decks the *lily* fair in flow'ry pride,
'Would, in the way His *Wisdom* sees the best,
'For *them* and for their *little ones* provide;
'But chiefly, in their hearts with *Grace divine* preside.'

XIX

From Scenes like these, old SCOTIA's grandeur springs,
That makes her lov'd at home, rever'd abroad:
Princes and lords are but the breath of kings,
'An honest man 's the noble work of GOD:'
And *certes*, in fair Virtue's heavenly road,
The *Cottage* leaves the *Palace* far behind:
What is a lordling's pomp? a cumbrous load,
Disguising oft the *wretch* of human kind,
Studied in arts of Hell, in wickedness refin'd!

XX

O SCOTIA! my dear, my native soil!
For whom my warmest wish to Heaven is sent!
Long may thy hardy sons of *rustic toil*
Be blest with health and peace and sweet content!
And O may Heaven their simple lives prevent
From *Luxury*'s contagion, weak and vile!
Then howe'er *crowns* and *coronets* be rent,
A *virtuous Populace* may rise the while,
And stand a wall of fire, around their much-lov'd ISLE.

XXI

O THOU! who pour'd the *patriotic tide*,
That stream'd thro' great, unhappy WALLACE' heart;
Who dar'd to, nobly, stem tyrannic pride,
Or *nobly die*, the second glorious part:
(The Patriot's GOD, peculiarly thou art,
His *friend*, *inspirer*, *guardian* and *reward*!)
O never, never SCOTIA's realm desert,
But still the *Patriot*, and the *Patriot-bard*,
In bright succession raise, her *Ornament* and *Guard*!

THE following POEM will, by many Readers, be well enough understood; but, for the sake of those who are unacquainted with the manners and traditions of the country where the scene is cast, Notes are added, to give some account of the principal Charms and Spells of that Night, so big with Prophecy to the Peasantry in the West of Scotland. The passion of prying into Futurity makes a striking part of the history of Human-nature, in it's rude state, in all ages and nations; and it may be some entertainment to a philosophic mind, if any such should honor the Author with a perusal, to see the remains of it, among the more unenlightened in our own.

73. *Halloween**

Yes! let the Rich deride, the Proud disdain,
The simple pleasures of the lowly train;
To me more dear, congenial to my heart,
One native charm, than all the gloss of art.
GOLDSMITH.

I

UPON that *night*, when Fairies light,
On *Cassilis Downans*† dance,
Or owre the lays, in splendid blaze,
On sprightly coursers prance;
Or for *Colean*, the rout is taen,
Beneath the moon's pale beams;
There, up the *Cove*,‡ to stray an' rove,
Amang the rocks an' streams
To sport that night.

II

Amang the bonie, winding banks,
Where *Doon* rins, wimplin, clear,
Where BRUCE|| ance rul'd the martial ranks,
An' shook his *Carrick* spear,

* Is thought to be a night when Witches, Devils, and other mischief-making beings, are all abroad on their baneful, midnight errands: particularly, those aerial people, the Fairies, are said, on that night, to hold a grand Anniversary.

† Certain little, romantic, rocky, green hills, in the neighbourhood of the ancient seat of the Earls of Cassilis.

‡ A noted cavern near Colean-house, called the Cove of Colean; which, as well as Cassilis Downans, is famed, in country story, for being a favourite haunt of Fairies.

|| The famous family of that name, the ancestors of ROBERT the great Deliverer of his country, were Earls of Carrick.

Some merry, friendly, countra folks,
  Together did convene,
To *burn* their nits, an' *pou* their stocks,
  An' haud their *Halloween*
      Fu' blythe that night.

III

The lasses feat, an' cleanly neat,
  Mair braw than when they're fine;
Their faces blythe, fu' sweetly kythe,
  Hearts leal, an' warm, an' kin':
The lads sae trig, wi' wooer-babs,
  Weel knotted on their garten,
Some unco blate, an' some wi' gabs,
  Gar lasses hearts gang startin
      Whyles fast at night.

IV

Then, first an' foremost, thro' the kail,
  Their *stocks** maun a' be sought ance;
They steek their een, an' grape an' wale,
  For muckle anes, an' straught anes.
Poor hav'rel *Will* fell aff the drift,
  An' wander'd thro' the *Bow-kail*,
An' pow't, for want o' better shift,
  A *runt* was like a sow-tail
      Sae bow't that night.

V

Then, straught or crooked, yird or nane,
  They roar an' cry a' throw'ther;
The vera *wee-things*, toddlan, rin,
  Wi' stocks out owre their shouther:

* The first ceremony of Halloween, is, pulling each a *Stock*, or plant of kail. They must go out, hand in hand, with eyes shut, and pull the first they meet with: its being big or little, straight or crooked, is prophetic of the size and shape of the grand object of all their Spells—the husband or wife. If any *yird*, or earth, stick to the root, that is *tocher*, or fortune; and the taste of the *custoc*, that is, the heart of the stem, is indicative of the natural temper and disposition. Lastly, the stems, or to give them their ordinary appellation, the *runts*, are placed somewhere above the head of the door; and the christian names of the people whom chance brings into the house, are, according to the priority of placing the *runts*, the names in question.

An' gif the *custock*'s sweet or sour,
Wi' joctelegs they taste them;
Syne coziely, aboon the door,
Wi' cannie care, they've plac'd them
To lye that night.

VI

The lasses staw frae 'mang them a',
To pou their *stalks o' corn*;*
But *Rab* slips out, an' jinks about,
Behint the muckle thorn:
He grippet *Nelly* hard an' fast;
Loud skirl'd a' the lasses;
But her *tap-pickle* maist was lost,
When kiutlan in the *Fause-house*†
Wi' him that night.

VII

The auld Guidwife's weel-hoordet *nits*‡
Are round an' round divided,
An' monie lads an' lasses fates
Are there that night decided:
Some kindle, couthie, side by side,
An' *burn* thegither trimly;
Some start awa, wi' saucy pride,
An' jump out owre the chimlie
Fu' high that night.

VIII

Jean slips in twa, wi' tentie e'e;
Wha 'twas, she wadna tell;
But this is *Jock*, an' this is *me*,
She says in to hersel:

* They go to the barn-yard, and pull each, at three several times, a stalk of Oats. If the third stalk wants the *top-pickle*, that is, the grain at the top of the stalk, the party in question will come to the marriage-bed any thing but a Maid.

† When the corn is in a doubtful state, by being too green, or wet, the Stack-builder, by means of old timber, *&c.* makes a large apartment in his stack, with an opening in the side which is fairest exposed to the wind: this he calls a *Fause-house*.

‡ Burning the nuts is a favourite charm. They name the lad and lass to each particular nut, as they lay them in the fire; and according as they burn quietly together, or start from beside one another, the course and issue of the Courtship will be.

He bleez'd owre her, an' she owre him,
As they wad never mair part,
Till fuff! he started up the lum,
An' *Jean* had e'en a sair heart
To see 't that night.

IX

Poor *Willie*, wi' his *bow-kail runt*,
Was *brunt* wi' primsie *Mallie*;
An' *Mary*, nae doubt, took the drunt,
To be compar'd to *Willie*:
Mall's nit lap out, wi' pridefu' fling,
An' her ain fit, it brunt it;
While *Willie* lap, an' swoor by *jing*,
'Twas just the way he wanted
To be that night.

X

Nell had the *Fause-house* in her min',
She pits hersel an' *Rob* in;
In loving bleeze they sweetly join,
Till white in ase they're sobbin:
Nell's heart was dancin at the view;
She whisper'd *Rob* to leuk for't;
Rob, stownlins, prie'd her bonie mou,
Fu' cozie in the neuk for't,
Unseen that night.

XI

But *Merran* sat behint their backs,
Her thoughts on *Andrew Bell*;
She lea'es them gashan at their cracks,
An' slips out by hersel:
She thro' the yard the nearest taks,
An' for the *kiln* she goes then,
An' darklins grapet for the *bauks*,
And in the *blue-clue** throws then,
Right fear't that night

* Whoever would, with success, try this spell, must strictly observe these directions. Steal out, all alone, to the *kiln*, and, darkling, throw into the *pot*, a clew of blue yarn: wind it in a new clew off the old one; and towards the latter end, something will hold the thread: demand, *wha hauds?* i.e. who holds? and answer will be returned from the kiln-pot, by naming the christian and sirname of your future Spouse.

XII

An' ay she *win't*, an' ay she swat,
  I wat she made nae jaukin;
Till something *held* within the *pat*,
  Guid L—d! but she was quaukin!
But whether 'twas the *Deil* himsel,
  Or whether 'twas a *bauk-en'*,
Or whether it was *Andrew Bell*,
  She did na wait on talkin
    To spier that night.

XIII

Wee Jenny to her Graunie says,
  'Will ye go wi' me Graunie?
'I'll *eat the apple** at the *glass*,
  'I gat frae uncle Johnie:'
She fuff't her pipe wi' sic a lunt,
  In wrath she was sae vap'rin,
She notic't na, an aizle brunt
  Her braw, new, worset apron
    Out thro' that night.

XIV

'Ye little Skelpie-limmer's-face!
  'I daur you try sic sportin,
'As seek the *foul Thief* onie place,
  'For him to spae your fortune:
'Nae doubt but ye may get a *sight*!
  'Great cause ye hae to fear it;
'For monie a ane has gotten a fright,
  'An' liv'd an' di'd deleeret,
    'On sic a night.

XV

'Ae Hairst afore the *Sherra-moor*,
  'I mind 't as weel 's yestreen,
'I was a gilpey then, I'm sure,
  'I was na past fyfteen:

* Take a candle, and go, alone, to a looking glass: eat an apple before it, and some traditions say you should comb your hair all the time: the face of your conjugal companion, *to be*, will be seen in the glass, as if peeping over your shoulder.

'The Simmer had been cauld an' wat,
'An' *Stuff* was unco green;
'An' ay a rantan *Kirn* we gat,
'An' just on *Halloween*
'It fell that night.

XVI

'Our *Stibble-rig* was *Rab M'Graen,*
'A clever, sturdy fallow;
'His Sin gat *Eppie Sim* wi' wean,
'That liv'd in Achmacalla:
'He gat *hemp-seed**, I mind it weel,
'An' he made unco light o't;
'But monie a day was *by himsel,*
'He was sae sairly frighted
'That vera night.'

XVII

Then up gat fechtan *Jamie Fleck,*
An' he swoor by his conscience,
That he could *saw hemp-seed* a peck;
For it was a' but nonsense:
The auld guidman raught down the pock,
An' out a handfu' gied him;
Syne bad him slip frae 'mang the folk,
Sometime when nae ane see'd him,
An' try't that night.

XVIII

He marches thro' amang the stacks,
Tho' he was something sturtan;
The *graip* he for a *harrow* taks,
An' haurls at his curpan:
And ev'ry now an' then, he says,
'Hemp-seed I saw thee,
'An' her that is to be my lass,
'Come after me an' draw thee
'As fast this night.'

* Steal out, unperceived, and sow a handful of hemp seed; harrowing it with any thing you can conveniently draw after you. Repeat, now and then, 'Hemp seed I saw thee, Hemp seed I saw thee, and him (or her) that is to be my true-love, come after me and pou thee.' Look over your left shoulder, and you will see the appearance of the person invoked, in the attitude of pulling hemp. Some traditions say, 'come after me and shaw thee,' that is, show thyself; in which case it simply appears. Others omit the harrowing, and say, 'come after me and harrow thee.'

XIX

He whistl'd up *lord Lenox' march*,
To keep his courage cheary;
Altho' his hair began to arch,
He was sae fley'd an' eerie:
Till presently he hears a squeak,
An' then a grane an' gruntle;
He by his showther gae a keek,
An' tumbl'd wi' a wintle
Out owre that night.

XX

He roar'd a horrid murder-shout,
In dreadfu' desperation!
An' young an' auld come rinnan out,
An' hear the sad narration:
He swoor 'twas hilchan *Jean M'Craw*,
Or crouchie *Merran Humphie*,
Till stop! she trotted thro' them a';
An' wha was it but *Grumphie*
Asteer that night?

XXI

Meg fain wad to the *Barn* gaen,
To *winn three wechts o' naething*;*
But for to meet the Deil her lane,
She pat but little faith in:
She gies the Herd a pickle nits,
An' twa red cheeket apples,
To watch, while for the *Barn* she sets,
In hopes to see *Tam Kipples*
That vera night.

* This charm must likewise be performed, unperceived and alone. You go to the *barn*, and open both doors; taking them off the hinges, if possible; for there is danger, that the Being, about to appear, may shut the doors, and do you some mischief. Then take that instrument used in winnowing the corn, which, in our country-dialect, we call a *wecht*; and go thro' all the attitudes of letting down corn against the wind. Repeat it three times; and the third time, an apparition will pass thro' the barn, in at the windy door, and out at the other, having both the figure in question and the appearance or retinue, marking the employment or station in life.

XXII

She turns the key, wi' cannie thraw,
  An' owre the threshold ventures;
But first on *Sawnie* gies a ca',
  Syne bauldly in she enters:
A *ratton* rattl'd up the wa',
  An' she cry'd, L—d preserve her!
An' ran thro' midden-hole an' a',
  An' pray'd wi' zeal and fervour,
      Fu' fast that night.

XXIII

They hoy't out Will, wi' sair advice;
  They hecht him some fine braw ane;
It chanc'd the *Stack* he *faddom't thrice*,*
  Was timmer-propt for thrawin:
He taks a swirlie, auld *moss-oak*,
  For some black, grousome *Carlin*;
An' loot a winze, an' drew a stroke,
  Till skin in blypes cam haurlin
      Aff 's nieves that night.

XXIV

A wanton widow *Leezie* was,
  As cantie as a kittlen;
But Och! that night, amang the shaws,
  She gat a fearfu' settlin!
She thro' the whins, an' by the cairn,
  An' owre the hill gaed scrievin,
Whare *three Lairds' lan's met at a burn*,†
  To dip her *left sark-sleeve* in,
      Was bent that night.

XXV

Whyles owre a linn the burnie plays,
  As thro' the glen it wimpl't;
Whyles round a rocky scar it strays;
  Whyles in a wiel it dimpl't;

* Take an opportunity of going, unnoticed, to a *Bear-stack*, and fathom it three times round. The last fathom of the last time, you will catch in your arms, the appearance of your future conjugal yoke-fellow.

† You go out, one or more, for this is a social spell, to a south-running spring or rivulet, where 'three Lairds' lands meet,' and dip your left shirt-sleeve. Go to bed in sight of a fire, and hang your wet sleeve before it to dry. Ly awake; and sometime near midnight, an apparition, having the exact figure of the grand object in question, will come and turn the sleeve, as if to dry the other side of it.

Whyles glitter'd to the nightly rays,
  Wi' bickerin, dancin dazzle;
Whyles cooket underneath the braes,
  Below the spreading hazle
      Unseen that night.

XXVI

Amang the brachens, on the brae,
  Between her an' the moon,
The Deil, or else an outler Quey,
  Gat up an' gae a croon:
Poor *Leezie*'s heart maist lap the hool;
  Near lav'rock-height she jumpet,
But mist a fit, an' in the *pool*,
  Out owre the lugs she plumpet,
      Wi' a plunge that night.

XXVII

In order, on the clean hearth-stane,
  The *Luggies** three are ranged;
And ev'ry time great care is taen,
  To see them duely changed:
Auld, uncle *John*, wha *wedlock's joys*,
  Sin' *Mar's-year* did desire,
Because he gat the toom dish thrice,
  He heav'd them on the fire,
      In wrath that night.

XXVIII

Wi' merry sangs, an' friendly cracks,
  I wat they did na weary;
And unco tales, an' funnie jokes,
  Their sports were cheap an' cheary:
Till *buttr'd So'ns*,† wi' fragrant lunt,
  Set a' their gabs a steerin;
Syne, wi' a social glass o' strunt,
  They parted aff careerin
      Fu' blythe that night.

* Take three dishes; put clean water in one, foul water in another, and leave the third empty: blindfold a person, and lead him to the hearth where the dishes are ranged; he (or she) dips the left hand: if by chance in the clean water, the future husband or wife will come to the bar of Matrimony, a Maid; if in the foul, a widow; if in the empty dish, it foretells, with equal certainty, no marriage at all. It is repeated three times; and every time the arrangement of the dishes is altered.

† Sowens, with butter instead of milk to them, is always the *Halloween Supper*.

74. [*The Mauchline Wedding*]

I

WHEN Eighty-five was seven month auld,
  And wearing thro' the aught,
When rotting rains and Boreas bauld
  Gied farmer-folks a faught;
Ae morning quondam Mason Will,
  Now Merchant Master Miller,
Gaed down to meet wi' Nansie Bell
  And her Jamaica siller,
      To wed, that day.—

2

The rising sun o'er Blacksideen*
  Was just appearing fairly,
When Nell and Bess† get up to dress
  Seven lang half-hours o'er early!
Now presses clink and drawers jink,
  For linnens and for laces;
But modest Muses only *think*
  What ladies' under dress is,
      On sic a day.—

3

But we'll suppose the stays are lac'd,
  And bony bosom steekit;
Tho', thro' the lawn—but guess the rest—
  An Angel scarce durst keekit:
Then stockins fine, o' silken twine,
  Wi' cannie care are drawn up;
And gartened tight, whare mortal wight—

. . . . .

. . . .

But now the gown wi' rustling sound,
  Its silken‡ pomp displays;
Sure there 's no sin in being vain
  O' siccan bony claes!

* a hill— † Miller's two sisters—
‡ The ladies' first silk gowns, got for the occasion

25 *Comment in MS*—As I never wrote it down, my recollection does not entirely serve me.—

Sae jimp the waist, the tail sae vast—
  Trouth, they were bony Birdies!
O Mither Eve, ye wad been grave
  To see their ample hurdies
        Sae large that day!!!

Then Sandy* wi 's red jacket bra'
  Comes, whip-jee-whoa! about,
And in he gets the bony twa—
  Lord send them safely out!
And auld John† Trot wi' sober phiz
  As braid and bra 's a Bailie,
His shouthers and his Sunday's giz
  Wi' powther and wi' ulzie
        Weel smear'd that day—

75. *The Auld Farmer's New-year-morning Salutation to his Auld Mare, Maggie, on giving her the accustomed ripp of corn to hansel in the New-year*

A *Guid New-year* I wish thee, Maggie!
Hae, there 's a ripp to thy auld baggie:
Tho' thou 's howe-backet, now, an' knaggie,
        I've seen the day,
Thou could hae gaen like ony staggie
        Out-owre the lay.

Tho' now thou 's dowie, stiff an' crazy,
An' thy auld hide as white 's a daisie,
I've seen thee dappl't, sleek an' glaizie,
        A bonie gray:
He should been tight that daur't to *raize* thee,
        Ance in a day.

Thou ance was i' the foremost rank,
A *filly* buirdly, steeve an' swank,
An' set weel down a shapely shank,
        As e'er tread yird;
An' could hae flown out-owre a stank,
        Like onie bird.

* Driver of the post chaise † M—'s father—

43 *Comment in MS* Against my Muse had come thus far, Miss Bess and I were once more in Unison, so I thought no more of the Piece.—

It 's now some nine-an'-twenty year,
Sin' thou was my *Guidfather's Meere*;
He gied me thee, o' tocher clear,
An' fifty mark;
Tho' it was sma', 'twas *weel-won* gear,
An' thou was stark.

When first I gaed to woo my *Jenny*,
Ye then was trottan wi' your Minnie:
Tho' ye was trickie, slee an' funnie,
Ye ne'er was donsie;
But hamely, tawie, quiet an' cannie,
An' unco sonsie.

That *day*, ye pranc'd wi' muckle pride,
When ye bure hame my bonie *Bride*:
An' sweet an' gracefu' she did ride
Wi' maiden air!
KYLE-STEWART I could bragged wide,
For sic a *pair*.

Tho' now ye dow but hoyte and hoble,
An' wintle like a saumont-coble,
That day, ye was a jinker noble,
For heels an' win'!
An' ran them till they a' did wauble,
Far, far behin'!

When thou an' I were young an' skiegh,
An' *Stable-meals* at Fairs were driegh,
How thou wad prance, an' snore, an' scriegh,
An' tak the road!
Towns-bodies ran, an' stood abiegh,
An' ca't thee mad.

When thou was corn't, an' I was mellow,
We took the road ay like a Swallow:
At *Brooses* thou had ne'er a fellow,
For pith an' speed;
But ev'ry tail thou pay't them hollow,
Whare'er thou gaed.

The sma', droop-rumpl't, hunter cattle,
Might aiblins waur't thee for a brattle;
But *sax Scotch mile*, thou try't their mettle,
An' gart them whaizle:
Nae whip nor spur, but just a wattle
O' saugh or hazle.

Thou was a noble *Fittie-lan'*,
As e'er in tug or tow was drawn!
Aft thee an' I, in aught hours gaun,
On guid March-weather,
Hae turn'd *sax rood* beside our han',
For days thegither.

Thou never braing't, an' fetch't, an' flisket,
But thy *auld tail* thou wad hae whisket,
An' spread abreed thy weel-fill'd *brisket*,
Wi' pith an' pow'r,
Till sprittie knowes wad rair't an' risket,
An' slypet owre.

When frosts lay lang, an' snaws were deep,
An' threaten'd *labor* back to keep,
I gied thy *cog* a wee-bit heap
Aboon the timmer;
I ken'd my *Maggie* wad na sleep
For that, or Simmer.

In *cart* or *car* thou never reestet;
The steyest brae thou wad hae fac't it;
Thou never lap, an' sten't, an' breastet,
Then stood to blaw;
But just thy step a wee thing hastet,
Thou snoov't awa.

My Pleugh is now thy *bairn-time* a';
Four gallant brutes, as e'er did draw;
Forby sax mae, I've sell't awa,
That thou hast nurst:
They drew me thretteen pund an' twa,
The vera warst.

Monie a sair daurk we twa hae wrought,
An' wi' the weary warl' fought!
An' monie an *anxious day*, I thought
We wad be beat!
Yet here to *crazy Age* we're brought,
Wi' something yet.

An' think na, my auld, trusty *Servan'*,
That now perhaps thou 's less deservin,
An' thy *auld days* may end in starvin',
For my last fow,
A heapet *Stimpart*, I'll reserve ane
Laid by for you.

We've worn to crazy years thegither;
We'll toyte about wi' ane anither;
Wi' tentie care I'll flit thy tether,
To some hain'd rig,
Whare ye may nobly rax your leather,
Wi' sma' fatigue.

76. *Address to the Deil*

O Prince, O chief of many throned pow'rs,
That led th' embattl'd Seraphim to war—
MILTON.

O THOU, whatever title suit thee!
Auld Hornie, Satan, Nick, or Clootie,
Wha in yon cavern grim an' sooty
Clos'd under hatches,
Spairges about the brunstane cootie,
To scaud poor wretches!

Hear me, *auld Hangie*, for a wee,
An' let poor, *damned bodies* bee;
I'm sure sma' pleasure it can gie,
Ev'n to a *deil*,
To skelp an' scaud poor dogs like me,
An' hear us squeel!

Great is thy pow'r, an' great thy fame;
Far ken'd, an' noted is thy name;
An' tho' yon *lowan heugh*'s thy hame,
Thou travels far;
An' faith! thou 's neither lag nor lame,
Nor blate nor scaur.

Whyles, ranging like a roaring lion,
For prey, a' holes an' corners tryin;
Whyles, on the strong-wing'd Tempest flyin,
Tirlan the *kirks*;
Whyles, in the human bosom pryin,
Unseen thou lurks.

I've heard my rev'rend *Graunie* say,
In lanely glens ye like to stray;
Or where auld, ruin'd castles, gray,
Nod to the moon,
Ye fright the nightly wand'rer's way,
Wi' eldritch croon.

When twilight did my *Graunie* summon,
To say her pray'rs, douse, honest woman,
Aft 'yont the dyke she 's heard you bumman,
Wi' eerie drone;
Or, rustling, thro' the boortries coman,
Wi' heavy groan.

Ae dreary, windy, winter night,
The stars shot down wi' sklentan light,
Wi' you, *mysel*, I gat a fright
Ayont the lough;
Ye, like a *rash-buss*, stood in sight,
Wi' waving sugh:

The cudgel in my nieve did shake,
Each bristl'd hair stood like a stake,
When wi' an eldritch, stoor, *quaick*, *quaick*,
Amang the springs,
Awa ye squatter'd like a *drake*,
On whistling wings.

Let *Warlocks* grim, an' wither'd *Hags*,
Tell, how wi' you, on ragweed nags,
They skim the muirs an' dizzy crags,
Wi' wicked speed;
And in kirk-yards renew their leagues,
Owre howcket dead.

Thence, countra wives, wi' toil an' pain,
May plunge an' plunge the *kirn* in vain;
For Och! the yellow treasure 's taen,
By witching skill;
An' dawtit, twal-pint *Hawkie* 's gane
As yell 's the Bill.

Thence, mystic knots mak great abuse,
On *Young-Guidmen*, fond, keen an' croose;
When the best *warklum* i' the house,
By cantraip wit,
Is instant made no worth a louse,
Just at the bit.

When thowes dissolve the snawy hoord,
An' float the jinglan icy boord,
Then, *Water-kelpies* haunt the foord,
By your direction,
An' nighted Trav'llers are allur'd
To their destruction.

An' aft your moss-traversing *Spunkies*
Decoy the wight that late an' drunk is;
The bleezan, curst, mischievous monkies
Delude his eyes,
Till in some miry slough he sunk is,
Ne'er mair to rise.

When MASONS' mystic *word* an' *grip*,
In storms an' tempests raise you up,
Some cock, or cat, your rage maun stop,
Or, strange to tell!
The *youngest Brother* ye wad whip
Aff straught to *H–ll*.

Lang syne in *Eden*'s bonie yard,
When youthfu' lovers first were pair'd,
An' all the Soul of Love they shar'd,
The raptur'd hour,
Sweet on the fragrant, flow'ry swaird,
In shady bow'r:

Then you, ye auld, snick-drawing dog!
Ye cam to Paradise incog,
An' play'd on a man a cursed brogue,
(Black be your fa'!)
An' gied the infant warld a shog,
'Maist ruin'd a'.

D'ye mind that day, when in a bizz,
Wi' reeket duds, an' reestet gizz,
Ye did present your smoutie phiz
'Mang better folk,
An' sklented on the *man of Uz*
Your spitefu' joke?

An' how ye gat him i' your thrall,
An' brak him out o' house an' hal',
While scabs an' botches did him gall,
Wi' bitter claw,
An' lows'd his ill-tongu'd, wicked *Scawl*
Was warst ava?

But a' your doings to rehearse,
Your wily snares an' fechtin fierce,
Sin' that day *MICHAEL did you pierce,
Down to this time,
Wad ding a' *Lallan* tongue, or *Erse*,
In Prose or Rhyme.

An' now, auld *Cloots*, I ken ye're thinkan,
A certain *Bardie*'s rantin, drinkin,
Some luckless hour will send him linkan,
To your black pit;
But faith! he'll turn a corner jinkan,
An' cheat you yet.

* Vide Milton, Book 6th.

But fare you weel, auld *Nickie-ben*!
O wad ye tak a thought an' men'!
Ye aiblins might—I dinna ken—
Still hae a *stake*—
I'm wae to think upo' yon den,
Ev'n for your sake.

77. *Scotch Drink*

Gie him strong Drink *until he wink,*
That's sinking in despair;
An' liquor *guid, to fire his bluid,*
That's prest wi' grief an' care:
There let him bowse an' deep carouse,
Wi' bumpers flowing o'er,
Till he forgets his loves *or* debts,
An' minds his griefs no more.
Solomon's Proverbs, Ch. 31st V. 6, 7.

LET other Poets raise a fracas
'Bout vines, an' wines, an' druken *Bacchus*,
An' crabbed names an' stories wrack us,
An' grate our lug,
I sing the juice *Scotch bear* can mak us,
In glass or jug.

O thou, my MUSE! guid, auld SCOTCH DRINK!
Whether thro' wimplin worms thou jink,
Or, richly brown, ream owre the brink,
In glorious faem,
Inspire me, till I *lisp* an' *wink*,
To sing thy name!

Let husky Wheat the haughs adorn,
And Aits set up their awnie horn,
An' Pease an' Beans, at een or morn,
Perfume the plain,
Leeze me on thee *John Barleycorn*,
Thou king o' grain!

On thee aft Scotland chows her cood,
In souple scones, the wale o' food!
Or tumbling in the boiling flood
Wi' kail an' beef;
But when thou pours thy strong *heart's blood*,
There thou shines chief.

Food fills the wame, an' keeps us livin:
Tho' life 's a gift no worth receivin,
When heavy-dragg'd wi' pine an' grievin;
But oil'd by thee,
The wheels o' life gae down-hill, scrievin,
Wi' rattlin glee.

Thou clears the head o' doited Lear;
Thou chears the heart o' drooping Care;
Thou strings the nerves o' Labor-sair,
At 's weary toil;
Thou ev'n brightens dark Despair,
Wi' gloomy smile.

Aft, clad in massy, siller weed,
Wi' Gentles thou erects thy head;
Yet, humbly kind, in time o' need,
The *poorman*'s wine,
His wee drap pirratch, or his bread,
Thou kitchens fine.

Thou art the life o' public haunts;
But thee, what were our fairs an' rants?
Ev'n goodly meetings o' the saunts,
By thee inspir'd,
When gaping they besiege the *tents*,
Are doubly fir'd.

That *merry night* we get the corn in
O sweetly, then, thou reams the horn in!
Or reekan on a *New-year-mornin*
In cog or bicker,
An' just a wee drap *sp'ritual burn* in,
An' *gusty sucker*!

When Vulcan gies his bellys breath,
An' Ploughmen gather wi' their graith,
O rare! to see thee fizz an' fraeth
I' the lugget caup!
Then *Burnewin* comes on like Death,
At ev'ry chap.

Nae mercy, then, for airn *or* steel;
The brawnie, banie, Ploughman-chiel
Brings hard owrehip, wi' sturdy wheel,
The strong forehammer,
Till block an' studdie ring an' reel
Wi' dinsome clamour.

When skirlin weanies see the light,
Thou maks the gossips clatter bright,
How fumbling coofs their dearies slight,
Wae worth the name!
Nae Howdie gets a social night,
Or plack frae them.

When neebors anger at a plea,
An' just as wud as wud can be,
How easy can the *barley-bree*
Cement the quarrel!
It 's ay the cheapest Lawyer's fee
To taste the barrel.

Alake! that e'er my *Muse* has reason
To wyte her countrymen wi' treason!
But mony daily weet their weason
Wi' liquors nice,
An' hardly, in a winter season,
E'er spier her price.

Wae worth that *Brandy*, burnan trash!
Fell source o' monie a pain an' brash!
Twins mony a poor, doylt, druken hash
O' half his days;
An' sends, beside, auld *Scotland*'s cash
To her warst faes.

Ye Scots wha wish auld Scotland well,
Ye chief, to you my tale I tell,
Poor, plackless devils like *mysel*,
It sets you ill,
Wi' bitter, dearthfu' *wines* to mell,
Or *foreign gill*.

May *Gravels* round his blather wrench,
An' *Gouts* torment him, inch by inch,
Wha twists his gruntle wi' a glunch
O' sour disdain,
Out owre a glass o' *Whisky-punch*
Wi' honest men!

O *Whisky*! soul o' plays an' pranks!
Accept a *Bardie*'s gratefu' thanks!
When wanting thee, what tuneless cranks
Are my poor Verses!
Thou comes—they rattle i' their ranks
At ither's arses!

Thee, *Ferintosh*! O sadly lost!
Scotland lament frae coast to coast!
Now colic-grips, an' barkin hoast,
May kill us a';
For loyal *Forbes' Charter'd boast*
Is taen awa!

Thae curst horse-leeches o' th' Excise,
Wha mak the *Whisky stills* their prize!
Haud up thy han' *Deil*! ance, twice, thrice!
There, sieze the blinkers!
An' bake them up in brunstane pies
For poor damn'd *Drinkers*.

Fortune, if thou'll but gie me still
Hale breeks, a scone, an' *Whisky gill*,
An' rowth o' *rhyme* to rave at will,
Tak a' the rest,
An' deal 't about as thy blind skill
Directs thee best.

78. *Brose and Butter*

JENNY sits up i' the laft,
Jockie wad fain a been at her;
But there cam a wind out o' the west
Made a' the winnocks to clatter.

O gie my love brose, lasses;
O gie my love brose and butter;
For nane in Carrick wi' him
Can gie a c—t its supper.

The laverock lo'es the grass,
  The paetrick lo'es the stibble:
And hey, for the gardiner lad,
  To gully awa wi' his dibble!
    O gie, &c.

My daddie sent me to the hill
  To pu' my minnie some heather;
An' drive it in your fill,
  Ye're welcome to the leather.
    O gie, &c.

The Mouse is a merry wee beast,
  The Moudiewart wants the een;
And O, for a touch o' the thing
  I had in my nieve yestreen.
    O gie, &c.

We a' were fou yestreen,
  The night shall be its brither;
And hey, for a roaring pin
  To nail twa wames thegither!
    O gie, &c.

79. *To J. S*****

Friendship, mysterious cement of the soul!
Sweet'ner of Life, and solder of Society!
I owe thee much—

BLAIR.

DEAR S****, the sleest, pawkie thief,
That e'er attempted stealth or rief,
Ye surely hae some warlock-breef
      Owre human hearts;
For ne'er a bosom yet was prief
      Against your arts.

For me, I swear by sun an' moon,
And ev'ry star that blinks aboon,
Ye've cost me twenty pair o' shoon
      Just gaun to see you;
And ev'ry ither pair that 's done,
      Mair taen I'm wi' you.

That auld, capricious carlin, *Nature*,
To mak amends for scrimpet stature,
She 's turn'd you off, a human-creature
On her *first* plan,
And in her freaks, on ev'ry feature,
She 's wrote, *the Man*.

Just now I've taen the fit o' rhyme,
My barmie noddle 's working prime,
My fancy yerket up sublime
Wi' hasty summon:
Hae ye a leisure-moment's time
To hear what 's comin?

Some rhyme a neebor's name to lash;
Some rhyme, (vain thought!) for needfu' cash;
Some rhyme to court the countra clash,
An' raise a din;
For me, an *aim* I never fash;
I rhyme for *fun*.

The star that rules my luckless lot,
Has fated me the russet coat,
An' damn'd my fortune to the groat;
But, in requit,
Has blest me with a *random-shot*
O' countra wit.

This while my notion 's taen a sklent,
To try my fate in guid, black *prent*;
But still the mair I'm that way bent,
Something cries, 'Hoolie!
'I red you, honest man, tak tent!
'Ye'll shaw your folly.

'There 's ither Poets, much your betters,
'Far seen in *Greek*, deep men o' *letters*,
'Hae thought they had ensur'd their debtors,
'A' future ages;
'Now moths deform in shapeless tatters,
'Their unknown pages.'

Then farewel hopes of Laurel-boughs,
To garland my poetic brows!
Henceforth, I'll rove where busy ploughs
Are whistling thrang,
An' teach the lanely heights an' howes
My rustic sang.

I'll wander on with tentless heed,
How never-halting moments speed,
Till fate shall snap the brittle thread;
Then, all unknown,
I'll lay me with th' *inglorious dead*,
Forgot and gone!

But why, o' Death, begin a tale?
Just now we 're living sound an' hale;
Then top and maintop croud the sail,
Heave *Care* o'er-side!
And large, before Enjoyment's gale,
Let 's tak the tide.

This life, sae far 's I understand,
Is a' enchanted fairy-land,
Where Pleasure is the Magic-wand,
That, wielded right,
Maks Hours like Minutes, hand in hand,
Dance by fu' light.

The *magic-wand* then let us wield;
For, ance that five an' forty 's speel'd,
See, crazy, weary, joyless Eild,
Wi' wrinkl'd face,
Comes hostan, hirplan owre the field,
Wi' creeping pace.

When ance *life's day* draws near the gloamin,
Then fareweel vacant, careless roamin;
An' fareweel chearfu' tankards foamin,
An' social noise;
An' fareweel dear, deluding woman,
The joy of joys!

O *Life*! how pleasant in thy morning,
Young Fancy's rays the hills adorning!
Cold-pausing Caution's lesson scorning,
    We frisk away,
Like school-boys, at th' expected warning,
    To joy and play.

We wander there, we wander here,
We eye the *rose* upon the brier,
Unmindful that the *thorn* is near,
    Among the leaves;
And tho' the puny wound appear,
    Short while it grieves.

Some, lucky, find a flow'ry spot,
For which they never toil'd nor swat;
They drink the *sweet* and eat the *fat*,
    But care or pain;
And haply, eye the barren hut,
    With high disdain.

With steady aim, some Fortune chase;
Keen hope does ev'ry sinew brace;
Thro' fair, thro' foul, they urge the race,
    And sieze the prey:
Then canie, in some cozie place,
    They close the *day*.

And others, like your humble servan',
Poor wights! nae rules nor roads observin;
To right or left, eternal swervin,
    They zig-zag on;
Till curst with Age, obscure an' starvin,
    They aften groan.

Alas! what bitter toil an' straining—
But truce with peevish, poor complaining!
Is Fortune's fickle *Luna* waning?
    E'en let her gang!
Beneath what light she has remaining,
    Let 's sing our Sang.

My pen I here fling to the door,
And kneel, ye *Pow'rs*, and warm implore,
'Tho' I should wander *Terra* o'er,
'In all her climes,
'Grant me but this, I ask no more,
'Ay rowth o' rhymes.

'Gie dreeping roasts to *countra Lairds*,
'Till icicles hing frae their beards;
'Gie fine braw claes to fine *Life-guards*,
'And *Maids of Honor*;
'And yill an' whisky gie to *Cairds*,
'Until they sconner.

'A *Title*, DEMPSTER merits it;
'A *Garter* gie to WILLIE PIT;
'Gie Wealth to some be-ledger'd Cit,
'In cent per cent;
'But give me real, sterling Wit,
'And I'm content.

'While ye are pleas'd to keep me hale,
'I'll sit down o'er my scanty meal,
'Be 't *water-brose*, or *muslin-kail*,
'Wi' chearfu' face,
'As lang 's the Muses dinna fail
'To say the grace.'

An anxious e'e I never throws
Behint my lug, or by my nose;
I jouk beneath Misfortune's blows
As weel 's I may;
Sworn foe to *sorrow*, *care*, and *prose*,
I rhyme away.

O ye, douse folk, that live by rule,
Grave, tideless-blooded, calm and cool,
Compar'd wi' you—O fool! fool! fool!
How much unlike!
Your hearts are just a standing pool,
Your lives, a dyke!

Nae hare-brain'd, sentimental traces,
In your unletter'd, nameless faces!
In *arioso* trills and graces
Ye never stray,
But *gravissimo*, solemn basses
Ye hum away.

Ye are sae *grave*, nae doubt ye're *wise*;
Nae ferly tho' ye do despise
The hairum-scairum, ram-stam boys,
The rattling squad:
I see ye upward cast your eyes—
—Ye ken the road—

Whilst I—but I shall haud me there—
Wi' you I'll scarce gang *ony where*—
Then *Jamie*, I shall say nae mair,
But quat my sang,
Content *with* You to mak a *pair*,
Whare'er I gang.

80. *The rantin dog the Daddie o't*

O Wha my babie-clouts will buy,
O Wha will tent me when I cry;
Wha will kiss me where I lie,
The rantin dog the daddie o't.

O Wha will own he did the faut,
O Wha will buy the groanin maut,
O Wha will tell me how to ca 't,
The rantin dog the daddie o't.

When I mount the Creepie-chair,
Wha will sit beside me there,
Gie me Rob, I'll seek nae mair,
The rantin dog the Daddie o't.

Wha will crack to me my lane;
Wha will mak me fidgin fain;
Wha will kiss me o'er again
The rantin dog the Daddie o't.

81. *The Author's Earnest Cry and Prayer**, *to the Right Honorable and Honorable, the Scotch Representatives in the House of Commons*

Dearest of Distillation! last and best!—
—How art thou lost!—
Parody on Milton.

YE IRISH LORDS, ye *knights* an' *squires*,
Wha represent our BRUGHS an' SHIRES,
An' dousely manage our affairs
In *Parliament*,
To you a simple Bardie's pray'rs
Are humbly sent.

Alas! my roupet *Muse* is haerse!
Your Honors' hearts wi' grief 'twad pierce,
To see her sittan on her arse
Low i' the dust,
An' scriechan out prosaic verse,
An' like to brust!

* This was wrote before the Act anent the Scotch Distilleries, of session 1786; for which Scotland and the Author return their most grateful thanks.

Tell them wha hae the chief direction,
Scotland and *me*'s in great affliction,
E'er sin' they laid that curst restriction
On AQUAVITÆ;
An' rouse them up to strong conviction,
An' move their pity.

Stand forth and tell yon PREMIER YOUTH
The honest, open, naked truth;
Tell him o' mine an' Scotland's drouth,
His servants humble:
The muckle devil blaw you south,
If ye dissemble!

Does ony *great man* glunch an' gloom?
Speak out an' never fash your thumb!
Let *posts* an' *pensions* sink or swoom
Wi' them wha grant them:
If honestly they canna come,
Far better want them.

In gath'rin votes ye were na slack,
Now stand as tightly by your tack:
Ne'er claw your lug, an' fidge your back,
An' hum an' haw,
But raise your arm, an' tell your crack
Before them a'.

Paint Scotland greetan owre her thrissle;
Her *mutchkin stowp* as toom 's a whissle;
An' damn'd Excise-men in a bussle,
Seizan a *Stell,*
Triumphant crushan 't like a muscle
Or laimpet shell.

Then on the tither hand present her,
A blackguard *Smuggler*, right behint her,
An', cheek-for-chow, a chuffie *Vintner*,
Colleaguing join,—
Picking her pouch as bare as Winter,
Of a' kind coin.

Is there, that bears the name o' SCOT,
But feels his heart's bluid rising hot,
To see his poor, auld Mither's *pot*,
Thus dung in staves;
An' plunder'd o' her hindmost groat,
By gallows knaves?

Alas! I'm but a nameless wight,
Trode i' the mire out o' sight!
But could I like MONTGOMERIES fight,
Or gab like BOSWEL,
There 's some *sark-necks* I wad *draw* tight,
An' *tye* some *hose* well.

God bless your Honors, can ye see 't,
The kind, auld, cantie Carlin greet,
An' no get warmly to your feet,
An' gar them hear it,
An' tell them, wi' a patriot-heat,
Ye winna bear it?

Some o' you nicely ken the laws,
To round the period an' pause,
An' with rhetoric clause on clause
To mak harangues;
Then echo thro' Saint Stephen's wa's
Auld Scotland's wrangs.

Dempster, a true-blue Scot I'se warran;
Thee, aith-detesting, chaste *Kilkerran*;
An' that glib-gabbet Highlan Baron,
The Laird o' *Graham*;
And ane, a chap that 's damn'd auldfarran,
Dundass his name.

Erskine, a spunkie norland billie;
True Campbels, *Frederic* an' *Ilay*;
An' Livistone, the bauld *Sir Willie*;
An' mony ithers,
Whom auld Demosthenes or Tully
Might own for brithers.

Arouse my boys! exert your mettle,
To get auld Scotland back her *kettle*!
Or faith! I'll wad my new pleugh-pettle,
Ye'll see 't or lang,
She'll teach you, wi' a reekan whittle,
Anither sang.

This while she 's been in crankous mood,
Her *lost Militia* fir'd her bluid;
(Deil na they never mair do guid,
Play'd her that pliskie!)
An' now she 's like to rin red-wud
About her *Whisky*.

An' L—d! if ance they pit her till 't,
Her tartan petticoat she'll kilt
An' durk an' pistol at her belt,
She'll tak the streets,
An' rin her whittle to the hilt,
I' th' first she meets!

For G–d-sake, Sirs! then speak her fair,
An' straik her cannie wi' the hair,
An' to the *muckle house* repair,
Wi' instant speed,
An' strive, wi' a' your Wit an' Lear,
To get remead.

Yon ill-tongu'd tinkler, *Charlie Fox*,
May taunt you wi' his jeers an' mocks;
But gie him 't het, my hearty cocks!
E'en cowe the cadie!
An' send him to his dicing box,
An' sportin lady.

Tell yon guid bluid of auld *Boconnock*'s,
I'll be his debt twa mashlum bonnocks,
An' drink his health in auld **Nanse Tinnock*'s
Nine times a week,
If he some scheme, like tea an' winnocks,
Wad kindly seek.

* A worthy old Hostess of the Author's in *Mauchline*, where he sometimes studies Politics over a glass of guid auld *Scotch Drink*.

Could he some *commutation* broach,
I'll pledge my aith in guid braid Scotch,
He need na fear their foul reproach
Nor erudition,
Yon mixtie-maxtie, queer hotch-potch,
The *Coalition.*

Auld Scotland has a raucle tongue;
She 's just a devil wi' a rung;
An' if she promise auld or young
To tak their part,
Tho' by the neck she should be strung,
She'll no desert.

And now, ye chosen FIVE AND FORTY,
May still your Mither's heart support ye;
Then tho' a *Minister* grow dorty,
An' kick your place,
Ye'll snap your fingers, poor an' hearty,
Before his face.

God bless your Honors, a' your days,
Wi' sowps o' kail an' brats o' claise,
In spite of a' the thievish kaes
That haunt St. *Jamie*'s!
Your humble Bardie sings an' prays
While *Rab* his name is.

Postcript

Let half-starv'd slaves in warmer skies,
See future wines, rich-clust'ring, rise;
Their lot auld Scotland ne'er envies,
But blyth an' frisky,
She eyes her freeborn, martial boys,
Tak aff their Whisky.

What tho' their Phebus kinder warms,
While Fragrance blooms and Beauty charms!
When wretches range, in famish'd swarms,
The scented groves,
Or hounded forth, *dishonor* arms,
In hungry droves.

Their *gun*'s a burden on their shouther;
They downa bide the stink o' *powther*;
Their bauldest thought 's a hank'ring swither,
To stan' or rin,
Till skelp—a shot—they're aff, a' throu'ther,
To save their skin.

But bring a SCOTCHMAN frae his hill,
Clap in his cheek a *highlan gill*,
Say, such is royal GEORGE's will,
An' there 's the foe,
He has nae thought but how to kill
Twa at a blow.

Nae cauld, faint-hearted doubtings tease him;
Death comes, with fearless eye he sees him;
Wi' bluidy hand a welcome gies him;
An' when he fa's,
His latest draught o' breathin lea'es him
In faint huzzas.

Sages their solemn een may steek,
An' raise a philosophic reek,
An' physically causes seek,
In *clime* an' *season*,
But tell me *Whisky*'s name in Greek,
I'll tell the reason.

SCOTLAND, my auld, respected Mither!
Tho' whyles ye moistify your leather,
Till when ye speak, ye aiblins blether;
Yet deil-mak-matter!
FREEDOM and WHISKY gang thegither,
Tak aff your whitter.

82. *Sketch*

HAIL, Poesie! thou nymph reserv'd!
In chase o' thee, what crowds hae swerv'd
Frae Common Sense, or sunk ennerv'd
'Mang heaps o' clavers;
And Och! o'er aft thy joes hae starv'd
'Mid a' thy favors!

Say, Lassie, why thy train amang,
While loud the trumps heroic clang,
And Sock and buskin skelp alang
To death or marriage;
Scarce ane has tried the Shepherd-sang
But wi' miscarriage?

In Homer's craft Jock Milton thrives;
Eschylus' pen Will Shakespeare drives;
Wee Pope, the knurlin, 'till him rives
Horatian fame;
In thy sweet sang, Barbauld, survives
E'en Sappho's flame.

But thee, Theocritus, wha matches?
They're no' Herd's ballats, Maro's catches;
Squire Pope but busks his skinklin patches
O' Heathen tatters:
I pass by hunders, nameless wretches,
That ape their betters.

In this braw age o' wit and lear,
Will nane the Shepherd's whistle mair
Blaw sweetly in his native air
And rural grace;
And wi' the far-fam'd Grecian share
A rival place?

Yes! there is ane; a Scotish callan!
There 's ane: come forrit, honest Allan!
Thou need na jouk behint the hallan,
A chiel sae clever;
The teeth o' Time may gnaw Tamtallan,
But thou 's for ever.

Thou paints auld Nature to the nines,
In thy sweet Caledonian lines;
Nae gowden stream thro' myrtles twines
Where Philomel,
While nightly breezes sweep the vines,
Her griefs will tell!

Thy rural loves are Nature's sel';
Nae bombast spates o' nonsense swell;
Nae snap conceits, but that sweet spell
O' witchin' loove,
That charm that can the strongest quell,
The sternest move.

In gowany glens thy burnie strays,
Where bonie lasses bleach their claes;
Or trots by hazelly shaws and braes
Wi' hawthorns gray,
Where blackbirds join the shepherd's lays
At close o' day.

83. *To a Louse, On Seeing one on a Lady's Bonnet at Church*

HA! whare ye gaun, ye crowlan ferlie!
Your impudence protects you sairly:
I canna say but ye strunt rarely,
Owre *gawze* and *lace*;
Tho' faith, I fear ye dine but sparely,
On sic a place.

Ye ugly, creepan, blastet wonner,
Detested, shunn'd, by saunt an' sinner,
How daur ye set your fit upon her,
Sae fine a *Lady*!
Gae somewhere else and seek your dinner,
On some poor body.

Swith, in some beggar's haffet squattle;
There ye may creep, and sprawl, and sprattle,
Wi' ither kindred, jumping cattle,
In shoals and nations;
Whare *horn* nor *bane* ne'er daur unsettle,
Your thick plantations.

Now haud you there, ye're out o' sight,
Below the fatt'rels, snug and tight,
Na faith ye yet! ye'll no be right,
Till ye've got on it,
The vera tapmost, towrin height
O' *Miss's bonnet*.

My sooth! right bauld ye set your nose out,
As plump an' gray as onie grozet:
O for some rank, mercurial rozet,
        Or fell, red smeddum,
I'd gie you sic a hearty dose o't,
        Wad dress your droddum!

I wad na been surpriz'd to spy
You on an auld wife's *flainen toy*;
Or aiblins some bit duddie boy,
        On 's *wylecoat*;
But Miss's fine *Lunardi*, fye!
    How daur ye do 't?

O *Jenny* dinna toss your head,
An' set your beauties a' abread!
Ye little ken what cursed speed
        The blastie 's makin!
Thae *winks* and *finger-ends*, I dread,
        Are notice takin!

O wad some Pow'r the giftie gie us
To see oursels as others see us!
It wad frae monie a blunder free us
        An' foolish notion:
What airs in dress an' gait wad lea'e us,
        And ev'n Devotion!

84. *Love and Liberty—A Cantata*

Recitativo—

WHEN lyart leaves bestrow the yird,
Or wavering like the Bauckie-bird[1],
  Bedim cauld Boreas' blast;
When hailstanes drive wi' bitter skyte,
And infant Frosts begin to bite,
  In hoary cranreuch drest;
Ae night at e'en a merry core
  O' randie, gangrel bodies,
In Poosie-Nansie's[2] held the splore,
  To drink their orra dudies:

[1] The old Scotch name for the Bat.

[2] The Hostess of a noted Caravansary in M——, well known to and much frequented by the lowest orders of Travellers and Pilgrims.

Wi' quaffing, and laughing,
They ranted an' they sang;
Wi' jumping, an' thumping,
The vera girdle rang.

First, niest the fire, in auld, red rags,
Ane sat; weel brac'd wi' mealy bags,
And knapsack a' in order;
His doxy lay within his arm;
Wi' USQEBAE an' blankets warm,
She blinket on her Sodger:
An' ay he gies the tozie drab
The tither skelpan kiss,
While she held up her greedy gab,
Just like an aumous dish:
Ilk smack still, did crack still,
Just like a cadger's whip;
Then staggering, an' swaggering,
He roar'd this ditty up—

Air. *Tune, Soldier's joy*

I AM a Son of Mars who have been in many wars,
  And show my cuts and scars wherever I come;
This here was for a wench, and that other in a trench,
  When welcoming the French at the sound of the drum.
    Lal de daudle &c.

My Prenticeship I past where my LEADER breath'd his last,
  When the bloody die was cast on the heights of ABRAM;
And I served out my TRADE when the gallant *game* was play'd,
  And the MORO low was laid at the sound of the drum.

I lastly was with Curtis among the *floating batt'ries*,
  And there I left for witness, an arm and a limb;
Yet let my Country need me, with ELLIOT to head me,
  I'd clatter on my stumps at the sound of a drum.

And now tho' I must beg, with a wooden arm and leg,
  And many a tatter'd rag hanging over my bum,
I'm as happy with my wallet, my bottle and my Callet,
  As when I us'd in scarlet to follow a drum.

What tho', with hoary locks, I must stand the winter shocks,
  Beneath the woods and rocks oftentimes for a home,
When the tother bag I sell and the tother bottle tell,
  I could meet a troop of HELL at the sound of a drum.

Recitativo—

He ended; and the kebars sheuk,
  Aboon the chorus roar;
While frighted rattons backward leuk,
  An' seek the benmost bore:
A fairy FIDDLER frae the neuk,
  He skirl'd out, ENCORE.
But up arose the martial CHUCK,
  An' laid the loud uproar—

Air. *Tune, Sodger laddie*

I ONCE was a Maid, tho' I cannot tell when,
And still my delight is in proper young men:
Some one of a troop of DRAGOONS was my dadie,
No wonder I'm fond of a SODGER LADDIE.
Sing lal de dal &c.

The first of my LOVES was a swaggering blade,
To rattle the thundering drum was his trade;
His leg was so tight and his cheek was so ruddy,
Transported I was with my SODGER LADDIE.

But the godly old Chaplain left him in the lurch,
The sword I forsook for the sake of the church;
He ventur'd the SOUL, and I risked the BODY,
'Twas then I prov'd false to my SODGER LADDIE.

Full soon I grew sick of my sanctified *Sot*,
The Regiment AT LARGE for a HUSBAND I got;
From the gilded SPONTOON to the FIFE I was ready;
I asked no more but a SODGER LADDIE.

But the PEACE it reduc'd me to beg in despair,
Till I met my old boy in a CUNNINGHAM fair;
His RAGS REGIMENTAL they flutter'd so gaudy,
My heart it rejoic'd at a SODGER LADDIE.

And now I have lived—I know not how long,
And still I can join in a cup and a song;
But whilst with both hands I can hold the glass steady,
Here 's to thee, MY HERO, MY SODGER LADDIE.

80 *An additional recitative and air, in Burns's holograph but written at a different time, follow in the Alloway MS (1786?):*

Recitative

Poor Merry-andrew, in $^{\text{the}}_{\text{a}}$ neuk,
  Sat guzzling wi' a Tinkler-hizzie;
They mind't na wha the chorus teuk,
  Between themsels they were sae busy:
At length wi' drink an' courting dizzy,
  He stoiter'd up an' made a face;
Then turn'd, an' laid a smack on Grizzie,
  Syne tun'd his pipes wi' grave grimace.

Air. Tune, Auld Sir Symon.

Sir Wisdom 's a fool when he 's fou;
  Sir Knave is a fool in a Session,
He 's there but a prentice, I trow,
  But I am a fool by profession.

My Grannie she bought me a beuk,
  An' I held awa to the school;
I fear I my talent misteuk,
  But what will ye hae of a fool.

For drink I would venture my neck;
  A hizzie 's the half of my Craft:
But what could ye other expect
  Of ane that 's avowedly daft.

I, ance, was ty'd up like a stirk,
  For civilly swearing and quaffing;
I, ance, was abus'd i' the kirk,
  For towsing a lass i' my daffin.

Poor Andrew that tumbles for sport,
  Let nae body name wi' a jeer;
There 's even, I'm tauld, i' the Court
  A Tumbler ca'd the Premier.

Observ'd ye yon reverend lad
  Mak faces to tickle the Mob;
He rails at our mountebank squad,
  Its rivalship just i' the job.

And now my conclusion I'll tell,
  For faith I'm confoundedly dry:
The chiel that 's a fool for himsel,
  Guid L—d, he 's far dafter than I.

Recitativo—

Then niest outspak a raucle Carlin,
Wha ken't fu' weel to cleek the Sterlin;
For mony a pursie she had hooked,
An' had in mony a well been douked:
Her LOVE had been a HIGHLAND LADDIE,
But weary fa' the waefu' woodie!
Wi' sighs an' sobs she thus began
To wail her braw JOHN HIGHLANDMAN—

Air. *Tune, O an' ye were dead Gudeman*

A HIGHLAND lad my Love was born,
The lalland laws he held in scorn;
But he still was faithfu' to his clan,
My gallant, braw JOHN HIGHLANDMAN.

Chorus—

Sing hey my braw John Highlandman!
Sing ho my braw John Highlandman!
There 's not a lad in a' the lan'
Was match for my John Highlandman.

With his Philibeg, an' tartan Plaid,
An' guid Claymore down by his side,
The ladies' hearts he did trepan,
My gallant, braw John Highlandman.
Sing hey &c.

We ranged a' from Tweed to Spey,
An' liv'd like lords an' ladies gay:
For a lalland face he feared none,
My gallant, braw John Highlandman.
Sing hey &c.

They banish'd him beyond the sea,
But ere the bud was on the tree,
Adown my cheeks the pearls ran,
Embracing my John Highlandman.
Sing hey &c.

But Och! they catch'd him at the last,
And bound him in a dungeon fast,
My curse upon them every one,
They've hang'd my braw John Highlandman.
Sing hey &c.

And now a Widow I must mourn
The Pleasures that will ne'er return;
No comfort but a hearty can,
When I think on John Highlandman.
Sing hey &c.

Recitativo—

A pigmy Scraper wi' his Fiddle,
Wha us'd to trystes an' fairs to driddle,
Her strappan limb an' gausy middle,
(He reach'd nae higher)
Had hol'd his HEARTIE like a riddle,
An' blawn 't on fire.

Wi' hand on hainch, and upward e'e,
He croon'd his gamut, ONE, TWO, THREE,
Then in an ARIOSO key,
The wee Apollo
Set off wi' ALLEGRETTO glee
His GIGA SOLO—

Air. *Tune, Whistle owre the lave o't*

LET me ryke up to dight that tear,
An' go wi' me an' be my DEAR;
An' then your every CARE an' FEAR
May whistle owre the lave o't.

Chorus—

I am a Fiddler to my trade,
An' a' the tunes that e'er I play'd,
The sweetest still to WIFE or MAID,
Was whistle owre the lave o't.

At KIRNS an' WEDDINS we'se be there,
An' O sae nicely 's we will fare!
We'll bowse about till Dadie CARE
Sing whistle owre the lave o't.
I am &c.

Sae merrily 's the banes we'll pyke,
An' sun oursells about the dyke;
An' at our leisure when ye like
We'll whistle owre the lave o't.
I am &c.

But bless me wi' your heav'n o' charms,
An' while I kittle hair on thairms
HUNGER, CAULD, an' a' sic harms
May whistle owre the lave o't.
I am &c.

Recitativo—

Her charms had struck a sturdy CAIRD,
As weel as poor GUTSCRAPER;
He taks the Fiddler by the beard,
An' draws a roosty rapier—
He swoor by a' was swearing worth
To speet him like a Pliver,
Unless he would from that time forth
Relinquish her for ever:

Wi' ghastly e'e poor TWEEDLEDEE
Upon his hunkers bended,
An' pray'd for grace wi' ruefu' face,
An' so the quarrel ended;
But tho' his little heart did grieve,
When round the TINKLER prest her,
He feign'd to snirtle in his sleeve
When thus the CAIRD address'd her—

Air. *Tune, Clout the Caudron*

MY bonie lass I work in brass,
A TINKLER is my station;
I've travell'd round all Christian ground
In this my occupation;
I've ta'en the gold an' been enroll'd
In many a noble squadron;
But vain they search'd when off I march'd
To go an' clout the CAUDRON.
I've ta'en the gold &c.

Despise that SHRIMP, that withered IMP,
  With a' his noise an' cap'rin;
An' take a share, with those that bear
  The *budget* and the *apron*!
And *by* that STOWP! my faith an' houpe,
  And *by* that dear KILBAIGIE*,
If e'er ye want, or meet with scant,
  May I ne'er weet my CRAIGIE!
      And by that Stowp, &c.

Recitativo—

The Caird prevail'd—th' unblushing fair
  In his embraces sunk;
Partly wi' LOVE o'ercome sae sair,
  An' partly she was drunk:
SIR VIOLINO with an air,
  That show'd a man o' spunk,
Wish'd UNISON between the PAIR,
  An' made the bottle clunk
      To their health that night.

But hurchin Cupid shot a shaft,
  That play'd a DAME a shavie—
The Fiddler RAK'D her, FORE AND AFT,
  Behint the Chicken cavie:
Her lord, a wight of HOMER's craft†,
  Tho' limpan wi' the Spavie,
He hirpl'd up an' lap like daft,
  An' shor'd them DAINTY DAVIE
      O' *boot* that night.

He was a care-defying blade,
  As ever BACCHUS listed!
Tho' Fortune sair upon him laid,
  His heart she ever miss'd it.
He had no WISH but—to be glad,
  Nor WANT but—when he thristed;
He hated nought but—to be sad,
  An' thus the Muse suggested
      His sang that night.

* A peculiar sort of Whiskie so called: a great favorite with Poosie Nansie's Clubs.

† Homer is allowed to be the eldest Ballad singer on record.

Air. *Tune, For a' that an' a' that*

I AM a BARD of no regard,
Wi' gentle folks an' a' that;
But HOMER LIKE the glowran byke,
Frae town to town I draw that.

Chorus—

For a' that an' a' that,
An' twice as muckle 's a' that,
I've lost but ANE, I've TWA behin',
I've WIFE ENEUGH for a' that.

I never drank the Muses' STANK,
Castalia's burn an' a' that,
But there it streams an' richly reams,
My HELICON I ca' that.
For a' that &c.

Great love I bear to all the FAIR,
Their humble slave an' a' that;
But lordly WILL, I hold it still
A mortal sin to thraw that.
For a' that &c.

In raptures sweet this hour we meet,
Wi' mutual love an' a' that;
But for how lang the FLIE MAY STANG,
Let INCLINATION law that.
For a' that &c.

Their tricks an' craft hae put me daft,
They've ta'en me in, an' a' that,
But clear your decks an' here 's the SEX!
I like the jads for a' that.
For a' that an' a' that
An' twice as muckle 's a' that,
My DEAREST BLUID to do them guid,
They're welcome till 't for a' that.

Recitativo—

So sung the BARD—and Nansie's waws
Shook with a thunder of applause
Re-echo'd from each mouth!
They toom'd their pocks, they pawn'd their duds,
They scarcely left to coor their fuds
To quench their lowan drouth:
Then owre again the jovial thrang
The Poet did request
To lowse his PACK an' wale a sang,
A BALLAD o' the best.
He, rising, rejoicing,
Between his TWA DEBORAHS,
Looks round him an' found them
Impatient for the Chorus.

Air. *Tune, Jolly Mortals fill your glasses*

SEE the smoking bowl before us,
Mark our jovial, ragged ring!
Round and round take up the Chorus,
And in raptures let us sing—

Chorus—

A fig for those by law protected!
LIBERTY 's a glorious feast!
Courts for Cowards were erected,
Churches built to please the PRIEST.

What is TITLE, what is TREASURE,
  What is REPUTATION's care?
If we lead a life of pleasure,
  'Tis no matter HOW or WHERE.
        A fig, &c.

With the ready trick and fable
  Round we wander all the day;
And at night, in barn or stable,
  Hug our doxies on the hay.
        A fig for &c.

Does the train-attended CARRIAGE
  Thro' the country lighter rove?
Does the sober bed of MARRIAGE
  Witness brighter scenes of love?
        A fig for &c.

Life is all a VARIORUM,
  We regard not how it goes;
Let them cant about DECORUM,
  Who have character to lose.
        A fig for &c.

Here's to BUDGETS, BAGS and WALLETS!
  Here's to all the wandering train!
Here's our ragged BRATS and CALLETS!
  One and all cry out, AMEN!
    A fig for those by LAW protected,
      LIBERTY's a glorious feast!
    COURTS for Cowards were erected,
      CHURCHES built to please the Priest.

III. Poems 1786

MOSSGIEL AND
EDINBURGH

85. *The Ordination*

For sense they little owe to frugal Heav'n—
To please the Mob they hide the little giv'n.

I

K********* Wabsters, fidge an' claw,
An' pour your creeshie nations;
An' ye wha leather rax an' draw,
Of a' denominations;
Swith to the *Laigh Kirk,* ane an' a',
An' there tak up your stations;
Then aff to *B–gb*—'s in a raw,
An' pour divine libations
For joy this day.

II

Curst Common-sense, that imp o' h–ll,
Cam in wi' Maggie Lauder*;
But O******* aft made her yell,
An' R***** sair misca'd her:
This day M'******* taks the flail,
An' he 's the boy will blaud her!
He'll clap a *shangan* on her tail,
An' set the bairns to daud her
Wi' dirt this day.

* Alluding to a scoffing ballad which was made on the admission of the late Reverend and worthy Mr L—— to the *Laigh Kirk.*

III

Mak haste an' turn king David owre,
  An' lilt wi' holy clangor;
O' double verse come gie us four,
  An' skirl up the Bangor:
This day the Kirk kicks up a stoure,
  Nae mair the knaves shall wrang her,
For Heresy is in her pow'r,
  And gloriously she'll whang her
      Wi' pith this day.

IV

Come, let a proper text be read,
  An' touch it aff wi' vigour,
How graceless *Ham** leugh at his Dad,
  Which made *Canaan* a niger;
Or *Phineas*† drove the murdering blade,
  Wi' wh–re-abhorring rigour;
Or *Zipporah*‡, the scauldin jad,
  Was like a bluidy tiger
      I' th' inn that day.

V

There, try his mettle on the creed,
  And bind him down wi' caution,
That *Stipend* is a carnal weed
  He takes but for the fashion;
And gie him o'er the flock, to feed,
  And punish each transgression;
Especial, *rams* that cross the breed,
  Gie them sufficient threshin,
      Spare them nae day.

VI

Now auld K*********, cock thy tail,
  An' toss thy horns fu' canty;
Nae mair thou 'lt rowte out-owre the dale,
  Because thy pasture 's scanty;
For lapfu's large o' *gospel kail*
  Shall fill thy crib in plenty,
An' *runts* o' *grace* the pick an' wale,
  No gi'en by way o' dainty
      But ilka day.

* Genesis, ch. ix. vers. 22. † Numbers, ch. xxv. vers. 8.
‡ Exodus, ch. iv. vers. 25.

VII

Nae mair by *Babel's streams* we'll weep,
  To think upon our *Zion*;
And hing our fiddles up to sleep,
  Like baby-clouts a-dryin:
Come, screw the pegs wi' tunefu' cheep,
  And o'er the thairms be tryin;
Oh, rare! to see our elbucks wheep,
  And a' like lamb-tails flyin
        Fu' fast this day!

VIII

Lang, *Patronage*, wi' rod o' airn,
  Has shor'd the Kirk's undoin,
As lately *F–nw–ck*, sair forfairn,
  Has proven to its ruin:
Our Patron, honest man! *Gl********,
  He saw mischief was brewin;
And like a godly, elect bairn,
  He 's wal'd us out a true ane,
        And sound this day.

IX

Now R******** harangue nae mair,
  But steek your gab for ever;
Or try the wicked town of A**,
  For there they'll think you clever;
Or, nae reflection on your lear,
  Ye may commence a Shaver;
Or to the *N–th–rt–n* repair,
  And turn a Carpet-weaver
        Aff-hand this day.

X

M***** and you were just a match,
  We never had sic twa drones;
Auld *Hornie* did the *Laigh Kirk* watch,
  Just like a winkin baudrons:
And ay he catch'd the tither wretch,
  To fry them in his caudrons;
But now his Honor maun detach,
  Wi' a' his brimstone squadrons,
        Fast, fast this day.

XI

See, see auld Orthodoxy's faes
  She 's swingein thro' the city!
Hark, how the nine-tail'd cat she plays!
  I vow it 's unco pretty:
There, Learning, with his Greekish face,
  Grunts out some Latin ditty;
And Common Sense is gaun, she says,
  To mak to *Jamie Beattie*
        Her plaint this day.

XII

But there 's Morality himsel,
  Embracing all opinions;
Hear, how he gies the tither yell,
  Between his twa companions!
See, how she peels the skin an' fell,
  As ane were peelin onions!
Now there, they're packed aff to h–ll,
  And banish'd our dominions,
        Henceforth this day.

XIII

O happy day! rejoice, rejoice!
  Come bouse about the porter!
Morality's demure decoys
  Shall here nae mair find quarter:
M'*******, R*****, are the boys
  That Heresy can torture;
They'll gie her on a rape a hoyse,
  And cowe her measure shorter
        By th' head some day.

XIV

Come, bring the tither mutchkin in,
  And here 's, for a conclusion,
To ev'ry *New-light** mother's son,
  From this time forth, Confusion:
If mair they deave us wi' their din,
  Or Patronage intrusion,
We'll light a spunk, and, ev'ry skin,
  We'll rin them aff in fusion
        Like oil, some day.

* *New-light* is a cant phrase, in the West of Scotland, for those religious opinions which Dr. Taylor of Norwich has defended so strenuously.

86. *The Inventory*

To Mr Robt Aiken in Ayr, in answer to his mandate requiring an account of servants, carriages, carriage-horses, riding horses, wives, children, &c.

SIR, as your mandate did request,
I send you here a faithfu' list,
O' gudes an' gear, an' a' my graith,
To which I'm clear to gi'e my aith.

Imprimis then, for carriage cattle,
I have four brutes o' gallant mettle,
As ever drew afore a pettle.
My **Lan' afore*'s a gude auld *has been*,
An' wight an' wilfu' a' his days been.
My †*Lan' ahin*'s a weel gaun fillie,
That aft has borne me hame frae Killie‡,
An' your auld burrough mony a time,
In days when riding was nae crime—
But ance whan in my wooing pride
I like a blockhead boost to ride,
The wilfu' creature sae I pat to,
(L—d pardon a' my sins an' that too!)
I play'd my fillie sic a shavie,
She 's a' bedevil'd wi' the spavie.
My §*Furr ahin*'s a wordy beast,
As e'er in tug or tow was trac'd.—
The fourth 's a Highland Donald hastie,
A d—n'd red wud Kilburnie blastie;
Foreby a *Cowt*, o' *Cowt's* the wale,
As ever ran afore a tail.
If he be spar'd to be a beast,
He'll draw me fifteen pun' at least.—
Wheel carriages I ha'e but few,
Three carts, an' twa are feckly new;
Ae auld wheelbarrow, mair for token,
Ae leg an' baith the trams are broken;
I made a poker o' the spin'le,
An' my auld mither brunt the trin'le.—
For men, I've three mischievous boys,
Run de'ils for rantin' an' for noise;

* The fore horse on the left-hand in the plough.
† The hindmost on the left-hand in the plough.
‡Kilmarnock.
§ The same on the right-hand in the plough.

A gaudsman ane, a thrasher t'other,
Wee Davock hauds the nowt in fother.
I rule them as I ought, discreetly,
An' aften labour them compleatly.
An' ay on Sundays duly nightly,
I on the questions *targe* them tightly;
Till faith, wee Davock 's turn'd sae gleg,
Tho' scarcely langer than your leg,
He'll screed you aff Effectual Calling,
As fast as ony in the dwalling.—
I've nane in female servan' station,
(L—d keep me ay frae a' temptation!)
I ha'e nae wife; and that my bliss is,
An' ye have laid nae tax on misses;
An' then if kirk folks dinna clutch me,
I ken the devils dare na touch me.
Wi' weans I'm mair than weel contented,
Heav'n sent me ane mae than I wanted.
My sonsie smirking dear-bought Bess,
She stares the daddy in her face,
Enough of ought ye like but grace;
But her, my bonny sweet wee lady,
I've paid enough for her already,
An' gin ye tax her or her mither,
B' the L—d! ye'se get them a' thegither.

And now, remember Mr. A–k–n,
Nae kind of licence out I'm takin';
Frae this time forth, I do declare,
I'se ne'er ride horse nor hizzie mair;
Thro' dirt and dub for life I'll paidle,
Ere I sae dear pay for a saddle;
My travel a' on foot I'll shank it,
I've sturdy bearers, Gude be thankit.—
The Kirk an' you may tak' you that,
It puts but little in your pat;
Sae dinna put me in your buke,
Nor for my ten white shillings luke.

This list wi' my ain han' I wrote it,
Day an' date as under notit,
Then know all ye whom it concerns,
Subscripsi huic,

ROBERT BURNS.

Mossgiel, February 22d, 1786.

87. *To Mr. John Kennedy*

Mossgiel, 3rd *March*, 1786.

Now Kennedy if foot or horse
E'er bring you in by Mauchline Corss,
L—d man there 's lasses there wad force
A hermit's fancy,
And down the gate in faith they're worse
And mair unchancy.

But as I'm sayin, please step to Dow's
And taste sic gear as Johnnie brews,
Till some bit callan bring me news
That you are there,
And if we dinna hae a bouze
Ise ne'er drink mair.

It 's no I like to sit an' swallow
Then like a swine to puke an' wallow,
But gie me just a true good fallow
Wi' right ingine,
And spunkie ance to make us mellow,
And then we'll shine.

Now if ye're ane o' warl's folk,
Wha rate the wearer by the cloak
An' sklent on poverty their joke
Wi' bitter sneer,
Wi' you no friendship I will troke
Nor cheap nor dear.

But if as I'm informed weel
Ye hate as ill 's the vera de'il
The flinty heart that canna feel—
Come Sir, here 's tae you:
Hae there 's my haun', I wiss you weel
And Gude be wi' you.

88. *Adam A——'s Prayer*

GUDE pity me, because I'm little,
For though I am an elf o' mettle,
And can, like ony wabster's shuttle,
Jink there or here;
Yet, scarce as lang 's a gude kail whittle,
I'm unco queer.

And now thou kens our waefu' case,
For *Geordie's Jurr* we're in disgrace,
Because we've stang'd her through the place,
And hurt her spleuchan,
For which we darena show our face
Within the clachan.

And now we're dern'd in dens and hollows,
And hunted as was William Wallace,
Wi' Constables, those blackguard fallows,
And Sodgers baith;
But gude preserve us frae the gallows,
That shamefu' death!

Auld, grim, black-bearded Geordie's sell;
Oh, shake him o'er the mouth o' hell,
There let him hing, and roar, and yell,
Wi' hideous din,
And if he offers to rebel,
Then heave him in.

When Death comes in wi' glimmering blink,
And tips auld druken Nanz the wink,
May Satan gie her a— a clink
Within his yet,
And fill her up wi' brimstone drink
Red, reeking, het.

There 's Jockie and the hav'rel Jenny,
Some Devil seize them in a hurry,
And waff them in th' infernal wherry
Straught through the lake,
And gie their hides a noble curry,
Wi' oil of aik.

As for the *Jurr*, poor worthless body,
She 's got mischief enough already,
Wi' stanged hips, and buttocks bloody,
She 's suffer'd sair;
But may she wintle in a woodie,
If she w—e mair.

89. *Song. On Miss W. A.*

Tune, Ettrick banks

'TWAS ev'n, the dewy fields were green,
On ev'ry blade the pearls hang,
The Zephyr wanton'd round the bean,
And bore its fragrant sweets alang;
In ev'ry glen the Mavis sang,
All nature list'ning seem'd the while;
Except where greenwood Echos rang
Amang the braes o' Ballochmyle.

With careless step I onward stray'd,
My heart rejoic'd in Nature's joy,
When, musing in a lonely glade,
A Maiden fair I chanc'd to spy:

Her look was like the Morning's eye,
  Her air like Nature's vernal smile,
The lilies' hue and roses' die
  Bespoke the Lass o' Ballochmyle.

Fair is a morn in flow'ry May,
  And sweet an ev'n in Autumn mild;
When roving through the garden gay,
  Or wand'ring in the lonely wild;
But Woman, Nature's darling child,
  There all her charms she does compile,
And all her other works are foil'd
  By th' bony Lass o' Ballochmyle.

O if she were a country Maid,
  And I the happy country Swain!
Though shelt'red in the lowest shed
  That ever rose on Scotia's plain:
Through weary Winter's wind and rain,
  With joy, with rapture I would toil,
And nightly to my bosom strain
  The bony Lass o' Ballochmyle.

Then Pride might climb the slipp'ry steep
  Where fame and honors lofty shine:
And Thirst of gold might tempt the deep
  Or downward seek the Indian mine:
Give me the Cot below the pine,
  To tend the flocks or till the soil,
And ev'ry day has joys divine
  With th' bony Lass o' Ballochmyle.

90. *Letter to J——s T——t, Gl—nc——r*

AULD com'rade dear and brither sinner,
How 's a' the folk about Gl—nc——r;
How do ye this blae eastlin win',
That 's like to blaw a body blin':
For me my faculties are frozen,
My dearest member nearly dozen'd:
I've sent you here by Johnie Simson,
Twa sage Philosophers to glimpse on!

Smith, wi' his sympathetic feeling,
An' Reid, to common sense appealing.
Philosophers have fought an' wrangled,
An' meikle Greek an' Latin mangled,
Till with their Logic-jargon tir'd,
An' in the depth of science mir'd,
To common sense they now appeal,
What wives an' wabsters see an' feel;
But, hark ye, friend, I charge you strictly,
Peruse them an' return them quickly;
For now I'm grown sae cursed douse,
I pray an' ponder *butt* the house,
My shins, my lane, I there sit roastin,
Perusing Bunyan, Brown and Boston;
Till by an' by, if I haud on,
I'll grunt a real Gospel groan:
Already I begin to try it,
To cast my een up like a Pyet,
When by the gun she tumbles o'er,
Flutt'ring an' gasping in her gore:
Sae shortly you shall see me bright,
A burning an' a shining light.

My heart-warm love to guid auld Glen,
The ace an' wale of honest men;
When bending down with auld gray hairs,
Beneath the load of years and cares,
May he who made him still support him,
An' views beyond the grave comfort him.

His worthy fam'ly far and near,
God bless them a' wi' grace and gear.

My auld school-fellow, Preacher Willie,
The manly tar, my mason billie,
An' Auchenbay, I wish him joy;
If he 's a parent, lass or boy,
May he be dad, and Meg the mither,
Just five and forty years thegither!
An' no forgetting wabster Charlie,
I'm tauld he offers very fairly,
An' L—d, remember singing Sannock,
Wi' hale-breeks, saxpence an' a bannock;
An' next, my auld acquaintance, Nancy,
Since she is fitted to her fancy;

An' her kind stars hae airted till her,
A guid chiel wi' a pickle siller:
My kindest, best respects I sen' it,
To cousin Kate an' sister Janet,
Tell them frae me, wi' chiels be cautious;
For, faith, they'll ablins fin' them fashious:
To grant a heart is fairly civil,
But to grant a maidenhead 's the devil!
An' lastly, Jamie, for yoursel,
May guardian angels tak a spell,
An' steer you seven miles south o' hell;
But first, before you see heav'ns glory,
May ye get mony a merry story,
Mony a laugh and mony a drink,
An' ay aneugh o' needfu' clink.

Now fare ye well, an' joy be wi' you,
For my sake this I beg it o' you,
Assist poor Simson a' ye can,
Ye'll fin' him just an honest man:
Sae I conclude and quat my chanter,
Yours, saint or sinner,
RAB THE RANTER.

91. [*To Mrs. C——*]

THOU flattering mark of friendship kind
Still may thy pages call to mind
  The dear, the beauteous donor:
Though sweetly female every part
Yet such a head, and more the heart,
  Does both the sexes honor.
She showed her taste refined and just
  When she selected thee,
Yet deviating own I must,
  For so approving me.
    But kind still, I mind still,
      The giver in the gift;
    I'll bless her and wiss her
      A Friend aboon the Lift.

92. *To a Mountain-Daisy, On turning one down, with the Plough, in April — 1786*

WEE, modest, crimson-tipped flow'r,
Thou 's met me in an evil hour;
For I maun crush amang the stoure
Thy slender stem:
To spare thee now is past my pow'r,
Thou bonie gem.

Alas! it 's no thy neebor sweet,
The bonie *Lark*, companion meet!
Bending thee 'mang the dewy weet!
Wi 's spreckl'd breast,
When upward-springing, blythe, to greet
The purpling East.

Cauld blew the bitter-biting *North*
Upon thy early, humble birth;
Yet chearfully thou glinted forth
Amid the storm,
Scarce rear'd above the *Parent-earth*
Thy tender form.

The flaunting *flow'rs* our Gardens yield,
High-shelt'ring woods and wa's maun shield,
But thou, beneath the random bield
O' clod or stane,
Adorns the histie *stibble-field*,
Unseen, alane.

There, in thy scanty mantle clad,
Thy snawie bosom sun-ward spread,
Thou lifts thy unassuming head
In humble guise;
But now the *share* uptears thy bed,
And low thou lies!

Such is the fate of artless Maid,
Sweet *flow'ret* of the rural shade!
By Love's simplicity betray'd,
And guileless trust,
Till she, like thee, all soil'd, is laid
Low i' the dust.

Such is the fate of simple Bard,
On Life's rough ocean luckless starr'd!
Unskilful he to note the card
Of *prudent Lore*,
Till billows rage, and gales blow hard,
And whelm him o'er!

Such fate to *suffering worth* is giv'n,
Who long with wants and woes has striv'n,
By human pride or cunning driv'n
To Mis'ry's brink,
Till wrench'd of ev'ry stay but HEAV'N,
He, ruin'd, sink!

Ev'n thou who mourn'st the *Daisy*'s fate,
That fate is thine—no distant date;
Stern Ruin's *plough-share* drives, elate,
Full on thy bloom,
Till crush'd beneath the *furrow*'s weight,
Shall be thy doom!

93. *The Lament. Occasioned by the Unfortunate Issue of a Friend's Amour*

Alas! how oft does goodness wound itself!
And sweet Affection *prove the spring of Woe!*
HOME.

I

O THOU pale Orb, that silent shines,
While care-untroubled mortals sleep!
Thou seest a *wretch*, who inly pines,
And wanders here to wail and weep!
With Woe I nightly vigils keep,
Beneath thy wan, unwarming beam;
And mourn, in lamentation deep,
How *life* and *love* are all a dream!

II

I joyless view thy rays adorn,
The faintly-marked, distant hill:
I joyless view thy trembling horn,
Reflected in the gurgling rill.

My fondly-fluttering heart, be still!
  Thou busy pow'r, Remembrance, cease!
Ah! must the agonizing thrill,
  For ever bar returning Peace!

III

No idly-feign'd, poetic pains,
  My sad, lovelorn lamentings claim:
No shepherd's pipe—Arcadian strains;
  No fabled tortures, quaint and tame.
The *plighted faith;* the *mutual flame;*
  The *oft-attested Powers above;*
The *promis'd Father's tender name;*
  These were the pledges of my love!

IV

Encircled in her clasping arms,
  How have the raptur'd moments flown!
How have I wish'd for Fortune's charms,
  For her dear sake, and her's alone!
And, must I think it! is she gone,
  My secret-heart's exulting boast?
And does she heedless hear my groan?
  And is she ever, ever lost?

V

Oh! can she bear so base a heart,
  So lost to Honor, lost to Truth,
As from the *fondest lover* part,
  The *plighted husband* of her youth?
Alas! Life's path may be unsmooth!
  Her way may lie thro' rough distress!
Then, who her pangs and pains will sooothe,
  Her sorrows share and make them less?

VI

Ye winged Hours that o'er us past,
  Enraptur'd more, the more enjoy'd,
Your dear remembrance in my breast,
  My fondly-treasur'd thoughts employ'd.
That breast, how dreary now, and void,
  For her too scanty once of room!
Ev'n ev'ry *ray* of *Hope* destroy'd,
  And not a *Wish* to gild the gloom!

VII

The morn that warns th' approaching day,
  Awakes me up to toil and woe:
I see the hours, in long array,
  That I must suffer, lingering, slow.
Full many a pang, and many a throe,
  Keen Recollection's direful train,
Must wring my soul, ere Phoebus, low,
  Shall kiss the distant, western main.

VIII

And when my nightly couch I try,
  Sore-harass'd out, with care and grief,
My toil-beat nerves, and tear-worn eye,
  Keep watchings with the nightly thief:
Or if I slumber, Fancy, chief,
  Reigns, hagard-wild, in sore afright:
E'vn day, all-bitter, brings relief,
  From such a horror-breathing night.

IX

O! thou bright Queen, who, o'er th' expanse,
  Now highest reign'st, with boundless sway!
Oft has thy silent-marking glance
  Observ'd us, fondly-wand'ring, stray!
The time, unheeded, sped away,
  While Love's *luxurious pulse* beat high,
Beneath thy silver-gleaming ray,
  To mark the mutual-kindling eye.

X

Oh! scenes in strong remembrance set!
  Scenes, never, never to return!
Scenes, if in stupor I forget,
  Again I feel, again I burn!
From ev'ry joy and pleasure torn,
  Life's weary vale I'll wander thro';
And hopeless, comfortless, I'll mourn
  A faithless woman's broken vow.

94. *Despondency, an Ode*

I

OPPRESS'D with grief, oppress'd with care,
A burden more than I can bear,
  I set me down and sigh:
O Life! Thou art a galling load,
Along a rough, a weary road,
  To wretches such as I!
Dim-backward as I cast my view,
  What sick'ning Scenes appear!
What Sorrows *yet* may pierce me thro',
  Too justly I may fear!
    Still caring, despairing,
      Must be my bitter doom;
    My woes here, shall close ne'er,
      But with the *closing tomb*!

II

Happy! ye sons of Busy-life,
Who, equal to the bustling strife,
  No other view regard!
Ev'n when the wished *end* 's deny'd,
Yet while the busy *means* are ply'd,
  They bring their own reward:
Whilst I, hope-abandon'd wight,
  Unfitted with an *aim*,
Meet ev'ry sad-returning night,
  And joyless morn the same.
    You, bustling and justling,
      Forget each grief and pain;
    I, listless, yet restless,
      Find ev'ry prospect vain.

III

How blest the Solitary's lot,
Who, all-forgetting, all-forgot,
  Within his humble cell,
The cavern wild with tangling roots,
Sits o'er his newly-gather'd fruits,
  Beside his crystal well!

Or haply, to his ev'ning thought,
By unfrequented stream,
The *ways of men* are distant brought,
A faint-collected dream:
While praising, and raising
His thoughts to Heaven on high,
As wand'ring, meand'ring,
He views the solemn sky.

IV

Than I, no *lonely Hermit* plac'd
Where never human footstep trac'd,
Less fit to play the part,
The *lucky moment* to improve,
And *just* to stop, and *just* to move,
With *self-respecting* art:
But ah! those pleasures, Loves and Joys
Which I too keenly taste,
The *Solitary* can despise,
Can want, and yet be blest!
He needs not, he heeds not,
Or human love or hate;
Whilst I here, must cry here,
At perfidy ingrate!

V

Oh, enviable, early days,
When dancing thoughtless Pleasure's maze,
To Care, to Guilt unknown!
How ill exchang'd for riper times,
To feel the follies, or the crimes,
Of others, or my own!
Ye tiny elves that guiltless sport,
Like linnets in the bush,
Ye little know the ills ye court,
When Manhood is your wish!
The losses, the crosses,
That *active man* engage;
The fears all, the tears all,
Of dim declining *Age*!

95. *Jeremiah 15th Ch. 10 V.*

AH, woe is me, my Mother dear!
  A man of strife ye've born me:
For sair contention I maun bear,
  They hate, revile and scorn me.—

I ne'er could lend on bill or band,
  That five per cent might blest me;
And borrowing, on the tither hand,
  The de'il a ane wad trust me.—

Yet I, a coin-denied wight,
  By Fortune quite discarded,
Ye see how I am, day and night,
  By lad and lass blackguarded.—

96. *Epitaph on a Henpecked Country Squire*

AS father Adam first was fool'd,
  A case that 's still too common,
Here lyes a man a woman rul'd,
  The devil rul'd the woman.

97. *Epigram on said Occasion*

O DEATH, hadst thou but spar'd his life,
  Whom we, this day, lament!
We freely wad exchang'd the *wife*,
  An' a' been weel content.

Ev'n as he is, cauld in his graff,
  The *swap* we yet will do 't;
Tak thou the Carlin's carcase aff,
  Thou 'se get the *saul* o' *boot*.

98. *Another*

One Queen Artemisa, as old stories tell,
When depriv'd of her husband she loved so well,
In respect for the love and affection he 'd show'd her,
She reduc'd him to dust, and she drank up the Powder.

But Queen N**********, of a diff'rent complexion,
When call'd on to order the fun'ral direction,
Would have *eat* her dead lord, on a slender pretence,
Not to show her respect, but—*to save the expence.*

99. *Extempore— to Mr. Gavin Hamilton*

To you, Sir, this summons I've sent,
Pray whip till the pownie is fraething;
But if you demand what I want,
I honestly answer you, naething.—

Ne'er scorn a poor Poet like me,
For idly just living and breathing,
While people of every degree
Are busy employed about—naething.—

Poor Centum per centum may fast,
And grumble his hurdies their claithing;
He'll find, when the balance is cast,
He 's gane to the devil for—naething.—

The Courtier cringes and bows,
Ambition has likewise its plaything;
A Coronet beams in his brows,
And what is a Coronet? naething.—

Some quarrel the presbyter gown,
Some quarrel Episcopal graithing,
But every good fellow will own
Their quarrel is all about—naething.—

The lover may sparkle and glow,
Approaching his bonie bit gay thing;
But marriage will soon let him know,
He 's gotten a buskit up naething.—

The Poet may jingle and rhyme,
  In hopes of a laureate wreathing,
And when he has wasted his time,
  He 's kindly rewarded with naething.—

The thundering bully may rage,
  And swagger and swear like a heathen;
But collar him fast, I'll engage
  You'll find that his courage is naething.—

Last night with a feminine whig,
  A Poet she could na put faith in,
But soon we grew lovingly big,
  I taught her, her terrors were naething.—

Her whigship was wonderful pleased,
  But charmingly tickled wi' ae thing;
Her fingers I lovingly squeezed,
  And kissed her and promised her—naething.—

The Priest anathemas may threat,
  Predicament, Sir, that we 're baith in;
But when honor's reveillé is beat,
  The holy artillery 's naething.—

And now I must mount on the wave,
  My voyage perhaps there is death in;
But what of a watery grave!
  The drowning a Poet is naething.—

And now as grim death 's in my thought,
  To you, Sir, I make this bequeathing:
My service as lang as ye 've ought,
  And my friendship, by G—, when ye 've naething.—

100. *On a Scotch Bard Gone to the West Indies*

A' YE wha live by sowps o' drink,
A' ye wha live by crambo-clink,
A' ye wha live and never think,
          Come, mourn wi' me!
Our *billie* 's gien us a' a jink,
          An' owre the Sea.

Lament him a' ye rantan core,
Wha dearly like a random-splore;
Nae mair he 'll join the *merry roar*,
In social key;
For now he 's taen anither shore,
An' owre the Sea!

The bonie lasses weel may wiss him,
And in their dear *petitions* place him:
The widows, wives, an' a' may bless him,
Wi' tearfu' e'e;
For weel I wat they 'll sairly miss him
That 's owre the Sea!

O Fortune, they hae room to grumble!
Hadst thou taen aff some drowsy bummle,
Wha can do nought but fyke an' fumble,
'Twad been nae plea;
But he was gleg as onie wumble,
That 's owre the Sea!

Auld, cantie KYLE may weepers wear,
An' stain them wi' the saut, saut tear:
'Twill mak her poor, auld heart, I fear,
In flinders flee:
He was her *Laureat* monie a year,
That 's owre the Sea!

He saw Misfortune's cauld *Nor-west*
Lang-mustering up a bitter blast;
A Jillet brak his heart at last,
Ill may she be!
So, took a birth afore the mast,
An' owre the Sea.

To tremble under Fortune's cummock,
On scarce a bellyfu' o' *drummock*,
Wi' his proud, independant stomach,
Could ill agree;
So, row't his hurdies in a *hammock*,
An' owre the Sea.

He ne'er was gien to great misguidin,
Yet coin his pouches wad na bide in;
Wi' him it ne'er was *under hidin*;
He dealt it free:
The *Muse* was a' that he took pride in,
That 's owre the Sea.

Jamaica bodies, use him weel,
An' hap him in a cozie biel:
Ye 'll find him ay a dainty chiel,
An' fou o' glee:
He wad na wrang'd the vera *Diel*,
That 's owre the Sea.

Fareweel, my *rhyme-composing billie*!
Your native soil was right ill-willie;
But may ye flourish like a lily,
Now bonilie!
I'll toast ye in my hindmost *gillie*,
Tho' owre the Sea!

101. [*Second Epistle to Davie*]

AULD NIBOR,

I'M three times, doubly, o'er your debtor,
For your auld-farrent, frien'ly letter;
Tho' I maun say 't, I doubt ye flatter,
Ye speak sae fair;
For my puir, silly, rhymin' clatter
Some less maun sair.

Hale be your heart, hale be your fiddle;
Lang may your elbuck jink an' diddle,
Tae cheer you thro' the weary widdle
O' war'ly cares,
Till bairns' bairns kindly cuddle
Your auld, gray hairs.

But DAVIE, lad, I'm red ye're glaikit;
I'm tauld the Muse ye hae negleckit;
An' gif it 's sae, ye sud be licket
Until ye fyke;
Sic hauns as you sud ne'er be faikit,
Be hain't wha like.

For me, I'm on Parnassus brink,
Rivan the words tae gar them clink;
Whyles daez't wi' love, whyles daez't wi' drink,
Wi' jads or masons;
An' whyles, but ay owre late, I think
Braw sober lessons.

Of a' the thoughtless sons o' man,
Commen' me to the Bardie clan;
Except it be some idle plan
O' rhymin clink,
The devil-haet, that I sud ban,
They never think.

Nae thought, nae view, nae scheme o' livin',
Nae cares tae gie us joy or grievin':
But just the pouchie put the nieve in,
An' while ought 's there,
Then, hiltie, skiltie, we gae scrivin',
An' fash nae mair.

Leeze me on rhyme! it 's ay a treasure,
My chief, amaist my only pleasure,
At hame, a-fiel, at wark or leisure,
The Muse, poor hizzie!
Tho' rough an' raploch be her measure,
She 's seldom lazy.

Haud tae the Muse, my dainty Davie:
The warl' may play you [monie] a shavie;
But for the Muse, she 'll never leave ye,
Tho' e'er sae puir,
Na, even tho' limpan wi' the spavie
Frae door tae door.

102. [*To*] *Mr. Gavin Hamilton, Mauchline*

I HOLD it, Sir, my bounden duty
To warn you how that Master TOOTIE,
Alias, Laird Mcgawn,
Was here to hire yon lad away
'Bout which ye spak the ither day,
An' wad hae done 't aff han':

But lest he learn the callan tricks,
As faith I muckle doubt him,
Like scrapin out auld Crummies' nicks,
An' tellin lies about them;
As lieve then I'd have then,
Your CLERKSHIP he should sair;
If sae be ye may be
Not fitted otherwhere.—

Altho' I say 't, he 's gleg enough,
An' 'bout a HOUSE that 's rude an' rough,
The boy might learn to SWEAR;
But then wi' you, he'll be sae taught,
An' get sic fair EXAMPLE straught,
I hae na ony fear.
Ye'll catechize him, ev'ry quirk,
An' shore him weel wi' HELL;
An' gar him follow to the kirk—
—Ay, when ye gang YOURSEL.
If ye then maun be then
Frae hame, this comin Friday,
Then please Sir, to lea'e Sir,
The orders wi' your LADY.—

My word of HONOR I hae gien,
In PAISLEY JOHN's, that night at een,
To meet the WARLD'S WORM;
To try to get the twa to gree,
An' name the airles, an' the fee,
In legal mode an' form:
I ken, he weel a SNICK can draw,
When simple bodies let him;
An' if a DEVIL be at a',
In faith, he 's sure to get him.—
To phrase you, an' praise you,
Ye ken your LAUREAT scorns:
The PRAY'R still, you share still,
Of grateful MINSTREL BURNS.

Mossgaville
Wednesday 3d May
1786.

103. *A Dedication To G**** H******* Esq;*

EXPECT na, Sir, in this narration,
A fleechan, fleth'ran *Dedication*,
To roose you up, an' ca' you guid,
An' sprung o' great an' noble bluid;
Because ye're sirnam'd like *His Grace*,
Perhaps related to the race:
Then when I'm tir'd—and sae are *ye*,
Wi' monie a fulsome, sinfu' lie,
Set up a face, how I stop short,
For fear your modesty be hurt.

This may do—maun do, Sir, wi' them wha
Maun please the Great-folk for a wamefou;
For me! sae laigh I need na bow,
For, LORD be thanket, *I can plough;*
And when I downa yoke a naig,
Then, LORD be thanket, *I can beg;*
Sae I shall say, an' that 's nae flatt'rin,
It 's just *sic Poet* an' *sic Patron.*

The Poet, some guid Angel help him,
Or else, I fear, some *ill ane* skelp him!
He may do weel for a' he 's done yet,
But only—he 's no just begun yet.

The Patron, (Sir, ye maun forgie me,
I winna lie, come what will o' me)
On ev'ry hand it will allow'd be,
He 's just—nae better than he should be.

I readily and freely grant,
He downa see a poor man want;
What 's no his ain, he winna tak it;
What ance he says, he winna break it;
Ought he can lend he'll no refus 't,
Till aft his guidness is abus'd;
And rascals whyles that do him wrang,
Ev'n *that*, he does na mind it lang:
As Master, Landlord, Husband, Father,
He does na fail his part in either.

But then, nae thanks to him for a' that;
Nae *godly symptom* ye can ca' that;
It 's naething but a milder feature,
Of our poor, sinfu', corrupt Nature:
Ye'll get the best o' moral works,
'Mang black *Gentoos*, and Pagan *Turks*,
Or Hunters wild on *Ponotaxi*,
Wha never heard of Orth–d–xy.
That he 's the poor man's friend in need,
The GENTLEMAN in word and deed,
It 's no through terror of D–mn–t–n;
It 's just a carnal inclination.

Morality, thou deadly bane,
Thy tens o' thousands thou hast slain!
Vain is his hope, whase stay an' trust is,
In *moral* Mercy, Truth and Justice!

No—stretch a point to catch a plack;
Abuse a Brother to his back;
Steal thro' the *winnock* frae a wh–re,
But point the Rake that taks the *door*;
Be to the Poor like onie whunstane,
And haud their noses to the grunstane;
Ply ev'ry art o' *legal* thieving;
No matter—stick to *sound believing*.

Learn three-mile pray'rs, an' half-mile graces,
Wi' weel spread looves, an' lang, wry faces;
Grunt up a solemn, lengthen'd groan,
And damn a' Parties but your own;
I'll warrant then, ye're nae Deceiver,
A steady, sturdy, staunch *Believer*.

O ye wha leave the springs o' C–lv–n,
For *gumlie dubs* of your ain delvin!
Ye sons of Heresy and Error,
Ye'll *some day* squeel in quaking terror!
When vengeance draws the sword in wrath,
And in the fire throws the *sheath*;
When Ruin, with his sweeping *besom*,
Just frets till Heav'n commission gies him;
While o'er the *Harp* pale Misery moans,
And strikes the ever-deep'ning tones,
Still louder shrieks, and heavier groans!

Your pardon, Sir, for this digression,
I maist forgat my *Dedication*;
But when Divinity comes cross me,
My readers still are sures lose me.

So Sir, you see 'twas nae daft vapour,
But I maturely thought it proper,
When a' my works I did review,
To *dedicate* them, Sir, to You:
Because (ye need na tak it ill)
I thought them something like *yoursel*.

Then patronize them wi' your favor,
And your Petitioner shall ever—
I had amaist said, *ever pray*,
But that's a word I need na say:
For prayin I hae little skill o't;
I'm baith dead-sweer, an' wretched ill o't;
But I'se repeat each poor man's *pray'r*,
That kens or hears about you, Sir—

'May ne'er Misfortune's gowling bark,
'Howl thro' the dwelling o' the Clerk!
'May ne'er his gen'rous, honest heart,
'For that same gen'rous spirit smart!
'May K******'s far-honor'd name
'Lang beet his hymeneal flame,
'Till H*******'s, at least a diz'n,
'Are frae their nuptial labors risen:
'Five bonie Lasses round their table,
'And sev'n braw fellows, stout an' able,
'To serve their King an' Country weel!
'By word, or pen, or pointed steel!
'May Health and Peace, with mutual rays,
'Shine on the ev'ning o' his days;
'Till his wee, curlie *John*'s ier-oe,
'When ebbing life nae mair shall flow,
'The last, sad, mournful rites bestow!'

I will not wind a lang conclusion,
With complimentary effusion:
But whilst your wishes and endeavours,
Are blest with Fortune's smiles and favours,
I am, Dear Sir, with zeal most fervent,
Your much indebted, humble servant.

But if, which Pow'rs above prevent,
That iron-hearted Carl, *Want*,
Attended, in his grim advances,
By *sad mistakes*, and *black mischances*,
While hopes, and joys, and pleasures fly him,
Make you as poor a dog as I am,
Your *humble servant* then no more;
For who would humbly serve the Poor?
But by a poor man's hopes in Heav'n!
While recollection's pow'r is giv'n,
If, in the vale of humble life,
The victim sad of Fortune's strife,
I, through the tender-gushing tear,
Should recognise my *Master dear*,
If friendless, low, we meet together,
Then, Sir, your hand—my FRIEND and BROTHER.

104. *A Bard's Epitaph*

Is there a whim-inspir'd fool,
Owre fast for thought, owre hot for rule,
Owre blate to seek, owre proud to snool,
Let him draw near;
And o'er this grassy heap sing dool,
And drap a tear.

Is there a Bard of rustic song,
Who, noteless, steals the crouds among,
That weekly this area throng,
O, pass not by!
But with a frater-feeling strong,
Here, heave a sigh.

Is there a man whose judgment clear,
Can others teach the course to steer,
Yet runs, himself, life's mad career,
Wild as the wave,
Here pause—and thro' the starting tear,
Survey this grave.

The poor Inhabitant below
Was quick to learn and wise to know,
And keenly felt the friendly glow,
And *softer flame*;
But thoughtless follies laid him low,
And stain'd his name!

Reader attend—whether thy soul
Soars fancy's flights beyond the pole,
Or darkling grubs this earthly hole,
In low pursuit,
Know, prudent, cautious, *self-controul*
Is Wisdom's root.

105. *Epistle to a Young Friend*

May — 1786.

I

I LANG hae thought, my youthfu' friend,
A Something to have sent you,
Tho' it should serve nae other end
Than just a kind memento;
But how the subject theme may gang,
Let time and chance determine;
Perhaps it may turn out a Sang;
Perhaps, turn out a Sermon.

II

Ye'll try the world soon my lad,
And ANDREW dear believe me,
Ye'll find mankind an unco squad,
And muckle they may grieve ye:
For care and trouble set your thought,
Ev'n when your end 's attained;
And a' your views may come to nought,
Where ev'ry nerve is strained.

III

I'll no say, men are villains a';
The real, harden'd wicked,
Wha hae nae check but *human law*,
Are to a few restricked:

But Och, mankind are unco weak,
  An' little to be trusted;
If *Self* the wavering balance shake,
  It 's rarely right adjusted!

IV

Yet they wha fa' in Fortune's strife,
  Their fate we should na censure,
For still th' *important end* of life,
  They equally may answer:
A man may hae an *honest heart*,
  Tho' Poortith hourly stare him;
A man may tak a neebor's part,
  Yet hae nae *cash* to spare him.

V

Ay free, aff han', your story tell,
  When wi' a bosom crony;
But still keep something to yoursel
  Ye scarcely tell to ony.
Conceal yoursel as weel 's ye can
  Frae critical dissection;
But keek thro' ev'ry other man,
  Wi' sharpen'd, sly inspection.

VI

The *sacred lowe* o' weel plac'd love,
  Luxuriantly indulge it;
But never tempt th' *illicit rove*,
  Tho' naething should divulge it:
I wave the quantum o' the sin;
  The hazard of concealing;
But Och! it hardens *a' within*,
  And petrifies the feeling!

VII

To catch Dame Fortune's golden smile,
  Assiduous wait upon her;
And gather gear by ev'ry wile,
  That 's justify'd by Honor:
Not for to *hide* in it a *hedge*,
  Nor for a *train-attendant*;
But for the glorious priviledge
  Of being *independant*.

VIII

The *fear o' Hell*'s a hangman's whip,
  To haud the wretch in order;
But where ye feel your *Honor* grip,
  Let that ay be your border:
It's slightest touches, instant pause—
  Debar a' side-pretences;
And resolutely keep it's laws,
  Uncaring consequences.

IX

The great CREATOR to revere,
  Must sure become the *Creature*;
But still the preaching cant forbear,
  And ev'n the rigid feature:
Yet ne'er with Wits prophane to range,
  Be complaisance extended;
An *atheist-laugh* 's a poor exchange
  For *Deity offended*!

X

When ranting round in Pleasure's ring,
  Religion may be blinded;
Or if she gie a *random-fling*,
  It may be little minded;
But when on Life we're tempest-driven,
  A Conscience but a canker—
A correspondence fix'd wi' Heav'n,
  Is sure a noble *anchor*!

XI

Adieu, dear, amiable Youth!
  Your *heart* can ne'er be wanting!
May Prudence, Fortitude and Truth
  Erect your brow undaunting!
In *ploughman phrase* 'GOD send you speed,'
  Still daily to grow wiser;
And may ye better reck the *rede*,
  Than ever did th' *Adviser*!

106. [*Lines written on a Bank-note*]

Wae worth thy pow'r, thou cursed leaf!
Fell source of all my woe and grief!
For lake o' thee I've lost my lass;
For lake o' thee I scrimp my glass;
I see the children of Affliction
Unaided, thro' thy curst restriction;
I've seen th' Oppressor's cruel smile
Amid his hapless victim's spoil;
And for thy potence vainly wish'd
To crush the Villain in the dust:
For lake o' thee I leave this much-lov'd shore,
Never perhaps to greet old Scotland more!

R. B.—Kyle.

107. *Highland Lassie O —*

To its own tune —

NAE gentle dames tho' ne'er sae fair
Shall ever be my Muse's care;
Their titles a' are empty show,
Gie me my Highland Lassie, O.—

Chorus—

Within the glen sae bushy, O,
Aboon the plain sae rashy, O,
I set me down wi' right gude will
To sing my Highland Lassie, O.—

O were yon hills and vallies mine,
Yon palace and yon gardens fine;
The world then the love should know
I bear my Highland Lassie, O.—
Within the glen &c.

But fickle Fortune frowns on me,
And I maun cross the raging sea;
But while my crimson currents flow,
I love my Highland Lassie, O.—
Within the glen &c.

Altho' thro' foreign climes I range,
I know her heart will never change;
For her bosom burns with honor's glow,
My faithful Highland Lassie, O.—
Within the glen &c.

For her I'll dare the billow's roar;
For her I'll trace a distant shore;
That Indian wealth may lustre throw
Around my Highland Lassie, O.—
Within the glen &c.

She has my heart, she has my hand,
By secret Truth and Honor's band:
Till the mortal stroke shall lay me low,
I'm thine, my Highland Lassie, O.—
Farewel, the glen sae bushy! O
Farewel, the plain sae rashy! O
To other lands I now must go
To sing my Highland Lassie, O.—

108. [*Address of Beelzebub*]

To the R^{t} Honble JOHN, EARL OF BREADALBANE, President of the R^{t} Honble the HIGHLAND SOCIETY, which met, on the 23^{d} of May last, at the Shakespeare, Covent garden, to concert ways and means to frustrate the designs of FIVE HUNDRED HIGHLANDERS who, as the Society were informed by M^{r} McKenzie of Applecross, were so audacious as to attempt an escape from theire lawful lords and masters whose property they are by emigrating from the lands of M^{r} McDonald of Glengary to the wilds of CANADA, in search of that fantastic thing—LIBERTY—

LONG LIFE, My lord, an' health be yours,
Unskaith'd by hunger'd HIGHLAN BOORS!
Lord grant, nae duddie, desp'rate beggar,
Wi' durk, claymore, or rusty trigger
May twin auld SCOTLAND O' a LIFE,
She likes—as BUTCHERS like a KNIFE!

Faith, you and Applecross were right
To keep the highlan hounds in sight!
I doubt na! they wad bid nae better
Than let them ance out owre the water;
Then up amang thae lakes an' seas
They'll mak what rules an' laws they please.

Some daring Hancocke, or a Frankline,
May set their HIGHLAN bluid a ranklin;
Some Washington again may head them,
Or some MONTGOMERY, fearless, lead them;
Till, God knows what may be effected,
When by such HEADS an' HEARTS directed:
Poor, dunghill sons of dirt an' mire,
May to PATRICIAN RIGHTS ASPIRE;
Nae sage North, now, nor sager Sackville,
To watch an' premier owre the pack vile!
An' whare will ye get Howes an' Clintons
To bring them to a right repentance,
To cowe the rebel generation,
An' save the honor o' the NATION?
THEY! an' be d–mn'd! what right hae they
To Meat, or Sleep, or light o' day,
Far less to riches, pow'r, or freedom,
But what your lordships PLEASE TO GIE THEM?

But, hear me, my lord! Glengary hear!
Your HAND 'S OWRE LIGHT ON THEM, I fear:
Your FACTORS, GREIVES, TRUSTEES an' BAILIES,
I canna say but they do gailies;
They lay aside a' tender mercies
An' tirl the HALLIONS to the BIRSIES;
Yet, while they're only poin'd, and herriet,
They'll keep their stubborn Highlan spirit.
But smash them! crush them a' to spails!
An' rot the DYVORS i' the JAILS!
The young dogs, swinge them to the labour,
Let WARK an' HUNGER mak them sober!
The HIZZIES, if they're oughtlins fausont,
Let them in Drury lane be lesson'd!
An' if the wives, an' dirty brats,
Come thiggan at your doors an' yets,
Flaffan wi' duds, an' grey wi' beese,
Frightan awa your deucks an' geese;
Get out a HORSE-WHIP, or a JOWLER,
The langest thong, the fiercest growler,
An' gar the tatter'd gipseys pack
Wi' a' their bastarts on their back!

Go on, my lord! I lang to meet you
An' in my HOUSE AT HAME to greet you;
Wi' COMMON LORDS ye shanna mingle,
The benmost newk, beside the ingle
At my right hand, assign'd your seat
'Tween Herod's hip, an' Polycrate;
Or, if ye on your station tarrow,
Between Almagro and Pizarro;
A seat, I'm sure ye're weel deservin 't;
An' till ye come—your humble servant

Beelzebub.

Hell 1st June Anno Mundi 5790

109. *Libel Summons* —

IN Truth and Honour's name—AMEN—
Know all men by these Presents plain:—

This fourth o' June, at Mauchline given,
The year 'tween eighty five and seven,
WE, Fornicators by profession,
As per extractum from each Session,
In way and manner here narrated,
Pro bono Amor congregated;
And by our brethren constituted,
A COURT OF EQUITY deputed.—
WITH special authoris'd direction
To take beneath our strict protection,
The stays-out-bursting, quondam maiden,
With GROWING LIFE and anguish laden;
Who by the rascal is deny'd,
That led her thoughtless steps aside.—
He who disowns the ruin'd Fair-one,
And for her wants and woes does care none;
The wretch that can refuse subsistence
To those whom he has given existence;
He who when at a lass's by-job,
Defrauds her wi' a fr–g or dry-b–b;
The coof that stands on clishmaclavers
When women haflins offer favors:—
All who in any way or manner
Distain the Fornicator's honor,
We take cognisance thereanent,
The proper Judges competent.—

FIRST, POET B—s he takes the chair,
Allow'd by a', his title 's fair;
And pass'd nem. con. without dissension,
He has a DUPLICATE pretension.—
Next, Merchant SMITH, our worthy FISCAL,
To cow each pertinaceous rascal;
In this, as every other state,
His merit is conspicuous great:
RICHMOND the third, our trusty CLERK,
The minutes regular to mark,

And sit dispenser of the law,
In absence of the former twa;
The fourth our MESSENGER AT ARMS,
When failing all the milder terms,
HUNTER, a hearty, willing brother,
Weel skill'd in *dead and living leather.—
Without PREAMBLE less or more said,
WE, body politic aforesaid,
With legal, due WHEAREAS, and WHEREFORE,
We are appointed here to care for
The interests of our constituents,
And punish contraveening truants,
Keeping a proper regulation
Within the lists of FORNICATION.—

WHEREAS, our FISCAL, by petition,
Informs us there is strong suspicion,
You, Coachman †Dow, and Clockie‡ BROWN,
Baith residenters in this town;
In other words, you, JOCK, and, SANDY,
Hae been at wark at HOUGHMAGANDIE;
And now when facts are come to light,
The matter ye deny outright.—

FIRST, YOU, JOHN BROWN, there 's witness borne,
And affidavit made and sworn,
That ye hae bred a hurly-burly
'Bout JEANY MITCHEL's tirlie-whirlie,
And blooster'd at her regulator,
Till a' her wheels gang clitter-clatter.—
And farther still, ye cruel Vandal,
A tale might even in hell be scandal!
That ye hae made repeated trials
Wi' drugs and draps in doctor's phials,
Mixt, as ye thought, wi' fell infusion,
Your ain begotten wean to poosion.—
And yet ye are sae scant o' grace,
Ye daur to lift your brazen face,
And offer for to take your aith,
Ye never lifted JEANY's claith.—
But tho' ye should yoursel manswear,
Laird Wilson's sclates can witness bear,

* A Tanner. † A coachman. ‡ A Clockmaker.

Ae e'ening of a MAUCHLINE fair,
That JEANY's masts they saw them bare;
For ye had furl'd up her sails,
And was at play—at heads and tails.—

NEXT, SANDY DOW, you're here indicted
To have, as publickly you're wyted,
Been clandestinely upward whirlin
The petticoats o' MAGGY BORELAN,
And giein her canister a rattle,
That months to come it winna settle.—
And yet, ye offer your protest,
Ye never herried Maggy's nest;
Tho', it 's weel ken'd that at her gyvel
Ye hae gien mony a kytch and kyvel.—

THEN BROWN AND DOW, before design'd,
For clags and clauses there subjoin'd,
WE, Court aforesaid, cite and summon,
That on the fifth o' July comin,
The hour o' cause, in our Court-ha',
At Whitefoord's arms, ye answer LAW!

[BUT, as reluctantly we PUNISH,
An' rather, mildly would admonish:
Since Better PUNISHMENT prevented,
Than OBSTINACY sair repented.—

THEN, for that ANCIENT SECRET'S SAKE,
You have the honor to partake;
An' for that NOBLE BADGE you wear,
YOU, SANDIE DOW, our BROTHER dear,
We give you as a MAN an' MASON,
This private, sober, friendly lesson.—

YOUR CRIME, a manly deed we view it,
As MAN ALONE, can only do it;
But, in denial persevering,
Is to a SCOUNDREL'S NAME adhering.
The BEST O' MEN, hae been surpris'd;
The BEST O' WOMEN been advis'd:
NAY, CLEVEREST LADS hae haen a TRICK O'T,
AN', BONNIEST LASSES taen a LICK O'T.—

Then Brother Dow, if you're asham'd
In such a QUORUM to be nam'd,
Your conduct much is to be blam'd.
See, ev'n HIMSEL—there 's GODLY BRYAN,
The auld WHATRECK he has been tryin;
When such as he put to their han',
What man on CHARACTER need stan'?
Then Brother dear, lift up your brow,
And, like yoursel, the TRUTH avow;
Erect a dauntless face upon it,
An' say, 'I am the man has done it;
'I SANDIE DOW GAT MEG WI' WEAN,
'An 's fit to do as much again.'
Ne'er mind their solemn rev'rend faces,
Had they—in proper times an' places,
But SEEN AN' FUN'—I mukle dread it,
They just would done as you an' WE did.—
To TELL THE TRUTH 's a manly lesson,
An' doubly proper in A MASON.—

YOU MONSIEUR BROWN, as it is proven,
JEAN MITCHEL's wame by you was hoven;
Without you by a quick repentance
Acknowledge Jean's an' your acquaintance,
Depend on 't, this shall be your sentence.—
Our beadles to the Cross shall take you,
And there shall mither naked make you;
Some canie grip near by your middle,
They shall it bind as tight 's a fiddle;
The raep they round the PUMP shall tak
An' tye your han's behint your back;
Wi' just an' ell o' string allow'd
To jink an' hide you frae the croud:
There ye shall stan', a legal seizure,
In during Jeanie Mitchel's pleasure;
So be, her pleasure dinna pass
Seven turnings of a half-hour glass:
Nor shall it in her pleasure be
To louse you out in less than THREE.—

THIS, our futurum esse DECREET,
We mean it not to keep a secret;
But in OUR SUMMONS here insert it,
And whoso dares, may controvert it.—]

THIS, mark'd before the date and place is,
SIGILLUM EST, PER,
B—S THE PRESES.

This Summons and the signet mark,
EXTRACTUM EST, PER,
RICHMOND, CLERK.

AT MAUCHLINE, idem date of June,
'Tween six and seven, the afternoon,
You twa, in propria personæ,
Within design'd, SANDY and JOHNY,
This SUMMONS legally have got,
As vide witness underwrote:
Within the house of JOHN DOW, vinter,
NUNC FACIO HOC,
GULLELMUS HUNTER.

110. *Epitaph on John Dove, Innkeeper, Mauchline*

HERE lies Johnny Pidgeon,
What was his religion,
Whae'er desires to ken,
To some other warl
Maun follow the carl,
For here Johnny Pidgeon had nane.

Strong ale was ablution,
Small beer persecution,
A dram was *memento mori*;
But a full flowing bowl,
Was the saving his soul,
And Port was celestial glory.

111. *Epitaph on a Wag in Mauchline*

LAMENT 'im Mauchline husbands a',
He aften did assist ye;
For had ye staid whole weeks awa'
Your wives they ne'er had miss'd ye.

Ye Mauchline bairns as on ye pass,
To school in bands thegither,
O tread ye lightly on his grass,
Perhaps he was your father.

112. [*On Willie Chalmers*]

Madam,

Wi' braw new branks in mickle pride,
And eke a braw new brechan,
My Pegasus I'm got astride,
And up Parnassus pechin;
Whiles owre a bush wi' downward crush,
The doited beastie stammers;
Then up he gets, and off he sets,
For sake o' *Willie Chalmers.*

I doubt na, lass, that weel kenned name
May cost a pair o' blushes;
I am nae stranger to your fame,
Nor his warm-urged wishes.
Your bonnie face sae mild and sweet,
His honest heart enamours,
And faith ye'll no be lost a whit,
Tho' waired on *Willie Chalmers.*

Auld Truth hersel' might swear ye're fair,
And Honour safely back her,
And Modesty assume your air,
And ne'er a ane mistak' her:
And sic twa love-inspiring e'en,
Might fire even holy Palmers;
Nae wonder then they've fatal been
To honest *Willie Chalmers.*

I doubt na Fortune may you shore
Some mim-mou'd pouthered priestie,
Fu' lifted up wi' Hebrew lore,
And band upon his breastie;
But oh! what signifies to you
His lexicons and grammars;
The feeling heart 's the royal blue,
And that 's wi' *Willie Chalmers.*

Some gapin' glowrin' countra laird,
  May warsle for your favour;
May claw his lug, and straik his beard,
  And host up some palaver.
My bonie maid, before ye wed
  Sic clumsy-witted hammers,
Seek Heaven for help, and barefit skelp
  Awa' wi' *Willie Chalmers.*

Forgive the Bard! my fond regard
  For ane that shares my bosom,
Inspires my muse to gie 'm his dues,
  For de'il a hair I roose him.
May powers aboon unite you soon,
  And fructify your amours,—
And every year come in mair dear
  To you and *Willie Chalmers.*

113. *A Dream*

Thoughts, words and deeds, the Statute blames with reason;
But surely Dreams *were ne'er indicted Treason.*

On reading, in the public papers, the Laureate's Ode, with the other parade of June 4th, 1786, the Author was no sooner dropt asleep, than he imagined himself transported to the Birth-day Levee; and, in his dreaming fancy, made the following Address.

I

GUID-MORNIN to your MAJESTY!
  May heaven augment your blisses,
On ev'ry new *Birth-day* ye see,
  A humble Poet wishes!
My Bardship here, at your Levee,
  On sic a day as this is,
Is sure an uncouth sight to see,
  Amang thae Birth-day dresses
      Sae fine this day.

II

I see ye're complimented thrang,
  By many a *lord* an' *lady*;
'God save the King' 's a cukoo sang
  That 's unco easy said ay:

The *Poets* too, a venal gang,
Wi' rhymes weel-turn'd an' ready,
Wad gar you trow ye ne'er do wrang,
But ay unerring steady,
On sic a day.

III

For me! before a Monarch's face,
Ev'n *there* I winna flatter;
For neither Pension, Post, nor Place,
Am I your humble debtor:
So, nae reflection on Your Grace,
Your Kingship to bespatter;
There 's monie *waur* been o' the Race,
And aiblins *ane* been better
Than You this day.

IV

'Tis very true, my sovereign King,
My skill may weel be doubted;
But *Facts* are cheels that winna ding,
An' downa be disputed:
Your *royal nest*, beneath *Your* wing,
Is e'en right reft an' clouted,
And now the third part o' the string,
An' less, will gang about it
Than did ae day.

V

Far be 't frae me that I aspire
To blame your Legislation,
Or say, ye wisdom want, or fire,
To rule this mighty nation;
But faith! I muckle doubt, my Sire,
Ye've trusted 'Ministration,
To chaps, wha, in a *barn* or *byre*,
Wad better fill'd their station
Than *courts* yon day.

VI

And now Ye've gien auld *Britain* peace,
Her broken shins to plaister;
Your sair taxation does her fleece,
Till she has scarce a tester:

For me, thank God, my life 's a *lease*,
Nae *bargain* wearing faster,
Or faith! I fear, that, wi' the geese,
I shortly boost to pasture
I' the craft some day.

VII

I'm no mistrusting *Willie Pit*,
When taxes he enlarges,
(An' *Will* 's a true guid fallow's get,
A Name not Envy spairges)
That he intends to pay your *debt*,
An' lessen a' your *charges*;
But, G–d-sake! let nae *saving-fit*
Abridge your bonie *Barges*
An' *Boats* this day.

VIII

Adieu, my LIEGE! may Freedom geck
Beneath your high protection;
An' may Ye rax Corruption's neck,
And gie her for dissection!
But since I'm here, I'll no neglect,
In loyal, true affection,
To pay your QUEEN, with due respect,
My fealty an' subjection
This great Birth-day.

IX

Hail, *Majesty most Excellent!*
While Nobles strive to please Ye,
Will Ye accept a Compliment,
A simple Poet gies Ye?
Thae bonie Bairntime, Heav'n has lent,
Still higher may they heeze Ye
In bliss, till Fate some day is sent,
For ever to release Ye
Frae Care that day.

X

For you, young Potentate o' W—,
I tell your *Highness* fairly,
Down Pleasure's stream, wi' swelling sails,
I'm tauld ye're driving rarely;

But some day ye may gnaw your nails,
An' curse your folly sairly,
That e'er ye brak *Diana*'s *pales*,
Or rattl'd dice wi' *Charlie*
By night or day.

XI

Yet aft a ragged *Cowte* 's been known,
To mak a noble *Aiver*;
So, ye may dousely fill a Throne,
For a' their clish-ma-claver:
There, Him at *Agincourt* wha shone,
Few better were or braver;
And yet, wi' funny, queer *Sir* John*,
He was an unco shaver
For monie a day.

XII

For you, right rev'rend O———,
Nane sets the *lawn-sleeve* sweeter,
Altho' a ribban at your lug
Wad been a dress compleater:
As ye disown yon paughty dog,
That *bears* the Keys of Peter,
Then swith! an' get a *wife* to hug,
Or trouth! ye'll stain the *Mitre*
Some luckless day.

XIII

Young, royal TARRY-BREEKS, I learn,
Ye've lately come athwart her;
A glorious† *Galley*, stem and stern,
Weel rigg'd for *Venus barter*;
But first hang out that she'll discern
Your *hymeneal Charter*,
Then heave aboard your *grapple airn*,
An', large upon her *quarter*,
Come full that day.

* Sir John Falstaff, Vide Shakespeare.
† Alluding to the Newspaper account of a certain royal Sailor's Amour

XIV

Ye lastly, bonie blossoms a',
  Ye *royal Lasses* dainty,
Heav'n mak you guid as weel as braw,
  An' gie you *lads* a plenty:
But sneer na *British-boys* awa;
  For Kings are unco scant ay,
An' German-Gentles are but *sma'*,
  They're better just than *want ay*
      On onie day.

XV

God bless you a'! consider now,
  Ye're unco muckle dautet;
But ere the *course* o' life be through,
  It may be bitter sautet:
An' I hae seen their *coggie* fou,
  That yet hae tarrow't at it,
But or the *day* was done, I trow,
  The laggen they hae clautet
      Fu' clean that day.

114. [*To Dr. John Mackenzie*]

FRIDAY first 's the day appointed
By our Right Worshipful Anointed,
  To hold our grand Procession,
To get a blade o' Johnie's Morals,
And taste a swatch o' Manson's barrels,
  I' the way of our Profession:
Our Master and the Brotherhood
  Wad a' be glad to see you;
For me, I wad be mair than proud
  To share the MERCIES wi' you.
    If Death then wi' skaith then
      Some mortal heart is hechtin,
    Inform him, an' storm him,
      That SATURDAY ye'll fecht him.

115. *The Farewell. To the Brethren of St. James's Lodge, Tarbolton*

Tune, Goodnight and joy be wi' you a'

I

ADIEU! a heart-warm, fond adieu!
  Dear brothers of the *mystic tye*!
Ye favour'd, ye enlighten'd Few,
  Companions of my social joy!
Tho' I to foreign lands must hie,
  Pursuing Fortune's slidd'ry ba',
With melting heart, and brimful eye,
  I'll mind you still, tho' far awa'.

II

Oft have I met your social Band,
  And spent the chearful, festive night;
Oft, honor'd with supreme command,
  Presided o'er the *Sons of light*:
And by that *Hieroglyphic* bright,
  Which none but *Craftsmen* ever saw!
Strong Mem'ry on my heart shall write
  Those happy scenes when far awa'!

III

May Freedom, Harmony and Love
  Unite you in the *grand Design*,
Beneath th' Omniscient Eye above,
  The glorious ARCHITECT Divine!

That you may keep th' *unerring line*,
  Still rising by the *plummet's law*,
Till *Order* bright, completely shine,
  Shall be my Pray'r when far awa'.

IV

And *You*, farewell! whose merits claim,
  Justly that *highest badge* to wear!
Heav'n bless your honor'd, noble Name,
  To Masonry and Scotia dear!
A last request, permit me here,
  When yearly ye assemble a',
One *round*, I ask it with a *tear*,
  To him, *the Bard, that 's far awa'*.

116. *The Farewell*

The valiant, in himself, what can he suffer?
Or what does he regard his single woes?
But when, alas! he multiplies himself,
To dearer selves, to the lov'd tender fair,
To those whose bliss, whose beings hang upon him,
To helpless children,—then, Oh then he feels
The point of misery festering in his heart,
And weakly weeps his fortunes like a coward:
Such, such am I!—undone!

Thomson's *Edward and Eleanora.*

Farewell, old Scotia's bleak domains,
Far dearer than the torrid plains,
  Where rich ananas blow!
Farewell, a mother's blessing dear!
A brother's sigh! a sister's tear!
  My Jean's heart-rending throe!
Farewell, my Bess! tho' thou'rt bereft
  Of my paternal care,
A faithful brother I have left,
  My part in him thou'lt share!
    Adieu too, to you too,
      My Smith, my bosom frien';
    When kindly you mind me,
      O then befriend my Jean!

What bursting anguish tears my heart;
From thee, my Jeany, must I part!
  Thou, weeping, answ'rest—'No!'
Alas! misfortune stares my face,
And points to ruin and disgrace,
  I for thy sake must go!
Thee, Hamilton, and Aiken dear,
  A grateful, warm adieu:
I, with a much-indebted tear,
  Shall still remember you!
    All-hail then, the gale then,
      Wafts me from thee, dear shore!
    It rustles, and whistles
      I'll never see thee more!

117. *Tam Samson's* Elegy*

An honest man's the noblest work of God—
POPE.

HAS auld K********* seen the Deil?
Or Great M'*******† thrawn his heel?
Or R********‡ again grown weel,
    To preach an' read?
'Na, waur than a'!' cries ilka chiel,
    '*Tam Samson* 's dead!'

K********* lang may grunt an' grane,
An' sigh an' sab, an' greet her lane,
An' cleed her bairns, man, wife, an' wean,
    In mourning weed;
To Death she 's dearly pay'd the kane,
    Tam Samson 's dead!

* When this worthy old Sportsman went out last muir-fowl season, he supposed it was to be, in Ossian's phrase, 'the last of his fields;' and expressed an ardent wish to die and be buried in the muirs. On this hint the Author composed his Elegy and Epitaph.

† A certain Preacher, a great favourite with the Million. *Vide* the ORDINATION, p. [170].

‡ Another Preacher, an equal favourite with the Few, who was at that time ailing. For him see also the ORDINATION, stanza IX.

The Brethren o' the mystic *level*
May hing their head in wofu' bevel,
While by their nose the tears will revel,
Like ony bead;
Death 's gien the Lodge an unco devel,
Tam Samson 's dead!

When Winter muffles up his cloak,
And binds the mire like a rock;
When to the loughs the Curlers flock,
Wi' gleesome speed,
Wha will they station at the *cock*,
Tam Samson 's dead?

He was the king of a' the Core,
To guard, or draw, or wick a bore,
Or up the rink like *Jehu* roar
In time o' need;
But now he lags on Death's *hog-score*,
Tam Samson 's dead!

Now safe the stately Sawmont sail,
And Trouts bedropp'd wi' crimson hail,
And Eels weel kend for souple tail,
And Geds for greed,
Since dark in Death's *fish-creel* we wail
Tam Samson dead!

Rejoice, ye birring Paitricks a';
Ye cootie Moorcocks, crousely craw;
Ye Maukins, cock your fud fu' braw,
Withoutten dread;
Your mortal Fae is now awa',
Tam Samson 's dead!

That woefu' morn be ever mourn'd
Saw him in shootin graith adorn'd,
While pointers round impatient burn'd,
Frae couples freed;
But, Och! he gaed and ne'er return'd!
Tam Samson 's dead!

In vain Auld-age his body batters;
In vain the Gout his ancles fetters;
In vain the burns cam down like waters,
An acre-braid!
Now ev'ry auld wife, greetin, clatters,
'Tam Samson 's dead!'

Owre mony a weary hag he limpit,
An' ay the tither shot he thumpit,
Till coward Death behind him jumpit,
Wi' deadly feide;
Now he proclaims, wi'tout o' trumpet,
Tam Samson 's dead!

When at his heart he felt the dagger,
He reel'd his wonted bottle-swagger,
But yet he drew the mortal trigger
Wi' weel-aim'd heed;
'L—d, five!' he cry'd, an' owre did stagger;
Tam Samson 's dead!

Ilk hoary Hunter mourn'd a brither;
Ilk Sportsman-youth bemoan'd a father;
Yon auld gray stane, amang the heather,
Marks out his head,
Whare *Burns* has wrote, in rhyming blether,
Tam Samson 's dead!

There, low he lies, in lasting rest;
Perhaps upon his mould'ring breast
Some spitefu' muirfowl bigs her nest,
To hatch an' breed:
Alas! nae mair he'll them molest!
Tam Samson 's dead!

When August winds the heather wave,
And Sportsmen wander by yon grave,
Three vollies let his mem'ry crave
O' pouther an' lead,
Till Echo answer frae her cave,
Tam Samson 's dead!

Heav'n rest his saul, whare'er he be!
Is th' wish o' mony mae than me:
He had twa fauts, or may be three,
Yet what remead?
Ae social, honest man want we:
Tam Samson 's dead!

THE EPITAPH

Tam Samson's weel-worn clay here lies,
Ye canting Zealots, spare him!
If Honest Worth in heaven rise,
Ye'll mend or ye win near him.

PER CONTRA

Go, Fame, an' canter like a filly
Thro' a' the streets an' neuks o' *Killie*,*
Tell ev'ry social, honest billie
To cease his grievin,
For yet, unskaith'd by Death's gleg gullie,
Tam Samson 's livin!

118. [*To John Kennedy*]

FAREWEL D . .r Friend! may Guid-luck hit you,
And 'mang her favorites admit you!
If e'er Detraction shore to smit you,
May nane believe him!
And ony deil that thinks to get you,
Good Lord deceive him!!!

119A. [*Epistle from a Taylor to* Robert Burns]

[WHAT waefu' news is this I hear,
Frae greeting I can scarce forbear,
Folk tells me, ye 're gawn aff this year,
Out o'er the sea,
And lasses wham ye lo'e sae dear
Will greet for thee.

* *Killie* is a phrase the country-folks sometimes use for the name of a certain town in the West.

Weel wad I like war ye to stay,
But Robin since ye will away,
I ha'e a word yet mair to say,
And maybe twa;
May he protect us night an' day,
That made us a'.

Whar thou art gaun, keep mind frae me,
Seek him to bear thee companie,
And, Robin, whan ye come to die,
Ye'll won aboon,
An' live at peace an' unity
Ayont the moon.

Some tell me, Rab, ye dinna fear
To get a wean, an' curse an' swear,
I'm unco wae, my lad, to hear
O' sic a trade,
Cou'd I persuade ye to forbear,
I wad be glad.

Fu' weel ye ken ye'll gang to *hell*,
Gin ye persist in doin' ill—
Waes me! ye're hurlin' down the hill
Withouten dread,
An' ye'll get leave to swear your fill
After ye're dead.

There,* walth o' women ye'll get near,
But gettin' weans ye will forbear,
Ye'll never say, my bonnie dear
Come, gie 's a kiss—
Nae kissing there—ye'll girn an' sneer,
An' ither hiss.

O Rab! lay by thy foolish tricks,
An' steer nae mair the female sex,
Or some day ye'll come through the pricks,
An' that ye'll see;
Ye'll fin' hard living wi' Auld Nicks;
I'm wae for thee.

But what 's this comes wi' sic a knell,
Amaist as loud as ony bell,
While it does mak' my conscience tell
Me what is true,
I'm but a ragget cowt mysel',
Owre sib to you!

* In hell.

We're owre like those wha think it fit,
To stuff their noddles fu' o' wit,
An' yet content in darkness sit,
Wha shun the light,
To let them see down to the pit,
That lang dark night.

But fareweel, Rab, I maun awa',
May he that made us keep us a',
For that wad be a dreadfu' fa'
And hurt us sair,
Lad, ye wad never mend ava,
Sae, Rab, tak' care.]

119B. *Robert Burns' Answer*

WHAT ails ye now, ye lousie b—h,
To thresh my back at sic a pitch?
Losh man! hae mercy wi' your natch,
Your bodkin 's bauld,
I did na suffer ha'f sae much
Frae Daddie Auld.

What tho' at times when I grow crouse,
I gi'e their wames a random pouse,
Is that enough for you to souse
Your servant sae!
Gae mind your seam, ye prick the louse,
An' jag the flae.

King David o' poetic brief,
Wrought 'mang the lasses sic mischief
As fill'd his after life wi' grief
An' bloody rants,
An' yet he 's rank'd amang the chief
O' lang syne saunts.

And maybe, Tam, for a' my cants,
My wicked rhymes, an' drucken rants,
I'll gie auld cloven Clooty's haunts
An unco slip yet,
An' snugly sit amang the saunts
At Davie's hip yet.

But fegs, the Session says I maun
Gae fa' upo' anither plan,

Than garren lasses cowp the cran
Clean heels owre body,
And sairly thole their mither's ban,
Afore the howdy.

This leads me on, to tell for sport,
How I did wi' the Session sort—
Auld Clinkum at the inner port
Cry'd three times, 'Robin!'
'Come hither lad, an' answer for 't,
'Ye're blam'd for jobbin'.'

Wi' pinch I put a Sunday's face on,
An' snoov'd awa' before the Session—
I made an open fair confession,
I scorn'd to lie;
An' syne Mess John, beyond expression,
Fell foul o' me.

A furnicator lown he call'd me,
An' said my fau't frae bliss expell'd me;
I own'd the tale was true he tell'd me,
'But what the matter,'
Quo' I, 'I fear unless ye geld me,
'I'll ne'er be better.'

'Geld you!' quo' he, 'and whatfore no,
'If that your right hand, leg or toe,
'Should ever prove your sp'ritual foe,
'You shou'd remember
'To cut it aff, an' whatfore no,
'Your dearest member.'

'Na, na,' quo' I, 'I'm no for that,
'Gelding 's nae better than 'tis ca't,
'I'd rather suffer for my faut,
'A hearty flewit,
'As sair owre hip as ye can draw 't!
'Tho' I should rue it.

'Or gin ye like to end the bother,
'To please us a', I've just ae ither,
'When next wi' yon lass I forgather,
'Whate'er betide it,
'I'll frankly gi'e her 't a' thegither,
'An' let her guide it.'

But, Sir, this pleas'd them warst ava,
An' therefore, Tam, when that I saw,
I said 'Gude night', and cam' awa',
And left the Session;
I saw they were resolved a'
On my oppression.

120. *The Brigs of Ayr, a Poem. Inscribed to J. B*********, Esq; Ayr*

THE simple Bard, rough at the rustic plough,
Learning his tuneful trade from ev'ry bough;
The chanting linnet, or the mellow thrush,
Hailing the setting sun, sweet, in the green thorn bush,
The soaring lark, the perching red-breast shrill,
Or deep-ton'd plovers, grey, wild-whistling o'er the hill;

The Brigs of Ayr. In the Burns Chronicle, *1926, pp. 61–2, is a transcript of a MS containing what were probably experiments in a dedication to Ballantine:*

Sir,
[recto] think not with a mercenary view
Some servile Sycophant approaches you.
To you my Muse would sing these simple lays,
To you my heart its grateful homage pays,
I feel the weight of all your kindness past,
But thank you not as wishing it to last:
Scorn'd be the wretch whose earth-born grov'lling soul
Would in his ledger-hopes his Friends enroll.
Tho I, a lowly nameless, rustic Bard,
Who ne'er must hope your goodness to reward,
Yet man to man, Sir, let us fairly meet,
And like masonic Level, equal greet.
How poor the balance! ev'n what Monarch's plan,
Between two noble creatures such as Man.
That to your Friendship I am strongly tied
I still shall own it, Sir, with grateful pride,
When haply roaring seas between us tumble wide.

[verso] Or if among so many cent'ries waste,
Thro the long vista of dark ages past,
Some much-lov'd honor'd name a radiance cast,
Perhaps some Patriot of distinguish'd worth,
I'll match him if My Lord will please step forth.
Or Gentleman and Citizen combine,
And I shall shew his peer in Ballantine:
Tho' honest men were parcell'd out for sale,
He might be shown a sample for the hale.

Shall he, nurst in the Peasant's lowly shed,
To hardy Independence bravely bred,
By early Poverty to hardship steel'd,
And train'd to arms in stern Misfortune's field,
Shall he be guilty of their hireling crimes,
The servile, mercenary Swiss of rhymes?
Or labour hard the panegyric close,
With all the venal soul of dedicating Prose?
No! though his artless strains he rudely sings,
And throws his hand uncouthly o'er the strings,
He glows with all the spirit of the Bard,
Fame, honest fame, his great, his dear reward.
Still, if some Patron's gen'rous care he trace,
Skill'd in the secret, to bestow with grace;
When B********* befriends his humble name,
And hands the rustic Stranger up to fame,
With heartfelt throes his grateful bosom swells,
The godlike bliss, to give, alone excels.

'Twas when the stacks get on their winter-hap,
And thack and rape secure the toil-won crap;
Potatoe-bings are snugged up frae skaith
Of coming Winter's biting, frosty breath;
The bees, rejoicing o'er their summer-toils,
Unnumber'd buds, an' flow'rs' delicious spoils,
Seal'd up with frugal care in massive, waxen piles,
Are doom'd by Man, that tyrant o'er the weak,
The death o' devils, smoor'd wi' brimstone reek:
The thund'ring guns are heard on ev'ry side,
The wounded coveys, reeling, scatter wide;
The feather'd field-mates, bound by Nature's tie,
Sires, mothers, children, in one carnage lie:
(What warm, poetic heart but inly bleeds,
And execrates man's savage, ruthless deeds!)
Nae mair the flow'r in field or meadow springs;
Nae mair the grove with airy concert rings,
Except perhaps the Robin's whistling glee,
Proud o' the height o' some bit half-lang tree:
The hoary morns precede the sunny days,
Mild, calm, serene, wide-spreads the noon-tide blaze,
While thick the gossamour waves wanton in the rays.

'Twas in that season; when a simple Bard,
Unknown and poor, simplicity's reward,
Ae night, within the ancient brugh of *Ayr*,
By whim inspir'd, or haply prest wi' care,
He left his bed and took his wayward rout,
And down by *Simpson*'s* wheel'd the left about:
(Whether impell'd by all-directing Fate,
To witness what I after shall narrate;
Or whether, rapt in meditation high,
He wander'd out he knew not where nor why)
The drowsy *Dungeon-clock*† had number'd two,
And *Wallace Tow'r*† had sworn the fact was true:
The tide-swoln Firth, with sullen-sounding roar,
Through the still night dash'd hoarse along the shore:
All else was hush'd as Nature's closed e'e;
The silent moon shone high o'er tow'r and tree:
The chilly Frost, beneath the silver beam,
Crept, gently-crusting, o'er the glittering stream.—

When, lo! on either hand the list'ning Bard,
The clanging sugh of whistling wings is heard;
Two dusky forms dart thro' the midnight air,
Swift as the *Gos*‡ drives on the wheeling hare;
Ane on th' *Auld Brig* his airy shape uprears,
The ither flutters o'er the *rising piers*:
Our warlock Rhymer instantly descry'd
The Sprites that owre the *Brigs of Ayr* preside.
(That Bards are second-sighted is nae joke,
And ken the lingo of the sp'ritual folk;
Fays, Spunkies, Kelpies, a', they can explain them,
And ev'n the vera deils they brawly ken them.)
Auld Brig appear'd of ancient Pictish race,
The vera wrinkles Gothic in his face:
He seem'd as he wi' Time had warstl'd lang,
Yet, teughly doure, he bade an unco bang.
New Brig was buskit in a braw, new coat,
That he, at *Lon'on*, frae ane *Adams* got;
In 's hand five taper staves as smooth 's a bead,
Wi' virls an' whirlygigums at the head.
The Goth was stalking round with anxious search,
Spying the time-worn flaws in ev'ry arch;

* A noted tavern at the *Auld Brig* end. † The two steeples.
‡ The gos-hawk, or falcon.

It chanc'd his new-come neebor took his e'e,
And e'en a vex'd and angry heart had he!
Wi' thieveless sneer to see his modish mien,
He, down the water, gies him this guid-een—

AULD BRIG

I doubt na, frien', ye'll think ye're nae sheep-shank,
Ance ye were streekit owre frae bank to bank!
But gin ye be a Brig as auld as me,
Tho' faith, that day, I doubt, ye'll never see;
There'll be, if that date come, I'll wad a boddle,
Some fewer whigmeleeries in your noddle.

NEW BRIG

Auld Vandal, ye but show your little mense,
Just much about it wi' your scanty sense;
Will your poor, narrow foot-path of a street,
Where twa wheel-barrows tremble when they meet,
Your ruin'd, formless bulk o' stane and lime,
Compare wi' bonie *Brigs* o' modern time?
There 's men of taste wou'd tak the *Ducat-stream*,*
Tho' they should cast the vera sark and swim,
Ere they would grate their feelings wi' the view
Of sic an ugly, Gothic hulk as you.

AULD BRIG

Conceited gowk! puff'd up wi' windy pride!
This mony a year I've stood the flood an' tide;
And tho' wi' crazy eild I'm sair forfairn,
I'll be a *Brig* when ye're a shapeless cairn!
As yet ye little ken about the matter,
But twa-three winters will inform ye better.
When heavy, dark, continued, a'-day rains
Wi' deepening deluges o'erflow the plains;
When from the hills where springs the brawling *Coil*,
Or stately *Lugar*'s mossy fountains boil,
Or where the *Greenock* winds his moorland course,
Or haunted *Garpal*† draws his feeble source,

* A noted ford, just above the Auld Brig.

† The banks of *Garpal Water* is one of the few places in the West of Scotland where those fancy-scaring beings, known by the name of *Ghaists*, still continue pertinaciously to inhabit.

Arous'd by blustering winds an' spotting thowes,
In mony a torrent down the snaw-broo rowes;
While crashing ice, borne on the roaring speat,
Sweeps dams, an' mills, an' brigs, a' to the gate;
And from *Glenbuck*,* down to the *Ratton-key*,†
Auld *Ayr* is just one lengthen'd, tumbling sea;
Then down ye'll hurl, deil nor ye never rise!
And dash the gumlie jaups up to the pouring skies.
A lesson sadly teaching, to your cost,
That Architecture's noble art is lost!

NEW BRIG

Fine *architecture*, trowth, I needs must say 't o't!
The L—d be thankit that we've tint the gate o't!
Gaunt, ghastly, ghaist-alluring edifices,
Hanging with threat'ning jut like precipices;
O'er-arching, mouldy, gloom-inspiring coves,
Supporting roofs fantastic, stony groves:
Windows and doors in nameless sculptures drest,
With order, symmetry, or taste unblest;
Forms like some bedlam Statuary's dream,
The craz'd creations of misguided whim;
Forms might be worshipp'd on the bended knee,
And still the *second dread command* be free,
Their likeness is not found on earth, in air, or sea.
Mansions that would disgrace the building-taste
Of any mason reptile, bird, or beast;
Fit only for a doited Monkish race,
Or frosty maids forsworn the dear embrace,
Or Cuifs of latter times, wha held the notion,
That sullen gloom was sterling, true devotion:
Fancies that our guid Brugh denies protection,
And soon may they expire, unblest with resurrection!

AULD BRIG

O ye, my dear-remember'd, ancient yealings,
Were ye but here to share my wounded feelings!
Ye worthy *Proveses*, an' mony a *Bailie*,
Wha in the paths o' righteousness did toil ay;
Ye dainty *Deacons*, an' ye douce *Conveeners*,
To whom our moderns are but causey-cleaners;

* The source of the river of Ayr.
† A small landing-place above the large key.

Ye godly *Councils* wha hae blest this town;
Ye godly *Brethren* o' the sacred gown,
Wha meekly gae your *hurdies* to the *smiters*;
And (what would now be strange) ye *godly Writers*:
A' ye douce folk I've borne aboon the broo,
Were ye but here, what would ye say or do!
How would your spirits groan in deep vexation,
To see each melancholy alteration;
And, agonising, curse the time and place
When ye begat the base, degen'rate race!
Nae langer Rev'rend Men, their country's glory,
In plain, braid Scots hold forth a plain, braid story:
Nae langer thrifty Citizens, an' douce,
Meet owre a pint, or in the Council-house;
But staumrel, corky-headed, graceless Gentry,
The herryment and ruin of the country;
Men, three-parts made by Taylors and by Barbers,
Wha waste your weel-hain'd gear on d——d *new Brigs* and *Harbours*!

NEW BRIG

Now haud you there! for faith ye've said enough,
And muckle mair than ye can mak to through.
As for your Priesthood, I shall say but little,
Corbies and *Clergy* are a shot right kittle:
But, under favor o' your langer beard,
Abuse o' Magistrates might weel be spar'd;
To liken them to your auld-warld squad,
I must needs say, comparisons are odd.
In *Ayr*, Wag-wits nae mair can have a handle
To mouth 'A Citizen', a term o' scandal:
Nae mair the Council waddles down the street,
In all the pomp of ignorant conceit;
Men wha grew wise priggin owre hops an' raisins,
Or gather'd lib'ral views in Bonds and Seisins.
If haply Knowledge, on a random tramp,
Had shor'd them with a glimmer of his lamp,
And would to Common-sense for once betray'd them,
Plain, dull Stupidity stept kindly in to aid them.

What farther clishmaclaver might been said,
What bloody wars, if Sprites had blood to shed,

No man can tell; but, all before their sight,
A fairy train appear'd in order bright:
Adown the glittering stream they featly danc'd;
Bright to the moon their various dresses glanc'd:
They footed o'er the wat'ry glass so neat,
The infant ice scarce bent beneath their feet:
While arts of Minstrelsy among them rung,
And soul-ennobling Bards heroic ditties sung.

O had *M'Lauchlan**, thairm-inspiring Sage,
Been there to hear this heavenly band engage,
When thro' his dear *Strathspeys* they bore with Highland rage;
Or when they struck old Scotia's melting airs,
The lover's raptur'd joys or bleeding cares;
How would his Highland lug been nobler fir'd,
And ev'n his matchless hand with finer touch inspir'd!
No guess could tell what instrument appear'd,
But all the soul of Music's self was heard;
Harmonious concert rung in every part,
While simple melody pour'd moving on the heart.

The Genius of the Stream in front appears,
A venerable Chief advanc'd in years;
His hoary head with water-lilies crown'd,
His manly leg with garter tangle bound.
Next came the loveliest pair in all the ring,
Sweet Female Beauty hand in hand with Spring;
Then, crown'd with flow'ry hay, came Rural Joy,
And Summer, with his fervid-beaming eye:
All-chearing Plenty, with her flowing horn,
Led yellow Autumn wreath'd with nodding corn;
Then Winter's time-bleach'd locks did hoary show,
By Hospitality with cloudless brow.
Next follow'd Courage with his martial stride,
From where the *Feal* wild-woody coverts hide:
Benevolence, with mild, benignant air,
A female form, came from the tow'rs of *Stair*:
Learning and Worth in equal measures trode,
From simple *Catrine*, their long-lov'd abode:

* A well known performer of Scottish music on the violin.

Last, white-rob'd Peace, crown'd with a hazle wreath,
To rustic Agriculture did bequeath
The broken, iron instruments of Death,
At sight of whom our Sprites forgat their kindling wrath.

121. *Wrote on the blank leaf of a copy of my first Edition, which I sent to an old Sweetheart, then married—*

ONCE fondly lov'd, and still rememb'red dear,
  Sweet early Object of my youthful vows,
Accept this mark of friendship, warm, sincere,
  Friendship—'tis all cold duty now allows.

And while you read the simple, artless rhymes,
  One friendly sigh for him—he asks no more,
Who, distant, burns in flaming torrid climes,
  Or haply lies beneath th' Atlantic roar.

'TWAS the girl I mention in my letter to D[r] Moore, where I speak of taking the sun's altitude.—Poor Peggy! Her husband is my old acquaintance and a most worthy fellow.—When I was taking leave of my Carrick relations intending to go to the West Indies, when I took farewel of her, neither she nor I could speak a syllable.—Her husband escorted me three miles on my road, and we both parted with tears.—

122. *Song*

Tune, Roslin Castle

I

THE gloomy night is gath'ring fast,
Loud roars the wild, inconstant blast,
Yon murky cloud is foul with rain,
I see it driving o'er the plain;
The Hunter now has left the moor,
The scatt'red coveys meet secure,
While here I wander, prest with care,
Along the lonely banks of *Ayr*.

II

The Autumn mourns her rip'ning corn
By early Winter's ravage torn;
Across her placid, azure sky,
She see the scowling tempest fly:

Chill runs my blood to hear it rave,
I think upon the stormy wave,
Where many a danger I must dare,
Far from the bonie banks of *Ayr*.

III

'Tis not the surging billow's roar,
'Tis not that fatal, deadly shore;
Tho' Death in ev'ry shape appear,
The Wretched have no more to fear:
But round my heart the ties are bound,
That heart transpierc'd with many a wound;
These bleed afresh, those ties I tear,
To leave the bonie banks of *Ayr*.

IV

Farewell, old *Coila*'s hills and dales,
Her heathy moors and winding vales;
The scenes where wretched Fancy roves,
Pursuing past, unhappy loves!
Farewell, my friends! farewell, my foes!
My peace with these, my love with those—
The bursting tears my heart declare,
Farewell, the bonie banks of *Ayr*!

123. *The Northern Lass*

She raise and loot me in

THOUGH cruel Fate should bid us part,
  Far as the Pole and Line,
Her dear idea round my heart
  Should tenderly entwine:

Though mountains rise, and desarts howl,
  And oceans roar between;
Yet dearer than my deathless soul
  I still would love my Jean.—

124. *A Fragment*—

Chorus

GREEN grow the rashes O,
Green grow the rashes O,
The lasses they hae wimble bores,
The widows they hae gashes O.

1

In sober hours I am a priest;
  A hero when I'm tipsey, O;
But I'm a king and ev'ry thing,
  When wi' a wanton Gipsey, O.
    Green grow &c.

2

'Twas late yestreen I met wi' ane,
  An' wow, but she was gentle, O!
Ae han' she pat roun' my cravat,
  The tither to my p—— O.
    Green grow &c.

3

I dought na speak—yet was na fley'd—
  My heart play'd duntie, duntie, O;
An' ceremony laid aside,
  I fairly fun' her c–ntie, O.—
      Green grow &c.

Multa desunt—

125. *The Calf*

To the Rev. Mr——, on his text, MALACHI, ch. iv. vers. 2. 'And they shall go forth, and grow up, like CALVES of the stall.'

RIGHT, Sir! your text I'll prove it true,
  Tho' Heretics may laugh;
For instance, there 's yoursel just now,
  God knows, an unco *Calf*!

And should some Patron be so kind,
  As bless you wi' a kirk,
I doubt na, Sir, but then we'll find,
  Ye're still as great a *Stirk*.

But, if the Lover's raptur'd hour
  Shall ever be your lot,
Forbid it, ev'ry heavenly Power,
  You e'er should be a *Stot*!

Tho', when some kind, connubial Dear
  Your But-and-ben adorns,
The like has been that you may wear
  A noble head of *horns*.

And, in your lug, most reverend J——,
To hear you roar and rowte,
Few men o' sense will doubt your claims
To rank amang the *Nowte*.

And when ye're number'd wi' the dead,
Below a grassy hillock,
Wi' justice they may mark your head—
'Here lies a famous *Bullock*!'

126. *Nature's Law*

Humbly inscribed to Gavin Hamilton, Esq.

'Great Nature spoke; observant man obey'd'—POPE.

LET other heroes boast their scars,
The marks of sturt and strife;
And other poets sign of wars,
The plagues of human life;
Shame fa' the fun; wi' sword and gun
To slap mankind like lumber!
I sing his name, and nobler fame,
Wha multiplies our number.

Great Nature spoke, with air benign,
'Go on, ye human race;
This lower world I you resign;
Be fruitful and increase.
The liquid fire of strong desire
I've pour'd it in each bosom;
Here, on this hand, does Mankind stand,
And there, is Beauty's blossom.'

The Hero of these artless strains,
A lowly bard was he,
Who sung his rhymes in Coila's plains,
With meikle mirth an' glee;
Kind Nature's care had given his share
Large, of the flaming current;
And, all devout, he never sought
To stem the sacred torrent.

He felt the powerful high behest
  Thrill, vital, thro' and thro';
And sought a correspondent breast,
  To give obedience due:
Propitious Powers screen'd the young flow'rs,
  From mildews of abortion;
And lo! the Bard—a great reward—
  Has got a double portion!

Auld cantie Coil may count the day,
  As annual it returns,
The third of Libra's equal sway,
  That gave another Burns,
With future rhymes, an' other times,
  To emulate his sire,
To sing auld Coil in nobler style,
  With more poetic fire.

Ye Powers of peace, and peaceful song,
  Look down with gracious eyes;
And bless auld Coila, large and long,
  With multiplying joys;
Lang may she stand to prop the land,
  The flow'r of ancient nations;
And Burnses spring, her fame to sing,
  To endless generations!

127. *Extempore Verses on Dining with Lord Daer*

Mossgiel, October 25th.

THIS wot all ye whom it concerns,
I, rhymer Rab, alias BURNS,
          October twenty-third,
A ne'er to be forgotten day!
Sae far I sprachl'd up the brae,
          I dinner'd wi' a LORD.

I've been at drucken Writers' feasts;
Nay, been bitch fou 'mang godly Priests;
          (Wi' rev'rence be it spoken!)
I've even join'd the honour'd jorum,
When mighty Squireships o' the Quorum,
          Their hydra drouth did sloken.

But wi' a LORD!—stand out my shin!
A LORD—a PEER—an EARL'S SON—
Up higher yet, my bonnet!
An' such a LORD—lang Scotch ell twa;
Our PEERAGE he looks o'er them a',
As I look o'er my sonnet.

But, O! for Hogarth's magic pow'r,
To shew Sir Bardie's willyart glowr,
An' how he star'd an' stammer'd!
When goavan 's he'd been led wi' branks,
An' stumpan on his ploughman shanks,
He in the parlour hammer'd.

To meet good Stuart little pain is
Or Scotia's sacred Demosthenes,
Thinks I, they are but men!
But Burns, my Lord—Guid G–d! I doited!
My knees on ane anither knoited,
As faultering I gaed ben!

I sidling shelter'd in a neuk,
An' at his Lordship staw a leuk,
Like some portentous omen;
Except GOOD SENSE, an' SOCIAL GLEE,
An' (what surpris'd me) MODESTY,
I marked nought uncommon.

I watch'd the symptoms o' the GREAT,
The GENTLE PRIDE, the LORDLY STATE,
The arrogant assuming;
The fient a pride, nae pride had he,
Nor sauce, nor state, that I could see,
Mair than an honest Ploughman.

Then from his Lordship I shall learn,
Henceforth to meet with unconcern,
One rank as well 's another;
Nae honest, worthy man need care,
To meet wi' NOBLE, youthfu' DAER,
For he but meets a BROTHER.

128. *The Sons of old Killie*

Tune—Shawnboy

YE sons of old Killie, assembled by Willie,
  To follow the noble vocation;
Your thrifty old mother has scarce such another
  To sit in that honoured station.
I've little to say, but only to pray,
  As praying 's the ton of your fashion;
A prayer from the muse you well may excuse,
  'Tis seldom her favourite passion.

Ye powers who preside o'er the wind and the tide,
  Who marked each element's border;
Who formed this frame with beneficent aim,
  Whose sovereign statute is order;
Within this dear mansion may wayward contention
  Or withered envy ne'er enter;
May secresy round be the mystical bound,
  And brotherly love be the centre.

The Sons of old Killie. Cunningham prints a note from Burns's MS: This song, wrote by Mr. Burns, was sung by him in the Kilmarnock Kilwinning Lodge, in 1786, and given by him to Mr. Parker, who was Master of the Lodge.

129. *Epistle to Captn. Willm. Logan at Park—*

Oct: 30th, 1786.

HAIL, thairm-inspirin, rattlin Willie!
Though Fortune's road be rough an' hilly
To ev'ry fiddling, rhyming billie,
We never heed;
But tak it like th' unbacked Fillie,
Proud o' her speed.

When idly goavin whyles we saunter,
Yirr, Fancy barks,—awa we canter,
Up-hill, down-brae, till some mishanter,
Some black Bog-hole,
Arreest us; then the scathe an' banter
We're forc'd to thole.

Hale be your HEART! Hale be your FIDDLE!
Lang may your elbuck jink an' didle,
To chear you through the weary widdle
O' this vile Warl:
Until ye on a cummock dridle,
A gray-hair'd Carl!

Come WEALTH, come POORTITH, late or soon,
Heav'n send your HEART-STRINGS ay IN TUNE!
An' screw your TEMPER-PINS aboon,
A FIFTH or mair,
The melancholious, sairie croon
O' cankrie CARE!

May still your Life, from day to day,
Nae LENTE LARGO, in the play,
But ALLEGRETTO FORTE, gay,
Harmonious flow:
A sweeping, kindling, bauld STRATHSPEY,
Encore! Bravo!

A' blessins on the cheary *gang*
Wha dearly like a Jig or sang;
An' never balance RIGHT and WRANG
By square and rule,
But as the CLEGS O' FEELING stang,
Are wise or fool!

My hand-wal'd CURSE keep hard in chase
The harpy, hoodock, purse-proud RACE,
Wha count on POORTITH as disgrace!
Their tuneless hearts,
May FIRE-SIDE DISCORDS jar a BASS
To a' their PARTS!

But come—your hand—my careless brither—
I' th' tither WARLD, if there 's anither,
An' that there is, I've little swither
About the matter;
We cheek for-chow shall jog the gither,
I 'se ne'er bid better.

We've fauts an' failins,—granted clearly:
We're frail, backsliding Mortals meerly:
Eve's bonie SQUAD, Priests wyte them sheerly,
For our grand fa':
But still—but still—I like them dearly;
GOD bless them a'!

Ochon! for poor CASTALIAN DRINKERS,
When they fa' foul o' earthly Jinkers!
The witching, curst, delicious blinkers
Hae put me hyte;
An' gart me weet my waukrife winkers,
Wi' girnan spite.

But by yon Moon! an' that 's high swearin;
An' every Star within my hearin!
An' by her een! wha was a dear ane,
I'll ne'er forget;
I hope to gie the JADS a clearin
In fair play yet!

My loss I mourn, but not repent it:
I'll seek my pursie whare I tint it:
Ance to the Indies I were wonted,
Some cantraip hour,
By some sweet Elf I may be dinted,
Then, VIVE L'AMOUR!

Faites mes BAISEMAINS respectueuse,
To sentimental Sister Susie,
An' honest LUCKY; no to roose ye,
Ye may be proud,
That sic a couple Fate allows ye
To grace your blood.

Nae mair, at present, can I measure;
An' trowth my rhymin ware 's nae treasure;
But when in Ayr, some half hour's leisure,
Be 't light, be 't dark,
Sir Bard will do himsel the pleasure
To call at PARK.

130. *A Winter Night*

Poor naked wretches, wheresoe'er you are,
That bide the pelting of this pityless storm!
How shall your houseless heads, and unfed sides,
Your loop'd and window'd raggedness, defend you
From seasons such as these—

SHAKESPEARE.

WHEN biting *Boreas*, fell and doure,
Sharp shivers thro' the leafless bow'r;
When *Phœbus* gies a short-liv'd glow'r,
Far south the lift,
Dim-dark'ning thro' the flaky show'r,
Or whirling drift.

Ae night the Storm the steeples rocked,
Poor Labour sweet in sleep was locked,
While burns, wi' snawy wreeths up-choked,
Wild-eddying swirl,
On thro' the mining outlet bocked,
Down headlong hurl.

List'ning, the doors an' winnocks rattle,
I thought me on the ourie cattle,
Or silly sheep, wha bide this brattle
O' winter war,
And thro' the drift, deep-lairing, sprattle,
Beneath a scar.

Ilk happing bird, wee, helpless thing!
That, in the merry months o' spring,
Delighted me to hear thee sing,
What comes o' thee?
Whare wilt thou cow'r thy chittering wing,
An' close thy e'e?

Ev'n you on murd'ring errands toil'd,
Lone from your savage homes exil'd,
The blood-stain'd roost, and sheep-cote spoil'd,
My heart forgets,
While pityless the tempest wild
Sore on you beats.

Now *Phœbe*, in her midnight reign,
Dark-muffl'd, view'd the dreary plain;
Still crouding thoughts, a pensive train,
Rose in my soul,
When on my ear this plaintive strain,
Slow-solemn, stole—

'Blow, blow ye Winds, with heavier gust!
'And freeze, thou bitter-biting Frost!
'Descend, ye chilly, smothering Snows!
'Not all your rage, as now, united shows
'More hard unkindness, unrelenting,
'Vengeful malice, unrepenting,
'Than heaven-illumin'd Man on brother Man bestows!

'See stern Oppression's iron grip,
'Or mad Ambition's gory hand,
'Sending, like blood-hounds from the slip,
'Woe, Want, and Murder o'er a land!
'Ev'n in the peaceful rural vale,
'Truth, weeping, tells the mournful tale,
'How pamper'd Luxury, Flatt'ry by her side,
'The parasite empoisoning her ear,
'With all the servile wretches in the rear,
'Looks o'er proud Property, extended wide;
'And eyes the simple, rustic Hind,
'Whose toil upholds the glitt'ring show,
'A creature of another kind,
'Some coarser substance, unrefin'd,
'Plac'd for her lordly use thus far, thus vile, below!

'Where, where is Love's fond, tender throe,
'With lordly Honor's lofty brow,
'The pow'rs you proudly own?
'Is there, beneath Love's noble name,
'Can harbour, dark, the selfish aim,
'To bless himself alone!
'Mark Maiden-innocence a prey
'To love-pretending snares,
'This boasted Honor turns away,
'Shunning soft Pity's rising sway,
'Regardless of the tears, and unavailing pray'rs!
'Perhaps, this hour, in Mis'ry's squalid nest,
'She strains your infant to her joyless breast,
'And with a Mother's fears shrinks at the rocking blast!

'Oh ye! who sunk in beds of down,
'Feel not a want but what yourselves create,
'Think, for a moment, on his wretched fate,
'Whom friends and fortune quite disown!
'Ill-satisfy'd, keen Nature's clam'rous call,
'Stretch'd on his straw he lays himself to sleep,
'While thro' the ragged roof and chinky wall,
'Chill, o'er his slumbers, piles the drifty heap!
'Think on the dungeon's grim confine,
'Where Guilt and poor Misfortune pine!
'Guilt, erring Man, relenting view!
'But shall thy legal rage pursue
'The Wretch, already crushed low
'By cruel Fortune's undeserved blow?
'Affliction's sons are brothers in distress;
'A Brother to relieve, how exquisite the bliss!'

I heard nae mair, for *Chanticleer*
Shook off the pouthery snaw,
And hail'd the morning with a cheer,
A cottage-rousing craw.

But deep this truth impress'd my mind—
Thro' all his works abroad,
The heart benevolent and kind
The most resembles GOD.

131. [*Extempore Reply to an Invitation*]

SIR,
Yours this moment I unseal,
And faith I'm gay and hearty!
To tell the truth and shame the deil,
I am as fou as Bartie:
But Foorsday, sir, my promise leal,
Expect me o' your partie,
If on a beastie I can speel
Or hurl in a cartie.
Yours,
ROBERT BURNS.

MAUCHLIN,
Monday Night, 10 o'clock

132. *Lying at a Reverend Friend's house one night, the Author left the following* Verses *in the room where he slept:—*

I

O THOU dread Pow'r, who reign'st above!
I know Thou wilt me hear;
When for this scene of peace and love,
I make my pray'r sincere.

II

The hoary Sire—the mortal stroke,
Long, long be pleas'd to spare;
To bless his little filial flock,
And show what good men are.

III

She, who her lovely Offspring eyes
With tender hopes and fears,
O bless her with a Mother's joys,
But spare a Mother's tears!

IV

Their hope, their stay, their darling youth,
  In manhood's dawning blush;
Bless him, Thou God of love and truth,
  Up to a Parent's wish.

V

The beauteous, seraph Sister-band,
  With earnest tears I pray,
Thou know'st the snares on ev'ry hand,
  Guide Thou their steps alway.

VI

When soon or late they reach that coast,
  O'er life's rough ocean driven,
May they rejoice, no wand'rer lost,
  A Family in Heaven!

133. [*The Night was still*]

THE night was still, and o'er the hill
  The moon shone on the castle wa';
The mavis sang, while dew-drops hang
  Around her on the castle wa'.

Sae merrily they danc'd the ring,
  Frae e'enin till the cocks did craw,
And aye the owerword o' the spring
  Was Irvine's bairns are bonnie a'.

134. [*Rusticity's ungainly Form*]

RUSTICITY's ungainly form
  May cloud the highest mind;
But when the heart is nobly warm,
  The good excuse will find.

Propriety's cold cautious rules
  Warm Fervour may o'erlook;
But spare poor Sensibility
  The ungentle harsh rebuke.

135. *Address to Edinburgh*

I

EDINA! *Scotia*'s darling seat!
  All hail thy palaces and tow'rs,
Where once beneath a Monarch's feet,
  Sat Legislation's sov'reign pow'rs!
From marking wildly-scatt'red flow'rs,
  As on the banks of *Ayr* I stray'd,
And singing, lone, the ling'ring hours,
  I shelter in thy honor'd shade.

II

Here Wealth still swells the golden tide,
  As busy Trade his labours plies;
There Architecture's noble pride
  Bids elegance and splendor rise;
Here Justice, from her native skies,
  High wields her balance and her rod;
There Learning, with his eagle eyes,
  Seeks Science in her coy abode.

III

Thy Sons, *Edina*, social, kind,
  With opens arms the Stranger hail;
Their views enlarg'd, their lib'ral mind,
  Above the narrow, rural vale:
Attentive still to Sorrow's wail,
  Or modest Merit's silent claim;
And never may their sources fail!
  And never envy blot their name!

IV

Thy Daughters bright thy walks adorn,
  Gay as the gilded summer sky,
Sweet as the dewy, milk-white thorn,
  Dear as the raptur'd thrill of joy!
Fair B—— strikes th' adoring eye,
  Heav'n's beauties on my fancy shine;
I see the *Sire of Love* on high,
  And own his work indeed divine!

V

There, watching high the least alarms,
  Thy rough, rude Fortress gleams afar;
Like some bold Vet'ran, gray in arms,
  And mark'd with many a seamy scar:
The pond'rous wall and massy bar,
  Grim-rising o'er the rugged rock,
Have oft withstood assailing War,
  And oft repell'd th' Invader's shock.

VI

With awe-struck thought, and pitying tears,
  I view that noble, stately Dome,
Where *Scotia*'s kings of other years,
  Fam'd heroes! had their royal home:
Alas, how chang'd the times to come!
  Their royal Name low in the dust!
Their hapless Race wild-wand'ring roam!
  Tho' rigid Law cries out, 'twas just!

VII

Wild-beats my heart, to trace your steps,
  Whose ancestors, in days of yore,
Thro' hostile ranks and ruin'd gaps
  Old *Scotia*'s bloody lion bore:
Ev'n *I* who sing in rustic lore,
  Haply *my Sires* have left their shed,
And fac'd grim Danger's loudest roar,
  Bold-following where your Fathers led!

VIII

Edina! Scotia's darling seat!
  All hail thy palaces and tow'rs,
Where once, beneath a Monarch's feet,
  Sat Legislation's sov'reign pow'rs!
From marking wildly-scatt'red flow'rs,
  As on the banks of *Ayr* I stray'd,
And singing, lone, the ling'ring hours,
  I shelter in thy honor'd shade.

136. *To a Haggis*

FAIR fa' your honest, sonsie face,
Great Chieftan o' the Puddin-race!
Aboon them a' ye tak your place,
Painch, tripe, or thairm:
Weel are ye wordy of a *grace*
As lang 's my arm.

The groaning trencher there ye fill,
Your hurdies like a distant hill,
Your *pin* wad help to mend a mill
In time o' need,
While thro' your pores the dews distil
Like amber bead.

His knife see Rustic-labour dight,
An' cut you up wi' ready slight,
Trenching your gushing entrails bright
Like onie ditch;
And then, O what a glorious sight,
Warm-reekin, rich!

Then, horn for horn they stretch an' strive,
Deil tak the hindmost, on they drive,
Till a' their weel-swall'd kytes belyve
Are bent like drums;
Then auld Guidman, maist like to rive,
Bethankit hums.

Is there that owre his French *ragout*,
Or *olio* that wad staw a sow,
Or *fricassee* wad mak her spew
Wi' perfect sconner,
Looks down wi' sneering, scornfu' view
On sic a dinner?

Poor devil! see him owre his trash,
As feckless as a wither'd rash,
His spindle shank a guid whip-lash,
His nieve a nit;
Thro' bluidy flood or field to dash,
O how unfit!

But mark the Rustic, *haggis-fed*,
The trembling earth resounds his tread,
Clap in his walie nieve a blade,
He'll mak it whissle;
An' legs, an' arms, an' heads will sned,
Like taps o' thrissle.

Ye Pow'rs wha mak mankind your care,
And dish them out their bill o' fare,
Auld Scotland wants nae skinking ware
That jaups in luggies;
But, if ye wish her gratefu' pray'r,
Gie her a *Haggis*!

137. *Verses intended to be written below a noble Earl's picture*

WHOSE is that noble, dauntless brow?
And whose that eye of fire?
And whose that generous, Princely mien,
Ev'n rooted Foes admire?

Stranger, to justly show that brow,
And mark that eye of fire,
Would take HIS hand, whose vernal tints,
His other Works admire.

Bright as a cloudless Summer-sun,
With stately port he moves;
His guardian Seraph eyes with awe
The noble Ward he loves.

Among th' illustrious Scottish Sons
That Chief thou may'st discern,
Mark Scotia's fond-returning eye,
It dwells upon GLENCAIRN.

138. *Song*

Tune, Jockey's Gray Breeks

I

AGAIN rejoicing Nature sees
  Her robe assume its vernal hues,
Her leafy locks wave in the breeze
  All freshly steep'd in morning dews.

CHORUS*

And maun I still on Menie† *doat,*
  And bear the scorn that 's in her e'e!
For it 's jet, jet black, an' it 's like a hawk,
  An' it winna let a body be!

II

In vain to me the cowslips blaw,
  In vain to me the vi'lets spring;
In vain to me, in glen or shaw,
  The mavis and the lintwhite sing.
    And maun I still, &c.

* This Chorus is part of a song composed by a gentleman in Edinburgh, a particular friend of the Author's.

† *Menie* is the common abbreviation of *Marianne*.

III

The merry Ploughboy cheers his team,
  Wi' joy the tentie Seedsman stalks,
But life to me 's a weary dream,
  A dream of ane that never wauks.
        And maun I still, &c.

IV

The wanton coot the water skims,
  Amang the reeds the ducklings cry,
The stately swan majestic swims,
  And ev'ry thing is blest but I.
        And maun I still, &c.

V

The Sheep-herd steeks his faulding slap,
  And owre the moorlands whistles shill,
Wi' wild, unequal, wand'ring step
  I meet him on the dewy hill.
        And maun I still, &c.

VI

And when the lark, 'tween light and dark,
  Blythe waukens by the daisy's side,
And mounts and sings on flittering wings,
  A woe-worn ghaist I hameward glide.
        And maun I still, &c.

VII

Come Winter, with thine angry howl,
  And raging bend the naked tree;
Thy gloom will soothe my chearless soul,
  When Nature all is sad like me!

And maun I still on Menie *doat,*
  And bear the scorn that 's in her e'e!
For it 's jet, jet black, an' it 's like a hawk,
  An' it winna let a body be.

IV. Poems 1787

EDINBURGH; BORDER TOUR;
HIGHLAND TOURS

139. *To Miss L——,*

With BEATTIE'S POEMS *for a New-Year's Gift.* Jan. 1. 1787.

AGAIN the silent wheels of time
  Their annual round have driv'n,
And you, tho' scarce in maiden prime,
  Are so much nearer Heav'n.

No gifts have I from Indian coasts
  The infant year to hail;
I send you more than India boasts
  In *Edwin*'s simple tale.

Our Sex with guile and faithless love
  Is charg'd, perhaps too true;
But may, dear Maid, each Lover prove
  An *Edwin* still to you.

140. [*There was a lad*]

Tune, Daintie Davie

THERE was a lad was born in Kyle,
But what na day o' what na style,
I doubt it 's hardly worth the while
To be sae nice wi' Robin.
Robin was a rovin' Boy,
Rantin' rovin', rantin' rovin';
Robin was a rovin' Boy,
Rantin' rovin' Robin.

Our monarch's hindmost year but ane
Was five-and-twenty days begun,
'Twas then a blast o' Janwar' Win'*
Blew hansel in on Robin.

The Gossip keekit in his loof,
Quo' scho wha lives will see the proof,
This waly boy will be nae coof,
I think we'll ca' him Robin.

* Jan. 25th 1759. the date of my Bardship's vital existence.—

He'll hae misfortunes great and sma',
But ay a heart aboon them a';
He'll be a credit till us a',
  We'll a' be proud o' Robin.

But sure as three times three mak nine,
I see by ilka score and line,
This chap will dearly like our kin',
  So leeze me on thee, Robin.

Guid faith quo' scho I doubt you Stir,
Ye'll gar the lasses lie aspar;
But twenty fauts ye may hae waur—
  So blessins on thee, Robin.

141. *Elegy on the Death of Robert Ruisseaux*

Now Robin lies in his last lair,
He'll gabble rhyme, nor sing nae mair,
Cauld poverty, wi' hungry stare,
    Nae mair shall fear him;
Nor anxious fear, nor cankert care
    E'er mair come near him.

To tell the truth, they seldom fash't him,
Except the moment that they crush't him;
For sune as chance or fate had hush't 'em
    Tho' e'er sae short,
Then wi' a rhyme or song he lash't 'em,
    And thought it sport.

Tho' he was bred to kintra wark,
And counted was baith wight and stark,
Yet that was never Robin's mark
    To mak a man;
But tell him, he was learn'd and clark,
    Ye roos'd him then!

142. *Epitaph. Here lies Robert Fergusson, Poet*

Born, September 5th, 1751—Died 16th October, 1774

No sculptur'd marble here, nor pompous lay,
'No story'd urn nor animated bust;'
This simple stone directs pale Scotia's way
To pour her sorrows o'er her Poet's dust.

[She mourns, sweet, tuneful youth, thy hapless fate,
Tho' all the pow'rs of song thy fancy fir'd;
Yet Luxury and Wealth lay by in state,
And thankless starv'd what they so much admir'd.

This humble tribute with a tear he gives,
A brother Bard, he can no more bestow;
But dear to fame thy Song immortal lives,
A nobler monument than Art can show.]

[*On Fergusson*]

143.

Curse on ungrateful man, that can be pleas'd,
And yet can starve the author of the pleasure!

O thou, my elder brother in Misfortune,
By far my elder Brother in the muse,
With tears I pity thy unhappy fate!
Why is the Bard unfitted for the world,
Yet has so keen a relish of its Pleasures?

144.

Ill-fated Genius! Heaven-taught Fergusson,
What heart that feels and will not yield a tear,
To think Life's sun did set e'er well begun
To shed its influence on thy bright career.

O why should truest Worth and Genius pine
Beneath the iron grasp of Want and Woe,
While titled knaves and idiot-greatness shine
In all the splendour Fortune can bestow?

145. *To a Painter*

DEAR —, I'll gie ye some advice,
You'll tak it no uncivil:
You shouldna paint at angels, man,
But try and paint the Devil.

To paint an angel's kittle wark,
Wi' Nick there's little danger;
You'll easy draw a lang-kent face,
But no sae weel a stranger.
R. B.

146. *To Mr E—— on his translation of and commentaries on Martial*

O THOU, whom Poesy abhors,
Whom Prose has turned out of doors;
Heard'st thou yon groan?—proceed no further!
'Twas laurell'd Martial calling, Murther!

147A. [*The Guidwife of Wauchope-House, to Robert Burns, the Airshire Bard. Feb. 1787*]

[MY canty, witty, rhyming ploughman,
I haffiins doubt, it is na' true, man,
That ye between the stilts was bred,
Wi' ploughman school'd, wi' ploughman fed.
I doubt it sair, ye've drawn your knowledge
Either frae grammar school, or colledge.
Guid troth, your saul and body baith
War' better fed, I'd gie my aith,
Than theirs, who sup sour milk and parritch,
An' bummil thro' the single caritch.

Whaever heard the ploughman speak,
Could tell gif Homer was a Greek?
He'd flee as soon upon a cudgel,
As get a single line of Virgil.
An' then sae slee ye crack your jokes
O' Willie P—t and Charlie F–x.
Our great men a' sae weel descrive,
An' how to gar the nation thrive,
Ane maist wad swear ye dwalt amang them,
An' as ye saw them, sae ye sang them.
But be ye ploughman, be ye peer,
Ye are a funny blade, I swear.
An' tho' the cauld I ill can bide,
Yet twenty miles, an' mair, I'd ride,
O'er moss, an' muir, an' never grumble,
Tho' my auld yad shou'd gae a stumble,
To crack a winter-night wi' thee,
An' hear thy sangs, an' sonnets slee.
A guid saut herring, an' a cake
Wi' sic a chiel a feast wad make.
I'd rather scour your rumming yill,
Or eat o' cheese and bread my fill,
Than wi' dull lairds on turtle dine,
An' ferlie at their wit and wine.
O, gif I kend but whare ye baide,
I'd send to you a marled plaid;
'Twad haud your shoulders warm and braw,
An' douse at kirk, or market shaw.
Far south, as weel as north, my lad,
A' honest Scotsmen lo'e the *maud.*
Right wae that we're sae far frae ither;
Yet proud I am to ca' ye brither.

Your most obed. E. S.]

147B. *The Answer*

GUIDWIFE,

I MIND it weel in early date,
When I was beardless, young and blate,
An' first cou'd thresh the barn,
Or haud a yokin at the pleugh,
An' tho' fu' foughten sair eneugh,
Yet unco proud to learn.

When first amang the yellow corn
    A man I reckon'd was;
An' with the lave ilk merry morn
    Could rank my rig and lass;
        Still shearing and clearing
        The tither stooked raw;
        With clavers and haivers
        Wearing the time awa':

Ev'n then a wish (I mind its power)
A wish, that to my latest hour
    Shall strongly heave my breast;
That I for poor auld Scotland's sake
Some useful plan, or book could make,
    Or sing a sang at least.

The rough bur-thistle spreading wide
    Amang the bearded bear,
I turn'd my weeding heuk aside,
    An' spar'd the symbol dear.
        No nation, no station
        My envy e'er could raise:
        A Scot still, but blot still,
        I knew no higher praise.

But still the elements o' sang
In formless jumble, right an' wrang,
    Wild floated in my brain;
Till on that hairst I said before,
My partner in the merry core,
    She rous'd the forming strain.

I see her yet, the sonsy quean,
    That lighted up my jingle;
Her pauky smile, her kittle een,
    That gar't my heart-strings tingle.
        So tiched, bewitched,
        I rav'd ay to mysel;
        But bashing and dashing,
        I kend na how to tell.

Hale to the sex, ilk guid chiel says,
Wi' merry dance in winter-days,
    An' we to share in common:

The gust o' joy, the balm of woe,
The saul o' life, the heav'n below,
Is rapture-giving woman.

Ye surly sumphs, who hate the name,
Be mindfu' o' your mither:
She, honest woman, may think shame
That ye're connected with her.
Ye're wae men, ye're nae men,
That slight the lovely dears:
To shame ye, disclaim ye,
Ilk honest birkie swears.

For you, na bred to barn and byre,
Wha sweetly tune the Scottish lyre,
Thanks to you for your line.
The marled plaid ye kindly spare,
By me should gratefully be ware;
'Twad please me to the Nine.

I'd be mair vauntie o' my hap,
Douse hingin o'er my curple,
Than ony ermine ever lap,
Or proud imperial purple.
Farewell then, lang hale then,
An' plenty be your fa':
May losses and crosses
Ne'er at your hallan ca'.

March, 1787. R. BURNS.

148. [*To Miss Isabella Macleod*]

THE crimson blossom charms the bee,
The summer sun the swallow;
So dear this tuneful gift to me
From lovely Isabella.

Her portrait fair upon my mind
Revolving Time shall mellow;
And Mem'ry's latest effort find
The lovely Isabella.

No Bard nor Lover's rapture this,
  In fancies vain and shallow;
She is, so come my soul to bliss!
  The lovely Isabella.

149. *Extempore, in the Court of S——*

Tune, Gillicrankie

Lord A——te

He clench'd his pamphlets in his fist,
  He quoted and he hinted,
Till in a declamation-mist,
  His argument he tint it:
He gaped for 't, he graped for 't,
  He fand it was awa, man;
And what his common sense came short,
  He eked out wi' law, man.

M[r] Er——ne—

Collected, Harry stood awee,
  Then open'd out his arm, man;
His lordship sat wi' ruefu' e'e,
  And ey'd the gathering storm, man:
Like wind-driv'n hail it did assail,
  Or torrents owre a lin, man;
The Bench sae wise lift up their eyes,
  Half-wauken'd wi' the din, man.

150. *Extempore Epistle to M^r. Mc Adam of Craigengillan, (wrote in Nanse Tinnock's, Mauchline) in answer to an obliging letter he sent in the commencement of my poetic career—*

Sir, o'er a gill I gat your card,
  I trow it made me proud;
See wha taks notice o' the Bard!
  I lap and cry'd fu' loud.—

Now diel-ma-care about their jaw,
  The senseless, gawky million;
I'll cock my nose aboon them a',
  I'm roos'd by Craigengillan.—

'Twas noble, Sir; 'twas like yoursel,
  To grant your high protection:
A great man's smile ye ken fu' well,
  Is ay a blest infection.—

Tho', by his* banes wha in a tub
  Match'd Macedonian Sandy!
On my ain legs thro' dirt and dub,
  I independant stand ay.—

And when those legs to gude, warm kail
  Wi' welcome canna bear me;
A lee dyke-side, a sybow-tail,
  And barley-scone shall chear me.—

Heaven spare you lang to kiss the breath
  O' mony flowery simmers!
And bless your bonie lasses baith,
  I'm tald they're loosome kimmers!

And God bless your Dunaskin's laird,
  The blossom of our gentry!
And may he wear an auld man's beard,
  A credit to his country!

151. *Prologue*

Spoken by Mr. W*oods on his Benefit night, Monday,* 16*th April,* 1787.

When by a generous Public's kind acclaim,
That dearest meed is granted—honest fame;
When *here* your favour is the *actor*'s lot,
Nor even the *man* in *private life* forgot;
What breast so dead to heav'nly Virtue's glow,
But heaves impassion'd with the grateful throe.

* Diogenes

Poor is the task to please a barb'rous throng,
It needs no Siddons' powers in Southern's song;
But here an ancient nation fam'd afar,
For genius, learning high, as great in war—
Hail, CALEDONIA, name for ever dear!
Before whose sons I'm honour'd to appear!
Where every science—every nobler art—
That can inform the mind, or mend the heart,
Is known; as grateful nations oft have found
Far as the rude barbarian marks the bound.
Philosophy, no idle pedant dream,
Here holds her search by heaven-taught Reason's beam;
Here History paints, with elegance and force,
The tide of Empire's fluctuating course;
Here Douglas forms wild Shakespeare into plan,
And Harley* rouses all the god in man.
When well-form'd taste, and sparkling wit unite,
With manly lore, or female beauty bright,
(Beauty, where faultless symmetry and grace,
Can only charm us in the second place,)
Witness my heart, how oft with panting fear,
As on this night, I've met these judges here!
But still the hope Experience taught to live,
Equal to judge—you're candid to forgive.
No hundred-headed Riot here we meet,
With decency and law beneath his feet;
Nor Insolence assumes fair Freedom's name;
Like CALEDONIANS, you applaud or blame.

O thou, dread Power! whose empire-giving hand
Has oft been stretch'd to shield the honour'd land!
Strong may she glow with all her ancient fire;
May every son be worthy of his sire;
Firm may she rise with generous disdain
At Tyranny's, or direr Pleasure's chain;
Still self-dependent in her native shore,
Bold may she brave grim Danger's loudest roar,
Till Fate the curtain drop on worlds to be no more.

* The Man of Feeling, wrote by Mr. M'Kenzie.

152. *Epistle to Mr. Tytler of Woodhouselee, Author of a Defence of Mary Queen of Scots—*

May — 1787

REVERED Defender of beauteous Stuart,
  Of Stuart!—a Name once respected,
A Name which to love was the mark of a true heart,
  But now 'tis despis'd and neglected.

Tho' something like moisture conglobes in my eye,
  Let no man misdeem me disloyal;
A poor, friendless wand'rer may well claim a sigh,
  Still more if that Wand'rer were royal.

My Fathers that *name* have rever'd on a throne,
  My Fathers have died to right it;
Those Fathers would spurn their degenerate Son
  That NAME should he scoffingly slight it.

Still in pray'rs for King G—— I most cordially join,
  The Queen and the rest of the gentry:
Be they wise, be they foolish, 'tis nothing of mine,
  Their title 's allow'd in the Country.

But why of that Epocha make such a fuss,
  That brought us th' Electoral Stem?
If bringing them over was lucky for *us*,
  I'm sure 'twas as lucky for *them*!

But Politics, truce! we're on dangerous ground;
  Who knows how the fashions may alter:
The doctrines today that are loyalty sound,
  Tomorrow may bring us a halter.

I send you a trifle, a head of a bard,
  A trifle scarce worthy your care;
But accept it, good sir, as a mark of regard,
  Sincere as a saint's dying prayer.

Now life's chilly evening dim shades on your eye,
  And ushers the long dreary night;
But you like the star that athwart gilds the sky,
  Your course to the latest is bright.

153. [*To Miss Ainslie, in Church*]

FAIR maid, you need not take the hint,
Nor idle texts pursue;
'Twas only sinners that he meant,
Not angels such as you.

154. [*To William Creech*]

Selkirk 13th. May 1787

AULD chuckie REEKIE 's sair distrest,
Down droops her ance weel-burnish'd crest,
Nae joy her bonie buskit nest
Can yield ava;
Her darling bird that she loes best,
Willie 's awa.—

O Willie was a witty wight,
And had o' things an unco slight;
Auld Reekie ay he keepit tight,
And trig and braw:
But now they'll busk her like a fright,
Willie 's awa.—

The stiffest o' them a' he bow'd,
The bauldest o' them a' he cow'd,
They durst nae mair than he allow'd,
That was a law:
We've lost a birkie weel worth gowd,
Willie 's awa.—

Now gawkies, tawpies, gowks and fools,
Frae colleges and boarding-schools,
May sprout like simmer puddock-stools
In glen or shaw;
He wha could brush them down to mools
Willie 's awa.—

The brethren o' the commerce-chaumer
May mourn their loss wi' doolfu' clamour;
He was a dictionar and grammar
Amang them a':
I fear they'll now mak mony a stammer,
Willie 's awa.—

Nae mair we see his levee door
Philosophers and Poets pour,
And toothy Critics by the score
In bloody raw;
The Adjutant of a' the core
Willie 's awa.—

Now worthy Greg'ry's latin face,
Tytler's and Greenfield's modest grace,
Mckenzie, Stuart, such a brace
As Rome ne'er saw;
They a' maun meet some ither place,
Willie 's awa.—

Poor BURNS—even Scotch Drink canna quicken,
He cheeps like some bewilder'd chicken,
Scar'd frae its minnie and the cleckin
By hoodie-craw:
Grief 's gien his heart an unco kickin,
Willie 's awa.—

Now ev'ry sour-mou'd, girnin blellum,
And Calvin's folk are fit to fell him;
Ilk self-conceited, critic skellum
His quill may draw;
He wha could brawlie ward their bellum
Willie 's awa.—

Up wimpling, stately Tweed I've sped,
And Eden scenes on chrystal Jed,
And Ettrick banks now roaring red
While tempests blaw;
But ev'ry joy and pleasure 's fled,
Willie 's awa.—

May I be Slander's common speech;
A text for Infamy to preach;
And lastly, streekit out to bleach
In winter snaw
When I forget thee, WILLIE CREECH,
Tho' far awa!—

May never wicked Fortune touzle him,
May never wicked men bamboozle him,
Until a pow as auld 's Methusalem
He canty claw:
Then to the blessed, new Jerusalem
Fleet-wing awa.—

155. [*To Symon Gray*]

I

SYMON Gray,
You're dull to-day.

II

DULNESS, with redoubted sway,
Has seized the wits of Symon Gray.

III

DEAR Cimon Gray,
The other day,
When you sent me some rhyme,
I could not then just ascertain
Its worth, for want of time.

But now today, good Mr. Gray,
I've read it o'er and o'er,
Tried all my skill, but find I'm still
Just where I was before.

We auld wives' minions gie our opinions,
Solicited or no;
Then of its fau'ts my honest thoughts
I'll give—and here they go.

Such d——'d bombast no time that 's past
Will show, or time to come,
So, Cimon dear, your song I'll tear,
And with it wipe my [bum].

156. [*To Renton of Lamerton*]

YOUR billet, Sir, I grant receipt;
Wi' you I'll canter ony gate;
Tho' 'twere a trip to yon blue warl
Whare Birkies march on burning marl.
Then, Sir, God willing, I'll attend ye;
An' to His goodness I commend ye—
R. Burns.

157. *Bonie Dundee*

'O WHAR did ye get that hauver-meal bannock?'
O silly blind body, O dinna ye see;
I gat it frae a young brisk Sodger Laddie,
Between Saint Johnston and bonie Dundee.

O gin I saw the laddie that gae me 't!
  Aft has he doudl'd me upon his knee;
May Heaven protect my bonie Scots laddie,
  And send him safe hame to his babie and me.

My blessins upon thy sweet, wee lippie!
  My blessins upon thy bonie e'e brie!
Thy smiles are sae like my blyth Sodger laddie,
  Thou 's ay the dearer, and dearer to me!
But I'll big a bow'r on yon bonie banks,
  Whare Tay rins wimplin by sae clear;
And I'll cleed thee in the tartan sae fine,
  And mak thee a man like thy dadie dear.

158. [*At Roslin Inn*]

My blessings on ye, honest wife,
  I ne'er was here before;
Ye've wealth o' gear for spoon and knife—
  Heart could not wish for more.

Heav'n keep you clear o' sturt and strife,
  Till far ayont fourscore,
And by the Lord o' death and life,
  I'll ne'er gae by your door!

159. *Epigram*

Whoe'er he be that sojourns here,
  I pity much his case,
Unless he come to wait upon
  The Lord their God, his Grace.

There 's naething here but Highland pride,
  And Highland scab and hunger;
If Providence has sent me here,
  'Twas surely in an anger.

Epigram. Note in Stewart (1801): Burns, accompanied by a friend, having gone to Inverary at a time when some company were there on a visit to his Grace the Duke of Argyll, finding himself and his companion entirely neglected by the Inn-keeper, whose whole attention seemed to be occupied with the visitors of his Grace, expressed his disapprobation of the incivility with which they were treated in the following lines

160. *On the death of Sir J. Hunter Blair—*

THE lamp of day, with ill-presaging glare,
  Dim, cloudy, sunk beyond the western wave:
Th' inconstant blast howl'd thro' the darkening air,
  And hollow whistled in the rocky cave.

Lone as I wander'd by each cliff and dell,
  *Once the lov'd haunts of Scotia's royal train;
Or mus'd where limpid streams, once hallow'd, well;
  Or mouldering ruins mark the sacred Fane.†

Th' increasing blast roar'd round the beetling rocks;
  The clouds, swift-wing'd, flew o'er the starry sky;
The groaning trees, untimely, shed their locks,
  And shooting meteors caught the startled eye.—

The paly moon rose in the livid east,
  And 'mong the cliffs disclos'd a stately Form,
In weeds of woe, that frantic beat her breast,
  And mix'd her wailings with the raving storm.—

Wild to my heart the filial pulses glow;
  'Twas CALEDONIA's trophy'd shield I view'd;
Her form majestic droop'd in pensive woe,
  The lightening of her eye in tears embu'd.—

Revers'd that spear, redoubtable in war,
  Reclin'd that banner, erst in fields unfurl'd,
That like a deathful meteor gleam'd afar,
  And brav'd the mighty monarchs of the world.—

'My patriot-Son fills an untimely grave!'
  With accent wild and lifted arms she cry'd;
'Low lies the hand that oft was stretch'd to save,
  'Low lies the heart that swell'd with honor's pride.—

'A weeping Country joins a Widow's tear,
  'The helpless Poor mix with the Orphans' cry;
'The drooping arts surround their Patron's bier,
  'And grateful Science heaves the heart-felt sigh.—

* The king's park at Holyroodhouse.—
† St Anthony's well and chapel.—

'I saw my Sons resume their ancient fire;
'I saw fair Freedom's blossoms richly blow:
'But ah, how hope is born but to expire!
'Relentless Fate has laid their Guardian low.—

'My Patriot falls—but shall he lie unsung,
'While empty Greatness saves a worthless name?
'No: every Muse shall join her tuneful tongue,
'And future ages hear his growing fame.—

'And I will join a Mother's tender cares,
'Thro' future times to make his virtues last,
'That distant years may boast of other BLAIRS—'
She said, and vanish'd with the sweeping blast.

161. [*To Miss Ferrier*]

MADAM

NAE Heathen Name shall I prefix,
Frae Pindus or Parnassus;
AULD REEKIE dings them a' to sticks
For rhyme-inspiring Lasses.—

Jove's tunefu' Dochters three times three
Made Homer deep their debtor;
But gien the body half an e'e,
Nine FERRIERS wad done better.—

Last day my mind was in a bog,
Down George's street I stoited;
A creeping, cauld PROSAIC fog
My vera senses doited.—

Do what I dought to set her free,
My Muse lay in the mire;
Ye turn'd a neuk—I saw your e'e—
She took the wing like fire.—

The mournfu' Sang I here inclose,
In GRATITUDE I send you;
And pray in rhyme, sincere as prose,
A' GUDE THINGS MAY ATTEND YOU.

ROBt BURNS

St James' Square
Saturday even:

162. *On reading, in a Newspaper, the Death of J—— M'L——, Esq. Brother to a Young Lady, a particular Friend of the Author's*

SAD thy tale, thou idle page,
And rueful thy alarms:
Death tears the brother of her love
From Isabella's arms.

Sweetly deckt with pearly dew
The morning rose may blow;
But cold successive noontide blasts
May lay its beauties low.

Fair on Isabella's morn
The sun propitious smil'd;
But, long ere noon, succeeding clouds
Succeeding hopes beguil'd.

Fate oft tears the bosom chords
That Nature finest strung:
So Isabella's heart was form'd,
And so that heart was wrung.

Dread Omnipotence, alone,
Can heal the wound He gave;
Can point the brimful grief-worn eyes
To scenes beyond the grave.

Virtue's blossoms there shall blow,
And fear no withering blast;
There Isabella's spotless worth
Shall happy be at last.

163. *Yon wild mossy mountains—*

Yon wild, mossy mountains sae lofty and wide,
That nurse in their bosom the youth o' the Clyde;
Where the grous lead their coveys thro' the heather to feed,
And the sheepherd tents his flock as he pipes on his reed.

Not Gowrie's rich valley, nor Forth's sunny shores,
To me hae the charms o' yon wild, mossy moors:
For there, by a lanely, sequestered stream,
Resides a sweet Lassie, my thought and my dream.—

Amang thae wild mountains shall still be my path,
Ilk stream foaming down its ain green, narrow strath;
For there, wi' my Lassie, the day-lang I rove,
While o'er us, unheeded, flee the swift hours o' Love.—

She is not the fairest, altho' she is fair;
O' nice education but sma' is her skair;
Her parentage humble as humble can be;
But I loe the dear Lassie because she loes me.—

To Beauty what man but maun yield him a prize,
In her armour of glances, and blushes, and sighs;
And when Wit and Refinement hae polish'd her darts,
They dazzle our een, as they flie to our hearts.—

But Kindness, sweet Kindness, in the fond-sparkling e'e,
Has lustre outshining the diamond to me;
And the heart beating love as I'm clasped in her arms,
O, these are my Lassie's all-conquering charms.—

164. *My Harry was a Gallant gay*

Tune, Highlander's Lament

My Harry was a gallant gay,
  Fu' stately strade he on the plain;
But now he 's banish'd far awa,
  I'll never see him back again.

Chorus

O for him back again,
  O for him back again,
I wad gie a' Knockhaspie's land
  For Highland Harry back again.

When a' the lave gae to their bed,
  I wander dowie up the glen;
I set me down and greet my fill,
  And ay I wish him back again.
    O for him &c.

O were some villains hangit high,
  And ilka body had their ain!
Then I might see the joyfu' sight,
  My Highlan Harry back again.
    O for him &c.

165. *Verses written on a window of the Inn at Carron*

WE cam' na here to view your warks,
  In hopes to be mair wise,
But only, lest we gang to hell,
  It may be nae surprise:
But whan we tirl'd at your door,
  Your porter dought na bear us;
Sae may, shou'd we to hell's yetts come,
  Your billy Satan sair us!

166. [*Lines on Stirling*]

[A] Written by Somebody in the window of an inn at Stirling on seeing the Royal Palace in ruins.

HERE Stewarts once in triumph reign'd,
And laws for Scotland's weal ordain'd;
But now unroof'd their Palace stands,
Their sceptre 's fall'n to other hands;
Fallen indeed, and to the earth,
Whence grovelling reptiles take their birth.—
The injur'd STEWART-line are gone,
A Race outlandish fill their throne;
An idiot race, to honor lost;
Who know them best despise them most.—

[B] These imprudent lines were answered, very petulantly, by somebody, I believe a Rev[d] M[r] Hamilton.—In a M.S.S. where I met with the answer, I wrote below—

WITH Esop's lion, Burns says, sore I feel
Each other blow, but d–mn that ass's heel!

[C] The Reproof

RASH mortal, and slanderous Poet, thy name
Shall no longer appear in the records of fame;
Dost not know that old Mansfield, who writes like the Bible,
Says the more 'tis a truth, Sir, the more 'tis a libel?

167. *On a Schoolmaster in Cleish Parish, Fifeshire*

HERE lie Willie M—hie's banes,
  O Satan, when ye tak him,
Gie him the schulin' o' your weans;
  For clever Deils he'll mak 'em!

168. *Strathallan's Lament*

THICKEST night, surround my dwelling!
  Howling tempests, o'er me rave!
Turbid torrents, wintry swelling,
  Roaring by my lonely cave.
Chrystal streamlets gently flowing,
  Busy haunts of base mankind,
Western breezes softly blowing,
  Suit not my distracted mind.

In the cause of Right engaged,
  Wrongs injurious to redress,
Honor's war we strongly waged,
  But the heavens deny'd success:
Ruin's wheel has driven o'er us,
  Not a hope that dare attend,
The wide world is all before us—
  But a world without a friend!

169. *Written with a Pencil over the Chimney-piece, in the Parlour of the Inn at Kenmore, Taymouth*

ADMIRING Nature in her wildest grace,
These northern scenes with weary feet I trace;
O'er many a winding dale and painful steep,
Th' abodes of coveyed grouse and timid sheep,
My savage journey, curious, I pursue,
Till fam'd Breadalbaine opens to my view.—
The meeting cliffs each deep-sunk glen divides,
The woods, wild-scattered, clothe their ample sides;
Th' outstretching lake, imbosomed 'mong the hills,
The eye with wonder and amazement fills;
The Tay meandering sweet in infant pride,
The palace rising on his verdant side;
The lawns wood-fringed in Nature's native taste;
The hillocks dropt in Nature's careless haste;
The arches striding o'er the new-born stream;
The village glittering in the noontide beam—

* * * * * *

Poetic ardours in my bosom swell,
Lone wandring by the hermit's mossy cell:
The sweeping theatre of hanging woods;
Th' incessant roar of headlong tumbling floods—

* * * * * *

Here Poesy might wake her heaven taught lyre,
And look through Nature with creative fire;
Here, to the wrongs of Fate half reconcil'd,
Misfortune's lightened steps might wander wild;
And Disappointment, in these lonely bounds,
Find balm to soothe her bitter rankling wounds:
Here heart-struck Grief might heavenward stretch her scan,
And injured Worth forget and pardon Man.

* * * * * *

170. *The birks of Aberfeldey.—Composed on the spot*

Tune, Birks of Abergeldie

Chorus

BONY lassie will ye go, will ye go, will ye go;
Bony lassie will ye go to the birks of Aberfeldey.—

I

Now Simmer blinks on flowery braes,
And o'er the chrystal streamlets plays;
Come let us spend the lightsome days
  In the birks of Aberfeldey.—

2

The little birdies blythely sing
While o'er their heads the hazels hing,
Or lightly flit on wanton wing
  In the birks of Aberfeldey.—

3

The braes ascend like lofty wa's,
The foamy stream deep-roaring fa's
O'erhung wi' fragrant-spreading shaws,
  The birks of Aberfeldey.—

4

The hoary cliffs are crown'd wi' flowers,
White o'er the linns the burnie pours
And rising weets wi' misty showers
  The birks of Aberfeldey.—

5

Let Fortune's gifts at random flee,
They ne'er shall draw a wish frae me;
Supremely blest wi' love and thee
  In the birks of Aberfeldey.—

171. [*Amang the trees*]

Tune—The King of France, he rade a race

AMANG the trees, where humming bees
  At buds and flowers were hinging, O!
Auld Caledon drew out her drone,
  And to her pipe was singing, O!

'Twas Pibroch, Sang, Strathspey, or Reels,
She dirl'd them aff, fu' clearly, O!
When there cam a yell o' foreign squeels,
That dang her tapsalteerie, O!

Their capon craws, and queer ha ha's,
They made our lugs grow eerie, O!
The hungry bike did scrape and pike
Till we were wae and weary; O!
But a royal ghaist, wha ance was cas'd
A prisoner aughteen year awa,
He fir'd a fiddler in the North
That dang them tapsalteerie, O!

172. *The Humble Petition of Bruar Water* to the Noble Duke of Athole*

My Lord, I know, your noble ear
Woe ne'er assails in vain;
Embolden'd thus, I beg you'll hear
Your humble slave complain,
How saucy Phebus' scorching beams,
In flaming summer-pride,
Dry-withering, waste my foamy streams,
And drink my crystal tide.

The lightly-jumping, glowrin trouts,
That thro' my waters play,
If, in their random, wanton spouts,
They near the margin stray;
If, hapless chance! they linger lang,
I'm scorching up so shallow,
They're left, the whitening stanes amang,
In gasping death to wallow.

Last day I grat wi' spite and teen,
As Poet B**** came by,
That, to a Bard, I should be seen
Wi' half my channel dry:

* Bruar Falls, in Athole, are exceedingly picturesque and beautiful; but their effect is much impaired by the want of trees and shrubs.

A panegyric rhyme, I ween,
  Even as I was he shor'd me;
But, had I in my glory been,
  He, kneeling, wad ador'd me.

Here, foaming down the skelvy rocks,
  In twisting strength I rin;
There, high my boiling torrent smokes,
  Wild-roaring o'er a linn:
Enjoying large each spring and well
  As Nature gave them me,
I am, altho' I say 't mysel,
  Worth gaun a mile to see.

Would then my noble master please
  To grant my highest wishes,
He'll shade my banks wi' towering trees,
  And bonie spreading bushes.
Delighted doubly then, my Lord,
  You'll wander on my banks,
And listen mony a grateful bird
  Return you tuneful thanks.

The sober laverock, warbling wild,
  Shall to the skies aspire;
The gowdspink, Music's gayest child,
  Shall sweetly join the choir;
The blackbird strong, the lintwhite clear,
  The mavis mild and mellow;
The robin pensive Autumn chear,
  In all her locks of yellow.

This too, a covert shall ensure,
  To shield them from the storm;
And coward maukin sleep secure,
  Low in her grassy form:
Here shall the shepherd make his seat,
  To weave his crown of flowers;
Or find a sheltering, safe retreat,
  From prone-descending showers.

And here, by sweet endearing stealth,
  Shall meet the loving pair,
Despising worlds with all their wealth
  As empty idle care:

The flowers shall vie in all their charms
The hour of heaven to grace,
And birks extend their fragrant arms
To screen the dear embrace.

Here haply too, at vernal dawn,
Some musing bard may stray,
And eye the smoking, dewy lawn,
And misty mountain, gray;
Or, by the reaper's nightly beam,
Mild-chequering thro' the trees,
Rave to my darkly dashing stream,
Hoarse-swelling on the breeze.

Let lofty firs, and ashes cool,
My lowly banks o'erspread,
And view, deep-bending in the pool,
Their shadows' wat'ry bed:
Let fragrant birks, in woodbines drest,
My craggy cliffs adorn;
And, for the little songster's nest,
The close embowering thorn.

So may, Old Scotia's darling hope,
Your little angel band
Spring, like their fathers, up to prop
Their honour'd native land!
So may, thro' Albion's farthest ken,
To social-flowing glasses
The grace be—'Athole's honest men,
'And Athole's bonnie lasses!'

173. A Verse composed and repeated by *Burns*, to the Master of the house, on taking leave at a place in the Highlands, where he had been hospitably entertained

WHEN death's dark stream I ferry o'er,
A time that surely shall come;
In Heaven itself, I'll ask no more,
Than just a Highland welcome.

174. *Written with a Pencil, standing by the Fall of Fyers, near Loch-Ness*

AMONG the heathy hills and ragged woods
The roaring Fyers pours his mossy floods;
Till full he dashes on the rocky mounds,
Where, thro' a shapeless breach, his stream resounds.
As high in air the bursting torrents flow,
As deep recoiling surges foam below,
Prone down the rock the whitening sheet descends,
And viewless Echo's ear, astonish'd, rends.
Dim-seen, through rising mists and ceaseless showers,
The hoary cavern, wide-surrounding, lowers.
Still thro' the gap the struggling river toils,
And still, below, the horrid caldron boils—

* * * * * *

175. *Castle Gordon*—intended to be sung to Morag—

[1]

STREAMS that glide in orient plains,
Never bound by Winter's chains;
Glowing here on golden sands,
There immixed with foulest stains
From Tyranny's empurpled hands:
These, their richly gleaming waves,
I leave the tyrants and their slaves,
Give me the stream that sweetly laves
The banks by CASTLE GORDON.—

2

Torrid forests, every gay,
Shading from the burning ray
Hapless wretches sold to toil;
Or the ruthless Native's way,
Bent on slaughter, blood and spoil:
Woods that ever verdant wave,
I leave the tyrant and the slave,
Give me the groves that lofty brave
The storms, by CASTLE GORDON.—

3

Wildly here without control,
Nature reigns and rules the whole;
In that sober, pensive mood,
Dearest to the feeling soul,
She plants the forest, pours the flood:
Life's poor day I'll musing rave,
And find at night a sheltering cave,
Where waters flow and wild woods wave
By bonny CASTLE GORDON.—

176. *The young Highland Rover*

Tune—Morag—

LOUD blaw the frosty breezes,
The snaws the mountains cover;
Like winter on me seizes
Since my young Highland rover
Far wanders nations over.

Chorus

Where'er he go, where'er he stray,
May Heaven be his warden;
Return him safe to fair Strathspey
And bonie Castle-Gordon.—

The trees now naked groaning
Shall soon wi' leaves be hinging,
The birdies dowie moaning
Shall a' be blythely singing,
And every flower be springing.

Chorus

Sae I'll rejoice the lee-lang day,
When by his mighty Warden
My Youth 's return'd to fair Strathspey
And bonie Castle-Gordon.

177. *Theniel Menzies' bony Mary—*

Tune, Ruffian's rant—

IN comin by the brig o' Dye,
  At Darlet we a blink did tarry;
As day was dawin in the sky
  We drank a health to bonie Mary.—

Chorus

Theniel Menzies' bonie Mary,
Theniel Menzies' bonie Mary,
Charlie Grigor tint his plaidie
Kissin Theniel's bonie Mary.—

Her een sae bright, her brow sae white,
  Her haffet locks as brown 's a berry;
And ay they dimpl't wi' a smile,
  The rosy cheeks o' bonie Mary.—
    Theniel Menzies' &c.

We lap and danc'd the lee-lang day,
  Till Piper lads were wae and weary;
But Charlie gat the spring to pay
  For kissin Theniel's bonie Mary.—
    Theniel Menzies' &c.

178. *Lady Onlie—*

Tune, Ruffian's rant

A' THE lads o' Thornie-bank
  When they gae to the shore o' Bucky,
They'll step in and tak a pint
  Wi' Lady Onlie, honest lucky.—

Chorus—

Lady Onlie, honest lucky,
Brews gude ale at shore o' Bucky;
I wish her sale for her gude ale,
The best on a' the shore o' Bucky.—

Her house sae bien, her curch sae clean,
  I wat she is a dainty Chuckie!
And cheary blinks the ingle gleede
  O' Lady Onlie, honest lucky.—
    Lady Onlie, &c.

179. *Song.—Composed at Auchtertyre on Miss Euphemia Murray of Lentrose—*

Tune, Andrew an' his cutty gun

BY Oughtertyre grows the aik,
  On Yarrow banks the birken shaw;
But Phemie was a bonier lass
  Than braes o' Yarrow ever saw.—

Chorus

Blythe, blythe and merry was she,
  Blythe was she but and ben:
Blythe by the banks of Ern,
  And blythe in Glenturit glen.—

2

Her looks were like a flower in May,
  Her smile was like a simmer morn,
She tripped by the banks of Ern
  As light 's a bird upon a thorn.—

3

Her bony face it was as meek
  As ony lamb upon a lee;
The evening sun was ne'er sae sweet
  As was the blink o' Phemie's e'e.—

4

The Highland hills I've wander'd wide,
  And o'er the lawlands I hae been;
But Phemie was the blythest lass
  That ever trode the dewy green.—

180. *On scaring some Water-Fowl in Loch-Turit, a wild scene among the Hills of Oughtertyre*

WHY, ye tenants of the lake,
For me your watry haunt forsake?
Tell me, fellow-creatures, why
At my presence thus you fly?
Why disturb your social joys,
Parent, filial, kindred ties?
Common friend to you and me,
Nature's gifts to all are free:
Peaceful keep your dimpling wave,
Busy feed, or wanton lave;
Or, beneath the sheltering rock,
Bide the surging billow's shock.

Conscious, blushing for our race,
Soon, too soon, your fears I trace:
Man, your proud usurping foe,
Would be lord of all below:
Plumes himself in Freedom's pride,
Tyrant stern to all beside.

The eagle, from the cliffy brow,
Marking you his prey below,
In his breast no pity dwells,
Strong Necessity compels.
But Man, to whom alone is given
A ray direct from pitying Heaven,
Glories in his heart humane—
And creatures for his pleasure slain.

In these savage, liquid plains,
Only known to wandering swains,
Where the mossy riv'let strays,
Far from human haunts and ways;
All on Nature you depend,
And life's poor season peaceful spend.

Or, if man's superior might
Dare invade your native right,
On the lofty ether borne,
Man with all his powers you scorn;
Swiftly seek, on clanging wings,
Other lakes and other springs;
And the foe you cannot brave,
Scorn at least to be his slave.

40 *Note in Glenriddell MS:* This was the production of a solitary forenoon's walk from Oughtertyre-house.—I lived there, Sir William's guest, for two or three weeks, and was much flattered by my hospitable reception.—What a pity that the mere emotions of gratitude are so impotent in this world! 'Tis lucky that, as we are told, they will be of some avail in the world to come.—

181. *My Peggy's face*

MY Peggy's face, my Peggy's form,
The frost of hermit age might warm;
My Peggy's worth, my Peggy's mind,
Might charm the first of human kind.
I love my Peggy's angel air,
Her face so truly heav'nly fair,
Her native grace so void of art,
But I adore my Peggy's heart.

The lily's hue, the rose's die,
The kindling lustre of an eye;
Who but owns their magic sway,
Who but knows they all decay!
The tender thrill, the pitying tear,
The generous purpose nobly dear,
The gentle look that Rage disarms,
These are all Immortal charms.

182. *Where braving angry Winter's storms*

Tune, Neil Gow's lament for Abercairny

WHERE braving angry Winter's storms
  The lofty Ochels rise,
Far in their shade, my Peggy's charms
  First blest my wondering eyes.—

As one who by some savage stream
  A lonely gem surveys,
Astonish'd doubly marks it beam
  With art's most polish'd blaze.—

Blest be the wild, sequester'd glade
  And blest the day and hour,
Where Peggy's charms I first survey'd,
  When first I felt their pow'r.—

The tyrant Death with grim controul
  May seize my fleeting breath,
But tearing Peggy from my soul
  Must be a stronger death.—

183. *The banks of the Devon—*

Tune, Bhannerach dhon na chri—

How pleasant the banks of the clear-winding Devon,
  With green-spreading bushes, and flowers blooming fair!
But the bonniest flower on the banks of the Devon
  Was once a sweet bud on the braes of the Ayr.
Mild be the sun on this sweet-blushing Flower,
  In the gay, rosy morn as it bathes in the dew;
And gentle the fall of the soft, vernal shower,
  That steals on the evening each leaf to renew!

O spare the dear blossom, ye orient breezes,
  With chill, hoary wing as ye usher the dawn!
And far be thou distant, thou reptile that seizest
  The verdure and pride of the garden or lawn!
Let Bourbon exult in his gay, gilded Lillies,
  And England triumphant display her proud Rose;
A fairer than either adorns the green vallies
  Where Devon, sweet Devon meandering flows.—

184. [*Epitaph for William Nicol*]

Ye maggots, feed on Willie's brains,
  For few sic feasts ye've gotten;
An' fix your claws into his heart,
  For fient a bit o't 's rotten.

185. *Ca' the ewes—* [*A*]

Chorus

Ca' the ewes to the knowes,
Ca' them whare the heather grows,
Ca' them whare the burnie rowes,
  My bonie Dearie.—

As I gaed down the water-side
There I met my Shepherd-lad,
He row'd me sweetly in his plaid,
  And he ca'd me his Dearie.—
    Ca' the &c.

Will ye gang down the water-side
And see the waves sae sweetly glide
Beneath the hazels spreading wide,
  The moon it shines fu' clearly.—
    Ca' the &c.

I was bred up at nae sic school,
My Shepherd-lad, to play the fool;
And a' the day to sit in dool,
  And naebody to see me.—
    Ca' the &c.

Ca' the ewes. For a later version of the song see **456**.

Ye sall get gowns and ribbons meet,
Cauf-leather shoon upon your feet,
And in my arms ye 'se lie and sleep,
And ye sall be my Dearie.—
Ca' the &c.

If ye'll but stand to what ye've said,
I'se gang wi' you, my Shepherd-lad,
And ye may rowe me in your plaid,
And I sall be your Dearie.—
Ca' the &c.

While waters wimple to the sea;
While Day blinks in the lift sae hie;
Till clay-cauld Death sall blin' my e'e,
Ye sall be my Dearie.—
Ca' the ewes &c.

186. *On the death of the late Lord President Dundas—*

LONE on the bleaky hills, the straying flocks
Shun the fierce storms among the sheltering rocks;
Down foam the rivulets, red with dashing rains,
The gathering floods burst o'er the distant plains;
Beneath the blast the leafless forests groan,
The hollow caves return a sullen moan.—

Ye hills, ye plains, ye forests and ye caves,
Ye howling winds, and wintry-swelling waves,
Unheard, unseen, by human ear or eye,
Sad to your sympathetick glooms I fly;
Where to the whistling blast and waters' roar,
Pale Scotia's recent wound I may deplore.—

O heavy loss thy Country ill could bear!
A loss these evil days can ne'er repair!
Justice, the high vicegerent of her God,
Her doubtful balance ey'd and sway'd her rod;
Hearing the tidings of the fatal blow,
She sunk abandon'd to the wildest woe.—

Wrongs, Injuries, from many a darksome den,
Now gay in hope explore the paths of men:
See from his cavern grim Oppression rise,
And throw on Poverty his cruel eyes;
Keen on the helpless victim see him fly,
And stifle, dark, the feebly-bursting cry.—
Mark ruffian Violence, distain'd with crimes,
Rousing elate in these degenerate times;
View unsuspecting Innocence a prey,
As guileful Fraud points out the erring way:
While subtle Litigation's pliant tongue
The life-blood equal sucks of Right and Wrong.—
Hark, injur'd Want recounts th' unlisten'd tale,
And much-wrong'd Misery pours th' unpitied wail!

Ye dark, waste hills, ye brown, unsightly plains,
Congenial scenes! ye soothe my mournful strains:
Ye tempests, rage; ye turbid torrents, roll;
Ye suit the joyless tenor of my soul:
Life's social haunts and pleasures I resign,
Be nameless wilds and lonely wanderings mine,
To mourn the woes my Country must endure,
That wound degenerate ages cannot cure.—

187. [*Answer to Clarinda*]

[From Clarinda on Mr B——'s saying that he had 'nothing else to do'.—

WHEN first you saw Clarinda's charms
  What raptures in your bosom grew!
Her heart was shut to love's alarms,
  But then—you'd nothing else to do.—

Apollo oft had lent his harp,
  But now 'twas strung from Cupid's bow;
You sung, it reach'd Clarinda's heart,
  She wish'd—you'd nothing else to do.—

40 *Foot-note in Huntington Library MS:* The foregoing Poem has some tolerable lines in it, but the incurable wound of my pride will not suffer me to correct, or even peruse it.—I sent a copy of it, with my best prose letter, to the Son of the Great Man the theme of the Piece, by the hands too of one of the noblest men in God's world, Alexi Wood, Surgeon—when behold, his Solicitorship took no more notice of my Poem or me than I had been a strolling Fiddler who had made free with his lady's name over the head of a silly new-reel! Did the gentleman think I look'd for any dirty gratuity!

Fair Venus smil'd, Minerva frown'd,
  Cupid observ'd, the arrow flew:
Indifference (ere a week went round)
  Shew'd—you'd had nothing else to do.—

Christmas eve Clarinda—]

Answer to the foregoing—Extempore

WHEN dear Clarinda, matchless fair,
  First struck Sylvander's raptur'd view,
He gaz'd, he listen'd to despair,
  Alas! 'twas all he dar'd to do.—

Love, from Clarinda's heavenly eyes,
  Transfix'd his bosom thro' and thro';
But still in Friendship's guarded guise,
  For more the demon fear'd to do.—

That heart, already more than lost,
  The imp beleaguer'd all perdue;
For frowning Honor kept his post,
  To meet that frown he shrunk to do.—

His pangs the Bard refus'd to own,
  Tho' half he wish'd Clarinda knew:
But Anguish wrung th' unweeting groan—
  Who blames what frantic Pain must do?

That heart, where motely follies blend,
  Was sternly still to Honor true:
To prove Clarinda's fondest friend,
  Was what a Lover sure might do.—

The Muse his ready quill employ'd,
  No dearer bliss he could pursue;
That bliss Clarinda cold deny'd—
  'Send word by Charles how you do!'—

The chill behest disarm'd his muse,
  Till Passion all impatient grew:
He wrote, and hinted for excuse,
  'Twas 'cause he'd nothing else to do.'—

But by those hopes I have above!
And by those faults I dearly rue!
The deed, the boldest mark of love,
For thee that deed I dare to do!—

O, could the Fates but name the price,
Would bless me with your charms and you!
With frantic joy I'd pay it thrice,
If human art or power could do!

Then take, Clarinda, friendship's hand,
(Friendship, at least, I may avow;)
And lay no more your chill command,
I'll write, whatever I've to do.—
Sylvander——

188. *Scots Ballad—*

Tune—Mary weep no more for me—

MY heart is wae and unco wae,
  To think upon the raging sea,
That roars between her gardens green,
  And th' bonie lass of ALBANIE.—

This lovely maid 's of noble blood,
  That ruled Albion's kingdoms three;
But Oh, Alas! for her bonie face!
  They hae wrang'd the lass of ALBANIE!—

In the rolling tide of spreading Clyde
  There sits an isle of high degree;
And a town of fame whose princely name
  Should grace the lass of ALBANIE.—

But there is a youth, a witless youth,
  That fills the place where she should be,
We'll send him o'er to his native shore,
  And bring our ain sweet ALBANIE.—

Alas the day, and woe the day,
  A false Usurper wan the gree,
That now commands the towers and lands,
  The royal right of ALBANIE.—

We'll daily pray, we'll nightly pray,
  On bended knees most ferventlie,
That the time may come, with pipe and drum,
  We'll welcome home fair ALBANIE.—

189. *A Birth-day Ode. December 31st 1787.*

AFAR th' illustrious Exile roams,
    Whom kingdoms on this day should hail!
  An Inmate of the casual shed;
    On transient Pity's bounty fed;
  Haunted by busy Mem'ry's bitter tale!
  Beasts of the forest have their savage homes,
    But He who should imperial purple wear
  Owns not the lap of earth where rests his royal head:
    His wretched refuge, dark Despair,

While ravening Wrongs and Woes pursue,
And distant far the faithful Few
Who would his sorrows share!
False flatterer, Hope, away!
Nor think to lure us as in days of yore:
We solemnize this sorrowing natal day,
To prove our loyal truth—we can no more;
And, owning Heaven's mysterious sway,
Submissive, low adore.

Ye honor'd, mighty Dead
Who nobly perish'd in the glorious cause,
Your King, your Country and her Laws;
From great Dundee who smiling Victory led,
And fell a martyr in her arms,
(What breast of northern ice but warms)
To bold Balmerino's undying name,
Whose soul of fire, lighted at Heaven's high flame,
Deserves the brightest wreath departed heroes claim;
Not unreveng'd your fate shall lie;
It only lags, the fatal hour:
Your blood shall with incessant cry
Awake at last th' unsparing Power!
As from the cliff with thundering course
The snowy ruin smokes along,
With doubling speed and gathering force,
Till deep it crashing whelms the cottage in the vale;
So Vengeance' arm, ensanguin'd, strong,
Shall with resistless might assail:
Usurping Br–ns—ck's head shall lowly lay,
And St—rt 's wrongs and yours with tenfold weight repay.

Perdition, baleful child of Night,
Rise and revenge the injur'd right
Of St—rt's Royal Race!
Lead on th' unmuzzled hounds of Hell
Till all the frighted Echoes tell
The blood-notes of the chace!
Full on the quarry point their view,
Full on the base, usurping crew,
The tools of Faction, and the Nation's curse:
Hark! how the cry grows on the wind;
They leave the lagging gale behind;

Their savage fury pitiless they pour,
With murdering eyes already they devour:
See, Br–ns—ick spent, a wretched prey;
His life, one poor, despairing day
Where each avenging hour still ushers in a worse!
Such Havock, howling all abroad,
Their utter ruin bring;
The base Apostates to their God,
Or Rebels to their KING!

190. *Hunting Song*

Tune—I rede you beware at the hunting

THE heather was blooming, the meadows were mawn,
Our lads gaed a-hunting, ae day at the dawn,
O'er moors and o'er mosses and mony a glen,
At length they discovered a bonie moor-hen.

I rede you beware at the hunting, young men;
I rede you beware at the hunting, young men;
Tak some on the wing, and some as they spring,
But cannily steal on a bonie moor-hen.

Sweet brushing the dew from the brown heather bells,
Her colors betray'd her on yon mossy fells;
Her plumage outlustred the pride o' the spring,
And O! as she wantoned gay on the wing.

Auld Phœbus himsel, as he peep'd o'er the hill,
In spite at her plumage he tryed his skill;
He levell'd his rays where she bask'd on the brae—
His rays were outshone, and but mark'd where she lay.

They hunted the valley, they hunted the hill;
The best of our lads wi' the best o' their skill;
But still as the fairest she sat in their sight,
Then, whirr! she was over, a mile at a flight.

191. [*On Johnson's Opinion of Hampden*]

FOR shame!
Let Folly and Knavery
Freedom oppose:
'Tis suicide, Genius,
To mix with her foes.

V. Poems 1788

EDINBURGH AND ELLISLAND

192. *Song*

ANNA, thy charms my bosom fire,
  And waste my soul with care;
But ah! how bootless to admire,
  When fated to despair!

Yet in thy presence, lovely Fair,
  To hope may be forgiven;
For sure 'twere impious to despair
  So much in sight of Heaven.

193. *An Extemporaneous Effusion on being appointed to the Excise*

SEARCHING auld wives' barrels,
  Ochon, the day!
That clarty barm should stain my laurels;
  But—what'll ye say!
These muvin' things ca'd wives and weans
Wad muve the very hearts o' stanes!

194. *To the Weaver's gin ye go*

MY heart was ance as blythe and free,
  As simmer days were lang,
But a bonie, westlin weaver lad
  Has gart me change my sang.

Cho:

To the weaver's gin ye go, fair maids,
  To the weaver's gin ye go,
I rede you right, gang ne'er at night,
  To the weaver's gin ye go.

My mither sent me to the town
  To warp a plaiden wab;
But the weary, weary warpin o't
  Has gart me sigh and sab.
    To the weaver's &c.

A bonie, westlin weaver lad
  Sat working at his loom;
He took my heart as wi' a net
  In every knot and thrum.
    To the weaver's &c.

I sat beside my warpin-wheel,
  And ay I ca'd it roun';
But every shot and every knock,
  My heart it gae a stoun.
    To the weaver's &c.

The moon was sinking in the west
  Wi' visage pale and wan,
As my bonie, westlin weaver lad
  Convoy'd me thro' the glen.
    To the weaver's &c.

But what was said, or what was done,
  Shame fa' me gin I tell;
But Oh! I fear the kintra soon
  Will ken as weel 's mysel!
    To the weaver's &c.

195. *I'm o'er young to Marry Yet*

I AM my mammy's ae bairn,
  Wi' unco folk I weary, Sir,
And lying in a man's bed,
  I'm fley'd it make me irie, Sir.
    I'm o'er young, I'm o'er young,
      I'm o'er young to marry yet;
    I'm o'er young, 'twad be a sin
      To tak me frae my mammy yet.

Hallowmass is come and gane,
  The nights are lang in winter, Sir;
And you an' I in ae bed,
  In trowth, I dare na venture, Sir.
    I'm o'er young &c.

Fu' loud and shill the frosty wind
  Blaws thro' the leafless timmer, Sir;
But if ye come this gate again,
  I'll aulder be gin simmer, Sir.
    I'm o'er young &c.

196. *Mc Pherson's Farewell*

FAREWELL, ye dungeons dark and strong,
  The wretch's destinie!
Mc Pherson's time will not be long,
  On yonder gallows-tree.

Chorus

Sae rantingly, sae wantonly,
  Sae dauntingly gae'd he:
He play'd a spring, and danc'd it round
  Below the gallows-tree.

O what is death but parting breath?
  On many a bloody plain
I've dar'd his face, and in this place
  I scorn him yet again!
    Sae rantingly, &c.

Untie these bands from off my hands,
  And bring to me my sword;
And there 's no a man in all Scotland,
  But I'll brave him at a word.
    Sae rantingly, &c.

I've liv'd a life of sturt and strife;
  I die by treacherie:
It burns my heart I must depart
  And not avenged be.
    Sae rantingly, &c.

Now farewell, light, thou sunshine bright,
  And all beneath the sky!
May coward shame distain his name,
  The wretch that dares not die!
    Sae rantingly, &c.

197. *Stay, my Charmer, can you leave me?*

Tune, An Gille dubh ciar dhubh

STAY, my Charmer, can you leave me;
Cruel, cruel to deceive me!
Well you know how much you grieve me:
  Cruel Charmer, can you go!
  Cruel Charmer, can you go!

By my love so ill requited;
By the faith you fondly plighted;
By the pangs of Lovers slighted;
  Do not, do not leave me so!
  Do not, do not leave me so!

198. *What will I do gin my Hoggie die*

WHAT will I do gin my Hoggie die,
  My joy, my pride, my Hoggie;
My only beast, I had nae mae,
  And vow but I was vogie.—

The lee-lang night we watch'd the fauld,
  Me and my faithfu' doggie;
We heard nought but the roaring linn
  Amang the braes sae scroggie.—

But the houlet cry'd frae the Castle-wa',
The blitter frae the boggie,
The tod reply'd upon the hill,
I trembled for my Hoggie.—

When day did daw and cocks did craw,
The morning it was foggie;
An unco tyke lap o'er the dyke
And maist has kill'd my Hoggie.—

199. *Jumpin John*

HER Daddie forbad, her Minnie forbad;
Forbidden she wadna be:
She wadna trow't, the browst she brew'd
Wad taste sae bitterlie.

Chorus

The lang lad they ca' jumpin John
Beguil'd the bonie lassie,
The lang lad they ca' jumpin John
Beguil'd the bonie lassie.

A cow and a cauf, a yowe and a hauf,
And thretty gude shillins and three;
A vera gude tocher, a cotter-man's dochter,
The lass wi' the bonie black e'e.

200. *Up in the Morning Early*

CAULD blaws the wind frae east to west,
  The drift is driving sairly;
Sae loud and shill 's I hear the blast,
  I'm sure it 's winter fairly.
Up in the morning 's no for me,
  Up in the morning early;
When a' the hills are cover'd wi' snaw,
  I'm sure it is winter fairly.

The birds sit chittering in the thorn,
  A' day they fare but sparely;
And lang 's the night frae e'en to morn,
  I'm sure it 's winter fairly.
    Up in the morning 's, &c.

201. *Dusty Miller*

HEY the dusty Miller,
  And his dusty coat;
He will win a shilling
  Or he spend a groat:
Dusty was the coat,
  Dusty was the colour;
Dusty was the kiss
  That I got frae the Miller.—

Hey the dusty Miller,
  And his dusty sack;
Leeze me on the calling
  Fills the dusty peck:
Fills the dusty peck,
  Brings the dusty siller;
I wad gie my coatie
  For the dusty Miller.

202. *Duncan Davison*

THERE was a lass, they ca'd her Meg,
  And she held o'er the moors to spin;
There was a lad that follow'd her,
  They ca'd him Duncan Davison.
The moor was driegh, and Meg was skiegh,
  Her favour Duncan could na win;
For wi' the rock she wad him knock,
  And ay she shook the temper-pin.

As o'er the moor they lightly foor,
  A burn was clear, a glen was green,
Upon the banks they eas'd their shanks,
  And ay she set the wheel between:
But Duncan swoor a haly aith
  That Meg should be a bride the morn,
Then Meg took up her spinnin-graith,
  And flang them a' out o'er the burn.

We will big a wee, wee house,
  And we will live like king and queen;
Sae blythe and merry 's we will be,
  When ye set by the wheel at e'en.
A man may drink and no be drunk,
  A man may fight and no be slain:
A man may kiss a bony lass,
  And ay be welcome back again.

203. *Where Helen Lies*

O THAT I were where Helen lies,
Night and day on me she cries;
O that I were where Helen lies
  In fair Kirkconnel lee.—
O Helen fair beyond compare,
A ringlet of thy flowing hair,
I'll wear it still for ever mair
  Untill the day I die.—

Curs'd be the hand that shot the shot,
And curs'd the gun that gave the crack!
Into my arms bird Helen lap,
  And died for sake o' me!

O think na ye but my heart was sair;
My Love fell down and spake nae mair;
There did she swoon wi' meikle care
On fair Kirkconnel lee.—

I lighted down, my sword did draw,
I cutted him in pieces sma';
I cutted him in pieces sma'
On fair Kirkconnel lee.—
O Helen chaste, thou wert modest,
If I were with thee I were blest
Where thou lies low and takes thy rest
On fair Kirkconnel lee.—

I wish my grave was growing green,
A winding sheet put o'er my e'en,
And I in Helen's arms lying
In fair Kirkconnel lee!
I wish I were where Helen lies!
Night and day on me she cries:
O that I were where Helen lies
On fair Kirkconnel lee.

204. *Duncan Gray—*

WEARY fa' you, Duncan Gray,
Ha, ha the girdin o't,
Wae gae by you, Duncan Gray,
Ha, ha the girdin o't;
When a' the lave gae to their play,
Then I maun sit the lee-lang day,
And jeeg the cradle wi' my tae
And a' for the bad girdin o't.—

Bonie was the lammas moon,
Ha, &c.
Glowrin a' the hills aboon,
Ha, &c.
The girdin brak, the beast cam down,
I tint my curch and baith my shoon,
And Duncan ye're an unco loon;
Wae on the bad girdin o't.—

But Duncan gin ye'll keep your aith,
  Ha, &c.
I'se bless you wi' my hindmost breath,
  Ha, &c.
Duncan gin ye'll keep your aith,
The beast again can bear us baith,
And auld Mess John will mend the skaith
  And clout the bad girdin o't.—

205. *The Ploughman*

THE Ploughman he 's a bony lad,
  His mind is ever true, jo,
His garters knit below his knee,
  His bonnet it is blue, jo.

Chorus

Then up wi't a', my Ploughman lad,
  And hey, my merry Ploughman;
Of a' the trades that I do ken,
  Commend me to the Ploughman.

My Ploughman he comes hame at e'en,
  He 's aften wat and weary:
Cast off the wat, put on the dry,
  And gae to bed, my Dearie.
    Up wi't a' &c.

I will wash my Ploughman's hose,
  And I will dress his o'erlay;
I will mak my Ploughman's bed,
  And chear him late and early.
    Up wi't a' &c.

I hae been east, I hae been west,
  I hae been at Saint Johnston,
The boniest sight that e'er I saw
  Was th' Ploughman laddie dancin.
    Up wi't a' &c.

Snaw-white stockins on his legs,
  And siller buckles glancin;
A gude blue bannet on his head,
  And O but he was handsome!
    Up wi't a' &c.

Commend me to the Barn yard,
  And the Corn-mou, man;
I never gat my Coggie fou
  Till I met wi' the Ploughman.
    Up wi't a' &c.

206. *Hey tuti tatey—*

LANDLADY count the lawin,
The day is near the dawin,
Ye're a' blind drunk, boys,
  And I'm jolly fou.—

Chorus—

Hey tuti tatey, How tuti taiti,
Hey tuti taiti, wha 's fou now.—

Cog an ye were ay fou,
Cog an ye were ay fou;
I wad sit and sing to you,
If ye were ay fou.—
Hey tuti &c.

Weel may we a' be,
Ill may we never see!
God bless the king
And the Companie!
Hey tuti &c.

207. *Raving winds around her blowing*

Tune, M^c^Grigor of Roro's Lament

RAVING winds around her blowing,
Yellow leaves the woodlands strowing,
By a river hoarsely roaring
Isabella stray'd deploring.
Farewell, hours that late did measure
Sunshine days of joy and pleasure;
Hail, thou gloomy night of sorrow,
Cheerless night that knows no morrow.

O'er the Past too fondly wandering,
On the hopeless Future pondering;
Chilly Grief my life-blood freezes,
Fell Despair my fancy seizes.
Life, thou soul of every blessing,
Load to Misery most distressing,
Gladly how would I resign thee,
And to dark Oblivion join thee!

208. *Musing on the roaring Ocean*

Tune, Druimionn dubh

MUSING on the roaring ocean
  Which divides my Love and me,
Wearying Heaven in warm devotion
  For his weal where'er he be;
Hope and Fear's alternate billow
  Yielding late to Nature's law,
Whisp'ring spirits round my pillow
  Talk of him that 's far awa.—

Ye whom Sorrow never wounded,
  Ye who never shed a tear,
Care-untroubled, joy-surrounded,
  Gaudy Day to you is dear:
Gentle Night do thou befriend me:
  Downy Sleep the curtain draw;
Spirits kind again attend me,
  Talk of him that 's far awa!

209. *To daunton me—*

THE blude-red rose at Yule may blaw,
The simmer lilies bloom in snaw,
The frost may freeze the deepest sea,
But an auld man shall never daunton me.—

Chorus—

To daunton me, to daunton me,
An auld man shall never daunton me.—

2

To daunton me, and me sae young,
Wi' his fause heart and his flattering tongue,
That is the thing you shall never see
For an auld man shall never daunton me.—
To daunton me, &c.

3

For a' his meal and a' his maut,
For a' his fresh beef and his saut,
For a' his gold and white monie,
An auld man shall never daunton me.—
To daunton me, &c.

4

His gear may buy him kye and yowes,
His gear may buy him glens and knowes,
But me he shall not buy nor fee,
For an auld man shall never daunton me.—
To daunton me, &c.

5

He hirples twa-fauld as he dow,
Wi' his teethless gab and his auld beld pow,
And the rain rins down frae his red-blear'd e'e,
That auld man shall never daunton me.—
To daunton me, &c.

210. [*Interpolation*]

YOUR friendship much can make me blest,
Oh, why that bliss destroy!
Why urge the only, one request
You know I will deny!

Your thought, if love must harbour there,
Conceal it in that thought;
Nor cause me from my bosom tear
The very friend I sought.

211. *O'er the water to Charlie—*

COME boat me o'er, come row me o'er,
Come boat me o'er to Charlie;
I'll gie John Ross anither bawbee
To boat me o'er to Charlie.—

Chorus

We'll o'er the water, we'll o'er the sea,
We'll o'er the water to Charlie;
Come weal, come woe, we'll gather nda go,
And live or die wi' Charlie.—

Interpolation. Added to Talk not of love *by 'Clarinda'*

I lo'e weel my Charlie's name,
  Tho' some there be abhor him:
But O, to see auld Nick gaun hame,
  And Charlie's faes before him!
    We'll o'er &c.

I swear and vow by moon and stars,
  And sun that shines so early!
If I had twenty thousand lives,
  I'd die as aft for Charlie.—
    We'll o'er &c.

212. *Up and warn a' Willie—*

Up and warn a' Willie,
  Warn, warn a';
To hear my cantie Highland sang,
  Relate the thing I saw, Willie.—

When we gaed to the braes o' Mar,
  And to the wapon-shaw, Willie,
Wi' true design to serve the king
  And banish whigs awa, Willie.—
Up and warn a', Willie,
  Warn, warn a';
For Lords and lairds came there bedeen
  And wow but they were braw, Willie.—

But when the standard was set up
Right fierce the wind did blaw, Willie;
The royal nit upon the tap
Down to the ground did fa', Willie.—
Up and warn a', Willie,
Warn, warn a';
Then second-sighted Sandie said
We'd do nae gude at a', Willie.—

But when the army join'd at Perth,
The bravest ere ye saw, Willie,
We didna doubt the rogues to rout,
Restore our king and a', Willie.
Up and warn a' Willie,
Warn, warn a';
The pipers play'd frae right to left
O whirry whigs awa, Willie.—

But when we march'd to Sherramuir
And there the rebels saw, Willie;
Brave Argyle attack'd our right,
Our flank and front and a', Willie.—
Up and warn a', Willie,
Warn, warn a';
Traitor Huntly soon gave way
Seaforth, St Clair and a' Willie.—

But brave Glengary on our right,
The rebel's left did claw, Willie,
He there the greatest slaughter made
That ever Donald saw, Willie.—
Up and warn a', Willie,
Warn, warn a',
And Whittam sh–t his breeks for fear
And fast did rin awa', Willie.—

For he ca'd us a Highland mob
And soon he'd slay us a', Willie;
But we chas'd him back to Stirling brig
Dragoons and foot and a', Willie.—
Up and warn a' Willie,
Warn, warn a',
At length we rallied on a hill
And briskly up did draw, Willie.—

But when Argyle did view our line,
And them in order saw, Willie,
He streight gaed to Dumblane again
And back his left did draw, Willie.—
Up and warn a' Willie,
Warn warn a',
Then we to Auchterairder march'd
To wait a better fa' Willie.—

Now if ye spier wha wan the day,
I've tell'd you what I saw, Willie,
We baith did fight and baith did beat
And baith did rin awa, Willie.
Up and warn a', Willie,
Warn, warn a' Willie,
For second sighted Sandie said
We'd do nae gude at a', Willie.—

213. *The Rosebud—*

A ROSEBUD by my early walk,
Adown a corn-enclosed bawk,
Sae gently bent its thorny stalk
All on a dewy morning.—

Ere twice the shades o' dawn are fled,
In a' its crimson glory spread,
And drooping rich the dewy head,
  It scents the early morning.—

Within the bush her covert nest
A little linnet fondly prest,
The dew sat chilly on her breast
  Sae early in the morning.—

She soon shall see her tender brood
The pride, the pleasure o' the wood,
Amang the fresh green leaves bedew'd,
  Awauk the early morning.—

So thou, dear bird, young Jeany fair,
On trembling string or vocal air,
Shalt sweetly pay the tender care
  That tents thy early morning.—

So thou, sweet Rosebud, young and gay,
Shalt beauteous blaze upon the day,
And bless the Parent's evening ray
  That watch'd thy early morning.—

214. [*Revision for Clarinda*]

Go on, sweet bird, and soothe my care,
Thy tuneful notes will hush Despair;
Thy plaintive warblings void of art
Thrill sweetly thro' my aching heart.
Now chuse thy mate, and fondly love,
And all the charming transport prove;
While I a lovelorn exile live,
Nor transport or receive or give.

For thee is laughing Nature gay;
For thee she pours the vernal day:
For me in vain is Nature drest,
While joy 's a stranger to my breast!

These sweet emotions all enjoy;
Let love and song thy hours employ!
Go on, sweet bird, and soothe my care;
Thy tuneful notes will hush Despair.

215. *And I'll kiss thee yet, yet*

Tune, Braes o' Balquhidder

AN I'll kiss thee yet, yet,
  An I'll kiss thee o'er again;
An I'll kiss thee yet, yet,
  My bony Peggy Alison.
[Ilk Care and Fear, when thou art near,
  I ever mair defy them, O;
Young kings upon their hansel throne
  Are no sae blest as I am, O!]

And I'll kiss thee yet, yet. Burns's note in Hastie MS: The chorus is the first, or lowest part of the tune—Each verse must be repeated twice to go through the high, or 2[d] part—

When in my arms, wi' a' thy charms,
  I clasp my countless treasure, O!
I seek nae mair o' Heav'n to share,
  Than sic a moment's pleasure, O!

And by thy een sae bony blue,
  I swear I'm thine forever O!
And on thy lips I seal my vow,
  And break it shall I never O!

216. *Rattlin, roarin Willie*

O RATTLIN, roarin Willie,
  O he held to the fair,
An' for to sell his fiddle
  And buy some other ware;
But parting wi' his fiddle,
  The saut tear blin't his e'e;
And Rattlin, roarin Willie,
  Ye're welcome hame to me.

O Willie, come sell your fiddle,
  O sell your fiddle sae fine;
O Willie, come sell your fiddle,
  And buy a pint o' wine;
If I should sell my fiddle,
  The warl' would think I was mad,
For mony a rantin day
  My fiddle and I hae had.

As I cam by Crochallan
  I cannily keekit ben,
Rattlin, roarin Willie
  Was sitting at yon boord-en',
Sitting at yon boord-en',
  And amang guid companie;
Rattlin, roarin Willie,
  Ye're welcome hame to me!

217. *Clarinda*

CLARINDA, mistress of my soul,
  The measur'd time is run!
The wretch beneath the dreary pole,
  So marks his latest sun.

To what dark cave of frozen night
  Shall poor Sylvander hie;
Depriv'd of thee, his life and light,
  The Sun of all his joy.

We part—but by these precious drops,
  That fill thy lovely eyes!
No other light shall guide my steps,
  Till thy bright beams arise.

She, the fair Sun of all her sex,
  Has blest my glorious day:
And shall a glimmering Planet fix
  My worship to its ray?

218. *The Winter it is Past*

THE winter it is past, and the summer 's come at last,
  And the small birds sing on ev'ry tree;
The hearts of these are glad, but mine is very sad,
  For my Lover has parted from me.

The rose upon the brier, by the waters running clear,
  May have charms for the linnet or the bee;
Their little loves are blest and their little hearts at rest,
  But my Lover is parted from me.

My love is like the sun, in the firmament does run,
  For ever constant and true;
But his is like the moon that wanders up and down,
  And every month it is new.

All you that are in love and cannot it remove,
  I pity the pains you endure:
For experience makes me know that your hearts are full of woe,
  A woe that no mortal can cure.

219. [*To Clarinda*]

FAIR Empress of the Poet's soul,
  And Queen of Poetesses;
Clarinda, take this little boon,
  This humble pair of Glasses.

And fill them high with generous juice,
  As generous as your mind;
And pledge me in the generous toast—
  'The whole of Humankind!'

'To those who love us!'—second fill;
  But not to those whom we love,
Lest we love those who love not us:—
  A third—'to thee and me, Love!'

Long may we live! Long may we love!
  And long may we be happy!!!
And may we never want a Glass,
  Well charg'd with generous Nappy!!!!

220. *Song—*

Tune—Captain Okean—

I

THE small birds rejoice in the green leaves returning,
  The murmuring streamlet winds clear thro' the vale;
The primroses blow in the dews of the morning,
  And wild-scattered cowslips bedeck the green dale;

But what can give pleasure, or what can seem fair,
  When the lingering moments are numbered by Care?
No birds sweetly singing, nor flowers gayly springing,
  Can sooth the sad bosom of joyless Despair.—

2

The deed that I dared, could it merit their malice,
  A KING and a FATHER to place on his throne;
His right are these hills, and his right are these vallies,
  Where wild beasts find shelter but I can find none:
But 'tis not my sufferings, thus wretched, forlorn,
  My brave, gallant friends, 'tis your ruin I mourn;
Your faith proved so loyal in hot, bloody trial,
  Alas, can I make it no sweeter return!

221. *Epitaph on R. Muir—*

WHAT Man could esteem, or what Woman could love,
  Was He who lies under this sod:
If Such Thou refusest admittance above,
  Then whom wilt thou favor, Good God!

222. *Epistle to Hugh Parker*

IN this strange land, this uncouth clime,
A land unknown to prose or rhyme;
Where words ne'er crost the muse's heckles,
Nor limpet in poetic shackles;
A land that prose did never view it,
Except when drunk he stacher't thro' it;
Here, ambush'd by the chimla cheek,
Hid in an atmosphere of reek,
I hear a wheel thrum i' the neuk,
I hear it—for in vain I leuk.—
The red peat gleams, a fiery kernel,
Enhusked by a fog infernal:
Here, for my wonted rhyming raptures,
I sit and count my sins by chapters;
For lief and spunk like ither Christians,
I'm dwindled down to mere existence,
Wi' nae converse but Gallowa' bodies,
Wi' nae kend face but Jenny Geddes.

Jenny, my Pegasean pride!
Dowie she saunters down Nithside,
And ay a westlin leuk she throws,
While tears hap o'er her auld brown nose!
Was it for this, wi' canny care,
Thou bure the Bard through many a shire?
At howes or hillocks never stumbled,
And late or early never grumbled?—
O, had I power like inclination,
I'd heeze thee up a constellation,
To canter with the Sagitarre,
Or loup the ecliptic like a bar;
Or turn the pole like any arrow;
Or, when auld Phebus bids good-morrow,
Down the zodiac urge the race,
And cast dirt on his godship's face;
For I could lay my bread and kail
He'd ne'er cast saut upo' thy tail.—
Wi' a' this care and a' this grief,
And sma', sma' prospect of relief,
And nought but peat reek i' my head,
How can I write what ye can read?—
Tarbolton, twenty-fourth o' June,
Ye'll find me in a better tune;
But till we meet and weet our whistle,
Tak this excuse for nae epistle.

ROBERT BURNS.

223. [*A*] *Written in Friar's Carse Hermitage on the banks of Nith— June—1788*

THOU whom chance may hither lead,
Be thou clad in russet weed,
Be thou deckt in silken stole,
Grave these maxims on thy soul.—

Life is but a day at most,
Sprung from night, in darkness lost;
Hope not sunshine every hour,
Fear not clouds will always lour.—
Happiness is but a name,
Make CONTENT and EASE thy aim.—

Ambition is a meteor gleam,
Fame a restless, airy dream;
Pleasures, insects on the wing
Round Peace, the tenderest flower of spring;
Those that sip the dew alone,
Make the butterflies thy own;
Those that would the bloom devour,
Crush the locusts, save the flower.—
For the FUTURE be prepar'd,
Guard, wherever thou canst guard,
But thy utmost duly done,
Welcome what thou canst not shun:—
Follies past, give thou to air;
Make their consequence thy care:
Keep the name of MAN in mind,
And dishonor not thy kind.—
Reverence with lowly heart
Him whose wondrous work thou art;
Keep his Goodness still in view,
Thy trust—and thy example too.—

Stranger, go! Heaven be thy guide!
Quod, the BEADSMAN ON NID-SIDE.—

223. [*B*] *Altered from the foregoing—Dec— 1788*

THOU whom chance may hither lead,
Be thou clad in russet-weed,
Be thou deckt in silken stole,
Grave these counsels on thy soul.—

Life is but a day at most,
Sprung from Night, in darkness lost,
Hope not sunshine every hour,
Fear not clouds will always lour.—

As Youth and Love with sprightly dance
Beneath thy morning star advance,
Pleasure with her siren air
May delude the thoughtless pair;
Let Prudence bless Enjoyment's cup,
Then, raptur'd, sip and sip it up.—

As thy day grows warm and high,
Life's meridian flaming nigh,
Dost thou spurn the humble vale?
Life's proud summits would'st thou scale?
Check thy climbing step elate,
Evils lurk in felon-wait;
Dangers, eagle-pinion'd, bold,
Soar around each cliffy hold,
While chearful Peace, with linnet-song,
Chants the lowly dells among.—

As the shades of evening close,
Beckoning thee to long repose,
As life itself becomes disease,
Seek the chimney-nook of Ease:
There, ruminate with sober thought
On all thou 'st seen, and heard, and wrought;
And teach the sportive Younkers round,
Saws of Experience, sage and sound.—
Say, Man's true, genuine estimate,
The grand criterion of his fate,
Is not, art thou High, or Low?
Did thy fortune ebb or flow?
Did many talents gild thy span?
Or frugal Nature grudge thee, One?
Tell them, and press it on their mind,
As thou thyself must shortly find,
The smile, or frown, of awful Heaven,
To Virtue, or to Vice, is given:
Say, to be just, and kind, and wise,
There solid Self-enjoyment lies;
That foolish, selfish, faithless ways,
Lead to be wretched, vile and base.—

Thus, resigned and quiet, creep
To thy bed of lasting sleep:
Sleep, whence thou shalt ne'er awake,
Night, where dawn shall never break,
Till Future Life, future no more,
To light and joy the Good restore,
To light and joy unknown before.—

Stranger, go! Heaven be thy guide!
Quod, the BEADSMAN OF NITH-SIDE.—

224. *The Fête Champetre—*

Tune, Gillicrankie—

I

O WHA will to Saint Stephen's house,
  To do our errands there, man;
O wha will to Saint Stephen's house,
  O' th' merry lads of Ayr, man?
Or will we send a Man-o'-law,
  Or will we send a Sodger?
Or him wha led o'er Scotland a'
  The meikle URSA MAJOR?

2

Come, will ye court a noble Lord,
  Or buy a score o' Lairds, man?
For Worth and Honor pawn their word
  Their vote shall be Glencaird's, man?
Ane gies them coin, ane gies them wine,
  Anither gies them clatter;
Anbank, wha guess'd the ladies' taste,
  He gies a Fête Champetre.—

3

When Love and Beauty heard the news,
  The gay green-woods amang, man,
Where gathering flowers and busking bowers
  They heard the blackbird's sang, man;
A vow they seal'd it with a kiss
  Sir Politicks to fetter,
As their's alone, the Patent-bliss,
  To hold a Fête Champetre.—

4

Then mounted Mirth, on gleesome wing,
  O'er hill and dale she flew, man;
Ilk wimpling burn, ilk chrystal spring,
  Ilk glen and shaw she knew, man:
She summonn'd every SOCIAL SPRITE,
  That sports by wood or water,
On th' bony Banks of Ayr to meet,
  And keep this Fête Champetre.—

5

Cauld Boreas, wi' his boisterous crew,
  Were bound to stakes like kye, man;
And Cynthia's car, o' silver fu',
  Clamb up the starry sky, man:
Reflected beams dwell in the streams,
  Or down the current shatter;
The western breeze steals thro' the trees,
  To view this Fête Champetre.—

6

How many a robe sae gayly floats!
  What sparkling jewels glance, man!
To HARMONY's enchanting notes
  As moves the mazy dance, man!
The echoing wood, the winding flood,
  Like Paradise did glitter,
When Angels met, at Adam's yett,
  To hold their Fête Champetre.—

7

When Politics cam there, to mix
  And make his ether-stane, man,
He circl'd round the magic ground,
  But entrance found he nane, man:
He blush'd for shame, he quat his name,
  Forswore it every letter,
Wi' humble prayer to join and share
  This festive Fête Champetre.—

225. [*To Alexander Cunningham*]

MY godlike Friend—nay do not stare,
  You think the phrase is odd like;
But, 'God is love,' the Saints declare,
  Then surely thou art Godlike.

And is thy Ardour still the same?
  And kindled still at Anna?
Others may boast a partial flame,
  But thou art a Volcano.—

Even Wedlock asks not Love beyond
  Death's tie-dissolving Portal;
But thou, omnipotently fond,
  May'st promise Love Immortal.—

Prudence, the Bottle and the Stew
  Are fam'd for Lovers' curing:
Thy Passion nothing can subdue,
  Nor Wisdom, Wine, nor Whoring.—

Thy Wounds such healing powers defy;
  Such Symptoms dire attend them;
That last, great Antihectic try,
  Marriage, perhaps, may mend them.—

Sweet Anna has an air, a grace,
  Divine magnetic touching!
She takes, she charms—but who can trace
  The process of BEWITCHING?

226. *O Mally's meek, Mally's sweet*

Chorus

O MALLY 's meek, Mally 's sweet,
  Mally 's modest and discreet,
Mally 's rare, Mally 's fair,
  Mally 's ev'ry way compleat.

As I was walking up the street,
  A barefit maid I chanc'd to meet,
But O, the road was very hard
  For that fair maiden's tender feet.
      Chorus, Mally 's meek &c.

It were mair meet, that those fine feet
  Were weel lac'd up in silken shoon,
And twere more fit that she should sit
  Within yon chariot gilt aboon.
      Chorus, Mally 's meek &c.

Her yellow hair, beyond compare,
  Comes trinkling down her swan white neck,
And her two eyes like stars in skies
  Would keep a sinking ship frae wreck.

227. *I love my Jean*

Tune—Miss admiral Gordon's Strathspey—

OF a' the airts the wind can blaw,
  I dearly like the West;
For there the bony Lassie lives,
  The Lassie I lo'e best:

There 's wild-woods grow, and rivers row,
  And mony a hill between;
But day and night my fancy's flight
  Is ever wi' my Jean.—

I see her in the dewy flowers,
  I see her sweet and fair;
I hear her in the tunefu' birds,
  I hear her charm the air:
There 's not a bony flower, that springs
  By fountain, shaw, or green;
There 's not a bony bird that sings
  But minds me o' my Jean.—

228. *O, were I on Parnassus Hill*

Tune, My love is lost to me

O WERE I on Parnassus hill;
Or had o' Helicon my fill;
That I might catch poetic skill,
  To sing how dear I love thee.

But Nith maun be my Muses well,
My Muse maun be thy bonie sell;
On Corsincon I'll glowr and spell,
 And write how dear I love thee.

Then come, sweet Muse, inspire my lay!
For a' the lee-lang simmer's day,
I coudna sing, I coudna say,
 How much, how dear, I love thee.
I see thee dancing o'er the green,
Thy waist sae jimp, thy limbs sae clean,
Thy tempting lips, thy roguish een—
 By Heaven and Earth I love thee.

By night, by day, a-field, at hame,
The thoughts o' thee my breast inflame;
And ay I muse and sing thy name,
 I only live to love thee.
Tho' I were doom'd to wander on,
Beyond the sea, beyond the sun,
Till my last, weary sand was run;
 Till then—and then I love thee.

229. *The Banks of Nith*

Tune, Robie donna gorach

THE Thames flows proudly to the sea,
 Where royal cities stately stand;
But sweeter flows the Nith, to me,
 Where Cummins ance had high command:

When shall I see that honor'd Land,
  That winding Stream I love so dear!
Must wayward Fortune's adverse hand
  For ever, ever keep me here.

How lovely, Nith, thy fruitful vales,
  Where bounding hawthorns gayly bloom;
And sweetly spread thy sloping dales
  Where lambkins wanton through the broom!
Tho' wandering, now, must be my doom,
  Far from thy bonie banks and braes,
May there my latest hours consume,
  Amang the friends of early days!

230. *To Robt. Graham of Fintry Esqr, with a request for an Excise Division—*

Ellisland—Sept. 8th 1788

WHEN Nature her great Masterpiece designed,
And framed her last, best Work, The Human Mind,
Her eye intent on all the mazy Plan,
She forms of various stuff the various Man.—
The USEFUL MANY first, she calls them forth,
Plain, plodding Industry, and sober Worth:
Thence Peasants, Farmers, native sons of earth,
And Merchandise' whole genus take their birth:
Each prudent Cit a warm existence finds,
And all Mechanics' many-aproned kinds.—
Some other, rarer Sorts are wanted yet,
The lead and buoy are needful to the net.—
The caput mortuum of Gross Desires,
Makes a material for mere knights and squires:
The Martial Phosphorus is taught to flow;
She kneads the lumpish Philosophic dough;
Then marks th' unyielding mass with grave Designs,
Law, Physics, Politics and deep Divines:
Last, she sublimes th' Aurora of the Poles,
The flashing elements of Female Souls.—

The ordered System fair before her stood,
Nature, well-pleased, pronounced it very good;

Yet, ere she gave creating labor o'er,
Half-jest, she tryed one curious labor more.—
Some spumy, fiery, ignisfatuus matter,
Such as the slightest breath of air might scatter,
With arch-alacrity, and conscious glee,
(Nature may have her whim as well as we;
Her Hogarth-art perhaps she meant to show it)
She forms the Thing, and christens it—A POET.—
Creature, tho' oft the prey of Care and Sorrow,
When blest today, unmindful of tomorrow;
A being formed t' amuse his graver friends,
Admired and praised—and there the wages ends;
A mortal quite unfit for Fortune's strife,
Yet oft the sport of all the ills of life;
Prone to enjoy each pleasure riches give,
Yet haply wanting wherewithall to live;
Longing to wipe each tear, to heal each groan,
Yet frequent all-unheeded in his own.—

But honest Nature is not quite a Turk;
She laught at, first, then felt for her poor Work:
Viewing the propless Climber of mankind,
She cast about a Standard-tree to find;
In pity for his helpless woodbine-state,
She clasp'd his tendrils round THE TRULY GREAT:
A title, and the only one I claim,
To lay strong hold for help on generous GRAHAM.—

Pity the tuneful Muses' hapless train,
Weak, timid Landsmen on life's stormy main!
Their hearts no selfish, stern, absorbent stuff
That never gives—tho' humbly takes enough;
The little Fate allows they share as soon,
Unlike sage, proverbed Wisdom's hard-wrung boon:
The world were blest, did bliss on them depend,
Ah, that the FRIENDLY e'er should want a FRIEND!

Let Prudence number o'er each sturdy son
Who life and wisdom at one race begun,
Who feel by reason and who give by rule,
(Instinct 's a brute, and Sentiment a fool!)
Who make poor, 'Will do,' wait upon, 'I should,'
We own they're prudent—but who owns they're good?

Ye Wise Ones, hence! ye hurt the social eye;
God's image rudely etch'd on base alloy!
But come, ye who the godlike pleasure know,
Heaven's attribute distinguished,—to bestow,
Whose arms of love would grasp all human-race;
Come, thou who givest with all a courtier's grace,
Friend of my life! (true Patron of my rhymes)
Prop of my dearest hopes for future times.—

Why shrinks my soul, half-blushing, half-afraid,
Backward, abashed, to ask thy friendly aid?
I know my need, I know thy giving hand,
I tax thy friendship at thy kind command:
But, there are such, who court the tuneful Nine,
Heavens, should the branded character be mine!
Whose verse in manhood's pride sublimely flows,
Yet vilest reptiles in their begging prose.
Mark, how their lofty, independant spirit
Soars on the spurning wing of injured Merit!
Seek you the proofs in private life to find?—
Pity, the best of words should be but wind!
So to heaven's gates the lark's shrill song ascends,
But grovelling on the earth the carol ends.—
In all the clamorous cry of starving Want
They dun Benevolence with shameless front:
Oblidge them, patronize their tinsel lays,
They persecute you all your future days.—

E'er my poor soul such deep damnation stain,
My horny fist, assume the Plough again;
The pie-bald jacket, let me patch once more;
On eighteenpence a week I've lived before.—
Tho', thanks to Heaven! I dare even that last shift,
I trust, meantime, my boon is in thy gift:
That, placed by thee upon the wished-for height,
Where Man and Nature fairer in her sight,
My Muse may imp her wing for some sublimer flight.

231. *The seventh of November—*

THE day returns, my bosom burns,
The blissful day we twa did meet:
Tho' Winter wild, in tempest toil'd,
Ne'er simmer-sun was half sae sweet.
Than a' the pride that loads the tide,
And crosses o'er the sultry Line;
Than kingly robes, than crowns and globes,
Heaven gave me more—it made thee mine.—

While day and night can bring delight,
Or Nature aught of pleasure give;
While Joys Above, my mind can move,
For Thee and Thee alone I live!
When that grim foe of life below
Comes in between to make us part;
The iron hand that breaks our Band,
It breaks my bliss—it breaks my heart!

232. *The blue-eyed Lassie*

I GAED a waefu' gate, yestreen,
  A gate, I fear, I'll dearly rue;
I gat my death frae twa sweet een,
  Twa lovely e'en o' bonie blue.
'Twas not her golden ringlets bright,
  Her lips like roses, wat wi' dew,
Her heaving bosom, lily-white,
  It was her een sae bonie blue.

She talk'd, she smil'd, my heart she wyl'd,
  She charm'd my soul I wist na how;
And ay the stound, the deadly wound,
  Cam frae her een sae bonie blue.
But spare to speak, and spare to speed;
  She'll aiblins listen to my vow:
Should she refuse, I'll lay my dead
  To her twa een sae bonie blue.

233. *A Mother's Lament for the loss of her only Son—*

'FATE gave the word, the arrow sped,'
  And pierc'd my Darling's heart;
And with him all the joys are fled,
  Life can to me impart.—

By cruel hands the Sapling drops,
  In dust dishonor'd laid:
So fell the pride of all my hopes,
  My age's future shade.—

The mother-linnet in the brake
  Bewails her ravish'd young;
So I, for my lost Darling's sake,
  Lament the live day long.—

Death! oft, I've fear'd thy fatal blow;
  Now, fond, I bare my breast;
O, do thou come and lay me low,
  With him I love at rest!

234. *The lazy mist*

THE lazy mist hangs from the brow of the hill,
Concealing the course of the dark winding rill;
How languid the scenes, late so sprightly, appear,
As Autumn to Winter resigns the pale year.
The forests are leafless, the meadows are brown,
And all the gay foppery of Summer is flown:
Apart let me wander, apart let me muse,
How quick Time is flying, how keen Fate pursues.

How long I have liv'd—but how much liv'd in vain;
How little of life's scanty span may remain:
What aspects, old Time, in his progress, has worn;
What ties, cruel Fate, in my bosom has torn.
How foolish, or worse, till our summit is gain'd!
And downward, how weaken'd, how darken'd, how pain'd!
Life is not worth having with all it can give,
For something beyond it poor man sure must live.

235. *Whistle o'er the lave o't—*

FIRST when Maggy was my care,
Heaven, I thought, was in her air;
Now we're married—spier nae mair—
  Whistle o'er the lave o't.—

Meg was meek, and Meg was mild,
Sweet and harmless as a child—
Wiser men than me 's beguil'd;
  Whistle o'er the lave o't.—

How we live, my Meg and me,
How we love and how we gree;
I carena by how few may see,
  Whistle o'er the lave o't.—

Wha I wish were maggots' meat,
Dish'd up in her winding-sheet;
I could write—but Meg maun see 't—
  Whistle o'er the lave o't.—

236. *Tam Glen—*

Tune, Merry beggars—

My heart is a breaking, dear Tittie,
Some counsel unto me come len';
To anger them a' is a pity,
But what will I do wi' Tam Glen?—

I'm thinking, wi' sic a braw fellow,
In poortith I might mak a fen':
What care I in riches to wallow,
If I mauna marry Tam Glen.—

There 's Lowrie the laird o' Dumeller,
'Gude day to you brute' he comes ben:
He brags and he blaws o' his siller,
But when will he dance like Tam Glen.—

My Minnie does constantly deave me,
And bids me beware o' young men;
They flatter, she says, to deceive me,
But wha can think sae o' Tam Glen.—

My Daddie says, gin I'll forsake him,
He'll gie me gude hunder marks ten:
But, if it 's ordain'd I maun take him,
O wha will I get but Tam Glen?

Yestreen at the Valentines' dealing,
My heart to my mou gied a sten;
For thrice I drew ane without failing,
And thrice it was written, Tam Glen.—

The last Halloween I was waukin
My droukit sark-sleeve, as ye ken;
His likeness cam up the house staukin,
And the very grey breeks o' Tam Glen!

Come counsel, dear Tittie, don't tarry;
  I'll gie you my bonie black hen,
Gif ye will advise me to Marry
  The lad I lo'e dearly, Tam Glen.—

237. *To the beautiful Miss Eliza J——n, on her principles of Liberty and Equality—*

How Liberty, girl, can it be by thee
    nam'd?
Equality too! hussey, art not asham'd:
FREE AND EQUAL indeed; while mankind
    thou enchainest,
And over their hearts a proud DESPOT
    so reignest.—

238. [*Sketch for an Elegy*]

CRAIGDARROCH, fam'd for speaking art
And every virtue of the heart,
Stops short, nor can a word impart
  To end his sentence,
When mem'ry strikes him like a dart
  With auld acquaintance.

Black James—whase wit was never laith,
But, like a sword had tint the sheath,
Ay ready for the work o' death—
  He turns aside,
And strains wi' suffocating breath
  His grief to hide.

Even Philosophic Smellie tries
To choak the stream that floods his eyes:
So Moses wi' a hazel-rice
  Came o'er the stane;
But, tho' it cost him speaking twice,
  It gush'd amain.

Go to your marble graffs, ye great,
In a' the tinkler-trash of state!
But by thy honest turf I'll wait,
Thou man of worth,
And weep the ae best fallow's fate
E'er lay in earth!

239. *Elegy on Capt. M—— H——, A* Gentleman *who held the Patent for his Honours immediately from Almighty God!*

But now his radiant course is run,
For Matthew's course was bright;
His soul was like the glorious sun,
A matchless Heavenly Light!

O DEATH! thou tyrant fell and bloody!
The meikle devil wi' a woodie
Haurl thee hame to his black smiddie,
O'er hurcheon hides,
And like stock-fish come o'er his studdie
Wi' thy auld sides!

He 's gane! he 's gane! he 's frae us torn,
The ae best fellow e'er was born!
Thee, Matthew, Nature's sel shall mourn
By wood and wild,
Where, haply, Pity strays forlorn,
Frae man exil'd.

Ye hills, near neebors o' the starns,
That proudly cock your cresting cairns;
Ye cliffs, the haunts of sailing yearns,
Where Echo slumbers:
Come join, ye Nature's sturdiest bairns,
My wailing numbers.

Mourn, ilka grove the cushat kens;
Ye hazly shaws and briery dens;
Ye burnies, wimplin down your glens,
Wi' toddlin din,
Or foaming, strang, wi' hasty stens,
Frae lin to lin.

Mourn, little harebells o'er the lee;
Ye stately foxgloves fair to see;
Ye woodbines hanging bonnilie,
In scented bowers;
Ye roses on your thorny tree,
The first o' flowers.

At dawn, when every grassy blade
Droops with a diamond at his head,
At even, when beans their fragrance shed,
I' th' rustling gale,
Ye maukins whiddin thro' the glade,
Come join my wail.

Mourn, ye wee songsters o' the wood;
Ye grouss that crap the heather bud;
Ye curlews calling thro' a clud;
Ye whistling plover;
And mourn, ye whirring paitrick brood;
He 's gane for ever!

Mourn, sooty coots, and speckled teals;
Ye fisher herons, watching eels;
Ye duck and drake, wi' airy wheels
Circling the lake:
Ye bitterns, till the quagmire reels,
Rair for his sake.

Mourn, clamouring craiks at close o' day,
'Mang fields o' flowering claver gay;
And when ye wing your annual way
Frae our cauld shore,
Tell thae far warlds, wha lies in clay,
Wham we deplore.

Ye houlets, frae your ivy bower,
In some auld tree, or eldritch tower,
What time the moon, wi' silent glowr,
Sets up her horn,
Wail thro' the dreary midnight hour
Till waukrife morn.

O, rivers, forests, hills, and plains!
Oft have ye heard my canty strains:
But now, what else for me remains
But tales of woe;
And frae my een the drapping rains
Maun ever flow.

Mourn, Spring, thou darling of the year;
Ilk cowslip cup shall kep a tear:
Thou, Simmer, while each corny spear
Shoots up its head,
Thy gay, green, flowery tresses shear,
For him that 's dead.

Thou, Autumn, wi' thy yellow hair,
In grief thy sallow mantle tear;
Thou, Winter, hurling thro' the air
The roaring blast,
Wide o'er the naked world declare
The worth we 've lost.

Mourn him thou Sun, great source of light;
Mourn, Empress of the silent night:
And you, ye twinkling starnies bright,
My Matthew mourn;
For through your orbs he 's taen his flight,
Ne'er to return.

O, H********! the man! the brother!
And art thou gone, and gone for ever!
And hast thou crost that unknown river,
Life's dreary bound!
Like thee, where shall I find another,
The world around!

Go to your sculptur'd tombs, ye Great,
In a' the tinsel trash o' state!
But by thy honest turf I'll wait,
Thou man of worth!
And weep the ae best fellow's fate
E'er lay in earth.

THE EPITAPH

Stop, passenger! my story 's brief,
  And truth I shall relate, man;
I tell nae common tale o' grief,
  For Matthew was a great man.

If thou uncommon merit hast,
  Yet spurn'd at Fortune's door, man;
A look of pity hither cast,
  For Matthew was a poor man.

If thou a noble sodger art,
  That passest by this grave, man;
There moulders here a gallant heart,
  For Matthew was a brave man.

If thou on men, their works and ways,
  Canst throw uncommon light, man;
Here lies wha weel had won thy praise,
  For Matthew was a bright man.

If thou at Friendship's sacred ca'
  Wad life itself resign, man;
Thy sympathetic tear maun fa',
  For Matthew was a kind man.

If thou art staunch without a stain,
  Like the unchanging blue, man;
This was a kinsman o' thy ain,
  For Matthew was a true man.

If thou hast wit, and fun, and fire,
  And ne'er gude wine did fear, man;
This was thy billie, dam, and sire,
  For Matthew was a queer man.

If ony whiggish whingin sot,
  To blame poor Matthew dare, man;
May dool and sorrow be his lot,
  For Matthew was a rare man.

240. *Auld lang syne*

SHOULD auld acquaintance be forgot
  And never brought to mind?
Should auld acquaintance be forgot,
  And auld lang syne!

Chorus

  For auld lang syne, my jo,
    For auld lang syne,
  We'll tak a *cup o' kindness yet
    For auld lang syne.

And surely ye'll be your pint stowp!
  And surely I'll be mine!
And we'll tak a cup o' kindness yet,
  For auld lang syne.
      For auld, &c.

We twa hae run about the braes,
  And pou'd the gowans fine;
But we've wander'd mony a weary fitt,
  Sin auld lang syne.
      For auld, &c.

We twa hae paidl'd in the burn,
  Frae morning sun till dine;
But seas between us braid hae roar'd,
  Sin auld lang syne.
      For auld, &c.

* Some Sing, Kiss, in place of Cup.

And there's a hand, my trusty fiere!
  And gie's a hand o' thine!
And we'll tak a right gude-willie-waught,
  For auld lang syne.
    For auld, &c.

241. *Epitaph for J. H. Writer in Ayr*

HERE lies a Scots mile of a chiel,
If he's in heaven, L—d, fill him weel!

242. *My bony Mary*

GO fetch to me a pint o' wine,
  And fill it in a silver tassie;
That I may drink, before I go,
  A service to my bonie lassie:
The boat rocks at the Pier o' Lieth,
  Fu' loud the wind blaws frae the Ferry,
The ship rides by the Berwick-law,
  And I maun leave my bony Mary.

The trumpets sound, the banners fly,
  The glittering spears are ranked ready,
The shouts o' war are heard afar,
  The battle closes deep and bloody.
It 's not the roar o' sea or shore,
  Wad make me langer wish to tarry;
Nor shouts o' war that 's heard afar—
  It 's leaving thee, my bony Mary!

243. *Ode, Sacred to the Memory of Mrs. —— of ——*

DWELLER in yon dungeon dark,
Hangman of creation, mark!
Who in widow weeds appears,
Laden with unhonoured years,
Noosing with care a bursting purse,
Baited with many a deadly curse?

STROPHE

View the wither'd beldam's face—
Can thy keen inspection trace
Aught of Humanity's sweet melting grace?
Note that eye, 'tis rheum o'erflows,
Pity's flood there never rose.
See those hands, ne'er stretch'd to save,
Hands that took—but never gave.
Keeper of Mammon's iron chest,
Lo, there she goes, unpitied and unblest,
She goes, but not to realms of everlasting rest!

ANTISTROPHE

Plunderer of Armies, lift thine eyes,
(A while forbear, ye torturing fiends),
Seest thou whose step, unwilling, hither bends?
No fallen angel, hurled from upper skies;
'Tis thy trusty *quondam Mate*,
Doomed to share thy fiery fate,
She, tardy, hell-ward plies.

EPODE

And are they of no more avail,
Ten thousand glittering pounds a year?
In other worlds can Mammon fail,
Omnipotent as he is here?
O, bitter mockery of the *pompous bier*,
While down the wretched *vital part* is driven!
The cave-lodged beggar, with a conscience clear,
Expires in rags, unknown, and goes to Heaven.

244. [*Versicles on Sign-posts*]

The everlasting surliness of a lion, Saracen's head, &c. or the unchanging blandness of the Landlord welcoming a Traveller, on some Sign-posts, would be no bad similies of the constant affected fierceness of a Bully, or the eternal simper of a Frenchman or a Fiddler.—

He looked
Just as your Sign-post lions do,
As fierce, and quite as harmless too—

Patient Stupidity
So, heavy, passive to the tempest's shocks,
Dull on the Sign-post stands the stupid Ox—

His face with smile eternal drest
Just like the Landlord to his guest,
High as they hang with creaking din
To index out the country Inn—

A head pure, sinless quite of brain or soul,
The very image of a Barber's Poll;
Just shews a human face and wears a wig,
And looks when well-friseur'd, amazing big—

245. *To Mr. John Taylor*

WITH Pegasus upon a day
  Apollo, weary flying,
(Thro' frosty hills the journey lay)
  On foot the way was plying.—

Poor, slip-shod, giddy Pegasus
  Was but a sorry walker,
To Vulcan then Apollo gaes
  To get a frosty calker.—

Oblidging Vulcan fell to wark,
  Threw by his coat and bonnet;
And did Sol's business in a crack,
  Sol pay'd him with a sonnet.—

Ye Vulcan's Sons of Wanlockhead,
  Pity my sad disaster,
My Pegasus is poorly shod,
  I'll pay you like my Master.—

246. *A Sonnet upon Sonnets*

FOURTEEN, a sonneteer thy praises sings;
What magic myst'ries in that number lie!
Your hen hath fourteen eggs beneath her wings
That fourteen chickens to the roost may fly.
Fourteen full pounds the jockey's stone must be;
His age fourteen—a horse's prime is past.
Fourteen long hours too oft the Bard must fast;
Fourteen bright bumpers—bliss he ne'er must see!
Before fourteen, a dozen yields the strife;
Before fourteen—e'en thirteen's strength is vain.
Fourteen good years—a woman gives us life;
Fourteen good men—we lose that life again.
What lucubrations can be more upon it?
Fourteen good measur'd verses make a sonnet.

247. *The Cares o' Love*

HE

THE cares o' Love are sweeter far
  Than onie other pleasure;
And if sae dear its sorrows are
  Enjoyment, what a treasure!

SHE

I fear to try, I dare na try
  A passion sae ensnaring;
For light 's her heart and blythe 's her song
  That for nae man is caring.

248. *Louis what reck I by thee*

LOUIS, what reck I by thee,
  Or Geordie on his ocean:
Dyvor, beggar louns to me,
  I reign in Jeanie's bosom.

Let her crown my love her law,
  And in her breast enthrone me:
Kings and nations, swith awa!
  Reif randies I disown ye!—

* * * * *

VI. Poems 1789

ELLISLAND

249. *Sketch. New Year's Day. To Mrs. Dunlop*

THIS day, Time winds th' exhausted chain,
To run the twelvemonth's length again:—
I see the old, bald-pated fellow,
With ardent eyes, complexion sallow,
Adjust the unimpair'd machine,
To wheel the equal, dull routine.

The absent lover, minor heir,
In vain assail him with their prayer,
Deaf as my friend, he sees them press,
Nor makes the hour one moment less.
Will you (the Major 's with the hounds,
The happy tenants share his rounds;
Coila 's fair Rachel's care to day*,
And blooming Keith 's engaged with Gray;)
From housewife cares a minute borrow—
—That grandchild's cap will do to-morrow—
And join with me a moralizing,
This day 's propitious to be wise in.

First, what did yesternight deliver?
'Another year is gone for ever.'
And what is this day's strong suggestion?
'The passing moment 's all we rest on!'
Rest on—for what? what do we here?
Or why regard the passing year?

* This young lady was drawing a picture of Coila from *The Vision.*

Will time, amus'd with proverb'd lore,
Add to our date one minute more?
A few days may—a few years must—
Repose us in the silent dust.
Then is it wise to damp our bliss?
Yes—all such reasonings are amiss!
The voice of nature loudly cries,
And many a message from the skies,
That something in us never dies:
That on this frail, uncertain state,
Hang matters of eternal weight:
That future life in worlds unknown
Must take its hue from this alone;
Whether as heavenly glory bright,
Or dark as misery's woeful night—
Since then, my honor'd, first of friends,
On this poor being all depends;
Let us th' important *now* employ,
And live as those who never die.
Tho' you, with days and honors crown'd,
Witness that filial circle round,
(A sight life's sorrows to repulse,
A sight pale envy to convulse)
Others now claim your chief regard;
Yourself, you wait your bright reward.

250. *Elegy on the Year 1788*

FOR Lords or kings I dinna mourn,
E'en let them die—for that they're born!
But oh! prodigious to reflect,
A *Towmont*, Sirs, is gane to wreck!
O *Eighty-eight*, in thy sma' space
What dire events ha'e taken place!
Of what enjoyments thou hast reft us!
In what a pickle thou hast left us!

The Spanish empire 's tint a head,
An' my auld teethless Bawtie 's dead;
The toolzie 's teugh 'tween Pitt an' Fox,
An' our gudewife's wee birdy cocks;

The tane is game, a bluidy devil,
But to the *hen-birds* unco civil;
The tither 's dour, has nae sic breedin',
But better stuff ne'er claw'd a midden!

Ye ministers, come mount the pupit,
An' cry till ye be haerse an' rupit;
For *Eighty-eight* he wish'd you weel,
An' gied you a' baith gear an' meal;
E'en mony a plack, an' mony a peck,
Ye ken yoursels, for little feck!

Ye bonny lasses, dight your een,
For some o' you ha'e tint a frien';
In *Eighty-eight*, ye ken, was ta'en
What ye'll ne'er ha'e to gi'e again.

Observe the very nowt an' sheep,
How dowff an' dowie now they creep;
Nay, even the yirth itsel' does cry,
For Embro' wells are grutten dry.

O *Eighty-nine*, thou 's but a bairn,
An' no owre auld, I hope to learn!
Thou beardless boy, I pray tak' care,
Thou now has got thy Daddy's chair,
Nae hand-cuff'd, mizl'd, haff-shackl'd *Regent*,
But, like himsel', a full free agent.
Be sure ye follow out the plan
Nae war than he did, honest man!
As muckle better as you can.

January 1, 1789.

251. *Robin shure in hairst*

Chorus

ROBIN shure in hairst,
  I shure wi' him;
Fint a heuk had I,
  Yet I stack by him.

Song

I gaed up to Dunse,
  To warp a wab o' plaiden;
At his daddie's yet,
  Wha met me but Robin.
    Robin shure &c.

Was na Robin bauld,
  Tho' I was a cotter,
Play'd me sic a trick
  And me the Eller's dochter!
    Robin shure &c.

Robin promis'd me
  A' my winter vittle;
Fient haet he had but three
  Goos feathers and a whittle.
    Robin shure &c.

252. [*Come rede me, dame*]

To its ain tune—

I

'COME rede me, dame, come tell me, dame,
'My dame come tell me truly,
'What length o' graith, when weel ca'd hame,
'Will sair a woman duly?'
The carlin clew her wanton tail,
Her wanton tail sae ready—
I learn'd a sang in Annandale,
Nine inch will please a lady.—

2

But for a koontrie c–nt like mine,
In sooth, we're nae sae gentle;
We'll tak tway thumb-bread to the nine,
And that 's a sonsy p–ntle:
O Leeze me on my Charlie lad,
I'll ne'er forget my Charlie!
Tway roarin handfu's and a daud,
He nidge't it in fu' rarely.—

3

But weary fa' the laithron doup,
And may it ne'er be thrivin!
It 's no the length that maks me loup,
But it 's the double drivin.—
Come nidge me, Tam, come nudge me, Tam,
Come nidge me o'er the nyvel!
Come lowse and lug your battering ram,
And thrash him at my gyvel!

253. [*Caledonia*]

Tune—Caledonian Hunt's delight—

THERE was on a time, but old Time was then young,
That brave Caledonia, the chief of her line,
From some of your northern deities sprung,
(Who knows not that brave Caledonia 's divine)

From Tweed to the Orcades was her domain,
  To hunt, or to pasture, or do what she would;
Her heavenly relations there fixed her reign,
  And pledged their godheads to warrant it good.—

A lambkin in peace, but a lion in war,
  The pride of her kindred the Heroine grew;
Her grandsire, old Odin, triumphantly swore,
  'Who e'er shall provoke thee th' encounter shall rue!'
With tillage or pasture at times she would sport,
  To feed her fair flocks by her green-rustling corn;
But chiefly the woods were her fav'rite resort,
  Her darling amusement the hounds and the horn.—

Long quiet she reigned, till thitherward steers
  A flight of bold eagles from Adria's strand;
Repeated, successive, for many long years,
  They darkened the air and they plunder'd the land.
Their pounces were murder, and horror their cry,
  They'd ravag'd and ruin'd a world beside;
She took to her hills and her arrows let fly,
  The daring invaders they fled or they di'd.—

The Camelon Savage disturb'd her repose
  With tumult, disquiet, rebellion and strife;
Provok'd beyond bearing, at last she arose,
  And robb'd him at once of his hopes and his life.
The Anglian lion, the terror of France,
  Oft prowling ensanguin'd the Tweed's silver flood;
But taught by the bright Caledonian lance,
  He learned to fear in his own native wood.—

The fell Harpy-raven took wing from the North,
  The scourge of the seas and the dread of the shore;
The wild Scandinavian boar issu'd forth,
  To wanton in carnage and wallow in gore:
O'er countries and kingdoms their fury prevail'd,
  No arts could appease them, no arms could repel;
But brave Caledonia in vain they assail'd,
  As Largs well can witness, and Loncartie tell.—

Thus bold, independant, unconquer'd and free,
  Her bright course of glory for ever shall run;
For brave Caledonia immortal must be,
  I'll prove it from Euclid as clear as the sun:

Rectangle-triangle the figure we'll chuse,
  The Upright is Chance, and old Time is the Base;
But brave Caledonia 's the Hypothenuse,
  Then, Ergo, she'll match them, and match them always.

254. [*At Whigham's Inn, Sanquar*]

ENVY, if thy jaundiced eye,
Through this window chance to spy,
To thy sorrow thou shalt find,
All that 's generous, all that 's kind,
Friendship, virtue, every grace,
Dwelling in this happy place.

255. [*To William Stewart*]

Brownhill Monday even:
DEAR Sir,

IN honest Bacon's ingle-neuk,
  Here maun I sit and think;
Sick o' the warld and warld's fock,
  And sick, d–mn'd sick o' drink!

I see, I see there is nae help,
  But still down I maun sink;
Till some day, *laigh enough*, I yelp,
  'Wae worth that cursed drink!'

Yestreen, alas! I was sae fu',
  I could but yisk and wink;
And now, this day, sair, sair I rue,
  The weary, weary drink.—

Satan, I fear thy sooty claws,
  I hate thy brunstane stink,
And ay I curse the luckless cause,
  The wicked soup o' drink.—

In vain I would forget my woes
  In idle rhyming clink,
For past redemption d–mn'd in Prose
  I can do nought but drink.—

For you, my trusty, well-try'd friend,
May Heaven still on you blink;
And may your life flow to the end,
Sweet as a dry man's drink!

ROBT. BURNS.

256. [*Lines written in the Kirk of Lamington*]

As cauld a wind as ever blew;
A caulder kirk, and in 't but few;
As cauld a minister 's ever spak;
Ye 'se a' be het or I come back.

257. *Afton Water*

FLOW gently, sweet Afton, among thy green braes,
Flow gently, I'll sing thee a song in thy praise;
My Mary 's asleep by thy murmuring stream,
Flow gently, sweet Afton, disturb not her dream.

Thou stock dove whose echo resounds thro' the glen,
Ye wild whistling blackbirds in yon thorny den,
Thou green crested lapwing thy screaming forbear,
I charge you disturb not my slumbering Fair.

How lofty, sweet Afton, thy neighbouring hills,
Far mark'd with the courses of clear, winding rills;
There daily I wander as noon rises high,
My flocks and my Mary's sweet Cot in my eye.

How pleasant thy banks and green vallies below,
Where wild in the woodlands the primroses blow;
There oft as mild ev'ning weeps over the lea,
The sweet scented birk shades my Mary and me.

Thy chrystal stream, Afton, how lovely it glides,
And winds by the cot where my Mary resides;
How wanton thy waters her snowy feet lave,
As gathering sweet flowerets she stems thy clear wave.

Flow gently, sweet Afton, among thy green braes,
Flow gently, sweet River, the theme of my lays;
My Mary 's asleep by thy murmuring stream,
Flow gently, sweet Afton, disturb not her dream.

258. *Ode to the departed Regency-bill—1789*

DAUGHTER of Chaos' doting years,
Nurse of ten thousand hopes and fears;
Whether thy airy, unsubstantial Shade
(The rites of sepulture now duly paid)
  Spread abroad its hideous form
  On the roaring Civil Storm,
  Deafening din and warring rage
  Factions wild with factions wage;
Or underground, deep-sunk, profound,
  Among the demons of the earth,
With groans that make the mountains shake,
  Thou mourn thy ill-starred, blighted birth;
Or in the uncreated Void,
  Where seeds of future-being fight,
With lightened step thou wander wide,
  To greet thy Mother—Ancient Night,
  And as each jarring, monster mass is past,
  Fond recollect what once thou wast:

In manner due, beneath this sacred oak,
Hear, Spirit hear! thy presence I invoke!
By a Monarch's heaven-struck fate!
By a disunited State!
By a generous Prince's wrongs!
By a Senate's strife of tongues!
By a Premier's sullen pride,
Louring on the changing tide!
By dread Thurlow's powers to awe,
Rhetoric, blasphemy and law!
By the turbulent ocean,
A Nation's commotion!
By the harlot-caresses
Of borough-addresses!
By days few and evil!
Thy portion, poor devil!
By Power, Wealth, Show! the gods by men adored!
By Nameless Poverty! their hell abhorred!
By all they hope! By all they fear!
Hear!!! And Appear !!!

Stare not on me, thou ghastly Power;
Nor grim with chained defiance lour:
No Babel-structure would *I* build
Where, Order exiled from his native sway,
Confusion may the REGENT-sceptre wield,
While all would rule and none obey:
Go, to the world of Man relate
The story of thy sad, eventful fate;
And call Presumptuous Hope to hear,
And bid him check his blind career;
And tell the sore-prest Sons of Care,
Never, never to despair.—

Paint CHARLES's speed on wings of fire,
The object of his fond desire;
Beyond his boldest hopes, at hand:
Paint all the triumph of the Portland Band:
Mark how they lift the joy-exulting voice;
And how their numerous Creditors rejoice:
But just as hopes to warm enjoyment rise,
Cry, CONVALESCENCE! and the vision flies.—

Then next pourtray a darkening twilight gloom
  Eclipsing, sad, a gay, rejoicing morn,
While proud Ambition to th' untimely tomb
  By gnashing, grim, despairing fiends is borne:
Paint ruin, in the shape of high D——
  Gaping with giddy terror o'er the brow;
In vain he struggles, the Fates behind him press,
  And clamorous hell yawns for her prey below:
How fallen That, whose pride late scaled the skies!
And This, like Lucifer, no more to rise!
  Again pronounce the powerful word;
See Day, triumphant from the night, restored.—

Then know this truth, ye Sons of Men!
  (Thus end thy moral tale)
Your darkest terrors may be vain,
  Your brightest hopes may fail.—

259. *On Seeing a Wounded Hare limp by me, which a Fellow had just shot at*

INHUMAN man! curse on thy barb'rous art,
  And blasted be thy murder-aiming eye;
  May never pity soothe thee with a sigh,
Nor ever pleasure glad thy cruel heart!

Go live, poor wanderer of the wood and field,
  The bitter little that of life remains:
  No more the thickening brakes and verdant plains
To thee shall home, or food, or pastime yield.

Seek, mangled wretch, some place of wonted rest,
  No more of rest, but now thy dying bed!
  The sheltering rushes whistling o'er thy head,
The cold earth with thy bloody bosom prest.

Oft as by winding Nith I, musing, wait
  The sober eve, or hail the chearful dawn,
  I'll miss thee sporting o'er the dewy lawn,
And curse the ruffian's aim, and mourn thy hapless fate.

N

260. *A new Psalm for the Chapel of Kilmarnock, on the thanksgiving-day for his Majesty's recovery—*

O, SING a new Song to the L——!
  Make, all and every one,
A joyful noise, ev'n for the king
  His Restoration.—

The Sons of Belial in the land
  Did set their heads together;
Come, let us sweep them off, said they,
  Like an o'erflowing river.—

They set their heads together, I say,
  They set their heads together:
On right, and left, and every hand,
  We saw none to deliver.—

Thou madest strong two chosen Ones,
  To quell the Wicked's pride:
That Young Man, great in Issachar
  The burden-bearing Tribe.—

And him, among the Princes chief
  In our Jerusalem,
The Judge that 's mighty in thy law,
  The Man that fears thy name.—

Yet they, even they, with all their might,
  Began to faint and fail;
Even as two howling, ravening wolves
  To dogs do turn their tail:—

Th' Ungodly o'er the Just prevail'd,
  For so thou hadst appointed,
That thou might'st greater glory give
  Unto thine own Annointed.—

And now thou hast restor'd our State,
  Pity our kirk also,
For she by tribulations
  Is now brought very low!—

Consume that High-Place, PATRONAGE,
  From off thine holy hill;
And in thy fury burn the book
  Even of that man, M^c^GILL.—

Now hear our Prayer, accept our Song,
  And fight thy Chosen's battle:
We seek but little, L——, from thee,
  Thou kens we get as little.—

261. *To M^r^ M^c^Murdo, with a pound of Lundiefoot Snuff—*

O COULD I give thee India's wealth
  As I this trifle send!
Because thy joy in both would be—
  To share them with thy Friend.—

But Golden Sands, Alas, ne'er grace
  The Heliconian stream:
Then take, what Gold shall never buy—
  An honest Bard's esteem.—

262. *Sketch. Inscribed to The R^t^ Hon. Ch. J. Fox Esq.—*

HOW Wisdom and Folly meet, mix and unite;
How Virtue and Vice blend their black and their white;
How Genius, th' illustrious father of fiction,
Confounds rule and law, reconciles contradiction,
I sing; if these mortals, the Critics, should bustle,
I care not, not I, let the Critics go whistle!

But now for a Patron, whose name and whose glory
At once may illustrate and honour my story.—

Thou, first of our orators, first of our wits,
Yet whose parts and acquirements seem just lucky hits;
With knowledge so vast, and with judgement so strong,
No man, with the half of 'em, e'er could go wrong;

With passions so potent, and fancies so bright,
No man with the half of 'em e'er could go right;
A sorry, poor, misbegot son of the Muses,
For using thy name offers fifty excuses.—

Good l—d, what is man! for as simple he looks,
Do but try to develope his hooks and his crooks,
With his depths and his shallows, his good and his evil,
All in all, he 's a problem must puzzle the devil.—

On his one ruling Passion Sir Pope warmly labours,
That, like th' old Hebrew walking switch, eats up its neighbours;
Human nature 's his Show-box—your friend, would you know him?
Pull the string Ruling Passion, the picture will show him.—
What pity in rearing so beauteous a system,
One trifling particular, Truth, should have missed him!
For spite of his fine theoretic positions,
Mankind is a science defies definitions.—

Some sort all our qualities each to its tribe,
And think Human-nature they truly describe.
Have you found this or t'other! theres more in the wind,
As by one drunken fellow his comrades you'll find.—
But such is the flaw, or the depth of the plan
In the make of that wonderful creature called MAN,
No two virtues whatever relation they claim,
Nor even two different shades of the same,
Though like as was ever twin brother to brother,
Possessing the one must imply you've the other.—

But truce with abstraction, and truce with a muse,
Whose rhymes you'll perhaps, Sir, ne'er deign to peruse:
Will you leave your justings, your jars and your quarrels,
Contending with Billy for proud-nodding laurels?
(My much-honor'd Patron, believe your poor Poet,
Your courage much more than your prudence you show it;
In vain with Squire Billy for laurels you struggle,
He'll have them by fair trade, if not, he will smuggle;
Not cabinets even of kings would conceal 'em,
He'd up the back-stairs and by G— he would steal 'em!
Then feats like Squire Billy's you ne'er can atchieve 'em,
It is not, outdo him, the task is, outthieve him.)—

263. [*To Peter Stuart*]

DEAR Peter, dear Peter,
We poor sons of metre
Are often negleckit, ye ken;
For instance, your sheet, man,
(Tho' glad I'm to see 't, man),
I get it no ae day in ten.

R. B.

264. *The Kirk of Scotland's Garland— a new Song*

I

ORTHODOX, Orthodox, who believe in John Knox,
Let me sound an alarm to your conscience;
A heretic blast has been blawn i' the West—
That what is not Sense must be Nonsense, Orthodox,
That what is not Sense must be Nonsense.—

2

Doctor Mac*, Doctor Mac, ye should streek on a rack,
To strike Evildoers with terror;
To join FAITH and SENSE upon any pretence
Was heretic, damnable error, &c.

3

Town of Ayr, Town of Ayr, it was rash, I declare,
To meddle wi' mischief a brewing;
Provost John† is still deaf to the Church's relief,
And Orator Bob‡ is its ruin, &c.

4

D'rymple mild§, D'rymple mild, tho' your heart 's like a child,
And your life like the new-driven snaw;
Yet that winna save ye, auld Satan maun have ye,
For preaching that three 's ane and twa, &c.

* Doctor McGill, Ayr—
† Provost Ballantine—
‡ Mr Aiken—
§ Dr Dalrymple, Ayr—

5

Calvin's Sons, Calvin's Sons, seize your spiritual guns—
  Ammunition ye never can need;
Your HEARTS are the stuff will be POWDER enough,
  And your SCULLS are a storehouse o' LEAD, &c.

6

Rumble John*, Rumble John, mount the steps with a groan,
  Cry, the BOOK is with heresy cramm'd;
Then lug out your ladle, deal brimstone like aidle,
  And roar ev'ry note o' the D–MN'D, &c.

7

Simper James†, Simper James, leave the fair Killie dames,
  There 's a holier chase in your view:
I'll lay on your head that the PACK ye'll soon lead,
  For PUPPIES like you there 's but few, &c.

8

Singet Sawnie‡, Singet Sawnie, are ye herding the PENNIE,
  Unconscious what danger awaits?
With a jump, yell and howl, alarm ev'ry soul,
  For Hannibal 's just at your gates, &c.

9

Poet Willie§, Poet Willie, gie the Doctor a volley
  Wi' your 'liberty's chain' and your wit:
O'er Pegasus' side ye ne'er laid a stride,
  Ye only stood by where he sh—, &c.

10

Andréw Gowk||, Andrew Gowk, ye may slander the BOOK,
  And the BOOK nought the waur, let me tell ye:
Ye're rich and look big, but lay by hat and wig—
  And ye'll hae a CALF'S-HEAD o' sma' value, &c.

* John Russel, Kilmarnock— † Ja[s] M[c]Kindlay, Kilm[ck]—

‡ A. Moodie, Riccartoun—

§ Will[m] Peebles in Newton upon Ayr, a Poetaster, who, among many other things, published an Ode on the Centenary of the Revolution in which was this line—'And bound in liberty's endearing chain'—

|| D[r] Andrew Mitchel, Monkton—

11

Barr Steenie*, Barr Steenie, what mean ye, what mean ye?
If ye'll meddle nae mair wi' the matter,
Ye may hae some pretence, man, to havins and sense, man,—
Wi' people that ken you nae better, &c.

12

Jamie Goose†, Jamie Goose, ye hae made but toom roose
O' hunting the wicked Lieutenant;
But the Doctor 's your mark, for the L—d's holy ark
He has couper'd and ca'd a wrang pin in, &c.

13

Davie Rant‡, Davie Rant, wi' a face like a saunt,
And a heart that wad poison a hog;
Raise an impudent roar, like a breaker lee-shore,
Or the KIRK will be tint in a bog, &c.

14

Cessnock-side§, Cessnock-side, wi' your turkey-cock pride,
O' manhood but sma' is your share;
Ye've the figure, it 's true, even your faes maun allow,
And your friends dare na say ye hae mair, &c.

15

Muirland Jock||, Muirland Jock, whom the L—d made a rock
To crush Common sense for her sins;
If ill-manners were Wit, there 's no mortal so fit
To confound the poor Doctor at ance, &c.

16

Daddie Auld¶, Daddie Auld, there 's a tod i' the fauld,
A tod meikle waur than the CLERK:
Tho' ye do little skaith ye'll be in at the death,
For if ye canna bite ye can bark, &c.

* Stephen Young, Barr—

† Ja^{s} Young in New Cumnock, who had lately been foiled in an ecclesiastic prosecution against a Lieut^{t} Mitchel—

‡ Dav^{d} Grant, Ochiltree—

§ George Smith, Galston—

|| John Shepherd, Muirkirk—

¶ Willm Auld, Mauchlin; for the Clerk, See, Holy Willie's prayer—

17

Holy Will*, Holy Will, there was wit i' your skull,
When ye pilfer'd the alms o' the poor;
The timmer is scant, when ye're ta'en for a saint,
Wha should swing in a rape for an hour, &c.

18

Poet Burns, Poet Burns, wi' your priest-skelping turns,
Why desert ye your auld native shire?
Tho' your Muse is a gipsey, yet were she even tipsey,
She could ca' us nae waur than we are, Poet Burns,
She could ca' us nae waur than we are.—

[19*a*]

[Afton's Laird, Afton's Laird, when your pen can be spar'd,
A copy o' this I bequeath,
On the same sicker score as I mention'd before,
To that trusty auld Worthy, Clackleith, Afton's Laird,
To that trusty auld Worthy, Clackleith.]

[19*b*]

[Factor John, Factor John, whom the Lord made alone,
And ne'er made another thy peer,
Thy poor servant, the Bard, in respectful regard,
Presents thee this token sincere, Factor John,
Presents thee this token sincere.]

265. *To Mr Graham of Fintry, On being appointed to my Excise Division—*

I CALL no goddess to inspire my strains,
A fabled Muse may suit a Bard that feigns:
'Friend of my life!' my ardent spirit burns,
And all the tribute of my heart returns,
For boons accorded, goodness ever new,
The Gift still dearer, as the Giver YOU.—

* An E[lder] in M[auchlin]e—

Thou Orb of Day! Thou Other Paler Light!
And all ye many-sparkling Stars of Night!
If aught that Giver from my mind efface;
If I that Giver's bounty e'er disgrace;
Then roll, to me, along your wandering spheres,
Only to number out A VILLAIN'S YEARS!

I lay my hand upon my swelling breast,
And grateful would—but cannot speak the rest.—

266. *A Grace before dinner, Extempore*

O, THOU, who kindly dost provide
For every creature's want!
We bless thee, God of nature wide,
For all thy goodness lent:
And, if it please thee heavenly guide,
May never worse be sent;
But whether granted or denied,
Lord bless us with content!
Amen!!!

267. *Grace after Meat*

O THOU, in whom we live and move,
Who mad'st the sea and shore,
Thy goodness constantly we prove,
And grateful would adore.

And if it please thee, Pow'r above,
Still grant us with such store;
The *Friend* we *trust;* the *Fair* we *love;*
And we desire no more.

268. *Willie brew'd a peck o' maut*

O WILLIE brew'd a peck o' maut,
And Rob and Allan cam to see;
Three blyther hearts, that lee lang night,
Ye wad na found in Christendie.

Chorus

We are na fou, we're nae that fou,
But just a drappie in our e'e;
The cock may craw, the day may daw,
And ay we'll taste the barley bree.

Here are we met, three merry boys,
Three merry boys I trow are we;
And mony a night we've merry been,
And mony mae we hope to be!
Cho[s] We are na fou, &c.

It is the moon, I ken her horn,
  That 's blinkin in the lift sae hie;
She shines sae bright to wyle us hame,
  But by my sooth she'll wait a wee!
    Cho^{s} We are na fou, &c.

Wha first shall rise to gang awa,
  A cuckold, coward loun is he!
Wha first beside his chair shall fa',
  He is the king amang us three!
    Cho^{s} We are na fou, &c.

269. *The Five Carlins—A Ballad—Tune, Chevy chase*

Written during the contested Election between Sir James Johnston and Captn Miller for the Dumfries district of Boroughs.—

THERE was five Carlins in the South,
  They fell upon a scheme,
To send a lad to London town
  To bring them tidings hame.—

Not only bring them tidings hame,
  But do their errands there;
And aiblins gowd and honor baith
  Might be that laddie's share.—

There was Maggy by the banks o' Nith*,
  A dame wi' pride enough;
And Marjory o' the mony lochs†,
  A Carlin auld and teugh:

* Dumfries   † Lochmaben

And blinkin Bess of Annandale*
  That dwelt on Solway-side;
And Brandy Jean that took her gill†
  In Galloway sae wide:

And black Jöan frae Crighton-peel‡
  O' gipsey kith and kin:
Five wighter Carlins were na found
  The South Coontrie within.—

To send a lad to London town,
  They met upon a day;
And mony a knight and mony a laird
  That errand fain wad gae.—

O mony a knight and mony a laird
  That errand fain wad gae;
But nae ane could their fancy please,
  O ne'er a ane but tway.—

The first ane was a belted knight,
  Bred of a Border band,
And he wad gae to London town,
  Might nae man him withstand.—

And he wad do their errands weel,
  And meikle he wad say;
And ilka ane at London Court
  Wad bid to him, Gude-day!

The niest came in a Sodger-boy
  And spak wi' modest grace,
And he wad gang to London town,
  If sae their pleasure was.—

He wad na hecht them courtly gifts,
  Nor meikle speech pretend;
But he wad hecht an honest heart
  Wad ne'er desert his friend.—

Now wham to chuse, and wham refuse,
  At strife thir Carlins fell;
For some had Gentle Folk to please,
  And some wad please themsel.—

* Annan
† Kircudbright
‡ Sanquhar (Crighton old Castle, or, Peel—

Then up spak mim-mou'd Meg o' Nith,
  And she spak up wi' pride,
And she wad send the Sodger-lad
  Whatever might betide.—

For the Auld Gudeman o' London Court,
  She didna care a pin;
But she wad send the Sodger-lad,
  To greet his eldest son.—

Then started Bess of Annandale,
  A deadly aith she 's taen,
That she wad vote the Border-knight,
  Tho' she should vote her lane.—

'For far-off fowls hae feathers fair,
  'And fools o' change are fain;
'But I hae try'd this Border-knight,
  'I'll try him yet again.'—

Says black Jöan frae Crighton-peel,
  A Carlin stoor and grim;
'The Auld Gudeman, or the Young Gudeman,
  'For me may sink or swim.

'For fools will prate o' Right, and Wrang,
  'While knaves laugh them to scorn;
'But the Sodger's friends hae blawn the best,
  'So he shall bear the horn.'—

Then Brandy Jean spak o'er her drink,
  'Ye weel ken, kimmers a',
'The Auld Gudeman o' London Court,
  'His back 's been at the wa':

'And mony a friend that kiss'd his caup,
  'Is now a fremit wight;
'But it 's ne'er be sae wi' Brandy Jean,
  'We'll send the Border-knight.'—

Then slaw rase Marjory o' the lochs,
  And wrinkled was her brow;
Her ancient weed was russet-grey,
  Her auld Scots heart was true.—

'There 's some Great Folk set light by me,
'I set as light by them;
'But I will send to London town
'Whom I lo'e best at hame.'—

So how this weighty plea may end,
Nae mortal wight can tell:
God grant the king, and ilka man,
May look weel to themsel.—

270. *The Laddies by the Banks o' Nith*

Tune, Up and waur them a', Willie

THE Laddies by the banks o' Nith
Wad trust his Grace wi' a', Jamie;
But he'll sair them, as he sair'd the King—
Turn tail and rin awa, Jamie.

Up and waur them a', Jamie,
Up and waur them a';
The Johnstones hae the guidin o't,
Ye turncoat Whigs awa!

The Laddies by the Banks o' Nith. *Another version:*

As I cam doon the banks o' Nith
And by Glenriddell's ha', man,
There I heard a piper play
Turn-coat Whigs awa, man.

Drumlanrig's towers hae tint the powers
That kept the lands in awe, man:
The eagle 's dead, and in his stead
We've gotten a hoodie-craw, man.

The turn-coat Duke his King forsook,
When his back was at the wa', man:
The rattan ran wi' a' his clan
For fear the house should fa', man.

The lads about the banks o' Nith,
They trust his Grace for a', man:
But he'll sair them as he sair't his King,
Turn tail and rin awa, man.

The day he stude his country's friend,
  Or gied her faes a claw, Jamie,
Or frae puir man a blessin wan,
  That day the Duke ne'er saw, Jamie.
    Up and waur them, &c.

But wha is he, his country's boast?
  Like him there is na twa, Jamie;
There 's no a callant tents the kye,
  But kens o' Westerha', Jamie.
    Up and waur them, &c.

To end the wark, here 's Whistlebirk,
  Lang may his whistle blaw, Jamie;
And Maxwell true, o' sterling blue;
  And we'll be Johnstones a', Jamie.
    Up and waur them, &c.

271. *To Miss C*********, a very young Lady*

Written on the blank leaf of a Book, presented to her by the Author.

BEAUTEOUS rose-bud, young and gay,
Blooming on thy early May,
Never may'st thou, lovely Flower,
Chilly shrink in sleety shower!
Never Boreas' hoary path,
Never Eurus' pois'nous breath,
Never baleful stellar lights,
Taint thee with untimely blights!
Never, never reptile thief
Riot on thy virgin leaf!
Nor even Sol too fiercely view
Thy bosom blushing still with dew!

  Mayst thou long, sweet crimson gem,
Richly deck thy native stem;
Till some evening, sober, calm,
Dropping dews, and breathing balm,
While all around the woodland rings,
And every bird thy requiem sings;

Thou, amid the dirgeful sound,
Shed thy dying honours round,
And resign to Parent Earth
The loveliest form she e'er gave birth.

272. *The Whistle. A Ballad*

As the authentic *Prose* history of the WHISTLE is curious, I shall here give it.—In the train of Anne of Denmark, when she came to Scotland with our James the Sixth, there came over also a Danish gentleman of gigantic stature and great prowess, and a matchless champion of Bacchus. He had a little ebony Whistle, which, at the commencement of the orgies, he laid on the table; and whoever was last able to blow it, every body else being disabled by the potency of the bottle, was to carry off the Whistle as a trophy of victory.— The Dane produced credentials of his victories, without a single defeat, at the courts of Copenhagen, Stockholm, Moscow, Warsaw, and several of the petty courts in Germany; and challenged the Scots Bacchanalians to the alternative of trying his prowess, or else of acknowledging their inferiority. —After many overthrows on the part of the Scots, the Dane was encountered by Sir Robert Lowrie of Maxwelton, ancestor to the present worthy baronet of that name; who, after three days and three nights' hard contest, left the Scandinavian under the table, 'And blew on the Whistle his requiem shrill.'

Sir Walter, son to Sir Robert before mentioned, afterwards lost the Whistle to Walter Riddel of Glenriddel, who had married a sister of Sir Walter's.—On Friday, the 16th October 1789, at Friars-Carse, the Whistle was once more contended for, as related in the Ballad, by the present Sir Robert Lowrie of Maxwelton; Robert Riddel, Esq. of Glenriddel, lineal descendant and representative of Walter Riddel, who won the Whistle, and in whose family it had continued; and Alexander Ferguson, Esq. of Craigdarroch, likewise descended of the great Sir Robert, which last gentleman carried off the hard-won honours of the field.

I SING of a Whistle, a Whistle of worth,
I sing of a Whistle, the pride of the North,
Was brought to the court of our good Scottish king,
And long with this Whistle all Scotland shall ring.

Old Loda*, still rueing the arm of Fingal,
The god of the bottle sends down from his hall—
'This Whistle 's your challenge, to Scotland get o'er,
'And drink them to hell, Sir! or ne'er see me more!'

Old poets have sung, and old chronicles tell,
What champions ventured, what champions fell;
The son of great Loda was conqueror still,
And blew on the Whistle their requiem shrill.

Till Robert, the lord of the Cairn and the Scaur,
Unmatched at the bottle, unconquered in war,
He drank his poor god-ship as deep as the sea,
No tide of the Baltic e'er drunker than he.

Thus Robert, victorious, the trophy has gained,
Which now in his house has for ages remained;
Till three noble chieftains, and all of his blood,
The jovial contest again have renewed.

* See Ossian's Caric-thura.

Three joyous good fellows with hearts clear of flaw;
Craigdarroch so famous for wit, worth, and law;
And trusty Glenriddel, so skilled in old coins;
And gallant Sir Robert, deep-read in old wines.

Craigdarroch began with a tongue smooth as oil,
Desiring Glenriddel to yield up the spoil;
Or else he would muster the heads of the clan,
And once more, in claret, try which was the man.

'By the gods of the ancients!' Glenriddel replies,
'Before I surrender so glorious a prize,
'I'll conjure the ghost of the great Rorie More*,
'And bumper his horn with him twenty times o'er.'

Sir Robert, a soldier, no speech would pretend,
But he ne'er turned his back on his foe—or his friend,
Said, toss down the Whistle, the prize of the field,
And knee-deep in claret he'd die or he'd yield.

To the board of Glenriddel our heroes repair,
So noted for drowning of sorrow and care;
But for wine and for welcome not more known to fame,
Than the sense, wit, and taste of a sweet lovely dame.

A bard was selected to witness the fray,
And tell future ages the feats of the day;
A bard who detested all sadness and spleen,
And wished that Parnassus a vineyard had been.

The dinner being over, the claret they ply,
And every new cork is a new spring of joy;
In the bands of old friendship and kindred so set,
And the bands grew the tighter the more they were wet.

Gay Pleasure ran riot as bumpers ran o'er;
Bright Phoebus ne'er witnessed so joyous a corps,
And vowed that to leave them he was quite forlorn,
Till Cynthia hinted he'd see them next morn.

Six bottles a-piece had well wore out the night,
When gallant Sir Robert, to finish the fight,
Turned o'er in one bumper a bottle of red,
And swore 'twas the way that their ancestor did.

* See Johnson's tour to the Hebrides.

Then worthy Glenriddel, so cautious and sage,
No longer the warfare, ungodly, would wage;
A high ruling elder to wallow in wine!
He left the foul business to folks less divine.

The gallant Sir Robert fought hard to the end;
But who can with Fate and Quart Bumpers contend?
Though Fate said, a hero should perish in light;
So uprose bright Phoebus—and down fell the knight.

Next uprose our Bard, like a prophet in drink:—
'Craigdarroch, thou'lt soar when creation shall sink!
'But if thou would flourish immortal in rhyme,
'Come—one bottle more—and have at the sublime !

'Thy line, that have struggled for freedom with Bruce,
'Shall heroes and patriots ever produce:
'So thine be the laurel, and mine be the bay;
'The field thou hast won, by yon bright god of day!'

272A. [*Answer to an Invitation*]

THE King's most humble servant, I
Can scarcely spare a minute;
But I'll be wi' you by an' bye,
Or else the deil 's be in it.

273A. [*From Dr. Blacklock*]

Edinburgh, 24*th August*, 1789.

[DEAR Burns, thou brother of my heart,
Both for thy virtues and thy art;
If art it may be call'd in thee,
Which Nature's bounty large and free,
With pleasure on thy breast diffuses,
And warms thy soul with all the Muses.

72 *Additional stanza in the Alloway MS, presenting the poem to* Mr Cairns, Junr, of Torr, Dumfries:

But one sorry quill, and that worn to the core;
No Paper, but such as I shew it:
But such as it is, will the good laird of TORE
Accept, & excuse the poor POET.—

Whether to laugh with easy grace,
Thy numbers move the sage's face,
Or bid the softer passions rise,
And ruthless souls with grief surprise,
'Tis Nature's voice distinctly felt,
Thro' thee her organ, thus to melt.

Most anxiously I wish to know,
With thee of late how matters go;
How keeps thy much lov'd Jean her health?
What promises thy farm of wealth?
Whether the Muse persists to smile,
And all thy anxious cares beguile?
Whether bright fancy keeps alive?
And how thy darling infants thrive?

For me with grief and sickness spent,
Since I my journey homeward bent,
Spirits depress'd no more I mourn,
But vigour, life and health return.
No more to gloomy thoughts a prey,
I sleep all night, and live all day;
By turns my book and friend[s] enjoy,
And thus my circling hours employ;
Happy while yet these hours remain,
If Burns could join the cheerful train,
With wonted zeal, sincere and fervent,
Salute once more his humble servant,

THO. BLACKLOCK.]

273B. [*To Dr. Blacklock*]

My Rev^{d} and dear Friend

WOW, but your letter made me vauntie!
And are ye hale, and weel, and cantie?
I kend it still your wee bit jauntie
Wad bring ye to:
Lord send you ay as weel 's I want ye,
And then ye'll do.—

The *Ill-thief* blaw the *Heron* south!
And never drink be near his drouth!
He tald mysel, by word o' mouth,
He'd tak my letter;
I lippen'd to the chiel in trouth,
And bade nae better.—

But aiblins honest Master Heron
Had at the time some dainty *Fair One*,
To ware his theologic care on,
    And holy study:
And tired o' *Sauls* to waste his lear on,
    E'en tried the *Body*.—

But what d'ye think, my trusty Fier,
I'm turn'd a Gauger—Peace be here!
Parnassian *Quines* I fear, I fear,
    Ye'll now disdain me,
And then my fifty pounds a year
    Will little gain me.—

Ye glaiket, gleesome, dainty Damies,
Wha by Castalia's wimplin streamies
Lowp, sing, and lave your pretty limbies,
    Ye ken, Ye ken,
That strang Necessity supreme is
    'Mang sons o' Men.—

I hae a wife and twa wee laddies,
They maun hae brose and brats o' duddies;
Ye ken yoursels my heart right proud is,
    I need na vaunt;
But I'll sned boosoms and thraw saugh-woodies
    Before they want.—

Lord help me thro' this warld o' care!
I'm weary sick o't late and air!
No but I hae a richer share
    Than mony ithers;
But why should ae man better fare,
    And a' Men brithers!

Come, *Firm Resolve* take thou the van,
Thou stalk o' carl-hemp in man!
And let us mind, faint heart ne'er wan
    A lady fair:
Wha does the utmost that he can,
    Will whyles do mair.—

But to conclude my silly rhyme,
(I'm scant o' verse and scant o' time,)
To make a happy fireside clime
To weans and wife,
That 's the true *Pathos* and *Sublime*
Of Human life.—

My Compliments to Sister Beckie;
And eke the same to honest Lucky,
I wat she is a dainty Chuckie
As e'er tread clay!
And gratefully my gude auld Cockie
I'm yours for ay.—
ROB.T BURNS

Ellisland
21st Oct. 1789

274. *A Song*—

Captn Cook's death

I

THOU lingering Star with lessening ray
  That lovest to greet the early morn,
Again thou usherest in the day
  My Mary from my Soul was torn—
O Mary! dear, departed Shade!
  Where is thy place of blissful rest?
Seest thou thy Lover lowly laid?
  Hearest thou the groans that rend his breast?

2

That sacred hour can I forget,
  Can I forget the hallowed grove,
Where by the winding Ayr we met,
  To live one day of Parting Love?
Eternity can not efface
  Those records dear of transports past;
Thy image at our last embrace,
  Ah, little thought we 'twas our last!

3

Ayr gurgling kissed his pebbled shore,
  O'erhung with wild-woods, thick'ning, green;
The fragrant birch, and hawthorn hoar,
  Twined, am'rous, round the raptured scene:
The flowers sprang wanton to be prest,
  The birds sang love on ev'ry spray;
Till too, too soon the glowing west
  Proclaimed the speed of winged day.—

4

Still o'er these scenes my mem'ry wakes,
  And fondly broods with miser-care;
Time but th' impression stronger makes,
  As streams their channels deeper wear:
My Mary, dear, departed Shade!
  Where is thy place of blissful rest!
Seest thou thy Lover lowly laid!
  Hearest thou the groans that rend his breast!

275. *On the Late Captain Grose's Peregrinations thro' Scotland, collecting the Antiquities of that Kingdom*

HEAR, Land o' Cakes, and brither Scots,
Frae Maidenkirk to Johny Groats!—
If there 's a hole in a' your coats,
I rede you tent it:
A chield 's amang you, taking notes,
And, faith, he'll prent it.

If in your bounds ye chance to light
Upon a fine, fat, fodgel wight,
O' stature short, but genius bright,
That 's he, mark weel—
And wow! he has an unco slight
O' cauk and keel.

By some auld, houlet-haunted, biggin*,
Or kirk deserted by its riggin,
It 's ten to ane ye'll find him snug in
Some eldritch part,
Wi' deils, they say, L—d safe 's! colleaguin
At some black art.—

Ilk ghaist that haunts auld ha' or chamer,
Ye gipsy-gang that deal in glamor,
And you, deep-read in hell's black grammar,
Warlocks and witches;
Ye'll quake at his conjuring hammer,
Ye midnight b—es.

It 's tauld he was a sodger bred,
And ane wad rather fa'n than fled;
But now he 's quat the spurtle-blade,
And dog-skin wallet,
And taen the—*Antiquarian trade*,
I think they call it.

* Vide his Antiquities of Scotland.

He has a fouth o' auld nick-nackets:
Rusty airn caps and jinglin jackets*,
Wad haud the Lothians three in tackets,
A towmont gude;
And parritch-pats, and auld saut-backets,
Before the Flood.

Of Eve's first fire he has a cinder;
Auld Tubalcain's fire-shool and fender;
That which distinguished the gender
O' Balaam's ass;
A broom-stick o' the witch of Endor,
Weel shod wi' brass.

Forbye, he'll shape you aff fu' gleg
The cut of Adam's philibeg;
The knife that nicket Abel's craig
He'll prove you fully,
It was a faulding jocteleg,
Or lang-kail gullie.—

But wad ye see him in his glee,
For meikle glee and fun has he,
Then set him down, and twa or three
Gude fellows wi' him;
And *port, O port!* shine thou a wee,
And THEN ye'll see him!

Now, by the Powers o' Verse and Prose!
Thou art a dainty chield, O Grose!—
Whae'er o' thee shall ill suppose,
They sair misca' thee;
I'd take the rascal by the nose,
Wad say, Shame fa' thee.

276. *Written under the picture of the celebrated Miss Burns*

CEASE, ye prudes, your envious railing,
Lovely Burns has charms—*confess;*
True it is, she had one failing,
Had ae woman ever less?

* Vide his treatise on ancient armour and weapons.

277. *Song—*

Tune—Auld Sir Symon

I'LL tell you a tale of a Wife,
And she was a Whig and a Saunt;
She liv'd a most sanctify'd life,
But whyles she was fash'd wi' her —.—
Fal lal &c.

2

Poor woman! she gaed to the Priest,
And till him she made her complaint;
'There 's naething that troubles my breast
'Sae sair as the sins o' my —.—

3

'Sin that I was herdin at hame,
'Till now I'm three score and ayont,
'I own it wi' sin and wi' shame
'I've led a sad life wi' my —.—

4

He bade her to clear up her brow,
And no be discourag'd upon 't;
For holy gude women enow
Were mony times waur't wi' their —.—

Song. A stanza quoted casually in a letter to Ainslie, 29 July 1787, is apparently an alternative to ll. 41–4:

Then hey, for a merry good fellow,
And hey, for a glass of good strunt;
May never WE SONS OF APOLLO
E'er want a good friend and a —.

5

It 's naught but Beelzebub's art,
  But that 's the mair sign of a saunt,
He kens that ye 're pure at the heart,
  Sae levels his darts at your —.—

6

What signifies Morals and Works,
  Our works are no wordy a runt!
It 's Faith that is sound, orthodox,
  That covers the fauts o' your —.—

7

Were ye o' the Reprobate race
  Created to sin and be brunt,
O then it would alter the case
  If ye should gae wrang wi' your —.—

8

But you that is Called and Free
  Elekit and chosen a saunt,
Will 't break the Eternal Decree
  Whatever ye do wi' your —?—

9

And now with a sanctify'd kiss
  Let 's kneel and renew covenant:
It 's this—and it 's this—and it 's this—
  That settles the pride o' your —.—

10

Devotion blew up to a flame;
  No words can do justice upon 't;
The honest auld woman gaed hame
  Rejoicing and clawin her —.—

11

Then high to her memory charge;
  And may he who takes it affront,
Still ride in Love's channel at large,
  And never make port in a —!!!

278. *Prologue—*

No song nor dance I bring from yon great city,
That queens it o'er our taste—the more 's the pity:
Tho' by the bye, abroad why will you roam?
Good sense and taste are natives here at home;
But not for panegyric I appear,
I come to wish you all a good new year!
Old Father Time deputes me here before ye,
Not for to preach, but tell his simple story:
The sage grave ancient cough'd, and bade me say,
'You're one year older this important day,'
If *wiser too*—he hinted some suggestion,
But 'twould be rude, you know, to ask the question;
And with a would-be-roguish leer and wink,
He bade me on you press this one word—'THINK!'

Ye sprightly youths, quite flush with hope and spirit,
Who think to storm the world by dint of merit,
To you the dotard has a deal to say,
In his sly, dry, sententious, proverb way!
He bids you mind, amid your thoughtless rattle
That the first blow is ever half the battle;
That tho' some by the skirt may try to snatch him,
Yet by the forelock is the hold to catch him;
That whether doing, suffering, or forbearing,
You may do miracles by persevering.

Last, tho' not least in love, ye youthful fair,
Angelic forms, high Heaven's peculiar care!
To you old Bald-pate smooths his wrinkled brow,
And humbly begs you'll mind the important—Now!
To crown your happiness he asks your leave,
And offers, bliss to give and to receive.

For our sincere, tho' haply weak endeavours,
With grateful pride we own your many favors;
And howsoe'er our tongues may ill reveal it,
Believe our glowing bosoms truly feel it.

279. *Nithsdale's welcome hame—*

THE noble Maxwels and their powers
  Are coming o'er the border,
And they'll gae big Terreagles' towers
  And set them a' in order:
And they declare, Terreagles fair,
  For their abode they chuse it;
There 's no a heart in a' the land
  But 's lighter at the news o't.—

Tho' stars in skies may disappear,
  And angry tempests gather;
The happy hour may soon be near
  That brings us pleasant weather:
The weary night o' care and grief
  May hae a joyfu' morrow,
So dawning day has brought relief,
  Fareweel our night o' sorrow.—

280. *Green Sleeves—*

GREEN sleeves and tartan ties
Mark my truelove where she lies;
I'll be at her or she rise,
My fiddle and I thegither.—

Be it by the chrystal burn,
Be it by the milk-white thorn,
I shall rouse her in the morn,
My fiddle and I thegither.—

281. [*To Alexander Findlater*]

Ellisland Saturday morning

DEAR Sir,
our Lucky humbly begs
Ye'll prie her caller, new-laid eggs:
L—d grant the Cock may keep his legs,
Aboon the Chuckies;
And wi' his kittle, forket clegs,
Claw weel their dockies!

Had Fate that curst me in her ledger,
A Poet poor, and poorer Gager,
Created me that feather'd Sodger,
A generous Cock,
How I wad craw and strut and r–ger
My kecklin Flock!

Buskit wi' mony a bien, braw feather,
I wad defied the warst o' weather:
When corn or bear I could na gather
To gie my burdies;
I'd treated them wi' caller heather,
And weel-knooz'd hurdies

Nae cursed CLERICAL EXCISE
On honest Nature's laws and ties;
Free as the vernal breeze that flies
At early day,
We'd tasted Nature's richest joys,
But stint or stay.—

But as this subject 's something kittle,
Our wisest way 's to say but little;
And while my Muse is at her mettle,
I am, most fervent,
Or may I die upon a whittle!
Your Friend and Servant—
Robt Burns.

VII. Poems 1790

ELLISLAND

282. [*To a Gentleman who had sent him a News-paper, and offered to continue it free of expense*]

KIND Sir, I've read your paper through,
And faith, to me, 'twas really new!
How guessed ye, Sir, what maist I wanted?
This mony a day I've grain'd and gaunted,
To ken what French mischief was brewin;
Or what the drumlie Dutch were doin;
That vile doup-skelper, Emperor Joseph,
If Venus yet had got his nose off;
Or how the collieshangie works
Atween the Russians and the Turks;
Or if the Swede, before he halt,
Would play anither Charles the twalt:
If Denmark, any body spak o't;
Or Poland, wha had now the tack o't;
How cut-throat Prussian blades were hingin;
How libbet Italy was singin;
If Spaniard, Portuguese, or Swiss,
Were sayin or takin aught amiss:
Or how our merry lads at hame,
In Britain's court kept up the game:
How royal George, the Lord leuk o'er him!
Was managing St. Stephen's quorum;
If sleekit Chatham Will was livin,
Or glaikit Charlie got his nieve in;
How daddie Burke the plea was cookin,
If Warren Hastings' neck was yeukin;

How cesses, stents, and fees were rax'd,
Or if bare a—s yet were tax'd;
The news o' princes, dukes, and earls,
Pimps, sharpers, bawds, and opera-girls;
If that daft buckie, Geordie W***s,
Was threshin still at hizzies' tails,
Or if he was grown oughtlins douser,
And no a perfect kintra cooser,
A' this and mair I never heard of;
And but for you I might despair'd of.
So gratefu', back your news I send you,
And pray, a' gude things may attend you!

Ellisland, Monday morning

283. *Elegy on Peg Nicholson—*

Tune, Chevy Chase

PEG Nicholson was a good bay mare,
  As ever trode on airn;
But now she 's floating down the Nith,
  And past the Mouth o' Cairn.

Peg Nicholson was a good bay mare,
  And rode thro' thick and thin;
But now she 's floating down the Nith,
  And wanting even the skin.

Peg Nicholson was a good bay mare,
  And ance she bore a priest;
But now she 's floating down the Nith,
  For Solway fish a feast.

Peg Nicholson was a good bay mare,
  And the priest he rode her sair:
And much oppressed and bruised she was—
  As priest-rid cattle are, &c. &c.

284. *I love my Love in secret*

My Sandy gied to me a ring,
Was a' beset wi' diamonds fine;
But I gied him a far better thing,
I gied my heart in pledge o' his ring.

My Sandy O, my Sandy O,
My bony, bony Sandy O;
Tho' the love that I owe to thee I dare na show,
Yet I love my love in secret my Sandy O.

My Sandy brak a piece o' gowd,
While down his cheeks the saut tears row'd;
He took a hauf and gied it to me,
And I'll keep it till the hour I die.
My Sandy O &c.

285. *Tibbie Dunbar*

Tune Johny McGill

O WILT thou go wi' me, sweet Tibbie Dunbar;
O wilt thou go wi' me, sweet Tibbie Dunbar:
Wilt thou ride on a horse, or be drawn in a car,
Or walk by my side, O sweet Tibbie Dunbar.—

I care na thy daddie, his lands and his money;
I care na thy kin, sae high and sae lordly:
But say thou wilt hae me for better for waur,
And come in thy coatie, sweet Tibbie Dunbar.—

286. *The Taylor fell thro' the bed, &c.*

Beware of the ripells

THE Taylor fell thro' the bed, thimble an' a',
The Taylor fell thro' the bed thimble an' a';
The blankets were thin and the sheets they were sma',
The Taylor fell thro' the bed, thimble an' a'.

The sleepy bit lassie she dreaded nae ill,
The sleepy bit lassie she dreaded nae ill;
The weather was cauld and the lassie lay stili,
She thought that a Taylor could do her nae ill.

Gie me the groat again, cany young man,
Gie me the groat again, cany young man;
The day it is short and the night it is lang,
The dearest siller that ever I wan.

There 's somebody weary wi' lying her lane,
There 's somebody weary wi' lying her lane,
There 's some that are dowie, I trow wad be fain
To see the bit Taylor come skippin again.

287. *Ay waukin O*

SIMMER 's a pleasant time,
  Flowers of every colour;
The water rins o'er the heugh,
  And I long for my true lover!
    Chorus
  Ay waukin, Oh,
    Waukin still and weary:
  Sleep I can get nane,
    For thinking on my Dearie.—

When I sleep I dream,
  When I wauk I'm irie;
Sleep I can get nane,
  For thinking on my Dearie.—
    Ay waukin &c.

Lanely night comes on,
  A' the lave are sleepin:
I think on my bonie lad,
  And I bleer my een wi' greetin.—
      Ay waukin &c.

288. *Beware o' bonie Ann*

YE gallants bright I red you right,
  Beware o' bonie Ann;
Her comely face sae fu' o' grace,
  Your heart she will trepan.
Her een sae bright, like stars by night,
  Her skin is like the swan;
Sae jimply lac'd her genty waist,
  That sweetly ye might span.

Youth, grace and love attendant move,
  And pleasure leads the van:
In a' their charms and conquering arms,
  They wait on bonie Ann.

The captive bands may chain the hands,
  But loove enslaves the man:
Ye gallants braw, I red you a',
  Beware o' bonie Ann.

289. *My Wife's a wanton, wee thing*

MY wife 's a wanton, wee thing,
My wife 's a wanton, wee thing,
My wife 's a wanton, wee thing,
  She winna be guided by me.

She play'd the loon or she was married,
She play'd the loon or she was married,
She play'd the loon or she was married,
  She'll do it again or she die.

She sell'd her coat and she drank it,
She sell'd her coat and she drank it,
She row'd hersell in a blanket,
  She winna be guided for me.

She mind't na when I forbade her,
She mind't na when I forbade her,
I took a rung and I claw'd her,
  And a braw gude bairn was she.

290. [*Lassie lie near me*]

LANG hae we parted been,
  Lassie my dearie;
Now we are met again,
  Lassie lie near me.
    Cho:s Near me, near me,
      Lassie lie near me;
      Lang hast thou lien thy lane,
      Lassie lie near me.

A' that I hae endur'd,
  Lassie, my dearie,
Here in thy arms is cur'd,
  Lassie lie near me.
    Cho:s Near me, &c.

291. *The Gardener wi' his paidle—or, The Gardener's March—*

WHEN rosy May comes in wi' flowers
To deck her gay, green, spreading bowers;
Then busy, busy are his hours,
  The Gardener wi' his paidle.—

The chrystal waters gently fa';
The merry birds are lovers a';
The scented breezes round him blaw,
  The Gardener wi' his paidle.—

When purple morning starts the hare
To steal upon her early fare;
Then thro' the dews he maun repair,
  The Gardener wi' his paidle.—

When Day, expiring in the west,
The curtain draws of Nature's rest;
He flies to her arms he lo'es the best,
  The Gardener wi' his paidle.—

292. *On a bank of Flowers*

On a bank of flowers in a summer day,
  For summer lightly drest,
The youthful blooming Nelly lay,
  With love and sleep opprest.
When Willie wand'ring thro' the wood,
  Who for her favour oft had su'd;
He gaz'd, he wish'd, he fear'd, he blush'd,
  And trembled where he stood.

Her closed eyes like weapons sheath'd
  Were seal'd in soft repose;
Her lips, still as she fragrant breath'd
  It richer dy'd the rose.
The springing lilies sweetly prest,
  Wild, wanton kiss'd her rival breast;
He gaz'd, he wish'd, he fear'd, he blush'd,
  His bosom ill at rest.

Her robes light waving in the breeze,
  Her tender limbs embrace;
Her lovely form, her native ease,
  All harmony and grace:

Tumultuous tides his pulses roll,
  A faltering, ardent kiss he stole;
He gaz'd, he wish'd, he fear'd, he blush'd,
  And sigh'd his very soul.

As flies the partridge from the brake
  On fear-inspired wings,
So Nelly starting, half-awake,
  Away affrighted springs:
But Willy follow'd,—as he should,
  He overtook her in the wood;
He vow'd, he pray'd, he found the maid
  Forgiving all and good.

293. *My love she 's but a lassie yet—*

My love she 's but a lassie yet,
My love she 's but a lassie yet;
We'll let her stand a year or twa,
  She'll no be half sae saucy yet.—

I rue the day I sought her O,
I rue the day I sought her O,
Wha gets her needs na say he 's woo'd,
  But he may say he 's bought her O.—

Come draw a drap o' the best o't yet,
Come draw a drap o' the best o't yet:
Gae seek for Pleasure whare ye will,
  But here I never misst it yet.—

We're a' dry wi' drinking o't,
We're a' dry wi' drinking o't:
The minister kisst the fidler's wife,
  He could na preach for thinkin o't.—

294. *Cauld frosty morning*

'TWAS past ane o'clock in a cauld frosty morning,
  When cankert November blaws over the plain,
I heard the kirk-bell repeat the loud warning,
  As, restless, I sought for sweet slumber in vain:

Then up I arose, the silver moon shining bright;
  Mountains and valleys appearing all hoary white;
Forth I would go, amid the pale, silent night,
  And visit the Fair One, the cause of my pain.—

Sae gently I staw to my lovely Maid's chamber,
  And rapp'd at her window, low down on my knee;
Begging that she would awauk from sweet slumber,
  Awauk from sweet slumber and pity me:
For, that a stranger to a' pleasure, peace and rest,
  Love into madness had fired my tortur'd breast;
And that I should be of a' men the maist unblest,
  Unless she would pity my sad miserie!

My True-love arose and whispered to me,
  (The moon looked in, and envy'd my Love's charms;)
'An innocent Maiden, ah, would you undo me!'
  I made no reply, but leapt into her arms:
Bright Phebus peep'd over the hills and found me there;
  As he has done, now, seven lang years and mair:
A faithfuller, constanter, kinder, more loving Pair,
  His sweet-chearing beam nor enlightens nor warms.

295. *Jamie come try me*

JAMIE come try me,
  Jamie come try me,
If thou would win my love
  Jamie come try me.

If thou should ask my love,
Could I deny thee?
If thou would win my love,
Jamie come try me.

If thou should kiss me, love,
Wha could espy thee?
If thou wad be my love,
Jamie come try me.
Jamie come &c.

296. *The Captain's Lady*

Mount your baggage

O MOUNT and go,
Mount and make you ready,
O mount and go,
And be the Captain's Lady.

When the drums do beat,
And the cannons rattle,
Thou shalt sit in state,
And see thy love in battle.
Cho:[s] O mount and go &c.

When the vanquish'd foe
Sues for peace and quiet,
To the shades we'll go
And in love enjoy it.
Cho:[s] O Mount &c.

297. *Johnie Cope*

SIR John Cope trode the north right far,
Yet ne'er a rebel he cam naur,
Until he landed at Dunbar
Right early in a morning.
  Hey Johnie Cope are ye wauking yet,
  Or are ye sleeping I would wit;
  O haste ye get up for the drums do beat,
  O fye Cope rise in the morning.

He wrote a challenge from Dunbar,
Come fight me Charlie an ye daur;
If it be not by the chance of war
I'll give you a merry morning.
  Hey Johnie Cope &c.

When Charlie look'd the letter upon
He drew his sword the scabbard from—
'So Heaven restore to me my own,
'I'll meet you, Cope, in the morning.'
  Hey Johnie Cope &c.

Cope swore with many a bloody word
That he would fight them gun and sword,
But he fled frae his nest like an ill scar'd bird,
And Johnie he took wing in the morning.
Hey Johnie Cope &c.

It was upon an afternoon,
Sir Johnie march'd to Preston town;
He says, my lads come lean you down,
And we'll fight the boys in the morning.
Hey Johnie Cope &c.

But when he saw the Highland lads
Wi' tartan trews and white cokauds,
Wi' swords and guns and rungs and gauds,
O Johnie he took wing in the morning.
Hey Johnie Cope &c.

On the morrow when he did rise,
He look'd between him and the skies;
He saw them wi' their naked thighs,
Which fear'd him in the morning.
Hey Johnie Cope &c.

O then he flew into Dunbar,
Crying for a man of war;
He thought to have pass'd for a rustic tar,
And gotten awa in the morning.
Hey Johnie Cope &c.

Sir Johnie into Berwick rade,
Just as the devil had been his guide;
Gien him the warld he would na stay'd
To foughten the boys in the morning.
Hey Johnie Cope &c.

Says the Berwickers unto Sir John,
O what's become of all your men,
In faith, says he, I dinna ken,
I left them a' this morning.
Hey Johnie Cope &c.

Says Lord Mark Car, ye are na blate,
To bring us the news o' your ain defeat;
I think you deserve the back o' the gate,
Get out o' my sight this morning.
  Hey Johnie Cope &c.

298. [*O dear Minny, what shall I do?*]

O DEAR minny, what shall I do?
O dear minny, what shall I do?
O dear minny, what shall I do?
Daft thing, doylt thing, do as I do.—

If I be black, I canna be lo'ed;
If I be fair, I canna be gude;
If I be lordly, the lads will look by me:
O dear minny, what shall I do.—
  O dear minny &c.

299. [*Carl an the king come*]

Chorus

CARL an the king come,
Carl an the king come;
Thou shalt dance and I will sing,
Carl an the king come.

An somebodie were come again,
Then somebodie maun cross the main,
And every man shall hae his ain,
Carl an the king come.
  Cho[s] Carl an &c.

I trow we swapped for the warse,
We gae the boot and better horse;
And that we'll tell them at the cross,
Carl and the king come.
  Cho[s] Carl an &c.

Coggie an the king come,
Coggie an the king come,
I'se be fou and thou 'se be toom,
Coggie an the king come.
  Cho[s] Coggie an &c.

300. *There's a youth in this City*

A Gaelic Air

I

THERE 's a youth in this city, it were a great pity
  That he from our lasses should wander awa;
For he 's bony and braw, weel-favour'd with a',
  And his hair has a natural buckle and a'.—
His coat is the hue of his bonnet sae blue;
  His facket is white as the new-driven snaw;
His hose they are blae, and his shoon like the slae;
  And his clear siller buckles they dazzle us a'.—

2

For beauty and fortune the laddie 's been courtin;
  Weel-featur'd, weel-tocher'd, weel-mounted and braw;
But chiefly the siller, that gars him gang till her;
  The Pennie 's the jewel that beautifies a'.—
There 's Meg wi' the mailin that fain wad a haen him;
  And Susie whase daddy was laird o' the Ha':
There 's lang-tocher'd Nancy maist fetters his fancy—
  But th' laddie's dear sel he lo'es dearest of a'.—

301. *My heart 's in the Highlands*

Tune, Failte na miosg

My heart 's in the Highlands, my heart is not here;
My heart 's in the Highlands a chasing the deer;
Chasing the wild deer, and following the roe;
My heart 's in the Highlands, wherever I go.—

Farewell to the Highlands, farewell to the North;
The birth-place of Valour, the country of Worth:
Wherever I wander, wherever I rove,
The hills of the Highlands for ever I love.—

Farewell to the mountains high cover'd with snow;
Farewell to the Straths and green vallies below:
Farewell to the forests and wild-hanging woods;
Farewell to the torrents and loud-pouring floods.—

My heart 's in the Highlands, my heart is not here,
My heart 's in the Highlands a chasing the deer:
Chasing the wild deer, and following the roe;
My heart 's in the Highlands, wherever I go.—

302. *John Anderson my Jo*

JOHN Anderson my jo, John,
  When we were first acquent;
Your locks were like the raven,
  Your bony brow was brent;
But now your brow is beld, John,
  Your locks are like the snaw;
But blessings on your frosty pow,
  John Anderson my Jo.

John Anderson my jo, John,
  We clamb the hill the gither;
And mony a canty day, John,
  We've had wi' ane anither:
Now we maun totter down, John,
  And hand in hand we'll go;
And sleep the gither at the foot,
  John Anderson my Jo.

303. *Awa whigs awa*

AWA whigs awa,
Awa whigs awa,
Ye're but a pack o' traitor louns,
Ye'll do nae gude at a'.

Our thrissles flourish'd fresh and fair,
And bonie bloom'd our roses;
But whigs cam like a frost in June,
And wither'd a' our posies.
Cho.s Awa whigs &c.

Our ancient crown 's fa'n in the dust;
Deil blin' them wi' the stoure o't,
And write their names in his black beuk
Wha gae the whigs the power o't!
Cho.s Awa whigs &c.

Our sad decay in church and state
Surpasses my descriving:
The whigs cam o'er us for a curse,
And we hae done wi' thriving.
Cho.s Awa whigs &c.

Grim Vengeance lang has taen a nap,
But we may see him wauken:
Gude help the day when royal heads
Are hunted like a maukin.
Cho.s Awa whigs &c.

304. *I'll mak you be fain to follow me*

As late by a sodger I chanced to pass,
I heard him a courtin a bony young lass;
My hinny, my life, my dearest, quo he,
I'll mak you be fain to follow me.
Gin I should follow you, a poor sodger lad,
Ilk ane o' my cummers wad think I was mad;
For battles I never shall lang to see,
I'll never be fain to follow thee.

To follow me, I think ye may be glad,
A part o' my supper, a part o' my bed,
A part o' my bed, wherever it be,
I'll mak you be fain to follow me.
Come try my knapsack on your back,
Alang the king's high-gate we'll pack;
Between Saint Johnston and bony Dundee,
I'll mak you be fain to follow me.

305. *Merry hae I been teethin a heckle*

Tune, Boddich na' mbrigs, or Lord Breadalbine's March

O MERRY hae I been teethin a heckle,
  An' merry hae I been shapin a spoon:
O merry hae I been cloutin a kettle,
  An' kissin my Katie when a' was done.
O, a' the lang day I ca' at my hammer,
  An' a' the lang day I whistle and sing;
O, a' the lang night I cuddle my kimmer,
  An' a' the lang night as happy 's a king.

Bitter in dool I lickit my winnins
  O' marrying Bess, to gie her a slave:
Blest be the hour she cool'd in her linnens,
  And blythe be the bird that sings on her grave!
Come to my arms, my Katie, my Katie,
  An' come to my arms and kiss me again!
Druken or sober, here 's to thee, Katie!
  And blest be the day I did it again.

306. *The White Cockade*

My love was born in Aberdeen,
The boniest lad that e'er was seen,
But now he makes our hearts fu' sad,
He takes the field wi' his White Cockade.

O he 's a ranting, roving lad,
He is a brisk an' a bonny lad,
Betide what may, I will be wed,
And follow the boy wi' the White Cockade.

I'll sell my rock, my reel, my tow,
My gude gray mare and hawkit cow;
To buy mysel a tartan plaid,
To follow the boy wi' the White Cockade.
Cho^s O he 's a ranting, roving lad.

307. *My Eppie*

Chorus

An O, my Eppie,
My Jewel, my Eppie!
Wha wad na be happy
  Wi' Eppie Adair!

I

By Love, and by Beauty;
By Law, and by Duty;
I swear to be true to
  My Eppie Adair!

2

A' Pleasure exile me;
Dishonour defile me,
If e'er I beguile thee,
  My Eppie Adair!

308. *The Battle of Sherra-moor*

Tune, Cameronian Rant

O CAM ye here the fight to shun,
  Or herd the sheep wi' me, man,
Or were ye at the Sherra-moor,
  Or did the battle see, man.
I saw the battle sair and teugh,
And reekin-red ran mony a sheugh,
My heart for fear gae sough for sough,
To hear the thuds, and see the cluds
O' Clans frae woods, in tartan duds,
Wha glaum'd at kingdoms three, man.
        Cho[s] la la la, &c.

The red-coat lads wi' black cockauds
  To meet them were na slaw, man,
They rush'd, and push'd, and blude outgush'd,
  And mony a bouk did fa', man:
The great Argyle led on his files,
I wat they glanc'd for twenty miles,
They hough'd the Clans like nine-pin kyles,

They hack'd and hash'd while braid swords clash'd,
And thro' they dash'd, and hew'd and smash'd,
Till fey men di'd awa, man.
Cho[s] la la la, &c.

But had ye seen the philibegs
And skyrin tartan trews, man,
When in the teeth they dar'd our Whigs,
And covenant Trueblues, man;
In lines extended lang and large,
When baiginets o'erpower'd the targe,
And thousands hasten'd to the charge;
Wi' Highland wrath they frae the sheath
Drew blades o' death, till out o' breath
They fled like frighted dows, man.
Cho[s] la la la, &c.

O how deil Tam can that be true,
The chace gaed frae the north, man;
I saw mysel, they did pursue
The horse-men back to Forth, man;
And at Dunblane in my ain sight
They took the brig wi' a' their might,
And straught to Stirling wing'd their flight,
But, cursed lot! the gates were shut
And mony a huntit, poor Red-coat
For fear amaist did swarf, man.
Cho[s] la la la, &c.

My sister Kate cam up the gate
Wi' crowdie unto me, man;
She swoor she saw some rebels run
To Perth and to Dundee, man:
Their left-hand General had nae skill;
The Angus lads had nae gude will,
That day their neebour's blude to spill;
For fear by foes that they should lose
Their cogs o' brose, they scar'd at blows
And hameward fast did flee, man.
Cho[s] la la la, &c.

They've lost some gallant gentlemen
Amang the Highland clans, man;
I fear my Lord Panmuir is slain,
Or in his en'mies hands, man:

Now wad ye sing this double flight,
Some fell for wrang and some for right,
And mony bade the warld gudenight;
Say pell and mell, wi' muskets knell
How Tories fell, and Whigs to h–ll
Flew off in frighted bands, man.
Cho.[s] la la la, &c.

309. *Sandy and Jockie*

TWA bony lads were Sandy and Jockie;
Jockie was lo'ed but Sandy unlucky;
Jockie was laird baith of hills and of vallies,
But Sandy was nought but the king o' gude fellows.

Jockie lo'ed Madgie, for Madgie had money,
And Sandie lo'ed Mary, for Mary was bony:
Ane wedded for Love, ane wedded for treasure,
So Jockie had siller, and Sandy had pleasure.

310. *Young Jockey was the blythest lad*

Young Jockey was the blythest lad
  In a ' our town or here awa;
Fu' blythe he whistled at the gaud,
  Fu' lightly danc'd he in the ha'.
He roos'd my een sae bonie blue,
  He roos'd my waist sae genty sma;
An ay my heart came to my mou,
  When ne'er a body heard or saw.

My Jockey toils upon the plain
  Thro' wind and weet, thro' frost and snaw;
And o'er the lee I leuk fu' fain
  When Jockey 's owsen hameward ca'.

An ay the night comes round again
  When in his arms he taks me a';
An ay he vows he'll be my ain
  As lang 's he has a breath to draw.

311. *A waukrife Minnie*

WHARE are you gaun, my bony lass,
  Whare are you gaun, my hiney.
She answer'd me right saucilie,
  An errand for my minnie.

O whare live ye, my bony lass,
  O whare live ye, my hiney.
By yon burn-side, gin ye maun ken,
  In a wee house wi' my minnie.

But I foor up the glen at e'en,
  To see my bony lassie;
And lang before the grey morn cam,
  She was na hauf sae saucey.

O weary fa' the waukrife cock,
  And the foumart lay his crawin!
He wauken'd the auld wife frae her sleep,
  A wee blink or the dawin.

An angry wife I wat she raise,
  And o'er the bed she brought her;
And wi' a meikle hazel rung
  She made her a weel pay'd dochter.

O fare thee weel, my bony lass!
  O fare thee weel, my hinnie!
Thou art a gay and a bony lass,
  But thou has a waukrife minnie.

312. *Song*

Tune, For a' that an' a' that

THO' women's minds, like winter winds,
May shift, and turn an' a' that,
The noblest breast adores them maist,
A consequence I draw that.

Chorus

For a' that, an' a' that,
An' twice as meikle 's a' that,
My dearest bluid to do them guid,
They're welcome till 't for a' that.

Great love I bear to all the Fair,
Their humble slave an' a' that;
But lordly WILL, I hold it still
A mortal sin to thraw that.
For a' that, &c.

In rapture sweet this hour we meet,
Wi' mutual love an' a' that,
But for how lang the flie may stang,
Let Inclination law that.
For a' that, &c.

Their tricks and craft hae put me daft,
They've taen me in, an' a' that,
But clear your decks, and here 's, the SEX!
I like the jads for a' that!
For a' that, an' a' that!
An' twice as meikle 's a' that,
My dearest bluid to do them guid,
They're welcome till 't for a' that.

313. *Killiecrankie*

WHARE hae ye been sae braw, lad!
  Whare hae ye been sae brankie O?
Whare hae ye been sae braw, lad?
  Cam ye by Killiecrankie O?

An ye had been whare I hae been,
  Ye wad na been sae cantie O;
An ye had seen what I hae seen,
  I' th' braes o' Killiecrankie O.

I faught at land, I faught at sea,
  At hame I faught my Auntie, O;
But I met the Devil and Dundee
  On th' braes o' Killiecrankie, O.
    An ye had been, &c.

The bauld Pitcur fell in a furr,
  An' Clavers gat a clankie, O;
Or I had fed an Athole Gled
  On th' braes o' Killiecrankie, O.
    An ye had been, &c.

314. *The Campbells are comin*

THE Campbells are comin, Oho, Oho!
The Campbells are comin, Oho, Oho!
The Campbells are comin to bonie Lochleven,
The Campbells are comin Oho, Oho!

Upon the Lomonds I lay, I lay,
Upon the Lomonds I lay, I lay,
I looked down to bonie Lochleven,
And saw three bonie perches play—
The Campbells &c.

Great Argyle he goes before,
He maks his cannons and guns to roar,
Wi' sound o' trumpet, pipe and drum
The Campbells are comin Oho, Oho!
The Campbells are &c.

The Campbells they are a' in arms
Their loyal faith and truth to show,
Wi' banners rattling in the wind
The Campbells are comin Oho, Oho!

The Campbells are comin. Note in Scots Musical Museum, Index Said to be composed on the imprisonment of Mary Queen of Scots in Lochleven Castle.

315. *Scots Prologue*, For Mrs. Sutherland's Benefit Night, *Spoken at the Theatre Dumfries*

WHAT needs this din about the town o' Lon'on?
How this new Play, and that new Sang is comin?
Why is outlandish stuff sae meikle courted?
Does Nonsense mend, like Brandy, when imported—
Is there nae Poet, burning keen for Fame,
Will bauldly try to gie us Plays at hame?
For Comedy abroad he need na toil,
A Knave an' Fool are plants of ev'ry soil:
Nor need he hunt as far as Rome or Greece,
To gather matter for a serious piece;
There 's themes enow in Caledonian story,
Wad shew the Tragic Muse in a' her glory.
Is there no daring Bard will rise and tell
How glorious Wallace stood, how hapless fell?
Where are the Muses fled, that should produce
A *drama* worthy of the name of Bruce?
How on *this* spot he first unsheath'd the sword
'Gainst mighty England and her guilty Lord,
And after many a bloody, deathless doing,
Wrench'd his dear country from the jaws of Ruin!
O! for a Shakespeare or an Otway scene,
To paint the lovely hapless Scottish Queen!
Vain ev'n the omnipotence of Female charms,
'Gainst headlong, ruthless, mad Rebellion's arms.
She fell—but fell with spirit truly Roman,
To glut that direst foe,—*a vengeful woman;*
A *woman*—tho' the phrase may seem uncivil,
As able—and as wicked as the devil!
[One Douglas lives in Home's immortal page,
But Douglases were heroes every age:
And tho' your fathers, prodigal of life,
A Douglas followed to the martial strife,
Perhaps, if bowls row right, and Right succeeds,
Ye yet may follow where a Douglas leads!]

As ye have generous done, if a' the land
Would take the Muses' servants by the hand,
Not only hear—but patronise—defend them,
And where ye justly can commend—commend them;

And aiblins when they winna stand the test,
Wink hard and say, 'The folks hae done their best.'
Would a' the land do this, then I'll be caition,
Ye'll soon hae Poets o' the Scottish nation,
Will gar Fame blaw until her trumpet crack,
And warsle Time, and lay him on his back.

For us and for our Stage, should ony spier,
'Whase aught thae Chiels maks a' this bustle here?'
My best leg foremost, I'll set up my brow,
We have the honor to belong to you!
We're your ain bairns, e'en guide us as ye like,
But, like guid mothers, shore before ye strike;
And grateful still, I trust, ye'll ever find us:
For gen'rous patronage, and meikle kindness,
We've got frae a' professions, sorts, an' ranks:
God help us!—we're but poor—ye 'se get but thanks!

316. *Lament of Mary Queen of Scots on the Approach of Spring*

Now Nature hangs her mantle green
  On every blooming tree,
And spreads her sheets o' daisies white
  Out o'er the grassy lea:
Now Phœbus chears the crystal streams,
  And glads the azure skies;
But nought can glad the weary wight
  That fast in durance lies.

Now laverocks wake the merry morn,
  Aloft on dewy wing;
The merle, in his noontide bower,
  Makes woodland echoes ring;
The mavis mild wi' many a note,
  Sings drowsy day to rest:
In love and freedom they rejoice,
  Wi' care nor thrall opprest.

Now blooms the lily by the bank,
  The primrose down the brae;
The hawthorn 's budding in the glen,
  And milk-white is the slae:
The meanest hind in fair Scotland
  May rove their sweets amang;
But I, the Queen of a' Scotland,
  Maun lie in prison strang.

I was the Queen o' bonie France,
  Where happy I hae been;
Fu' lightly rase I on the morn,
  As blythe lay down at e'en:
And I'm the sovereign of Scotland,
  And mony a traitor there;
Yet here I lie in foreign bands,
  And never ending care.

But as for thee, thou false woman,
  My sister and my fae,
Grim vengeance, yet, shall whet a sword
  That thro' thy soul shall gae:
The weeping blood in woman's breast
  Was never known to thee;
Nor th' balm that draps on wounds of woe
  Frae woman's pitying e'e.

My son! my son! may kinder stars
  Upon thy fortune shine!
And may those pleasures gild thy reign,
  That ne'er wad blink on mine!
God keep thee frae thy mother's faes,
  Or turn their hearts to thee:
And where thou meet'st thy mother's friend,
  Remember him for me!

O! soon, to me, may summer-suns
  Nae mair light up the morn!
Nae mair, to me, the autumn winds
  Wave o'er the yellow corn!
And in the narrow house o' death
  Let winter round me rave;
And the next flowers, that deck the spring,
  Bloom on my peaceful grave.

317. *Song—*

Tune, Cornwallis lament for Coln! Moorhouse

SENSIBILITY how charming,
  Dearest Nancy, thou canst tell;
But distress with horrors arming,
  Thou hast also known too well.—

Fairest flower, behold the lily,
  Blooming in the sunny ray.
Let the blast sweep o'er the valley,
  See it prostrate on the clay.—

Hear the woodlark charm the forest,
  Telling o'er his little joys:
Hapless bird! a prey the surest
  To each pirate of the skies.—

Dearly bought the hidden treasure,
  Finer Feelings can bestow:
Chords that vibrate sweetest pleasure,
  Thrill the deepest notes of woe.—

318. *Epistle to Rob*t *Graham Esq: of Fintry on the Election for the Dumfries string of Boroughs, Anno 1790—*

FINTRY, my stay in worldly strife,
Friend o' my Muse, Friend o' my Life,
    Are ye as idle 's I am?
Come then, wi' uncouth, kintra fleg,
O'er Pegasus I'll fling my leg,
    And ye shall see me try him.—

I'll sing the zeal Drumlanrig bears,
Wha left the all-important cares
    Of fiddles, wh–res and hunters;
And, bent on buying Borough-towns,
Cam shaking hands wi' wabster-louns,
    And kissin barefit bunters.—

Confusion thro' our Boroughs rode,
Whistling his roaring pack abroad
    Of mad, unmuzzled lions;
As Queensberry BUFF AND BLUE unfurled,
And Westerha and Hopeton hurled
    To every whig defiance.—

But cautious Queensberry left the war,
Th' unmanner'd dust might soil his star,
    Besides, he hated *Bleeding*:
But left behind him heroes bright,
Heroes in Cesarean fight,
    Or Ciceronian pleading.—

O, for a throat like huge Monsmeg,
To muster o'er each ardent Whig,
    Beneath Drumlanrig's banner!
Heroes and heroines commix,
All in the field of Politics
    To win immortal honor.—

Mcmurdo* and his lovely Spouse,
(Th' enamour'd laurels kiss her brows)
Led on the Loves and Graces:
She won each gaping Burgess' heart,
While he, sub rosa, play'd his part
Among their wives and lasses.—

Craigdarroch led a light-arm'd Core,
Tropes, metaphors and figures pour
Like Hecla streaming thunder:
Glenriddel†, skill'd in rusty coins,
Blew up each Tory's dark designs,
And bar'd the treason under.—

In either wing two champions fought;
Redoubted STAIG‡, who set at nought
The wildest savage Tory:
While WELSH§, who never flinch'd his ground,
High-wav'd his magnum bonum round
With Cyclopean fury.—

Miller‖ brought up th' artillery ranks,
The many-pounders of the banks,
Resistless desolation!
While Maxwelton¶, that baron bold,
'Mid LAWSON's** port entrench'd his hold,
And threaten'd worse damnation.—

To these what Tory hosts oppos'd,
With these what Tory warriors clos'd,
Surpasses my descriving:
Squadrons, extended long and large,
With headlong speed rush to the charge,
Like furious devils driving.—

What Verse can sing, or Prose narrate,
The butcher deeds of bloody Fate,
Amid this mighty tulzie!
Grim Horror girn'd; pale Terror roar'd,
As Murder at his thrapple shor'd;
And Hell mix'd in the brulzie.—

* The Duke's Factor and Cousin †Robt Riddel Esqr of Glenriddel
‡ Provost of Dumfries and Director of the Bank of Scotland
§ Sherriff Substitute
‖ Patrick Miller Esqr of Dalswinton the Candidate's father
¶ Sir Robt Lowrie ** A famous wine Mercht

As Highland craigs by thunder cleft,
When lightenings fire the stormy lift,
Hurl down wi' crashing rattle;
As flames among a hundred woods,
As headlong foam a hundred floods,
Such is the rage of battle.—

The stubborn Tories dare to die,
As soon the rooted oaks would fly
Before th' approaching fellers:
The Whigs come on like ocean's roar,
When all his wintry billows pour
Against the Buchan bullers.—

Lo, from the shades of Death's deep night,
Departed Whigs enjoy the fight,
And think on former daring:
The muffled Murtherer of CHARLES*
The Magna charta flag unfurls,
All deadly gules it 's bearing.—

Nor wanting ghosts of Tory fame;
Bold SCRIMGEOUR† follows gallant GRAHAM‡,
Auld Covenanters shiver!
(Forgive, forgive! much wrong'd Montrose!
Now, Death and Hell engulph thy foes,
Thou liv'st on high for ever.)

Still o'er the field the combat burns,
The Tories, Whigs, give way by turns,
But Fate the word has spoken:
For Woman's wit, and strength of Man,
Alas! can do but what they can;
The Tory ranks are broken.—

O, that my een were flowing burns!
My voice, a lioness that mourns
Her darling cub's undoing!
That I might greet, that I might cry,
While Tories fall, while Tories fly
From furious whigs pursuing.—

* Charles 1st. was executed by a man in a mask.—
† Viscount Dundee ‡ Montrose—

What Whig but melts for good SIR JAMES!
Dear to his Country by the names,
Friend, Patron, Benefactor!
Not Pulteney's wealth can Pulteney save;
And Hopeton falls, the generous, brave;
And STEWART* bold as Hector!

Thou, Pit, shalt rue this overthrow,
And Thurlow growl a curse of woe,
And Melville melt in wailing:
How Fox and Sheridan rejoice!
And Burke shall shout, O Prince, arise!
Thy power is all-prevailing!

For your poor friend, the Bard, afar
He hears and sees the distant war,
A cool Spectator purely:
So, when the storm the forest rends,
The Robin in the hedge descends,
And patient chirps securely.—

Now, for my friends' and brethren's sakes,
And for my native LAND-o'-CAKES,
I pray with holy fire;
Lord, send a rough-shod troop o' hell,
O'er a', wad Scotland buy, or sell,
And grind them in the mire!!!
I am, &c.

319. *On the Birth of a Posthumous Child, born in peculiar circumstances of Family-Distress*

SWEET floweret, pledge o' meikle love,
And ward o' mony a prayer,
What heart o' stane wad thou na move,
Sae helpless, sweet, and fair.

* Wm. Stuart of Hill-side Esqr.

On the Birth of a Posthumous Child. The Glenriddell MS is headed: Extempore nearly—On the birth of Monsr. Henri, posthumous child to a Monsr. Henri, a Gentleman of family and fortune from Switzerland; who died in three days illness, leaving his lady, a sister of Sir Thos. Wallace, in her sixth month of this her first child.—The lady and her Family were particular friends of the Author. —The child was born in November —90—

November hirples o'er the lea,
  Chill, on thy lovely form;
And gane, alas! the sheltering tree,
  Should shield thee frae the storm.

May HE who gives the rain to pour,
  And wings the blast to blaw,
Protect thee frae the driving shower,
  The bitter frost and snaw.

May HE, the friend of woe and want,
  Who heals life's various stounds,
Protect and guard the mother plant,
  And heal her cruel wounds.

But late she flourished, rooted fast,
  Fair on the summer morn:
Now, feebly bends she, in the blast,
  Unsheltered and forlorn.

Blest be thy bloom, thou lovely gem,
  Unscathed by ruffian hand!
And from thee many a parent stem
  Arise to deck our land.

320. *Song—*

Tune, Banks of Banna

I

YESTREEN I had a pint o' wine,
  A place where body saw na;
Yestreen lay on this breast o' mine
  The gowden locks of Anna.—
The hungry Jew in wilderness
  Rejoicing o'er his manna,
Was naething to my hiney bliss
  Upon the lips of Anna.—

2

Ye Monarchs take the East and West,
  Frae Indus to Savannah!
Gie me within my straining grasp
  The melting form of Anna.—
There I'll despise Imperial charms,
  An Empress or Sultana,
While dying raptures in her arms
  I give and take with Anna!!!

3

Awa, thou flaunting god o' day!
  Awa, thou pale Diana!
Ilk star, gae hide thy twinkling ray!
  When I'm to meet my Anna.—
Come, in thy raven plumage, Night;
  Sun, moon and stars withdrawn a';
And bring an angel pen to write
  My transports wi' my Anna.—

321. *Tam o' Shanter. A Tale*

Of Brownyis and of Bogillis full is this buke.
GAWIN DOUGLAS.

WHEN chapman billies leave the street,
And drouthy neebors, neebors meet,
As market-days are wearing late,
An' folk begin to tak the gate;
While we sit bousing at the nappy,
And getting fou and unco happy,
We think na on the lang Scots miles,
The mosses, waters, slaps, and styles,
That lie between us and our hame,
Whare sits our sulky sullen dame,
Gathering her brows like gathering storm,
Nursing her wrath to keep it warm.

  This truth fand honest *Tam o' Shanter*,
As he frae Ayr ae night did canter,
(Auld Ayr, wham ne'er a town surpasses,
For honest men and bonny lasses.)

  O *Tam*! hadst thou but been sae wise,
As ta'en thy ain wife *Kate*'s advice!
She tauld thee weel thou was a skellum,
A blethering, blustering, drunken blellum;
That frae November till October,
Ae market-day thou was nae sober;

Tam o' Shanter. Introductory note in the Glenriddell MS: When Captain Grose was at Friars-Carse in Summer 1790 Collecting materials for his Scottish Antiquities he applied to M[r] Burns then living in the neighbourhood to write him an account of the Witches Meetings at Aloway Church near Ayr who complied with his request and wrote for him the following Poem.

That ilka melder, wi' the miller,
Thou sat as lang as thou had siller;
That every naig was ca'd a shoe on,
The smith and thee gat roaring fou on;
That at the L—d 's house, even on Sunday,
Thou drank wi' Kirkton Jean till Monday.
She prophesied that late or soon,
Thou would be found deep drown'd in Doon;
Or catch'd wi' warlocks in the mirk,
By *Alloway*'s auld haunted kirk.

Ah, gentle dames! it gars me greet,
To think how mony counsels sweet,
How mony lengthen'd sage advices,
The husband frae the wife despises!

But to our tale: Ae market-night,
Tam had got planted unco right;
Fast by an ingle, bleezing finely,
Wi' reaming swats, that drank divinely;
And at his elbow, Souter *Johnny*,
His ancient, trusty, drouthy crony;
Tam lo'ed him like a vera brither;
They had been fou for weeks thegither.
The night drave on wi' sangs and clatter;
And ay the ale was growing better:
The landlady and *Tam* grew gracious,
Wi' favours, secret, sweet, and precious:
The Souter tauld his queerest stories;
The landlord's laugh was ready chorus:
The storm without might rair and rustle,
Tam did na mind the storm a whistle.

Care, mad to see a man sae happy,
E'en drown'd himsel amang the nappy:
As bees flee hame wi' lades o' treasure,
The minutes wing'd their way wi' pleasure:
Kings may be blest, but *Tam* was glorious,
O'er a' the ills o' life victorious!

But pleasures are like poppies spread,
You seize the flower, its bloom is shed;
Or like the snow falls in the river,
A moment white—then melts for ever;

Or like the borealis race,
That flit ere you can point their place;
Or like the rainbow's lovely form
Evanishing amid the storm.—
Nae man can tether time or tide;
The hour approaches *Tam* maun ride;
That hour, o' night's black arch the key-stane,
That dreary hour he mounts his beast in;
And sic a night he taks the road in,
As ne'er poor sinner was abroad in.

The wind blew as 'twad blawn its last;
The rattling showers rose on the blast;
The speedy gleams the darkness swallow'd;
Loud, deep, and lang, the thunder bellow'd:
That night, a child might understand,
The Deil had business on his hand.

Weel mounted on his gray mare, *Meg*,
A better never lifted leg,
Tam skelpit on thro' dub and mire,
Despising wind, and rain, and fire;
Whiles holding fast his gude blue bonnet;
Whiles crooning o'er some auld Scots sonnet;
Whiles glowring round wi' prudent cares,
Lest bogles catch him unawares:
Kirk-Alloway was drawing nigh,
Whare ghaists and houlets nightly cry.—

By this time he was cross the ford,
Whare, in the snaw, the chapman smoor'd;
And past the birks and meikle stane,
Whare drunken *Charlie* brak 's neck-bane;
And thro' the whins, and by the cairn,
Whare hunters fand the murder'd bairn;
And near the thorn, aboon the well,
Whare *Mungo*'s mither hang'd hersel.—
Before him *Doon* pours all his floods;
The doubling storm roars thro' the woods;
The lightnings flash from pole to pole;
Near and more near the thunders roll:
When, glimmering thro' the groaning trees,
Kirk-Alloway seem'd in a bleeze;
Thro' ilka bore the beams were glancing;
And loud resounded mirth and dancing.—

Inspiring bold *John Barleycorn*!
What dangers thou canst make us scorn!
Wi' tippeny, we fear nae evil;
Wi' usquabae, we'll face the devil!—
The swats sae ream'd in *Tammie* 's noddle,
Fair play, he car'd na deils a boddle.
But *Maggie* stood right sair astonish'd,
Till, by the heel and hand admonish'd,
She ventured forward on the light;
And, vow! *Tam* saw an unco sight!
Warlocks and witches in a dance;
Nae cotillion brent new frae *France*,
But hornpipes, jigs, strathspeys, and reels,
Put life and mettle in their heels.
A winnock-bunker in the east,
There sat auld Nick, in shape o' beast;
A towzie tyke, black, grim, and large,
To gie them music was his charge:
He screw'd the pipes and gart them skirl,
Till roof and rafters a' did dirl.—
Coffins stood round, like open presses,
That shaw'd the dead in their last dresses;
And by some devilish cantraip slight
Each in its cauld hand held a light.—
By which heroic *Tam* was able
To note upon the haly table,
A murderer's banes in gibbet airns;
Twa span-lang, wee, unchristen'd bairns;
A thief, new-cutted frae a rape,
Wi' his last gasp his gab did gape;
Five tomahawks, wi' blude red-rusted;
Five scymitars, wi' murder crusted;
A garter, which a babe had strangled;
A knife, a father's throat had mangled,
Whom his ain son o' life bereft,
The grey hairs yet stack to the heft;
Wi' mair o' horrible and awefu',
Which even to name wad be unlawfu'.

142 *Additional lines in MSS:*

Three Lawyers' tongues, turn'd inside out,
Wi' lies seam'd like a beggar's clout;
Three Priests' hearts, rotten, black as muck,
Lay stinking, vile, in every neuk.—

As *Tammie* glow'rd, amaz'd, and curious,
The mirth and fun grew fast and furious:
The piper loud and louder blew;
The dancers quick and quicker flew;
They reel'd, they set, they cross'd, they cleekit,
Till ilka carlin swat and reekit,
And coost her duddies to the wark,
And linket at it in her sark!

Now, *Tam*, O *Tam*! had thae been queans,
A' plump and strapping in their teens,
Their sarks, instead o' creeshie flannen,
Been snaw-white seventeen hunder linnen!
Thir breeks o' mine, my only pair,
That ance were plush, o' gude blue hair,
I wad hae gi'en them off my hurdies,
For ae blink o' the bonie burdies!

But wither'd beldams, auld and droll,
Rigwoodie hags wad spean a foal,
Lowping and flinging on a crummock,
I wonder didna turn thy stomach.

But *Tam* kend what was what fu' brawlie,
There was ae winsome wench and wawlie,
That night enlisted in the core,
(Lang after kend on *Carrick* shore;
For mony a beast to dead she shot,
And perish'd mony a bony boat,
And shook baith meikle corn and bear,
And kept the country-side in fear:)
Her cutty sark, o' Paisley harn,
That while a lassie she had worn,
In longitude tho' sorely scanty,
It was her best, and she was vauntie.—
Ah! little kend thy reverend grannie,
That sark she coft for her wee Nannie,
Wi' twa pund Scots, ('twas a' her riches),
Wad ever grac'd a dance of witches!

But here my Muse her wing maun cour;
Sic flights are far beyond her pow'r;
To sing how Nannie lap and flang,
(A souple jade she was, and strang),

And how *Tam* stood, like ane bewitch'd,
And thought his very een enrich'd;
Even Satan glowr'd, and fidg'd fu' fain,
And hotch'd and blew wi' might and main:
Till first ae caper, syne anither,
Tam tint his reason a' thegither,
And roars out, 'Weel done, Cutty-sark!'
And in an instant all was dark:
And scarcely had he Maggie rallied,
When out the hellish legion sallied.

As bees bizz out wi' angry fyke,
When plundering herds assail their byke;
As open pussie's mortal foes,
When, pop! she starts before their nose;
As eager runs the market-crowd,
When 'Catch the thief!' resounds aloud;
So Maggie runs, the witches follow,
Wi' mony an eldritch skreech and hollow.

Ah, *Tam*! Ah, *Tam*! thou'll get thy fairin!
In hell they'll roast thee like a herrin!
In vain thy *Kate* awaits thy comin!
Kate soon will be a woefu' woman!
Now, do thy speedy utmost, Meg,
And win the key-stane* of the brig;
There at them thou thy tail may toss,
A running stream they dare na cross.
But ere the key-stane she could make,
The fient a tail she had to shake!
For Nannie, far before the rest,
Hard upon noble Maggie prest,
And flew at *Tam* wi' furious ettle;
But little wist she Maggie's mettle—
Ae spring brought off her master hale,
But left behind her ain gray tail:
The carlin claught her by the rump,
And left poor Maggie scarce a stump.

Now, wha this tale o' truth shall read,
Ilk man and mother's son, take heed:

* It is a well known fact that witches, or any evil spirits, have no power to follow a poor wight any farther than the middle of the next running stream.—It may be proper likewise to mention to the benighted traveller, that when he falls in with *bogles*, whatever danger may be in his going forward, there is much more hazard in turning back.

Whene'er to drink you are inclin'd,
Or cutty-sarks run in your mind,
Think, ye may buy the joys o'er dear,
Remember Tam o' Shanter's mare.

322. [*Ken ye ought o' Captain Grose?*]

Written in a wrapper inclosing a letter to Captn Grose, to be left with Mr Cardonnel Antiquarian—

Tune, Sir John Malcolm—

KEN ye ought o' Captain Grose?
  Igo and ago—
If he 's amang his friends or foes?
  Iram coram dago.—

Is he South, or is he North?
  Igo and ago—
Or drowned in the river Forth?
  Iram coram dago.—

Is he slain by Highland bodies?
  Igo and ago—
And eaten like a wether-haggis?
  Iram coram dago.—

Is he to Abram's bosom gane?
  Igo and ago—
Or haudin Sarah by the wame?
  Iram coram dago.—

Whare'er he be, the Lord be near him!
  Igo and ago—
As for the deil, he daur na steer him,
  Iram coram dago.—

But please transmit th' inclosed letter,
  Igo and ago—
Which will oblidge your humble debtor,
  Iram coram dago.—

So may ye hae auld Stanes in store,
  Igo and ago—
The very Stanes that Adam bore;
  Iram coram dago.—

So may ye get in glad possession,
  Igo and ago—
The coins o' Satan's Coronation!
  Iram coram dago.—

323. *Epigram on Capt. Francis Grose, The Celebrated Antiquary*

The following epigram, written in a moment of festivity by Burns, was so much relished by Grose, that he made it serve as an excuse for prolonging the convivial occasion that gave it birth to a very late hour.

THE Devil got notice that GROSE was a-dying,
So whip! at the summons, old Satan came flying;
But when he approach'd where poor FRANCIS lay moaning,
And saw each bed-post with its burden a-groaning,
Astonished! confounded! cry'd Satan, by G–d,
I'll want 'im, ere I take such a d——ble load.

Epigram on Capt. Francis Grose. Stewart's note on line 4: Mr. Grose was exceedingly corpulent, and used to rally himself, with the greatest good humour, on the singular rotundity of his figure.

VIII. Poems 1791

ELLISLAND AND DUMFRIES

324. *A Fragment, which was meant for the beginning of an Elegy on the late Miss Burnet of Monboddo—*

LIFE ne'er exulted in so rich a prize,
As Burnet lovely from her native skies;
Nor envious Death so triumph'd in a blow,
As that which laid th' accomplish'd Burnet low.—

Thy form and mind, sweet Maid! can I forget,
In richest ore the brightest jewel set!
In thee, what Heaven above, was truest shown,
For by his noblest work the Godhead best is known.—

In vain ye flaunt in summer's pride, ye groves;
Thou crystal streamlet with thy flowery shore,
Ye woodland choir that chant your idle loves,
Ye cease to charm, Eliza is no more.—

Ye heathy wastes immix'd with reedy fens,
Ye mossy streams with sedge and rushes stor'd,
Ye rugged cliffs o'erhanging dreary glens,
To you I fly, ye with my soul accord.—

Princes whose cumbrous pride was all their worth,
Shall venal lays their pompous exit hail;
And thou, sweet Excellence! forsake our earth,
And not a Muse in honest grief bewail!

We saw thee shine in youth and beauty's pride,
And virtue's light that beams beyond the spheres;
But like the sun eclips'd at morning tide,
Thou left'st us darkling in a world of tears.—

The Parent's heart that nestled fond in thee,
  That heart how sunk a prey to grief and care!
So deckt the woodbine sweet yon aged tree;
  So, rudely ravish'd, left it bleak and bare.—

325. *To Terraughty, on his birth-day*

HEALTH to the Maxwels' veteran Chief!
Health, ay unsour'd by care or grief:
Inspired, I turn'd Fate's sybil leaf,
    This natal morn,
I see thy life is stuff o' prief,
    Scarce quite half-worn.—

This day thou metes threescore eleven,
And I can tell that bounteous Heaven
(The Second-sight, ye ken, is given
    To ilka Poet)
On thee a tack o' seven times seven
    Will yet bestow it.—

If envious buckies view wi' sorrow
Thy lengthen'd days on this blest morrow,
May DESOLATION's lang-teeth'd harrow,
    Nine miles an hour,
Rake them like Sodom and Gomorrah
    In brunstane stoure.—

But for thy friends, and they are mony,
Baith honest men and lasses bony,
May couthie fortune, kind and cany,
    In social glee,
Wi' mornings blythe and e'enings funny
    Bless them and thee:—

Fareweel, auld birkie! Lord be near ye,
And then the deil he daur na steer ye:
Your friends ay love, your faes ay fear ye!
    For me, Shame fa' me,
If neist my heart I dinna wear ye,
    While BURNS they ca' me.

326. *There'll never be peace till Jamie comes hame—*

Slowish

BY yon castle wa' at the close of the day,
I heard a man sing tho' his head it was grey;
And as he was singing the tears down came,
There'll never be peace till Jamie comes hame.—
The Church is in ruins, the State is in jars,
Delusions, oppressions, and murderous wars:
We dare na weel say 't, but we ken wha 's to blame,
There'll never be peace till Jamie comes hame.—

My seven braw sons for Jamie drew sword,
And now I greet round their green beds in the yerd;
It brak the sweet heart of my faithfu' auld Dame,
There'll never be peace till Jamie comes hame.—

Now life is a burden that bows me down,
Sin I tint my bairns, and he tint his crown;
But till my last moments my words are the same,
There'll never be peace till Jamie comes hame.—

327. *I look to the North—*

OUT over the Forth, I look to the North,
  But what is the North and its Highlands to me;
The South, nor the East, gie ease to my breast,
  The far foreign land, or the wide rolling sea:
But I look to the West, when I gae to rest,
  That happy my dreams and my slumbers may be;
For far in the West lives he I lo'e best,
  The man that is dear to my babie and me.—

* * * * * *

328. *The Banks o' Doon* [*A*]

Cambdelmore

YE flowery banks o' bonie Doon,
  How can ye blume sae fair;
How can ye chant, ye little birds,
  And I sae fu' o' care!

Thou'll break my heart, thou bonie bird
  That sings upon the bough;
Thou minds me o' the happy days
  When my fause luve was true.

Thou'll break my heart, thou bonie bird
  That sings beside thy mate;
For sae I sat, and sae I sang,
  And wist na o' my fate.

Aft hae I rov'd by bonie Doon,
  To see the wood-bine twine,
And ilka bird sang o' its love,
  And sae did I o' mine.

Wi' lightsome heart I pu'd a rose
  Frae aff its thorny tree,
And my fause luver staw the rose,
  But left the thorn wi' me.

Wi' lightsome heart I pu'd a rose,
  Upon a morn in June:
And sae I flourish'd on the morn,
  And sae was pu'd or noon!

The Banks o' Doon [*B*]

YE banks and braes o' bonie Doon,
  How can ye bloom sae fresh and fair;
How can ye chant, ye little birds,
  And I sae weary, fu' o' care!
Thou'll break my heart, thou warbling bird,
  That wantons thro' the flowering thorn:
Thou minds me o' departed joys,
  Departed, never to return.—

Oft hae I rov'd by bonie Doon,
  To see the rose and woodbine twine;
And ilka bird sang o' its Luve,
  And fondly sae did I o' mine.—

Wi' lightsome heart I pu'd a rose,
  Fu' sweet upon its thorny tree;
And my fause Luver staw my rose,
  But, ah! he left the thorn wi' me.—

329. *On Mr. James Gracie*

GRACIE, thou art a man of worth,
  O be thou Dean for ever!
May he be damn'd to hell henceforth,
  Who fauts thy weight or measure!

330. *Orananaoig, or, The Song of death*

A Gaelic Air

FAREWELL, thou fair day; thou green earth; and ye skies,
  Now gay with the broad setting sun!
Farewell, loves and friendships, ye dear tender ties!
  Our race of existence is run.

Thou grim king of terrors, thou life's gloomy foe,
  Go frighten the coward and slave!
Go teach them to tremble, fell tyrant! but know,
  No terrors hast thou to the Brave.

Thou strik'st the dull peasant, he sinks in the dark,
  Nor saves e'en the wreck of a name:
Thou strik'st the young hero, a glorious mark!
  He falls in the blaze of his fame.
In the field of proud honor, our swords in our hands,
  Our King and our Country to save,
While victory shines on life's last ebbing sands,
  O, who would not die with the Brave!

331. *Address, To the Shade of Thomson, on crowning his Bust, at* Ednam, Roxburgh-shire, *with Bays*

WHILE virgin Spring, by Eden's flood,
  Unfolds her tender mantle green,
Or pranks the sod in frolic mood,
  Or tunes Eolian strains between.

While Summer with a matron grace
  Retreats to Dryburgh's cooling shade,
Yet oft, delighted, stops to trace
  The progress of the spiky blade.

While Autumn, benefactor kind,
  By Tweed erects his aged head,
And sees, with self-approving mind,
  Each creature on his bounty fed.

While maniac Winter rages o'er
  The hills whence classic Yarrow flows,
Rousing the turbid torrent's roar,
  Or sweeping, wild, a waste of snows.

So long, sweet Poet of the Year,
  Shall bloom that wreath thou well hast won;
While Scotia, with exulting tear,
  Proclaims that *Thomson* was her son.

332. *Extempore—on some Commemorations of Thomson*

DOST thou not rise, indignant Shade,
  And smile wi' spurning scorn,
When they wha wad hae starv'd thy life,
  Thy senseless turf adorn.—

They wha about thee mak sic fuss
  Now thou art but a name,
Wad seen thee d–mn'd ere they had spar'd
  Ae plack to fill thy wame.—

Helpless, alane, thou clamb the brae,
  Wi' meikle, meikle toil,
And claught th' unfading garland there,
  Thy sair-won, rightful spoil.—

And wear it there! and call aloud,
  This axiom undoubted—
'Wouldst thou hae Nobles' patronage,
  First learn to live without it!'

To whom hae much, shall yet be given,
  Is every Great man's faith;
But he, the helpless, needful wretch,
  Shall lose the mite he hath.—

333. *Lovely Davies*

Tune, Miss Muir

O HOW shall I, unskilfu', try
The Poet's occupation?
The tunefu' Powers, in happy hours,
That whisper, inspiration,

Even they maun dare an effort mair
Than aught they ever gave us,
Or they rehearse in equal verse
The charms o' lovely DAVIES.—

Each eye it chears when she appears,
Like Phebus in the morning,
When past the shower, and every flower
The garden is adorning:
As the wretch looks o'er Siberia's shore,
When winter-bound the wave is;
Sae droops our heart when we maun part
Frae charming, lovely DAVIES.—

Her smile's a gift frae boon the lift,
That maks us mair than princes;
A scepter'd hand, a king's command,
Is in her darting glances:
The man in arms 'gainst female charms,
Even he her willing slave is;
He hugs his chain, and owns the reign
Of conquering lovely DAVIES.—

My Muse to dream of such a theme,
Her feeble powers surrender;
The eagle's gaze alane surveys;
The sun's meridian splendor:
I wad in vain essay the strain,
The deed too daring brave is;
I'll drap the lyre, and, mute, admire
The charms o' lovely DAVIES.—

334. *Lament for James, Earl of Glencairn*

THE wind blew hollow frae the hills,
By fits the sun's departing beam
Look'd on the fading yellow woods
That wav'd o'er Lugar's winding stream:
Beneath a craigy steep, a Bard,
Laden with years and meikle pain,
In loud lament bewail'd his lord,
Whom death had all untimely taen.

He lean'd him to an ancient aik,
  Whose trunk was mould'ring down with years;
His locks were bleached white with time,
  His hoary cheek was wet wi' tears;
And as he touch'd his trembling harp,
  And as he tuned his doleful sang,
The winds, lamenting thro' their caves,
  To echo bore the notes alang.

'Ye scatter'd birds that faintly sing,
  'The reliques of the vernal quire;
'Ye woods that shed on a' the winds
  'The honours of the aged year:
'A few short months, and glad and gay,
  'Again ye'll charm the ear and e'e;
'But nocht in all-revolving time
  'Can gladness bring again to me.

'I am a bending aged tree,
  'That long has stood the wind and rain;
'But now has come a cruel blast,
  'And my last hald of earth is gane:
'Nae leaf o' mine shall greet the spring,
  'Nae simmer sun exalt my bloom;
'But I maun lie before the storm,
  And ithers plant them in my room.

'I've seen sae mony changefu' years,
  'On earth I am a stranger grown;
'I wander in the ways of men,
  'Alike unknowing and unknown:
'Unheard, unpitied, unreliev'd,
  'I bear alane my lade o' care,
'For silent, low, on beds of dust,
  'Lie a' that would my sorrows share.

'And last, (the sum of a' my griefs!)
  'My noble master lies in clay;
'The flower amang our barons bold,
  'His country's pride, his country's stay:
'In weary being now I pine,
  'For all the life of life is dead,
'And hope has left my aged ken,
  'On forward wing for ever fled.

'Awake thy last sad voice, my harp!
'The voice of woe and wild despair!
'Awake, resound thy latest lay,
'Then sleep in silence evermair!
'And thou, my last, best, only friend,
'That fillest an untimely tomb,
'Accept this tribute from the Bard
'Thou brought from fortune's mirkest gloom.

'In Poverty's low barren vale,
'Thick mists, obscure, involv'd me round;
'Though oft I turned the wistful eye,
'Nae ray of fame was to be found:
'Thou found'st me, like the morning sun
'That melts the fogs in limpid air,
'The friendless Bard and rustic song,
'Became alike thy fostering care.

'O! why has Worth so short a date?
'While villains ripen grey with time!
'Must thou, the noble, generous, great,
'Fall in bold manhood's hardy prime!
'Why did I live to see that day?
'A day to me so full of woe?
'O! had I met the mortal shaft
'Which laid my benefactor low!

'The bridegroom may forget the bride,
'Was made his wedded wife yestreen;
'The monarch may forget the crown
'That on his head an hour has been;
'The mother may forget the child
'That smiles sae sweetly on her knee;
'But I'll remember thee, Glencairn,
'And a' that thou hast done for me!'

334A. *Lines, sent to Sir John Whiteford, of Whiteford, Bart. with the foregoing Poem*

THOU, who thy honour as thy God rever'st,
Who, save thy *mind's reproach*, nought earthly fear'st,
To thee this votive off'ring I impart,
The tearful tribute of a broken heart.

The *Friend* thou valued'st, I, the *Patron*, lov'd;
His worth, his honour, all the world approv'd.
We'll mourn till we too go as he has gone,
And tread the shadowy path to that dark world unknown.

335. *To R***** G***** of F*****, Esq.*

LATE crippled of an arm, and now a leg,
About to beg a *pass* for leave to beg;
Dull, listless, teased, dejected, and deprest,
(Nature is adverse to a cripple's rest);
Will generous G***** list to his Poet's wail?
(It soothes poor Misery, heark'ning to her tale),
And hear him curse the light he first surveyed,
And doubly curse the luckless rhyming trade?

Thou, Nature, partial Nature, I arraign;
Of thy caprice maternal I complain.
The lion and the bull thy care have found,
One shakes the forest, and one spurns the ground:
Thou giv'st the ass his hide, the snail his shell,
Th' envenomed wasp, victorious, guards his cell.—
Thy minions, kings, defend, controul, devour,
In all th' omnipotence of rule and power.—
Foxes and statesmen, subtile wiles ensure;
The cit and polecat stink, and are secure.
Toads with their poison, doctors with their drug,
The priest and hedgehog in their robes, are snug.
Even silly woman has her warlike arts,
Her tongue and eyes, her dreaded spear and darts.

But O! thou bitter step-mother and hard,
To thy poor, fenceless, naked child—the Bard!
A thing unteachable in world's skill,
And half an idiot too, more helpless still.
No heels to bear him from the opening dun;
No claws to dig, his hated sight to shun;
No horns, but those by luckless Hymen worn,
And those, alas! not Amalthea's horn:
No nerves olfact'ry, Mammon's trusty cur,
Clad in rich Dulness' comfortable fur.
In naked feeling, and in aching pride,
He bears the unbroken blast from every side:

Vampyre booksellers drain him to the heart,
And scorpion Critics cureless venom dart.

Critics—appalled, I venture on the name,
Those cut-throat bandits in the paths of fame:
Bloody dissectors, worse than ten Monroes;
He hacks to teach, they mangle to expose.

His heart by causeless wanton malice wrung,
By blockheads' daring into madness stung;
His well-won bays, than life itself more dear,
By miscreants torn, who ne'er one sprig must wear:
Foiled, bleeding, tortured, in the unequal strife,
The hapless Poet flounders on thro' life.
Till fled each hope that once his bosom fired,
And fled each Muse that glorious once inspired,
Low-sunk in squalid, unprotected age,
Dead, even resentment, for his injured page,
He heeds or feels no more the ruthless Critic's rage!

So, by some hedge, the generous steed deceased,
For half-starved snarling curs a dainty feast;
By toil and famine wore to skin and bone,
Lies, senseless of each tugging bitch's son.

55 *Additional lines* (*character-sketches of William Creech and William Smellie*) *follow in an early MS:*

A little, upright, pert, tart, tripping wight,
And still his precious Self his dear delight;
Who loves his own smart shadow in the streets
Better than e'er the fairest fair/she he meets.
Much specious lore, but little understood,
Fineering oft outshines the solid wood:
A man of fashion too, he made his tour,
Learn'd vive la bagatelle et vive l'amour;
So travell'd monkies their grimace improve,
Polish their grin, nay sigh for ladies' love:
His meddling Vanity, a busy fiend,
Still making work his Selfish-craft must mend—

Crochallan came;
The old cock'd hat, the brown surtout the same;
His grisly beard just bristling in its might,
'Twas four long nights and days from shaving-night;
His uncomb'd, hoary locks, wild-staring, thatch'd,
A head for thought profound and clear unmatch'd:
Yet, tho' his caustic wit was biting rude,
His heart was warm, benevolent and good.

O Dulness! portion of the truly blest!
Calm sheltered haven of eternal rest!
Thy sons ne'er madden in the fierce extremes
Of Fortune's polar frost, or torrid beams.
If mantling high she fills the golden cup,
With sober selfish ease they sip it up:
Conscious the bounteous meed they well deserve,
They only wonder 'some folks' do not starve.
The grave sage hern thus easy picks his frog,
And thinks the Mallard a sad worthless dog.
When disappointment snaps the clue of hope,
And thro' disastrous night they darkling grope,
With deaf endurance sluggishly they bear,
And just conclude that 'fools are fortune's care.'
So, heavy, passive to the tempest's shocks,
Strong on the sign-post stands the stupid ox.

Not so the idle Muses' mad-cap train,
Nor such the workings of their moon-struck brain;
In equanimity they never dwell,
By turns in soaring heaven, or vaulted hell.

I dread thee, Fate, relentless and severe,
Will all a poet's, husband's, father's fear!
Already one strong hold of hope is lost,
Glencairn, the truly noble, lies in dust;
(Fled, like the sun eclips'd as noon appears,
And left us darkling in a world of tears:)
O! hear my ardent, grateful, selfish prayer!
F*****, my other stay, long bless and spare!
Thro' a long life his hopes and wishes crown;
And bright in cloudless skies his sun go down!
May *bliss domestic* smooth his private path;
Give energy to life; and soothe his latest breath,
With many a filial tear circling the bed of death!

336. *Gloomy December*

ANCE mair I hail thee, thou gloomy December!
  Ance mair I hail thee, wi' sorrow and care;
Sad was the parting thou makes me remember,
  Parting wi' Nancy, Oh, ne'er to meet mair!
Fond lovers' parting is sweet, painful pleasure,
  Hope beaming mild on the soft parting hour,
But the dire feeling, 'O, farewell for ever!'
  Anguish unmingl'd and agony pure.—

Wild as the winter now tearing the forest,
  Till the last leaf o' the summer is flown,
Such is the tempest has shaken my bosom
  Till my last hope and last comfort is gone:

Still as I hail thee, thou gloomy December,
  Still shall I hail thee wi' sorrow and care;
For sad was the parting thou makes me remember,
  Parting wi' Nancy, Oh, ne'er to meet mair.—

337. *Song—*

Tune, Rory Dall's port

Ae fond kiss, and then we sever;
Ae fareweel, and then for ever!
Deep in heart-wrung tears I'll pledge thee,
Warring sighs and groans I'll wage thee.—

Who shall say that Fortune grieves him,
While the star of hope she leaves him:
Me, nae chearful twinkle lights me;
Dark despair around benights me.—

I'll ne'er blame my partial fancy,
Naething could resist my Nancy:
But to see her, was to love her;
Love but her, and love for ever.—

Had we never lov'd sae kindly,
Had we never lov'd sae blindly!
Never met—or never parted,
We had ne'er been broken-hearted.—

Fare-thee-weel, thou first and fairest!
Fare-thee-weel, thou best and dearest!
Thine be ilka joy and treasure,
Peace, Enjoyment, Love and Pleasure!—

Ae fond kiss, and then we sever!
Ae fareweel, Alas, for ever!
Deep in heart-wrung tears I'll pledge thee,
Warring sighs and groans I'll wage thee.—

IX. Poems 1792

DUMFRIES

338. [*There was twa Wives*]

Tak your auld cloak about you

THERE was twa wives, and twa witty wives,
  As e'er play'd houghmagandie,
And they coost oot, upon a time,
  Out o'er a drink o' brandy;
Up Maggy rose, and forth she goes,
  And she leaves auld Mary flytin,
And she f–rted by the byre-en'
  For she was gaun a sh–ten.

She f–rted by the byre-en',
  She f–rted by the stable;
And thick and nimble were her steps
  As fast as she was able:

Till at yon dyke-back the hurly brak,
  But raxin for some dockins,
The beans and pease cam down her thighs,
  And she cackit a' her stockins.

339. *O saw ye bonie Lesley*

The collier's dochter

O SAW ye bonie Lesley,
  As she gaed o'er the Border?
She 's gane, like Alexander,
  To spread her conquests farther.

To see her is to love her,
  And love but her for ever;
For Nature made her what she is
  And never made anither.

Thou art a queen, fair Lesley,
  Thy subjects we, before thee:
Thou art divine, fair Lesley,
  The hearts o' men adore thee.

The deil he could na scaith thee,
  Or aught that wad belang thee:
He'd look into thy bonie face,
  And say, 'I canna wrang thee!'

The Powers aboon will tent thee,
  Misfortune sha'na steer thee;
Thou'rt like themsels sae lovely,
  That ill they'll ne'er let near thee.

Return again, fair Lesley,
  Return to Caledonie!
That we may brag, we hae a lass
  There 's nane again sae bonie.

340. *Craigieburn-wood—A Song—*

I

SWEET closes the evening on Craigieburn-wood,
  And blythely awaukens the morrow;
But the pride o' the spring in the Craigieburn-wood
  Can yield me nought but sorrow.—

2

I see the spreading leaves and flowers,
  I hear the wild birds singing;
But pleasure they hae nane for me
  While care my heart is wringing.

3

I can na tell, I maun na tell,
  I dare na for your anger:
But secret love will break my heart,
  If I conceal it langer.

4

I see thee gracefu', straight and tall,
  I see thee sweet and bonie;
But Oh, what will my torments be,
  If thou refuse thy Johnie!

5

To see thee in another's arms,
  In love to lie and languish:
'Twad be my dead, that will be seen,
  My heart wad brust wi' anguish!

6

But Jeanie, say thou wilt be mine,
  Say thou loes nane before me;
And a' my days o' life to come
  I'll gratefully adore thee.

Old Chorus

Beyond thee, Dearie, beyond thee, Dearie,
  And Oh to be lying beyond thee!
O sweetly, soundly, weel may he sleep,
  That 's laid in the bed beyond thee.—

341. *Frae the friends and Land I love*

Tune, Carron Side

FRAE the friends and Land I love,
  Driven by Fortune's felly spite,
Frae my best Beloved I rove,
  Never mair to taste delight.—
Never mair maun hope to find
  Ease frae toil, relief frae care:
When Remembrance wracks the mind,
  Pleasures but unveil Despair.—

Brightest climes shall mirk appear,
  Desart ilka blooming shore;
Till the Fates, nae mair severe,
  Friendship, Love and Peace restore.—
Till Revenge, wi' laurell'd head,
  Bring our Banished hame again;
And ilk loyal, bonie lad
  Cross the seas and win his ain.—

342. *Hughie Graham*

OUR lords are to the mountains gane,
  A hunting o' the fallow deer;
And they hae gripet Hughie Graham
  For stealing o' the bishop's mare.—

And they hae tied him hand and foot,
  And led him up thro' Stirling town;
The lads and lasses met him there,
  Cried, Hughie Graham thou art a loun.—

O lowse my right hand free, he says,
  And put my braid sword in the same;
He 's no in Stirling town this day,
  Daur tell the tale to Hughie Graham.—

Up then bespake the brave Whitefoord,
  As he sat by the bishop's knee;
Five hundred white stots I'll gie you,
  If ye'll let Hughie Graham gae free.—

O haud your tongue, the bishop says,
  And wi' your pleading let me be;
For tho' ten Grahams were in his coat,
  Hughie Graham this day shall die.—

Up then bespake the fair Whitefoord,
  As she sat by the bishop's knee;
Five hundred white pence I'll gie you,
  If ye'll gie Hughie Graham to me.—

O haud your tongue now lady fair,
  And wi' your pleading let me be;
Altho' ten Grahams were in his coat,
  Its for my honor he maun die.—

They've taen him to the gallows knowe,
  He looked to the gallows tree,
Yet never color left his cheek,
  Nor ever did he blin' his e'e.—

At length he looked round about,
  To see whatever he could spy;
And there he saw his auld father,
  And he was weeping bitterly.—

O haud your tongue, my father dear,
  And wi' your weeping let it be;
Thy weeping 's sairer on my heart,
  Than a' that they can do to me.—

And ye may gie my brother John
  My sword that 's bent in the middle clear,
And let him come at twelve o'clock
  And see me pay the bishop's mare.—

And ye may gie my brother James
My sword that 's bent in the middle brown;
And bid him come at four o'clock,
And see his brother Hugh cut down.—

Remember me to Maggy my wife,
The niest time ye gang o'er the moor;
Tell her, she staw the bishop's mare,
Tell her, she was the bishop's whore.

And ye may tell my kith and kin,
I never did disgrace their blood;
And when they meet the bishop's cloak,
To mak it shorter by the hood.—

343. *John come kiss me now*—

Chorus

O JOHN, come kiss me now, now, now;
O John, my luve, come kiss me now;
O John, come kiss me by and by,
For weel ye ken the way to woo.—

O some will court and compliment,
  And ither some will kiss and daut;
But I will mak o' my gudeman,
  My ain gudeman, it is nae faute.—
    O John &c.

O some will court and compliment,
  And ither some will prie their mou,
And some will hause in ithers arms,
  And that 's the way I like to do.—
    O John &c.

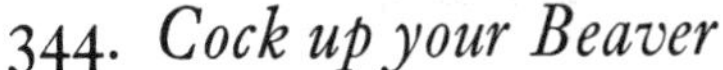

344. *Cock up your Beaver*

Slowish

WHEN first my brave Johnie lad came to this town,
He had a blue bonnet that wanted the crown,
But now he has gotten a hat and a feather,
Hey, brave Johnie lad, cock up your beaver.

Cock up your beaver, and cock it fu' sprush;
We'll over the border and gie them a brush;
There 's somebody there we'll teach better behaviour,
Hey, brave Johnie lad, cock up your beaver.

345. *My Tochers the Jewel*

O MEIKLE thinks my Luve o' my beauty,
  And meikle thinks my Luve o' my kin;
But little thinks my Luve, I ken brawlie,
  My tocher 's the jewel has charms for him.
It 's a' for the apple he'll nourish the tree;
  It 's a' for the hiney he'll cherish the bee;
My laddie 's sae meikle in love wi' the siller,
  He canna hae luve to spare for me.

Your proffer o' luve 's an airle-penny,
  My tocher 's the bargain ye wad buy;
But an ye be crafty, I am cunnin,
  Sae ye wi' anither your fortune maun try.
Ye're like to the timmer o' yon rotten wood,
  Ye're like to the bark o' yon rotten tree,
Ye'll slip frae me like a knotless thread,
  And ye'll crack your credit wi' mae nor me.

346. *Then Guidwife count the lawin*

GANE is the day and mirk 's the night,
But we'll ne'er stray for faute o' light,
For ale and brandy 's stars and moon,
And blude-red wine 's the rysin Sun.

Chorus

Then guidwife count the lawin, the lawin, the lawin,
Then guidwife count the lawin, and bring a coggie mair.

There 's wealth and ease for gentlemen,
And semple-folk maun fecht and fen;
But here we're a' in ae accord,
For ilka man that 's drunk 's a lord.
Cho.s Then goodwife count &c.

My coggie is a haly pool,
That heals the wounds o' care and dool;
And pleasure is a wanton trout,
An' ye drink it a', ye'll find him out.
Cho.s Then goodwife count &c.

347. *What can a young lassie do wi' an auld man*

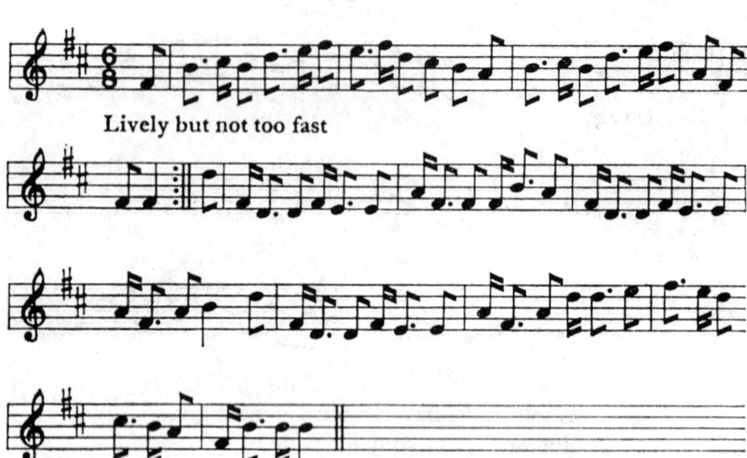

WHAT can a young lassie, what shall a young lassie,
  What can a young lassie do wi' an auld man?
Bad luck on the pennie, that tempted my Minnie
  To sell her poor Jenny for siller and lan'!

He 's always compleenin frae morning to e'enin,
  He hosts and he hirpls the weary day lang:
He 's doyl't and he 's dozin, his blude it is frozen,
  O, dreary 's the night wi' a crazy auld man!

He hums and he hankers, he frets and he cankers,
  I never can please him, do a' that I can;
He 's peevish, and jealous of a' the young fallows,
  O, dool on the day I met wi' an auld man!

My auld auntie Katie upon me taks pity,
  I'll do my endeavour to follow her plan;
I'll cross him, and wrack him untill I heartbreak him,
  And then his auld brass will buy me a new pan.—

348. *The bonie lad that 's far awa*

O HOW can I be blythe and glad,
Or how can I gang brisk and braw,
When the bonie lad that I loe best,
Is o'er the hills and far awa.—
[When the &c.]

[It 's no the frosty winter wind,
It 's no the driving drift and snaw;
But ay the tear comes in my e'e,
To think on him that 's far awa.—
But the &c.]

My father pat me frae his door,
My friends they hae disown'd me a';
But there is ane will tak my part,
The bonie lad that 's far awa.—
[But there &c.]

A pair o' gloves he bought to me,
And silken snoods he gae me twa,
And I will wear them for his sake,
The bonie lad that 's far awa.—
[And I will &c.]

O weary winter soon will pass,
And spring will cleed the birken shaw:
And my young babie will be born,
And he'll be hame that 's far awa.—
[And my &c.]

349. *I do confess thou art sae fair—*

I DO confess thou art sae fair,
  I wad been o'er the lugs in luve;
Had I na found, the slightest prayer
  That lips could speak, thy heart could muve.—

I do confess thee sweet, but find,
  Thou art sae thriftless o' thy sweets,
Thy favors are the silly wind
  That kisseth ilka thing it meets.—

See yonder rose-bud, rich in dew,
  Amang its native briers sae coy,
How sune it tines its scent and hue,
  When pu'd and worn a common toy!

Sic fate ere lang shall thee betide;
  Tho' thou may gayly bloom a while,
Yet sune thou shalt be thrown aside,
  Like ony common weed and vile.—

350. *Galloway Tam*

O Galloway Tam came here to woo,
I'd rather we'd gin him the brawnit cow;
For our lass Bess may curse and ban
The wanton wit o' Galloway Tam.

O Galloway Tam came here to shear,
I'd rather we'd gin him the gude gray mare;
He kist the gudewife and strack the gudeman,
And that 's the tricks o' Galloway Tam.

351. *Song—*

As I cam down by yon castle wa',
And in by yon garden green,
O there I spied a bony bony lass,
But the flower-borders were us between.

A bony bony lassie she was,
As ever mine eyes did see:
O five hundred pounds would I give,
For to have such a pretty bride as thee.

To have such a pretty bride as me,
Young man ye are sairly mista'en;
Tho' ye were king o' fair Scotland,
I wad disdain to be your queen.

Talk not so very high, bony lass,
O talk not so very, very high:
The man at the fair that wad sell,
He maun learn at the man that wad buy.

I trust to climb a far higher tree,
And herry a far richer nest:
Tak this advice o' me, bony lass,
Humility wad set thee best.

352. *Lord Ronald my Son—*

O WHERE hae ye been, Lord Ronald, my son?
O where hae ye been, Lord Ronald, my son?
I hae been wi' my sweetheart, mother, make my bed soon;
For I'm weary wi' the hunting, and fain wad lie down.—

What got ye frae your sweetheart, Lord Ronald, my son?
What got ye frae your sweetheart, Lord Ronald, my son?
I hae got deadly poison, mother, make my bed soon;
For life is a burden that soon I'll lay down.—

* * * * * *

353. *Bonie laddie, Highland laddie*

Tune, The old Highland laddie

I HAE been at Crookieden,
  My bonie laddie, Highland laddie,
Viewing Willie and his men,
  My bonie laddie, Highland laddie.—
There our faes that brunt and slew,
  My bonie laddie, Highland laddie,
There, at last, they get their due,
  My bonie laddie, Highland laddie.—

Satan sits in his black neuk,
  My bonie &c.
Breaking sticks to roast the Duke,
  My bonie &c.
The bloody monster gae a yell,
  My bonie &c.
And loud the laugh gaed round a' hell!
  My bonie &c.

354. *It is na, Jean, thy bonie face*

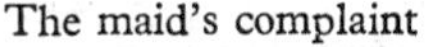

IT is na, Jean, thy bonie face,
  Nor shape that I admire,
Altho' thy beauty and thy grace
  Might weel awauk desire.—

Something in ilka part o' thee
  To praise, to love, I find,
But dear as is thy form to me,
  Still dearer is thy mind.—

Nae mair ungen'rous wish I hae,
  Nor stronger in my breast,
Than, if I canna mak thee sae,
  At least to see thee blest.

Content am I, if Heaven shall give
  But happiness to thee:
And as wi' thee I'd wish to live,
  For thee I'd bear to die.

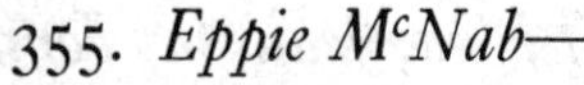

355. *Eppie McNab—*

Slow

O SAW ye my dearie, my Eppie Mcnab?
O saw ye my dearie, my Eppie Mcnab?
She 's down in the yard, she 's kissin the Laird,
She winna come hame to her ain Jock Rab.—

O come thy ways to me, my Eppie Mcnab;
O come thy ways to me, my Eppie Mcnab;
What-e'er thou has done, be it late, be it soon,
Thou 's welcome again to thy ain Jock Rab.—

What says she, my dearie, my Eppie Mcnab?
What says she, my dearie, my Eppie Mcnab?
She lets thee to wit, that she has thee forgot,
And for ever disowns thee, her ain Jock Rab.—

O had I ne'er seen thee, my Eppie M^cnab!
O had I ne'er seen thee, my Eppie M^cnab!
As light as the air, and fause as thou 's fair,
Thou 's broken the heart o' thy ain Jock Rab!

356. *Wha is that at my bower door?*

WHA is that at my bower-door?
  O wha is it but Findlay;
Then gae your gate, ye 'se nae be here!
  Indeed maun I, quo' Findlay.—

What mak ye, sae like a thief?
  O come and see, quo' Findlay;
Before the morn ye'll work mischief;
  Indeed will I, quo' Findlay.—

Gif I rise and let you in,
  Let me in, quo' Findlay;
Ye'll keep me waukin wi' your din;
  Indeed will I, quo' Findlay.—

In my bower if ye should stay,
  Let me stay, quo' Findlay;
I fear ye'll bide till break o' day;
  Indeed will I, quo' Findlay.—

Here this night if ye remain,
  I'll remain, quo' Findlay;
I dread ye'll learn the gate again;
  Indeed will I, quo' Findlay.—

What may pass within this bower,
  Let it pass, quo' Findlay;
Ye maun conceal till your last hour;
  Indeed will I, quo' Findlay.—

357. *The bonny wee thing*

Chorus

BONIE wee thing, canie wee thing,
  Lovely wee thing, was thou mine;
I wad wear thee in my bosom,
  Least my Jewel I should tine.—

Wishfully I look and languish
  In that bonie face o' thine;
And my heart it stounds wi' anguish,
  Least my wee thing be na mine.—
    Bonie wee &c.

The bonny wee thing. Subscription in MS Note the first part of the music is repeated, for the Chorus—

Wit, and Grace, and Love, and Beauty,
  In ae constellation shine;
To adore thee is my duty,
  Goddess o' this soul o' mine!

358. *Geordie—An old Ballad*

THERE was a battle in the north,
  And nobles there was many,
And they hae kill'd Sir Charlie Hay,
  And they laid the wyte on Geordie.

O he has written a lang letter,
  He sent it to his lady;
Ye maun cum up to Enbrugh town
  To see what words o' Geordie.

When first she look'd the letter on,
  She was baith red and rosy;
But she had na read a word but twa,
  Till she wallow't like a lily.

Gar get to me my gude grey steed,
  My menzie a' gae wi' me;
For I shall neither eat nor drink,
  Till Enbrugh town shall see me.

And she has mountit her gude grey steed,
  Her menzie a' gaed wi' her;
And she did neither eat nor drink
  Till Enbrugh town did see her.

And first appear'd the fatal block,
  And syne the aix to head him;
And Geordie cumin down the stair,
  And bands o' airn upon him.

But tho' he was chain'd in fetters strang,
  O' airn and steel sae heavy,
There was na ane in a' the court,
  Sae bra' a man as Geordie.

O she 's down on her bended knee,
  I wat she 's pale and weary,
O pardon, pardon, noble king,
  And gie me back my Dearie!

I hae born seven sons to my Geordie dear,
  The seventh ne'er saw his daddie:
O pardon, pardon, noble king,
  Pity a waefu' lady!

Gar bid the headin-man mak haste!
  Our king reply'd fu' lordly:
O noble king, tak a' that 's mine,
  But gie me back my Geordie.

The Gordons cam and the Gordons ran,
  And they were stark and steady;
And ay the word amang them a'
  Was, Gordons keep you ready.

An aged lord at the king's right hand
  Says, noble king, but hear me;
Gar her tell down five thousand pound
  And gie her back her Dearie.

Some gae her marks, some gae her crowns,
  Some gae her dollars many;
And she 's tell'd down five thousand pound,
  And she 's gotten again her Dearie.

She blinkit blythe in her Geordie's face,
  Says, dear I've bought thee, Geordie:
But there sud been bluidy bouks on the green,
  Or I had tint my laddie.

He claspit her by the middle sma',
  And he kist her lips sae rosy:
The fairest flower o' woman-kind
  Is my sweet, bonie Lady!

359. *As I was a wand'ring*

Tune, Rinn m'eudial mo mhealladh—

A Gaelic air—

As I was a wand'ring ae midsummer e'enin,
  The pipers and youngsters were makin their game,
Amang them I spyed my faithless fause luver,
  Which bled a' the wounds o' my dolour again.—

Chorus

Weel, since he has left me, may pleasure gae wi' him;
I may be distress'd, but I winna complain:
I'll flatter my fancy I may get anither,
My heart it shall never be broken for ane.—

I could na get sleepin till dawin, for greetin;
The tears trickl'd down like the hail and the rain:
Had I na got greetin, my heart wad a broken,
For Oh, luve forsaken 's a tormenting pain!
Weel since he has &c.

Although he has left me for greed o' the siller,
I dinna envy him the gains he can win:
I rather wad bear a' the lade o' my sorrow,
Than ever hae acted sae faithless to him.—
Weel, since he has &c.

360. *The weary Pund o' Tow*

Chorus

THE weary pund, the weary pund,
The weary pund o' tow;
I think my wife will end her life,
Before she spin her tow.—

I bought my wife a stane o' lint,
  As gude as e'er did grow;
And a' that she has made o' that
  Is ae poor pund o' tow.—
    The weary &c.

There sat a bottle in a bole,
  Beyont the ingle low;
And ay she took the tither souk,
  To drouk the stourie tow.—
    The weary &c.

Quoth I, for shame, ye dirty dame,
  Gae spin your tap o' tow!
She took the rock, and wi' a knock,
  She brak it o'er my pow.—
    The weary &c.

At last her feet, I sang to see 't,
  Gaed foremost o'er the knowe;
And or I wad anither jad,
  I'll wallop in a tow.—
    The weary &c.

361. *I hae a wife o' my ain*

I HAE a wife o' my ain,
  I'll partake wi' naebody;
I'll tak Cuckold frae nane,
  I'll gie Cuckold to naebody.—

I hae a penny to spend,
  There, thanks to naebody;
I hae naething to lend,
  I'll borrow frae naebody.—

I am naebody's lord,
  I'll be slave to naebody;
I hae a gude braid sword,
  I'll tak dunts frae naebody.—

I'll be merry and free,
  I'll be sad for naebody;
Naebody cares for me,
  I care for naebody.—

362. *When she cam ben she bobbed*

O WHEN she cam ben she bobbed fu' law,
O when she cam ben she bobbed fu' law;
And when she cam ben she kiss'd Cockpen,
  And syne deny'd she did it at a'.—

And was na Cockpen right saucy witha',
And was na Cockpen right saucy witha',
In leaving the dochter of a lord,
  And kissin a Collier-lassie an' a'.—

O never look down, my lassie at a',
O never look down, my lassie at a';
Thy lips are as sweet and thy figure compleat,
  As the finest dame in castle or ha'.—

Tho' thou has nae silk and holland sae sma,
Tho' thou has nae silk and holland sae sma,
Thy coat and thy sark are thy ain handywark
  And Lady Jean was never sae braw.—

363. *O, for ane and twenty Tam*

Tune, The Moudiewort

An O, for ane and twenty Tam!
  An hey, sweet ane and twenty, Tam!
I'll learn my kin a rattlin sang,
  An I saw ane and twenty, Tam.

They snool me sair, and haud me down,
  And gar me look like bluntie, Tam;
But three short years will soon wheel roun',
  And then comes ane and twenty, Tam.
    An O, for &c.

A gleib o' lan', a claut o' gear,
  Was left me by my Auntie, Tam;
At kith or kin I need na spier,
  An I saw ane and twenty, Tam.
    An O, for &c.

They'll hae me wed a wealthy coof,
  Tho' I mysel hae plenty, Tam;
But hearst thou, laddie, there 's my loof,
  I'm thine at ane and twenty, Tam!
    An O, for &c.

R

364. *O Kenmure's on and awa, Willie*

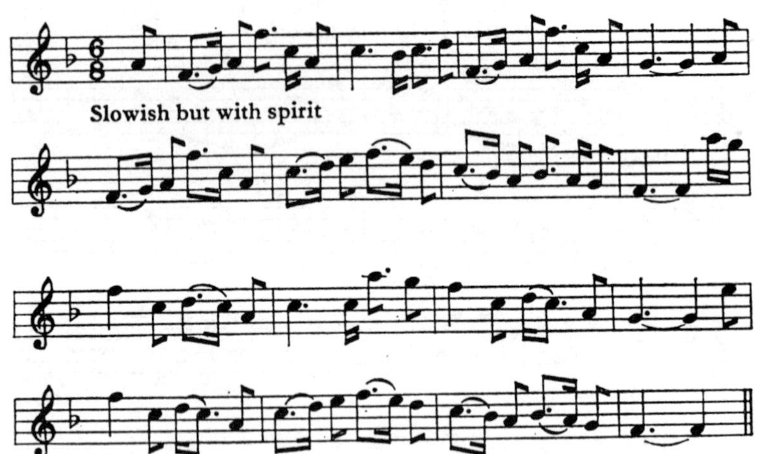

O KENMURE 's on and awa, Willie,
O Kenmure 's on and awa;
An Kenmure's Lord 's the bravest Lord
That ever Galloway saw.

Success to Kenmure's band, Willie!
Success to Kenmure's band,
There 's no a heart that fears a Whig
That rides by Kenmure's hand.

Here 's Kenmure's health in wine, Willie,
Here 's Kenmure's health in wine,
There ne'er was a coward o' Kenmure's blude,
Nor yet o' Gordon's Line.

O Kenmure's lads are men, Willie,
O Kenmure's lads are men,
Their hearts and swords are metal true,
And that their faes shall ken.

They'll live, or die wi' fame, Willie,
They'll live, or die wi' fame,
But soon wi' sounding victorie
May Kenmure's Lord come hame.

Here 's Him that 's far awa, Willie,
  Here 's Him that 's far awa,
And here 's the flower that I lo'e best,
  The rose that 's like the snaw.

365. *Bessy and her spinning wheel*

O LEEZE me on my spinnin-wheel,
And leeze me on my rock and reel;
Frae tap to tae that cleeds me bien,
And haps me fiel and warm at e'en!
I'll set me down and sing and spin,
While laigh descends the simmer sun,
Blest wi' content, and milk and meal,
O leeze me on my spinnin-wheel.—

On ilka hand the burnies trot,
And meet below my theekit cot;
The scented birk and hawthorn white
Across the pool their arms unite,

Alike to screen the birdie's nest,
And little fishes' callor rest:
The sun blinks kindly in the biel'
Where, blythe I turn my spinnin wheel.—

On lofty aiks the cushats wail,
And Echo cons the doolfu' tale;
The lintwhites in the hazel braes,
Delighted, rival ithers lays:
The craik amang the claver hay,
The pairtrick whirrin o'er the ley,
The swallow jinkin round my shiel,
Amuse me at my spinnin wheel.—

Wi' sma' to sell, and less to buy,
Aboon distress, below envy,
O wha wad leave this humble state,
For a' the pride of a' the Great?
Amid their flairing, idle toys,
Amid their cumbrous, dinsome joys,
Can they the peace and pleasure feel
Of Bessy at her spinnin wheel!

366. *My Collier laddie—*

WHARE live ye, my bonie lass,
  And tell me how they ca' ye?
My name, she says, is Mistress Jean,
  And I follow my Collier laddie.
My name, she says, is Mistress Jean,
  And I follow my Collier laddie.

See you not yon hills and dales
  The sun shines on sae brawlie?
They a' are mine and they shall be thine,
  Gin ye'll leave your Collier laddie.
They a' are &c.

Ye shall gang in gay attire,
  Weel buskit up sae gaudy;
And ane to wait on every hand,
  Gin ye'll leave your Collier laddie.
And ane to wait on every &c.

Tho' ye had a' the sun shines on,
  And the earth conceals sae lowly;
I wad turn my back on you and it a',
  And embrace my Collier laddie.
I wad turn &c.

I can win my five pennies in a day
  And spen 't at night fu' brawlie;
And make my bed in the Collier's neuk,
  And lie down wi' my Collier laddie.
And make my bed &c.

Loove for loove is the bargain for me,
  Tho' the wee Cot-house should haud me;
And the warld before me to win my bread,
  And fair fa' my Collier laddie!
And the warld before me to win my bread,
  And fair fa' my Collier laddie!

367. *The Shepherd's Wife*

THE Shepherd's wife cries o'er the knowe,
  Will ye come hame, will ye come hame;
The Shepherd's wife cries o'er the knowe,
  Will ye come hame again een, jo?

What will I get to my supper,
  Gin I come hame, gin I come hame?
What will I get to my supper,
  Gin I come hame again een, jo?

Ye 'se get a panfu' o' plumpin parridge,
  And butter in them, and butter in them,
Ye 'se get a panfu' o' plumpin parridge,
  Gin ye'll come hame again een, jo.—

Ha, ha, how! that 's naething that dow,
  I winna come hame, I canna come hame;
Ha, ha, how! that 's naething that dow,
  I winna come hame gin een, jo.—

The Shepherd's wife &c.
What will I get &c.

A reekin fat hen, weel fryth'd i' the pan,
  Gin ye'll come hame, gin ye'll come hame,
A reekin fat hen weel fryth'd i' the pan,
  Gin ye'll come hame again een jo.—

Ha, ha, how! &c.
The Shepherd's wife &c.
What will I get &c.

A weel made bed and a pair o' clean sheets,
  Gin ye'll come hame, gin ye'll come hame,
A weel made bed and a pair o' clean sheets,
  Gin ye'll come hame again een jo.—

Ha, ha, how! &c.
The Shepherd's wife &c.
What will I get &c.

A luving wife in lily-white linens,
  Gin ye'll come hame, gin ye'll come hame,
A luving wife in lily-white linens,
  Gin ye'll come hame again een, jo.—

Ha, ha, how! that 's something that dow,
  I will come hame, I will come hame;
Ha, ha, how! that 's something that dow,
  I will come hame again een, jo.—

368. *Johnie Blunt*—

THERE liv'd a man in yonder glen,
  And John Blunt was his name, O;
He maks gude maut, and he brews gude ale,
  And he bears a wondrous fame, O.—

The wind blew in the hallan ae night,
  Fu' snell out o'er the moor, O;
'Rise up, rise up, auld Luckie,' he says,
  'Rise up and bar the door, O.'—

They made a paction tween them twa,
  They made it firm and sure, O,
Whae'er sud speak the foremost word,
  Should rise and bar the door, O.—

Three travellers that had tint their gate,
  As thro' the hills they foor, O,
They airted by the line o' light
  Fu' straught to Johnie Blunt's door, O.—

They haurl'd auld Luckie out o' her bed,
  And laid her on the floor, O;
But never a word auld Luckie wad say,
  For barrin o' the door, O.—

'Ye've eaten my bread, ye hae druken my ale,
  'And ye'll mak my auld wife a whore, O—'
Aha, Johnie Blunt! ye hae spoke the first word,
  Get up and bar the door, O.—

369. *Country Lassie—*

IN simmer when the hay was mawn,
  And corn wav'd green in ilka field,
While claver blooms white o'er the lea,
  And roses blaw in ilka bield;

Blythe Bessie, in the milkin-shiel,
  Says, I'll be wed come o't what will;
Outspak a dame in wrinkled eild,
  O' gude advisement comes nae ill.—

Its ye hae wooers mony ane,
  And lassie ye're but young ye ken;
Then wait a wee, and canie wale,
  A routhie butt, a routhie ben:
There 's Johnie o' the Buskieglen,
  Fu' is his barn, fu' is his byre;
Tak this frae me, my bonie hen,
  It 's plenty beets the luver's fire.—

For Johnie o' the Buskieglen,
  I dinna care a single flie;
He loes sae weel his craps and kye,
  He has nae loove to spare for me:
But blythe 's the blink o' Robie's e'e,
  And weel I wat he loes me dear;
Ae blink o' him I wad na gie
  For Buskieglen and a' his gear.—

O thoughtless lassie, life 's a faught,
  The canniest gate, the strife is sair;
But ay fu'-han't is fechtin best,
  A hungry care 's an unco care:
But some will spend, and some will spare,
  An' wilfu' folk maun hae their will;
Syne as ye brew, my maiden fair,
  Keep mind that ye maun drink the yill.—

O gear will buy me rigs o' land,
  And gear will buy me sheep and kye;
But tender heart o' leesome loove,
  The gowd and siller canna buy:
We may be poor, Robie and I,
  Light is the burden Loove lays on;
Content and Loove brings peace and joy,
  What mair hae queens upon a throne.—

370. *Fair Eliza*

TURN again, thou fair Eliza,
  Ae kind blink before we part;
Rew on thy despairing Lover,
  Canst thou break his faithfu' heart!
Turn again, thou fair Eliza,
  If to love thy heart denies,
For pity hide the cruel sentence
  Under friendship's kind disguise!

Thee, sweet maid, hae I offended?
  The offence is loving thee:
Canst thou wreck his peace for ever,
  Wha for thine wad gladly die!
While the life beats in my bosom,
  Thou shalt mix in ilka throe:
Turn again, thou lovely maiden,
  Ae sweet smile on me bestow.—

Not the bee upon the blossom,
  In the pride o' sinny noon;
Not the little sporting fairy,
  All beneath the simmer moon;
Not the Poet in the moment
  Fancy lightens in his e'e,
Kens the pleasure, feels the rapture,
  That thy presence gies to me.—

371. *Ye Jacobites by name—*

YE Jacobites by name, give an ear, give an ear;
Ye Jacobites by name, give an ear;
Ye Jacobites by name
Your fautes I will proclaim,
Your doctrines I maun blame,
You shall hear.—

What is Right, and what is Wrang, by the law, by the law?
What is Right, and what is Wrang, by the law?
What is Right, and what is Wrang?
A short Sword, and a lang,
A weak arm, and a strang
For to draw.—

What makes heroic strife, fam'd afar, fam'd afar?
What makes heroic strife, fam'd afar?
What makes heroic strife?
To whet th' Assassin's knife,
Or hunt a Parent's life
Wi' bludie war.—

Then let your schemes alone, in the State, in the State,
Then let your schemes alone in the State,
Then let your schemes alone,
Adore the rising sun,
And leave a Man undone
To his fate.—

372. *The Posie*

O LUVE will venture in where it daur na weel be seen,
O luve will venture in where wisdom ance has been;
But I will down yon river rove, amang the woods sae green,
  And a' to pu' a posie to my ain dear May.—

The primrose I will pu', the firstling o' the year;
And I will pu' the pink, the emblem o' my Dear,
For she is the pink o' womankind, and blooms without a peer;
  And a' to be a posie to my ain dear May.—

I'll pu' the budding rose when Phebus peeps in view,
For it 's like a baumy kiss o' her sweet, bonie mou;
The hyacinth 's for constancy, wi' its unchanging blue,
  And a' to be a posie to my ain dear May.—

The lily it is pure, and the lily it is fair,
And in her lovely bosom I'll place the lily there;
The daisy 's for simplicity and unaffected air,
  And a' to be a posy to my ain dear May.—

The hawthorn I will pu', wi' its locks o' siller grey,
Where like an aged man it stands at break o' day;
But the songster's nest within the bush I winna tak away;
  And a' to be a posie to my ain dear May.—

The woodbine I will pu' when the e'ening star is near,
And the diamond draps o' dew shall be her een sae clear;
The violet 's for modesty which weel she fa's to wear,
  And a' to be a posie to my ain dear May.—

I'll tie the posie round wi' the silken band o' luve,
And I'll place it in her breast, and I'll swear by a' abuve,
That to my latest draught o' life the band shall ne'er remuve,
  And this will be a posie to my ain dear May.—

373. *Song—Sic a wife as Willie's wife—*

WILLIE Wastle dwalls on Tweed,
  The spot they ca' it Linkumdoddie;
A creeshie wabster till his trade,
  Can steal a clue wi' ony body:
He has a wife that 's dour and din,
  Tinkler Madgie was her mither;
Sic a wife as Willie's wife,
  I wadna gie a button for her.—

She has an e'e, she has but ane,
  Our cat has twa, the very colour;
Five rusty teeth, forbye a stump,
  A clapper-tongue wad deave a miller:
A whiskin beard about her mou,
  Her nose and chin they threaten ither;
Sic a wife as Willie's wife,
  I wad na gie a button for her.—

She 's bow-hough'd, she 's hem-shin'd,
Ae limpin leg a hand-bread shorter;
She 's twisted right, she 's twisted left,
To balance fair in ilka quarter:
She has a hump upon her breast,
The twin o' that upon her shouther;
Sic a wife as Willie's wife,
I wad na gie a button for her.—

Auld baudrans by the ingle sits,
An wi' her loof her face a washin;
But Willie's wife is nae sae trig,
She dights her grunzie wi' a hushian:
Her waly nieves like midden-creels,
Her feet wad fyle the Logan-water;
Sic a wife as Willie's wife,
I wad na gie a button for her.—

374. *My bonie laddie's young but he's growin yet—*

O LADY Mary Ann looks o'er the castle-wa',
She saw three bonie boys playin at the ba',
The youngest he was the flower amang them a',
My bonie laddie 's young but he 's growin yet.—

O Father, O Father, an ye think it fit,
We'll send him a year to the College yet,
We'll sew a green ribban round about his hat,
And that will let them ken he 's to marry yet.—

Lady Mary Ann was a flower in the dew,
Sweet was its smell and bonie was its hue,
And the langer it blossom'd, the sweeter it grew,
For the lily in the bud will be bonier yet.—

Young Charlie Cochran was the sprout of an aik,
Bonie, and bloomin and straught was its make,
The sun took delight to shine for its sake,
And it will be the brag o' the forest yet.—

The Simmer is gane when the leaves they were green,
And the days are awa that we hae seen,
But far better days I trust will come again,
For my bonie laddie 's young but he 's growin yet.—

375. *Such a parcel of rogues in a nation—*

FAREWEEL to a' our Scotish fame,
  Fareweel our ancient glory;
Fareweel even to the Scotish name,
  Sae fam'd in martial story!

Now Sark rins o'er the Solway sands,
And Tweed rins to the ocean,
To mark whare England's province stands,
Such a parcel of rogues in a nation!

What force or guile could not subdue,
Thro' many warlike ages,
Is wrought now by a coward few,
For hireling traitors' wages.
The English steel we could disdain,
Secure in valor's station;
But English gold has been our bane,
Such a parcel of rogues in a nation!

O would, or I had seen the day
That treason thus could sell us,
My auld grey head had lien in clay,
Wi' BRUCE and loyal WALLACE!
But pith and power, till my last hour,
I'll mak this declaration;
We're bought and sold for English gold,
Such a parcel of rogues in a nation!

376. *Kellyburnbraes—*

THERE lived a carl in Kellyburnbraes,
Hey and the rue grows bonie wi' thyme;
And he had a wife was the plague o' his days,
And the thyme it is wither'd and rue is in prime;
And he had a wife was the plague o' his days,
And the thyme it is wither'd and rue is in prime.—

Ae day as the carl gaed up the lang-glen,
  Hey &c.
He met wit the d–v–l, says, how do ye fen?
  And &c.

I've got a bad wife, Sir, that 's a' my complaint,
  Hey &c.
For, saving your presence, to her ye're a saint,
  And &c.

It 's neither your stot nor your staig I shall crave,
  Hey &c.
But gie me your wife, man, for her I must have,
  And &c.

O, welcome most kindly! the blythe carl said;
  Hey &c.
But if ye can match her—ye're waur than ye're ca'd,
  And &c.

The d–v–l has got the auld wife on his back,
  Hey &c.
And like a poor pedlar he 's carried his pack,
  And &c.

He 's carried her hame to his ain hallan-door,
  Hey &c.
Syne bade her gae in for a b—ch and a wh—,
  And &c.

Then straight he makes fifty, the pick o' his band,
  Hey &c.
Turn out on her guard in the clap of a hand,
  And &c.

The carlin gaed thro' them like onie wud bear,
  Hey &c.
Whae'er she gat hands on, cam near her nae mair,
  And &c.

A reekit, wee devil looks over the wa',
  Hey &c.
O help, Master, help! or she'll ruin us a',
  And &c.

The d–v–l he swore by the edge o' his knife,
  Hey &c.
He pitied the man that was ty'd to a wife,
  And &c.

The d–v–l he swore by the kirk and the bell,
  Hey &c.
He was not in wedlock, thank Heaven, but in h—,
  And &c.

Then Satan has travell'd again wi' his pack,
  Hey &c.
And to her auld husband he 's carried her back,
  And &c.

I hae been a d–v–l the feck o' my life,
  Hey and the rue grows bonie wi' thyme;
But ne'er was in h–ll till I met wi' a wife,
  An' the thyme it is wither'd, and rue is in prime.
But ne'er was in h–ll till I met wi' a wife,
  An' the thyme it is wither'd and rue is in prime.

377. [*Jockey fou and Jenny fain*]

[—ITHERS seek they kenna what,
Features, carriage, and a' that,
Gie me loove in her I court;
Loove to loove maks a' the sport.—]

Let loove sparkle in her e'e;
Let her loe nae man but me;
That 's the tocher gude I prize,
There the Luver's treasure lies.—

378. *The Slave's Lament*—

IT was in sweet Senegal that my foes did me enthrall
For the lands of Virginia-ginia O;
Torn from that lovely shore, and must never see it more,
And alas! I am weary, weary O!
Torn from &c.

All on that charming coast is no bitter snow and frost,
Like the lands of Virginia-ginia O;
There streams for ever flow, and there flowers for ever blow,
And alas! I am weary, weary O!
There streams &c.

The burden I must bear, while the cruel scourge I fear,
In the lands of Virginia-ginia O;
And I think on friends most dear with the bitter, bitter tear,
And Alas! I am weary, weary O!
And I think &c.

379. *Bonie Bell*

THE smiling spring comes in rejoicing,
  And surly winter grimly flies;
Now crystal clear are the falling waters,
  And bonny blue are the sunny skies.
Fresh o'er the mountains breaks forth the morning,
  The ev'ning gilds the Ocean's swell;
All Creatures joy in the sun's returning,
  And I rejoice in my Bonie Bell.

The flowery Spring leads sunny Summer,
  And yellow Autumn presses near,
Then in his turn comes gloomy Winter,
  Till smiling Spring again appear.
Thus seasons dancing, life advancing,
  Old Time and Nature their changes tell,
But never ranging, still unchanging,
  I adore my Bonie Bell.

380. *The gallant Weaver*

WHERE Cart rins rowin to the sea,
By mony a flower and spreading tree,
There lives a lad, the lad for me,
  He is a gallant Weaver.—

Oh I had wooers aught or nine,
They gied me rings and ribbans fine;
And I was fear'd my heart wad tine
  And I gied it to the Weaver.—

My daddie sign'd my tocher-band
To gie the lad that has the land,
But to my heart I'll add my hand
  And give it to the Weaver.—

While birds rejoice in leafy bowers,
While bees delight in opening flowers,
While corn grows green in simmer showers
  I love my gallant Weaver.—

381. *Hey Ca' thro'*

Up wi' the carls of Dysart,
And the lads o' Buckhiven,
And the Kimmers o' Largo,
And the lasses o' Leven.
Hey ca' thro' ca' thro'
For we hae mickle a do,
Hey ca' thro' ca' thro'
For we hae mickle a do.

We hae tales to tell,
And we hae sangs to sing;
We hae pennies to spend,
And we hae pints to bring.
Hey ca' thro' &c.

We'll live a' our days,
And them that comes behin',
Let them do the like,
And spend the gear they win.
Hey ca' thro' &c.

382. *Can ye labor lea—*

Chorus

O CAN ye labor lea, young man,
  O can ye labor lea;
Gae back the gate ye came again,
  Ye 'se never scorn me.—

I fee'd a man at martinmass,
  Wi' airle-pennies three;
But a' the faute I had to him,
  He could na labor lea.—
    O can ye &c.

O clappin 's gude in Febarwar,
  An kissin 's sweet in May;
But what signifies a young man's love,
  An 't dinna last for ay.—
    O can ye &c.

O kissin is the key o' luve,
  An clappin is the lock,
An makin-of 's the best thing,
  That e'er a young Thing got.—
    O can ye &c.

383. *The deuks dang o'er my daddie—*

THE bairns gat out wi' an unco shout,
  The deuks dang o'er my daddie, O,
The fien-ma-care, quo' the feirrie auld wife,
  He was but a paidlin body, O.—
He paidles out, an' he paidles in,
  An' he paidles late and early, O;
This seven lang year I hae lien by his side,
  An he is but a fusionless carlie, O.—

O had your tongue, my feirrie auld wife,
  O had your tongue, now Nansie, O:
I've seen the day, and sae hae ye,
  Ye wad na been sae donsie, O.—
I've seen the day ye butter'd my brose,
  And cuddled me late and early, O;
But downa do's come o'er me now,
  And, Oh, I find it sairly, O!

384. *As I went out ae May morning*

As I went out ae may morning,
  A may morning it chanc'd to be;
There I was aware of a weelfar'd Maid
  Cam linkin' o'er the lea to me.—

O but she was a weelfar'd maid,
  The boniest lass that 's under the sun;
I spier'd gin she could fancy me,
  But her answer was, I am too young.—

To be your bride I am too young,
  To be your loun wad shame my kin,
So therefore pray young man begone,
  For you never, never shall my favor win.—

But amang yon birks and hawthorns green,
  Where roses blaw and woodbines hing,
O there I learn'd my bonie lass
  That she was not a single hour too young.—

The lassie blush'd, the lassie sigh'd,
  And the tear stood twinklin in her e'e;
O kind Sir, since ye hae done me this wrang,
  It 's pray when will ye marry me.—

It 's of that day tak ye nae heed,
  For that 's ae day ye ne'er shall see;
For ought that pass'd between us twa,
  Ye had your share as weel as me.—

She wrang her hands, she tore her hair,
  She cried out most bitterlie,
O what will I say to my mammie,
  When I gae hame wi' my big bellie!

O as ye maut, so maun ye brew,
  And as ye brew, so maun ye tun;
But come to my arms, my ae bonie lass,
  For ye never shall rue what ye now hae done!—

385. *She's fair and fause &c.*

The lads of Leith

SHE 's fair and fause that causes my smart,
  I lo'ed her meikle and lang;
She 's broken her vow, she 's broken my heart,
  And I may e'en gae hang.—
A coof cam in wi' routh o' gear,
And I hae tint my dearest dear;
But woman is but warld's gear,
  Sae let the bonie lass gang.—

Whae'er ye be that woman love,
  To this be never blind;
Nae ferlie 'tis tho' fickle she prove,
  A woman has 't by kind:
O woman, lovely woman fair!
An angel form 's faun to thy share;
'Twad been o'er meikle to gien thee mair,
  I mean an angel mind.

386. *The De'il's awa wi' th' Exciseman*

THE deil cam fiddlin thro' the town,
  And danc'd awa wi' th' Exciseman;
And ilka wife cries, auld Mahoun,
  I wish you luck o' the prize, man.

Chorus

The deil 's awa the deil 's awa
  The deil 's awa wi' th' Exciseman,
He 's danc'd awa he 's danc'd awa
    He 's danc'd awa wi' th' Exciseman.

We'll mak our maut and we'll brew our drink,
  We'll laugh, sing, and rejoice, man;
And mony braw thanks to the meikle black deil,
  That danc'd awa wi' th' Exciseman.
    The deil 's awa &c.

There 's threesome reels, there 's foursome reels,
  There 's hornpipes and strathspeys, man,
But the ae best dance e'er cam to the Land
  Was, the deil 's awa wi' th' Exciseman.
    The deil 's awa &c.

387. *Song*

Tune, Ewe bughts Marion

I

WILL ye go to the Indies, my Mary,
  And leave auld Scotia's shore;
Will ye go to the Indies, my Mary,
  Across th' Atlantic roar.

2

O sweet grows the lime and the orange
  And the apple on the pine;
But a' the charms o' the Indies
  Can never equal thine.

3

I hae sworn by the Heavens to my Mary,
  I hae sworn by the Heavens to be true;
And sae may the Heavens forget me,
  When I forget my vow!

4

O plight me your faith, my Mary,
  And plight me your lily-white hand;
O plight me your faith, my Mary,
  Before I leave Scotia's strand.

5

We hae plighted our truth, my Mary,
  In mutual affection to join:
And curst be the cause that shall part us,
  The hour, and the moment o' time!!!

388. *My wife 's a winsome wee thing*

SHE is a winsome wee thing,
She is a handsome wee thing,
She is a lo'esome wee thing,
  This sweet wee wife o' mine,

2

I never saw a fairer,
I never lo'ed a dearer;
And neist my heart I'll wear her,
  For fear my jewel tine.

3

She is a winsome wee thing,
She is a handsome wee thing,
She is a lo'esome wee thing,
  This dear wee wife o' mine.

4

The warld's wrack we share o't,
The warstle and the care o't;
Wi' her I'll blythely bear it,
And think my lot divine.

389. *Highland Mary—*

Tune, Katharine Ogie—

Ye banks, and braes, and streams around
The castle o' Montgomery,
Green be your woods, and fair your flowers,
Your waters never drumlie!
There Simmer first unfald her robes,
And there the langest tarry:
For there I took the last Fareweel
O' my sweet Highland Mary.

How sweetly bloom'd the gay, green birk,
How rich the hawthorn's blossom;
As underneath their fragrant shade,
I clasp'd her to my bosom!

The golden Hours, on angel wings,
  Flew o'er me and my Dearie;
For dear to me as light and life
  Was my sweet Highland Mary.

Wi' mony a vow, and lock'd embrace,
  Our parting was fu' tender;
And pledging aft to meet again,
  We tore oursels asunder:
But Oh, fell Death's untimely frost,
  That nipt my Flower sae early!
Now green 's the sod, and cauld 's the clay,
  That wraps my Highland Mary!

O pale, pale now, those rosy lips
  I aft hae kiss'd sae fondly!
And clos'd for ay, the sparkling glance,
  That dwalt on me sae kindly!
And mouldering now in silent dust,
  That heart that lo'ed me dearly!
But still within my bosom's core
  Shall live my Highland Mary.

390. *The Rights of Woman—Spoken by Miss Fontenelle on her benefit night*

WHILE Europe's eye is fixed on mighty things,
The fate of Empires, and the fall of Kings;
While quacks of State must each produce his plan,
And even children lisp The Rights of Man;
Amid this mighty fuss, just let me mention,
The Rights of Woman merit some attention.—

First, in the Sexes' intermixed connection,
One sacred Right of Woman is, Protection.
The tender flower that lifts its head, elate,
Helpless, must fall before the blasts of Fate,
Sunk on the earth, defaced its lovely form,
Unless *your Shelter* ward th' impending storm.

Our second Right—but needless here is caution,
To keep that Right inviolate 's the fashion.
Each man of sense has it so full before him
He'd die before he'd wrong it—'tis Decorum.—

There was, indeed, in far less polished days,
A time when rough, rude man had naughty ways:
Would swagger, swear, get drunk, kick up a riot,
Nay even thus invade a lady's quiet.—
Now, thank our Stars! these Gothic times are fled,
Now well-bred men (and you are all well-bred)
Most justly think (and we are much the gainers)
Such conduct neither spirit, wit, nor manners.—

For Right the third, our last, our best, our dearest,
That Right to fluttering Female hearts the nearest,
Which even the Rights of Kings, in low prostration,
Most humbly own—'tis dear, dear Admiration!
[In that blest sphere alone we live and move;
There taste that life of life—immortal love.—]
Smiles, glances, sighs, tears, fits, flirtations, airs;
'Gainst such an host, what flinty savage dares.—
When aweful Beauty joins in all her charms,
Who is so rash as rise in rebel arms?

But truce with kings, and truce with Constitutions,
With bloody armaments, and Revolutions;
Let MAJESTY your first attention summon,
Ah, ça ira! THE MAJESTY OF WOMAN!!!

391. *Here's a Health to them that's awa*

HERE 's a health to them that 's awa,
Here 's a health to them that 's awa;
And wha winna wish gude luck to our cause,
May never gude luck be their fa'!
It 's gude to be merry and wise,
It 's gude to be honest and true,
It 's gude to support Caledonia's cause,
And bide by the Buff and the Blue.

Here 's a health to them that 's awa,
Here 's a health to them that 's awa;
Here 's a health to Charlie, the chief o' the clan,
Altho' that his band be sma'.
May Liberty meet wi' success!
May Prudence protect her frae evil!
May Tyrants and Tyranny tine i' the mist,
And wander their way to the devil!

Here 's a health to them that 's awa,
Here 's a health to them that 's awa;
Here 's a health to Tammie, the Norland laddie,
That lives at the lug o' the law!
Here 's freedom to him that wad read,
Here 's freedom to him that wad write!
There 's nane ever fear'd that the Truth should be heard,
But they whom the Truth wad indite.

Here 's a health to them that 's awa,
An' here 's to them that 's awa!
Here 's to Maitland and Wycombe! Let wha does na like 'em
Be built in a hole in the wa'!
Here 's timmer that 's red at the heart,
Here 's fruit that is sound at the core;
And may he that wad turn the buff and blue coat
Be turn'd to the back o' the door!

Here 's a health to them that 's awa,
Here 's a health to them that 's awa;
Here 's Chieftan M^c^leod, a chieftan worth gowd
Tho' bred amang mountains o' snaw!
Here 's friends on baith sides o' the Forth,
And friends on baith sides o' the Tweed;
And wha wad betray old Albion's right,
May they never eat of her bread!

392. *The lea-rig—*

WHEN o'er the hill the eastern star
  Tells bughtin-time is near, my jo,
And owsen frae the furrowed field
  Return sae dowf and weary O:
Down by the burn where scented birks
  Wi' dew are hanging clear, my jo,
I'll meet thee on the lea-rig,
  My ain kind Dearie O.

At midnight hour, in mirkest glen,
  I'd rove and ne'er be irie O,
If thro' that glen I gaed to thee,
  My ain kind Dearie O:
Altho' the night were ne'er sae wet,
  And I were ne'er sae weary O,
I'd meet thee on the lea-rig,
  My ain kind Dearie O.

The hunter lo'es the morning sun,
  To rouse the mountain deer, my jo,
At noon the fisher takes the glen,
  Adown the burn to steer, my jo;

Gie me the hour o' gloamin grey,
  It maks my heart sae cheary O
To meet thee on the lea-rig
  My ain kind Dearie O.

393. *Auld Rob Morris*

THERE 's auld Rob Morris that wons in yon glen,
He 's the king o' gude fellows, and wale of auld men;
He has gowd in his coffers, he has owsen and kine,
And ae bonie lassie, his dawtie and mine.

She 's fresh as the morning, the fairest in May;
She 's sweet as the e'enin amang the new hay;
As blythe and as artless as the lambs on the lea,
And dear to my heart as the light to my e'e.

But oh, she 's an Heiress, auld Robin 's a laird;
And my daddie has nocht but a cot-house and yard:
A wooer like me maunna hope to come speed;
The wounds I must hide that will soon be my dead.

The day comes to me, but delight brings me nane;
The night comes to me, but my rest it is gane:
I wander my lane like a night-troubled ghaist,
And I sigh as my heart it wad burst in my breast.

O had she but been of a laigher degree,
I then might hae hop'd she wad smil'd upon me!
O, how past descriving had then been my bliss,
As now my distraction no words can express!

394. *Duncan Gray*

DUNCAN GRAY cam here to woo,
  Ha, ha, the wooing o't,
On blythe Yule night when we were fu',
  Ha, ha, the wooing o't.
Maggie coost her head fu' high,
Look'd asklent and unco skiegh,
Gart poor Duncan stand abiegh;
  Ha, ha, the wooing o't.

Duncan fleech'd, and Duncan pray'd;
  Ha, ha, the wooing o't.
Meg was deaf as Ailsa craig,
  Ha, ha, the wooing o't.
Duncan sigh'd baith out and in,
Grat his een baith bleer't an' blin',
Spak o' lowpin o'er a linn;
  Ha, ha, the wooing o't.

Time and Chance are but a tide,
  Ha, ha, the wooing o't.
Slighted love is sair to bide,
  Ha, ha, the wooing o't.
Shall I, like a fool, quoth he,
For a haughty hizzie die?
She may gae to —— France for me!
  Ha, ha, the wooing o't.

How it comes let Doctors tell,
  Ha, ha, the wooing o't.
Meg grew sick as he grew heal,
  Ha, ha, the wooing o't.
Something in her bosom wrings,
For relief a sigh she brings;
And O her een, they spak sic things!
  Ha, ha, the wooing o't.

Duncan was a lad o' grace,
  Ha, ha, the wooing o't.
Maggie's was a piteous case,
  Ha, ha, the wooing o't.
Duncan could na be her death,
Swelling Pity smoor'd his Wrath;
Now they're crouse and canty baith,
  Ha, ha, the wooing o't.

395. [*Why should na poor folk mowe*]

WHEN Princes and Prelates and het-headed zealots
  All Europe hae set in a lowe,
The poor man lies down, nor envies a crown,
  And comforts himsel with a mowe.—

Chorus

  And why shouldna poor folk mowe, mowe, mowe,
    And why shouldna poor folk mowe:
  The great folk hae siller, and houses and lands,
    Poor bodies hae naething but mowe.—

2

When Br–nsw–ck's great Prince cam a cruising to Fr–nce
  Republican billies to cowe,
Bauld Br–nsw–c's great Prince wad hae shawn better sense,
  At hame with his Princess to mowe.—
    And why should na &c.—

3

Out over the Rhine proud Pr–ss–a wad shine,
  To *spend* his best blood he did vow;
But Frederic had better ne'er forded the water,
  But *spent* as he docht in a mowe.—
    And why &c.—

4

By sea and by shore! the Emp–r–r swore,
In Paris he'd kick up a row;
But Paris sae ready just leugh at the laddie
And bade him gae tak him a mowe.—
And why &c.—

5

Auld Kate laid her claws on poor Stanislaus,
And Poland has bent like a bow:
May the deil in her a— ram a huge pr–ck o' brass!
And damn her in h–ll with a mowe!
And why &c.—

6

But truce with commotions and new-fangled notions,
A bumper I trust you'll allow:
Here 's George our gude king and Charlotte his queen,
And lang may they tak a gude mowe!

396. *Here awa', there awa'*

HERE awa', there awa' wandering, Willie,
Here awa', there awa', haud awa' hame;
Come to my bosom, my ae only deary,
Tell me thou bring'st me my Willie the same.

Loud tho' the winter blew cauld on our parting,
'Twas na the blast brought the tear in my e'e:
Welcome now Simmer, and welcome my Willie;
The Simmer to Nature, my Willie to me.

Rest, ye wild storms, in the cave o' your slumbers,
  How your dread howling a lover alarms!
Wauken, ye breezes! row gently, ye billows!
  And waft my dear Laddie ance mair to my arms.

But oh, if he 's faithless, and minds na his Nanie,
  Flow still between us, thou wide roaring main:
May I never see it, may I never trow it,
  But, dying, believe that my Willie 's my ain!

X. Poems 1793

DUMFRIES

397. *Galla Water*

BRAW, braw lads on Yarrow braes,
  Rove among the blooming heather;
But Yarrow braes, nor Ettrick shaws,
  Can match the lads o' Galla water.

But there is ane, a secret ane,
  Aboon them a' I loe him better;
And I'll be his, and he'll be mine,
  The bonie lad o' Galla water.

Altho' his daddie was nae laird,
  And tho' I hae na meikle tocher,
Yet rich in kindest, truest love,
  We'll tent our flocks by Galla water.

It ne'er was wealth, it ne'er was wealth,
  That coft contentment, peace, or pleasure;
The bands and bliss o' mutual love,
  O that 's the chiefest warld's treasure!

398. *Song—*

Tune, Cauld kail in Aberdeen

O POORTITH cauld, and restless love,
  Ye wrack my peace between ye;
Yet poortith a' I could forgive
  An 'twere na for my Jeanie.

Chorus

O why should Fate sic pleasure have,
  Life's dearest bands untwining?
Or why sae sweet a flower as love,
  Depend on Fortune's shining?

This warld's wealth when I think on,
  Its pride, and a' the lave o't;
My curse on silly coward man,
  That he should be the slave o't.
    O why &c.

Her een sae bonie blue betray,
  How she repays my passion;
But Prudence is her o'erword ay,
  She talks o' rank and fashion.
    O why &c.

O wha can prudence think upon,
And sic a lassie by him:
O wha can prudence think upon,
And sae in love as I am?
O why &c.

How blest the wild-wood Indian's fate,
He wooes his simple Dearie:
The silly bogles, Wealth and State,
Did never make them eerie.
O why &c.

399. *Lord Gregory—*

O MIRK, mirk is this midnight hour,
And loud the tempest's roar:
A waefu' wanderer seeks thy tower,
Lord Gregory ope thy door.

An exile frae her father's ha',
And a' for loving thee;
At least some pity on me shaw,
If love it may na be.

Lord Gregory, mind'st thou not the grove,
  By bonie Irwine-side,
Where first I own'd that virgin-love
  I lang, lang had denied.

How aften didst thou pledge and vow,
  Thou wad for ay be mine;
And my fond heart, itsel sae true,
  It ne'er mistrusted thine.

Hard is thy heart, Lord Gregory,
  And flinty is thy breast:
Thou dart of Heaven that flashest by,
  O wilt thou give me rest!

Ye mustering thunders from above
  Your willing victim see!
But spare, and pardon my fause Love,
  His wrangs to Heaven and me!

400. *Sonnet—On hearing a thrush sing on a morning walk in January*

SING on, sweet thrush, upon the leafless bough,
Sing on, sweet bird, I'll listen to thy strain;
See aged Winter 'mid his surly reign
At thy blythe carol clears his furrowed brow.—

Thus in bleak Poverty's dominion drear
Sits meek Content, with light, unanxious heart,
Welcomes the rapid moments, bids them part,
Nor asks if they bring aught to hope, or fear.—

I thank thee, Author of this opening day,
Thou whose bright sun now gilds yon orient skies.
Riches denied, thy boon was purer joys,
What Wealth could never give, nor take away!—

But come, thou child of Poverty and Care,
The mite high Heaven bestowed, that mite with thee I'll share.

401. *Address to General Dumourier*

YOU'RE welcome to Despots, Dumourier;
You're welcome to Despots, Dumourier.—
  How does Dampiere do?
  Aye, and Bournonville too?
Why did they not come along with you, Dumourier?

I will fight France with you, Dumourier,—
I will fight France with you, Dumourier:—
  I will fight France with you,
  I will take my chance with you;
By my soul I'll dance a dance with you, Dumourier.

Then let us fight about, Dumourier;
Then let us fight about, Dumourier;
  Then let us fight about,
  'Till freedom's spark is out,
Then we'll be d–mned no doubt—Dumourier.

402. [*A Toast*]

At a meeting of the Dumfriesshire Volunteers, held to commemorate the anniversary of Rodney's Victory, April 12th, 1782, BURNS was called upon for a Song, instead of which he delivered the following lines extempore.

INSTEAD of a song, boys, I'll give you a toast,
Here 's the memory of those on the twelfth that we lost;
That we lost, did I say, nay, by heav'n that we found,
For their fame it shall last while the world goes round.
The next in succession, I'll give you the King,
Whoe'er wou'd betray him, on high may he swing;
And here 's the grand fabric, our free Constitution,
As built on the base of the great Revolution;
And longer with Politics, not to be cramm'd,
Be Anarchy cur'sd, and be Tyranny damn'd;
And who wou'd to Liberty e'er prove disloyal,
May his son be a hangman, and he his first trial.

403. *Open the door to me Oh*

OH, open the door, some pity to shew,
  If love it may na be, Oh;
Tho' thou hast been false, I'll ever prove true,
  Oh, open the door to me, Oh.

Cauld is the blast upon my pale cheek,
  But caulder thy love for me, Oh:
The frost that freezes the life at my heart,
  Is nought to my pains frae thee, Oh.

The wan moon sets behind the white wave,
  And time is setting with me, Oh:
False friends, false love, farewell! for mair
  I'll ne'er trouble them, nor thee, Oh.

She has open'd the door, she has open'd it wide,
  She sees his pale corse on the plain, Oh:
My true love! she cried, and sank down by his side,
  Never to rise again, Oh.

404. *Jessie—A new Scots song*

To the tune—Bonie Dundee

TRUE-HEARTED was he, the sad swain o' the Yarrow,
  And fair are the maids on the banks o' the Ayr;
But by the sweet side o' the Nith's winding river,
  Are lovers as faithful, and maidens as fair:
To equal young Jessie, seek Scotia all over;
  To equal young Jessie, you seek it in vain:
Grace, Beauty and Elegance fetter her lover,
  And maidenly modesty fixes the chain.

Fresh is the rose in the gay, dewy morning,
And sweet is the lily at evening close;
But in the fair presence o' lovely, young Jessie,
Unseen is the lily, unheeded the rose.
Love tits in her smile, a wizard ensnaring;
Enthron'd in her een he delivers his law:
And still to her charms she alone is a stranger,
Her modest demeanor 's the jewel of a'.

405. *Song—*

Nansy 's to the green-wood gane

FAREWELL, thou stream that winding flows
Around Eliza's dwelling;
O mem'ry, spare the cruel throes
Within my bosom swelling:
Condemn'd to drag a hopeless chain,
And yet in secret languish;
To feel a fire in every vein,
Nor dare disclose my anguish.—

Love's veriest wretch, unseen, unknown
  I fain my griefs would cover;
The bursting sigh, th' unweeting groan,
  Betray the hapless lover:
I know thou doom'st me to despair,
  Nor wilt, nor canst relieve me;
But, Oh Eliza, hear one prayer,
  For pity's sake forgive me!

The music of thy voice I heard,
  Nor wist while it enslav'd me;
I saw thine eyes, yet nothing fear'd,
  Till fears no more had sav'd me:
Th' unwary Sailor thus, aghast,
  The wheeling torrent viewing,
Mid circling horrors sinks at last
  In overwhelming ruin.—

406. *When wild War's deadly Blast was blawn*

The Mill, Mill O

When wild War's deadly blast was blawn,
  And gentle Peace returning,
Wi' mony a sweet babe fatherless,
  And mony a widow mourning:
I left the lines, and tented field,
  Where lang I'd been a lodger,
My humble knapsack a' my wealth,
  A poor and honest sodger.

A leal, light heart was in my breast,
  My hand unstain'd wi' plunder;
And for fair Scotia, hame again
  I cheery on did wander.
I thought upon the banks of Coil,
  I thought upon my Nancy,
And ay I mind't the witching smile
  That caught my youthful fancy.

At length I reach'd the bonny glen,
  Where early life I sported;
I pass'd the mill and trysting thorn,
  Where Nancy aft I courted:
Wha spied I but my ain dear maid,
  Down by her mother's dwelling!
And turn'd me round to hide the flood
  That in my een was swelling.

Wi' alter'd voice, quoth I, sweet lass,
  Sweet as yon hawthorn's blossom,
O! happy, happy may he be
  That 's dearest to thy bosom:
My purse is light, I've far to gang,
  And fain wad be thy lodger;
I've serv'd my king and country lang,
  Take pity on a sodger!

Sae wistfully she gaz'd on me,
  And lovelier was than ever;
Quo' she, a sodger ance I lo'ed,
  Forget him shall I never:
Our humble cot, and hamely fare,
  Ye freely shall partake it,
That gallant badge, the dear cockade,
  Ye're welcome for the sake o't.

She gaz'd—she redden'd like a rose,—
  Syne pale like ony lily,
She sank within my arms, and cried,
  Art thou my ain dear Willie?—
By Him who made yon sun and sky,
  By whom true love 's regarded,
I am the man—and thus may still
  True lovers be rewarded!

The wars are o'er, and I'm come hame,
  And find thee still true-hearted;
Tho' poor in gear, we're rich in love,
  And mair,—we'se ne'er be parted!
Quo' she, my grandsire left me gowd,
  A mailin plenish'd fairly;
And come, my faithful sodger lad,
  Thou'rt welcome to it dearly!

For gold the merchant ploughs the main,
  The farmer ploughs the manor;
But glory is the sodger's prize,
  The sodger's wealth is honour;
The brave poor sodger ne'er despise,
  Nor count him as a stranger;
Remember, he 's his country's stay
  In day and hour of danger.

407A. *O ken ye what Meg o' the mill has gotten*

O KEN ye what Meg o' the mill has gotten,
An' ken ye what Meg o' the mill has gotten;
A braw new naig wi' the tail o' a rottan,
And that 's what Meg o' the mill has gotten.

O ken ye what Meg o' the mill loes dearly,
An' ken ye what Meg o' the mill loes dearly;
A dram o' gude strunt in a morning early,
And that 's what Meg o' the mill loes dearly.

O ken ye how Meg o' the mill was married,
An' ken ye how Meg o' the mill was married;
The Priest he was oxter'd, the Clerk he was carried,
And that 's how Meg o' the mill was married.

O ken ye how Meg o' the mill was bedded,
An' ken ye how Meg o' the mill was bedded;
The groom gat sae fu' he fell awald beside it,
And that 's how Meg o' the mill was bedded.

407B. *Ken ye what Meg o' the mill has gotten—*

O KEN ye what Meg o' the mill has gotten,
An ken ye what Meg o' the mill has gotten?
She 's gotten a coof wi' a claut o' siller,
And broken the heart o' the barley Miller.—

The Miller was strappin, the Miller was ruddy,
A heart like a lord, and a hue like a lady;
The Laird was a widdefu', bleerit knurl;
She 's left the gude-fallow and taen the churl.—

The Miller he hecht her, a heart leal and luving,
The Laird did address her wi' matter mair muving,
A fine pacing horse wi' a clear chainet bridle,
A whip by her side, and a bony side-sadle.

O wae on the siller, it is sae prevailing,
And wae on the luve that 's fix'd on a mailin!
A tocher 's nae word in a true luver's parle,
But, gie me my luve, and a fig for the warl!

408. *Song—*

Tune, Liggeram cosh—

BLYTHE hae I been on yon hill,
As the lambs before me;
Careless ilka thought and free,
As the breeze flew o'er me:

Now nae langer sport and play,
  Mirth or sang can please me;
Lesley is sae fair and coy,
  Care and anguish seize me.

Heavy, heavy is the task,
  Hopeless love declaring:
Trembling, I dow nocht but glowr,
  Sighing, dumb, despairing!
If she winna ease the thraws,
  In my bosom swelling;
Underneath the grass-green sod
  Soon maun be my dwelling.

409. *Song—*

Tune Logan Water—

O, LOGAN, sweetly didst thou glide,
The day I was my Willie's bride;
And years sinsyne hae o'er us run,
Like Logan to the simmer sun.

But now thy flowery banks appear
Like drumlie Winter, dark and drear,
While my dear lad maun face his faes,
Far, far frae me and Logan braes.—

Again the merry month o' May
Has made our hills and vallies gay;
The birds rejoice in leafy bowers,
The bees hum round the breathing flowers:
Blythe Morning lifts his rosy eye,
And Evening's tears are tears of joy:
My soul, delightless, a' surveys,
While Willie 's far frae Logan braes.—

Within yon milkwhite hawthorn bush,
Amang her nestlings sits the thrush;
Her faithfu' Mate will share her toil,
Or wi' his song her cares beguile:
But, I wi' my sweet nurslings here,
Nae Mate to help, nae Mate to cheer,
Pass widowed nights and joyless days,
While Willie 's far frae Logan braes.—

O wae upon you, Men o' State,
That brethren rouse in deadly hate!
As ye make mony a fond heart mourn,
Sae may it on your heads return!
How can your flinty hearts enjoy
The widow's tears, the orphan's cry:
But soon may Peace bring happy days
And Willie, hame to Logan braes!

410. *On being asked why God had made Miss D—— so little and Mrs A—— so big—*

ASK why God made the GEM so small,
  And why so huge the granite?
Because God meant, mankind should set
  That higher value on it.—

411A. [*On*] *Maxwell of Cardoness*—

BLESS J–s–s Ch——, O Cardoness,
With grateful lifted eyes;
Who taught that not the soul alone,
But body too shall rise.

For had he said, the soul alone
From death I will deliver:
Alas, alas, O Cardoness!
Then hadst thou lain forever!

411B. *Extempore—On being shown a beautiful Country seat belonging to the same*—

WE grant they're thine, those beauties all,
So lovely in our eye:
Keep them, thou eunuch, C——ss,
For others to enjoy!

412. [*Annotations in Verse*]

[A] WISDOM and Science—honor'd Powers!
Pardon the truth a sinner tells;
I owe my dearest, raptured hours
To FOLLY with her cap and bells.—

[B] GRANT me, indulgent Heaven, that I may live
To see the miscreants feel the pains they give:
Deal Freedom's sacred treasures free as air,
Till SLAVE and DESPOT be but *things which were!*

[C] PERISH their names, however great or brave,
Who in the DESPOT's cursed errands bleed!
But who for FREEDOM fills a hero's grave,
Fame with a Seraph-pen, record the glorious deed!

[D] LOVE's records, written on a heart like mine,
Not Time's last effort can efface a line.

R. B.

413. *O were my Love yon Lilack fair*

O WERE my Love yon Lilack fair,
  Wi' purple blossoms to the Spring;
And I, a bird to shelter there,
  When wearied on my little wing.

How I wad mourn, when it was torn
  By Autumn wild, and Winter rude!
But I wad sing on wanton wing,
  When youthfu' May its bloom renew'd.

[O gin my love were yon red rose,
  That grows upon the castle wa'!
And I mysel' a drap o' dew,
  Into her bonnie breast to fa'!

Oh, there beyond expression blesst
  I'd feast on beauty a' the night;
Seal'd on her silk-saft faulds to rest,
  Till fley'd awa by Phebus' light!]

414. *A Ballad*

THERE was a lass and she was fair,
  At kirk and market to be seen;
When a' our fairest maids were met,
  The fairest maid was bonie Jean.

And ay she wrought her Mammie's wark,
  And ay she sang sae merrilie;
The blythest bird upon the bush
  Had ne'er a lighter heart than she.

But hawks will rob the tender joys
  That bless the little lintwhite's nest;
And frost will blight the fairest flowers,
  And love will break the soundest rest.

Young Robie was the brawest lad,
  The flower and pride of a' the glen;
And he had owsen, sheep and kye,
  And wanton naigies nine or ten.

He gaed wi' Jeanie to the tryste,
  He danc'd wi' Jeanie on the down;
And lang e'er witless Jeanie wist,
  Her heart was tint, her peace was stown.

As in the bosom o' the stream
  The moon-beam dwells at dewy e'en;
So, trembling, pure, was tender love
  Within the breast o' bonie Jean.

And now she works her Mammie's wark,
  And ay she sighs wi' care and pain;
Yet wist na what her ail might be,
  Or what wad mak her weel again.

But did na Jeanie's heart lowp light,
  And did na joy blink in her e'e;
As Robie tauld a tale o' love,
  Ae e'enin on the lily lea.

The sun was sinking in the west,
  The birds sang sweet in ilka grove:
His cheek to hers he fondly laid,
  And whisper'd thus his tale o' love.

O Jeanie fair, I loe thee dear;
  O canst thou think to fancy me!
Or wilt thou leave thy Mammie's cot,
  And learn to tent the farms wi' me.

At barn or byre thou shalt na drudge,
  Or naething else to trouble thee;
But stray amang the heather-bells,
  And tent the waving corn wi' me.

Now what could artless Jeanie do?
  She had na will to say him na:
At length she blush'd a sweet consent,
  And love was ay between them twa.

415. [*Epigrams on Lord Galloway*]

[A] On seeing the beautiful country-seat of lord G——

WHAT dost thou in that mansion fair,
  Flit, G——! and find
Some narrow, dirty, dungeon cave,
  The picture of thy mind.—

[B] On the same n–blem–n—

No St–w–rt art thou, G——,
  The St——ts all were brave:
Besides, the St——ts were but *fools*,
  Not one of them a *knave*.—

[C] On the same—

BRIGHT ran thy LINE, O G——,
  Thro' many a far-fam'd sire:
So ran the far-fam'd ROMAN WAY,
  So ended in a MIRE.—

[D] To the same, on the Author being threatened with his resentment—

SPARE me thy vengeance, G——.
  In quiet let me live:
I ask no kindness at thy hand,
  —For thou hast none to give.—

416. [*On the death of Echo, a Lap-dog*]

[A]

IN wood and wild, ye warbling throng,
  Your heavy loss deplore;
Now half extinct your powers of song,
  Sweet Echo is no more.

Ye jarring, screeching things around,
Scream your discordant joys;
Now half your din of tuneless sound
With Echo silent lies.

[B]

Ye warblers of the vocal grove,
Your heavy loss deplore;
Now half your melody is lost,
Sweet Echo is no more.

Each shrieking, screaming bird and beast,
Exalt your tuneless voice;
Half your deformity is hid,
Here Echo silent lies.

417. *On J–hn M–r–ne, laird of L–gg–n—*

When M–r–ne, deceased, to the devil went down,
'Twas nothing would serve him but Satan's own crown:
Thy fool's head, quoth Satan, that crown shall wear never;
I grant thou'rt as wicked—but not quite so clever.—

418. *Phillis the fair—*

Tune Robin Adair—

WHILE larks with little wing
  Fann'd the pure air,
Viewing the breathing spring,
  Forth I did fare:
Gay the sun's golden eye
Peep'd o'er the mountains high;
Such thy morn! did I cry,
  Phillis the fair.

In each bird's careless song,
  Glad, I did share;
While yon wild flowers among
  Chance led me there:
Sweet to the opening day,
Rosebuds bent the dewy spray;
Such thy bloom, did I say,
  Phillis the fair.

Down in a shady walk,
  Doves cooing were;
I mark'd the cruel hawk,
  Caught in a snare:
So kind may Fortune be,
Such make his destiny!
He who would injure thee,
  Phillis the fair.

419. *Song*

HAD I a cave on some wild, distant shore,
Where the winds howl to the waves' dashing roar:
  There would I weep my woes,
  There seek my lost repose,
  Till Grief my eyes should close,
    Ne'er to wake more.

Falsest of womankind, canst thou declare,
All thy fond plighted vows—fleeting as air!
  To thy new lover hie,
  Laugh o'er thy perjury—
  Then in thy bosom try,
    What peace is there!

420. *Song—*

O WHISTLE, and I'll come to ye, my lad,
O whistle, and I'll come to ye, my lad;
Tho' father, and mother, and a' should gae mad,
  Thy JEANIE will venture wi' ye, my lad.

But warily tent, when ye come to court me,
And come nae unless the back-yett be a-jee;
Syne up the back-style and let naebody see,
  And come as ye were na comin to me—
  And come as ye were na comin to me.—
    O whistle &c.

At kirk, or at market whene'er ye meet me,
Gang by me as tho' that ye car'd nae a flie;
But steal me a blink o' your bonie black e'e,
  Yet look as ye were na lookin at me—
  Yet look as ye were na lookin at me.—
    O whistle &c.

Ay vow and protest that ye care na for me,
And whyles ye may lightly my beauty a wee;
But court nae anither, tho' jokin ye be,
  For fear that she wyle your fancy frae me—
  For fear that she wyle your fancy frae me.—

421. *Song—*

Tune—Geordie's byre—

I

ADOWN winding Nith I did wander,
  To mark the sweet flowers as they spring;
Adown winding Nith I did wander,
  Of Phillis to muse and to sing.—

Chorus

Awa wi' your Belles and your Beauties,
  They never wi' her can compare:
Wha-ever has met wi' my Phillis,
  Has met wi' the Queen o' the Fair.—

2

The Daisy amus'd my fond fancy,
  So artless, so simple, so wild:
Thou emblem, said I, o' my Phillis,
  *For she is simplicity's child.—
    Awa &c.—

* Here the *Poet* trusts that he shall also be found a *Prophet*; and that this charming feature will ever be a distinguishing trait in his Heroine.

3

The Rose-bud 's the blush o' my Charmer,
  Her sweet balmy lip when 'tis prest:
How fair and how pure is the lily,
  But fairer and purer her breast.—
    Awa &c.—

4

Yon knot of gay flowers in the arbour,
  They ne'er wi' my Phillis can vie:
Her breath is the breath o' the woodbine,
  Its dew-drop o' diamond, her eye.—
    Awa &c.—

5

Her voice is the songs of the morning,
  That wake thro' the green-spreading grove;
When Phebus peeps over the mountains
  On music, and pleasure, and love.—
    Awa &c.

6

But Beauty, how frail and how fleeting,
  The bloom of a fine summer's day;
While Worth in the mind of my Phillis
  Will flourish without a decay.—
    Awa &c.—

422. *Allan Water*

By Allan-side I chanc'd to rove,
While Phebus sank beyond Benledi*;
The winds were whispering thro' the grove,
The yellow corn was waving ready:
I listen'd to a lover's sang,
And thought on youthfu' pleasures mony;
And ay the wild-wood echoes rang—
O dearly do I lo'e thee, Annie.—

O happy be the woodbine bower,
Nae nightly bogle make it eerie;
Nor ever sorrow stain the hour,
The place and time I met my Dearie!
Her head upon my throbbing breast,
She, sinking, said, 'I'm thine for ever!'
While mony a kiss the seal imprest,
The sacred vow, we ne'er should sever.—

* A mountain west of Strathallan 3009 feet high.

The haunt o' Spring 's the primrose-brae,
The Simmer joys the flocks to follow;
How cheery, thro' her shortening day,
Is Autumn in her weeds o' yellow:
But can they melt the glowing heart,
Or chain the soul in speechless pleasure,
Or thro' each nerve the rapture dart,
Like meeting HER, our bosom's treasure.

423. *Song*

Tune, Cauld kail

COME, let me take thee to my breast,
And pledge we ne'er shall sunder;
And I shall spurn, as vilest dust,
The warld's wealth and grandeur:
And do I hear my Jeanie own,
That equal transports move her?
I ask for dearest life alone
That I may live to love her.

Thus in my arms, wi' a' thy charms,
I clasp my countless treasure;
I seek nae mair o' Heaven to share,
Than sic a moment's pleasure:
And by thy een, sae bonie blue,
I swear I'm thine for ever!
And on thy lips I seal my vow,
And break it shall I never!

424. *Dainty Davie*

NOW rosy May comes in wi' flowers,
To deck her gay, green spreading bowers;
And now comes in my happy hours,
To wander wi' my Davie.—

Chorus

Meet me on the warlock knowe,
Dainty Davie, Dainty Davie;
There I'll spend the day wi' you,
My ain dear dainty Davie.—

The crystal waters round us fa',
The merry birds are lovers a',
The scented breezes round us blaw,
Awandering wi' my Davie.—
Meet me &c.

As purple morning starts the hare,
To steal upon her early fare,
Then through the dews I will repair,
To meet my faithfu' Davie.—
Meet me &c.

When day, expiring in the west,
The curtain draws o' Nature's rest,
I'll flee to his arms I lo'e the best,
And that 's my ain dear Davie.—

Chorus

Meet me on the warlock knowe,
Bonie Davie, dainty Davie;
There I'll spend the day wi' you,
My ain dear dainty Davie.—

425. *Robert Bruce's March to Bannockburn—*

To its ain tune—[no. **206**]

SCOTS, wha hae wi' WALLACE bled,
Scots, wham BRUCE has aften led,
Welcome to your gory bed,—
Or to victorie.—

Now 's the day, and now 's the hour;
See the front o' battle lour;
See approach proud EDWARD's power,
Chains and Slaverie.—

Wha will be a traitor-knave?
Wha can fill a coward's grave?
Wha sae base as be a Slave?
—Let him turn and flie:—

Wha for SCOTLAND's king and law,
Freedom's sword will strongly draw,
FREE-MAN stand, or FREE-MAN fa',
Let him follow me.—

By Oppression's woes and pains!
By your Sons in servile chains!
We will drain our dearest veins,
  But they *shall* be free!

Lay the proud Usurpers low!
Tyrants fall in every foe!
LIBERTY's in every blow!
  Let us DO—OR DIE!!!

426. *To Maria*—

Epigram—On Lord Buchan's assertion, that 'Women ought always to be flattered grossly, or not spoken to at all'——

'PRAISE Woman still!' his Lordship says,
  'Deserved, or not, no matter,'
But thee, Maria, while I praise,
  There Flattery cannot flatter.—

Maria, all my thought and dream,
  Inspires my vocal shell:
The more I praise my lovely Theme
  The more the truth I tell.—

427. *Down the burn Davie*

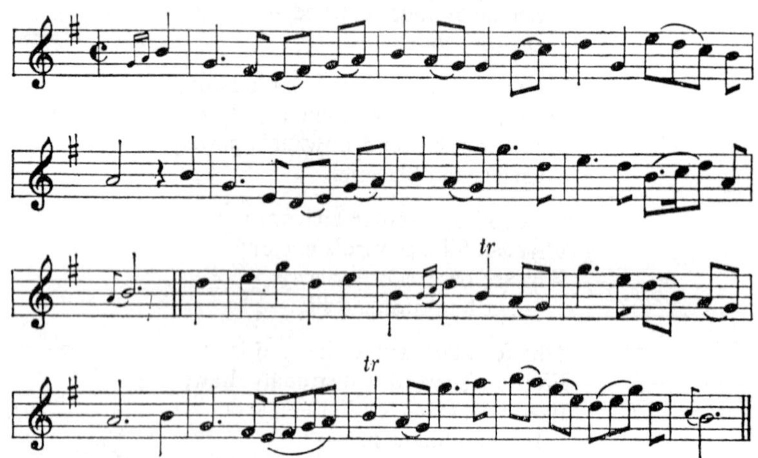

As down the burn they took their way,
  And thro' the flowery dale;
His cheek to hers he aft did lay,
  And love was ay the tale.—

With 'Mary, when shall we return,
  Sic pleasure to renew;'
Quoth Mary, Love, I like the burn,
  And ay shall follow you.—

428. [*Passion's Cry*]

'I cannot but remember such things were,
'And were most dear to me'—

In vain would Prudence, with decorous sneer,
Point out a cens'ring world, and bid me fear:
Above that world on wings of love I rise:
I know its worst and can that worst despise.—
'Wronged, injured, shunned, unpitied, unredrest;
'The mocked quotation of the scorner's jest'—
Let Prudence' direst bodements on me fall,
Clarinda, rich reward! o'erpays them all.—
As low-borne mists before the sun remove,
So shines, so reigns unrivalled mighty Love.—
In vain the laws their feeble force oppose;
Chained at his feet, they groan Love's vanquished foes;
In vain Religion meets my shrinking eye;
I dare not combat, but I turn and fly:
Conscience in vain upbraids th' unhallowed fire;
Love grasps his scorpions, stifled they expire:
Reason drops headlong from his sacred throne,
Thy dear idea reigns, and reigns alone;
Each thought intoxicated homage yields,
And riots wanton in forbidden fields.—

By all on High, adoring mortals know!
By all the conscious villain fears below!
By, what, Alas! much more my soul alarms,
My doubtful hopes once more to fill thy arms!
E'en shouldst thou, false, forswear each guilty tie,
Thine, and thine only, I must live and die!!!

429. *The Primrose—*

Tune, Todlin Hame—

Dost ask me, why I send thee here,
This firstling of the infant year?
Dost ask me, what this primrose shews,
Bepearled thus with morning dews?—

I must whisper to thy ears,
The sweets of love are wash'd with tears.

This lovely native of the dale
Thou seest, how languid, pensive, pale:
Thou seest this bending stalk so weak,
That each way yielding doth not break?

I must tell thee, these reveal,
The doubts and fears that lovers feel.

430. *Thou hast left me ever*

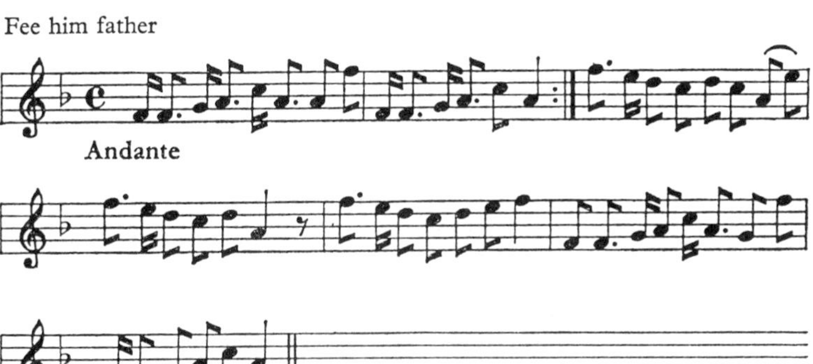

THOU hast left me ever, Jamie,
  Thou hast left me ever.
Thou hast left me ever, Jamie,
  Thou hast left me ever.
Aften hast thou vow'd that Death,
  Only should us sever:
Now thou 's left thy lass for ay—
  I maun see thee never, Jamie,
    I'll see thee never.—

Thou hast me forsaken, Jamie,
  Thou hast me forsaken:
Thou hast me forsaken, Jamie,
  Thou hast me forsaken.
Thou canst love anither jo,
  While my heart is breaking:
Soon my weary een I'll close—
  Never mair to waken, Jamie,
    Ne'er mair to waken.

431. *Song*—

Tune, Oran gaoil—

BEHOLD the hour, the boat arrive;
  Thou goest, thou darling of my heart:
Severed from thee, can I survive,
  But Fate has willed—and we must part.
I'll often greet this surging swell,
  Yon distant Isle will often hail:
'E'en here, I took the last farewell;
  'There, latest marked her vanished sail.'

Along the solitary shore,
  While flitting sea-fowl round me cry,
Across the rolling, dashing roar
  I'll west-ward turn my wistful eye:
Happy, thou Indian grove, I'll say,
  Where now my Nancy's path may be!
While through thy sweets she loves to stray,
  O tell me, does she muse on me!

432. *Fair Jenny—*

Tune, The grey cock

WHERE are the joys I have met in the morning,
  That danc'd to the lark's early song?
Where is the peace that awaited my wandring,
  At evening the wild-woods among?

No more a winding the course of yon river,
  And marking sweet flowerets so fair:
No more I trace the light footsteps of Pleasure,
  But Sorrow and sad-sighing Care.—

Is it that Summer 's forsaken our vallies,
  And grim, surly Winter is near?
No, no! the bees humming round the gay roses
  Proclaim it the pride of the year.—

Fain would I hide, what I fear to discover,
  Yet long, long too well have I known:
All that has caused this wreck in my bosom,
  Is Jenny, fair Jenny alone.—

Time cannot aid me, my griefs are immortal,
  Not Hope dare a comfort bestow:
Come then, enamour'd and fond of my anguish,
  Enjoyment I'll seek in my woe.—

433. *On Captn. W—— R–dd–ck of C–rb—ton—*

LIGHT lay the earth on Billy's breast,
His chicken heart so tender:
But build a castle on his head,
His scull will prop it under.—

434. *Thine am I, my Chloris fair*

THINE am I, my Chloris fair,
Well thou may'st discover;
Every pulse along my veins
Tells the ardent Lover.

To thy bosom lay my heart,
There to throb and languish:
Tho' Despair had wrung its core,
That would heal its anguish.

Take away these rosy lips,
Rich with balmy treasure:
Turn away thine eyes of love,
Lest I die with pleasure!

What is Life when wanting Love?
Night without a morning:
Love 's the cloudless summer sun,
Nature gay adorning.

435. [*Bonie Mary*]

Tune, Minnie's ay glowerin o'er me—

Chorus

COME cowe me, minnie, come cowe me;
Come cowe me, minnie, come cowe me;
The hair o' my a— is grown into my c—t,
And they canna win to, to m–we me.

I

When Mary cam over the Border,
When Mary cam over the Border;
As eith 'twas approachin the C—t of a hurchin,
Her a— was in sic a disorder.—

2

But wanton Wattie cam west on't,
But wanton Wattie cam west on't,
He did it sae tickle, he left nae as meikle
'S a spider wad bigget a nest on't.—

3

And was nae Wattie a Clinker,
He m–w'd frae the Queen to the tinkler,
Then sat down, in grief, like the Macedon chief
For want o' mae warlds to conquer.—

4

And O, what a jewel was Mary!
And O, what a jewel was Mary!
Her face it was fine, and her bosom divine,
And her c–nt it was theekit wi' glory.—
  Come cowe &c.—

436. *Act Sederunt of the Session—A Scots Ballad—*

Tune—O'er the muir amang the heather—

In Edinburgh town they've made a law,
  In Edinburgh at the Court o' Session,
That standing pr–cks are fauteors a',
  And guilty of a high transgression.—

Chorus

Act Sederunt o' the Session,
Decreet o' the Court o' Session,
That standing pr–cks are fauteors a',
And guilty of a high transgression.

2

And they've provided dungeons deep,
  Ilk lass has ane in her possession;
Untill the wretches wail and weep,
  They there shall lie for their transgression.—

Chorus

Act Sederunt o' the Session,
Decreet o' the Court o' Session,
The rogues in pouring tears shall weep,
By act Sederunt o' the Session.—

437. *To Captn G——, on being asked why I was not to be of the party with him and his brother K–nm–re at Syme's—*

DOST ask, dear Captain, why from Syme
I have no invitation,
When well he knows he has with him
My first friends in the nation?

Is it because I love to toast,
And round the bottle hurl?
No! there conjecture wild is lost,
For *Syme* by God 's no churl!—

Is 't lest with bawdy jests I bore,
As oft the matter of fact is?
No! *Syme* the theory can't abhor—
Who loves so well the practice.—

Is it a fear I should avow
Some heresy seditious?
No! *Syme* (but this is entre nous)
Is quite an old Tiresias.—

In vain Conjecture thus would flit
Thro' mental clime and season:
In short, dear Captain, Syme 's a Wit—
Who asks of Wits a reason?—

Yet must I still the sôrt deplore
That to my griefs adds one more,
In balking me the social hour
With you and noble Kenmure.—

438. *Impromptu, on Mrs. W. Riddell's Birthday, 4th Novr. 1793*

OLD Winter, with his frosty beard,
Thus once to Jove his prayer prefered.
What have I done of all the year,
To bear this hated doom severe?
My chearless suns no pleasure know;
Night's horrid car drags, dreary, slow:
My dismal months no joys are crowning,
But spleeny English, hanging, drowning.

Now, Jove, for once be mighty civil;
To counter balance all this evil;
Give me, and I've no more to say,
Give me MARIA's natal day!
That brilliant gift will so enrich me,
Spring, Summer, Autumn, cannot match me.

'Tis done!!! says Jove: so ends my story,
And Winter once rejoiced in glory.

439. *Occasional Address, Spoken by Miss Fontenelle, on her Benefit-Night, Decr. 4th. 1793.—Written by Mr Burns—*

STILL anxious to secure your partial favor,
And not less anxious sure, this night than ever,
A Prologue, Epilogue, or some such matter,
'Twould vamp my Bill, thought I, if nothing better;
So, sought a Poet, roosted near the skies,
Told him, I came to feast my curious eyes;
Said, nothing like his works was ever printed,
And last, my Prologue-business, slily hinted.

Ma'am, let me tell you, quoth my Man of RHYMES,
I know your bent—these are no laughing times;
Can you, but Miss, I own I have my fears,
Dissolve in pause—and sentimental tears—

With laden sighs, and solemn-rounded sentence,
Rouse from his sluggish slumbers, fell Repentance;
Paint Vengeance, as he takes his horrid stand,
Waving on high the desolating brand,
Calling the storms to bear him o'er a guilty Land!

I could no more—askance the creature eyeing,
D'ye think, said I, this face was made for crying?
I'll laugh, that 's pos—nay more, the world shall know it;
And so, your servant, gloomy Master Poet.

Firm as my creed, Sirs, 'tis my fix'd belief,
That Misery 's another word for Grief:
I also think—so may I be a Bride!
That so much laughter, so much life enjoy'd.

Thou man of crazy care, and ceaseless sigh,
Still under bleak Misfortune's blasting eye;
Doom'd to that sorest task of man alive—
To make three guineas do the work of five;
Laugh in Misfortune's face—the beldam witch!
Say, you'll be merry—tho' you can't be rich.

Thou other man of care, the wretch in love,
Who long with jiltish arts and airs hast strove;
Who, as the boughs all temptingly project,
Measur'st, in desp'rate thought—a rope—thy neck—
Or, where the beetling cliffs o'erhang the deep
Peerest, to meditate the healing leap:
[For shame! for shame! I tell thee, thou art no man:
This for a giddy, vain, capricious woman?
A creature, though I say 't, you know, that should not;
Ridiculous with her idiot, 'Would and Would not.']
Wouldst thou be cur'd, thou silly, moping elf?
Laugh at her follies; laugh e'en at thyself:
Learn to despise those frowns, now so terrific;
And love a kinder—that 's your grand specific!

To sum up all—be merry! I advise;
And as we're merry, may we still be wise.

440. *On seeing Miss Fontenelle in a Favourite Character*

SWEET naïveté of feature,
  Simple, wild, enchanting elf,
Not to thee, but thanks to nature,
  Thou art acting but thyself.

Wert thou awkward, stiff, affected,
  Spurning nature, torturing art;
Loves and graces all rejected,
  Then indeed thou 'd'st act a part.

441. *English song*

To the tune—My joe Janet—

HUSBAND, husband, cease your strife,
  Nor longer idly rave, Sir:
Tho' I am your wedded wife,
  Yet I am not your slave, Sir.

'One of two must still obey,
  'Nancy, Nancy;
'Is it Man or Woman, say,
  'My Spouse Nancy.'

If 'tis still the lordly word,
  Service and obedience;
I'll desert my Sov'reign lord,
  And so, good b'ye, Allegiance!

'Sad will I be, so bereft,
  'Nancy, Nancy;
'Yet I'll try to make a shift,
  'My Spouse Nancy.'—

My poor heart then break it must,
  My last hour I am near it:
When you lay me in the dust,
  Think how you will bear it.—

'I will hope and trust in Heaven,
  'Nancy, Nancy;
'Strength to bear it will be given,
  'My Spouse Nancy.'—

Well, Sir, from the silent dead,
  Still I'll try to daunt you;
Ever round your midnight bed
  Horrid sprites shall haunt you.—

'I'll wed another, like my Dear,
  'Nancy, Nancy;
'Then all hell will fly for fear,
  'My Spouse, Nancy.'—

XI. Poems 1794

DUMFRIES

442. *To Miss Graham of Fintray—*

HERE, where the Scotish Muse immortal lives,
In sacred strains and tuneful numbers join'd,
Accept the gift; though humble he who gives,
Rich is the tribute of the grateful mind.

So may no ruffian feeling in thy breast
Discordant jar thy bosom-chords among;
But Peace attune thy gentle soul to rest,
Or love ecstatic wake his seraph song.

Or Pity's notes, in luxury of tears,
As modest want the tale of woe reveals;
While conscious Virtue all the strain endears,
And heaven-born Piety her sanction seals.

443. *Monody on Maria—*

HOW cold is that bosom which folly once fired,
How pale is that cheek where the rouge lately glistened;
How silent that tongue which the echoes oft tired,
How dull is that ear which to flattery so listened.—

If sorrow and anguish *their* exit await,
From friendship and dearest affection removed;
How doubly severer, Maria, thy fate,
Thou diedst unwept, as thou livedst unloved.—

Loves, Graces, and Virtues, I call not on you;
So shy, grave and distant, ye shed not a tear:
But come, all ye offspring of folly so true,
And flowers let us cull for Maria's cold bier.—

We'll search through the garden for each silly flower,
We'll range through the forest for each idle weed;
But chiefly the nettle, so typical, shower,
For none e'er approached her but rued the rash deed.—

We'll sculpture the marble, we'll measure the lay;
Here Vanity* strums on her idiot lyre;
Here keen Indignation shall dart on his prey,
Which spurning Contempt shall redeem from his ire.—

THE EPITAPH—

Here lies, now a prey to insulting Neglect,
What once was a butterfly gay in life's beam:
Want only of wisdom denied her respect,
Want only of goodness denied her esteem.—

444. *Wilt thou be my Dearie*—

Tune, The Sutor's dochter—

* N.B. the lady affected to be a Poetess.

WILT thou be my Dearie;
When sorrow wrings thy gentle heart,
O wilt thou let me chear thee:
By the treasure of my soul,
That 's the love I bear thee!
I swear and vow, that only thou
Shalt ever be my Dearie—
Only thou, I swear and vow,
Shalt ever be my Dearie.—

Lassie, say thou lo'es me;
Or if thou wilt na be my ain,
Say na thou'lt refuse me:
If it winna, canna be,
Thou for thine may chuse me,
Let me, Lassie, quickly die,
Trusting that thou lo'es me—
Lassie, let me quickly die,
Trusting that thou lo'es me.—

445. *Sonnet, on the Death of Robert Riddel, Esq.* of Glen Riddel, April *1794*

NO more, ye warblers of the wood, no more,
Nor pour your descant, grating, on my soul:
Thou young-eyed spring, gay in thy verdant stole,
More welcome were to me grim winter's wildest roar.

How can ye charm, ye flow'rs, with all your dyes?
Ye blow upon the sod that wraps my friend:
How can I to the tuneful strain attend?
That strain flows round th' untimely tomb where Riddel lies.

Yes, pour, ye warblers, pour the notes of woe,
And soothe *the Virtues* weeping on this bier:
The *Man of Worth*, and has not left his peer,
Is in his 'narrow house' for ever darkly low.

Thee, Spring, again with joy shall others greet,
Me, mem'ry of my loss will only meet.

446. *On Robert Riddel*

To Riddel, much-lamented man,
  This ivied cot was dear;
Reader, dost value matchless worth?
  This ivied cot revere.

447. *Banks of Cree*

Here is the glen, and here the bower,
  All underneath the birchen shade;
The village-bell has told the hour,
  O what can stay my lovely maid.

'Tis not Maria's whispering call;
  'Tis but the balmy breathing gale,
Mixt with some warbler's dying fall
  The dewy star of eve to hail.

It is Maria's voice I hear;
  So calls the woodlark in the grove
His little, faithful Mate to chear,
  At once 'tis music—and 'tis love.

And art thou come! and art thou true!
  O welcome dear to love and me!
And let us all our vows renew
  Along the flowery banks of Cree.

448. *Pinned to Mrs R——'s carriage—*

If you rattle along like your Mistress's tongue,
  Your speed will outrival the dart:
But, a fly for your load, you'll break down on the road,
  If your stuff be as rotten 's her heart.—

449. *In answer to one who affirmed of a well-known Character here, Dr B ——, that there was Falsehood in his very looks—*

That there is Falsehood in his looks,
  I must and will deny;
They say, their Master is a Knave—
  —And sure they do not lie.—

450. *Extempore* [*on The* Loyal Natives' *Verses*]

[Ye sons of sedition give ear to my song,
Let Syme, Burns, and Maxwell pervade every throng,
With Craken the attorney, and Mundell the quack,
Send Willie the monger to hell with a smack.]

YE true 'Loyal Natives', attend to my song,
In uproar and riot rejoice the night long;
From *envy* and *hatred* your corps is exempt;
But where is your shield from the *darts of contempt?*

451. *Ode* [*For General Washington's Birthday*]

NO Spartan tube, no Attic shell,
No lyre Eolian I awake;
'Tis Liberty's bold note I swell,
Thy harp, Columbia, let me take.
See gathering thousands, while I sing,
A broken chain, exulting, bring,
And dash it in a tyrant's face!
And dare him to his very beard,
And tell him, he no more is feared,
No more the Despot of Columbia's race.
A tyrant's proudest insults braved,
They shout, a People freed! They hail an Empire saved.

Where is Man's godlike form?
Where is that brow erect and bold,
That eye that can, unmoved, behold
The wildest rage, the loudest storm,
That e'er created fury dared to raise!
Avaunt! thou caitiff, servile, base,
That tremblest at a Despot's nod,
Yet, crouching under th' iron rod,
Canst laud the arm that struck th' insulting blow!
Art thou of man's imperial line?
Dost boast that countenance divine?
Each sculking feature answers, No!
But come, ye sons of Liberty,
Columbia's offspring, brave as free,
In danger's hour still flaming in the van:
Ye know, and dare maintain, The Royalty of Man.

Alfred, on thy starry throne,
Surrounded by the tuneful choir,
The Bards that erst have struck the patriot lyre,
And roused the freeborn Briton's soul of fire,
No more thy England own.—
Dare injured nations form the great design,
To make detested tyrants bleed?
Thy England execrates the glorious deed!
Beneath her hostile banners waving,
Every pang of honor braving,
England in thunders calls—'The Tyrant's cause is mine!'
That hour accurst, how did the fiends rejoice,
And hell thro' all her confines raise th' exulting voice,
That hour which saw the generous English name
Linkt with such damned deeds of everlasting shame!

Thee, Caledonia, thy wild heaths among,
Famed for the martial deed, the heaven-taught song,
To thee, I turn with swimming eyes.—
Where is that soul of Freedom fled?
Immingled with the mighty Dead!
Beneath that hallowed turf where WALLACE lies!
Hear it not, Wallace, in thy bed of death!
Ye babbling winds in silence sweep;
Disturb not ye the hero's sleep,
Nor give the coward secret breath.—
Is this the ancient Caledonian form,
Firm as her rock, resistless as her storm?
Shew me that eye which shot immortal hate,
Blasting the Despot's proudest bearing:
Shew me that arm which, nerved with thundering fate,
Braved Usurpation's boldest daring!
Dark-quenched as yonder sinking star,
No more that glance lightens afar;
That palsied arm no more whirls on the waste of war.

452. *On W. R——, Esq.*

So vile was poor Wat, such a miscreant slave,
That the worms even damn'd him when laid in his grave.
In his scull there is famine!' a starv'd reptile cries;
And his heart it is poison!' another replies.

453. *A red red Rose*

Major Graham

O MY Luve 's like a red, red rose,
  That 's newly sprung in June;
O my Luve 's like the melodie
  That 's sweetly play'd in tune.—

As fair art thou, my bonie lass,
  So deep in luve am I;
And I will love thee still, my Dear,
  Till a' the seas gang dry.—

Till a' the seas gang dry, my Dear,
  And the rocks melt wi' the sun:
I will love thee still, my Dear,
  While the sands o' life shall run.—

And fare thee weel, my only Luve!
  And fare thee weel, a while!
And I will come again, my Luve,
  Tho' it were ten thousand mile!

454. *On the seas and far away—*

Tune, O'er the hills &c.

I

How can my poor heart be glad,
When absent from my Sailor lad;
How can I the thought forego,
He 's on the seas to meet the foe:
Let me wander, let me rove,
Still my heart is with my Love;
Nightly dreams and thoughts by day
Are with him that 's far away.

Chorus

On the seas and far away,
On stormy seas and far away,
Nightly dreams and thoughts by day
Are ay with him that 's far away.

2

[When in summer noon I faint,
As weary flocks around me pant,
Haply in this scorching sun
My Sailor 's thundering at his gun:

Bullets spare my only joy!
Bullets spare my darling boy!
Fate do with me what you may,
Spare but him that 's far away.

Chorus

On the seas and far away,
On stormy seas and far away,
Fate do with me what you may,
Spare but him that 's far away.]

3

At the starless midnight hour
When Winter rules with boundless power;
As the storms the forest tear,
And thunders rend the howling air:
Listening to the doubling roar,
Surging on the rocky shore,
All I can—I weep and pray
For his weal that 's far away.

Chorus

On the seas and far away,
On stormy seas and far away,
All I can—I weep and pray
For his weal that 's far away.

4

Peace thy olive wand extend,
And bid wild War his ravage end,
Man with brother Man to meet,
And as a brother kindly greet:
Then may Heaven with prosperous gales
Fill my Sailor's welcome sails,
To my arms their charge convey,
My dear lad that 's far away.

Chorus

On the seas and far away,
On stormy seas and far away,
To my arms their charge convey,
My dear lad that 's far away.

455. *To Dr Maxwell, on Miss Jessy Staig's recovery*

MAXWELL, if merit here you crave,
That merit I deny:
You save fair Jessy from the grave!
An ANGEL could not die.

456. *Ca' the yowes to the knowes [B]*

Chorus—
CA' the yowes to the knowes,
Ca' them whare the heather grows,
Ca' them whare the burnie rowes,
My bonie Dearie.

I

Hark, the mavis' evening sang
Sounding Clouden's woods amang;
Then a faulding let us gang,
My bonie Dearie.
Ca' the &c.

2

We'll gae down by Clouden side,
Through the hazels spreading wide
O'er the waves, that sweetly glide
To the moon sae clearly.
Ca' the &c.

3

Yonder Clouden's silent towers,
Where at moonshine midnight hours
O'er the dewy bending flowers
Fairies dance sae cheary.
Ca' the &c.

4

Ghaist nor bogle shalt thou fear;
Thou'rt to Love and Heaven sae dear,
Nocht of Ill may come thee near,
My bonie Dearie.
Ca' the &c.

5

Fair and lovely as thou art,
Thou hast stown my very heart;
I can die—but canna part,
My bonie Dearie.
Ca' the &c.

457. *She says she lo'es me best of a'—*

SAE flaxen were her ringlets,
Her eyebrows of a darker hue,
Bewitchingly o'erarching
Twa laughing een o' bonie blue.—
Her smiling, sae wyling,
Wad make a wretch forget his woe;
What pleasure, what treasure,
Unto these rosy lips to grow:
Such was my Chloris' bonie face,
When first her bonie face I saw;
And ay my Chloris' dearest charm,
She says, she lo'es me best of a'.—

Like harmony her motion;
Her pretty ancle is a spy,
Betraying fair proportion,
Wad make a saint forget the sky.—

Sae warming, sae charming,
  Her fauteless form and gracefu' air;
Ilk feature—auld Nature
  Declar'd that she could do nae mair:
Hers are the willing chains o' love,
  By conquering Beauty's sovereign law;
And ay my Chloris' dearest charm,
  She says, she lo'es me best of a'.—

Let others love the city,
  And gaudy shew at sunny noon;
Gie me the lonely valley,
  The dewy eve, and rising moon
Fair beaming, and streaming
  Her silver light the boughs amang;
While falling, recalling,
  The amorous thrush concludes his sang;
There, dearest Chloris, wilt thou rove
  By wimpling burn and leafy shaw,
And hear my vows o' truth and love,
  And say, thou lo'es me best of a'.—

458. *Saw ye my Phely* (*quasi dicat*, *Phillis*)

Tune, When she cam ben she bobbit—

O SAW ye my dearie, my Phely?
O saw ye my dearie, my Phely?
She 's down i' the grove, she 's wi' a new Love,
    She winna come hame to her Willy.—

What says she, my dearest, my Phely?
What says she, my dearest, my Phely?
She lets thee to wit that she has thee forgot,
    And for ever disowns thee her Willy.—

O had I ne'er seen thee, my Phely!
O had I ne'er seen thee, my Phely!
As light as the air, and fause as thou 's fair,
    Thou 's broken the heart o' thy Willy.—

459. *How lang and dreary is the night*

A Galick Air

How lang and dreary is the night,
  When I am frae my Dearie;
I restless lie frae e'en to morn,
  Though I were ne'er sae weary.—

Chorus

For Oh, her lanely nights are lang;
  And Oh, her dreams are eerie;
And Oh, her widow'd heart is sair,
  That 's absent frae her Dearie.—

When I think on the lightsome days
  I spent wi' thee, my Dearie;
And now what seas between us roar,
  How can I be but eerie.—
    For Oh, &c.

How slow ye move, ye heavy hours;
  The joyless day, how dreary:
It was na sae ye glinted by,
  When I was wi' my Dearie.—
    For Oh, &c.

460. *Song—*

Tune, Duncan Gray—

LET not Woman e'er complain
  Of inconstancy in love;
Let not Woman e'er complain,
  Fickle Man is apt to rove:
Look abroad through Nature's range,
Nature's mighty law is CHANGE;
Ladies would it not be strange
  Man should then a monster prove.—

Mark the winds, and mark the skies;
  Oceans ebb, and oceans flow:
Sun and moon but set to rise;
  Round and round the seasons go:
Why then ask of silly Man,
To oppose great Nature's plan?
We'll be constant while we can—
  You can be no more, you know.

461. *The auld man's winter thought—*

BUT lately seen in gladsome green
  The woods rejoiced the day,
Thro' gentle showers the laughing flowers
  In double pride were gay:

But now our joys are fled—
On winter blasts awa!
Yet maiden May, in rich array,
Again shall bring them a'.—

But my white pow—nae kindly thowe
Shall melt the snaws of Age;
My trunk of eild, but buss or beild,
Sinks in Time's wintry rage.—
Oh, Age has weary days!
And nights o' sleepless pain!
Thou golden time o' Youthfu' prime,
Why comes thou not again!

462. *The Lovers morning salute to his Mistress—*

Tune, Deil tak the wars

SLEEP'ST thou, or wauk'st thou, fairest creature;
Rosy morn now lifts his eye,
Numbering ilka bud which Nature
Waters wi' the tears o' joy.
Now, to the streaming fountain,
Or up the heathy mountain,
The hart, hind, and roe, freely, wanton stray;
In twining hazel bowers,
His lay the linnet pours;
The lavrock, to the sky
Ascends, wi' sangs o' joy:
While the sun and thou arise to bless the day.

Phebus, gilding the brow of morning,
Banishes ilk darksome shade,
Nature gladdening and adorning;
Such, to me, my lovely maid.
When frae my Chloris parted,
Sad, chearless, broken-hearted,
Then night's gloomy shades o'ercast my sky:
But when she charms my sight,
In pride of Beauty's light;
When through my very heart,
Her beaming glories dart;
'Tis then—'tis then I wake to life and joy!

463. *On seeing Mrs Kemble in Yarico—*

KEMBLE, thou cur'st my unbelief
Of Moses and his rod:
At Yarico's sweet notes of grief
The rock with *tears* had flow'd.—

464. *To the Honble Mr R. M——, of P–nm–re, on his high Phaeton*

THOU fool, in thy Phaeton towering,
Art proud when that Phaeton 's prais'd?
'Tis the pride of a Thief's exhibition
When higher his pillory 's rais'd.

465. *Song, altered from an old English one—*

It was the charming month of May,
When all the flowers were fresh and gay,
One morning, by the break of day,
  The youthful, charming Chloe;
From peaceful slumber she arose,
Girt on her mantle and her hose,
And o'er the flowery mead she goes,
  The youthful, charming Chloe.

Chorus

Lovely was she by the dawn,
  Youthful Chloe, charming Chloe,
Tripping o'er the pearly lawn,
  The youthful, charming Chloe.

The feather'd people, you might see,
Perch'd all around on every tree,
In notes of sweetest melody
  They hail the charming Chloe;
Till, painting gay the eastern skies,
The glorious sun began to rise,
Out-rivall'd by the radiant eyes
  Of youthful, charming Chloe.
    Lovely was she &c.

466. *Lassie wi' the lintwhite locks—*

Tune, Rothiemurche's rant

Chorus

LASSIE wi' the lintwhite locks,
  Bonie lassie, artless lassie,
Wilt thou wi' me tent the flocks,
  An wilt thou be my Dearie O.—

Now Nature cleeds the flowery lea,
And a' is young and sweet like thee,
O wilt thou share its joys wi' me,
  And say thou'lt be my Dearie O.—
    Lassie &c.—

The primrose bank, the wimpling burn,
The cuckoo on the milkwhite thorn,
The wanton lambs at rosy morn
  Shall glad thy heart, my Dearie O.
    Lassie &c.—

And when the welcome simmer shower
Has chear'd ilk drooping little flower,
We'll to the breathing woodbine bower
  At sultry noon, my Dearie O.
    Lassie, &c.—

As Cynthia lights, wi' silver ray,
The weary shearer's hameward way,
Through yellow waving fields we'll stray,
  And talk o' love, my Dearie O.
    Lassie &c.—

And should the howling wintry blast
Disturb my lassie's midnight rest,
I'll fauld thee to my faithfu' breast,
  And comfort thee, my Dearie O.
    Lassie &c.—

467. [*To Chloris*]

AH, Chloris, since it may not be,
  That thou of love wilt hear;
If from the lover thou maun flee,
  Yet let the *friend* be dear.

Altho' I love my Chloris, mair
  Than ever tongue could tell;
My passion I will ne'er declare—
  I'll say, I wish thee well.

Tho' a' my daily care thou art,
  And a' my nightly dream,
I'll hide the struggle in my heart,
  And say it is esteem.

468. *Song—*

Tune, The Sow's tail

He

O PHILLY, happy be that day
When roving through the gather'd hay,
My youthfu' heart was stown away,
  And by thy charms, my Philly.—

She

O Willy, ay I bless the grove
Where first I own'd my maiden love,
Whilst thou did pledge the Powers above
  To be my ain dear Willy.—

He

As Songsters of the early year
Are ilka day mair sweet to hear,
So ilka day to me mair dear
  And charming is my Philly.—

She

As on the brier the budding rose
Still richer breathes and fairer blows,
So in my tender bosom grows
  The love I bear my Willy.—

He

The milder sun and bluer sky
That crown my harvest cares wi' joy,
Were ne'er sae welcome to my eye
  As is a sight o' Philly.—

She

The little swallow's wanton wing,
Tho' wafting o'er the flowery Spring,
Did ne'er to me sic tydings bring,
  As meeting o' my Willy.—

He

The bee that thro the sunny hour
Sips nectar in the opening flower,
Compar'd wi' my delight is poor,
  Upon the lips o' Philly.—

She

The woodbine in the dewy weet
When evening shades in silence meet,
Is nocht sae fragrant or sae sweet
  As is a kiss o' Willy.—

He

Let Fortune's wheel at random run;
And Fools may tyne, and Knaves may win;
My thoughts are a' bound up on ane,
  And that 's my ain dear Philly.—

She

What 's a' the joys that gowd can gie?
I care na wealth a single flie;
The lad I love 's the lad for me,
  And that 's my ain dear Willy.—

469. *Can you leave me thus, my Katy*

Tune, Roy's Wife

Chorus

Canst thou leave me thus, my Katy,
Canst thou leave me thus, my Katy;
Well thou know'st my aching heart,
And canst thou leave me thus for pity.—

Is this thy plighted, fond regard,
  Thus cruelly to part, my Katy:
Is this thy faithful swain's reward—
  An aching broken heart, my Katy.—
    Canst thou &c.

Farewel! and ne'er such sorrows tear
  That fickle heart of thine, my Katy!
Thou mayest find those will love thee dear—
  But not a love like mine, my Katy.—
    Canst thou &c.

470. *Scotish Song*—

Tune, My lodging is on the cold ground

BEHOLD, my Love, how green the groves,
  The primrose banks how fair;
The balmy gales awake the flowers,
  And wave thy flaxen hair:
The lavrock shuns the palace gay,
  And o'er the cottage sings;
For Nature smiles as sweet, I ween,
  To shepherds as to kings.—

Let minstrels sweep the skillfu' string,
  In lordly, lighted ha';
The shepherd stops his simple reed,
  Blythe, in the birken shaw:
The princely revel may survey
  Our rustic dance wi' scorn,
But are their hearts as light as ours
  Beneath the milkwhite thorn.—

The shepherd, in the flowery glen,
  In shepherd's phrase will woo;
The courtier tells a finer tale,
  But is his heart as true:
These wild-wood flowers I've pu'd, to deck
  That spotless breast o' thine;
The courtier's gems may witness love—
  But 'tis na love like mine.—

471. *Song*—

CONTENTED wi' little, and cantie wi' mair,
Whene'er I forgather wi' Sorrow and Care,
I gie them a skelp, as they're creeping alang,
Wi' a cog o' gude swats and an auld Scotish sang.

I whyles claw the elbow o' troublesome thought;
But Man is a soger, and Life is a faught:
My mirth and gude humour are coin in my pouch,
And my FREEDOM 's my Lairdship nae monarch dare touch.

A towmond o' trouble, should that be my fa',
A night o' gude fellowship sowthers it a';
When at the blythe end of our journey at last,
Wha the deil ever thinks o' the road he has past.

Blind Chance, let her snapper and stoyte on her way;
Be 't to me, be 't frae me, e'en let the jade gae:
Come Ease, or come Travail; come Pleasure, or Pain;
My warst word is—'Welcome and welcome again!'

472. *My Nanie 's awa—*

Tune, There'll never be peace—

NOW in her green mantle blythe Nature arrays,
And listens the lambkins that bleat o'er the braes,
While birds warble welcomes in ilka green shaw;
But to me it 's delightless—my Nanie 's awa.—

The snawdrap and primrose our woodlands adorn,
And violets bathe in the weet o' the morn;
They pain my sad bosom, sae sweetly they blaw,
They mind me o' Nanie—and Nanie 's awa.—

Thou lavrock that springs frae the dews of the lawn
The shepherd to warn o' the grey-breaking dawn,
And thou mellow mavis that hails the night-fa',
Give over for pity—my Nanie 's awa.—

Come Autumn, sae pensive, in yellow and grey,
And soothe me wi' tydins o' Nature's decay:
The dark, dreary Winter, and wild-driving snaw,
Alane can delight me—now Nanie 's awa.—

473–479. [*Dumfries Epigrams*]

It was observed to R. B. that R—— of C—— face would make a good painting.

C——D faithful likeness, friend Painter,
  would'st seize?
Keep out Worth, Wit and Wisdom: Put in what
  you please.

474.

Extempore on Miss E. I——, a Lady of a figure indicating amazonian strength.

SHOULD he escape the slaughter of thine Eyes,
Within thy strong Embrace he struggling dies.

475.

To a Club in Dfrs. who styled themselves the Dumfries Loyal Natives and exhibited violent party work and intemperate Loyalty . . . 10th June 1794

PRAY, who are these *Natives* the Rabble so ven'rate?
They're our true ancient *Natives*, and they breed
    undegen'rate
The ignorant savage that weather'd the storm,
When the *man* and the Brute differed but in the form.

476.

On an old acquaintance who seemed to pass the Bard without notice

[i] DOST hang thy head, Billy, asham'd that thou
    knowest me?
'Tis paying in kind a just debt that thou owest me.

[ii] DOST blush, my dear Billy, asham'd of thyself,
  A Fool and a Cuckold together?
The fault is not thine, insignificant elf,
  Thou wast not consulted in either.

477.

Immediate extempore on being told by W L of the Customs Dublin that Com Goldie did not seem disposed to push the bottle.

FRIEND Commissar, since we're met and are happy,
Pray why should we part without having more nappy!
Bring in t'other bottle, for faith I am dry—
Thy drink thou can't part with and neither can I.

478.

On Mr. Burke by an opponent and a friend to Mr. Hastings.

OFT I have wonder'd that on Irish ground
No poisonous Reptile ever has been found:
Revealed the secret stands of great Nature's work:
She preserved her poison to create a Burke!

479.

At the election of Magistrates for Dumfries, 1794, John M'Murdo, Esqr., was chosen Provost and a Mr. Swan one of the Baillies; and at the Entertainment usually given on the occasion Burns, seeing the Provost's Supporters on the Bench, took his pencil and wrote the following.

BAILLIE Swan, Baillie Swan,
Let you do what you can,
God ha' mercy on honest Dumfries:
But e'er the year 's done,
Good Lord! Provost John
Will find that his *Swans* are but *Geese*.

480. *On Chloris requesting me to give her a spray of a sloe-thorn in full blossom—*

FROM the white-blossom'd sloe, my dear Chloris requested
A sprig, her fair breast to adorn:
No, by Heavens! I replied, let me perish for ever,
Ere I plant in that bosom a *thorn*!

XII. Poems 1795–1796

DUMFRIES

481. *Ode to Spring—*

Tune, The tither morn—

WHEN maukin bucks, at early f—s,
  In dewy glens are seen, Sir;
And birds, on boughs, take off their m—s,
  Amang the leaves sae green, Sir;
Latona's sun looks liquorish on
  Dame Nature's grand impètus,
Till his p–go rise, then westward flies
  To r–ger Madame Thetis.

Yon wandering rill that marks the hill,
  And glances o'er the brae, Sir,
Slides by a bower where many a flower
  Sheds fragrance on the day, Sir;
There Damon lay, with Sylvia gay,
  To love they thought no crime, Sir;
The wild-birds sang, the echoes rang,
  While Damon's a–se beat time, Sir.

First, wi' the thrush, his thrust and push
  Had compass large and long, Sir;
The blackbird next, his tuneful text,
  Was bolder, clear and strong, Sir:
The linnet's lay came then in play,
  And the lark that soar'd aboon, Sir;
Till Damon, fierce, mistim'd his a—,
  And f—'d quite out o' tune, Sir.

482. *Song—For a' that and a' that—*

Is there, for honest Poverty
    That hings his head, and a' that;
The coward-slave, we pass him by,
    We dare be poor for a' that!
  For a' that, and a' that,
    Our toils obscure, and a' that,
  The rank is but the guinea's stamp,
    The Man 's the gowd for a' that.—

What though on hamely fare we dine,
    Wear hoddin grey, and a' that.
Gie fools their silks, and knaves their wine,
    A Man 's a Man for a' that.
  For a' that, and a' that,
    Their tinsel show, and a' that;
  The honest man, though e'er sae poor,
    Is king o' men for a' that.—

Ye see yon birkie ca'd, a lord,
    Wha struts, and stares, and a' that,
Though hundreds worship at his word,
    He 's but a coof for a' that.
  For a' that, and a' that,
    His ribband, star and a' that,
  The man of independant mind,
    He looks and laughs at a' that.—

A prince can mak a belted knight,
    A marquis, duke, and a' that;
But an honest man' s aboon his might,
    Gude faith he mauna fa' that!

For a' that, and a' that,
Their dignities, and a' that,
The pith o' Sense, and pride o' Worth,
Are higher rank that a' that.—

Then let us pray that come it may,
As come it will for a' that,
That Sense and Worth, o'er a' the earth
Shall bear the gree, and a' that.
For a' that, and a' that,
Its comin yet for a' that,
That Man to Man the warld o'er,
Shall brothers be for a' that.—

483. *Sweet fa's the eve on Craigieburn*

SWEET fa's the eve on Craigieburn,
And blythe awakes the morrow,
But a' the pride o' Spring's return
Can yield me nocht but sorrow.—
I see the flowers and spreading trees,
I hear the wild birds singing;
But what a weary wight can please,
And Care his bosom wringing.—

Fain, fain would I my griefs impart,
Yet dare na for your anger;
But secret love will break my heart,
If I conceal it langer.
If thou refuse to pity me;
If thou shalt love anither;
When yon green leaves fade frae the tree,
Around my grave they'll wither.—

484. *The Dumfries Volunteers*

Tune, Push about the jorum

DOES haughty Gaul invasion threat,
  Then let the louns bewaure, Sir,
There 's WOODEN WALLS upon our seas,
  And VOLUNTEERS on shore, Sir:
The *Nith* shall run to *Corsincon*,*
  And *Criffell*† sink in *Solway*,
E'er we permit a Foreign Foe
  On British ground to rally.

O, let us not, like snarling tykes,
  In wrangling be divided,
Till, slap! come in an *unco loun*,
  And wi' a rung decide it!
Be BRITAIN still to BRITAIN true,
  Amang oursels united;
For never but by British hands
  Must British wrongs be righted.

The *kettle* o' the Kirk and State,
  Perhaps a clout may fail in 't;
But deil a foreign tinkler-loun
  Shall ever ca' a nail in 't:

* A high hill at the source of the Nith.
† A high hill at the confluence of the Nith with Solway Frith.

Our FATHERS' BLUDE the *kettle* bought,
  And wha wad dare to spoil it,
By Heavens, the sacreligious dog
  Shall fuel be to boil it!

The wretch that would a *Tyrant* own,
  And the wretch, his true-sworn brother,
Who'd set the *Mob* above the *Throne*,
  May they be damn'd together!
Who will not sing, GOD SAVE THE KING,
  Shall hang as high 's the steeple;
But while we sing, GOD SAVE THE KING,
  We'll ne'er forget THE PEOPLE!
Fal de ral &c.

485. *Let me in this ae night—*

Will ye lend me your loom Lass

Slowish

O LASSIE, art thou sleeping yet,
Or art thou wakin, I would wit,
For Love has bound me, hand and foot,
  And I would fain be in, jo.

Chorus

O let me in this ae night,
This ae, ae, ae, night;
For pity's sake this ae night
O rise and let me in, jo.

Thou hear'st the winter wind and weet,
Nae star blinks thro' the driving sleet;
Take pity on my weary feet,
And shield me frae the rain, jo.—
O let me in &c.

The bitter blast that round me blaws
Unheeded howls, unheeded fa's;
The cauldness o' thy heart 's the cause
Of a' my grief and pine, jo.—
O let me in &c.

HER ANSWER

O tell na me o' wind and rain,
Upbraid na me wi' cauld disdain,
Gae back the gate ye cam again,
I winna let ye in, jo.—

Chorus

I tell you now this ae night,
This ae, ae, ae night,
And ance for a' this ae night,
I winna let you in, jo.

The snellest blast, at mirkest hours,
That round the pathless wanderer pours,
Is nocht to what poor She endures,
That 's trusted faithless Man, jo.—
I tell you now &c.

The sweetest flower that deck'd the mead,
Now trodden like the vilest weed—
Let simple maid the lesson read,
The wierd may be her ain, jo.—
I tell you now &c.

The bird that charm'd his summer day,
And now the cruel Fowler's prey,
Let that to witless woman say
  The gratefu' heart o' man jo.—
    I tell you now &c.

486. *Fragment—Epistle from Esopus to Maria*

FROM these drear solitudes and frowzy Cells,
Where Infamy with sad repentance dwells;
Where Turnkeys make the jealous portal fast,
Then deal from iron hands the spare repast;
Where truant 'prentices, yet young in sin,
Blush at the curious stranger peeping in;
Where strumpets, relics of the drunken roar,
Resolve to drink—nay half, to whore—no more;
Where tiny thieves, not destined yet to swing,
Beat hemp for others riper for the string:—
From these dire scenes my wretched lines I date,
To tell Maria her Esöpus' fate.
  'Alas, I feel I am no actor here!'
'Tis *real* Hangmen *real* scourges bear.
Prepare, M****, for a horrid tale
Will turn thy very rouge to deadly pale;
Will make thy hair, tho erst from gypsey poll'd,
By Barber woven and by Barber sold,
Tho twisted smooth by *Harry*'s* nicest care,
Like Boary bristles to erect and stare.
The Hero of the mimic scene, no more
I start in Hamlet, in Othello roar;
Or haughty Chieftan, mid the din of arms,
In highland bonnet woo Malvina's charms;
While Sans Culotes stoop up the mountain high
And steal from me Maria's prying eye.

  Blest highland Bonnet! once my proudest dress!
Now, prouder still, Maria's temples press!
I see her wave thy tow'ring plumes afar,
And call each Coxcomb to the wordy war.
I see her face the first of Ireland's Sons,†
And even out-irish his Hibernian bronze.

* her Servant. † Captn. R. G.

The Crafty Colonel* leaves the tartan'd lines
For other wars, where He a hero shines:
The hopeful youth,† in Scottish Senate bred,
Who owns a B——y 's heart but not / without the head,
Comes, 'mid a string of coxcombs, to display
That veni, vidi, vici is his way.
The shrinking Bard‡ adown an alley sculks,
And dreads a meeting worse than Woolwich hulks—
Tho' there his heresies in Church and State
Might well award him Muir and Palmer's fate:
Still she, undaunted, reels and rattles on,
And dares the public like a noontide sun!

What scandal call'd Maria's janty stagger
The ricket reeling of a crooked swagger?
What slander nam'd her seeming want of art
The flimsey wrapper of a rotten heart—
Whose spite e'en worse than Burns's venom when
He dips in gall unmixed his eager pen,
And pours his vengeance in the burning line?
Who christen'd thus Maria's Lyre divine,
The idiot strum of vanity bemused,
And e'en th' abuse of poesy abused?
Who called her verse a parish workhouse, made
For motely, foundling fancies, stolen or strayed?

A Workhouse! ah, that sound awakes my woes,
And pillows on the thorn my racked repose!
In durance vile here must I wake and weep,
And all my frowzy Couch in sorrow steep;
That straw where many a rogue has lain of yore,
And vermin'd Gypseys litter'd heretofore.
Why, L——dale, thus thy wrath on Vagrants pour?
Must Earth no Rascal save thyself endure?
Must thou alone in crimes immortal swell,
And make a vast Monopoly of Hell?
Thou knowest the Virtues cannot hate thee worse;
The Vices also, must *they* club their curse?
Or must no tiny sin to others fall,
Because thy guilt 's supreme enough for all?

Maria, send me too thy griefs and cares;
In all of thee, sure, thy Esopus shares.

* Col. McD— † B. M—d ‡ R.B.

As thou at all mankind the flag unfurls,
Who on my fair one Satire's vengeance hurls?
Who calls thee pert, affected, vain Coquette,
A wit in folly and a fool in wit?
Who says that Fool alone is not thy due,
And quotes thy treacheries to prove it true?
Our force united on thy foes we'll turn,
And dare the war with all of woman born:
For who can write and speak as thou and I—
My periods that decyphering defy,
And thy still matchless tongue that conquers all reply?

487. *On Miss J. Scott, of Ayr*

OH! had each SCOT of ancient times,
Been, JEANY SCOTT, as thou art,
The bravest heart on English ground,
Had yielded like a coward.

488. *Song—*

Tune, We'll gang nae mair to yon town—[see no. **574**]

O WAT ye wha 's in yon town,
Ye see the e'enin Sun upon,
The dearest maid 's in yon town,
That e'enin Sun is shining on.

Now haply down yon gay green shaw
She wanders by yon spreading tree;
How blest ye flow'rs that round her blaw,
Ye catch the glances o' her e'e.
O wat ye wha 's, &c.

How blest ye birds that round her sing,
And welcome in the blooming year,
And doubly welcome be the spring,
The season to my Jeanie dear.
O wat ye wha 's, &c.

The sun blinks blyth on yon town,
Amang the broomy braes sae green;
But my delight in yon town,
And dearest pleasure, is my Jean.
  O wat ye wha 's, &c.

Without my fair, not a' the charms
O' Paradise could yeild me joy;
But gie me Jeanie in my arms,
And welcome Lapland's dreary sky.
  O wat ye wha s', &c.

My cave wad be a lovers' bow'r,
Tho' raging winter rent the air;
And she a lovely little flower,
That I wad tent and shelter there.
  O wat ye wha 's, &c.

O sweet is she in yon town,
The sinkin Sun 's gane down upon:
A fairer than 's in yon town,
His setting beam ne'er shone upon.
  O wat ye wha 's, &c.

If angry fate is sworn my foe,
And suffering I am doom'd to bear;
I careless quit aught else below,
But, spare me, spare me Jeanie dear.
  O wat ye wha 's, &c.

For while life's dearest blood is warm,
Ae thought frae her shall ne'er depart,
And she—as fairest is her form,
She has the truest kindest heart.
  O wat ye wha 's, &c.

489. *Song—(On Chloris being ill)*

Tune, Ay wakin O—

Chorus—

LONG, long the night,
  Heavy comes the morrow,
While my soul's delight
  Is on her bed of sorrow.—

I

Can I cease to care,
  Can I cease to languish,
While my darling Fair
  Is on the couch of anguish.—
    Long, &c.—

2

Ev'ry hope is fled;
  Ev'ry fear is terror;
Slumber even I dread,
  Ev'ry dream is horror.
    Long, &c.

3

Hear me, Powers Divine!
  Oh, in pity, hear me!
Take aught else of mine,
  But my Chloris spare me!
    Long, &c.

490. *Elegy on Mr. William Cruikshank A. M.*

NOW honest William 's gaen to Heaven,
  I wat na gin 't can mend him:
The fauts he had in Latin lay,
  For nane in English kend them.—

491–494. [*The Heron Ballads, 1795*]

[Tune, For a' that, and a' that]

WHAM will we send to London town,
  To Parliament, and a' that,
Wha maist in a' the country round,
  For worth and sense may fa' that.—
    For a' that, and a' that,
      Thro' Galloway and a' that,
    Whilk is the Laird, or belted Knight,
      That best deserves to fa' that?

2

Wha sees Kirouchtree's open yett,
 And wha is 't never saw that,
Or wha e'er wi' Kirouchtree met,
 That has a doubt of a' that?
  For a' that and a' that,
   Here 's Heron yet for a' that;
  The independant Patriot,
   The Honest Man, and a' that.

3

Tho' wit and worth, in either sex,
 Saint Mary's Isle can shaw that;
Wi' Lords and Dukes let Selkirk mix,
 For weel does Selkirk fa' that.
  For a' that and a' that,
   Here 's Heron yet for a' that;
  An independant Commoner
   Maun bear the gree and a' that.

4

To paughty Lordlings shall we jouk,
 And it against the law, that:
For even a Lord may be a gowk,
 Tho' sprung frae kings and a' that.
  For a' that and a' that,
   Here 's Heron yet for a' that;
  A lord may be a lousy loun,
   Wi' ribband, star and a' that.—

5

Yon beardless boy comes o'er the hills,
 Wi 's uncle's gowd, and a' that:
But we'll hae ane frae 'mang oursels
 A man we ken and a' that.—
  For a' that and a' that,
   Here 's Heron yet for a' that;
  We are na to the market come
   Like nowt and naigs and a' that.—

6

If we are to be knaves and fools,
 And bought and sauld and a' that,
A truant callan frae the schools
 It 's ne'er be said did a' that.

For a' that, and a' that,
Here 's Heron yet for a' that;
And Master Dicky, thou shalt get
A gird and stick to ca' that.—

[7]

[Then let us drink the *Stewartry*,
Kirochtree's Laird, and a' that,
Our Representative to be,
For weel he 's worthy a' that.
For a' that, and a' that,
Here 's Heron yet for a' that;
A House o' Commons such as he,
They wad be blest that saw that.]

492. *The Election: A New Song*

Tune—Fy, let us a' to the Bridal

Fy let us a' to K[IRKCUDBRIGHT],
For there will be bickerin there;
For *M——'s light horse* are to muster,
And O, how the heroes will swear!

And there will be *M——* commander,
  And *G——* the battle to win;
Like brothers they'll stand by each other,
  Sae knit in alliance and kin.

And there will be black-nebbit *Johnie*,
  The tongue o' the trump to them a';
An he get na H–ll for his haddin,
  The Deil gets nae justice ava.
And there will be *K——*'s birkie,
  A boy no sae black at the bane;
But as to his fine *Nabob* fortune,
  We'll e'en let the subject alane.

And there will be *W——*'s new *Sh——ff*,
  Dame Justice fu' brawlie has sped;
She 's gotten the heart of a *B——*,
  But Lord! what 's become o' the head?
And there will be *C——*, Esquire,
  Sae mighty in *C——*'s eyes;
A wight that will weather d–mn–tion,
  The Devil the prey will despise.

And there will be *——ses* doughty,
  New-christening towns far and near;
Abjuring their democrat doings
  By kissin the a— of a *Peer*.
And there will be *K——*, sae gen'rous,
  Whase honour is proof to the storm;
To save them from stark reprobation,
  He lent them his name to the *Firm*.

But we winna mention *R——stle*,
  The *body*, e'en let him escape:
He'd venture the gallows for siller,
  An 'twere na the cost o' the rape.
And where is our King's *L—— L——t*,
  Sae fam'd for his *gratefu'* return?
The billie is gettin his questions,
  To say in *S—nt St–ph–n's* the morn.

And there will be Lads o' the g–sp–l,
  M——, wha 's as *gude* as he 's *true*:
And there will be *B——'s Apostle*,
  Wha 's mair o' the *black* than the *blue*:

And there will be Folk frae *Saint* MARY's,
A *house* o' great merit and note;
The deil ane but honours them highly,
Tho' deil ane will gie them his vote.

And there will be wealthy young *RICHARD*—
Dame Fortune should hing by the neck
For prodigal thriftless bestowing—
His merit had won him respect.
And there will be rich brother *Nabobs*,
Tho' *Nabobs*, yet men of the first:
And there will be *C–ll–ston*'s whiskers,
And *Quintin*, o' lads not the warst.

And there will be *Stamp-office Johnie*,
Tak tent how ye purchase a dram:
And there will be gay *C–ss–ncary*,
And there will be gleg *Colonel Tam*.
And there will be trusty KIROCHTREE,
Whase honour was ever his law;
If the VIRTUES were packt in a parcel
His WORTH might be sample for a'.

And can we forget the auld MAJOR,
Wha 'll ne'er be forgot in the *Greys*;
Our flatt'ry we'll keep for some other,
HIM, only it 's justice to praise.
And there will be maiden *K–lk–rran*,
And also *B–rsk–m–n*'s gude Knight;
And there will be roaring *B–rtwhistle*,
Yet, luckily roars in the right.

And there, frae the *N–ddisd–le* border,
Will mingle the *M–xw–lls* in droves;
Teugh *Jockie*, staunch *Geordie*, and *Walie*,
That greens for the fishes and loaves.
And there will be *L–g–n M—d–w–l*,
Sculdudry—and he will be there;
And also the *Wild Scot o' Galloway*,
Sogering, gunpowder *Bl—r*.

Then hey the *chaste Int'rest* o' *B*——,
And hey for the blessins 'twill bring;
It may send *B*—— to the C——ns,
In S–d–m 'twould make him a King.

And hey for the sanctified *M*——,
Our land wha wi' Ch–p–ls has stor'd:
He founder'd his horse amang harlots,
But gied the auld naig to the L–rd!

493. *Johnie B——'s lament—*

Tune, The babes o' the wood

'TWAS in the seventeen hunder year
O' Christ and ninety-five,
That year I was the waest man
Of any man alive.—

On March, the three and twentieth morn,
The sun raise clear and bright,
But Oh, I was a waefu' man
Ere toofa' o' the night.—

Earl G——y lang did rule this land
With *equal* right and fame;
Fast knit in *chaste* and haly bands
Wi' B——n's noble name.—

Earl G——y's man o' men was I,
And chief o' B——n's host:
So twa blind beggars on a string
The faithfu' tyke will trust.—

But now Earl G——y's sceptre 's broke,
And B——n's wi' the slain;
And I my ancient craft may try,
Sen honestie is gane.—

'Twas on the bonie banks o' Dee,
  Beside K———t towers,
The St——t and the M——y there
  Did muster a' their powers.—

The M——y on his auld grey yad,
  Wi' *winged spurs*, did ride;
That auld grey yad, a' Nidsdale rade,
  He lifted by Nid-side.—

And there was B——ie, I ween,
  I' th' front rank he wad shine;
But B——ie had better been
  Drinking Madeira wine.—

And frae Gl–nk–ns cam to our aid
  A Chief o' doughty deed:
In case that WORTH should wanted be,
  O' K——re we had need.—

And by our banner march'd M——d,
  And B——le was na slack,
Whase haly Priest-hoods nane could stain,
  For wha can dye the BLACK.—

And there, sae grave, Squire C——ss
  Look'd on till a' was done:
So, in the tower o' C——ss
  A houlet sits at noon.—

And there led I the B——y clan;
  My *gamesome* billie WILL,
And my son M——nd, *wise* as *brave*,
  My footsteps followed still.—

The DOUGLAS and the HERON's name
  We set nocht to their score:
The DOUGLAS and the HERON's name
  Had felt our might before.—

Yet D——SES o' weight had we,
  The pair o' lusty lairds,
For building cot-houses sae fam'd,
  And christening kail-yards.—

And there R–dc–stle drew the sword
  That ne'er was stain'd wi' gore;
Save on a wanderer, lame and blind,
  To drive him frae his door.—

And last cam creeping C–l——n,
  Was mair in fear than wrath:
Ae KNAVE was constant in his mind,
  To keep that KNAVE frae scathe.—

* * * * * *

494. *Buy Braw Troggin. An Excellent New Song*

Tune—Buy broom Besoms

WHA will buy my Troggin,
  Fine ELECTION WARE;
Broken trade o' *BR*——
  A' in high repair.

Chorus

Buy braw Troggin,
  Frae the Banks o' *Dee*!
Wha want Troggin,
  Let them come to me.

Here 's a noble Earl's
  Fame and high renown,
For an auld sang—
  It 's thought the Gudes were stown.
    Buy braw Troggin, &c.

Here 's the Worth o' *BR*——,
  In a *needle's e'e*:
Here 's a reputation,
  Tint by *B*——.
    Buy braw Troggin, &c.

Here 's an HONEST CONSCIENCE,
  Might a Prince adorn,
Frae the *Downs o' T——*,
  —So was never worn.
    Buy braw Troggin, &c.

Here 's its Stuff and Lynin,
  C——ss's Head;
Fine for a Soger,
  A' the wale o' lead.
    Buy braw Troggin, &c.

Here 's a little Wadset,
  B—ttle's scrap o' Truth;
Pawn'd in a gin-shop,
  Quenching haly drouth.
    Buy braw Troggin, &c.

Here 's Armorial Bearings,
  Frae the Manse of ——;
The crest, an *auld crab-apple*,
  Rotten at the core.
    Buy braw Troggin, &c.

Here is Satan's Picture,
  Like a bizzard-gled,
Pouncing *poor R——tle*,
  Sprawlin as a tade.
    Buy braw Troggin, &c.

Here 's the Font where *D——*
  Stane and mortar names;
Lately us'd at *C——*,
  Christening *M——*'s crimes.
    Buy braw Troggin, &c.

Here 's the Worth and Wisdom
  C——n can boast;
By a *thievish Midge*
  They had been nearly lost.
    Buy braw Troggin, &c.

Here is *M——*'s Fragments
  O' the Ten Commands;
Gifted by BLACK JOCK
  —To get them off his hands.
    Buy braw Troggin, &c.

Saw ye e'er sic Troggin?
If to buy ye're slack,
HORNIE 's turning Chapman,
He'll buy a' the *Pack*!

Buy braw Troggin,
Frae the Banks o' *Dee*!
Wha want Troggin,
Let them come to me.

495. *Address to the woodlark—*

O STAY, sweet warbling woodlark stay,
Nor quit for me the trembling spray,
A hapless lover courts thy lay,
Thy soothing fond complaining.—

Again, again that tender part,
That I may catch thy melting art;
For surely that wad touch her heart
Wha kills me wi' disdaining.—

Say, was thy little mate unkind,
And heard thee as the careless wind?
Oh, nocht but love and sorrow join'd,
Sic notes o' woe could wauken!

Thou tells o' never-ending care;
O' speechless grief, and dark despair:
For pity's sake, sweet bird, nae mair!
Or my poor heart is broken!

496. *Song—*

THEIR groves o' sweet myrtle let Foreign Lands reckon,
  Where bright-beaming summers exalt the perfume,
Far dearer to me yon lone glen o' green breckan
  Wi' th' burn stealing under the lang, yellow broom:
Far dearer to me are yon humble broom bowers,
  Where the blue-bell and gowan lurk, lowly, unseen;
For there, lightly tripping amang the wild flowers,
  A listening the linnet, oft wanders my JEAN.

Tho' rich is the breeze in their gay, sunny vallies,
  And cauld, CALEDONIA's blast on the wave;
Their sweet-scented woodlands that skirt the proud palace,
  What are they? The haunt o' the TYRANT and SLAVE.
The SLAVE's spicy forests, and gold-bubbling fountains,
  The brave CALEDONIAN views wi' disdain;
He wanders as free as the winds of his mountains,
  Save LOVE's willing fetters, the chains o' his JEAN.

497. *Song—*

Tune, Laddie lie near me

'TWAS na her bonie blue e'e was my ruin;
Fair tho' she be, that was ne'er my undoing:
'Twas the dear smile when naebody did mind us,
'Twas the bewitching, sweet, stown glance o' kindness.

Sair do I fear that to hope is denied me,
Sair do I fear that despair maun abide me;
But tho' fell Fortune should fate us to sever,
Queen shall she be in my bosom for ever.

Chloris I'm thine wi' a passion sincerest,
And thou hast plighted me love o' the dearest!
And thou 'rt the angel that never can alter,
Sooner the sun in his motion would falter.

498. *Altered from an old English song—*

Tune, John Anderson my jo—

HOW cruel are the Parents
Who riches only prize,
And to the wealthy booby
Poor Woman sacrifice:

Meanwhile the hapless Daughter
Has but a choice of strife;
To shun a tyrant Father's hate,
Become a wretched Wife.—

The ravening hawk pursuing,
The trembling dove thus flies,
To shun impelling ruin
Awhile her pinions tries;
Till of escape despairing,
No shelter or retreat,
She trusts the ruthless Falconer
And drops beneath his feet.—

499. *Song*

Tune, Deil tak the wars—

Mark yonder pomp of costly fashion,
Round the wealthy, titled bride:
But when compar'd with real passion,
Poor is all that princely pride.
What are their showy treasures,
What are their noisy pleasures,
The gay, gaudy glare of vanity and art:
The polish'd jewel's blaze
May draw the wond'ring gaze,
And courtly grandeur bright
The fancy may delight,
But never, never can come near the heart.—

But did you see my dearest Chloris,
In simplicity's array;
Lovely as yonder sweet opening flower is,
Shrinking from the gaze of day.
O then, the heart alarming,
And all resistless charming,
In Love's delightful fetters, she chains the willing soul!
Ambition would disown
The world's imperial crown,
Even Av'rice would deny
His worshipp'd deity,
And feel thro' every vein love's raptures roll.—

500. *Address to the Tooth-Ache*

(*Written by the Author at a time when he was grievously tormented by that Disorder.*)

My curse on your envenom'd stang,
That shoots my tortur'd gums alang,
An' thro' my lugs gies mony a bang
Wi' gnawin vengeance;
Tearing my nerves wi' bitter twang,
Like racking engines.

A' down my beard the slavers trickle,
I cast the wee stools owre the meikle,
While round the fire the hav'rels keckle,
To see me loup;
I curse an' ban, an' wish a heckle
Were i' their doup.

Whan fevers burn, or agues freeze us,
Rheumatics gnaw, or colics squeeze us,
Our neebors sympathize, to ease us,
Wi' pitying moan;
But thou—the hell o' a' diseases,
They mock our groan.

O' a' the num'rous human dools,
Ill har'sts, daft bargains, *cutty-stools*,
Or worthy friends laid i' the mools,
Sad sight to see!
The tricks o' knaves, or fash o' fools,
Thou bear'st the gree.

Whare'er that place be, priests ca' hell,
Whare a' the tones o' mis'ry yell,
An' plagues in ranked number tell
In deadly raw,
Thou, *Tooth-ache*, surely bear'st the bell
Aboon them a'!

O ! thou grim mischief-makin chiel,
That gars the notes o' discord squeel,
Till human-kind aft dance a reel
In gore a shoe thick,
Gie a' the faes o' Scotland's weal
A Towmond's Tooth-Ache!

501. *English Song—*

Tune, Let me in this ae night—[see no. **485**]

FORLORN, my Love, no comfort near,
Far, far from thee I wander here;
Far, far from thee, the fate severe
At which I most repine, Love.—

Chorus

O wert thou, Love, but near me,
But near, near, near me;
How kindly thou wouldst chear me,
And mingle sighs with mine, Love.—

Around me scowls a wintry sky,
Blasting each bud of hope and joy;
And shelter, shade, nor home have I,
Save in these arms of thine, Love.
O wert &c.—

Cold, alter'd friends with cruel art
Poisoning fell Misfortune's dart;—
Let me not break thy faithful heart,
And say that fate is mine, Love.—
O wert &c.—

But dreary tho' the moments fleet,
O let me think we yet shall meet!
That only ray of solace sweet
Can on thy Chloris shine, Love!
O wert &c.—

502. *Scotch Song—*

NOW Spring has clad the grove in green,
And strewed the lea wi' flowers:
The furrow'd waving corn is seen
Rejoice in fostering showers.
While ilka thing in Nature join
Their sorrows to forego,
O why thus all alone are mine
The weary steps o' woe.—

The trout within yon wimpling burn
  That glides, a silver dart,
And safe beneath the shady thorn
  Defies the angler's art:
My life was ance that careless stream,
  That wanton trout was I;
But Love wi' unrelenting beam
  Has scorch'd my fountains dry.—

The little floweret's peaceful lot
  In yonder cliff that grows,
Which save the linnet's flight, I wot,
  Nae ruder visit knows,
Was mine; till Love has o'er me past,
  And blighted a' my bloom,
And now beneath the withering blast
  My youth and joy consume.—

The waken'd lav'rock warbling springs
  And climbs the early sky,
Winnowing blythe her dewy wings
  In morning's rosy eye;
As little reckt I sorrow's power,
  Until the flowery snare
O' witching love, in luckless hour,
  Made me the thrall o' care.—

O had my fate been Greenland snows,
  Or Afric's burning zone,
Wi' man and nature leagu'd my foes,
  So Peggy ne'er I'd known!
The wretch whase doom is, hope nae mair,
  What tongue his woes can tell;
Within whase bosom save Despair
  Nae kinder spirits dwell.—

503. *Scotish Ballad—*

Tune, the Lothian Lassie

LAST May a braw wooer cam down the lang glen,
  And sair wi' his love he did deave me;
I said, there was naething I hated like men,
  The deuce gae wi'm, to believe me, believe me,
  The deuce gae wi'm, to believe me.

He spak o' the darts in my bonie black een,
  And vow'd for my love he was dying;
I said, he might die when he liked for JEAN—
  The Lord forgie me for lying, for lying,
  The Lord forgie me for lying!

A weel-stocked mailen, himsel for the laird,
  And marriage aff-hand, were his proffers:
I never loot on that I kend it, or car'd,
  But thought I might hae waur offers, waur offers,
  But thought I might hae waur offers.

But what wad ye think? in a fortnight or less,
  The deil tak his taste to gae near her!
He up the lang loan to my black cousin, Bess,
  Guess ye how, the jad! I could bear her, could bear her,
  Guess ye how, the jad! I could bear her.

But a' the niest week as I petted wi' care,
  I gaed to the tryste o' Dalgarnock;
And wha but my fine, fickle lover was there,
  I glowr'd as I'd seen a warlock, a warlock,
  I glowr'd as I'd seen a warlock.

But owre my left shouther I gae him a blink,
  Least neebors might say I was saucy:
My wooer he caper'd as he'd been in drink,
  And vow'd I was his dear lassie, dear lassie,
  And vow'd I was his dear lassie.

I spier'd for my cousin fu' couthy and sweet,
  Gin she had recover'd her hearin,
And how her new shoon fit her auld shachl't feet;
  But, heavens! how he fell a swearin, a swearin,
  But, heavens! how he fell a swearin.

He begged, for Gudesake! I wad be his wife,
  Or else I wad kill him wi' sorrow:
So e'en to preserve the poor body in life,
  I think I maun wed him tomorrow, tomorrow,
  I think I maun wed him tomorrow.—

504. *Fragment*

Tune, The Caledonian Hunt's delight—

WHY, why tell thy lover,
  Bliss he never must enjoy;
Why, why undecieve him,
  And give all his hopes the lie?

O why, while fancy, raptured, slumbers,
  Chloris, Chloris all the theme,
Why, why would'st thou cruel
  Wake thy lover from his dream.

505. *Poetical Inscription, for an Altar to Independence At Kerrouchtry, the seat of Mr. Heron, written in Summer 1795*

THOU, of an independent mind
With soul resolv'd, with soul resigned;
Prepar'd pow'rs proudest frown to brave,
Who wilt not be, nor have a slave;

Virtue alone who dost revere,
Thy own reproach alone dost fear,
Approach this shrine, and worship here.

506. [*To Chloris*]

Written on the blank leaf of a copy of the last edition of my Poems, presented to the lady whom in so many fictitious reveries of Passion but with the most ardent sentiments of *real* friendship, I have so often sung under the name of—CHLORIS—

'TIS Friendship's pledge, my young, fair FRIEND;
Nor thou the gift refuse,
Nor with unwilling ear attend
The moralising Muse.

Since thou, in all thy youth and charms,
Must bid the world adieu,
(A world 'gainst Peace in constant arms)
To join the Friendly Few:

Since, thy gay morn of life o'ercast,
Chill came the tempest's lour;
(And ne'er Misfortune's eastern blast
Did nip a fairer flower:)

Since life's gay scenes must charm no more;
Still much is left behind,
Still nobler wealth hast thou in store,
THE COMFORTS OF THE MIND!

Thine is the self-approving glow,
On conscious Honor's part;
And (dearest gift of Heaven below)
Thine Friendship's truest heart.

The joys refin'd of Sense and Taste,
With every Muse to rove:
And doubly were the Poet blest
These joys could he improve.—

507. *Song—*

Tune, This is no my ain house—

O THIS is no my ain lassie,
  Fair tho' the lassie be:
O weel ken I my ain lassie,
  Kind love is in her e'e.

I see a form, I see a face,
Ye weel may wi' the fairest place:
It wants, to me, the witching grace,
  The kind love that 's in her e'e.

O this is no my ain lassie,
  Fair tho' the lassie be:
Weel ken I my ain lassie,
  Kind love is in her e'e.

She 's bonie, blooming, straight and tall;
And lang has had my heart in thrall;
And ay it charms my very saul,
  The kind love that 's in her e'e.
    O this is no &c.

A thief sae pawkie is my Jean
To steal a blink, by a' unseen;
But gleg as light are lovers' een,
  When kind love is in the e'e.
    O this is no &c.

It may escape the courtly sparks,
It may escape the learned clerks;
But weel the watching lover marks
  The kind love that 's in her e'e.

508. *Scotish Song—*

O BONIE was yon rosy brier,
  That blooms sae far frae haunt o' man;
And bonie she, and ah, how dear!
  It shaded frae the e'enin sun.—

Yon rosebuds in the morning dew
  How pure, amang the leaves sae green;
But purer was the lover's vow
  They witness'd in their shade yestreen.—

All in its rude and prickly bower
  That crimson rose how sweet and fair;
But love is far a sweeter flower
  Amid life's thorny path o' care.—

The pathless wild, and wimpling burn,
Wi' Chloris in my arms, be mine;
And I the warld nor wish nor scorn,
Its joys and griefs alike resign.—

509. *Song*

Tune, Morag—

O WAT ye wha that lo'es me,
And has my heart a keeping?
O sweet is she that lo'es me,
As dews o' summer weeping,
In tears the rosebuds steeping.—

Chorus—

O that 's the lassie o' my heart,
My lassie, ever dearer;
O that 's the queen o' womankind,
And ne'er a ane to peer her.—

If thou shalt meet a lassie
In grace and beauty charming,
That e'en thy chosen lassie,
Erewhile thy breast sae warming,
Had ne'er sic powers alarming.—
O that 's &c.—

If thou hast heard her talking,
  And thy attention 's plighted,
That ilka body talking
  But her, by thee is slighted;
  And thou art all delighted.—
    O that 's &c.—

If thou hast met this Fair One,
  When frae her thou hast parted,
If every other Fair One,
  But her, thou hast deserted,
  And thou art broken hearted.—
  O that 's the lassie o' my heart,
    My lassie, ever dearer:
  O that 's the queen o' womankind,
    And ne'er a ane to peer her.—

510. [*To John Syme*]

[A]. On refusing to dine with him, after having been promised the first of company, and the first of Cookery, 17th December, 1795.

No more of your guests, be they titled or not,
  And cook'ry the first in the nation:
Who is proof to thy personal converse and wit,
  Is proof to all other temptation.

[B] With a present of a dozen of Porter.

O HAD the malt thy strength of mind,
  Or hops the flavour of thy wit;
'Twere drink for first of human kind,
  A gift that e'en for S**e were fit.

Jerusalem Tavern, Dumfries.

511. *On Mr. Pit's hair-powder tax*

PRAY Billy Pit explain thy rigs,
  This new poll-tax of thine!
'I mean to mark the GUINEA PIGS
  'From other common SWINE.'

512. [*The Solemn League and Covenant*]

The Solemn League and Covenant
  Now brings a smile, now brings a tear.
But sacred Freedom, too, was theirs;
  If thou 'rt a slave, indulge thy sneer.

513. *The Bob o' Dumblane*

Lassie, lend me your braw hemp-heckle,
  And I'll lend you my thripplin kame:
My heckle is broken, it canna be gotten,
  And we'll gae dance the Bob o' Dumblane.—

Twa gaed to the wood, to the wood, to the wood,
  Twa gaed to the wood, three cam hame:
An 't be na weel bobbit, weel bobbit, weel bobbit,
  An 't be na weel bobbit, we'll bob it again.—

514. *Poem*

Addressed to Mr. Mitchell, Collector of Excise, Dumfries.

Friend o' the Poet, tried and leal,
Wha, wanting thee, might beg, or steal:
Alake! Alake! the meikle Deil
    Wi' a' his witches
Are at it, skelpin! jig and reel,
    In my poor pouches.

Fu' fain I, modestly, would hint it,
That One Pound, One, I sairly want it;
If wi' the hizzie down ye sent it,
    It would be kind;
And while my heart wi' life-blood dunted,
    I'd bear 't in mind.

So may the AULD YEAR gang out moaning,
To see the NEW come, laden, groaning,
With double plenty, o'er the loaning,
To THEE and THINE;
DOMESTIC PEACE and COMFORT crowning
The hail DESIGN.

Hogmanai eve: 1795.
R. Burns.

Postscript.

Ye've heard this while now I've been licket,
And by fell Death 'maist nearly nicket;
Grim loon! he gat me by the fecket,
And sair he sheuk;
But by good luck, I lap a wicket,
And turn'd a neuk.

But by that HEALTH, I've got a share o't!
And by that LIFE, I'm promis'd mair o't!
My hale and weel I'll take a care o't
A tentier way:
So fareweel, FOLLY, hilt and hair o't,
For ance and ay!

R. B.

515. *The Dean of Faculty—A new Ballad—*

Tune, The Dragon of Wantley

DIRE was the hate at old Harlaw
  That Scot to Scot did carry;
And dire the discord Langside saw,
  For beauteous, hapless Mary:
But Scot with Scot ne'er met so hot,
  Or were more in fury seen, Sir,
Than 'twixt HAL and BOB for the famous job—
  Who should be the FACULTY'S DEAN, Sir.—

This HAL for genius, wit and lore
  Among the first was number'd;
But pious BOB, 'mid Learning's store,
  Commandment the tenth remember'd.
Yet simple BOB the victory got,
  And wan his heart's desire;
Which shews that Heaven can boil the pot
  Though the devil piss in the fire.—

Squire HAL besides had in this case
  Pretensions rather brassy,
For talents to deserve a place
  Are qualifications saucy;
So their Worships of the Faculty,
  Quite sick of Merit's rudeness,
Chose one who should owe it all, d'ye see,
  To their gratis grace and goodness.—

As once on Pisgah purg'd was the sight
  Of a son of Circumcision,
So may be, on this Pisgah height,
  BOB's purblind, mental vision:
Nay, BOBBY's mouth may be opened yet
  Till for eloquence you hail him,
And swear he has the angel met
  That met the ass of Balaam.—

In your heretic sins may ye live and die,
  Ye heretic Eight and thirty!
But accept, ye Sublime Majority,
  My congratulations hearty.—
With your Honors and a certain King
  In your servants this is striking—
The more incapacity they bring,
  The more they're to your liking.—

516. *Hey for a lass wi' a tocher*

Tune, Balinamona and ora

AWA wi' your witchcraft o' beauty's alarms,
The slender bit beauty you grasp in your arms:
O, gie me the lass that has acres o' charms,
O, gie me the lass wi' the weel-stockit farms.

Chorus

Then hey, for a lass wi' a tocher, then hey, for
 a lass wi' a tocher,
Then hey, for a lass wi' a tocher; the nice
 yellow guineas for me.

Your beauty 's a flower, in the morning that blows,
And withers the faster the faster it grows;
But the rapturous charm o' the bonie green knowes,
Ilk Spring they're new deckit wi' bonie white yowes.
 Then hey &c.

And e'en when this Beauty your bosom has blest,
The brightest o' beauty may cloy, when possest;
But the sweet yellow darlings wi' Geordie imprest,
The langer ye hae them,—the mair they're carest!
 Then hey &c.

517. *Poem on Life*

Addressed to Colonel De Peyster, Dumfries, 1796.

My honored colonel, deep I feel
Your interest in the Poet's weal;
Ah! now sma' heart hae I to speel
The steep Parnassus,
Surrounded thus by bolus pill,
And potion glasses.

O what a canty warld were it,
Would pain and care, and sickness spare it;
And fortune favor worth and merit,
As they deserve:
(And aye a rowth, roast beef and claret;
Syne wha would starve?)

Dame life, tho' fiction out may trick her,
And in paste gems and frippery deck her;
Oh! flickering, feeble, and unsicker
I've found her still,
Ay wavering like the willow wicker,
'Tween good and ill.

Then that curst carmagnole, auld Satan,
Watches, like bawd'rons by a rattan,
Our sinfu' saul to get a claute on
Wi' felon ire;
Syne, whip! his tail ye'll ne'er cast saut on,
He 's off like fire.

Ah! Nick, ah Nick it is na fair,
First shewing us the tempting ware,
Bright wines and bonnie lasses rare,
To put us daft;
Syne weave, unseen, thy spider snare
O' hell's damned waft.

Poor man the flie, aft bizzes bye,
And aft as chance he comes thee nigh,
Thy auld damned elbow yeuks wi' joy,
And hellish pleasure;
Already in thy fancy's eye,
Thy sicker treasure.

Soon heels o'er gowdie! in he gangs,
And like a sheep-head on a tangs,
Thy girning laugh enjoys his pangs
And murdering wrestle,
As dangling in the wind he hangs
A gibbet's tassel.

But lest you think I am uncivil,
To plague you with this draunting drivel,
Abjuring a' intentions evil,
I quat my pen:
The Lord preserve us frae the devil!
Amen! Amen!

518. *Here 's a health to ane I lo'e dear*

Chorus

HERE 's a health to ane I lo'e dear,
Here 's a health to ane I lo'e dear;
Thou art sweet as the smile when fond lovers meet,
And soft as their parting tear—Jessy.

1

Although thou maun never be mine,
Although even hope is denied;
'Tis sweeter for thee despairing,
Than aught in the warld beside—Jessy.
Here 's a health &c.

2

I mourn thro' the gay, gaudy day,
As, hopeless, I muse on thy charms;
But welcome the dream o' sweet slumber,
For then I am lockt in thy arms—Jessy.
Here 's a health &c.

519–522. [*On Jessy Lewars*]

[A] TALK not to me of savages
From Afric's burning sun,
No savage e'er can rend my heart
As, Jessy, thou hast done.

But Jessy's lovely hand in mine,
A mutual faith to plight,
Not even to view the heavenly choir
Would be so blest a sight.

520.

[B] FILL me with the rosy wine,
Call a toast—a toast divine;
Give the Poet's darling flame,
Lovely Jessy be the name;
Then thou mayest freely boast,
Thou hast given a peerless toast.

521.

[C] SAY, sages, what 's the charm on earth
Can turn Death's dart aside?
It is not purity and worth,
Else Jessy had not died.

522.

[D] BUT rarely seen since Nature's birth,
The natives of the sky;
Yet still one seraph 's left on earth,
For Jessy did not die.

523. *To a Young Lady,* Miss Jessy L——, Dumfries; With Books which the Bard presented her

THINE be the volumes, Jessy fair,
And with them take the poet's prayer;
That fate may in her fairest page,
With every kindliest, best presage,
Of future bliss, enroll thy name:
With native worth, and spotless fame,

And wakeful caution still aware
Of ill—but chief, man's felon snare;
All blameless joys on earth we find,
And all the treasures of the mind—
These be thy guardian and reward;
So prays thy faithful friend, *the bard*.
ROBERT BURNS.

June 26th 1796

524. [*Oh wert thou in the cauld blast*]

OH wert thou in the cauld blast,
  On yonder lea, on yonder lea;
My plaidie to the angry airt,
  I'd shelter thee, I'd shelter thee:
Or did misfortune's bitter storms
  Around thee blaw, around thee blaw,
Thy bield should be my bosom,
  To share it a', to share it a'.

Or were I in the wildest waste,
  Sae black and bare, sae black and bare,
The desart were a paradise,
  If thou wert there, if thou wert there.
Or were I monarch o' the globe,
  Wi' thee to reign, wi' thee to reign;
The brightest jewel in my crown,
  Wad be my queen, wad be my queen.

525. *Song*

Tune, Rothiemurchie

Chorus

FAIREST maid on Devon banks,
Crystal Devon, winding Devon,
Wilt thou lay that frown aside,
And smile as thou wert wont to do.

I

Full well thou knowest I love thee dear,
Couldst thou to malice lend an ear!
O did not Love exclaim, 'Forbear,
'Nor use a faithful lover so.'—
Fairest maid &c.

2

Then come, thou fairest of the fair,
Those wonted smiles O let me share;
And by thy beauteous self I swear,
No love but thine my heart shall know.—

526. *To Mr. S. McKenzie—*

THE friend who wild from Wisdom's way
The fumes of wine infuriate send,
(Not moony madness more astray)
Who but deplores that hapless friend?

Mine was th' insensate, frenzied part,
(Ah! why did I those scenes outlive,
Scenes so abhorrent to my heart!)
'Tis thine to pity and forgive.—

Song. Thomson's note on MS: These I presume are the last verses which came from the great Bard's pen, as he died very soon after

To Mr. S. McKenzie. The recipient's note runs: Mr. Robt. Burns with a pretended excuse for having used my character ill—1796—Delivered to me by Mr. Syme,—opposite the Inn possessed by Mrs. Riddick, in Bank Street.

527. *A Fragment—On Glenriddel's Fox breaking his chain—*

Thou, Liberty, thou art my theme;
Not such as idle Poets dream,
Who trick thee up a Heathen goddess
That a fantastic cap and rod has:
Such stale conceits are poor and silly;
I paint thee out, a Highland filly,
A sturdy, stubborn, handsome dapple,
As sleek 's a mouse, as round 's an apple,
That when thou pleasest can do wonders;
But when thy luckless rider blunders,
Or if thy fancy should demur there,
Wilt break thy neck ere thou go further.—

These things premis'd, I sing a fox,
Was caught among his native rocks,
And to a dirty kennel chain'd,
How he his liberty regain'd.—

Glenriddel, a Whig without a stain,
A Whig in principle and grain,
Couldst thou enslave a free-born creature,
A native denizen of Nature?
How couldst thou with a heart so good,
(A better ne'er was sluic'd with blood)
Nail a poor devil to a tree,
That ne'er did harm to thine or thee?

The staunchest Whig Glenriddel was,
Quite frantic in his Country's cause;
And oft was Reynard's prison passing,
And with his brother Whigs canvassing
The Rights of Men, the Powers of Women,
With all the dignity of Freemen.—

Sir Reynard daily heard debates
Of Princes' kings' and Nations' fates;
With many rueful, bloody stories
Of tyrants, Jacobites and tories:
From liberty how angels fell,
That now are galley-slaves in hell;

How Nimrod first the trade began
Of binding Slavery's chains on Man;
How fell Semiramis, G–d d–mn her!
Did first with sacreligious hammer,
(All ills till then were trivial matters)
For Man dethron'd forge hen-peck fetters;
How Xerxes, that abandon'd tory,
Thought cutting throats was reaping glory,
Untill the stubborn Whigs of Sparta
Taught him great Nature's Magna charta;
How mighty Rome her fiat hurl'd,
Resistless o'er a bowing world,
And kinder than they did desire,
Polish'd mankind with sword and fire:
With much too tedious to relate,
Of Ancient and of Modern date,
But ending still how Billy Pit,
(Unlucky boy!) with wicked wit,
Has gagg'd old Britain, drain'd her coffer,
As butchers bind and bleed a heifer.—

Thus wily Reynard by degrees,
In kennel listening at his ease,
Suck'd in a mighty stock of knowledge,
As much as some folks at a college.—
Knew Britain's rights and constitution,
Her aggrandizement, diminution,
How fortune wrought us good from evil;
Let no man then despise the devil,
As who should say, I ne'er can need him;
Since we to scoundrels owe our freedom.—

528. [*To Captain Riddell*]

Ellisland: Monday Even:

YOUR News and Review, Sir, I've read through and through, Sir,
With little admiring or blaming:
The Papers are barren of home-news or foreign,
No murders or rapes worth the naming.—

Our friends the Reviewers, those Chippers and Hewers,
  Are judges of Mortar and Stone, Sir;
But of *meet*, or *unmeet*, in a *Fabrick* complete,
  I'll boldly pronounce they are none, Sir.—

My Goose-quill too rude is to tell all your goodness
  Bestowed on your servant, The Poet;
Would to God I had one like a beam of the Sun,
  And then all the World should know it!

ROBT. BURNS

529. [*Reply to Robert Riddell*]

[Dear Bard
        To ride this day is vain
For it will be a steeping rain
  So come and sit with me
Wee'l twa or three leaves fill up with scraps
And whiles fill up the time with Cracks
  And spend the day with glee.

R. R.]

Ellisland

DEAR Sir, at ony time or tide
I'd rather sit wi' you than ride,
  Tho' 'twere wi' royal Geordie:
And trowth your kindness soon and late
Aft gars me to mysel look blate—
  THE LORD IN HEAVEN REWARD YE!

R. BURNS.

530. [*Grim Grizzle*]

GRIM Grizzel was a mighty Dame
  Weel kend on Cluden-side:
Grim Grizzel was a mighty Dame
  O' meikle fame and pride.

When gentles met in gentle bowers
  And nobles in the ha',
Grim Grizzel was a mighty Dame,
  The loudest o' them a'.

Where lawless Riot rag'd the night
  And Beauty durst na gang,
Grim Grizzel was a mighty Dame
  Wham nae man e'er wad wrang.

Nor had Grim Grizzel skill alane
  What bower and ha' require;
But she had skill, and meikle skill,
  In barn and eke in byre.

Ae day Grim Grizzel walked forth,
  As she was wont to do,
Alang the banks o' Cluden fair,
  Her cattle for to view.

The cattle sh— o'er hill and dale
  As cattle will incline,
And sair it grieved Grim Grizzel's heart
  Sae muckle muck to tine.

And she has ca'd on John o' Clods,
  Of her herdsmen the chief,
And she has ca'd on John o' Clods,
  And tell'd him a' her grief:—

'Now wae betide thee, John o' Clods!
  I gie thee meal and fee,
And yet sae meikle muck ye tine
  Might a' be gear to me!

'Ye claut my byre, ye sweep my byre,
  The like was never seen;
The very chamber I lie in
  Was never half sae clean.

'Ye ca' my kye adown the loan
  And there they a' discharge:
My Tammy's hat, wig, head and a'
  Was never half sae large!

'But mind my words now, John o' Clods,
  And tent me what I say:
My kye shall sh— ere they gae out,
  That shall they ilka day.

'And mind my words now, John o' Clods,
  And tent now wha ye serve;
Or back ye 'se to the Colonel gang,
  Either to steal or starve.'

Then John o' Clods he lookèd up
  And syne he lookèd down;
He lookèd east, he lookèd west,
  He lookèd roun' and roun'.

His bonnet and his rownantree club
  Frae either hand did fa';
Wi' lifted een and open mouth
  He naething said at a'.

At length he found his trembling tongue,
  Within his mouth was fauld:—
'Ae silly word frae me, madam,
  Gin I daur be sae bauld.

'Your kye will at nae bidding sh—,
  Let me do what I can;
Your kye will at nae bidding sh—
  Of onie earthly man.

'Tho' ye are great Lady Glaur-hole,
  For a' your power and art
Tho' ye are great Lady Glaur-hole,
  They winna let a fart.'

'Now wae betide thee, John o' Clods!
  An ill death may ye die!
My kye shall at my bidding sh—,
  And that ye soon shall see.'

Then she 's ta'en Hawkie by the tail,
  And wrung wi' might and main,
Till Hawkie rowted through the woods
  Wi' agonising pain.

'Sh—, sh—, ye bitch,' Grim Grizzel roar'd,
  Till hill and valley rang;
'And sh—, ye bitch,' the echoes roar'd
  Lincluden wa's amang.

531. *Burns grace at Kirkudbright*

SOME have meat and cannot eat,
Some can not eat that want it:
But we have meat and we can eat,
Sae let the Lord be thankit.

532. [*Graces——at the Globe Tavern*]

Before Dinner

O LORD, when hunger pinches sore,
Do thou stand us in stead,
And send us from thy bounteous store
A tup- or wether-head!
Amen.

After Dinner.

[A]

O LORD, since we have feasted thus,
Which we so little merit,
Let Meg now take away the flesh,
And Jock bring in the spirit!
Amen.

[B]

L—D, we [thee] thank an' thee adore
For temp'ral gifts we little merit;
At present we will ask no more,
Let *William Hislop give the spirit.*

[*Lines* Written on windows of the Globe Tavern, Dumfries]

533. [A]

THE greybeard, old wisdom, may boast of his treasures,
Give me with gay folly to live;
I grant him his calm-blooded, time-settled pleasures,
But folly has raptures to give.

Lines. Title of 534 in Alloway MS On the great Recruiting in the year 17— during the American war.—Tune, Gillicrankie.—

534. [B] *Song—*

I MURDER hate by field or flood,
  Tho' glory's name may screen us;
In wars at home I'll spend my blood,
  Life-giving wars of Venus:
The deities that I adore
  Are social Peace and Plenty;
I'm better pleased *to make one more,*
  Than be the death of twenty.—

I would not die like Socrates,
  For all the fuss of Plato;
Nor would I with Leonidas,
  Nor yet would I with Cato:
The Zealots of the Church, or State,
  Shall ne'er my mortal foes be,
But let me have bold *ZIMRI's fate,
  Within the arms of COSBI!—

535. [C]

MY bottle is a holy pool,
That heals the wounds o' care an' dool;
And pleasure is a wanton trout,
An ye drink it, ye'll find him out.

536. [D]

IN politics if thou would'st mix,
  And mean thy fortunes be;
Bear this in mind, be deaf and blind,
  Let great folks hear and see.

* Vide. Numbers Chap. 25th. Verse 8th.—15th.—

537. *Lines* Written on a window, at the King's Arms Tavern, Dumfries

YE men of wit and wealth, why all this sneering
'Gainst poor Excisemen? give the cause a hearing:
What are your landlords' rent-rolls? taxing ledgers:
What premiers, what? even Monarchs' mighty gaigers:
Nay, what are priests? those seeming godly wisemen:
What are they, pray? but spiritual Excisemen.

538. [*You're welcome, Willie Stewart*]

[Chorus] YOU'RE welcome, Willie Stewart,
You're welcome, Willie Stewart;
There 's ne'er a flower that blooms in May
That 's half sae welcome 's thou art.

Come, bumpers high, express your joy,
The bowl we maun renew it;
The tappit-hen gae bring her ben,
To welcome Willie Stewart.

May foes be strang, and friends be slack,
Ilk action may he rue it;
May woman on him turn her back,
That wrangs thee, Willie Stewart.

539. [*At Brownhill Inn*]

AT Brownhill we always get dainty good cheer
And plenty of bacon each day in the year;
We've a' thing that 's nice, and mostly in season—
But why always *Bacon*?—come, tell me a reason.

540. *On W—— Gr–h–m Esq: of M–sskn–w*

'STOP thief!' dame Nature called to Death,
As Willie drew his latest breath:
How shall I make a fool again—
My choicest model thou hast ta'en.—

541. [*Epitaph on Mr. Burton*]

HERE, cursing swearing Burton lies,
  A buck, a beau, or *Dem my eyes!*
Who in his life did little good,
  And his last words were, *Dem my blood!*

542. *Epitaph on D—— C——*

HERE lies in earth a root of H–ll,
  Set by the Deil's ain dibble;
This worthless body d——d himsel,
  To save the L—d the trouble.

543. *Epitaph Extempore, On a person nicknamed the Marquis, who desired Burns to write one on him*

HERE lies a mock Marquis whose titles were shamm'd,
If ever he rise, it will be to be d——'d.

544. *Epitaph on J–hn B–shby—*

HERE lies J–hn B–shby, *honest man!*
Cheat him devil—if you can.—

545. *On Captn L——lles—*

WHEN L——lles thought fit from this world to depart,
Some friends warmly spoke of embalming his heart;
A bystander whispers—'Pray don't make so much o't,
'The subject is *poison*, no reptile will touch it.'—

546. [*On John M'Murdo*]

BLEST be M'Murdo to his latest day!
No envious cloud o'ercast his evening ray;
No wrinkle furrowed by the hand of care,
Nor ever sorrow add one silver hair!
O, may no son the father's honour stain,
Nor ever daughter give the mother pain!

547. [*On Gabriel Richardson*]

HERE brewer Gabriel's fire 's extinct,
  And empty all his barrels:
He 's blest—if as he brew'd he drink—
  In upright, honest morals.

548. *On Commissary Goldie's Brains*

LORD, to account who dares Thee call,
  Or e'er dispute Thy pleasure?
Else, why within so thick a wall
  Enclose so poor a treasure?

549. *The Hue and Cry of John Lewars*—

A poor man ruined and undone by Robbery and Murder. Being an aweful WARNING to the young men of this age, how they look well to themselves in this dangerous, terrible WORLD.—

A THIEF, AND A MURDERER! stop her who can!
  Look well to your lives and your goods!
Good people, ye know not the hazard you run,
  'Tis the far-famed and much-noted WOODS.—

While I looked at her eye, for the devil is in it,
  In a trice she whipt off my poor heart:
Her brow, cheek and lip—-in another sad minute,
  My peace felt her murderous dart.—

Her features, I'll tell you them over—but hold!
  She deals with your wizards and books;
And to peep in her face, if but once you're so bold,
  There 's witchery kills in her looks.—

But softly—I have it—her haunts are well known,
  At midnight so slily I'll watch her;
And sleeping, undrest, in the dark, all alone—
  Good lord! the dear THIEF HOW I'LL CATCH HER!

550. [*The Keekin' Glass*]

How daur ye ca' me 'Howlet-face,'
  Ye blear-e'ed, wither'd spectre?
Ye only spied the keekin' glass,
  An' there ye saw your picture.

551. [*Inscription on a Goblet*]

There's death in the cup—sae beware!
  Nay, more—there is danger in touching;
But wha can avoid the fell snare?
  The man and his wine 's sae bewitching!

552. [*On Andrew Turner*]

In Se'enteen Hunder 'n Forty-Nine
The Deil gat stuff to mak a swine,
  An' coost it in a corner;
But wilily he chang'd his plan,
An' shap'd it something like a man,
  An' ca'd it Andrew Turner.

553. [*The Toadeater*]

No more of your titled acquaintances boast,
  Nor of the gay groups you have seen;
A crab louse is but a crab louse at last,
  Tho' stack to the   of a Queen.

XIII. Last Songs for *The Scots Musical Museum*

554. *The lovely lass o' Inverness—*

THE luvely Lass o' Inverness,
  Nae joy nor pleasure can she see;
For e'en and morn she cries, Alas!
  And ay the saut tear blins her e'e:
Drumossie moor, Drumossie day,
  A waefu' day it was to me;
For there I lost my father dear,
  My father dear and brethren three!

The lovely lass o' Inverness. Thomson's note: Drumossie Muir, or Culloden Field, which proved so fatal to the Highland Clans, fighting under Prince CHARLES STUART, against the English army commanded by the Duke of CUMBERLAND

Their winding-sheet the bludy clay,
  Their graves are growing green to see;
And by them lies the dearest lad
  That ever blest a woman's e'e!
Now wae to thee, thou cruel lord,
  A bludy man I trow thou be;
For mony a heart thou has made sair
  That ne'er did wrang to thine or thee!

555. *Song—*

Tune, Cumnock Psalms—

As I stood by yon roofless tower,
  Where the wa'-flower scents the dewy air.
Where the houlet mourns in her ivy bower,
  And tells the midnight moon her care:

Chorus

A lassie all alone was making her moan,
  Lamenting our lads beyond the sea;
In the bluidy wars they fa', and our honor 's gane and a',
  And broken-hearted we maun die.—

The winds were laid, the air was still,
  The stars they shot alang the sky;
The tod was howling on the hill,
  And the distant-echoing glens reply.—
The lassie &c.

The burn, adown its hazelly path,
  Was rushing by the ruin'd wa',
    Hasting to join the sweeping Nith
  Whase roarings seem'd to rise and fa'.—
The lassie &c.

The cauld, blae north was streaming forth
  Her lights, wi' hissing, eerie din;
Athort the lift they start and shift,
  Like Fortune's favors, tint as win.—
The lassie &c.

Now, looking over firth and fauld,
  Her horn the pale-fac'd Cynthia rear'd,
When, lo, in form of Minstrel auld,
  A stern and stalwart ghaist appear'd.—
The lassie &c.

And frae his harp sic strains did flow,
  Might rous'd the slumbering Dead to hear;
But Oh, it was a tale of woe,
  As ever met a Briton's ear.—
The lassie &c.

He sang wi' joy his former day,
  He weeping wail'd his latter times:
But what he said it was nae play,
  I winna ventur 't in my rhymes.—
The lassie &c.

556. *The Wren's Nest*

THE Robin cam to the wren's nest
  And keekit in and keekit in,
O weel 's me on your auld pow,
  Wad ye be in, wad ye be in.
Ye 'se ne'er get leave to lie without,
  And I within, and I within,
As lang 's I hae an auld clout
  To row you in, to row you in.

* * * * * *

557. *O an ye were dead Gudeman—*

Chorus

O AN ye were dead gudeman,
A green turf on your head, gudeman,
I wad bestow my widowhood
Upon a rantin Highlandman.—

There 's sax eggs in the pan, gudeman,
There 's sax eggs in the pan, gudeman;
There 's ane to you, and twa to me,
And three to our John Highlandman.—
  O an ye &c.

A sheep-head 's in the pot, gudeman,
A sheep-head 's in the pot, gudeman;
The flesh to him the broo to me,
An the horns become your brow, gudeman.—

Chorus to the last verse—

Sing round about the fire wi' a rung she ran,
An rownd about the fire wi' a rung she ran:
Your horns shall tie you to the staw,
And I shall bang your hide, gudeman.—

558. *Tam Lin*

O I forbid you, maidens a'
That wear gowd on your hair,
To come, or gae by Carterhaugh,
For young Tom-lin is there.

There 's nane that gaes by Carterhaugh
But they leave him a wad;
Either their rings, or green mantles,
Or else their maidenhead.

Janet has kilted her green kirtle,
A little aboon her knee;
And she has broded her yellow hair
A little aboon her bree;
And she 's awa to Carterhaugh
As fast as she can hie.

When she cam to Carterhaugh
Tom-lin was at the well,
And there she fand his steed standing
But away was himsel.

She had na pu'd a double rose,
A rose but only tway,
Till up then started young Tom-lin,
Says, Lady, thou 's pu' nae mae.

Why pu's thou the rose, Janet,
And why breaks thou the wand?
Or why comes thou to Carterhaugh
Withoutten my command?

Carterhaugh it is my ain,
Ma daddie gave it me;
I'll come and gang by Carterhaugh
And ask nae leave at thee.

Janet has kilted her green kirtle
A little aboon her knee,
And she has snooded her yellow hair,
A little aboon her bree,
And she is to her father's ha,
As fast as she can hie.

Four and twenty ladies fair
Were playing at the ba,
And out then cam the fair Janet,
Ance the flower amang them a'.

Four and twenty ladies fair
Were playing at the chess,
And out then cam the fair Janet,
As green as onie glass.

Out then spak an auld grey knight,
Lay o'er the castle-wa,
And says, Alas, fair Janet for thee
But we'll be blamed a'.

Haud your tongue ye auld-fac'd knight,
Some ill death may ye die,
Father my bairn on whom I will,
I'll father nane on thee.

Out then spak her father dear,
And he spak meek and mild,
And ever alas, sweet Janet, he says,
I think thou gaes wi' child.

If that I gae wi' child, father,
Mysel maun bear the blame;
There 's ne'er a laird about your ha,
Shall get the bairn's name.

If my Love were an earthly knight,
  As he 's an elfin grey;
I wad na gie my ain true-love
  For nae lord that ye hae.

The steed that my true-love rides on,
  Is lighter than the wind;
Wi' siller he is shod before,
  Wi' burning gowd behind.

Janet has kilted her green kirtle
  A little aboon her knee;
And she has snooded her yellow hair
  A little aboon her brie;
And she 's awa to Carterhaugh
  As fast as she can hie.

When she cam to Carterhaugh,
  Tom-lin was at the well;
And there she fand his steed standing,
  But away was himsel.

She had na pu'd a double rose,
  A rose but only tway,
Till up then started young Tom-lin,
  Says, Lady thou pu's nae mae.

Why pu's thou the rose Janet,
  Amang the groves sae green,
And a' to kill the bonie babe
  That we gat us between.

O tell me, tell me, Tom-lin she says,
  For 's sake that died on tree,
If e'er ye was in holy chapel,
  Or Christendom did see.

Roxbrugh he was my grandfather,
  Took me with him to bide,
And ance it fell upon a day
  That wae did me betide.

Ance it fell upon a day,
  A cauld day and a snell,
When we were frae the hunting come
  That frae my horse I fell.

The queen o' Fairies she caught me,
  In yon green hill to dwell,
And pleasant is the fairy-land;
  But, an eerie tale to tell!

Ay at the end of seven years
  We pay a tiend to hell;
I am sae fair and fu' o flesh
  I'm fear'd it be mysel.

But the night is Halloween, lady,
  The morn is Hallowday;
Then win me, win me, an ye will,
  For weel I wat ye may.

Just at the mirk and midnight hour
  The fairy folk will ride;
And they that wad their truelove win,
  At Milescross they maun bide.

But how shall I thee ken, Tom-lin,
  O how my truelove know,
Amang sae mony unco knights
  The like I never saw.

O first let pass the black, Lady,
  And syne let pass the brown;
But quickly run to the milk-white steed,
  Pu ye his rider down:

For I'll ride on the milk-white steed,
  And ay nearest the town;
Because I was an earthly knight
  They gie me that renown.

My right hand will be glov'd, lady,
  My left hand will be bare;
Cockt up shall my bonnet be,
  And kaim'd down shall my hair;
And thae 's the tokens I gie thee,
  Nae doubt I will be there.

They'll turn me in your arms, lady,
  Into an ask and adder,
But hald me fast and fear me not,
  I am your bairn's father.

They'll turn me to a bear sae grim,
  And then a lion bold;
But hold me fast and fear me not,
  As ye shall love your child.

Again they'll turn me in your arms
  To a red het gaud of airn;
But hold me fast and fear me not,
  I'll do to you nae harm.

And last they'll turn me, in your arms,
  Into the burning lead;
Then throw me into well-water,
  O throw me in wi' speed!

And then I'll be your ain truelove,
  I'll turn a naked knight:
Then cover me wi' your green mantle,
  And cover me out o sight.

Gloomy, gloomy was the night,
  And eerie was the way,
As fair Jenny in her green mantle
  To Milescross she did gae.

About the middle o' the night
  She heard the bridles ring;
This lady was as glad at that
  As any earthly thing.

First she let the black pass by,
  And syne she let the brown;
But quickly she ran to the milk-white steed,
  And pu'd the rider down.

Sae weel she minded what he did say
  And young Tom-lin did win;
Syne cover'd him wi' her green mantle
  As blythe 's a bird in spring.

Out then spak the queen o' Fairies,
  Out of a bush o' broom;
Them that has gotten young Tom-lin,
  Has gotten a stately groom.

Out then spak the queen o' Fairies,
  And an angry queen was she;
Shame betide her ill-fard face,
  And an ill death may she die,
For she 's ta'en awa the boniest knight
  In a' my companie.

But had I kend, Tom-lin, she says,
  What now this night I see,
I wad hae taen out thy twa grey een,
  And put in twa een o' tree.

559. *Had I the wyte she bade me*

Come kiss with me

HAD I the wyte, had I the wyte,
  Had I the wyte, she bade me;
She watch'd me by the hie-gate-side,
  And up the loan she shaw'd me;
And when I wad na venture in,
  A coward loon she ca'd me:
Had Kirk and State been in the gate,
  I lighted when she bade me.—

Sae craftilie she took me ben,
  And bade me mak nae clatter;
'For our ramgunshoch, glum Goodman
  'Is o'er ayont the water:'
Whae'er shall say I wanted grace,
  When I did kiss and dawte her,
Let him be planted in my place,
  Syne, say, I was a fautor.—

Could I for shame, could I for shame,
  Could I for shame refus'd her;
And wad na Manhood been to blame,
  Had I unkindly us'd her:
He claw'd her wi' the ripplin-kame,
  And blae and bluidy bruis'd her;
When sic a husband was frae hame,
  What wife but wad excus'd her?

I dighted ay her een sae blue,
  And bann'd the cruel randy;
And weel I wat her willin mou
  Was e'en like succarcandie.
At glomin-shote it was, I wat,
  I lighted on the Monday;
But I cam thro' the Tiseday's dew
  To wanton Willie's brandy.—

560. *Comin thro' the rye*

COMIN thro' the rye, poor body,
  Comin thro' the rye,
She draigl't a' her petticoatie
  Comin thro' the rye.
    Oh Jenny 's a' weet, poor body,
      Jenny 's seldom dry;
    She draigl't a' her petticoatie
      Comin thro' the rye.

Gin a body meet a body
  Comin' thro' the rye,
Gin a body kiss a body
  Need a body cry.
    Chos. Oh Jenny 's a' weet, &c.

Gin a body meet a body
  Comin thro' the glen;
Gin a body kiss a body
  Need the warld ken!
    Chos. Oh Jenny's a' weet, &c.

561. *The rowin 't in her apron*

OUR young lady 's a huntin gane,
Sheets nor blankets has she ta'en,
But she 's born her auld son or she cam hame,
  And she 's row'd him in her apron.—

Her apron was o' the hollan fine,
Laid about wi' laces nine;
She thought it a pity her babie should tyne,
  And she 's row'd him in her apron.—

Her apron was o' the hollan sma,
Laid about wi' laces a',
She thought it a pity her babe to let fa,
  And she row'd him in her apron.—

* * * * * *

Her father says within the ha,
Amang the knights and nobles a,
I think I hear a babie ca,
  In the chamber amang our young ladies.—

O father dear it is a bairn,
I hope it will do you nae harm,
For the daddie I lo'ed, and he'll lo'e me again,
  For the rowin 't in my apron.—

O is he a gentleman, or is he a clown,
That has brought thy fair body down,
I would not for a' this town
  The rowin 't in thy apron.—

Young Terreagles he 's nae clown,
He is the toss of Edinborrow town,
And he'll buy me a braw new gown
  For the rowin 't in my apron.—

* * * * * *

Its I hae castles, I hae towers,
I hae barns, I hae bowers,
A' that is mine it shall be thine,
  For the rowin 't in thy apron.—

562. *Charlie he 's my darling*

'TWAS on a monday morning,
Right early in the year,
That Charlie cam to our town,
The young Chevalier.—

Chorus

An' Charlie he's my darling, my darling, my darling,
Charlie he 's my darling, the young Chevalier.—

As he was walking up the street,
  The city for to view,
O there he spied a bonie lass
  The window looking thro'.—
    An Charlie &c.

Sae light 's he jimped up the stair,
  And tirled at the pin;
And wha sae ready as hersel
  To let the laddie in.—
    An Charlie &c.

He set his Jenny on his knee,
  All in his Highland dress;
For brawlie weel he ken'd the way
  To please a bonie lass.—
    An Charlie &c.

Its up yon hethery mountain,
  And down yon scroggy glen,
We daur na gang a milking,
  For Charlie and his men.—
    An Charlie &c.

563. *The Lass of Ecclefechan*

GAT ye me, O gat ye me,
  O gat ye me wi' naethin,
Rock and reel and spinnin wheel
  A mickle quarter bason.

Bye attour, my Gutcher has
  A hich house and a laigh ane,
A' for bye, my bonnie sel,
  The toss of Ecclefechan.

O had your tongue now Luckie Laing,
  O had your tongue and jauner;
I held the gate till you I met,
  Syne I began to wander:
I tint my whistle and my sang,
  I tint my peace and pleasure;
But your green graff, now Luckie Laing,
  Wad airt me to my treasure.

564. *We'll hide the Couper behint the door—*

Tune, Bab at the bowster—

Chorus

We'll hide the Couper behint the door,
  Behint the door, behint the door;
We'll hide the Couper behint the door,
  And cover him under a mawn O.—

The Couper o' Cuddy cam here awa,
He ca'd the girrs out o'er us a';
And our gudewife has gotten a ca'
That 's anger'd the silly gudeman O.—
We'll hide &c.

He sought them out, he sought them in,
Wi', deil hae her! and, deil hae him!
But the body he was sae doited and blin',
He wist na whare he was gaun O.—
We'll hide &c.

They couper'd at e'en, they couper'd at morn,
Till our gudeman has gotten the scorn;
On ilka brow she 's planted a horn,
And swears that there they shall stan' O.—
We'll hide &c.

565. *Leezie Lindsay*

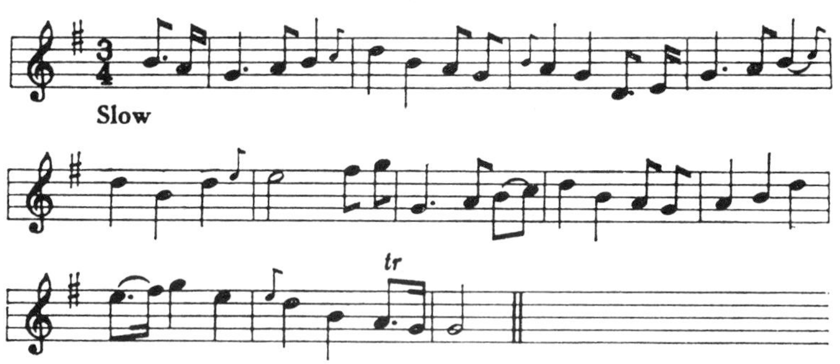

WILL ye go to the Highlands Leezie Lindsay,
Will ye go to the Highlands wi' me;
Will ye go to the Highlands Leezie Lindsay,
My pride and my darling to be.

* * * * * *

566. *For the sake o' Somebody—*

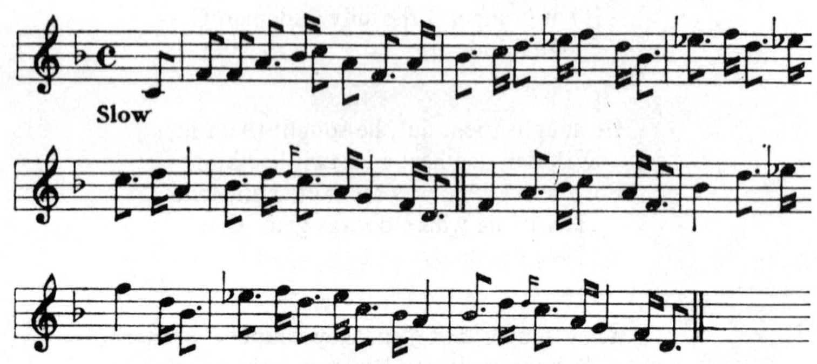

MY heart is sair, I dare na tell,
   My heart is sair for Somebody;
I could wake a winter-night
   For the sake o' Somebody.—
      Oh-hon! for Somebody!
      Oh-hey! for Somebody!
I could range the warld round,
   For the sake o' Somebody.—

Ye Powers that smile on virtuous love,
   O, sweetly smile on Somebody!
Frae ilka danger keep him free,
   And send me safe my Somebody.—
      Ohon! for Somebody!
      Ohey! for Somebody!
I wad do—what wad I not—
   For the sake o' Somebody!

567. *The cardin o't—*

I COFT a stane o' haslock woo,
To mak a wab to Johnie o't;
For Johnie is my onlie jo,
I lo'e him best of onie yet.—

Chorus—

The cardin o't, the spinnin o't,
The warpin o't, the winnin o't;
When ilka ell cost me a groat,
The taylor staw the lynin o't.—

For though his locks be lyart grey,
And though his brow be beld aboon,
Yet I hae seen him on a day
The pride of a' the parishon.—
The cardin &c.

568. *Sutors o' Selkirk—*

Its up wi' the Sutors o Selkirk,
  And down wi' the Earl o' Hume;
And here is to a' the braw laddies
  That wear the single sol'd shoon:
Its up wi' the Sutors o' Selkirk,
  For they are baith trusty and leal;
And up wi' the lads o' the Forest,
  And down wi' the Merse to the deil.—

* * * * * *

569. *Tibbie Fowler*

TIBBIE Fowler o' the glen,
  There 's o'er mony wooin at her,
Tibbie Fowler o' the glen,
  There 's o'er mony wooin at her.

Chorus

Wooin at her, pu'in at her,
  Courtin at her, canna get her:
Filthy elf, it 's for her pelf,
  That a' the lads are wooin at her.

Ten cam east, and ten cam west,
  Ten came rowin o'er the water;
Twa came down the lang dyke side,
  There 's twa and thirty wooin at her.
    Wooin at her, &c.

There 's seven but, and seven ben,
  Seven in the pantry wi' her;
Twenty head about the door,
  There 's ane and forty wooin at her.
    Wooin at her, &c.

She 's got pendles in her lugs,
  Cockle-shells wad set her better;
High-heel'd shoon and siller tags,
  And a' the lads are wooin at her.
    Wooin at her, &c.

Be a lassie e'er sae black,
  An she hae the name o' siller,
Set her upo' Tintock-tap,
  The wind will blaw a man till her.
    Wooin at her, &c.

Be a lassie e'er sae fair,
  An she want the pennie siller;
A flie may fell her in the air,
  Before a man be even till her.
    Wooin at her, &c.

570. *There's three true gude fellows*

THERE 's three true gude fellows,
There 's three true gude fellows,
There 's three true gude fellows
  Down ayont yon glen.

Its now the day is dawin,
But or night do fa' in,
Whase cock 's best at crawin,
  Willie thou sall ken.
    There 's three, &c.

571. *The bonie lass made the bed to me—*

WHEN Januar wind was blawing cauld
  As to the north I took my way,
The mirksome night did me enfauld,
  I knew na whare to lodge till day.—

By my gude luck a maid I met,
  Just in the middle o' my care;
And kindly she did me invite
  To walk into a chamber fair.—

I bow'd fu' low unto this maid,
  And thank'd her for her courtesie;
I bow'd fu' low unto this maid,
  And bade her mak a bed for me.—

She made the bed baith large and wide,
  Wi' twa white hands she spread it down;
She put the cup to her rosy lips
  And drank, 'Young man now sleep ye sound.'—

She snatch'd the candle in her hand,
  And frae my chamber went wi' speed;
But I call'd her quickly back again
  To lay some mair below my head.—

A cod she laid below my head,
  And served me wi' due respect;
And to salute her wi' a kiss,
  I put my arms about her neck.—

Haud aff your hands young man, she says,
  And dinna sae uncivil be:
Gif ye hae ony luve for me,
  O wrang na my virginitie!—

Her hair was like the links o' gowd,
  Her teeth were like the ivorie,
Her cheeks like lillies dipt in wine,
  The lass that made the bed to me.—

Her bosom was the driven snaw,
  Twa drifted heaps sae fair to see;
Her limbs the polish'd marble stane,
  The lass that made the bed to me.—

I kiss'd her o'er and o'er again,
  And ay she wist na what to say;
I laid her between me and the wa',
  The lassie thought na lang till day.—

Upon the morrow when we rase,
  I thank'd her for her courtesie:
But ay she blush'd, and ay she sigh'd,
  And said, Alas, ye've ruin'd me.—

I clasp'd her waist and kiss'd her syne,
  While the tear stood twinklin in her e'e;
I said, My lassie dinna cry,
  For ye ay shall mak the bed to me.—

She took her mither's holland sheets
  And made them a' in sarks to me:
Blythe and merry may she be,
  The lass that made the bed to me.—

The bonie lass made the bed to me,
  The braw lass made the bed to me;
I'll ne'er forget till the day that I die
  The lass that made the bed to me.—

572. *Sae far awa—*

O SAD and heavy should I part,
  But for her sake sae far awa;
Unknowing what my way may thwart,
  My native land sae far awa.—

Thou that of a' things Maker art,
  That form'd this Fair sae far awa,
Gie body strength, then I'll ne'er start
  At this my way sae far awa.—

How true is love to pure desert,
  So love to her, sae far awa:
And nocht can heal my bosom's smart,
  While Oh, she is sae far awa.—

Nane other love, nane other dart,
  I feel, but her's sae far awa;
But fairer never touch'd a heart
  Than her's, the Fair sae far awa.—

573. *The Reel o' Stumpie*

WAP and rowe, wap and row,
  Wap and row the feetie o't,
I thought I was a maiden fair,
  Till I heard the greetie o't.

My daddie was a Fiddler fine,
  My minnie she made mantie O;
And I mysel a thumpin quine,
  And danc'd the reel o' Stumpie O.

574. *I'll ay ca' in by yon town—*

Chorus

I'LL ay ca' in by yon town,
  And by yon garden green, again;
I'll ay ca' in by yon town,
  And see my bonie Jean again.—

There 's nane sall ken, there 's nane sall guess,
What brings me back the gate again,
But she, my fairest faithfu' lass,
And stownlins we sall meet again.—
I'll ay ca' &c.—

She'll wander by the aiken tree,
When trystin time draws near again;
And when her lovely form I see,
O haith, she 's doubly dear again!
I'll ay ca' &c.—

575. *The rantin laddie—*

AFTEN hae I play'd at the cards and the dice,
For the love of a bonie rantin laddie;
But now I maun sit in my father's kitchen neuk,
Below a bastart babie.—

For my father he will not me own,
And my mother she neglects me,
And a' my friends hae lightlyed me,
And their servants they do slight me.—

But had I a servant at my command,
As aft-times I've had many,
That wad rin wi' a letter to bonie Glenswood,
Wi' a letter to my rantin laddie.—

Oh, is he either a laird, or a lord,
  Or is he but a cadie,
That ye do him ca' sae aften by name,
  Your bonie, bonie rantin laddie.—

Indeed he is baith a laird and a lord,
  And he never was a cadie;
But he is the Earl o' bonie Aboyne,
  And he is my rantin laddie.—

O ye 'se get a servant at your command,
  As aft-times ye've had many,
That sall rin wi' a letter to bonie Glenswood,
  A letter to your rantin laddie.—

When lord Aboyne did the letter get,
  O but he blinket bonie;
But or he had read three lines of it,
  I think his heart was sorry.—

O wha is he daur be sae bauld,
  Sae cruelly to use my lassie?

* * * * *
* * * *

For her father he will not her know,
  And her mother she does slight her,
And a' her friends hae lightlied her,
  And their servants they neglect her.—

Go raise to me my five hundred men,
  Make haste and make them ready;
With a milkwhite steed under every ane,
  For to bring hame my lady.—

As they cam in thro Buchan shire,
  They were a company bonie,
With a gude claymore in every hand,
  And O, but they shin'd bonie.—

576. *O May thy morn*

O MAY, thy morn was ne'er sae sweet,
  As the mirk night o' December;
For sparkling was the rosy wine,
  And private was the chamber:
And dear was she, I dare na name,
  But I will ay remember.—
And dear was she, I dare na name,
  But I will ay remember.—

And here 's to them, that, like oursel,
  Can push about the jorum;
And here 's to them that wish us weel,
  May a' that 's gude watch o'er them:
And here 's to them, we dare na tell,
  The dearest o' the quorum.—
And here 's to them, we dare na tell,
  The dearest o' the quorum.—

577. *As I cam o'er the Cairney mount—*

As I cam o'er the Cairney mount,
  And down amang the blooming heather,
Kindly stood the milkin-shiel
  To shelter frae the stormy weather.—

Chorus

O my bonie Highland lad,
  My winsome, weelfar'd Highland laddie;
Wha wad mind the wind and rain,
  Sae weel row'd in his tartan plaidie.—

*   *   *   *   *

Now Phebus blinkit on the bent,
  And o'er the knowes the lambs were bleating:
But he wan my heart's consent,
  To be his ain at the neist meeting.—
    O my bonie &c.—

578. *Highland laddie*—

She

THE bonniest lad that e'er I saw,
  Bonie laddie, highland laddie,
Wore a plaid and was fu' braw,
  Bonie Highland laddie.

On his head a bonnet blue,
  Bonie &c.
His royal heart was firm and true,
  Bonie &c.

He

Trumpets sound and cannons roar,
  Bonie lassie, Lawland lassie,
And a' the hills wi' echoes roar,
  Bonie Lawland lassie.

Glory, Honor now invite
  Bonie &c.
For freedom and my King to fight
  Bonie &c.

She

The sun a backward course shall take,
  Bonie laddie &c.
Ere ought thy manly courage shake;
  Bonie laddie &c.

Go, for yoursel procure renown,
Bonie &c.
And for your lawful king his crown,
Bonie Highland laddie.

579. *Lovely Polly Stewart—*

Tune, Ye're welcome Charlie Stewart

Chorus

O LOVELY Polly Stewart!
O charming Polly Stewart!
There 's ne'er a flower that blooms in May
That 's hauf sae sweet as thou art.—

The flower it blaws, it fades, it fa's,
And art can ne'er renew it;
But Worth and Truth eternal youth
Will gie to Polly Stewart.—
O lovely &c.

May he, whase arms shall fauld thy charms,
Possess a leal and true heart!
To him be given, to ken the Heaven
He grasps in Polly Stewart!
O lovely &c.

580. *The Highland balou—*

HEE-balou, my sweet, wee Donald,
Picture o' the great Clanronald;
Brawlie kens our wanton Chief
Wha got my wee Highland thief.—

Leeze me on thy bonie craigie,
And thou live, thou'll steal a naigie,
Travel the country thro' and thro',
And bring hame a Carlisle cow.—

Thro' the Lawlands, o'er the Border,
Weel, my babie, may thou furder:
Herry the louns o' the laigh Countrie,
Syne to the Highlands hame to me.—

* * * * *

581. *Bannocks o' bear-meal—*

Chorus

Bannocks o' bear meal,
Bannocks o' barley,
Here 's to the Highlandman's bannocks o' barley.—

Wha, in a brulzie, will first cry a parley?
Never the lads wi' the bannocks o' barley.—
Bannocks o' &c.

Wha, in his wae days, were loyal to Charlie?
Wha but the lads wi' the bannocks o' barley.—
Bannocks o' &c.—

* * * * *

582. *Wae is my heart*

WAE is my heart, and the tear 's in my e'e;
Lang, lang joy 's been a stranger to me:
Forsaken and friendless my burden I bear,
And the sweet voice o' pity ne'er sounds in my ear.

Love, thou hast pleasures, and deep hae I loved;
Love thou hast sorrows, and sair hae I proved:
But this bruised heart that now bleeds in my breast,
I can feel by its throbbings will soon be at rest.—

O, if I were, where happy I hae been;
Down by yon stream and yon bonie castle-green:
For there he is wandring, and musing on me,
Wha wad soon dry the tear frae his Phillis's e'e.—

583A. *Here 's his health in water*

ALTHOUGH my back be at the wa',
And though he be the fautor,
Although my back be at the wa',
Yet here 's his health in water.—

O wae gae by his wanton sides,
Sae brawly 's he could flatter;
Till for his sake I'm slighted sair,
And dree the kintra clatter:
But though my back be at the wa',
Yet here 's his health in water.—

* * * * *

583B. *Here 's his health in water*

Tune—The job o' journey-wark

ALTHO' my back be at the wa',
An' tho' he be the fau'tor;
Altho' my back be at the wa',
I'll drink his health in water.
O wae gae by his wanton sides,
Sae brawly 's he cou'd flatter.

I for his sake am slighted sair,
An' dree the kintra clatter;
But let them say whate'er they like,
Yet, here 's his health in water.

He follow'd me baith out and in,
Thro' a' the nooks o' Killie;
He follow'd me baith out an' in,
Wi' a stiff stanin' p–llie.
But when he gat atween my legs,
We made an unco splatter;
An' haith, I trow, I soupled it,
Tho' bauldly he did blatter;
But now my back is at the wa',
Yet here 's his health in water.

584. *Gude Wallace*

O FOR my ain king, quo gude Wallàce,
The rightfu king o' fair Scotland;
Between me and my Sovereign Blude
I think I see some ill seed sawn.—

Wallàce out over yon river he lap,
And he has lighted low down on yon plain,
And he was aware of a gay ladie,
As she was at the well washing.—

What tydins, what tydins, fair lady, he says,
What tydins hast thou to tell unto me;
What tydins, what tydins, fair lady, he says,
What tydins hae ye in the South Countrie.—

Low down in yon wee Ostler house,
  There is fyfteen Englishmen,
And they are seeking for gude Wallàce,
  It 's him to take and him to hang.—

There 's nocht in my purse, quo gude Wallàce,
  There 's nocht, not even a bare pennie;
But I will down to yon wee Ostler house
  Thir fyfteen Englishmen to see.—

And when he cam to yon wee Ostler house,
  He bad benedicite be there;

* * * * * *
* * * * *

Where was ye born, auld crookit Carl,
  Where was ye born, in what countrie;
I am a true Scot born and bred,
  And an auld, crookit carl just sic as ye see.—

I wad gie fyfteen shilling to onie crookit carl,
  To onie crookit carl just sic as ye,
If ye will get me gude Wallàce,
  For he is the man I wad very fain see.—

He hit the proud Captain alang the chafft-blade,
  That never a bit o' meat he ate mair;
And he sticket the rest at the table where they sat,
  And he left them a' lyin sprawlin there.—

Get up, get up, gudewife, he says,
  And get to me some dinner in haste;
For it will soon be three lang days
  Sin I a bit o' meat did taste.—

The dinner was na weel readie,
  Nor was it on the table set,
Till other fyfteen Englishmen
  Were a' lighted about the yett.—

Come out, come out now, gude Wallàce,
  This is the day that thou maun die;
I lippen nae sae little to God, he says,
  Altho' I be but ill wordie.—

The gudewife had an auld gudeman,
  By gude Wallàce he stiffly stood,
Till ten o' the fyfteen Englishmen
  Before the door lay in their blude.—

The other five to the greenwood ran,
  And he hang'd these five upon a grain:
And on the morn wi' his merry men a'
  He sat at dine in Lochmaben town.—

585. *The auld man's mare 's dead—*

SHE was cut-luggit, painch-lippit,
Steel-waimit, staincher-fittit,
Chanler-chaftit, lang-neckit,
  Yet the brute did die.—

Chorus

The auld man's mare 's dead,
The poor man's mare 's dead,
The auld man's mare 's dead
  A mile aboon Dundee.—

Her lunzie-banes were knaggs and neuks,
She had the cleeks, the cauld, the crooks,
The jawpish and the wanton yeuks,
  And the howks aboon her e'e.—
    The auld &c.

My Master rade me to the town,
He ty'd me to a staincher round,
He took a chappin till himsel,
  But fient a drap gae me.

The auld man's mare 's dead,
The poor man's mare 's dead,
The peats and tours and a' to lead
And yet the bitch did die.

586. *The Taylor—*

THE Taylor he cam here to sew,
And weel he kend the way to woo,
For ay he pree'd the lassie's mou
As he gaed but and ben O.

Chorus

For weel he kend the way O
The way O, the way O,
For weel he kend the way O
The lassie's heart to win O.—

The Taylor rase and sheuk his duds,
The flaes they flew awa in cluds,
And them that stay'd gat fearfu' thuds,
The Taylor prov'd a man O.—

Chorus

For now it was the gloamin,
The gloamin, the gloamin,
For now it was the gloamin
When a' to rest are gaun O.—

* * * * *

587. *There grows a bonie brier-bush &c.*

THERE grows a bonie brier-bush in our kail-yard,
There grows a bonie brier-bush in our kail-yard;
And below the bonie brier-bush there 's a lassie and a lad,
And they're busy, busy courtin in our kail-yard.—

We'll court nae mair below the buss in our kail-yard,
We'll court nae mair below the buss in our kail-yard;
We'll awa to Athole's green, and there we'll no be seen,
Whare the trees and the branches will be our safe-guard.—

Will ye go to the dancin in Carlyle's ha',
Will ye go to the dancin in Carlyle's ha';
Whare Sandy and Nancy I'm sure will ding them a'?
I winna gang to the dance in Carlyle-ha'.

What will I do for a lad, when Sandy gangs awa?
What will I do for a lad, when Sandy gangs awa?
I will awa to Edinburgh and win a pennie fee,
And see an onie bonie lad will fancy me,—

He 's comin frae the North that 's to fancy me,
He 's comin frae the North that 's to fancy me;
A feather in his bonnet and a ribbon at his knee,
He 's a bonie, bonie laddie and yon be he.—

588. *Here 's to thy health my bonie lass*

Tune, Loggan burn

HERE 's to thy health, my bonie lass,
  Gudenight and joy be wi' thee:
I'll come nae mair to thy bower-door,
  To tell thee that I loe thee.
O dinna think, my pretty pink,
  But I can live without thee:
I vow and swear, I dinna care,
  How lang ye look about ye.

Thou'rt ay sae free informing me
  Thou hast nae mind to marry:
I'll be as free informing thee,
  Nae time hae I to tarry.
I ken thy friends try ilka means
  Frae wedlock to delay thee;
Depending on some higher chance,
  But fortune may betray thee.

I ken they scorn my low estate,
  But that does never grieve me;
For I'm as free as any he,
  Sma' siller will relieve me.
I'll count my health my greatest wealth,
  Sae lang as I'll enjoy it:
I'll fear nae scant, I'll bode nae want,
  As lang 's I get employment.

But far-off fowls hae feathers fair,
  And ay until ye try them:
Tho' they seem fair, still have a care,
  They may prove as bad as I am.
But at twal at night, when the moon shines bright,
  My dear, I'll come and see thee;
For the man that loves his mistress weel,
  Nae travel makes him weary.

589. *It was a' for our rightfu' king*

It was a' for our rightfu' king
  We left fair Scotland's strand;
It was a' for our rightfu' king,
  We e'er saw Irish land, my dear,
  We e'er saw Irish land.—

Now a' is done that men can do,
  And a' is done in vain:
My Love and Native Land fareweel,
  For I maun cross the main, my dear,
  For I maun cross the main.

He turn'd him right and round about,
  Upon the Irish shore,
And gae his bridle-reins a shake,
  With, Adieu for evermore, my dear,
  And adieu for evermore.

The soger frae the wars returns,
  The sailor frae the main,
But I hae parted frae my Love,
  Never to meet again, my dear,
  Never to meet again.

When day is gane, and night is come,
  And a' folk bound to sleep;
I think on him that 's far awa,
  The lee-lang night and weep, my dear,
  The lee-lang night and weep.—

590. *The Highland widow's lament*

OH, I am come to the low Countrie,
  Ochon, Ochon, Ochrie!
Without a penny in my purse
  To buy a meal to me.—

It was na sae in the Highland hills,
  Ochon, Ochon, Ochrie!
Nae woman in the Country wide
  Sae happy was as me.—

For then I had a score o' kye,
  Ochon, &c.—
Feeding on yon hill sae high,
  And giving milk to me.—

And there I had three score o' yowes,
  Ochon, &c.—
Skipping on yon bonie knowes,
  And casting woo to me.—

I was the happiest of a' the Clan,
  Sair, sair may I repine;
For Donald was the brawest man,
  And Donald he was mine.—

Till Charlie Stewart cam at last,
  Sae far to set us free;
My Donald's arm was wanted then
  For Scotland and for me.—

Their waefu' fate what need I tell,
  Right to the wrang did yield;
My Donald and his Country fell
  Upon Culloden field.—

Ochon, O, Donald, Oh!
  Ochon, &c.—
Nae woman in the warld wide
  Sae wretched now as me.—

591. *O steer her up and had her gaun*

O STEER her up and had her gaun,
  Her mither 's at the mill, jo;
An' gin she winna tak a man
  E'en let her tak her will, jo.

First shore her wi' a kindly kiss
  And ca' anither gill, jo;
An' gin she tak the thing amiss
  E'en let her flyte her fill, jo.

O steer her up and be na blate,
  An' gin she tak it ill, jo,
Then lea'e the lassie till her fate,
  And time nae langer spill, jo;
Ne'er break your heart for ae rebute,
  But think upon it still, jo,
That gin the lassie winna do 't,
  Ye'll fin' anither will, jo.

592. *Wee Willie Gray*

WEE Willie Gray, an' his leather wallet;
Peel a willie wand, to be him boots and jacket.
The rose upon the breer will be him trouse an' doublet,
The rose upon the breer will be him trouse an' doublet.

Wee Willie Gray, and his leather wallet;
Twice a lily-flower will be him sark and cravat;
Feathers of a flee wad feather up his bonnet,
Feathers of a flee wad feather up his bonnet.

593. *Gudeen to you kimmer*

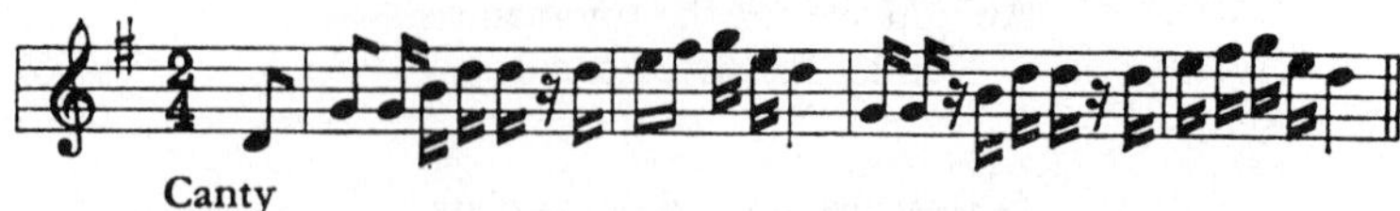

GUDEEN to you kimmer
 And how do ye do?
Hiccup, quo' kimmer,
 The better that I'm fou.

Chorus

 We're a' noddin, nid nid noddin,
  We're a' noddin at our house at hame,
 We're a' noddin, nid nid noddin,
  W'ere a' noddin at our house at hame.

Kate sits i' the neuk,
 Suppin hen-broo;
Deil tak Kate
 An' she be na noddin too!
  We're a' noddin &c.

How's a' wi' you, kimmer,
 And how do ye fare?
A pint o' the best o't,
 And twa pints mair.
  We're a' noddin &c.

How's a' wi' you, kimmer,
 And how do ye thrive;
How mony bairns hae ye?
 Quo' kimmer, I hae five.
  We're a' noddin &c.

Are they a' Johny's?
 Eh! atweel no:
Twa o' them were gotten
 When Johny was awa.
  We're a' noddin &c.

Cats like milk
  And dogs like broo;
Lads like lasses weel,
  And lasses lads too.
    We're a' noddin &c.

594. *O ay my wife she dang me*

Chorus

O AY my wife she dang me,
  An' aft my wife she bang'd me,
If ye gie a woman a' her will
  Gude faith she'll soon oergang ye.

On peace and rest my mind was bent,
  And fool I was I marry'd;
But never honest man's intent
  As cursedly miscarry'd.

Some sairie comfort still at last,
  When a' thir days are done, man,
My pains o' hell on earth is past,
  I'm sure o' bliss aboon, man.
    O ay my wife she &c.

595. *Scroggam*

THERE was a wife wonn'd in Cockpen,
Scroggam;
She brew'd gude ale for gentlemen,
Sing auld Cowl, lay you down by me,
Scroggam, my Dearie, ruffum.

The gudewife's dochter fell in a fever,
Scroggam;
The priest o' the parish fell in anither,
Sing auld Cowl, lay you down by me,
Scroggam, my Dearie, ruffum.

They laid the twa i' the bed thegither,
Scroggam;
That the heat o' the tane might cool the tither,
Sing auld Cowl, lay you down by me,
Scroggam, my Dearie, ruffum.

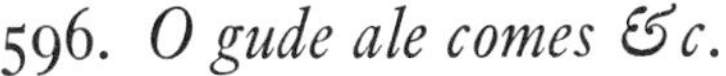

O GUDE ale comes and gude ale goes,
Gude ale gars me sell my hose,
Sell my hose and pawn my shoon,
Gude ale keeps my heart aboon.

I had sax owsen in a pleugh,
They drew a' weel eneugh,
I sald them a', ane by ane,
Gude ale keeps my heart aboon.

Gude ale hauds me bare and busy,
Gars me moop wi' the servant hizzie,
Stand i' the stool when I hae done,
Gude ale keeps my heart aboon.

O gude ale comes and gude ale goes,
Gude ale gars me sell my hose;
Sell my hose and pawn my shoon,
Gude ale keeps my heart aboon.

597. *My Lady's gown there 's gairs upon 't*

Chorus

MY Lady's gown there 's gairs upon 't,
And gowden flowers sae rare upon 't;
But Jenny's jimps and jirkinet
My Lord thinks meikle mair upon 't.

My Lord a hunting he is gane,
But hounds or hawks wi' him are nane;
By Colin's cottage lies his game,
If Colin's Jenny be at hame.
  My Lady's gown &c.

My Lady 's white, my Lady 's red
And kith and kin o' Cassillis' blude,
But her tenpund lands o' tocher gude
Were a' the charms his Lordship lo'ed.
  My Lady's gown &c.

Out o'er yon moor, out o'er yon moss,
Whare gor-cocks thro' the heather pass,
There wons auld Colin's bonie lass,
A lily in a wilderness.
  My Lady's gown &c.

Sae sweetly move her genty limbs,
Like music-notes o' Lovers hymns;
The diamond-dew in her een sae blue
Where laughing love sae wanton swims.
  My Lady's gown &c

My Lady 's dink, my Lady 's drest,
The flower and fancy o' the west;
But the Lassie that a man loes best,
O that 's the Lass to mak him blest.
  My Lady's gown &c

598. *Sweetest May*

Kinloch of Kinloch

SWEETEST May let love inspire thee;
Take a heart which he designs thee;
As thy constant slave regard it;
For its faith and truth reward it.

Proof o' shot to Birth or Money,
Not the wealthy, but the bonie;
Not high-born, but noble-minded,
In Love's silken band can bind it.

599. *Jockey 's ta'en the parting kiss*

JOCKEY 's ta'en the parting kiss,
  O'er the mountains he is gane;
And with him is a' my bliss,
  Nought but griefs with me remain.
Spare my love, ye winds that blaw,
  Plashy sleets and beating rain;
Spare my love, thou feath'ry snaw,
  Drifting o'er the frozen plain.

When the shades of evening creep
  O'er the day's fair, gladsome e'e,
Sound and safely may he sleep,
  Sweetly blythe his waukening be.
He will think on her he loves,
  Fondly he'll repeat her name;
For whare'er he distant roves
  Jockey's heart is still at hame.

600. *O lay thy loof in mine lass*

Chorus

O LAY thy loof in mine lass,
  In mine lass, in mine lass,
And swear on thy white hand lass,
  That thou wilt be my ain.

Song

A slave to love's unbounded sway,
  He aft has wrought me meikle wae;
But now, he is my deadly fae,
  Unless thou be my ain.
    O lay thy loof &c.

There 's monie a lass has broke my rest,
That for a blink I hae lo'ed best;
But thou art queen within my breast
For ever to remain.
O lay thy loof &c.

601. *Cauld is the e'enin blast*

CAULD is the e'enin blast
O' Boreas o'er the pool,
And dawin it is dreary,
When birks are bare at Yule.

O cauld blaws the e'enin blast
When bitter bites the frost,
And in the mirk and dreary drift
The hills and glens are lost.

Ne'er sae murky blew the night
That drifted o'er the hill,
But bonie Peg a Ramsey
Gat grist to her mill.

602. *There was a bonie lass*

THERE was a bonie lass,
And a bonie, bonie lass,
And she lo'ed her bonie laddie dear;
Till war's loud alarms
Tore her laddie frae her arms,
Wi' monie a sigh and a tear.

Over sea, over shore,
Where the cannons loudly roar;
He still was a stranger to fear:
And nocht could him quail,
Or his bosom assail,
But the bonie lass he lo'ed sae dear.

603. *There's news lasses news*

THERE 's news, lasses, news,
  Gude news I've to tell,
There 's a boatfu' o' lads
  Come to our town to sell.

Chorus The wean wants a cradle,
    An' the cradle wants a cod,
  An' I'll no gang to my bed
    Until I get a nod.

Father, quo' she, Mither, quo' she,
  Do what ye can,
I'll no gang to my bed
  Till I get a man.
    The wean &c.

I hae as gude a craft rig
  As made o' yird and stane;
And waly fa' the ley-crap
  For I maun till 't again.
    The wean &c.

604. *O that I had ne'er been Married*

O THAT I had ne'er been married,
I wad never had nae care,
Now I've gotten wife and bairns
An' they cry crowdie ever mair.
Ance crowdie, twice crowdie,
Three times crowdie in a day;
Gin ye crowdie ony mair,
Ye'll crowdie a' my meal away.

Waefu' Want and Hunger fley me,
Glowrin' by the hallan en';
Sair I fecht them at the door,
But ay I'm eerie they come ben.
Ance crowdie &c.

605. *The German lairdie*

WHAT merriment has taen the whigs,
  I think they be gaen mad, Sir,
Wi' playing up their whiggish jigs,
  Their dancin may be sad, Sir.—

Chorus

Sing heedle liltie, teedle liltie,
  Andum tandum tandie;
Sing fal de dal, de dal lal lal,
  Sing howdle liltie dandie.—

The Revolution principles
  Has put their heads in bees, Sir;
They're a' fa'n out amang themsels,
  Deil tak the first that grees, Sir.—
    Sing heedle, &c.

XIV. Undated Poems and *Dubia*

606. *Epitaph for H—— L——, Esq., of L——*

HERE lyes Squire Hugh —— ye harlot crew,
 Come mak' your water on him,
I'm sure that he weel pleas'd would be
 To think ye pish'd upon him.

607. *A Ballad—*

WHILE Prose-work and rhymes
 Are hunted for crimes,
And things are — the devil knows how;
 Aware o' my rhymes,
 In these kittle times,
The subject I chuse is a ——.

Some cry, Constitution!
 Some cry, Revolution!
And Politicks kick up a rowe;
 But Prince and Republic,
 Agree on the Subject,
No treason is in a good ——.

Th' Episcopal lawn,
 And Presbyter band,
Hae lang been to ither a cowe;
 But still the proud Prelate,
 And Presbyter zealot
Agree in an orthodox ——.

Poor Justice, 'tis hinted—
 Ill natur'dly squinted,
The Process—but mum—we'll allow—
 Poor Justice has ever
 For C—t had a favor,
While Justice could tak a gude ——.

Now fill to the brim—
To her, and to him,
Wha willingly do what they dow;
And ne'er a poor wench
Want a friend at a pinch,
Whase failing is only a ——.

608. *Muirland Meg*

Tune—Saw ye my Eppie M'Nab [see no. **355**]

AMANG our young lassies there 's Muirland Meg,
She'll beg or she work, and she'll play or she beg,
At thretteen her maidenhead flew to the gate,
And the door o' her cage stands open yet.—

Her kittle black een they wad thirl you thro',
Her rose-bud lips cry, kiss me now;
The curls and links o' her bonie black hair,
Wad put you in mind that the lassie has mair.—

An armfu' o' love is her bosom sae plump,
A span o' delight is her middle sae jimp;
A taper, white leg, and a thumpin thie,
And a fiddle near by, an ye play a wee!

Love 's her delight, and kissin 's her treasure;
She'll stick at nae price, an ye gie her gude measure.
As lang 's a sheep-fit, and as girt 's a goose-egg,
And that 's the measure o' Muirland Meg.

609. *The Patriarch*

Tune—The auld cripple Dow

As honest Jacob on a night,
Wi' his beloved beauty,
Was duly laid on wedlock' s bed,
And noddin' at his duty:
Tal de dal, &c.

'How lang, she says, ye fumblin' wretch,
  'Will ye be f——g at it?
'My eldest wean might die of age,
  'Before that ye could get it.

'Ye pegh, and grane, and groazle there,
  'And mak an unco splutter,
'And I maun ly and thole you here,
  'And fient a hair the better.'

Then he, in wrath, put up his graith,
  'The deevil 's in the hizzie!
'I m–w you as I m–w the lave,
  'And night and day I'm bisy.

'I've bairn'd the servant gypsies baith,
  'Forbye your titty Leah;
'Ye barren jad, ye put me mad,
  'What mair can I do wi' you.

'There 's ne'er a m–w I've gi'en the lave,
  'But ye ha'e got a dizzen;
'And d—n'd a ane ye 'se get again,
  'Altho' your c—t should gizzen.'

Then Rachel calm, as ony lamb,
  She claps him on the waulies,
Quo' she, 'ne'er fash a woman's clash,
  'In trowth, ye m–w me braulies.

'My dear 'tis true, for mony a m–w,
  'I'm your ungratefu' debtor;
'But ance again, I dinna ken,
  'We'll aiblens happen better.'

Then honest man! wi' little wark,
  He soon forgat his ire;
The patriarch, he coost the sark,
  And up and till 't like fire!!!

610. *The Trogger*

Tune—Gillicrankie

As I cam down by Annan side,
  Intending for the border,
Amang the Scroggie banks and braes,
  Wha met I but a trogger.
He laid me down upon my back,
  I thought he was but jokin,
Till he was in me to the hilts,
  O the deevil tak sic troggin!

What could I say, what could I do,
  I bann'd and sair misca'd him,
But whiltie-whaltie gae'd his a—e
  The mair that I forbade him:
He stell'd his foot against a stane,
  And doubl'd ilka stroke in,
Till I gaed daft amang his hands,
  O the deevil tak sic troggin!

Then up we raise, and took the road,
  And in by Ecclefechan,
Where the brandy-stoup we gart it clink,
  And the strang-beer ream the quech in.
Bedown the bents o' Bonshaw braes,
  We took the partin' yokin';
But I've claw'd a sairy c—t synsine,
  O the deevil tak sic troggin!

611. *Godly Girzie*

Tune—Wat ye wha I met yestreen

The night it was a haly night,
  The day had been a haly day;
Kilmarnock gleam'd wi' candle light,
  As Girzie hameward took her way.
A man o' sin, ill may he thrive!
  And never haly-meeting see!
Wi' godly Girzie met belyve,
  Amang the Cragie hills sae hie.

The chiel' was wight, the chiel' was stark,
He wad na wait to chap nor ca',
And she was faint wi' haly wark,
She had na pith to say him na.
But ay she glowr'd up to the moon,
And ay she sigh'd most piouslie;
'I trust my heart 's in heaven aboon,
'Whare'er your sinfu' p——e be.'

612. *The Jolly Gauger*

Tune—We'll gang nae mair a rovin'

THERE was a jolly gauger, a gauging he did ride,
And he has met a beggar down by yon river side.
An' we'll gang nae mair a rovin' wi' ladies to the wine,
When a beggar wi' her meal-pocks can fidge her tail sae fine.

Amang the broom he laid her; amang the broom sae green,
And he 's fa'n to the beggar, as she had been a queen.
An' we'll gang, &c.

My blessings on thee, laddie, thou 's done my turn sae weel,
Wilt thou accept, dear laddie, my pock and pickle meal?
An' we'll, &c.

Sae blyth the beggar took the bent, like ony bird in spring,
Sae blyth the beggar took the bent, and merrily did sing.
An' we'll, &c.

My blessings on the gauger, o' gaugers he 's the chief.
Sic kail ne'er crost my kettle, nor sic a joint o' beef.
An' we'll, &c.

613. *Wha'll m–w me now*

Tune—Comin' thro' the rye

O WHA'LL m–w me now, my jo,
An' wha'll m–w me now:
A sodger wi' his bandileers
Has bang'd my belly fu'.

O, I hae tint my rosy cheek,
Likewise my waste sae sma';
O wae gae by the sodger lown,
The sodger did it a'.
An' wha'll, &c.

Now I maun thole the scornfu' sneer
O' mony a saucy quine;
When, curse upon her godly face!
Her c—t 's as merry 's mine.
An' wha'll, &c.

Our dame hauds up her wanton tail,
As due as she gaes lie;
An' yet misca's [a] young thing,
The trade if she but try.
An' wha'll, &c.

Our dame can lae her ain gudeman,
An' m–w for glutton greed;
An' yet misca's a poor thing
That 's m—n' for its bread.
An' wha'll, &c.

Alake! sae sweet a tree as love,
Sic bitter fruit should bear!
Alake, that e'er a merry a—e,
Should draw a sa'tty tear.
An' wha'll, &c.

But deevil damn the lousy loun,
  Denies the bairn he got!
Or lea's the merry a—e he lo'ed
  To wear a ragged coat!
    An' wha'll, &c.

614. *O saw ye my Maggie—*

I

SAW ye my Maggie?
  Saw ye my Maggie?
Saw ye my Maggie?
  Comin oer the lea?

2

What mark has your Maggie,
What mark has your Maggie,
What mark has your Maggie,
  That ane may ken her be?

3

My Maggie has a mark,
Ye'll find it in the dark,
It 's in below her sark,
  A little aboon her knee.

4

What wealth has your Maggie,
What wealth has your Maggie,
What wealth has your Maggie,
  In tocher, gear, or fee?

5

My Maggie has a treasure,
A hidden mine o' pleasure,
I'll howk it at my leisure,
It 's alane for me.

6

How loe ye your Maggy,
How loe ye your Maggy,
How loe ye your Maggy,
An loe nane but she?

7

Ein that tell our wishes,
Eager glowing kisses,
Then diviner blisses,
In holy ecstacy!—

8

How meet you your Maggie,
How meet you your Maggie,
How meet you your Maggie,
When nane 's to hear or see?

9

Heavenly joys before me,
Rapture trembling o'er me,
Maggie I adore thee,
On my bended knee!!!

615. *Gie the lass her Fairin'*

Tune—Cauld kail in Aberdeen

O GIE the lass her fairin', lad,
O gie the lass her fairin',
An' something else she'll gie to you,
That 's waly worth the wearin';
Syne coup her o'er amang the creels,
When ye hae taen your brandy,
The mair she bangs the less she squeels,
An' hey for houghmagandie.

Then gie the lass a fairin', lad,
  O gie the lass her fairin',
An' she'll gie you a hairy thing,
  An' of it be na sparin';
But coup her o'er amang the creels,
  An' bar the door wi' baith your heels,
The mair she gets the less she squeels;
  An' hey for houghmagandie.

616. *The Book-Worms*

THROUGH and through the inspired leaves,
  Ye maggots, make your windings;
But, oh! respect his lordship's taste,
  And spare his golden bindings.

617. *On Marriage*

THAT hackney'd judge of human life,
  The Preacher and the King,
Observes: 'The man that gets a wife
  He gets a noble thing.'

But how capricious are mankind,
  Now loathing, now desirous!
We married men, how oft we find
  The best of things will tire us!

618. [*Here's, a bottle and an honest friend*]

HERE'S, a bottle and an honest friend!
  What wad ye wish for mair, man?
Wha kens, before his life may end,
  What his share may be of care, man.

The Book-Worms. There is a transcript of another version in Syme's MSS:

Free thro' the leaves ye maggots make
  your windings,
But for the Owners' sake oh spare the
  Bindings!

Then catch the moments as they fly,
 And use them as ye ought, man:—
Believe me, happiness is shy,
 And comes not ay when sought, man.

619. *Fragment*

HER flowing locks, the raven's wing,
Adown her neck and bosom hing;
How sweet unto that breast to cling,
 And round that neck entwine her!

Her lips are roses wat wi' dew,
O, what a feast, her bonie mou'!
Her cheeks a mair celestial hue,
 A crimson still diviner.

620. *A Tale—*

'TWAS where the birch and sounding thong are plyed,
The noisy domicile of Pedant-pride;
Where Ignorance her darkening vapour throws,
And Cruelty directs the thickening blows;
Upon a time, Sir Abece the great,
In all his pedagogic powers elate,
His awful Chair of state resolves to mount,
And call the tembling Vowels to account.—

First enter'd A; a grave, broad, solemn Wight,
But ah! deform'd, dishonest to the sight!
His twisted head look'd backward on his way,
And flagrant from the scourge he grunted, AI!

Reluctant, E stalk'd in; with piteous race
The jostling tears ran down his honest face!
That name, that well-worn name, and all his own,
Pale he surrenders at the tyrant's throne!
The Pedant stifles keen the Roman sound
Not all his mongrel diphthongs can compound;
And next the title following close behind,
He to the nameless, ghastly wretch assign'd.

The cob-webb'd, Gothic dome resounded, Y!
In sullen vengeance, I, disdain'd reply:
The Pedant swung his felon cudgel round,
And knock'd the groaning Vowel to the ground!

In rueful apprehension enter'd O,
The wailing minstrel of despairing woe;
Th' Inquisitor of Spain the most expert
Might there have learnt new mysteries of his art:
So grim, deform'd, with horrors, entering U,
His dearest friend and brother scarcely knew!

As trembling U stood staring all aghast,
The Pedant in his left hand clutch'd him fast;
In helpless infant's tears he dipp'd his right,
Baptiz'd him EU, and kick'd him from his sight.

621. *The Henpeck'd Husband*

CURS'D be the man, the poorest wretch in life,
The crouching vassal to the tyrant wife,
Who has no will but by her high permission;
Who has not sixpence but in her possession;
Who must to her his dear friend's secret tell;
Who dreads a curtain-lecture worse than hell.
Were such the wife had fallen to my part,
I'd break her spirit, or I'd break her heart;
I'd charm her with the magic of a switch,
I'd kiss her maids, and kick the perverse b—h.

622. *On a dog of Lord Eglintons*

I NEVER barked when out of season,
  I never bit without a reason;
I ne'er insulted weaker brother,
  Nor wronged by force or fraud another.
We brutes are placed a rank below;
  Happy for man could he say so.

623. [*Epitaph*]

LO worms enjoy the seat of bliss
Where Lords and Lairds afore did kiss.

624. *Delia*

FAIR the face of orient day,
Fair the tints of op'ning rose;
But fairer still my Delia dawns,
More lovely far her beauty blows.

Sweet the Lark's wild-warbled lay,
Sweet the tinkling rill to hear;
But, Delia, more delightful still,
Steal thine accents on mine ear.

The flower-enamour'd busy Bee
The rosy banquet loves to sip;
Sweet the streamlet's limpid lapse
To the sun-brown'd Arab's lip;

But, Delia, on thy balmy lips
Let me, no vagrant insect, rove!
O let me steal one liquid kiss!
For Oh! my soul is parch'd with love!

625. *The Tree of Liberty*

HEARD ye o' the tree o' France,
  I watna what 's the name o't;
Around it a' the patriots dance,
  Weel Europe kens the fame o't.
It stands where ance the Bastile stood,
  A prison built by kings, man,
When Superstition's hellish brood
  Kept France in leading strings, man.

Upo' this tree there grows sic fruit,
  Its virtues a' can tell, man;
It raises man aboon the brute,
  It maks him ken himsel, man.

Gif ance the peasant taste a bit,
He 's greater than a lord, man,
An' wi' the beggar shares a mite
O' a' he can afford, man.

This fruit is worth a' Afric's wealth,
To comfort us 'twas sent, man:
To gie the sweetest blush o' health,
An' mak us a' content, man.
It clears the een, it cheers the heart,
Maks high and low gude friends, man;
And he wha acts the traitor's part
It to perdition sends, man.

My blessings aye attend the chiel
Wha pitied Gallia's slaves, man,
And staw a branch, spite o' the deil,
Frae yont the western waves, man.
Fair Virtue water'd it wi' care,
And now she sees wi' pride, man,
How weel it buds and blossoms there,
Its branches spreading wide, man.

But vicious folks aye hate to see
The works o' Virtue thrive, man;
The courtly vermin 's banned the tree,
And grat to see it thrive, man;
King Loui' thought to cut it down,
When it was unco sma', man;
For this the watchman cracked his crown,
Cut aff his head and a', man.

A wicked crew syne, on a time,
Did tak a solemn aith, man,
It ne'er should flourish to its prime,
I wat they pledged their faith, man.
Awa' they gaed wi' mock parade,
Like beagles hunting game, man,
But soon grew weary o' the trade
And wished they'd been at hame, man.

For Freedom, standing by the tree,
Her sons did loudly ca', man;
She sang a sang o' liberty,
Which pleased them ane and a', man.

By her inspired, the new-born race
  Soon drew the avenging steel, man;
The hirelings ran—her foes gied chase,
  And banged the despot weel, man.

Let Britain boast her hardy oak,
  Her poplar and her pine, man,
Auld Britain ance could crack her joke,
  And o'er her neighbours shine, man.
But seek the forest round and round,
  And soon 'twill be agreed, man,
That sic a tree can not be found,
  'Twixt London and the Tweed, man.

Without this tree, alake this life
  Is but a vale o' woe, man;
A scene o' sorrow mixed wi' strife,
  Nae real joys we know, man.
We labour soon, we labour late,
  To feed the titled knave, man;
And a' the comfort we're to get
  Is that ayont the grave, man.

Wi' plenty o' sic trees, I trow,
  The warld would live in peace, man;
The sword would help to mak a plough,
  The din o' war wad cease, man.
Like brethren in a common cause,
  We'd on each other smile, man;
And equal rights and equal laws
  Wad gladden every isle, man.

Wae worth the loon wha wadna eat
  Sic halesome dainty cheer, man;
I'd gie my shoon frae aff my feet,
  To taste sic fruit, I swear, man.
Syne let us pray, auld England may
  Sure plant this far-famed tree, man;
And blythe we'll sing, and hail the day
  That gave us liberty, man.

626. *Broom Besoms* (*A*)

I MAUN hae a wife, whatsoe'er she be;
An she be a woman, that 's eneugh for me.

Chorus

Buy broom besoms! wha will buy them now;
Fine heather ringers, better never grew.

If that she be bony, I shall think her right:
If that she be ugly, where 's the odds at night?
Buy broom &c.

O, an she be young, how happy shall I be!
If that she be auld, the sooner she will die.
Buy broom &c.

If that she be fruitfu', O! what joy is there!
If she should be barren, less will be my care.
Buy broom &c.

If she like a drappie, she and I'll agree;
If she dinna like it, there 's the mair for me.
Buy broom &c.

Be she green or gray; be she black or fair;
Let her be a woman, I shall seek nae mair.
Buy broom &c.

627. *Broom Besoms* (*B*)

YOUNG and souple was I, when I lap the dyke;
Now I'm auld and frail, I douna step a syke.
Buy broom &c.

Young and souple was I, when at Lautherslack,
Now I'm auld and frail, and lie at Nansie's back.
Buy broom &c.

Had she gien me butter, when she gae me bread,
I wad looked baulder, wi' my beld head.
Buy broom &c.

628. [*Fragment*]

Now health forsakes that angel face,
  Nae mair my Dearie smiles;
Pale sickness withers ilka grace,
  And a' my hopes beguiles:
The cruel Powers reject the prayer
  I hourly mak for thee;
Ye Heavens how great is my despair,
  How can I see him die!

629. *Epigram on Rough Roads*

I'm now arrived—thanks to the gods!—
  Thro' pathways rough and muddy,
A certain sign that makin roads
  Is no this people's study:
Altho' I'm not wi' Scripture cram'd,
  I'm sure the Bible says
That heedless sinners shall be damn'd,
  Unless they mend their *ways*.

630. *On the Duchess of Gordon's Reel Dancing*

She kiltit up her kirtle weel
  To show her bonie cutes sae sma',
And walloped about the reel,
  The lightest louper o' them a'!

While some, like slav'ring, doited stots
  Stoit'ring out thro' the midden dub,
Fankit their heels amang their coats
  And gart the floor their backsides rub;

Gordon, the great, the gay, the gallant,
  Skip't like a maukin owre a dyke:
Deil tak me, since I was a callant,
  Gif e'er my een beheld the like!

631. *To the Memory of the Unfortunate Miss Burns 1791*

LIKE to a fading flower in May,
Which Gardner cannot save,
So Beauty must, sometime, decay
And drop into the grave.

Fair Burns, for long the talk and toast
Of many a gaudy Beau,
That Beauty has forever lost
That made each bosom glow.

Think, fellow sisters, on her fate!
Think, think how short her days!
Oh! think, and, e'er it be too late,
Turn from your evil ways.

Beneath this cold, green sod lies dead
That once bewitching dame
That fired Edina's lustful sons,
And quench'd their glowing flame.

632. [*Bonnie Peg*]

AS I cam in by our gate-end,
As day was waxen weary,
O wha cam tripping down the street
But bonnie Peg, my dearie!

Her air sae sweet, and shape complete,
Wi' nae proportion wanting,
The queen of love did never move
Wi' motion mair enchanting.

Wi' linked hands we took the sands
Adown yon winding river;
And, oh! that hour, and broomy bower,
Can I forget it ever!—

Cætera desunt.

GLOSSARY

(B) denotes Burns's glosses in the 1786 and 1787 editions. Other references are to Grose, *Dictionary of the Vulgar Tongue* (1796), Jamieson's Scottish *Dictionary* (1808), and Johnson's English *Dictionary* (1755).

A

a, *v. inf.* have (reduced form of **hae**).
a', *adj.*, *adv.*, *n.* all.
aback, *adv.* in the rear; 'away, aloof' (B).
abiegh, *adv.* aside, 'at a shy distance' (B).
ablins. See **aiblens**.
(a)boon, *adv.* up; *prep.* above, over. **Get aboon**, rejoice.
about, *adv.* here and there; alternately; *prep.* in the neighbourhood of.
abread, **abreed**, *adv.* wide, 'in breadth' (B); 'abroad, in sight' (B).
abus't, *v. pa. t.* abused.
acquaint, **acquent**, *ppl. adj.* familiar; acquainted with each other.
acre-braid, *n.* an acre in breadth (22 yards).
advices, *n.* counsels.
advisement, *n.* thought, deliberation.
ae, *adj.* one, a certain; one of two; only; emphatic before a superlative.
aff, *adv.*, *prep.* off, away.
aff-han(d), *adv.* at once, on the spur of the moment; in a free and easy way.
aff-loof, *adv.* 'unpremeditated' (B).
aff 's, off his.
a-fiel, *adv.* in the field, outside.
afore, *prep.* before; in front of.
aft(en), **aft(en)-times**, *adv.* often.
again, *prep.* ready for, before.
agley, *adv.* awry, wrong.
ahin(t), *prep.* behind. See **furr ahin**, **lan' ahin**.
aiblens, **a(i)blins**, *adv.* perhaps.
aidle, *n.* ditch water, byre wash.
aik, *n.* oak; **aiken**, *adj.*
ain, *adj.* own.
air, *adv.* early.
airles, *n.* payment made in token of employment; **airle-penny**, earnest money.
airn, *n.* iron; *pl.* fetters.
airt, *n.* quarter, direction; *v.* guide.
aith, *n.* oath.
aits, *n. pl.* oats.
aiver, *n.* 'an old horse' (B); carthorse.
aix, *n.* axe.
aizle, *n.* 'a hot cinder' (B); ember of tobacco.
a-jee, *adv.* ajar.
alake, *int.* alas.
alane, *adj.*, *adv.* alone.
alarms, *n. pl.* provocations; *ppl. adj.* **alarming**, exciting.
amaist, *adv.* almost.
amang, *prep.* among.
an('), *conj.* (1) and; (2) if; **an 't, if it.**
anathem, *v.* curse.
ance, *adv.* once.
ane, *adj.*, *pron.* one, a(n).
aneuch, *adj.*, *n.* enough.
anger, *v.* make angry; become angry.
anither, *adj.*, *pron.* another.
an's, and am; and is; and his.
aqua-fontis, *n.* spring water.
aqua-vitæ, *n.* alcohol, whisky.
arch, *v.* rise in a curve.
area, *n.* walled or railed court, churchyard.
ase, **auss**, *n.* ashes.
ask, *n.* eft, lizard.
asklent, *adv.* askew, on the side; askance.
aspar, *adv.* aspread, with legs apart.
asteer, *adj.* 'abroad, stirring' (B).
athort, *prep.* across.
attour. See **bye attour**.
atweel, *adv.* certainly, indeed.
atween, *prep.* between.
aught, *adj.* eight, eighth; **aughteen**, eighteen.
aught, *n.* anything.
aught, *pa. ppl.* possessed of.
auld, *adj.* old; **auld-fac'd**, ancient-looking.

auldfarran, auld-farrent, *adj.* old-fashioned, hence 'sagacious, cunning, prudent' (B); wise, witty.
auld-warld, *adj.* old-fashioned, antiquated.
aumous (dish), *n.* alms-dish.
auss. See **ase.**
ava, *adv. phr.* of all; at all.
awa, *adv.* away; *int.*
awald, *adv.* in a state of drunkenness. Prop. of a sheep lying on its back and unable to get up.
awauk, *v.* awake.
awe, *v.* owe.
awee, *adv.* for a moment.
awkart, *adj.* obstinate, cantankerous.
awnie, *adj.* having awns, bearded.
ayont, *prep., adv.* beyond, past.

B

ba', *n.* ball; game of handball.
babie-clouts, baby-clouts, *n. pl.* baby-linen.
backlins, *adv.* backwards; **backlins-comin,** *ppl. phr.* returning.
back-style, back-yett, *nn.* the stile, gate in the rear fence of the house. See **yett.**
bade. See **bid, bide.**
baggie, *n.* belly.
baiginets, *n. pl.* bayonets.
bail(l)ie, *n.* landlord's deputy; borough officer corresponding to alderman.
bair, *v.* uncover, clear.
bairn, *n.* child; *v.* get a woman with child.
bairn-time, *n.* all the offspring of one mother, 'a family of children, a brood' (B).
baith, *pron., adj., conj.* both.
bakes, *n. pl.* biscuits.
ballat, *n.* ballad, traditional verse tale.
ban, *v. tr.* curse; *intr.* swear; *n.* curse.
ban(d), *n.* (1) legal or money bond; (2) white linen strip attached to clerical collar.
bandileers, *n. pl.* bandoliers, cases containing charges for a musket; *fig.* 'balls', testicles.
banditti, *n. attrib.* treacherous, vicious.
bane, *n.* bone; bone-comb.
bang, *v.* thrash, thump, hammer; *transf.* copulate vigorously. These senses comb. in *pa. pple.* **613.** 4.
bang, *n.* blow, pain, 'effort' (B) **120.** 80 (in standing through the centuries).
banie, *adj.* bony, big-boned, 'stout' (B).
bannock, bonnock, *n.* round, flat girdle-baked cake of oatmeal, barley, pease, or flour.
bardie, *n.* minor poet.
barefit, *adj.* barefooted.
barley-bree, *n.* whisky.
barm, *n.* yeast; **barmie,** *adj.* passionate, fermenting with ideas.
barn, *n.* corn in the barn.
bashing, *pres. pple.* abashed, confused.
bastart, *n.* bastard.
batch, *n.* 'crew, gang' (B), set.
batts, *n.* colic, 'botts' (B).
bauckie-bird, *n.* bat.
baudrans, baudrons, bawd'rons, *n.* cat.
bauk, *n.* cross-beam, tying the rafters in a roof; **bauk-en',** *n.* end of a crossbeam.
bauld, *adj.* bold, audacious; stormy.
baumy, *adj.* balmy.
bawbee, *n.* coin of six pennies Scots originally struck in base silver by James V, a halfpenny.
baw'drons. See **baudrans.**
bawk, *n.* strip of unploughed land in a cultivated field, or between farms to mark a boundary.
baws'nt, *adj.* 'having a white stripe down the face' (B), brindled.
bawtie, *n.* name given to a dog.
be. See **let be.**
bead, *n.* drop of liquor.
bear, beir, *n.* barley.
bear, *v.* allow, suffer, admit
bearers, *n. pl.* legs.
beastie, *n.* horse.
beat. See **beet.**
beaver, *n.* beaver hat.
beck, *n.* obeisance, curtsey.
bedeen, *adv.* early, quickly, anon
bedlam, *adj.* fit for Bedlam, mad.
beese, *n.* vermin.
beet, beat, *v.* mend, kindle, 'add fuel to fire' (B).
befa', *v.* befall.

behin(t), *prep., adv.* behind.
beild. See **biel(d).**
beir. See **bear.**
belang, *v.* belong to (with indirect obj.)
beld, *adj.* bald.
bellum, *n.* rumpus, force, onslaught.
bellys, *n.* bellows.
belted, *adj.* descr. the distinctive belt of an earl or a knight.
belyve, *adv.* quickly, at once, soon.
ben, *adv., prep.* indoors, within, 'into the *spence* or parlour' (B); *n.* parlour, inner room. See **but(t) and ben.**
benmost, *adj.* furthest in, innermost.
benorth, *prep.* to the north of.
bent, *n.* sandy hillock or moor covered with bent-grass.
bent, *n.* (1) as prec., or (2) hillside, ridge of a hill **612**. 9.
beside our han'. See **han'.**
besouth, *prep.* to the south of.
bestead, *pa. pple.* placed, circumstanced.
bethankit, *pa. pple.* (God) be thanked, 'the grace after meat' (B).
beuk, *n.* book.
bevel, *n.* mason's rule; **in . . . bevel,** on the line set by the bevel, obliquely.
bewaure, *v.* beware.
beyont, *prep.* beyond, on the far side of.
bicker, *v.* rush, scurry; *n.* short rush, stagger.
bicker, *n.* wooden drinking vessel with one or two staves extended to form lugs.
bid, *v.* ask. desire; **bid to,** hail, salute.
bide, *v.* remain, await, stay for; stand, endure.
biel(d), beild, *n.* protection, shelter, cover.
bien, *adj.* cosy, comfortable, well-stocked; *adv.* **bien(ly),** comfortably, warmly.
big, *adj.* elated, passionate.
big, *v.* build; **biggin,** *n.* building, cottage.
bike. See **byke.**
bill, *n.* bull.
billie, billy, *n.* craft-brother; friend, comrade; fellow, lad.
bird(ies). See **burd.**
birdy, *adj.* chicken, poultry.
birk, *n.* birch tree; **birken,** *adj.*
birkie, *n.* lively, spry fellow.
birrin(g), *ppl. adj.* whirring, 'the noise of partridges, &c., when they spring' (B).
birsie, *n.* bristle, hair.
birth, *n.* berth, place on board ship.
bit, (1) *n.* 'crisis, nick of time' (B); (2) *quasi-adj.* by omission of *of*, indicating littleness, affection, contempt.
bitch, *n.* term of contempt; **bitch-fou,** *adj.* beastly drunk.
bizz, *v.* buzz; *n.* stir, flurry.
bizzard, *n.* buzzard; 'often, but wrongly, called *the bizzard gled*' (Jamieson). See **gled.**
black, *adj.* dark, swarthy; foul, ugly; wicked, malignant, sinister; disastrous.
blackguarding, *pres. pple.* roistering; *pa. pple.* reviled **95**. 12.
black-nebbit, *ppl. adj.* 'democratically inclined, or inimical to the present government' (Jamieson).
blade. See **blaud.**
blae, *adj.* blue, livid, bitter.
blast. *v.* blow, curse, wither; **blast(i)et,** *ppl. adj.* accursed, dwarfish; **blastie,** *n.* ill-tempered beast, ill-disposed creature.
blate, *adj.* bashful, diffident.
blather, *n.* bladder.
blatter, *v.* work vigorously, noisily.
blaud, blade, *n.* piece, specimen, selection.
blaud, *v.* slap, beat; *ppl. adj.* pelting.
blaw, *v.* (1) blow; (2) get breath back; (3) boast; **blawn,** *pa. pple.* (have) blown.
blaze, *n.* brilliance, display.
blear, bleer(i)t, *adj.* watery-eyed, bleary.
bleeze, *n., v.* blaze.
blellum, *n.* idle babbler; blusterer, railer.
blether, *v.* talk foolishly, babble, boast; **blethers,** *n. pl.*
blin,' *v., adj.* blind; **blin't** *pa. t.*
blink, *v.* glance fondly; leer flirtatiously; gleam, 'shine by fits' (B).
blink, *n.* 'a smiling look' (B); instant; short time, moment.

blinkers, *n. pl.* ogling, alluring girls; spies, cheats ('a term of contempt' (B)).
blitter, *n.* 'bleater', snipe.
blooster, *v.* blow gustily (of the wind); *pa. t.* stormed.
blude. See **bluid.**
blue-boram, *n.* pox.
blue-clue, *n.* ball of blue yarn used for divining.
blue-gown, *n. attrib.* 'one of those beggars who get annually, on the King's birthday, a blue cloke or gown with a badge' (B).
bluid, blude, *n.* blood; offspring; = semen **84.** 234; **bluidy,** *adj.*
bluntie, *n.* fool.
blype, *n.* 'a coat, a shred; applied to the skin . . . when it *peels* in coats, or is rubbed off, in shreds' (Jamieson).
bob, *v.* move up and down; curtsey; dance; *n.* dance.
bock, *v.* 'to vomit, to gush intermittently' (B).
bod(d)le, *n.* copper coin first struck by Charles I, equivalent to a sixth of an English penny.
bode, *v.* expect, look for.
bodie, body, *n.* person, fellow; *pl.* folk; **a body's sel,** oneself.
boggie, *n.* bog, marsh.
bogle, *n.* ghost, spectre, goblin.
bole, *n.* recess in wall, serving as shelf or cupboard.
bolus, *n.* large medicinal pill.
bon ton, good breeding.
bon(n)ie, bony, *adj.* fair, pretty, sweet; fine, splendid, handsome.
bonnock. See **bannock.**
boon. See **aboon.**
boord, *n.* surface, layer (of ice).
boord-en', *n.* end of a table.
boortree, *n.* 'the shrub elder planted much of old in hedges of barn-yards, &c.' (B).
boosom, *n.* besom, twig-broom.
boost, *v.* must, ought.
boot, o', into the bargain, as well.
bore, *n.* crevice, crack; curling term, passage between two guarding stones **117.** 26.
botch, *n.* 'an angry tumour' (B).
bother, *v.* fuss, give trouble.
bouk, *n.* body, carcase.
'bout, *prep.* about, concerning; around, in.
bow, *v.* bend; subdue; **bow't,** *ppl. adj.* crooked, bent.
bow-hough'd, *adj.* bandy-legged.
bow-kail, *n.* cabbage. See **kail.**
bowse, *v.* drink heavily; **b. about,** drink in turn; **bouze,** *n.* drinking-party.
bra'. See **braw.**
brachen, breckan, *n.* bracken, coarse fern.
brae, *n.* hill, hillside, high ground by a river.
brag, *v.* challenge; **bragged,** have challenged; *n.* boast, pride.
braid, *adj.* broad, plain; **b. money,** pieces of gold; **b. sword,** broad-bladed cutting sword.
braid-claith, *n.* broad-cloth.
braik, *n.* heavy harrow.
brainge, *v.* plunge, 'draw unsteadily' (B).
brak, *pa. t.* of *brek,* break; **brak's,** broke his.
brandy-stoup. See **stoup.**
brankie, *adj.* finely dressed.
branks, *n.* halter, bridle.
bran'y, *n.* brandy.
brash, *n.* 'a sudden illness' (B).
brat, *n.* child 'so called in contempt' (Johnson).
brats, *n. pl.* rags.
brattle, *n.* clatter; hurry; short race; noisy onset.
braw, bra', *adj.* fine, splendid; handsome; finely dressed; **braulies, brawlie, brawly,** *adv.* admirably, very much; *intensive* very.
brawds, *n. pl.* ruffians (?).
brawnit, *adj.* brindled.
braxies, *n. pl.* sheep that have died of braxy.
breastet, *v. pa. t.* pulled forward.
breastie, *n.* a little breast.
brechan, *n.* horse-collar made of, or lined with, straw.
breckan. See **brachen.**
bree, *n.* whisky.
bree, brie, *n.* brow.
breeks, *n.* breeches, trousers.
breer, brier, *n., adj.* briar.
brent, *adj.* smooth, unwrinkled.
brent, *ppl. adj.* branded, brand (new)

-brewn, *ppl. adj.* brewed.
brie. See **bree.**
brief, *n.* writing; literary skill. Cf. **warlock-breef.**
brier(-bush). See **breer.**
brig, *n.* bridge.
brisket, *n.* breast.
brither, *n.* brother.
brock, *n.* badger.
broded, *v. pa. pple.* braided.
brogue, *n.* trick, hoax.
broo, *n.* water, soup; **snaw-broo**, half-melted snow, slush.
broose, *n.* wedding race.
brose, *n.* oatmeal mixed with boiling water or milk, and salt and butter added.
browst, *n.* brew; *fig.* mischief, ill.
browster, *n.* brewer; **b. wives**, ale-wives, landladies.
brugh, *n.* borough.
brulzie, *n.* uproar, affray, quarrel.
brunstane, *n., adj.* brimstone.
brunt, *v.* burnt.
brush, *n.* onset, attack.
brust, *v.* burst.
buckie, *n.* (1) buck, 'gay debauchee'; (2) 'a perverse or refractory person' (Jamieson).
buckle, *n.* curliness; **buckl'd**, *ppl. adj.* 'crisped and curled by being kept long in the same state' (Johnson).
buckskin, *n., adj.* American.
budget, *n.* leather bag.
buff, *v.* thrash, beat.
bught, *v.* fold sheep; **bughtin-time**, time in the evening when ewes are milked.
buirdly, *adj.* stalwart, stately.
buller, *n.* loud roar; whirlpool.
bum, *v.* hum.; **bum-clock**, *n.* 'a humming beetle that flies in the evening' (B), cockchafer.
bummil, *v.* hum, mumble, stutter clumsily; **bummle**, *n.* idle, impotent bungler.
bunter, *n.* drab, 'half whore and half beggar' (Grose).
burd(ie), bird(ie), *n.* lady, girl.
bure, *v. pa. t.* bore, carried, won; **b. sic hands**, fought so vigorously.
burn(ie), *n.* water, stream; water used in brewing.
burnewin, *n.* burn-the-wind, blacksmith.
bur-thistle, *n.* spear-thistle.
busk, *v.* prepare, dress; dress up; *ppl. adj.* well-furnished, splendid.
buss, *n.* bush.
bussle, *n.* commotion, fuss.
but, *prep.* without; but that, other than that; lacking, less.
but(t), *prep., adv.* out, to the outer room; **butt the house**, in the kitchen; **but(t) and ben**, in the kitchen or outer room, and in the parlour or inner room of a cottage; backwards and forwards; *n. phr.* a cottage. See **ben.**
butching, *vbl. n.* butchering.
buttock-hire, *n.* ecclesiastical fine for fornication.
by, *prep., adv.* concerning, about (it); over, past; **by himself**, beside himself, 'lunatic, distracted' (B); **bye attour**, besides, in addition.
by-job, *n.* fornication.
byke, bike, *n.* hive; swarm, crowd.
byre, *n.* cowshed; **byre-en'**, *n.* outside end of the byre.

C

ca', *v.* (1) call, **ca't** *pa. t.*; name, **ca't**, name it, **ca'd** *pa. pple.*; (2) urge forward, drive; *intr.* be driven, plod on; (3) drive (in), knock, hammer; (4) *phr.* **ca' the crack**, gossip, talk; **ca' thro'**, work away, get work done.
ca', *n.* call; knock, blow.
cackit, *v. pa. t.* befouled with excrement.
cad(d)ie, *n.* fellow, ragamuffin, rascal.
cadger, *n.* travelling hawker.
caff, *n.* chaff.
caird, *n.* tinker, gipsy.
caition, *n.* surety
calces, *pl.* of **calx**, powder.
Caledon, *n.* Scotland.
calf-ward, *n.* 'a small enclosure for calves' (B), the churchyard.
callan(t), *n.* stripling, lad.
caller, callor, *adj.* fresh, cool.
callet, *n.* wench, trull.
cam, *pa. t.* of *come*.
canker, *v.* become peevish; **cankert, cankrie**, *adj.* ill-natured.

canna, *v.* cannot.

can(n)ie, can(n)y, *adj., adv.* (1) knowing, shrewd; careful, cautious, frugal **40.** 57; (2) favourable, lucky; (3) gentle, steady, kindly, pleasant.

cant, *n.* song, merry tale.

cantan, *ppl. adj.* whining, hypocritical.

cantie, canty, *adj., adv.* lively, cheerful(ly), pleasant(ly).

cantraip, *n.* magic, witching.

cape-stane, *n.* coping-stone.

cap'rin, *n.* capering.

car, *n.* crude cart without wheels; carriage.

card, *n.* chart.

care, *n.* sweetheart.

careerin, *pres. pple.* running this way and that.

careless, *adj.* free from anxiety, untroubled.

caretna by, cared nothing, not at all.

caritch, *n.* catechism.

carl(e), carlie, *n.* fellow, old man.

carl-hemp, *n.* seed-bearing hemp.

carlin, *n.* old woman, witch; old fellow.

carmagnole, *n.* rascal.

carte(s), *n.* card(s).

case, *v.* enclose, shut up.

cast out, *v.* fall out, quarrel.

catch'd, *v. pa. t.*; *pa. pple.* caught.

catch-the-plack, *n.* money-grubbing. See **plack.**

cattle, *n.* horses, beasts.

caudron, *n.* cauldron.

cauf, *n.* calf; **cauf-leather,** *adj.* calfskin.

cauk and keel, *n. phr.* drawing, sketching.

cauld, *n., adj.* cold.

caup, *n.* wooden bowl; **kiss his caup,** drink from the same vessel with him in token of friendship, loyalty.

cause, *n.* case, trial.

causey-cleaner, *n.* street-cleaner.

cavie, *n.* (hen-)coop.

cess, *n.* land-tax.

chafft-blade, *n.* jaw-bone.

chainet, *ppl. adj.* fitted, adorned with chains.

chamer, *n.* bed-chamber.

change-house, *n.* ale-house.

chanler-chaftit, *adj.* lantern-jawed.

chantan, *pres. pple.* singing.

chanter, *n.* the part of a bagpipe on which the melody is played; pastoral pipe.

chap, *n.* fellow.

chap, *n.* blow, stroke; *v.* knock, thrash, beat.

chap, chappin, *n.* liquid measure, half a Scots pint; drink of liquor.

chapman, *n.* pedlar.

chearfu', *adj.* cheerful.

cheek, *n.* side-piece.

cheek-for-chow (jow), *adv. phr.* cheek by jowl, side by side.

cheel, chiel(d), *n.* lad, young fellow, chap.

chimla, chimlie, *n.* fire-place, hearth.

chittering, *ppl. adj.* trembling, shivering.

chow, *v.* chew.

chuck(ie), *n.* mother hen; sweetheart, dear.

chuffie, *adj.* portly, 'fat-faced' (B).

cit, *n.* citizen, townsman.

clachan, *n.* village; *attrib.* ale-house **55.** 13.

claes, claise, claething, claith(ing), *n.* clothes, dress.

clag, *n.* 'an incumbrance, a burden lying on property; a forensic term' (Jamieson); a claim.

clamb, *v. pa. t.* climbed.

clankie, *n.* knock, blow.

clap, *v.* stroke fondly, caress; **clappin,** *n.*

clark, *adj.* scholarly; **clarket,** *pa. pple.* written up.

clarty, *adj.* sticky, dirty.

clash, *n.* chatter, 'an idle tale, the story of the day' (B); *v.* gossip, talk scandal.

class, *n.* division of society, electorate.

clatter, *n.* uproar, chatter, gossip.

claught. See **cleek.**

claut(e), *n.* clutch, grip; handful, lump; *v.* scrape, clean out.

claver, *n.* clover.

clavers, *n.* idle talk, chatter.

claw, *n.* scratching; blow, drubbing; *v.* scratch, beat, thrash; **clew,** *pa. t.* scratched gently.

claymore, *n.* two-handed Highland sword.

clean, *adj.* comely, shapely; empty; *adv.* quite, utterly.
clear, *adj.* quite free.
clearin, *n.* beating.
cleckin, *n.* brood.
cleed, *v.* clothe.
cleek, *v.* clutch, lay hold of, pilfer; link arms in the dance; **claught**, *pa. t.*; **claughtin 't**, gathering it.
cleeks, *n.* cramp in horses, which '*cleiks*, or as it were hooks up, their hinder-legs' (Jamieson), string-halt.
cleg, *n.* gad-fly.
clew. See **claw**.
clink, *n.* (1) cash; (2) jingle (of verse); (3) sharp stroke; *v.* (1) ring, rhyme; (2) sit down smartly.
clinker, *n.* lively rogue.
clips, *n.* shears, clippers.
clishmaclaver(s), *n.* wordy discourse, tittle-tattle, blethers.
clockin-time, *n.* hatching-time, child-bearing.
cloot, *n.* division of the hoof, the hoof; **Clooty, Cloots**, the (cloven-footed) Devil.
close, *adj.* constant, unrelieved.
clour, *n.* 'a bump or swellling after a blow' (B).
clout, *n.*, *v.* patch.
clud, *n.* cloud.
clunk, *v.* gurgle.
coat(ie), *n.* petticoat, skirt.
coaxin, *ppl. adj.* making a 'cokes' of, wheedling, flattering.
coble. See **saumont-coble**.
cock, *n.* (1) good fellow, chap; **cockie**, crony; (2) circle at which the stones are aimed in curling.
cod, *n.* pillow.
coff, *v.* buy; **coft**, *pa. t.*
cog(gie), *n.* wooden vessel made of staves and girded with metal bands, for drinking liquor; as a corn measure; *transf.* womb.
colleaguin, *v. pres. pple.* associating, conspiring.
collieshangie, *n.* dispute, uproar.
command, *n.* commandment.
commen', *v.* commend.
commerce-chaumer, *n.* chamber of commerce.
compleenin, *v. pres. pple.* complaining
conveener, *n.* president of a trades court.
cood, *n.* cud.
coof, cuif, *n.* fool, clown, lout.
cooket, *v. pa. t.* 'appeared and disappeared by fits' (B).
coor, *v.* cover, protect.
cooser, *n.* stallion; lecher.
coost, *v. pa. t.* cast, threw off, discarded (for battle); tossed; looped; **coost out**, fell out, disagreed.
cootie, *n.* (milk-)basin, (wash-)tub.
cootie, *adj.* with feathered legs.
corbie, *n.* raven.
core, *n.* band of dancers; party, merry company; team of curlers.
corn-mou, *n.* stack, pile, of corn.
corn't, *v. pa. pple.* fed with corn.
corss, *n.* (market-)cross, market-place.
cot(-house), *n.* cottage; **cot-folk**, cottagers.
cotillion, *n.* 18th-cent. French dance.
cotter(-man), *n.* farm tenant, cottager.
couldna, *v.* could not.
countra, *adj.* country, rustic. See **kintra**.
coup. See **cowp**.
couper, *n.* cooper; *v.* repair, *pa. t.* (transf.) copulated **564**. 13.
cour, cow'r, *v.* lower, fold; *ppl. adj.* **cowran**, cringing, timid.
court-day, *n.* rent-day.
couthie, couthy, *adj.* loving, kind.
cow(e), *v.* crop, trim (the hair); cut short; berate, scold, beat thoroughly, humiliate; *n.* trouncing.
cowe, *v.* terrify; *n.* terror, hobgoblin.
cowp, coup, *b.* upset, capsize; *pa. pple.* blown over, laid low **67**. 49; **coup the cran**, somersault, get ruined.
cowt(e), *n.* colt; *transf.* awkward fellow.
cozie, *adj.* snug, comfortable.
crabbet, *adj.* crabbed, ill-natured.
crack, *n.* gossip, chat, *pl.* jokes, talk; story, scandalous tale; *v.* talk, chat, make (a jest).
craft, *n.* croft, infield, land adjoining farm-house; *adj.* (sexual metaphor) **603**. 13.
craig, *n.* crag, cliff.

craig(ie), *n.* neck, throat, gullet.
craik, *n.* land-rail, corn-crake.
crambo-clink, crambo-jingle, *n.* doggerel verse.
cran, *n.* crane, tripod for a pot.
crankous, *adj.* fretful, captious, awkward.
crank, *n.* harsh sound, 'the noise of an ungreased wheel' (B); *pl.* grating lines.
cranreuch, *n.* hoar-frost.
crap, *n.* (1) top, head; (2) crop; *v.* crop.
craw, *n.* (1) crow; (2) cock's crow.
crazy, *adj.* crazed, infirm.
creel, *n.* wicker basket carried on the back; '*to have one's wits in a creel*, to be craz'd, to be fascinated' (B).
creepie-chair, *n.* three-legged stool, used as stool of repentance in church.
creeshie, *adj.* greasy, filthy.
crib, *n.* barred manger in a byre.
critic, *adj.* critical, practising criticism.
crock, *n.* old ewe past bearing.
crood, croud, *v.* coo.
crookit, *adj.* crooked, deformed.
crooks, *n.* disease of sheep, causing curvature of the neck.
croon, *n.* (1) moan, whine; (2) low, bellow; *v.* boom (of a bell), hum.
croose. See **crouse.**
cross, *prep.* across.
crouch, *v.* bend, cringe submissively.
crouchie, *adj.* hump-backed.
croud, *n.*, *v.* crowd. See **crood.**
crouse, croose, *adj.* merry, cocksure.
crowdie, *n.* oatmeal mixed with water and eaten raw; porridge; **crowdie-time**, *n.* breakfast-time.
crowlan, *ppl. adj.* creeping.
crummie, *n.* cow with crooked horns; a cow's name.
crummock, *n.* stick with crooked head, crook.
crump, *adj.* 'hard and brittle, *spoken of bread*' (B), baked dry.
crunt, *n.* 'a blow on the head with a cudgel' (B).
cry, *v.* call, summon; protest, claim.
cuif. See **coof.**
cummer. See **kimmer.**
cummock, *n.* 'a short staff with a crooked head' (B).
c–nt(ie), *n.* *pudendum muliebre*
curch, *n.* kerchief.
curchie, *n.* curtsey.
curler, *n.* player in curling.
curmurring, *n.* 'slight, rumbling noise' (B), flatulence.
curpan, *n.* rump.
curple, *n.* buttocks.
curry, *n.* dressing, beating.
cushat, *n.* wood-pigeon.
custoc(k), *n.* kale-stalk, cabbage stem.
cute, *n.* ankle.
cut-luggit, *adj.* crop-eared (for identification).
cutty, *adj.* short, brief; **cutty-stool**, *n.* stool of repentance in church, cf. **creepie-chair.**

D

dadie, *n.* father.
daez't, *ppl. adj.* stupefied, besotted.
daffin, *n.* fooling, frolic, flirtation, dallying.
daft, *adj.* silly, foolish; libertine; wild with excitement.
dail, *n.* dale.
dail, *n.* deal, fir- or pine-wood plank.
daimen-icker, *n.* occasional ear of corn.
dainty, *n.* treat; *adj.* (1) worthy, open-hearted; (2) 'pleasant, good-humoured, agreeable' (B); (3) stately.
dander, *v.* stroll, wander about.
dang. See **ding.**
darklins, *adv.* in the dark.
dashing, *pple.* cast down.
date, *n.* season, time of life.
daud, *v.* 'to thrash, abuse' (B), pelt. See **dawd.**
daunton, *v.* subdue, discourage, cast down.
daur, *v.* dare; *pa. t.* **daur't, durst,** dared (do).
daurk, *n.* day's labour. Cf. **han'-daurk.**
daut, dawt(e), *v.* fondle, caress, pet; *ppl. adj.* treasured, spoiled; **dawtie**, *n.* darling, pet.
daw, *v.* dawn; **dawin**, *n.*
dawd, daud, *n.* hunk, large piece.
deacon, *n.* president of a trade, and *ex officio* town councillor.

dead, *n.* death.
dead-sweer, *adj.* quite disinclined.
deal about, *v.* divide, distribute.
dearthfu', *adj.* costly.
deave, *v.* deafen.
decreet, *n.* judgment of a court of law.
deep-lairing, *ppl. adj.* sinking deep into the drifts.
deevil, de'il, diel, *n.* devil, the Devil.
de'il a (ane), not a (one), no (one) at all; **deil na, deil nor** (expressing strong negation); **deil-mak-matter,** no matter. See **hair, deil a, (deil-)haet.**
deleeret, deliret, *ppl. adj.* delirious, crazed.
delver, *n.* gardener, labourer; **delvin,** *n.* digging.
den, *n.* dean, dingle.
dern, *v.* hide.
design, *v.* designate.
detach, *v.* disengage.
deu(c)k, *n.* duck.
devel, *n.* violent blow.
devil-haet. See **haet.**
dibble, *n.* pointed stick for making holes in planting seedlings; *fig.* penis.
dictionar, *n.* dictionary.
did(d)le, *n.* jig, move jerkily, fiddle.
dight, *v.* make ready; wipe, rub down; wipe ready, dry, clean; winnow.
dimpl't, *v. pa. t.* dimpled.
din, *adj.* dark, dingy.
dine, *n.* dinner-time.
ding, *v.* overcome, weary; excel, beat; *neut. pass.* be shifted, be worn out **113.** 30; **dang,** *pa. t.* pushed, knocked, clouted; **dung in,** *pa. pple.* beaten into.
dink, *adj.* trim, finely dressed.
dinna, *v.* do not.
dinner, *v.* dine.
dinsome, *adj.* noisy.
dint, *n.* occasion, chance; *v.* pierce with an arrow.
dirl, *v.* shake, rattle; play vigorously, reel off; *as adv.* with a clatter, 'slight tremulous stroke or pain' (B), **55.** 95.
discover, *v.* disclose, reveal (pregnancy).
ditt(a)y, *n.* ground of indictment (Sc. law); **gat our d.,** received our reproof.
diz(ze)n, *n., adj.* dozen; hank, dozen 'cuts' (each 310 yards) of yarn, the standard of a day's spinning.
do, *v.* put up with, stand.
docht. See **dow.**
dochter, *n.* daughter.
dock(ie), *n.* backside.
dockin, *n.* dock(-leaf).
doit, *v.* to be crazed, enfeebled by age or drink; **doited,** *pa. t.* acted stupid, blundered, *trans.* enfeebled, dulled; **doytan,** *ppl. adj.* stumbling, blundering; **doited,** *ppl. adj.* muddled, 'stupified, hebetated' (B).
donsie, *adj.* hapless, unlucky; ill-tempered, unmanageable.
dool, *n.* sorrow, misery; **sing d.,** lament; **doolfu',** *adj.*
dorty, *adj.* supercilious, haughty.
doubt, *v.* fear, think, suspect, with the implication of probability.
douce, douse, *adj.* sedate, sober, prudent, kindly; **douse(ly),** circumspectly, decorously.
doudle, *v.* dandle.
dought. See **dow.**
douk, *v.* duck, dip.
douna. See **downa.**
doup, *n.* backside, buttocks; **doup-skelper,** *n.* lecher.
dour(e), dowr(e), *adj.* harsh, severe; pertinacious, unyielding; sullen.
douse. See **douce.**
dow, *n.* pigeon.
dow, *v.* be able, have courage (to do), dare; **docht, dought,** *pa. t.*
dowf(f), *adj.* listless, 'pithless, wanting force' (B), melancholy, dull.
dowie, *adj.* sad, dismal, melancholy; sickly, dejected.
downa, douna, *v.* cannot **81.** 158; **downa do,** *n. comb.* impotence.
down-brae, *adv.* downhill.
dowr(e). See **dour(e).**
doxy, *n.* beggar's wench.
doylt, *ppl. adj.* dazed, muddled, stupid.
doytan. See **doit.**
dozen, dozin, *ppl. adj.* impotent; **dozen'd,** *pa. pple.* made impotent.
draigle, *v.* bedraggle, bespatter.
drank, *v. pa. t.* ***intr.*** tasted.

drant, drunt, *n.* sulks.
drap, *n.* drop; amount of; **drappie,** *n.* (a little) liquor.
draunt, *v.* whine, drone out.
drave on, *v. pa. t.* passed.
dree, *v.* suffer, put up with.
dreeping, *ppl. adj.* dripping (with gravy).
dreigh, driegh, *adj.* slow, tedious, dreary.
dress. See **droddum.**
drid(d)le, *v.* dawdle, saunter; totter.
driegh. See **dreigh.**
drift, *n.* (1) flock, herd; (2) falling snow driven by the wind; hence **drifty,** *adj.*
droddum, *n.* backside; **dress your d.,** thrash you.
drone, *n.* (1) supplementary pipe (bass or tenor) of the bagpipe, sounding one continous note; (2) monotonous humming.
droop-rumpl't, *adj. comb.* with drooping haunches.
drouk, *v.* soak, drench; **droukit,** *ppl. adj.*
drouth, *n.* thirst; **drouthy,** *adj.*
dru(c)ken, *ppl. adj.* drunken, tipsy; *pa. pple.* drunk **368.** 21.
drumlie, *adj.* sedimented, cloudy; gloomy, thick-skulled; turbid, muddy; dark, sullen.
drummock, *n.* oatmeal and cold water.
drunt. See **drant.**
dry, *adj.* thirsty.
dry-b–b, *n.* copulation without emission.
duan, *n.* canto.
dub, *n.* stagnant pool, puddle, pond; mud, mire.
duddie, *adj.* ragged, tattered.
dud(d)ies, duds, *n. pl.* (1) clothes; (2) rags, tatters.
due, *adv.* fittingly, readily.
dung. See **ding.**
dunt, *n.* dull knock, blow; *v.* strike, thump, throb.
durk, *n.* short Highland dagger, worn in the belt.
durst. See **daur.**
dusht, *n. pa. pple.* 'pushed by a ram, ox, &c.' (B).
dwall, *v.* dwell; **dwalling,** *n.* dwelling, cottage.
dyke, *n.* low dry-stone wall.
dyvor, *n.* bankrupt.

E

eastlin, *adj.* easterly.
easy, *adv.* easily.
e'e, *n.* eye; **een, ein,** *pl.*
e'en, *n.* evening.
e'en, *adv.* even; just, simply.
eerie, irie, *adj.* (1) apprehensive, 'frighted, *dreading spirits*' (B); (2) weird, ghostly, uncanny; (3) gloomy, melancholy.
efter, *adv.* afterwards.
eild, *n.* old age.
ein. See e'e.
eith, *adj.* easy.
elbuck, *n.* elbow.
eldritch, *adj.* uncanny, unearthly; 'ghastly, frightful' (B), hideous; haunted.
eleckit, *pa. pple.* elected, chosen.
elf, *n.* dwarf; hideous creature; bewitching girl.
ell, *n.* unit of measurement (37·059 inches).
eller, *n.* (Presbyterian) elder.
Embro', Enbrugh, *n.* familiar forms of 'Edinburgh'.
eneuch, eneugh, *adj., adv.* enough.
enow, *adj.* enough, sufficient.
Erse, *adj.* Highland, Gaelic.
ether-stane, *n.* adder-stone, used as amulet.
ettle, *n.* purpose, aim.
even (till), *ppl. adj.* proposed as a partner for, matched with.
ev'n down, *adj. phr.* downright, sheer.
expeckit, *pa. pple.* (have) expected.
eydent, *adj.* assiduous, diligent.

F

fa', *v.* (1) fall; (2) befall; (3) come by, win, obtain, lay claim to, have a right to, deserve.
fa', *n.* (1) fortune; (2) turn of events; (3) the Fall.
facket, fecket, *n.* woollen waistcoat, vest.
factor, *n.* steward, agent of an estate.
faddom, *v.* measure by the fathom.

fae, *n.* foe.
faem, *n.* foam, froth.
faikit, *ppl. adj.* excused, given a respite.
fain, *adj.* glad, content; **fain o' ither,** fond of each other. See **fidge.**
fair, *adj.* easy; *adv.* fairly, openly; **fairly,** *adv.* clearly, indeed. **Fair fa',** good luck to.
fairin, *n.* present from a fair; in phr. **give, get, take a fairin,** reward, deserts, punishment.
fairy, *adj.* dwarfish.
faith ye, *int.* confound you.
fallow, *n.* fellow, chap.
famous, *adj.* grand, fine.
fa'n. See **fa'.**
fand. See **fin'.**
fank, *v.* entangle, ensnare, catch.
farina, *n.* flour, meal.
farl, *n.* quarter of the circular oaten **bannock.**
fash, *v.* bother, trouble; *pa. pple.* afflicted; **fash . . . thumb,** pay heed; *n.* trouble, annoyance.
fashious, *adj.* tricky, awkward, irksome.
Fasteneen, *n.* Shrove Tuesday (evening).
fatherly, *adv.* with a father's affection.
fatt'rels; *n. pl.* 'ribbon ends' (B).
faught. See **fecht.**
fauld, *v.* enfold, enclose, gather **579.** 9, *pa. pple.* **fauld;** *ppl. adj.* **faulding-(jocteleg),** clasp-(knife).
fauld, *n.* (sheep) fold; *v.* to gather in, pen; *vbl. n.* **a faulding;** *comb.* **faulding slap,** fold gate.
faun. See **fa'.**
fause, *adj.* false; *comb.* **fause-house,** *n.* **73.** 53 *n.*
fausont, fawsont, *ppl. adj.* respectable, 'decent, seemly' (B).
faut(e), fau't, *n.* fault, (sexual) failing; want, lack; **a' the f. I had to,** the only fault I could find with; *v.* find fault with.
faut(e)or, *n.* defaulter, wrong-doer.
fawsont. See **fausont.**
fear, *v.* frighten, scare; **fear'd, fear't,** *pa. pple.* and *ppl. adj.* frightened.
feat, *adj.* spruce, trim.
Febarwar, *n.* February.
fecht, *v.* fight; **faught,** *pa. t.*; **fechtan,** *ppl. adj.* fighting, disputatious; **fechtin, faught,** *nn.* fighting, struggle, strife.
feck, *n.* value, return, advantage; **the feck,** the majority, most; **feckly,** *adv.* for the most part, almost.
fecket. See **facket.**
fee, *v.* hire (as a servant); **fee(s),** *n.* servant's (half-yearly) wages.
feetie, *n. pl.* (*dim.*) feet (*sing.* **fit(tie),** foot).
feg, *n.* fig.
fegs, *int.* indeed! truly!
feide, *n.* enmity.
feirrie, *adj.* sturdy.
fell, *n.* cuticle above the flesh.
fell, *adj.* potent, pungent; harsh, cruel, keen; **felly,** *adj.* bitter.
fen', fend, *v.* support, fend (for themselves); **how do ye fen,** how do you do; *n.* shift, effort.
Ferintosh, *n.* a whisky.
ferlie, *v.* marvel, wonder; *n.* 'a term of contempt' (B) **83.** 1.
fetch, *v.* draw breath painfully, gasp; 'to stop suddenly in the draught, and then come on too hastily' (B).
fey, *adj.* doomed.
fidge, *v.* shrug, twitch, frisk; **fidge fu' fain,** twitch with excitement; **fidgean-fain, fidgin fain,** *adj. phr.* excited, eager.
fiel, *adv.* cosily, softly.
fi(e)nt a, *strong neg.* the devil a; **fien-ma-care,** *expr. unconcern*; **f. a hair,** see **hair**; **f. haet (o't).** See **haet.**
fier, *adj.* hearty, sound.
fier(e), *n.* companion, comrade.
fin', *v.* find; **fand,** *pa. t.*; **fun',** found, felt (sexually).
fint. See **fi(e)nt a.**
fire-shool. See **shool.**
fiscal, *n.* procurator fiscal, attorney (practising in the lower courts).
fish-creel. See **creel.**
fissle, *v.* make a rustling noise; bustle, get excited.
fit(t), *n.* foot; foothold. Cf. **feetie.**
fit, *n.* poem, strain of music.
fittie-lan', *n.* rear left-hand horse in the plough.

flae, *n.* flea.
flaff, *v.* flap, flutter; **flaffan,** *pres. pple.*
flainen, flannen, *n.* flannel.
flairing, *ppl. adj.* gaudy, extravagant.
flang. See **fling.**
flee, *v.* fly.
fleech, *v.* wheedle, coax, flatter; **fleechan,** *ppl. adj.*
fleesh, *n.* fleece.
fleet-wing, *either v.* fly swiftly, *or adv.* in swift flight.
fleg, *n.* blow, kick; fling.
fleth'ran, *ppl. adj.* wheedling, cajoling.
flewit, *n.* blow, slap.
fley, *v.* terrify, frighten.
flichter, *v.* 'to flutter *as young nestlings when their dam approaches*' (B).
flie, *n.* fly; hence, something of no value (*foll. a neg.*).
flinders, *n. pl.* fragments, smithereens.
fling, *v.* throw, kick; **flang,** *pa. t.*; *pres. pple.* capering; **fling,** *n.* jump; *comb.* **flingin-tree,** swingle of a flail, 'a flail' (B).
flisk, *v.* 'to fret at the yoke' (B).
flit, *v. tr.* shift, move; *intr.* go, depart; change abode.
flittering, *ppl. adj.* fluttering [f. **flit.**]
flyte, *v.* scold, rail.
fock(s), *n.* folk.
fodgel, *adj.* plump and good-humoured.
foggage, *n.* rank grass.
fool, play the, indulge in sexual dalliance.
foor, *v. pa. t.* fared, went, travelled.
Foorsday, *n.* Thursday.
for, *prep.* of **47.** 51.
forbear, *n.* ancestor, forefather.
for(e)by(e), *prep.* besides, as well as; *adv.* what is more.
forehammer, *n.* hammer with which the smith strikes first, sledge-hammer.
forfairn, *ppl. adj.* undone, exhausted, worn out.
forfoughten. See **foughten.**
forgather, *v.* assemble, congregate; encounter; **f. up,** take up with, keep company with.
forgie, *v.* forgive.
forjesket, *ppl. adj.* 'jaded with fatigue' (B), worn out.
forrit, *adv.* forward.
fother, *n.* fodder, hay.
fou, fow, fu', *adj.* full; drunk; *adv.* very, quite.
foughten, *pa. pple.* of **fecht,** *ppl. adj.* harassed, worn out; **forfoughten, fu' foughten,** utterly tired.
foumart, fulmart, *n.* pole-cat.
fouth, *n.* plenty, abundance.
fow, *n.* firlot ('fill', full measure). See **fou.**
frae, *prep.* from.
fraeth, *v.* foam, froth.
frank, *adj.* generous, lavish.
freak, *n.* odd notion, fancy.
free, *v.* clear, leap over.
fremit, *adj.* strange, aloof, cold.
frien', *n.* friend; **freens,** *pl.*
fr–g, *n.* sexual stimulation; *pres. pple.* rubbing.
fright, *n.* ridiculous creature; *v.* frighten, scare.
frythe, *v.* fry.
fu'. See **fou.**
fu'-han't, *comb.* being full-handed, having enough.
f—(k), *n.* copulation; *v.*
fud, *n.* backside; tail, scut.
fuff, *v.* puff, smoke.
fumble, *v.* act awkwardly, impotently **100.** 21.
fun, *n.* boisterous sport.
fun'. See **fin'.**
funny, *adj.* sportive, whimsical, facetious, merry.
furder, *v.* go on, progress; *n.* progress, good luck.
furm, *n.* form, bench.
furnicator, *n. attrib.* fornicating.
furr, *n.* furrow, ditch.
furr ahin, *n.* right-hand horse immediately in front of the plough.
fusion, *n.* fluidity caused by heat.
fusionless, *adj.* pithless, dry, weak.
fyke, *v.* fidget, 'to piddle, to be in a fuss about trifles' (B), fiddle, twitch; *n.* fuss, commotion.
fyle, *v.* defile, foul **373.** 30.

G

gab, *n.* (1) bold, entertaining chatter;

v. talk readily, eloquently; (2) mouth.
gae, *v.* go, walk; **gaen, gane,** *pa. pple.*; **gaun,** *pres. pple.*; **gaes lie,** goes to bed.
gae. See **gie.**
gaets. See **gate.**
gaiger. See **gauge.**
gailies, *adv.* tolerably, well enough.
gair, *n.* strip of cloth, gusset.
gait, *n.* goat.
gamesome, *adj.* merry, sportive.
gang, *v.* go, depart, walk.
gangrel, *n.* vagrant, tramp.
gar, *v.* make, cause, compel; **gart, gar't,** *pa. t., pa. pple.*; **garren,** *vbl. sb.*; **gar get,** have brought.
garten, *n.* garter; *v., pa. pple.* gartered.
gash, (1) *v.* chat volubly, prattle; (2) *adj.* shrewd, witty; smart, respectable, neat.
gat, *v. pa. t.* of *get*; begot, conceived; **gat the whissle:** see **groat.**
gate, *n.* road, way, fashion; **gaets,** *pl.* habits.
gaud, *n.* iron bar used in the forge, as weapon *pl.* **297.** 27; goad for driving cattle in the plough; **gaudsman,** *n.* boy who 'goads' the team.
gauge, *v.* measure the contents of a cask; **ga(u)ger,** *n.* exciseman.
gaun. See **gae.**
Gaun, *n.* **Gavin.**
gaunt, *v.* gape, gasp.
gausie, gawsy, *adj.* ample, jovial-looking; fine, full, showy; plump.
gawkie, *n.* booby, fool; **gawky,** *adj.* stupid, empty-headed.
gear, *n.* possessions, money, property; livestock; liquor.
geck, *v.* toss the head in scorn, scoff (at).
ged, *n.* pike.
gent, *n.* gentleman, fellow. See **genty.**
gentles, *n. pl.* 'great folks' (B), gentry.
gent(y), *adj.* dainty, graceful, slender.
Geordie, George, (yellow), *n.* guinea.
get, *n.* offspring, brat.
ghaist, *n.* ghost.
gie, *v.* give; **giein,** *pres. pple.*; **gae,** *pa. t.*; **gien,** *pa. pple.*, (have given) **385.** 15; **gies,** give us, give me; **gied,** *pa. t.*; **gie up,** offer for intercession **63.** 23.
gif, *conj.* if.
giftie, *n. dim.* of *gift*; power, talent **83.** 43.
giga, *n.* gigue, lively air.
gill, *n.* Scots measure, quarter-mutchkin (*c.* three-quarters of the imperial gill); **gillie,** vessel holding a gill.
gilpey, *n.* young girl.
gimmer(-pet), *n.* yearling ewe kept as pet.
gimp. See **jimp.**
gin, *prep., conj.* before, by (of time).
gin, *conj.* if, whether; that, O that! (after vbs. of wishing).
gird, *n.* boy's hoop; **girr,** hoop for a barrel.
girdin, *vbl. n.* (a) girthing, and (b) copulating.
girdle, *n.* griddle for baking scones.
girn, *v.* grin, snarl, 'twist the features in rage, agony, &c.' (B).
girr. See **gird.**
girt('s), *adj.* great (as).
giz(z), *n.* wig.
gizzen, *v.* warp, wither, shrivel through drought.
glaiket, glaikit, *adj.* careless, foolish, carefree, inattentive, irresponsible, giddy.
glaive, *n.* sword.
glaizie, *adj.* 'glittering, smooth like glass' (B), glossy.
glamor, *n.* enchantment, magic.
glaum, *v.* snatch, grab, lay hold of.
glaur-hole, *n.* mud-hole, mire; contemptuous nick-name.
gled, *n.* kite. See **bizzard.**
gleede, *n.* live coal, glowing fire.
gleesome, *adj.* cheerful, merry.
gleg, *adj.* quick, lively; quick-witted, smart; keen-edged.
gleib, *n.* portion of land.
glib-gabbet, *adj.* smooth-tongued.
glimpse, *v.* take a look (at).
glint, *v.* go quickly, slip (by).
gloamin, *n.* twilight, dusk.
glomin-shote, *n.* 'twilight interval [taken] before using lights' indoors (Jamieson).
glowr, (1) *v.* stare wide-eyed, gaze intently, *n.* **127.** 20; (2) gleam,

glowr, (2) (*cont.*):
shine out (of the sun, moon), *n.* **239.** 57; (3) *n.* scowl.

glunch, *v.*, *n.* look sullen, scowl, frown.

goave, *v.* stare stupidly, vacantly; **goavan's,** staring . . . as if.

goom, *n.* gum.

gor-cock, *n.* male of the red grouse.

gos, *n.* goshawk.

gossip, *n.* neighbour-woman.

gowan, *n.* 'the flower of the daisy, dandelion, hawkweed, &c.' (B).

gowd, *n.* gold; **gowden,** *adj.*; **gowdie,** *n.* (golden) head.

gowdspink, *n.* goldfinch.

gowff, *v.* hit with the open hand as in hand-ball or *gowf-the-ba'*; *pa. t.* struck.

gowk, *n.* cuckoo; fool, dolt.

gowling, *ppl. adj.* howling, yelling.

grace-prood, *adj.* smugly conscious of divine favour, sanctimonious.

gracious, *adj.* friendly, amiable.

graff, *n.* grave, tomb.

grain, *n.* branch of a tree.

grain. See **grane.**

graip, *n.* farm-yard and garden fork.

graith, *n.* (1) equipment, tools, ploughing gear, goods; (2) dress, habit; **graithing,** vestments; (3) *membrum virile.*

graizle, *v.* scrape, grind.

grane, grain, *n.*, *v.* groan.

grape, *v.* grope, feel for, search with the hands; *pa. t.* **grapet.**

grat. See **greet.**

Grannie, Graunie, *n.* grandmother.

gray-neck, *n.* a gambler, trimmer.

great, *adj.* 'thick', intimate, friendly.

gree, *n.* social degree, supremacy; hence **bear the g., carry the g.,** win first place, come off best.

gree, *v.* agree.

green, *v.* yearn, long (for).

greet, *v.* weep, cry; **grat,** *pa. t.*; **grutten,** *pa. pple.*; **greetie, greetin(g),** *nn.* crying.

greive, *n.* manager, farm-bailiff.

grip, *v.* grasp; **gripet,** *pa. pple.* apprehended, taken; *n.* sharp pain, *pl.* gripes.

grissle, *n.* gristle; stump of a quill pen.

groat, *n.* silver coin of small value, 3*d.* Scots; '*to get the whistle of one's groat*, to play a losing game' (B).

groazle, *v.* breathe heavily, grunt.

gr[o]usome, *adj.* horrible, 'loathsomely grim' (B).

grozet, *n.* gooseberry.

grumble, *v.* begrudge; **grumbling,** *ppl. adj.* mumbling, murmuring.

Grumphie, *n.* grumbler, the sow.

grun', *n.* the ground, earth.

grunstane, *n.* grindstone.

gruntle, *n.* grunt; snout, nose.

grunzie, *n.* snout.

grushie, *adj.* thriving, lusty, strong.

grusome. See **gr[o]usome.**

grutten. See **greet.**

gude, guid, *adj.*, *adv.*, *n.*, *v.* good; *substit. for* God. *Combs.*: **gu(i)deen,** good-evening; **guid-father,** *n.* father-in-law; **gudeman, guidman,** *n.* head of a household, master, husband; **guidwife,** *n.* mistress, wife; **gude-willy,** *adj.* generous; **gude-willie-waught,** cordial drink, 'cup of kindness' (see **waught**).

gullie, gully, *n.* large knife; *v.* dig, cut.

gulravage, *n.* romp, uproar, horse-play.

gumlie, *adj.* muddy.

gumption, *n.* common-sense, shrewdness.

gust, *n.* relish, flavour; **gusty,** *adj.* tasty, appetizing.

gutcher, *n.* grandfather.

gutscraper, *n.* fiddler.

gutty, *adj.* pot-bellied.

gyvel, *n.* gable; (*fig.*) *pudendum muliebre.*

H

ha' *n.* hall; **ha' folk,** *pl.* servants.

ha'. See **hae.**

ha'd, haddin. See **haud.**

hae, ha'(e), *v.* have; *imperat.* 'here!', 'take this!'; **haen,** *pa. pple.* See **hae't.**

haerse, *adj.* hoarse.

hae't, haet, have it; as neg. or imprec. in *phrs.* **de(v)il h., d–mn'd h., fien(t) haet (o't),** devil a bit, devil a one, 'damn all', nothing.

ha'f. See **hauf.**

haff-, *adv.* half-. See **hauf.**
haffet, *n.* temple; lock of hair growing on the temple.
haf(f)lins(-wise), *adv.* in half measure, partly, nearly.
hag(g), *n.* 'a scar or gulf in mosses and moors' (B), made by water-channels or peat-cutting.
haggis, *n.* a pudding of minced liver, meal, suet, onions, and spices, boiled in a sheep's stomach.
hail, *n.* small shot, pellets.
hail. See **hale.**
hain, *v.* save, spare; *ppl. adj.* enclosed, kept for hay; **weel-hain'd**, *ppl. adj.* well-preserved, hoarded.
hainch, *n.* haunch, hip.
hair, *n.* whit, trifle, trace; *phrs.* **deil a h., fien' a h.,** not a bit. Cf. **hae't.**
hairst, *n.* harvest.
hairum-scairum, *adj.* wild.
haith, 'a petty oath' (B).
haivers, *n. pl.* nonsense, gossip.
hal(d), *n.* hold, dwelling, refuge.
hale, hail, *adj.* healthy, sound; entire, whole.
hale, *n.* health.
half-lang, *adj.* half-length.
half-sarket. See **sark.**
hallan, *n.* partition (usually of mud or clay and stones) between a cottage door and fireplace to divert the draught, *or* between living-room and byre; **hallan en'**, angle between the hallan and the main wall.
hallion *n.* idler, rascal.
Halloween, *n.* eve of All Saints' Day; **Hallow-mass**, festival of All Saints.
haly, *adj.* holy.
hame, *n.*, *adv.* home; **hamely**, *adj.* familiar, plain, common, friendly; **hameward**, *adv.* homewards.
hammers, *n.pl.* noisy, clumsy fellows.
han(d), haun', *n.* hand, 'rare hands', artists **101.** 17; *phrs.* **beside our han'**, 'at our own hand', by, for ourselves; **'mang hands**, at intervals. *Combs.*: **han'-daurk**, *n.* labour of the hands (see **daurk**); **hand-bread**, *n.* hand's breadth; **hand-wal'd**, *adj.* hand-picked, choice (see **wale**).
hang(it). See **hing.**
Hangie, *n.* hangman; the Devil.
hanker, *v.* hang about, loiter, hesitate.
hansel, *n.* new-year or good-luck gift; **hansel in**, *v.* be a first gift for (the new year).
hap, *v.* cover, shield; *n.* plaid.
hap, *v.* hop, *ppl. adj.* **130.** 19; drop in quick succession.
happen, *v.* turn out, come off, manage.
happer, *n.* hopper (of a mill).
hap-step-an'-loup, *adv.* briskly.
hardy, *adj.* bold, foolhardy.
hark, *v.* listen (to); **harket**, *pa. pple.*
harn, *n.* coarse linen, sackcloth.
harpy, *n.*; *attrib.* rapacious, plundering.
har'sts. See **hairst.**
has been, *n.* one past his best.
hash, (1) *v.* hack, mangle, waste; (2) *n.* waster, impudent or dissolute fool.
haslock, *n.* wool on sheep's neck.
haud, ha'd, *v.* hold, keep; **haud aff**, keep away; **haud awa**, come away (cf. **held**); **h. in**, keep in, supply with; **h. on**, persist; **h. tae**, stick to; **haud you**, stay; **haddin**, *n.* inheritance, possession.
hauf, ha'f, *n.* half; **hauf-mutchkin**, see **mutchkin.**
haugh, *n.* level, fertile land by a river.
haun'. See **han(d).**
haurl, *v.* drag; *pres. pple.* peeling **73.** 206; haul off to punishment.
hause, *v.* embrace.
hauver, *n.* oat; *attrib.* **h.-meal**, oatmeal.
havins, *n. pl.* behaviour; good manners, sense.
hav[e]rel, *adj.*, *n.* simpleton, half-wit(ted.)
hawkie, *n.* cow with white face, pet name for a cow; **hawkit**, spotted or streaked with white.
head, *v.* behead; **headinman**, *n.* headsman, executioner.
heal, *adj.* healthy, well; **healsome**, *adj.* wholesome.
heapet, *ppl. adj.* heaped, well-filled.
hech, *int.* a sighing exclamation, 'Oh! strange!' (B).
hecht, *v.* promise, pledge, offer; *pres. pple.* threatening **114.** 12.

heckle, *n.* flax-comb.
hee-balou, *int.* hush!
heed, observation, care.
heeze, *v.* lift, exalt, elevate.
held (awa, to), *v. pa. t.* took (my) way; kept to **563.** 11.
hellim, *n.* helm, tiller.
hem-shin'd, *ppl. adj.* with shins shaped like *haims,* the curved pieces of wood or metal fixed over a draught-horse's collar.
hen, *n.*; used as term of endearment to a girl.
herd, *n.* herd-boy.
here awa, *adv.* (1) hereabouts, in this neighbourhood; (2) hither (and thither).
herry, *v.* harry, plunder; **herryment,** devastation, waste.
het, *adj.* hot, burning, excited; **h. and cauld,** *adv. phrs.* at all times.
heugh, *n.* (1) crag, steep bank; (2) ravine, pit.
heuk, *n.* hook, sickle.
hich, hie, *adj.* high; **high-gate,** *n.* highway; **h.-gate-side,** *n.* side of the high-road.
hilch, *v.* lurch, limp.
hilt and hair, (every) bit.
hiltie, skiltie, *adv.* pell-mell, heedlessly.
hindmost, *adj.* last, final.
hiney, hinnie, hinny, *n.* honey, sweetheart, darling; *adj.* sweet.
hing, *v.* hang, make (us) hang **51.** 3; **hang,** *pa. t.*; **hangit,** *pa. pple.*
hirple, *v.* limp, hobble, move unevenly (as a hare).
hissel, *n.* flock of sheep on one farm or in one shepherd's care.
histie, *adj.* dry, stony.
hit, *v.* manage, achieve, reach (it).
hizzie, *n.* wench; silly girl; trull, whore.
ho(a)st, *n., v.* cough.
hoddan, *pple.* jogging along, bumping in the saddle.
hoddin, *n.* coarse grey homespun cloth of mixed black and white wool.
hoggie, *n.* young sheep from time of weaning till the first fleece is sheared.
hog-score, *n.* distance-line in curling. See **score.**
hog-shouther, *v.* push about; 'a kind of horse play by jostling with the shoulder; to justle' (B).
Hollan(d), *n.* holland cloth, fine linen.
hollow, *n.* halloo.
hoodie-craw, *n.* the hooded or grey **crow,** black in the head, wings, and tail.
hoodock, *n.* the hooded crow; an avaricious person, *attrib.*
hool, *n.* membrane, pericardium.
hoolie, *adv. int.* gently, slowly, 'take leisure! stop!' (B).
hoord, *n.* hoard, drift; **hoordet,** *ppl. adj.* hoarded.
horn, *n.* horn vessel, horn spoon; **bear the horn,** carry off the prize; **Hornie,** *n.* the horned Devil.
host. See **ho(a)st.**
hotch, *v.* hitch, jerk about.
hough, *v.* disable, by cutting the tendons of the hough.
houghmagandie, *n.* fornication.
houlet, *n.* owl(et); **howlet-face,** *n.*
houpe, *n.* hope.
hove, *v.* rise; *tr.* make to swell, distend.
how deil, how the devil.
how(c)k, *v.* dig, delve; *ppl. adj.* dug up, exhumed **76.** 54.
howdie, howdy, *n.* midwife.
howe, *n.* hollow, valley, glen; *adj.* hollow, deep; *comb.* **howe-backet,** 'sunk in the back' (B).
howks, *n. pl.* a disease in animals affecting the eyes.
howlet-face. See **houlet.**
hoyse, *n.* hoist, 'a pull upwards' (B).
hoy't, *v. pa. t.* cried 'hoy!'
hoyte, *n.* 'a motion between a trot and a gallop' (B); hence *v.* move clumsily, waddle.
huff, *v.* scold, berate.
Hughoc, *n.* little Hugh.
hum, *v.* hoax, take in, humbug.
hum, *v.* mumble; **hum an' haw,** mutter inarticulately in hesitation.
Humphie, *n.* nick-name for a hunchback.
hunder, *num. adj.* and *n.* hundred; hundredth.
hung, *ppl. adj.* eloquent.
hunkers, *n. pl.* hams, haunches.

hurcheon, hurchin, *n.* hedgehog; mischievous child, urchin.
hurdies, *n. pl.* buttocks, backside.
hurl, *v.* trundle along, move violently; **hurly,** *n.* onrush, downward surge.
hushian, *n.* footless stocking.
hyte, *adj.* crazed, daft.

I

i', *prep.* in, into.
icker. See **daimen-icker.**
ier-oe, *n.* great-grandchild.
ilk(a), *adj.* each, every.
ill-, *adj., adv.* evil; **ill-taen,** *ppl. adj.* ill-taken, resented; **Ill-thief,** *n.* the Devil; **ill-willie,** *adj.* ill-disposed, malignant, ungenerous.
in during, *prep.* during.
in for 't, liable to punishment.
in to, *prep.* within, to.
indentin, *pres. pple.* pledging, engaging.
ingine, *n.* talent, genius, wit.
ingle, *n.* fire burning on a hearth; **ingle-cheek,** *n.* chimney-corner; **ingle-low(e),** *n.* firelight; **ingle-neuk,** *n.* chimney-corner; **ingle-side,** *n.* fireside.
irie. See **eerie.**
I'se, I shall. See **sall.**
ither, *adj.* other, another, further; *pron.* each other; **other,** *adv.* otherwise, else.
it 's, it shall. See **sall.**

J

jacket, *n.* coat of mail.
jad, *n.* mare; wench, hussy.
jag the flae, tailor.
Januar, Janwar', *n.* January.
jauk, *v.* 'to dally, to trifle' (B), waste time; **jaukin,** *n.* delay.
jauner, *n.* idle chatter.
jauntie, *n.* little trip, journey.
jaup, *v.* 'to jerk as agitated water' (B), splash; *n. pl.* **120.** 126.
jaw, *v.* pour, dash, throw.
jaw, *n.* chatter.
jawpish, *n.* urinary disease of horses, urethritis.
jee, *int. quasi-adv.* with a swing, sideways.
jeeg, *v.* jog, rock.
jillet, *n.* giddy wench, jilt.
jimp, *v.* jump.
jimp, gimp, *adj.* slender, graceful, neat; *adv.* closely.
jimps, *n. pl.* skirts.
jing, by, a mild expletive.
jink, *v.* dodge, dart, slip aside; move quickly, zig-zag; jerk; *n.* the act of eluding someone, the slip; **jinker,** *n.* a high-spirited beast, 'a gay, sprightly girl' (B).
jirkinet, *n.* 'substitute for stays, without whalebone' (Jamieson).
jirt, *n.* jerk.
jo(e), *n.* sweetheart.
job, *n.* intrigue, jobbery; **jobbin,** *n.* fornication. Cf. **by-job.**
jocteleg, *n.* clasp-knife.
jog, *v.* trudge.
jorum, *n.* drinking-vessel, punch-bowl.
jouk, *v.* dodge, duck; bow.
jow, *v.* toll; 'a verb, which includes both the swinging motion and pealing sound of a large bell' (B).
jowler, *n.* heavy-jawed dog, hound.
jundie, *v.* elbow, jostle.
jurr, *n.* servant-maid, skivvy.

K

kae, *n.* jackdaw, thief.
kail, *n.* (1) borecole, green kale; (2) vegetable broth, *fig.* **85.** 50; hence (3) semen **612.** 12: *combs.* **k.-blade,** leaf of kale; **k.-runt,** stalk stripped of leaves; **k. whittle,** knife with blade at right angles to the handle for cutting kale; **k.-yard,** kitchen- or cottage-garden. Cf. **bow-kail, muslin-kail.**
kaim, *v.* comb. See **ripplin-kame.**
kane, *n.* payment in kind, reckoning.
kebar, *n.* long pine pole; rafter.
kebbuck, *n.* home-made cheese; **k.-heel,** the hard end of a cheese.
keckle, *v.* cackle, giggle.
keek, *v.* peer, glance, peep (at); **keek,** *n.* cautious glance, sly glance; **keekin' glass,** *n.* mirror.
kelpie, *n.* water demon in the shape of a horse.
ken, *v.* (1) know, be aware of, learn; (2) be acquainted with, recognize, identify.
kennin, *vbl. n.* (a) little, trifle
kep, *v.* keep, catch.

ket, *n.* 'a matted, hairy fleece of wool' (B).
kettle, *n.* cauldron, pit; transf. *pudendum muliebre.*
kiaugh, *n.* 'carking anxiety' (B).
kiln, *n.* kiln for drying grain.
kilt, *v.* tuck up the skirts.
kimmer, cummer, *n.* (1) gossip, woman, wife (usually familiar or contemptuous); (2) lass, wench.
kin', kind, *n.* nature, innate disposition; *adj.* kindly, agreeable, winsome; *adv.* somewhat, rather **57**. 23.
king's-hood, *n.* second stomach in a ruminant; paunch.
kintra, koontrie, *adj.* country; *n.* country-side, country people.
kirk, *n.* church; **k.-hammer,** clapper of church bell.
kirn, *n.* churn.
kirn, *n.* harvest-home, merrymaking at end of harvest.
kirs'n *v.* christen; dilute with water.
kirtle, *n.* gown, skirts.
kist, *n.* chest, coffer.
kitchen, *v.* season, give relish to.
kith and kin, *hendiadys for* kinsfolk.
kittle, *v.* (1) tickle, excite, rouse; (2) **k. up,** tune up, play; *adj.* (1) likely, inclined; (2) fickle, ticklish, difficult, tricky; (3) dangerous, hard to resist, unsafe to meddle with.
kittlen, *n.* kitten.
kiutle . . . wi', *v.* 'to cuddle, to caress, to fondle' (B).
knag(g), *n.* knot, spur, stump; **knaggie,** *adj.* knobbly, bony.
knappin-hammer, *n.* hammer for breaking stones.
knoit, *v.* knock.
knowe, *n.* mound, hillock.
knurl, knurlin, *n.* dim. of *knur,* dwarf.
koontrie. See **kintra.**
kye, *n. pl.* cows, cattle.
kyles, *n. pl.* skittles.
kytch, *n.* toss, jerk, upward shove.
kyte, *n.* belly.
kythe, *v.* make known, discover, tell.
kyvel, *n.* thump, bang (?).

L

labo(u)r, *v.* belabour, thrash; work, cultivate.
lade, *n.* load.
lae, *v.* 'lay', lie down (to, with).
laft, *n.* loft.
lag, *adj.* laggard, backward.
laggen, *n.* angle between sides and bottom of a cask, dish.
laid (upon), *v. pa. t.* assailed.
laigh, *adj.* low; of a church which is not the main or earliest foundation in a place.
laik, lake, *n.* lack.
laimpet, *n.* limpet.
lair, *n.* bed, grave.
laird, *n.* landed proprietor, squire.
laith, *adj.* loath, unwilling, reluctant; **laithfu',** *adj.* 'bashful, sheepish' (B).
laithron, *adj.* lazy, inactive, sluggish.
lake. See **laik.**
lallan(d), *adj.* lowland; **lallans,** *n.* lowland Scots.
lambie, *n.* dim. of *lamb.*
Lammas, *n.* 1 August, harvest festival for the consecration of the new bread.
lan', *n.* land, country; untilled soil in **lan' afore, lan' ahin,** terms for plough-horses; *pl.* estates.
lane, lanely, *adj.* lonely, solitary; after *poss. prons.,* -self: **her lane,** by herself; **my lane, thy-lane.**
lang, *adj.* long; *combs.* **lang-kail,** *n.* borecole, Scotch kale (see **kail**); **lang-kent,** *ppl. adj.* familiar; **lang-mustering,** *ppl. adj.*; **lang-neckit,** *ppl. adj.*; **lang syne,** *attrib.* ancient (see **syne**); **lang-tocher'd,** *ppl. adj.* well-dowered (see **tocher**).
lank, *adj.* thin and languid.
lap, *v. pa. t.* of **loup**; leapt, leapt up.
lap, *v. pa. t.* enfolded, wrapped.
lave, *n.* rest, remainder, others.
laverock, lav'rock, *n.* lark; **l.-height,** the height of the lark's flight.
law, *v.* decree, determine.
lawin, *n.* tavern-bill, reckoning.
lawland, *n.* lowland.
lay, *v.* ascribe, attribute; allay, still.
lay, lea, lee, *n.* untilled ground left fallow, part of the outfield, pasture; *pudendum muliebre* **382**; *combs.* **ley-crap,** the first crop after grass;

lea-rig, ridge of unploughed grass between arable ridges, a **bawk.**
lead, *v.* lead in, cart.
lea'e, *v.* leave.
leal, *adj.* loyal, faithful, true.
lear, *n.* learning, lore.
lea-rig. See **lay, lea.**
learn, *v.* teach.
least, *conj.* lest, for fear.
leather, *n.* hide, skin; lining of the throat; *pudendum muliebre.*
leddy, *n.* colloq. short form of *lady.*
lee, *adj.* sheltered, protected from the wind. See **lay, lea.**
lee-lang, *adj.* live-long, whole, all day (night) through; **leesome,** *adj.* dear, tender, delightful; **leeze me on,** lief is me, I am delighted by; **as lieve,** *adv.* rather.
left-hand, *adj.* sinister.
leister, *n.* pronged spear used in salmon fishing, trident.
len', *v.* give, grant.
let, *v.* allow; let fly; **lets . . . wit,** informs; **let be,** 'to give over, to cease' (B).
leugh, *v. pa. t.* of *lauch,* laugh.
leuk, *v.* look, watch; *n.* appearance, expression, glance, *pl.* looks.
ley. See **lay, lea.**
libbet, *ppl. adj.* castrated.
lick, *n.* measure, little bit; *pl.* thrashing, punishment; *v.* **lick . . . winnings,** make the best of a bad job; wallop, thrash.
liein, *v. pres. pple.* telling lies.
lien, *v. pa. pple.* lain.
lieve, as. See **lee-lang.**
lift, *n.* sky, heavens.
lift, *n.* load, large amount; **l. aboon,** boost; **gie a l.,** give a helping hand.
light, *v.* alight.
lightly, *v.* slight, disparage.
like (to), *adj.* likely to, looking as if to; *adv.* as it were, as if.
lilt, *v.* lift up the voice.
limmer, *n.* rascal; jade, mistress, whore.
limpan, *v. pres. pple.* limping; *pa. t.* **limpet.**
lingo, *n.* foreign or unintelligible language.
link, *v.* trip, go briskly, skip.
lin(n), waterfall, cataract.
linnens, *n. pl.* grave cloths, winding-sheet.
lint, *n.* flax plant, flax for spinning; **lintwhite,** *adj.* white as flax, flaxen.
lintwhite, *n.* linnet.
lippen (to), *v.* trust, depend on.
lippie, *n.* dim. of *lip.*
list, *v.* enlist.
listen, *v. tr.* hear attentively.
loan, loaning, *n.* strip of grass running through arable ground, serving as pasture, milking-place, and driving road.
locked, *ppl. adj.* closely fastened.
lo'e, *v.* love; **loosome,** *adj.* sweet, charming.
logger, *adj.* thick, stupid.
loof, *n.* palm; hand given in pledge; paw. Cf. **aff-loof.**
loon, loun, lown, *n.* (1) rascal, rogue; (2) fellow; (3) wanton, whore.
loosome. See **lo'e.**
loot, *v. pa. t.* of *lat,* let, allowed; let out, uttered; **loot on,** showed, disclosed.
loove, *n.* love; **looves,** see **loof.**
losh, *int.* distortion of *Lord.*
lough, *n.* loch, lake.
loun, lown. See **loon.**
loup, lowp, *v.* leap, jump; **louper,** *n.* dancer.
lour, *v.* look threateningly.
louse, lowse, *v.* loose.
lowe, *n.* flame; *v.* blaze, rage. See **ingle.**
lucky, *n.* familiar term of address to an old woman; ale-wife.
lug, *v.* draw out.
lug, *n.* ear; **chimla lug,** side wall of chimney recess, chimney-corner; *ppl. adj.* **lugget (caup),** (shallow wooden dish) with handles (see **caup**); **luggie,** *n.* wooden dish with staves projecting to form handles.
lum, *n.* chimney.
lum. See **warklum.**
Lunardi, *n.* a kind of bonnet named after the Italian balloonist.
lunch, *n.* large slice, thick piece.
lunt, *v.* smoke (a pipe); *n.* puff of smoke; *n.* steam.
lunzie-banes, *n. pl.* haunch-bones.

lyart, *adj.* streaked with white, grizzled; grey; streaked, red and white **84**. 1.

M

madden, *v.* grow mad.
mae, *adj. quasi-n.* more.
Mahoun, *n.* the Devil.
mailen, mailin, *n.* piece of arable land held on lease, small-holding.
maingie, *adj.* having the mange, scabby.
mair, *adj., adv.* greater, more; **m. for token**, especially, in particular.
maist(ly), *adv.* mostly.
maist, *adv.* almost.
mak, *v.* make, do; **mak o'**, treat affectionately, fuss over; **makin-of**, *vbl. n.* petting, fondling; **mak to through**, see through, make good.
mamie, *n.* mother.
'mang, *prep.* among; **'mang hands**, see **han'**.
manswear, *v.* perjure (oneself).
manteele, *n.* mantle, cape.
mantie, *n.* gown; **made m.**, was a dress-maker.
mantling, *ppl. adj.* foaming, creaming.
mark, *n.* coin worth 13*s.* 4*d.* Scots, at this date $13\frac{1}{3}$*d.* sterling.
marled, *ppl. adj.* parti-coloured.
mashlum, *n.* maslin, mixed meal.
maskin-pat, *n.* pot for infusing (masking) tea.
mason, *n.* mason, freemason; *attrib.* masonic.
maud, *n.* shepherd's grey plaid.
maukin, *n.* the hare; **m. bucks**, buck hares.
maun, *auxil. v.* must; **maun(n)a**, must not.
maut(e), *n.* malt, barley prepared for brewing, ale; **groanin maut**, ale provided for visitors at a lying-in.
mavis, *n.* thrush.
maw, *v.* mow, reap.
mawn, *n.* maund, two-handled wicker basket.
meal-pocks. See **pock**.
meere, *n.* mare.
meikle, mickle, mu(c)kle, *adj.* great, plentiful, much; *adv.* much, greatly; **meikle corn**, oats; **mickle a do**, much to do.
melder, *n.* quantity of meal ground for a customer at one time; the occasion of grinding a customer's corn at the mill.
mell, *v.* consort, have friendly dealings; meddle, tamper.
melvie, *v.* 'to soil with meal' (B).
men', mend, *v. tr.* cure, heal; *intr.* mend one's ways, repent.
mense, *n.* decorum, sense, moderation, tact; **menseless**, *adj.* ill-bred, boorish.
menzie, *n.* armed company, retinue.
mercies, *n. pl.* liquor.
Merran, *n.* Marion.
Mess John, Mass J., [Maister of Arts], the priest, minister.
messan, *n.* lap-dog; cur.
mete, *v.* complete the full measure of.
mickle. See **meikle**.
midden-creel, *n.* manure-basket.
midden-hole, *n.* 'a gutter at the bottom of the dung-hill' (B).
milkin-shiel. See **shiel**.
mim, *adj., adv.* demure(ly); **mim-mou'd**, 'reserved in discourse, not communicative, implying the idea of affectation of modesty' (Jamieson).
min, min', *n.* mind, recollection.
mind, *v.* remind, remember; watch, take care of, see to; **mind't**, *ppl. adj.* disposed, inclined.
minnie, minny, *n.* familiar word for mother.
mirk, *n.* darkness, *adj.* dark; **mirksome**, *adj.*
misca', miska', *v.* abuse, malign.
mis(c)hanter, *n.* misadventure, mishap.
misguidin, *vbl. n.* mismanagement, squandering.
mislear'd, *ppl. adj.* unmannerly, mischievous.
miss, *n.* mistress, whore.
mist, *v. pa. t.* missed.
mistak', *v.* mistake; **misteuk**, *pa t.*; **mista'en**, *pa. pple.*
mite-horn, *n.* horn on the harvest-bug.
mither, *n.* mother.
mix(t)ie-max(t)ie, *adj.* jumbled, confused, incongruous.

mizl'd, *ppl. adj.* confused, mystified, misinformed.
mock, *n.* derision, abuse.
modewurk, moudiewart, *n.* mouldwarp, mole; *fig.* penis.
monie, mony, *adj., n.* many.
mool, *n.* earth, clod; grave-clods, grave.
moop, *v.* 'to nibble as a sheep' (B) **24.** 55; ? kiss, copulate.
morn, the, *adv.* tomorrow.
moss, *n.* swamp, peat-bog.
mottie, *adj.* full of specks, spotty, dusty.
mou', *n.* mouth.
moudiewart. See **modewurk.**
mow(e), *v.* copulate (with a woman); *n.* intercourse.
much about it, about the same.
mu(c)kle. See **meikle.**
muir, *n.* moor; **muirfowl,** *n.* red grouse; **muirland,** *adj.* from the moor.
muscle, *n.* mollusc, mussel.
musie, *n.* dim. *muse.*
muslin-kail, *n.* thin broth, of water, shelled barley, and greens only.
mutchkin, *n.* quarter pint (Scots), *c.* $\frac{3}{4}$ imperial pint.
muve, *v.* move; *ppl. adj.* affecting.
mysel, *pron.* myself; emphatic **76.** 39.

N

'n, *conj.* and.
na', nae, *adv., conj.* not, by no means. See **deil na, whatna.**
na(e), *adj.* no; **naebody,** *n.* no-one; **naething,** *n.* nothing.
naig, *n.* small horse, pony; **naigies,** *dim. pl.*
nail('t), *v.* clinch, prove (it).
nane, *pron., adj., adv.* none.
nappy, *n.* ale.
natch, *n.* notch; notching shears.
naur, *prep.* near.
near(-)hand, *adv.* almost.
neebo(u)r, nibor, *n.* neighbour.
negleckit, negleket, *pa. pple.* neglected.
neist. See **niest.**
neuk, newk, *n.* corner, recess.
new-ca'd, *ppl. adj.* newly calved.
nibor. See **neebo(u)r.**
nice, *adj.* fine, delightful; dainty, refined, fastidious, precise.
nick, *n.* cut; *v.* cut through, slit; *pres. pple.* cutting down, reaping; *pa. pple.* seized, nabbed **514.** 20.
Nick, Auld N., Nickie-ben, familiar names for the Devil.
nidge, *v.* push, thrust.
niest, neist, *adj., adv.* next.
nieve, *n.* fist, clenched hand; **nieve-fu',** *n.* handful.
niffer, *n.* 'an exchange; to exchange, to barter' (B); comparison.
niger, *n.* negro.
nightly, *adj.* appearing at night, travelling at night; *adv.* at night(s).
nine(s), to the, to the highest degree, to perfection.
nit, *n.* nut; standard boss **212.** 15.
no, *adv.* not; not that **87.** 13.
nocht, *n.* nothing; *adv.* not.
noddle, *n.* head, brain, pate.
nor, *conj.* than. See **deil nor.**
nor . . . nor, *conj.* neither . . . nor.
norland, *adj.* northern, from the north.
nor-west, *n.* north-west wind.
notion, *n.* understanding, fancy, desire.
nowt(e), *n.* cattle, oxen.
nyvel, *n.* navel.

O

och, *interj.* expressing surprise, sorrow, regret.
ochon, oh-hon, *interj.* alas.
o'er. See **owre.**
oergang, *v.* overcome, trample on
o'erlay, *n.* neck-tie.
o'erword. See **owerword.**
offer, *v.* promise, seem likely to turn out.
onie, ony, *adj., pron.* any.
or, *prep,* ere, before.
orra, *adj.* odd, spare, extra.
ostler house, *n,* hostelry, inn.
o't, of it.
other. See **ither.**
ought, *n.* anything (*var.* **aught**); **oughtlins,** *adv.* anything in the least, at all.
ourie, *adj.* poor, dreary, wretched.
oursel(ls), *pron. pl.* ourselves.
outcast, *n.* quarrel.

outler quey, *n.* young cow lying out at night.
out(-)owre, *prep.* over across, above, beyond; *adv.* over; **out thro',** *adv.* right through.
outspak, *v. pa. t.* spoke out, up.
owerword, o'erword, *n.* burden, refrain.
owre, ower, *adv., prep.* over; *adj., adv.* too; **o'er far,** too surely.
owrehip, *adv.* over the hip.
owsen, *n. pl.* oxen, cattle.
owther, *n.* author.
oxter'd, *pa. pple.* armed, carried under the arm.

P

pack (aff), *v.* go packing, depart.
pack, *adj.* 'intimate, familiar' (B).
paetrick. See **pai(r)trick.**
paidle, *v.* paddle, wade; dabble, fumble impotently.
paidle, *n.* paddle, hoe. Cf. **pattle.**
painch, *n.* belly, paunch; **painch-lippit,** *adj.* having lips like paunches.
pai(r)trick, paetrick, *n.* partridge; *fig.* girl.
palaver, *n.* idle chatter, nonsense.
pang, *v.* cram, stuff.
parishon, *n.* parish.
parle, *n.* speech, language (nonce-word).
(a) parliamentin, *ppl.* attending, serving in parliament.
parritch, pirratch, *n.* porridge; **p.-pat,** *n.* porridge-pot.
part's be, part, share shall be.
party-match, *n.* card contest.
pat, *n.* pot. See **pit.**
pattle, pettle, *n.* small long-handled spade used to clean the plough.
paughty, *adj.* proud, insolent.
pauky, pawkie, *adj.* cunning, crafty, sly.
pay, *v.* give deserts, flog; **pay't hollow,** beat thoroughly.
pech, pegh, *v.* 'to fetch the breath short *as in an asthma*' (B).
peel, *n.* palisade; castle, keep.
peer, *v.* equal, rank with.
pegh. See **pech.**
peghan, *n.* stomach.
p[e]go, *n.* penis.
pell [*and*] mell, *adv.* in violent disorder.
pendle, *n.* pendule, pendant.
pennie fee, penny-fee, *n.* wages paid in money.
penny-wheep, *n.* small beer.
pennyworths, *n. pl.* good bargain.
perish, *v.* make to perish, destroy.
pet, *v.* take the pet, sulk.
pettle. See **pattle.**
Phely, *n.* Phillis.
philibeg, *n.* kilt.
phiz, *n.* countenance, expression of face.
phrase, *v.* flatter (make a phrase about); **phraisin,** *adj.* exaggerating, extravagant.
pibroch, *n.* classical bagpipe music.
pickle, *n.* small quantity of.
pictur'd beuk, *n.* playing card.
pike, pyke, *v.* pick (at); pluck.
p[i]llie, *n.* pillicock, penis.
pin, *n.* skewer; gallows-peg; latch pin; *fig.* penis.
pinch, wi', *adv. phr.* reluctantly, complainingly.
pine, *n.* pain, sorrow.
p[intle], p[e]ntle, *n.* penis.
pint-stowp. See **stoup.**
pirratch. See **parritch.**
piss, pish, *v.* urinate; *ppl. adj.* soaked with urine.
pit, *v.* put, make; **pat,** *pa. t.*; **pat to,** put to it, drove.
placad, *n.* placard, summons, proclamation.
plack, *n.* small coin (4 pennies Scots), copper, farthing, nothing worth; **plackless,** *adj.* penniless.
plaid(ie), *n.* long piece of woollen cloth, chequered or tartan, used as a cloak; **plaiden,** *adj.* with check or tartan pattern, *n.* cloth of this kind.
plaister, *n., v.* plaster.
planted, *pa. pple.* settled in.
play, *n.* joy, pleasure, source of delight.
plea, *n.* action at law.
pleugh, plew, *n.* plough; ploughing-team; **p.-pettle** (see **pattle**).
pliskie, *n.* trick.
pliver, *n.* green plover; lapwing, peewit.
plumpet, *v. pa. t.* plunged, sank.

plumpin, *ppl. adj.* swelling, fattening.
plush, *adj.* long-knapped velvet.
poacher-court, *n.* kirk session.
pock, *n.* poke, bag.
poind, *v.* distrain, seize goods and sell them under warrant.
poortith, *n.* poverty.
Poosie, *adj.* pejorative term for a woman; **Poossie, puss(ie),** *n.* Puss, the hare.
poosion, *n.* poison.
pot, *n.* pot-still, to which heat is applied directly and not by a steam-jacket.
potatoe-bing, *n.* heap of potatoes for winter storage.
pou, pow, pu', *v.* pull.
pouchie, *n.* dim. *pouch.*
pouk, *v.* poke, prod.
pouse, *n.* push, thrust.
pouther, powther, *n.* powder; **pouthered,** *ppl. adj.*; **pouthery,** *adj.*
pow, *n.* head.
pownie, *n.* 'Pony, a little Scotch horse' (Bailey, 1730–6).
powt, *n.* poult, chicken.
powther. See **pouther.**
pree. See **prie.**
preen, *n.* pin; something of little value.
Premier, *n.* prime minister; *v.* play the prime minister (nonce-word).
prent, *n., v.* print.
presents, *n. pl.* (the) present document.
preses, *n.* president.
prest, *pa. pple.* oppressed.
pr[i]ck, *n.* phallus.
pride, *v.* make proud; **pridefu',** *adj.* proud.
prie, pree, *v.* try, taste; **p. (her) mou',** kiss (her).
prief, *n., adj.* proof; substance, quality.
priestie, *n.* priest (dim. used contemptuously).
priggin, *pres. pple.* chaffering, haggling.
primsie, *adj.* 'demure, precise' (B), affected.
proof. See **prie.**
proper, *adj.* handsome, elegant, fine.
proves, *n.* provost, chief magistrate.
pu'. See **pou.**
puddock-stool, *n.* toadstool.
puir, *adj.* poor.
pumps, *n. pl.* low-heeled shoes.
pun(d), *n. pl.* pounds.
pursie, *n.* little purse.
puss(ie). See **Poosie.**
pyet, *n.* magpie.
pyke. See **pike.**
pyle, *n.* spike, blade; grain, glume or pale of chaff.

Q

quarrel, *v.* dispute, challenge.
quat, *v.* (Engl. *quit*) leave, put by; *pa. t.* left, abandoned.
quaukin, *pres. pple.* quaking.
quean, quine, *n.* (1, Sc. sense) young girl, sturdy lass; (2, Engl. sense) jade, hussy.
quech, *n.* quaich, shallow drinking-vessel made usually of staves, with two handles.
queer, *adj.* (1) odd in appearance; (2) roguish.
queir, *n.* choir.
questions, *n. pl.* the catechism.
quey, *n.* 'a cow from one year to two years old' (B), heifer.
quietlenswise, *adv.* quietly.
quine. See **quean.**
quo, *pa. t.* of *quethe,* said.

R

racked, *ppl. adj.* excessive, extortionate.
rade, *v. pa. t.* rode; *fig.* served, copulated with.
raep, rape, *n.* rope.
ragged, *adj.* unkempt, shaggy.
ragouts, *n. pl.* highly seasoned dishes of stewed meat and vegetables.
ragweed, *n.* ragwort.
raible, *v.* gabble.
rair, *v.* roar, complain; **rair't,** *pa. pple.*
ra(i)se, *v. pa. t.* rose; **rais'd,** made . . . get up.
raize, *v.* provoke, rouse.
ramblan, *ppl. adj.* roving.
ramfeezl'd, *ppl. adj.* exhausted.
ramgunshoch, *adj.* ill-tempered.
ram-stam, *adj.* headstrong, reckless.
random-splore, *n.* careless frolic, carousal. See **splore.**

randy, *n.* rough, rude fellow; **randie,** *adj.* rude, coarse-tongued, riotous.
rant, *v.* make merry; **ranter,** *n.* riotous fellow, merry singer; **rant,** *n.* (1) spree, jollification, (2) tirade.
rap, *n.* knock.
rape. See **raep.**
raploch, *adj.* coarse, homely.
rarely, *adv.* unusually well, finely.
rase. See **ra(i)se.**
rash, *n.* rush; **r.-buss,** *n.* clump of rushes.
rattan, ratton, rottan, *n.* rat.
rattlin(g), *adj.* loquacious, lively in speech or manner.
raucle, *adj.* rough, coarse, rudely strong.
raught. See **ryke.**
raw, *n.* row, file.
rax, *v.* stretch; *ppl. adj.* elastic **68. 22.**
ream, *n.* cream, froth; *v.* foam.
reave. See **rief.**
rebute, *n.* rebuke, reproach.
reck, *v.* regard, care for, heed.
red(e), *v.* advise, counsel, warn.
red-wat-shod, *adj.* shod with wet blood. See **wat.**
red-wud, *adj.* violently distracted, stark mad. See **wud.**
reek, *n.* smoke; *ppl. adj.* **reekan,** dripping, bloody; *ppl. adj.* **reeket, reekit,** smoked, smoky; **reekin-red,** *adj.* steaming with warm blood; **warm-reekin,** *adj.*
reest, *v.* 'to stand restive' (B).
reestet, *ppl. adj.* smoke-dried, 'cured'.
reif. See **rief.**
remarkin, *vbl. n.* observation, entertainment.
remead, remeid, *n.* remedy, redress.
respeckit, *ppl. adj.* considered worthy.
ribban, *n.* riband, ribbon.
rice, *n.* branch.
rickle, *n.* pile of sheaves, stack.
rief, *n.* plunder; **reif,** *adj.* thieving, despoiling; **reave,** *v.*
rig, *n.* arable ridge; *fig. pudendum muliebre*; **riggin,** *n.* ridge, roof.
rig-woodie, *n.* ridge- or back-band for a cart-horse, made of twisted withes; *attrib.* abusive epithet, prob. withered, coarse, yellow.
rin, *v.* run.
ringer, *n.* circlet, binding.
ripp, *n.* 'a handful of unthreshed corn, &c.' (B).
ripple, *v.* draw flax through a comb to remove seed; **ripplin-kame,** *n.*
risk, *v.* 'to make a noise like the breaking of small roots with the plough' (B).
rive, *v.* break up; reave, take by force; burst, part asunder.
roaring, *adj.* brisk, vigorous, riotous.
rock, *n.* distaff; **rockin,** spinning party.
rood, *n.* quarter-acre.
r[o]ger, *n. fig.* penis; *v.* take sexually.
rook, *n. fig.* impudent cheat.
roon, *n.* round, circuit.
roose, rouse, *v.* stir up, agitate.
roose, *v.* praise; *n.* boast.
roosty, *adj.* rusty.
rottan. See **rattan.**
round, *adv.* confidently, roundly.
roupet, rupit, *ppl. adj.* husky, hoarse.
rouse. See **roose.**
rousing, *adj.* outrageous.
rout, *n.* road, course, way.
routh(ie). See **rowth.**
rove, *n.* ramble.
rowan (tree), *n.* mountain ash.
row(e), *v.* roll, wrap; **rowin't,** *vbl. n.* wrapping of it.
rowte, *v.* bellow, roar, low.
rowth, routh, *n.* abundance, plenty; **routhie,** *adj.* plentiful.
rozet, *n.* resin.
rumming, *adj.* ? drinking.
run(-)deil, *n.* complete, thorough-going devil.
rung, *n.* cudgel.
runkl'd, *ppl. adj.* wrinkled.
runt, *n.* cabbage stalk; *ppl. adj.* stunted.
rupit. See **roupet.**
ruth, *n.* pity.
ryke, *v.* reach; **raught,** *pa. t.*

S

's, shortened form of (1) **is,** is, are; (2) **as**; (3) **us**; (4) **sall,** shall.
sab, *v.* sob.
sae, *adv., conj.* so.
saft, *adj.* soft; silly, lax; soft to the touch.

sair, *v.* serve, treat; suffice, satisfy sexually; **sairs**, *pres. pl.* avail; **sair't**, *pa. pple.*

sair, *adj.*, *adv.* sore(ly); *adj.* sorry; sad, aching; hard, harsh, heavy; *adv.* severely, quite, desperately, violently; *combs.* **sairwark**, *n.* hardship, labour; **sair-won**, *adj.* hard-won.

sairie, **sairy**, *adj.* sorry, mean, wretched; afflicted, sore.

sal-alkali, *n.* soda-ash; **sal-marinum**, *n.* common salt.

sald, *v. pa. t.* sold; **sell't awa**, *pa. pple.* disposed of by sale.

sall, *v.* shall; reduced enclitic forms *-s(e)*, *-s'*, mis-written *-'s(e)*, **I'se**, **we'se**, **ye'se**, **it's**.

sample, *n.* example.

sang, *n.* song.

Sannock, **Sawnie**, *n.* abbreviations of *Alexander*.

sappy, *adj.* plump, succulent.

sark, *n.* shirt; chemise, shift; **half-sarket**, *ppl. adj.* half-clothed; **sark-necks**, *n. pl.* collars.

sa'tty. See **saut**.

saugh, *n.* sallow, willow; **s.-woodies**, *n. pl.* ropes of twisted sallow-withes.

saul, *n.* soul.

saumont, **sawmont**, *n.* salmon; **s.-coble**, *n.* flat-bottomed rowing-boat used in spearing salmon on the river, or in net-fishing by the coast.

saunt, *n.* saint; puritan, *pl.* the elect.

saut, *n.*, *adj.* salt; **sa'tty**, *adj.*; **sautet**, *ppl. adj.*; *comb.* **saut-backet**, *n.* small wooden box for holding salt water, kept near the kitchen fireplace.

saw, *v.* sow.

sawmont. See **saumont**.

Sawnie. See **Sannock**.

sax, *adj.*, *n.* six; **saxpence**, *n.*

scaith. See **skaith**.

scandal-potion, *n.* tea.

scant, *adj.* stinted, deficient, poor, scarce; *n.* dearth, poverty.

scar, *n.* cliff, bank, rock.

scar, *v.* scare, frighten off; **scaur**, *adj.* afraid.

scathe. See **skaith**.

scaud, *v.* scald.

scaur. See **scar**.

scawl, *n.* scolding, abusive woman; **scauldin**, *ppl. adj.*

scho, *pron.* she.

schulin', schooling.

sclates, *n. pl.* slates.

sconner, *v.* feel sick, feel disgust; *n.* disgust, revulsion.

score, *n.* indentation.

scow'r, *v.* roister; **scour'd**, *pa. t.* ran, ranged.

scraichan, *ppl. adj.* screaming.

scriegh, *v.* 'to cry shrilly' (B), neigh; **scriechan**, *pres. pple.* screeching.

screed, *n.* tear; *v.* repeat readily, rattle (off).

scri(e)ve, *v.* 'to glide swiftly along' (B).

scrimp, *v.* be sparing of, cut down on; **scrimpet**, *ppl. adj.* stunted; **scrimply**, *adv.* scarcely, barely.

scrivin'. See **scri(e)ve**.

scroggie, **scroggy**, *adj.* covered with stunted bushes.

sea-way, *n.* the progress of a ship through the waves.

see'd, *v. pa. t.* saw; **far seen**, *ppl. adj.* well versed.

se'enteen, *adj.* seventeen.

seisin, *n.* sasine, in Sc. law, 'an Instrument (of a settled Style) . . . setting forth that upon such a Day . . . the Disponee was seized and invested in the Feu in virtue of his Disposition' (Innes, *Idea Juris Scotici*, 1733).

sell't. See **sald**.

semple-folk, *n.* humble, common folk.

sen', *v.* send; **sen't**, send it.

sen. *See* **sin**.

sense, in a, in any respect.

servan', *adj.* servant, menial.

service, *n.* toast in homage.

set, *v.* set out, start off; suit, become; **sets . . . ill**, ill becomes; **s. light by**, value little, despise; **s. up a face**, put on a favourable appearance, make a pretence; **settlin'**, *vbl. n.* quieting, fixing.

shachl't, *ppl. adj.* shapeless, twisted by shuffling.

shaird, *n.* shard; fragment, remnant.

shangan, *n.* 'a stick cleft at one end for putting the tail of a dog, &c. into, by way of mischief, or to frighten him away' (B).

shank (it), *v.* walk.
shanna, sha'na, *v.* shan't.
shaul, *adj.* shallow.
shaver, *n.* barber; young wag, roisterer, joker; **shavie**, *n.* trick.
shaw, *n.* 'a small wood in a hollow place' (B).
shaw, *v.* show, reveal.
shear, *v.* reap with a sickle; **shure**, *pa. t.*
sheep-shank (bane), nae, *n.* person of no little importance.
sheerly, *adv.* wholly, entirely.
sheuch, sheugh, *n.* trench, ditch.
sheuk, *v. pa. t.* shook.
shiel, *n.* hut, shanty; **milkin-s.**, *n.* shed for milking cows or ewes.
shift, *v.* change places.
shill, *adj.* resonant, shrill.
sh[it], *v.* void excrement; a **sh–ten**, to shit.
shog, *n.* jog, shock.
shool. *n.* shovel; **fire-shool**, *n.*
shoon, *n. pl.* shoes.
shore, *v.* (1) threaten; (2) offer.
shot, *n.* single movement of the shuttle.
shouther, *n.* shoulder.
shure. See **shear.**
sib, *adj.* akin, closely related.
sic, *adj.* such; **siccan**, *adj.* such-like.
sicker, *adj.* secure, safe, steady; *adv.* effectively, severely.
sidelins, *adv.* sideways, obliquely; **sidling**, *pres. pple.* moving furtively, unobtrusively.
sie, *v.* see.
siller, *n.* silver, wealth.
silly, *adj.* poor, hapless, pitiful; frail, sorry, helpless, harmless; foolish; weak, feeble.
simmer, *n.* summer.
sin, sin', sen, *adv., prep., conj.* since, from the time that; **sinsyne**, *adv.* since then. See **syn(e).**
sin, *n.* son.
singet, *ppl. adj.* singed, parched, shrunken.
sinn, *n.* sun; **sinny**, *adj.*
sinsyne. See **sin.**
sirnam'd, *pa. pple.* surnamed.
skair, *n.* Sc. var. of *share.*
skaith, scaith, scathe, *n.* hurt, damage; *v.* harm.
skeigh, skiegh, *adj.* 'mettlesome, fiery, proud' (B), disdainful.
skellum, *n.* rascal, scoundrel.
skelp, (1) *v.* strike, beat, thrash; *ppl. adj.* smacking (kiss); *n.* slap; smack! bang!; (2) *v.* hurry, rush; **skelpie-limmer**, *n.* hussy, 'a technical term in female scolding' (B). See **limmer.**
skelvy, *adj.* shelfy, ledged.
skiegh. See **skeigh.**
skinking, *adj.* watery.
skinklin, *ppl. adj.* glittering, showy.
skirl, *v.* shriek, yell.
sklent, *v.* throw aslant, squint greedily, direct aslant with malice; *ppl. adj.* falling obliquely, slanting; *n.* side-look.
skouth, *n.* scope, liberty.
skyre, *v.* to shine; **skyrin**, *ppl. adj.* flaunting, bright-coloured.
skyte, *n.* 'a smart and sudden blow, so as to make what strikes rebound in a slanting direction' (Jamieson).
slade, *pa. t.* of *slide,* slip, steal away.
slae, *n.* the blackthorn, its fruit.
slap, *v.* cut, bring down; drive, strike; *adv.* directly, suddenly.
slap, *n.* gap in a dyke or fence; **faulding s.**, see **fauld.**
slaw, *adj., adv.* slow.
slee, *adj.* clever, wise, witty, sly; *superl.* **sleest.**
sleeket, sleekit, *ppl. adj.* smooth glossy; sly.
slight, *n.* skill, dexterity; artifice.
slip, *n.* quick-release leash.
sloken, *v.* slake, satisfy.
slype. *v.* 'to fall over *as a wet furrow from the plough*' (B).
sma', *adj.* little, slight; slender, narrow; *adv.* into little bits.
smeddum, *n.* fine powder used as medicine or insecticide.
smeek, *n.* smoke.
smiddie, *n.* smithy.
smirking, *ppl. adj.* smiling.
smit, *v.* smite.
smoke, *v.* give off vapour, spray.
smoor, *v.* smother; *pa. t.* was smothered **321.** 90.
smoutie, *adj.* 'smutty, obscene; ugly' (B).
smytrie, *n.* numerous collection.

snap, *adj.* quick, smart
snapper, *v.* stumble.
snash, *n.* abuse, insolence.
snaw, *n.* snow; **snawy,** *adj.*; *combs.* **snaw-drap,** *n.*; **snaw-broo,** see **broo.**
sned, *v.* cut off, lop, prune.
sneeshin (mill), *n.* snuff (box).
snell, *adj.* keen, bitter.
snick, *n.* latch, bar; **s.-drawing,** *ppl. adj.* crafty.
snirtle, *v.* laugh quietly, snigger.
snood, *n.* girl's hair-band; **snooded,** *pa. pple.* bound with a snood.
snool, *n.* 'one whose spirit is broken with oppressive slavery; [*v.*] to submit tamely, to sneak' (B); snub.
snoove, *v.* go steadily on.
snore, *v.* snort.
snowck, *v.* snuff, poke about with the nose.
snuff, *v.* sniff.
sobbin. See **sab.**
so(d)ger, *n.* soldier.
some(thing), *adv.* somewhat, a bit.
sonnet, *n.* song.
sonsie, sonsy, *adj.* good-natured, tractable; buxom, comely.
sort, *v.* meet together (with).
s(o)ugh, *n.* rushing sound of wind; deep breath.
souk, *n.* suck, swig.
soup(e), sowp, *n.* sup, drink, mouthful.
souple, *v.* soften; *adj.*, soft, pliant, supple.
sour-mou'd, *ppl. adj.* peevish, bitter-tongued.
souse, *v.* strike, beat.
s(o)uter, sutor, sowter, *n.* shoemaker, cobbler.
so(we)ns, *n.* sour pudding of oats and water.
sowp. See **soup(e).**
sowth, *v.* 'to try over a tune with a low whistle' (B).
sowther, *v.* solder, patch up.
spae, *v.* divine, foretell.
spail, *n.* spale, splinter.
spair, *v.* spare; *ppl. adj.* restrained, reticent.
spairge, *v.* plaster, sprinkle; bespatter.
spak, *v. pa. t.* spoke.
span-lang, *adj.* small (lit. the measure of the extended hand, 9 ins.)
spavie, *n.* spavin, tumour caused by inflammation of a horse's shank cartilage, or of the hock-bone; **spavet,** *ppl. adj.* spavined.
spean, *v.* wean.
speat, *n.* spate, flood.
speed, come s., *v.* prosper, attain a desire; **on . . . speed,** hurrying about; **speedy,** *adj.* quick, brief.
speel, *v.* climb.
speet, *v.* spit, transfix.
spell, *v.* study, contemplate.
spell, tak a, take turns at the work, work continuously.
speir. See **spier.**
spence, *n.* parlour, inner room.
spen't, spend it; **spent,** *pa. t.* spent (himself) sexually.
spier, speir, *v.* ask, inquire; **s. at,** ask of; **s. in,** ask within.
spill, *v.* destroy, waste.
spin'le, *n.* spindle, axle.
splatter, *v.* sputter, bespatter; *n.* splash, noisy splutter.
spleuchan, *n.* tobacco-pouch, purse; *fig. pudendum muliebre.*
splore, *n.* frolic, uproar, carousal. See **random-splore.**
sport, *v.* spend in pleasure, *pa. t.* **406.** 18; **sportin,** *vbl. n.* sexual fun, games, jesting; **sportin' lady,** *n.* whore.
spotting, *ppl. adj.* staining.
spout, *n.* spurt, dart.
sprachle, *v.* clamber.
sprattle, *v.* struggle, scramble.
sprawl, *v.* struggle, crawl.
spring, *n.* dance, lively tune.
sprittie, *adj.* 'rushy' (B).
sprush, *adv.* sprucely, smartly.
spunk, *n.* spark, match; **spunkie,** *adj.* spirited, mettlesome; *n.* (1) will o' the wisp, (2) spirits, whisky.
spurtle, *n.* wooden instrument for turning oat-cakes, porridge-stick; **s.-blade,** *n.* sword.
squad, *n.* company, party; set.
squatter, *v.* 'flutter in water' (B).
squattle, *v.* squat, nestle down.
stacher, *v.* toddle, totter, stagger.
stack, *pa. t.* of *stick.*
sta(i)g, *n.* young horse; *dim.* **staggie.**

staincher, stanchel, *n.* stanchion, iron bar; *ppl. adj.* **s.-fitted,** iron-footed.

stammer, *v.* stumble (of a horse).

stan' *v.* stand, stop, stick; **he wad stan't,** he would have stood; **standing, stanin',** *ppl. adj.* erect; **stan',** *n.* pause, halt.

stanchel. See **staincher.**

stane, *n.* stone; measure of weight.

stang, *n.* stake, wooden bar; **stang'd,** *v. pa. t.* made to ride the stang; *ppl. adj.* bruised on the stang.

stang, *n., v.* goad, sting.

stanin'. See **stan'.**

stank, *n.* pond, 'a pool of standing water' (B).

stap, *v.* stop; **stapple,** *n* stopper, bung.

stare, *v.* express clearly; stare in the face, confront.

stark, *adj.* strong, hardy; stiff, rigid.

starn, *n.* star; **starnies,** *n. pl.* little stars.

startle, *v.* take fright; 'to run *as cattle stung by the gadfly*' (B), caper.

statuary, *n.* sculptor.

staukin, *pres. pple.* stalking, walking stealthily.

staumrel, *adj.* stammering, half-witted, silly.

staw, *n.* stall; *v.* to satiate.

staw, *v. pa. t.* stole; crept, slipped away; **stown** *pa. pple.*; **stowlins,** *adv.* by stealth, secretly.

stay, *n.* hindrance, halt.

steek, *n.* stitch.

steek, *v.* shut; *pa. pple.* enclosed.

steel-waimit, *ppl. adj.* steel-bellied.

steer, *v.* stir, agitate, rouse; affect, afflict; **a steerin,** in motion.

steer, *v.* take one's way.

steeve, *adj.* firm, strong.

stegh, *v.* cram the stomach with food.

stell, *n.* still, apparatus for distillation; *pl.* **stills.**

stell, *v.* post, fix.

sten', *n.* leap, bound; **sten't,** *v. pa. t.* reared, turned.

stent, *n.* impost, duty.

stey, *adj.* steep, difficult.

stibble, *n.* stubble; *combs.* **s.-field, s.-rig,** stubble field, 'the reaper who takes the lead' (B).

stick, *n.* cudgel, splinter, fragment; **a' to sticks, s. an' stow,** *adv. phr.* utterly; *v.* stab.

stills. See **stell.**

stilt, *n.* plough handle; *v.* lift the legs high, prance.

stimpart, *n.* measure of grain, ¼-peck, 'heapet' or 'straiked'.

stir, *n.*; corruption of *sir.*

stirk, *n.* young bullock.

stock, *n.* plant, stem; see B's note on **73.** 29; *pl.* kindred, parties.

stoited, stoiter'd. See **stoyte.**

stomach, *n.* spirit, temper.

stook, *n.* set of corn sheaves placed on end in two rows, against each other, in the field.

stoor, *adj.* harsh, 'sounding hollow, strong and hoarse' (B); massive, stern. See **stoure.**

stops . . . o', *v.* keeps from, deprives of.

store, in, in plenty.

storm, *v.* rage at, tell peremptorily

stot, *n.* young bullock.

stoun(d), *n.* thrill of pleasure.

stoup, stowp(e), *n.* tankard, measure; *comb.* **pint-s.**

stoure, stoor, *n.* battle, tumult, storm; adversity; dust; **like s.,** *adv. phr.* swiftly; **stourie,** *adj.* dusty.

stow'd, *pa. pple.* (have) filled, crammed.

stown(lins). See **staw.**

stoyte, stoit(er), *v.* lurch, stagger.

strack, *v. pa. t.* struck.

strade, *v. pa. t.* strode.

strae, *n.* straw; **s.-death,** *n.* natural death in bed.

straik, *v.* stroke.

strak, *v. pa. t.* struck.

strang, *adj.* strong; violent; *comb.* **strang-beer,** *n.*

strappan, *ppl. adj.* strapping, sturdy.

straught, *v.* stretch (dead); *adj.* straight; *adv.*

streek, *v.* stretch.

striddle, *v.* straddle, stride.

string, *n.* string used as a measure.

stroan't, *v. pa. pple.* pissed.

strunt, *n.* liquor.

strunt, *v.* move with assurance.

stude, *v. pa. t.* stood.
studdie, *n.* stithy, anvil.
stuff, *n.* provision, store of corn, 'grain in whatever state; whether as growing, cut down, in the barn, or in the mill' (Jamieson).
stump, *v.* walk clumsily; **stumpie (pen)**, worn quill pen.
sturt, *v.* fret, trouble; *ppl. adj.* troubled, afraid; *n.* contention, quarrelling, violence, esp. in traditional allit. phr. **s. and strife.**
styme, see a, see at all.
sucker, *n.* sugar; **succar-candie**, *n.*
sud, *v.* should (have).
sugh. See **s(o)ugh.**
summon, *n.*; *obs. sg.* of summons
sumph, *n.* simpleton, sullen ass.
sune, *adv.* soon.
Suthron, *adj.*, *n. pl.* southerners, Englishmen.
sutor. See **s(o)uter.**
swaird, *n.* sward.
swank, *adj.* limber, agile; **swankie**, *n.* strapping lad.
swap, *v.* strike, strike a bargain; exchange.
swarf, *v.* swoon.
swat, *v. pa. t.* sweated.
swatch, *n.* sample.
swats, *n. pl.* new small beer.
swinge, *v.* flog.
swirl, *n.* 'a curve [71. 36], an eddying blast or pool, a knot in wood' (B); **swirlie**, *adj.* 'knaggy, full of knots' (B).
swith, *adv.*, *interj.* quickly!, away!
swither, *n.* state of agitation, flurry.
swoor, *v. pa. t.* swore.
sybow, *n.* spring onion; **s.-tail**, *n.*
syke, *n.* small stream, ditch.
syn(e), *adv.*, *conj.* then, since; **lang s.**, long since, long ago.

T

tack, *n.* leasehold, tenure.
tacket, *n.* hob-nail for boots.
tae, *n.* toe; *ppl. adj.* **three-tae'd.**
tae, *prep.*, *conj.* to.
taed, tade, *n.* toad.
ta'en. See **tak.**
taet, *n.* tuft, small handful.
tail, *n.* *pudendum muliebre.*
ta(i)rge, *v.* discipline, constrain.
tak(e), *v.* take, seize; take one's way; **tak aff**, drink off, up; carry away; **take off**, finish *or* mimic; **tak the gate**, take to the road, get home; **ta'en**, *pa. pple.* (have) taken.
tald. See **tell.**
tane . . . tither, *pron.*, *adj.* one . . . other.
tangle, *n.* sea-weed.
tangs, *n.* (*pl. form as sg.*) tongs.
tap, *n.* (1) top, head; (2) portion of lint put on the distaff; **tapma(i)st, tapmost**, *adj.* topmost; **tap-pickle**, *n.* the grain (*pickle*) at the end of a stalk of wheat, barley, oats.
taper, *adj.* tapering, slender.
tapetless, *adj.* 'heedless, foolish' (B).
tappit-hen, *n.* hen with a top-knot; drinking-vessel with a knobbed lid.
tapsalteerie, *adv. comb.* topsy-turvy, upside down, in disorder.
targe, *n.* light shield.
tarrow, *v.* hesitate, show reluctance; *pa. pple.* **tarrow't**, 'murmured' (B).
tarry-breeks, *n.* nickname for a sailor.
tassie, *n.* dim. of *tass*, silver goblet.
ta(u)ld. See **tell.**
tauted, tawtied, *ppl. adj.* matted, shaggy.
tawie, *adj.* (of a horse) 'that handles quietly' (B).
tawpie, *n.* senseless girl.
teen, *n.* vexation, chagrin.
teethin, *pres. pple.* putting fresh teeth into.
tell, *v.* relate, enumerate; count the price out (and drink off); **t. down**, count out, pay; **t. the tale to**, defy, defeat; **ta(u)ld**, *pa. t.* and *pa. pple.*
temper-pin, *n.* (1) tuning screw; (2) screw for regulating the movement of the spinning-wheel.
ten-hours bite, *comb.* 'a slight feed to the horses while in the yoke in the forenoon' (B); **tenpund**, *adj.* of the annual value of ten pounds.
tent, *n.* 'a field pulpit' (B).
tent, *v.* heed, care, tend; watch, take heed; *n.* caution, care; **tentie**, *adj* watchful, careful.

tester, *n.* sixpence.
tether, *n.* rope, noose.
teugh, *adj.* tough, hardy, violent.
thack, *n.* thatching.
thae, *dem. pron., adj.* those; **thae's,** those are.
thairm, *n.* intestine; *pl.* fiddle strings; **th.-inspirin(g),** *adj.* gifted on the fiddle.
thanket, thankit, *pa. pple.* thanked.
theek, *v.* collateral form of *thatch*; **theekit,** *pa. pple.* and *ppl. adj.*
thegither, *adv.* together; at a time, continuously.
thick, *adj.* (1) familiar, intimate; (2) going in quick succession, rapid.
thie, *n.* thigh.
thieveless, *adj.* cold, without warmth.
thig, *v.* take, accept; beg.
thir, *dem. adj.* these.
thirl, *v.* pierce, penetrate.
thole, *v.* endure, suffer.
thou's(e), *v.* thou art, thou hast, thou shalt. Cf. **I'se, ye'se.** See **sall.**
thowe, *n.* thaw.
thowless, *adj.* spiritless.
thrang, *n.* crowd, press of people; *adj.* crowding, in a crowd, busy; **thick an' thrang,** closely engaged together; *v.* crowd in, jostle; *adv.* busily, earnestly.
thrapple, *n.* throat.
thrash. See **thresh.**
thrave, *n.* two **stooks** of corn, hence a measure of straw, &c.
thraw, *v.* turn, twist; worst, frustrate; *n.* twist, turn; **for thrawin,** to prevent warping; *n. pl.* throes, pangs.
threap, *v.* argue obstinately, 'maintain by dint of assertion' (B).
three-tae'd. See **tae.**
thresh, *v.* beat, belabour; **thrash,** *v.* flail, strike (sexually); **threshin,** *vbl. n.* beating.
thretteen, *adj.* thirteen.
thretty, *adj.* thirty.
thripplin, *ppl. adj.* apparently f. **ripple.**
thrissle, thristle, *n.* thistle.
thrist, *v.* thirst.
through, mak to. See **mak.**
(a') throw'ther, a' throu'ther, *adv. phr.* 'through each other', in confusion, disorder.
thrum, *n.* an end of warp-thread left unwoven on the loom when the web is cut off.
thrum, *v.* sound monotonously, hum.
thumb-bread, *n. pl.* thumb's breadths.
thummart, *n.* polecat **52. 31.**
thump, *v.* strike; *pa. t.* fired; **thumpin,** *ppl. adj. fig.* (*colloq.*) exceptionally large, fine.
thysel, *pron.* yourself.
tiched, *ppl. adj.* touched, affected.
tickle, *v.* rouse; please, amuse.
tiend, *n.* tythe, tax, due.
tight, *adj.* (1) neat, shapely; (2) tidy, cosy, snug; (3) capable, able, ready, virile **77. 71**; *adv.* closely, strictly.
till, *prep.* to; **till't,** to it.
till't, *v.* cultivate it **603. 16.**
timmer, *n.* timber; trees; material; wooden edge **75. 76.**
tine, tyne, *v.* lose, get lost; **tint,** *pa. t., pa. pple.*
tinkler, *n.* itinerant mender of pots and pans, usually a gipsy; low rascal; *combs.* **t.-gipsey, t.-hizzie** (see **hizzie**), **t.-trash,** gipsy trumpery.
tint. See **tine.**
tip. See **toop.**
tippence, *n.* twopence; **tippeny,** *n.* ale originally sold at 2*d.* a Scots pint (3 imperial pts.).
tipt . . . off, *pa. t.* passed, given.
tirl, *v.* strip, uncover, unthatch.
tirl, *v.* rattle at a door, by turning or lifting the latch.
tirlie-whirlie, *n. pudendum muliebre.*
Tiseday, *n.* Tuesday.
tither (the), *pron., adj.* the other (of two), the other (day).
tittie, titty, *n.* (*colloq.*) sister.
tittlan, *ppl. adj.* tattling, whispering.
tocher, *n.* dowry; **t.-band,** *n.* marriage settlement; *v.* furnish with a dowry.
tod, *n.* fox.
toddlan, todlin, *pres. pple.* toddling; walking unsteadily; *ppl. adj.* hurrying, pattering.
toddy, *n.* whisky, hot water, and sugar.
ton, *n.* fashion, mode.
toofa', *n.* falling-to, beginning (of night).

toolzie. See **tulzie.**
toom, *adj., v.* empty.
toop, tip, tup, *n.* ram.
toss, *n.* toast, belle.
touch, a wee, a very little.
toun, town, *n.* village, farm, town; *combs.* **t.-en',** *n.* end of a village; **towns-bodies,** *n. pl.*
tour, *n.* turf, sod.
tout, *n.* blast (of a trumpet); *v.*
touzle, *v.* ruffle, handle roughly; **towsing,** *vbl. n.* rumpling, handling indelicately; **towzie,** *adj.* unkempt, shaggy.
tow, *n.* bell-rope; rope; gallows-rope.
tow, *n.* fibre of flax prepared for spinning.
towmond, towmont, *n.* twelve-month, year.
towns-bodies. See **toun.**
towsing, towzie. See **touzle.**
toy, *n.* close-fitting cap, 'a very old fashion of female head dress' (B).
toyte, *v.* 'walk like old age' (B), totter.
tozie, *adj.* warm, cosy, tipsy.
trac'd, *pa. pple.* harnessed.
tram, *n.* cart or barrow shaft.
transmugrify'd, *ppl. adj.* transformed, metamorphosed.
trashtrie, *n.* trashery, rubbish.
tread, *v. pa. t.* trod.
tree, *n.* timber, wood.
trepan, *v.* inveigle, beguile.
trews, trouse, *n.* close-fitting trousers, worn with stockings.
trick, *n.* habit, turn; **trickie,** *adj.* crafty, deceitful.
trig, *adj.* trim, smart.
trinkle, *v.* trickle, flow.
trin'le, *n.* wheel of a barrow.
trogger, *n.* trucker, pedlar; **troggin,** *vbl. n.* pedlar's ware, *fig.* **610.** 8; **troke,** *v.* barter, deal for.
trot, *v.* run, bustle (of a stream).
trouse. See **trews.**
trow, *v.* trust; believe; **trow't,** believe it; **in trouth, trowth,** *adv., interj.* truly, indeed.
trustee, *n.* administrator.
tryst(e), *n.* meeting, assembly; cattle-fair, market; **trysted,** *ppl. adj.* appointed; **trystin(g),** *ppl. adj.*
tug, *n.* 'raw hide, *of which, in olden times, plough-traces were frequently made*' (B).
tulzie, toolzie, *n.* quarrel, contest, brawl.
tun, *v.* put into a tun, cask.
tup. See **toop.**
twa(y), *numeral adj., n.* two; **twa-fauld,** *adv.* bent double; **twa-three,** *adj.* two or three, a few.
'twad. See **wad.**
twal, *numeral adj., n.* twelve, mid-night; **t. hundred,** woven in a reel of 1,200 divisions; **twalpennie,** *attrib.* shilling('s); **t.-pint,** *adj.* giving 12 pints at a milking; **twalt,** *adj.* twelfth.
twa-three. See **twa(y),**
twin, *v.* separate (from), deprive (of).
twine, *n.* thread.
twissle, *n.* wrench, twist.
tyke, *n.* dog, cur, mongrel.
tyne. See **tine.**
tyta, *n.* pet name for 'father'

U

ulzie, *n.* oil.
unchancy, *adj.* ill-omened; dangerous. Cf. **wanchancie.**
unco, *adj.* odd, strange; *adv.* very; **uncos,** *n. pl.* strange tales, news.
under hidin, in hiding.
unkenn'd, unkend-of, *ppl. adj.* unknown, unnoticed. See **ken.**
unsicker, *adj.* unsure, fickle. See **sicker.**
unskaith'd, *ppl. adj.* unscathed. See **skaith.**
upo', *prep.* upon.
up wi', here's to; **up wi't a',** here's to (you).
urinus-spiritus, *n.* spirit of urine.
use't, *p. pple.* used, treated; **us'd,** *ppl. adj.* experienced 47. 49.
usquabae, usquebae, *n.* whisky.

V

vapour, *n.* fancy, whimsy; **vap'rin,** *ppl. adj.* blustering, fuming.
vauntie, *adj.* vain, proud.
vend, *v.* sell; advance, utter.
vera, *adj.* very, actual; true, real.
viewin, *vbl. n.* view, sight.
virl, *n.* band of metal or ivory.
vittel, vittle, *n.* grain, fodder.

vogie, *adj.* vain.
vow, *interj.* See **wow.**

W

wa', **waw**, *n.* wall.
wab, *n.* web, woven fabric.
wabster, *n.* weaver; *comb.* **w.-loun** (see **loun**).
wad, *v.* covenant; wager, stake; wed, marry; *n.* pledge, forfeit.
wad, *v.* would (have); (who) would; **wadna**, would not; **'twad**, it would (have).
wadset, *n.* something pledged; in Sc. law the conveyance of land in pledge for, or in satisfaction of, a debt or obligation.
wae, woe; (1) *interj.*, *adv.* **waes**, woe is (me), alas; **wae sucks** (sakes), alas; **wae gae by**, **w. on**, **w. worth**, may evil befall, cursed be; (2) *n.* misery, misfortune; **wae(fu')**, *adj.* bringing misery **84**. 86; *superl.* **waest**, most wretched.
waff, **waft**, *v.* carry by water; *n.* sea-trip.
waft, *n.* weft in a web, *fig.*
wag, *v.* nod, shake; **w.-wits**, *n. pl.* scandal-mongers, jokers.
wail, *v. tr.* bewail.
wair, **ware**, *v.* spend, lay out, bestow.
wale, *n.* choice, choicest one (kind); *v.* choose, pick out.
walie, **wa(w)ly**, **waulie**, *adj.* handsome, fine, ample; *adv.* amply, fully; **waly fa'**, good luck to **603**. 15; *n. pl.* genitals **609**. 26.
wallop, *v.* kick the heels, thrash about, be hanged; *n.* leap, violent beat.
wallow, *v.* wither, fade, grow pale.
waly fa'. See **walie.**
wame, *n.* belly, stomach; *pudendum muliebre*, uterus; **wamefou**, *n.* belly-full, meal.
wan, *v. pa. t.* won.
wanchancie, *adj.* dangerous, unlucky.
wand, *n.* branch, slender stem.
wanrestfu', *adj.* restless.
wap, *v.* wrap.
wapon-shaw, *n.* muster, review of men under arms in a lordship.
war. See **wa(u)r.**
ware, *pa. pple.* worn.
wark, *n.* work, labour; combat, business in hand; *pl.* (iron) works **165**. 1.
warklum, *n.* instrument, tool for work; *fig.* penis.
warl(d), *n.* world; **w.'s worm**, low creature of earth; **warly**, *adj.* worldly.
warlock, *n.* witch, wizard; **w.-breef**, *n.* charter conveying magical powers, charm.
warly. See **warl(d).**
warp, *v.* weave; **warpin**, *vbl. n.* **w.-wheel**, *n.*
warran, *v.* warrant, guarantee.
warsle, *v.* wrestle, struggle, contend (with); **warstle**, *n.* struggle, strife.
was, *v. pa. t.* were.
wastrie, *n.* wastefulness, extravagance.
waste, *n.* waist.
wat, *adj.* wet; *pa. pple.*
wat, *v.* know, be aware of, be sure; **watna**, don't know.
water, *n.* urine; **w.-brose**, *n.* **brose** made with water; **w.-fit**, *n.* mouth of a river; **w.-kelpie**, see **kelpie.**
watna. See **wat.**
wattle, *n.* wand, stick.
wauble, *v.* 'to swing' (B), move unsteadily from side to side.
waught, *n.* draught, heavy drink.
wauk, **wauken**, *v. intr.* be or stay awake, wake up; *tr.* wake, arouse **70**. 165; *pres. pple.* staying awake to keep watch (on), **236**. 25; *ppl. adj.* **waukin**, awake, sleepless; **waukrife**, *adj.* wakeful, vigilant.
wauket, *ppl. adj.* made callous, horny.
waulies. See **walie.**
wa(u)r, *adj.*, *adv.* worse; *v.* worst, excel, surpass.
wa(u)rst, *adj.*, *adv.* worst.
wavering, *pres. pple.* wandering, fluttering.
waw. See **wa'.**
wawly. See **walie.**
wean, *n.* child; **weanies**, *dim. pl* infants.
wearing, *pres. pple.* passing (of time); *vbl. n.* possessing, enjoying.

weary, *v.* grow weary, bored; *adj.* tiring, toilsome; *adv.* utterly, miserably; *phr.* **weary fa'**, a curse on.

weason, *n.* gullet.

wecht, *n.* sieve (cf. B's note, **73**. 182).

wee, *n., adj.* little bit, while; **w.-bit,** *quasi-adj.* little bit of a; **(a) w. thing,** *adv. phr.* a little; **w.-thing,** *n.* child, infant.

weel, *adv., adj.* well, fine, satisfied; *n.* well-being, welfare, prosperity; **as w.'s,** as well as; **w.'s me on,** a blessing on (cf. **leeze me on**); **weelfar'd,** *ppl. adj.* well-favoured, handsome; **w.-gaun,** *ppl. adj.* good-going, active (see **gae**); **w.-hain'd,** see **hain**; **w.-hoordet,** *ppl. adj.* closely hoarded; **w.-knooz'd,** *ppl. adj.* well-pummelled, drubbed; **w.-swall'd,** *ppl. adj.* fully stretched; **w.-tocher'd,** *ppl. adj.* well-dowered (see **tocher**).

weepers, *n. pl.* cuffs.

weet, *v., adj.* wet; *n.* dew, rain.

wenching, *ppl. adj.* whoring.

we'se, *v.* we'll. See **sall.**

westlin, *adj.* west(ern), westerly; west country; westward.

wether, *n.* castrated ram; *combs.* **w.-haggis,** *n.* **haggis** made in a wether's stomach; **w.-head.**

wha, whae(v)er, *pron.* who; **wham,** whom; **whase,** *pron.* whose; **whase,** who is.

whaizle, *v.* 'to wheez' (B).

whalp, *v.* whelp.

wham. See **wha.**

whan, *adv.* when.

whang, *n.* thick slice of cheese; *v.* to beat (as with a thong), flog.

whare, wha(u)r, *adv., conj.* where.

whase. See **wha.**

whatfore no, why not?

whatn(a), (on, by) what (a).

whatreck, *interrog. phr.* what does it matter; *adv.* (*parenthetic*) nevertheless; *adv.* (*used substantivally*) fornication **109**. 121.

whatt, *v.pa. t.* whetted, put an edge on.

whaup, *n.* curlew.

whaur. See **whare.**

wheep, *v.* jerk, jig.

whid, *n.* word (thieves' cant); a lie.

whid, *v.* move nimbly and noiselessly (of a hare); *n.* 'the motion of a hare running but not frightened' (B).

whig, *n.* Puritan, hypocrite; **whiggish,** *adj.* rigid, precisian.

whigmeleerie, *n.* whimsical ornament.

whiles. See **whyles.**

whin, *n.* gorse, furze-bush.

whinge, *v.* whine; *ppl. adj.* canting, complaining.

whin-rock, whunstane, *n.* whinstone, hard dark rock (e.g. greenstone, basalt).

whipper-in, *n.* huntsman responsible for keeping the hounds in pack.

whirl, *n.* rush, rapid trip.

whirlygigums, *n. pl.* fantastic ornaments.

whirry, *v.* hurry, drive.

whist, held my, kept silent.

whissle, gat the. See **groat.**

whitter, *n.* draught of liquor.

whittle, *n.* knife used as a weapon; clasp-knife; surgical knife; **kail-wh.,** see **kail.**

whunstane. See **whin-rock.**

whyle, whiles (*n., adv. gen.*) *adv.* at times, sometimes; **wh. . . . wh.,** now . . . then, at times . . . at times.

wi', *prep,* with; **wi'm, wi's, wi't,** with him, his, it.

wick (a bore), *v.* 'to strike a stone in an oblique direction, *a term in curling*' (B).

wicker, *n.* branch.

widdefu'. See **woodie.**

widdle, *n.* strife, trouble.

wiel, *n.* eddy.

wierd, *n.* fate, fortune.

wifie, *n. dim.* wife, 'a fondling term' (Jamieson).

wight, *n.* creature, fellow.

wight, *adj.* strong, stout.

wil-cat, *n.* wild-cat.

willie, *n.* willow,

willyart, *adj.* shy, awkward.

wi'm. See **wi'.**

wimble, wumble, *n.* gimlet; *fig.* phallus.

wimple, *v.* meander; *ppl. adj.* twisting, turning.

win, *v.* reach, gain, get; **win,** *pa. pple.* **555**. 20; earn.

win', *v.* wind; **win't**, *pa. t.* wound; *vbl. n.* **567**. 6.
win', *n.* wind, breath.
winkers, *n. pl.* eye-lashes, eyes.
winn, *v.* winnow.
winna, *v.* will not, won't.
winnock, *n.* window; **w.-bunker**, *n.* window-seat.
win't. See **win'**.
winter-hap, *n.* covering for the winter. See **hap**.
wintle, *v.* swing from side to side, roll; *n.* 'a wavering, swinging motion' (B).
winze, *n.* curse.
wi's. See **wi'**.
wiss, *v.* wish.
wit, *v.* know.
wi't. See **wi'**.
witchin(g), *ppl. adj.* bewitching, fascinating.
withoutten, *prep.* without.
witty, *adj.* jocular, merry.
won, *v.* dwell.
wonner, *n.* wonder, marvel, fine specimen (contemptuous).
wonted, *pa. pple.* habituated, accustomed.
woo', **woo**, *n.* wool.
woodie, **woody**, *n.* withy, rope, halter for hanging; **widdefu'**, *adj.* deserving hanging, rascally.
wooer-bab, *n.* garter at the knee tied with two loops and worn by a suitor.
woor, *pa. t.* wore out.
wordie, *n.* little word; **words**, *n. pl.* news.
wordie, **wordy**, *adj.* worthy.
worms, *n. pl.* long spiral tubes at the head of a whisky still, in which the vapour is condensed.
worset, *adj.* worsted, woollen fabric, *attrib.*
wow, **vow**, *interj.* (emphatic).
wrack, *n.* wreckage, waste washed on a flood; *v.* wreck, destroy.
wrack, *n.* rubbish; worldly possessions.
wrack, *v.* torment, punish.
wraith, *n.* 'a spirit, a ghost; an apparition exactly like a living person, whose appearance is said to forbode the person's approaching death' (B).
wrang, *n.*, *v.*, *adj.* wrong; *pa. pple.* (have) wronged **100**. 53.
wreeth, *n.* snow-drift.
write, *n.* writing; **w.-(chiel)**, *n.* lawyer; **wrote**, *pa. pple.* written.
wud, *adj.* enraged, angry. Cf. **red-wud**.
wumble. See **wimble**.
wyle, *v.* lure; *pa. t.* beguiled.
wylecoat, *n.* 'a flannel vest' (B).
wyte, *v.* blame, reproach (with, for).

Y

yad, *n.* mare, old horse.
yard, *n.* garden; **yerd**, *n.* church yard. See **kail-yard**.
yealing, *n.* contemporary in age.
year, *n. pl.* years.
yearn, *n.* eagle.
yell, *adj.* barren; milkless, dry.
yerd. See **yard**.
yerk, *v.* lash, stir up.
ye'se, *v.* you shall. See **sall**.
yestreen, *adv.* yesterday even(ing).
yet(t), *n.* gate.
yeuk, *v.* itch; **yeuks**, *n. pl.* itch.
yill, *n.* ale; *comb.* **y.-caup**, see **caup**.
yird, **yirth**, *n.* earth.
yirr, *n.* a bark.
yirth. See **yird**.
yisk, *v.* hiccup, belch.
yokin, *vbl. n.* contest, turn; sexual bout, coupling.
'yont, *prep.* beyond, on the far side of.
youngkers, *n. pl.* young folk.
yoursel, *pron.* yourself, -selves.
yowe, *n.* ewe; *dim.* **yowie**, ewe-lamb.
Yule, *n.* Christmas.

INDEX OF AIRS

[*References are to the numbers of the songs for which the airs are transcribed. The commoner alternative titles are included*]

INDEX OF SHORT TITLES

[*Poems entitled 'Ballad', 'Song', or with first-line titles only, are omitted. References are to numbers, not pages*]

INDEX OF FIRST LINES